STALIN'S
SECRET WAR

by the same author
VICTIMS OF YALTA
THE HALF-MAD LORD

Nikolai Tolstoy

STALIN'S SECRET WAR

JONATHAN CAPE

THIRTY BEDFORD SQUARE LONDON

First published 1981
Copyright © Nikolai Tolstoy 1981

Jonathan Cape Ltd, 30 Bedford Square, London WC1

British Library Cataloguing in Publication Data

Tolstoy, Nikolai
Stalin's secret war.
1. Russia – Politics and government – 1936–1953
I. Title
354.4707'2'09   JN6524

ISBN 0-224-01665-2

Photoset by Rowland Phototypesetting Ltd
Bury St Edmunds, Suffolk
and printed in Great Britain by The Anchor Press Ltd
and bound by Wm Brendon & Son Ltd
both of Tiptree, Essex

This book is dedicated to my dear wife
Georgina

Рыжим татарином рыщет вольность,
С прахом равняя алтарь и трон.
Над пепелищами-рев застольный
Беглых солдат и неверных жен.

Contents

Acknowledgments

This book could not have been written without the generous help of industrious friends all over the world. I would like to take this opportunity of expressing my thanks and respects, especially perhaps to those who have themselves been victims of the terrible events I have had to describe:

Mr John Antonevics; Baltiska Humanistiska Forbundet, Stockholm; Mr W. Bolubash; Mr Andrew Boyle; Mr and Mrs Philip C. Brooks; Herr Ortwin Buchbender; Mr Keith Bush (Radio Free Europe); Centre d'Études Russes de Meudon; Mr and Mrs Vladimir Czugunow; Mr O. Dīkis; Professor Colonel Gerald Draper; Miss Liz Dribben; the Estonian Information Centre, Stockholm; the Estonian Legation, London; M. le capitaine Patrick Ferrant; Mr Stanley W. Frolick; the Rev. Pranas Gaida; Mr Patrick Janson-Smith; Mrs Anna Petrovna Jekabsons; Mr Josef Josten; Mr Indulis Kažocinš; Mr Arnis Keksis; Professor Robin Kemball; Mr Leo Labedz; the Latvian Legation, London; Lettiska Nationella Fonden, Stockholm; Lithuanian American Council; Lithuanian Association in Great Britain; Lithuanian Consulate General, Toronto; the staff of the London Library; Mr Ulick Loring; Mr Michael Lüsis; Sir Fitzroy Maclean, Bart.; Mr Eric Major; Mr David Martin; Mrs Jill Merrill; the staff of the National Archives, Washington; Dr Michael Parrish; Mr Edward Pearce; Professor Vladimir Petrov; Mr Vilis Pomelnieks; Dr V. Poremsky; the Rev. J. Prunskis; the staff of the Public Record Office, London; Mr John Reed; Mrs Lucy Roberts; Sir John Russell; Captain Z. Salnajs; Dr Ehrenfried Schütte; M. Charles Sellier; Mr J. Šimanis; Mr V. Sokolov-Samarin; Mr Peter Solly-Flood; the Tartu Institute, Toronto; Mr Robert K. G. Temple; Mr A. Teteris; Professor Hugh Thomas; Professor Vladimir Tolstoy-Miloslavsky; Mr Arnold Tonska; Mr and Mrs Mallory Walker; Dr Alfred M. de Zayas; Mr Constantine Zelenko.

Transcripts of Crown-copyright records in the Public Record Office appear by permission of the Controller of H.M. Stationery Office. For permission to print the endpaper map, which is based on a map originally published by the Free Trade Union Committee of the American Federation of Labor, I am grateful to the American Federation of Labor and Congress of Industrial Organizations.

Note on Abbreviations

In the home of the acronym, certain institutions formed an integral part of the Soviet system. These security, espionage and related services were established by Lenin at the outset of Soviet rule, and changed thereafter in little but their size and nomenclature.

The state security apparatus began life on 20 December 1917 as the Cheka, so called from the initials of the Extraordinary Commission (*Chrezvychainaia Kommissia*), whose full title was the Всероссійская Чрезвычайная Коммиссія по Борьбе съ Контр-революціей (ЧК): 'The All-Russian Extraordinary Commission for Combating Counter-revolution'.

On 6 February 1922 the Cheka was replaced by the GPU, subsequently (in 1923) the OGPU, known by the initials of the *Obedinnoe Gosudarstvennoe Politicheskoe Upravlenie*: 'United State Political Administration (ОГПУ: Объединенное Государственное Политическое Управление). The change in name appears to have taken place in response to widespread dread and hatred aroused by the organization at home and abroad. For the same reason the OGPU in turn became on 10 July 1934 the striking arm of the NKVD, by which name the security forces were subsequently known. NKVD are the initials of the *Narodny Kommissariat Vnutrennikh Del*: 'People's Commissariat for Internal Affairs' (НКВД: Народный Комиссариат Внутренних Дел).

In 1941 the political police was officially hived off from the NKVD, becoming the NKGB, *Narodny Komissariat Gosudarstvennoi Bezopasnosti*: 'People's Commissariat for State Security' (НКГБ: Народный Комиссариат Государственной Безопасности).

In 1934 all corrective labour camps and colonies were turned over to the administration of GULAG, a subordinate division of the NKVD. GULAG is the acronym of the *Glavnoe Upravlenie Ispravitelno-Trudovikh Lagerei*: 'Main Administration of Corrective-

Labour Camps' (ГУЛаг: Главное Управление Исправительно-Трудовых Лагерей).

During and after the war of 1941–5 a special branch of the security administration was established under the name SMERSH, popularized (anachronistically) by Ian Fleming in a 'James Bond' novel. SMERSH is the acronym of *Smert shpionam*: 'Death to Spies' (СМЕРШ:-Смерть шпионам).

Throughout the period covered by this book the parallel espionage and subversion wing of the Red Army was termed GRU, *Glavnoe Razvedyvatelnoe Upravlenie*: 'Chief Intelligence Directorate' (ГРУ:-Главное Разведывательное Управление).

Introduction

Stalin's Secret War is neither a life of Joseph Stalin nor a history of Soviet Russia's role in the Second World War. Nothing can yet replace Adam B. Ulam's superb biography, and Professor John Erickson is on the point of completing his magisterial history of military operations on the Eastern Front. The present work is primarily an attempt to interpret Soviet policy, internal and external, during the crucial years 1938 to 1945. Above all, I have tried to lay bare how Stalin himself saw events and reacted to them. For there has probably never been a ruler in history whose power was as absolute as Stalin's. Though autocracy has its limitations, it is true to say that in all essentials Soviet policy was simply Stalin's policy.

This being so, I believe that what Stalin *did* and what Stalin *said* are of paramount importance. None of his actions or words was straightforward, but his actions at least were consistent, whilst his words were very revealing of his changing hopes and fears. These may have been unreal or unwise, but they were the mainsprings of his policy-making and have to be understood.

Thus I believe the evidence suggests that Stalin lived throughout this period in real fear of an internal collapse of the Soviet regime, similar in suddenness to that which had engulfed the Provisional Government of Kerensky in 1917. Such a likelihood may well seem to have been remote, so debilitated was the population at large and so great were the police resources of the Soviet state. But the point is not the validity of such a fear, but its existence and the reactions which it provoked.

Again, Soviet policy cannot be understood out of its social context. The gap between the privileged class and the rest of the population was so great as to be virtually unprecedented in history, and the weaponry deployed to maintain this divide so vast as to appear paranoid were it not for its very real necessity. Below the 'free' population lay the fifteen million or more slaves of GULAG, a further source of fear and hate.

Much writing on Soviet Russia appears to be vitiated by considering these aspects in isolation. There are excellent books describing Soviet diplomacy and military history. There are others detailing Stalin's amazing private life, and yet more relating the savage horrors of GULAG and Katyn, L'vov and Vinnitsa. It seems to me that it is necessary from time to time to link all these factors into a continuous narrative.

The Katyn Massacre, for example, was more than just a hideous example of Soviet barbarity. It was a para-military operation, involving a month's large-scale disruption of major sections of the Soviet strategic railway system, at a time when the international situation seemed to place the USSR in deadly peril. Why did Stalin choose just *that* moment for the operation? Similarly the timing of purges in the Baltic States, Poland and Bessarabia in 1940 and later is all-important.

Stalin's relationship with Hitler forms another absorbing aspect of the story. All the evidence suggests that the Nazi-Soviet alliance of 1939–41 was very close to Stalin's heart. In June 1945 Stalin told a delegation of Poles that 'In Poland the sacrifices of the people during the German occupation have brought forth the possibility of changes within Poland, and created a better ground for understanding with Soviet Russia.'[1] Here was an allusion to German actions following Hitler's direction to Himmler in 1939 to ensure that the SS 'liquidate Poland's upper class wherever it was to be found',[2] and to Stalin's own abandonment of risen Warsaw in 1944.

Stalin was perceptive enough to see how closely his and Hitler's interests coincided, but not how dangerous was the alliance. Everything indicates that the pact with Hitler was eagerly welcomed, whilst the subsequent wartime alliance with Britain and the United States was regarded with fear and suspicion. All this becomes perfectly intelligible when it is seen that Stalin's prime concern was with the internal stability of the Soviet Union. Foreign policy always remained secondary to this overriding consideration, even in the most dangerous and extraordinary circumstances. In the first week of the German invasion the slaughter of prisoners in Lithuanian and Ukrainian gaols took precedence over the supply of crucial munitions to the Red Army on the frontier. Hundreds of thousands of well-equipped troops guarded the camps of GULAG in preference to stemming the onslaught of the Wehrmacht.

Many other intriguing aspects of those turbulent years receive a fresh look. How far did British and French Communists go in helping Hitler in 1940? What is the true story of Russia's 'twenty million war dead', a figure trotted out regularly by Soviet spokesmen to still Western criticisms? What induced Russians to fight so bravely after 1941 for a regime that had virtually made war on them for more than twenty years? How did Hitler succeed in deceiving Stalin on the eve of Barbarossa? Could incipient Cold War attitudes have been avoided in 1945?

Finally, the failure of British and American diplomacy, outwitted by Stalin at almost every turn, is examined. This happened against the background of a ground swell of pro-Soviet public opinion in the West. Much of this stemmed from generous, if irrational, impulses, and much again from sensations of personal or public guilt. Less respectable motives swayed fellow-travellers and Communists, many of whom fell prey to feelings of personal inadequacy resulting in sadistic impulses indulged at the expense of the long-suffering Russian people. Their mentality in many ways reflected that of Stalin himself. The sinister role of the traitor is glimpsed on occasions, and men who betrayed their countries and came near to bringing civilization to ruin live on in well-pensioned and decorated retirement in Britain and the United States.

Also with us still is the Soviet Union, essentially the same forty years on in its institutions, ambitions and fears. In Eastern Europe it preserves the only living memorial of the Third Reich: the occupation of the Baltic States, eastern Poland and northern Romania, granted by Hitler to Stalin in the Moscow Award of 1939. Solzhenitsyn warns us that

> Today the Western world faces a greater danger than that which threatened it in 1939 . . . So much has been ceded, surrendered, and traded away that today even a fully united Western world can no longer prevail except by allying itself with the captive peoples of the communist world.[3]

This perilous situation springs from the events of 1939–45, and we still live with the inheritance of Stalin and Hitler. A closer look at those crucible years may help us to understand the nature of the danger, and even provide intimations of the remedy. Understanding, patience, resolve and self-sacrifice are the qualities civilization requires if it is to survive. The KGB possesses all the resources of its predecessor the NKVD, and the rumble of lorries in darkened streets and the 3 a.m. knock at the door can come as easily in Washington as in Warsaw.

Part One

I

The New Society

Karl Marx argued that if only the contradictions of capitalist society could be abolished and man be brought to come to terms with his condition, life and politics would merge into a fully satisfying sense of oneness with the social environment.[1] It is difficult to relate this vague concept to any likely real world, and Marx rarely went much further into his vision of the future. When he did, the dream seemed oddly simple. In *The German Ideology*, he wrote:

> In communist society, where nobody has one exclusive sphere of activity but each can become accomplished in any branch he wishes, society regulates the general production and thus makes it possible to do one thing today and another tomorrow, to hunt in the morning, fish in the afternoon, rear cattle in the evening, criticise after dinner, just as I have a mind, without becoming hunter, fisherman, shepherd or critic.[2]

Lenin was an enthusiastic apostle of this coming New Harmony and, as a practical revolutionary, was more specific in his description of its workings. Every citizen would be responsible for running the state, work which he would perform for workingmen's wages. There would be no standing army; instead the masses would themselves be armed and stand guard over their hard-won heritage. The bureaucracy, police and law-courts would become superfluous, as man's competitive instincts became transformed into a spirit of voluntary co-operation. In short, the state would wither away, leaving a body of citizens who would find the exercise of their unexploited labour so deeply fulfilling that they would work productively for the sheer pleasure of doing so, thus doing away with any motive for social antagonism.[3] This concept is of course wholly in accordance with Marx's prescription. He emphatically stressed that communist society, *ipso facto*, 'would have no need of bourgeois institutions such as representative political bodies (which invariably gave rise to bureaucracies alienated from the public) and rules of law safeguarding civil liberties.'[4]

In the meantime, laws, so far as they were necessary at all, existed to suppress the resistance of classes hostile to the interests of the proletariat. In fact, of course, such a concept meant there was no law other than what the Party leadership considered to be such. This view is explicit throughout Lenin's writings, in his advocacy of the 'dictatorship of the proletariat' as the necessary prelude to the future communist state: 'The scientific term "dictatorship" means nothing more nor less than authority untrammelled by any laws, absolutely unrestricted by any rules whatever, and based directly on violence. The term "dictatorship" has *no other meaning but this* – mark this well . . . '[5] Lenin firmly believed that the Party leadership, as the proletariat's vanguard, must be hampered by no institutional checks whatever. Instructions to his followers to 'use both corruption and the threat of general extermination' and (of some possible saboteurs) to 'kill off all of them' ensured the effectiveness of the new dictatorship.[6]

Stalin's continuation and extension of the use of terror as the Party's chief weapon was a logical development of the same policy. There was much that was wild and irrational about his purges, but they too were consistent with the essential lawlessness of Communist rule. To guarantee the extinction of opposition, it was necessary to stir the pot continually, anticipating the aggregation of lumps of resistance.[7]

Thus Soviet Russia was from the beginning an avowed dictatorship, in which the successive manifestations of the political police could and did rove at will throughout society, unchallenged by any legal or customary restrictions, directing the people in whatever direction the dictatorship saw fit. As Milovan Djilas succinctly expresses it:

> Of course, Russia under Stalin had 'laws' and 'institutions' on the statute books, and often these were even respected in matters such as driving on the correct side of the road, regulating the electricity supply of Tomsk, or the alcoholic content of vodka. But in all things pertaining to man's spiritual and intellectual freedom, Russia under Stalin was a lawless land. What the Prince says, goes – and nothing else.[8]

Nevertheless there lay over this unrestricted apparatus of coercion and terror a palimpsest of legal institutions. The first Soviet Constitution of 1918 frankly declared its objective to be the establishment of 'a dictatorship of the proletariat, a powerful centralized government'. Accepting this stipulation, however, far-ranging guarantees of liberty were established for that section of the population which Lenin and the Party decided to be the proletariat. They included freedom of speech, of the press, of association, of assembly, of conscience, and so forth. The constituent republics of the Union, several of which had recently been conquered by force of arms, were given the right to secede should they desire. The All-Russian Congress of Soviets consisted of delegates theoretically chosen by popular election, the franchise being qualified in order to assign a predominant voice to the urban proletariat. A revised Constitution ratified in 1924 confirmed and clarified these provisions, creating a Supreme Court and formally increasing judicial independence.

In 1936 Stalin promulgated with great éclat an entirely new Constitution. This was based on the premise that at last, hostile classes having been totally eliminated, there was no longer any need to restrict the franchise to any one class. Henceforward there was to be universal adult suffrage, together with a secret ballot. Local and national government were to be entirely democratic and representative in character. All imaginable rights (work, rest and leisure, education, association, freedom of the press and religious observance, etc.) were expressly guaranteed. Privacy of correspondence and inviolability of the person were established, as was the right to unrestricted ownership and inheritance of home and property.[9]

It is hardly necessary to point out that none of these rights existed in reality, and all were violated on so consistently wide a scale as to confirm their non-existence. The expensive and troublesome charade was designed to cloak the exercise of naked, unfettered power, seized and maintained by brute force. Immediately after his accession to power, Lenin, who was extremely frank about his aims and methods, began to appreciate the widespread revulsion his assaults on liberty were arousing. He was 'conscious of the daily erosion of what few democratic institutions remained, but wished from time to time to invoke the virtuous-sounding name of democracy.'[10] Thus the constitution of 1924 paraded parliamentary and democratic forms, 'but the springs of power in the Soviet system

were concealed'.[11] At local level, for example, the Congress of
Soviets of an *oblast* (province) was mere window-dressing for the
local Party apparatus, and had no legislative or executive capacity
whatever. The role of the Supreme Soviet was similarly 'ornamental
and decorative', conveying 'the impression of a well-rehearsed
theatrical spectacle from which almost all elements of conflict have
been eliminated . . . The task of the Supreme Soviet is not to question but to execute, to clothe the Party thesis in the garb of constitutional legality.' The absence of refractoriness or opposed views
is understandable; as a former officer of the Kremlin Guard has
revealed, 'to guard against any sudden subversive tendencies on
the part of the hand-picked delegates, an armed Guard officer sits at
every table of fifteen or twenty delegates. There is an armed Guard
officer, also, for every twelve persons in the gallery.'[12]

The realities of dictatorship under Lenin and Stalin lay crudely
concealed behind a plasterboard façade of traditional liberal legalities
and constitutional procedure. The purpose of this fictional parade
was to clothe the apparatus of despotism in garments of respectability, and to 'legalize' government administration. Elections, with
their predictable 99.7 per cent favourable results, had the additional
function of periodically drumming up popular participation in the
regime's workings, and registering the solidarity of the people with
their Party and Government. Still more important was the obvious
intent to deceive gullible foreigners, and to facilitate the propaganda
work of foreign Communist Parties. The 'Stalin Constitution' of
1936, in particular, with its uncommunistic concession to the existence of private property, coincided with the Popular Front policy of
uniting world socialists against fascism. It was effective in predictable circles: Stephen Spender decided that the new Constitution had
'removed the . . . terror', a view shared by the depressing congeries
of Harold Laski, Walter Duranty, Anna Louise Strong, *et al.*[13]

This amazing dichotomy between fact and fable in the USSR naturally produced a schizophrenic effect on the population, to which
they gradually adjusted themselves. People had to

'believe without believing', and it was this state of mind that the
party sought to create and maintain in its own members and, as far
as possible, in the whole population. Half-starved people, lacking
the bare necessities of life, attended meetings at which they repeated the government's lies about how well off they were, and in

a bizarre way they half-believed what they were saying. They all knew what it was 'right' to say, i.e. what was demanded of them, and in a curious way they confused this 'rightness' with truth. Truth, they knew, was a party matter, and therefore lies became true even if they contradicted the plain facts of experience. The condition of thus living in separate worlds was one of the most remarkable achievements of the Stalinist system.[14]

However fanciful Lenin's ideological views, he was eminently a realist when it came to measures essential to the survival of his regime. Like Hitler, he was a keen student of Gustave Lebon's classic work on the behaviour of crowds, *La Psychologie de la Foule*. (Hitler in turn revealed that he had 'studied revolutionary technique in the works of Lenin and Trotsky and other Marxists'.)[15] Lenin, and Stalin after him, appreciated that Bolshevik ruthlessness was repellent to many, and that to be made acceptable the dictatorship must be partially hidden behind a semblance of democratic procedure. They had to concede that what people wanted desperately were not abstract concepts of 'freedom', still less equality, but tangible protection in the form of elective representation, impartial courts of justice, rights of property and other constitutional devices for the preservation of liberty characteristic of the nineteenth-century bourgeois state vilified by Karl Marx.

The Soviet parade of liberal institutions greatly impressed people at all levels of intelligence and influence in foreign countries. This was indeed its main purpose. But as far as material conditions went, the overwhelming majority of the population of Russia lived in conditions of such appalling poverty as to make life under the Tsarist government, harsh as it had been for the poor, seem tolerable in comparison.[16]

In 1937 a Soviet official noted that the average housing space in Smolensk had fallen to *three square metres per person*. It was in consequence quite normal to find up to fifteen families living in a single flat, 'with an overflow of "house workers" (servants) sleeping on boxes in the corridor, on the kitchen floor, on the common oven'. To have a roof over one's head at all was an expensive privilege: an American Communist reporter in Moscow had to pay a *deposit* of 1,500 dollars in order to live with his family in half a disused stable. 'The house was without a foundation, and as the winter thawed into spring, the walls began to sweat. Great leprous patches along the floor line and on the ceiling spread slowly but surely.' The place was swarming with vermin: one may scarcely conceive how less privileged people lived.[17] Outside the favoured Siberian town of Stalinsk (formerly Kuznetsk),

> . . . vast barracks colonies had mushroomed outward from the fringes of the old city. The overflow population, thousands of families, lived in the damp dugouts in the ground we called *zemlyanki*. These crude holes in the ground, covered with handmade gabled roofs, were pathetically familiar sights around new enterprises in the Soviet Union where housing could not keep pace with new population. They were usually sixteen or eighteen feet long, eight or ten feet wide and six or eight feet deep – about enough to sleep two persons.

Many of these new arrivals were peasants, driven by the policy of collectivization from the countryside to seek food in the towns. Most of them died of starvation in the streets, and there were cases of cannibalism on the part of people driven mad with hunger.[18] Food was even more difficult to obtain than adequate housing. Queues formed outside shops on the faintest expectation of obtaining something to eat; people would sit all night on the pavement in hopes of buying a herring the next day.

In April 1940 the American Ambassador saw in 'most of the towns where I stopped [in south Russia] long lines of people were waiting to buy bread and other foodstuffs. At the important port of Odessa this condition was particularly noticeable, food lines being so continuous on the main street that thousands of people were visible from a single point.' He believed this arose from poor distribution, rather than an actual shortage of food. Another, Russian-speaking, observer in the same year

> . . . said that conditions have grown steadily worse, that women often get up at 2.00 in the morning (at 48 below in the depth of winter) to be first in line to buy whatever there may be. More often than not the store has sold out of everything by the time they reach their turn. Then they go home dog-tired and try again the next day. They are not the least bit concerned about what it is on sale . . . The Army and the new upper class is pampered, but no one else in the whole country has any rights or privileges that cannot be withdrawn without notice.

After a year in Moscow, the witness concluded that

> Not very much leadership would be required to start a counter-Stalinist revolution . . . Many people have come to believe if Germany turned eastward she could find enough people in Russia who were fed up with the present rulers to welcome any outside aid, even from the Germans.[19]

Discipline in factories was draconian. Lenin had laid down that 'the masses *unquestioningly obey the single will* of the leaders of the labour process', whilst Trotsky urged the 'militarization of labour', whereby workmen would become totally at the disposition of the state.[20] It fell to Stalin to complete his predecessors' recommendations. In 1932 internal passports were introduced to prevent workers shifting their employment without permission; if they did so they were deprived of ration cards and living quarters. This was followed in 1938 by a 'labour book', containing a full record of a worker's career, without which he could not gain employment at all. 'A decree issued in June 1940 made employees who were more than twenty minutes late for work without a valid medical excuse subject to a penalty of compulsory labor at their usual place of work with a deduction of up to 25 per cent of their wages, and repetition of the offense carried more drastic penalties.'

Finally, in June 1940, 'all workers were frozen on their jobs. Changes of employment required the express permission of management, and departures from employment without such authorization were punished by imprisonment.' Conditions as rigid as this verged in some respects on slavery. The helpless workers recognized their total submission to their employers in a fatalistic proverb: 'Let the *natshalniks* (bosses) think it over; they read the newspapers, talk on the telephone and drink tea with *sugar*.'[21]

All this and much more information on the real situation of workers in the Soviet Union was readily available to all who wished to know. Andrew Smith, an American Communist, went to work in Russia as a volunteer in factories from 1932 to 1935. On his return he published a lengthy memoir,[22] which in its English edition passed through seven impressions in two months. In it he described in detail the horrific living conditions of his fellow-workers; the transparent, if elaborate, measures taken to deceive foreign visitors; the iron control of the GPU police; the squalid luxury and immorality of the new ruling class; the purges, kidnappings and other grim aspects of Soviet life.

But one of the most disheartening aspects of the Russian people's suffering was the widespread indifference with which it was regarded in the free and relatively luxurious West. This indifference with some seemed to develop into a positive hatred and contempt for the Russians. Walter Duranty, an American journalist, could dismiss millions of deaths, caused by the forced famine, in a phrase which came readily to many Western liberals: 'But they're only Russians . . . ' The Webbs and American authors Lincoln Steffens and Upton Sinclair expressed similar views, and a host of other fellow-travellers were anxious that the Marxist experiment should be performed on primitive Russians, who apparently enjoyed suffering.[23]

The absence of condemnation by the West becomes even more significant when one considers that huge section of the Russian people living in conditions immeasurably worse than that of the ordinary poor just described. Solzhenitsyn's indictment of *The Gulag Archipelago* awoke the world to the existence of Soviet Russia's most remarkable institution. Yet, magnificent as is Solzhenitsyn's achievement, there are virtually no facts of importance in it which could not have been drawn from numerous first-hand accounts published in every Western language since Lenin authorized the first punitive camps in January 1918. In this way Western observers were in a much better position to know the truth about the GULAG system of forced-labour camps than was the Russian public itself, which had no access to literature of any kind on the subject.[24]

It was as soon after the Revolution as January 1918 that Lenin declared his aim of 'purging the Russian land of all kinds of harmful insects'; i.e. people opposed to his seizure of power. To accomplish this he suggested various measures, all more or less brutal, including 'punishment at forced labour of the hardest kind'.[25] By the beginning of the 1930s the prison and concentration camp population was growing at such a speed that Stalin, perhaps influenced by the suggestion of a former prisoner serving in the NKVD (political police), adopted the idea of utilizing the prisoners as a major factor in the country's labour force.[26] There were several advantages in this scheme. The prisoners, who were all actual or potential enemies of the regime, could be dispatched to extremely inhospitable regions unlikely to attract free labour. The casualty rate was likely to be high, but this too was an advantage, since potential opposition would be continually drained off, whilst the remaining 'free' population provided a near inexhaustible source of fresh human material.

Though forced labour was necessarily a very wasteful and inefficient form of production, it occupied nevertheless a major place in the Soviet economy until the late 1950s. Indeed, considering the colossal work-force at its disposal and the varied industrial sources of production with which it was concerned, it bore a fair claim to being *the* major factor in the Soviet economy.[27]

In the war the Germans captured a printed copy of *The State Plan for the Development of the National Economy of the USSR for 1941*. The NKVD appropriation comprised about 18 per cent of the whole, but as gold production (almost exclusively mined by slaves) and other commodities were omitted from the report, it is clear that slave-labour accounted for at least 25 per cent of the Soviet Union's economy. When the war began to use up enormous supplies of Russian manpower, the NKVD followed the Red Army into occupied neighbouring states to dispatch back to the camps further millions of foreign slaves.[28]

Though the Communist revival of slavery might appear a reactionary measure, it was in many ways an entirely novel evolution. In particular, it was immeasurably harsher in important respects than the well-known slave communities of the ancient world, and that of the Negroes in the United States.

Firstly, climatic conditions were generally much more grim for slaves in the Soviet Union, whether in the Arctic camps or those of the Central Asian deserts. Secondly, Soviet slaves were invariably separated from their wives and children and prevented from perpetuating new relationships. Thirdly, Soviet slaves normally lived in places remote from the rest of society. Fourthly, Soviet slaves suffered from a scourge which was by general consensus worse than that of their guards. This was the camp criminal community, which, with the guards' connivance, preyed day and night on the suffering prisoners. Fifthly, treatment of Soviet slaves was rendered more than habitually cruel because they were not regarded as merely a supply of cheap work, but also as enemies of the nation.

The only mitigating factor that might be urged is that in pre-Soviet slave societies the slaves lived and died in a state of bondage, whereas under Lenin and Stalin they were sentenced to specific terms. However, in view of the enormous death-rate, and the fact that sentences were liable to be arbitrarily extended for further terms, this limitation proved to be scant consolation.

All these factors resulted in a death-rate which, it may safely be estimated even in the absence of exact statistics, was far beyond that of other slave societies.

Estimates vary considerably as to the numbers held at any one time in GULAG. Very careful records were kept at headquarters, and Vyshinsky was probably telling the truth when he boasted to the Polish Ambassador that 'we have records of everybody, living or dead'.[29] Though it is unlikely that these will see the light of day before Soviet power is dissolved, many observers, particularly prisoners, found convincing methods of arriving at overall figures.

In 1938 many leading GULAG officials were purged and gaoled. An imprisoned German Communist learned at the time that

. . . these G.U.L.A.G. officials knew the arrest figures every month. In Kiev and subsequently in Moscow I met comrades who had been in the same cells with them. Their figures exceeded ours by between 10 and 15 per cent. We arrived at a grand total of nine million arrests and we deducted two million for criminals, which left us seven million 'politicals' for 1937 and 1938. We must now add about a million for those who were already in prison in 1936.[30]

But a prisoner working in the statistical section of the White Sea-Baltic Combine in 1934 was able even at that early date to 'estimate the total population in the Concentration Camps at not less than five millions, and this is probably a conservative figure'.[31]

By 1940 prisoners making elaborate calculations based on known prison populations in Leningrad arrived at a total of 'between eighteen and twenty-five million', and a Cossack prisoner five years later suggested similar figures.[32] Calculations provided by NKVD guards and officials tended to be lower: twelve to fifteen million.[33] But official figures may well have been kept artificially low in order to allow for the colossal wastage. For all we know, the total of prisoners at its peak (probably in 1945–6, when floods of new prisoners flowed in from conquered territories, together with returning Russians from liberated Europe) was higher still.

Other intelligent former inmates concluded that there were no less than forty to forty-five million people held under GULAG authority, and though this estimate must surely be exaggerated, it certainly reflects the impact of first-hand experience of what was almost literally 'a nation in the mines'. Here is a glimpse of just one transit camp, where prisoners were preparing for embarkation to Kolyma:

> When we came out on to the immense field outside the camp I witnessed a spectacle that would have done justice to a Cecil B. De-Mille production. As far as the eye could see there were columns of prisoners marching in one direction or another like armies on a battlefield. A huge detachment of security officers, soldiers, and signal corps men with field telephones and motor-cycles kept in touch with headquarters, arranging the smooth flow of these human rivers . . . 100,000 were part of the scene before us. One could see endless columns of women, of cripples, of old men and even teenagers, all in military formation, five in a row, going through the huge field, and directed by whistles and flags.[34]

Discrepancies in estimation must in part be due to the fact that strict calculation formed only one factor in drawing up figures, and it is possible that other considerations played their part.

For instance, roughly half a million people were held in the Kolyma gold-fields; but to maintain this total it was necessary for the NKVD to top it up each year with a further eighty to a hundred thousand.[35] In this way the recorded population of a camp in a given year could vary by a fifth according to which way one regarded the numbers.

Then again, enormous numbers were perpetually being shifted in cattle-trucks from prison to transit camp, and from transit camp to work camp. 'At the lowest estimate there are a million and a half prisoners being moved by rail in Soviet Russia at any given moment.' And amongst these there were great numbers who never reached the camps proper. In wintertime there were many deaths on the journey long before any prisoner ever saw a camp. Unheated, overcrowded cattle trucks, travelling often for weeks on end through the snow, caused an awesome casualty rate. A German woman saw sixty workmen being removed after one such journey, their bodies frozen stiff as wooden planks. In 1941 a whole trainload of 1,650 Poles was frozen to death, together with 110 NKVD guards.[36]

For the hundreds of thousands travelling annually to Kolyma there was the further ordeal of the voyage across the Sea of Okhotsk. The steamer *Dzhurma* was caught in pack-ice on its maiden voyage near Wrangel Island. It was not freed until after the next spring, by which time every one of its 12,000 prisoners had frozen to death.

Other disasters, almost as horrific, occurred often; and on every journey numbers died through overcrowding, starvation, or cruelties at the hands of guards and criminals.[37]

Many survived, merely to die soon after arrival in the transit camps. In Vladivostok transit camp, for example, where prisoners were gathered before travelling by sea to the Kolyma gold-field, 'tens of thousands' in 1938 alone were carried off by a frightful spotted-typhus epidemic. The pestilence cut swathes through crowded barracks.

> The camp infirmary was so crowded with the sick, who lay on every cot and along all the floors of the wards and corridors, that any kind of care was impossible. Some of the women from our barrack were called in to act as nurses. Their chief occupation was counting the dead who had escaped the misery of the gold mines which awaited the others. In silence we stared through the barbed wire at the hearses which drove out of the camp every night. Piled high with naked bodies, the load tied on with cord and covered with canvas, the trucks drove out, carrying the victims to eternal freedom.

In the absence of any sort of hygiene the place was infested with lice, which swarmed over the prisoners in such numbers that there was nothing to be done but suffer the torment. 'Now and then we would reach under our blouses', wrote a woman prisoner, 'when we could no longer endure the itching, fish out a handful of the vermin, and throw them away. As often as not they landed not on the floor, but on other prisoners.'[38]

But the most savage annual death toll was yet to come: in the labour camps themselves. A reliable Polish inmate noted that he 'never came across a prisoner who had worked in the forest for more than two years. As a rule they left after a year, with incurable disease of the heart, and were transferred to brigades engaged at lighter work; from these they soon "retired" – to the mortuary.' A comrade who worked in the camp death-registration office remembered that 'in the office stood two cupboards the height of a normal man; one was filled with three vertical stacks of death certificates, the other contained only two and a half such stacks. Dead prisoners were brought into the office, each with his personal data written on a slip of paper tied round his ankle.' A copy of each certificate was sent to GULAG – but not to the dead man's family.[39]

In Kolyma the annual death-rate rose swiftly to more than 50 per cent. Men simply collapsed where they stood. In the gold-fields,

A man pushing a wheelbarrow up the high runway to the panning apparatus would suddenly halt, sway for a moment, and fall down from a height of twenty-four to thirty feet. And that was the end. Or a man, loading a barrow, prodded by the shouts of a foreman or a guard, unexpectedly would sink to the ground, blood would gush from his mouth – and everything was over.

Poles and other foreigners arriving in later years died in even greater proportions: 60 or 70 per cent. By 1941 the intake of 1937–8 had virtually vanished.[40]

From the chimneys of the Lubianka daily arose smoke from the corpse incinerator, wafting the ashes of the dead over the houses of the living.[41] Within ten years Russia was fast becoming a colossal graveyard; all along the endless railway networks lay corpses, frozen in the snows of the north, or picked clean by kites in the deserts of Central Asia; while the archipelago of camps was ringed by a community of the dead which soon outnumbered that of the living. Until 1948, every corpse was brought to the camp guardroom for registration. A sentry thrust his bayonet through the silent heart, to ensure that no one living left the camp, and the naked bodies were piled on to an oxcart for transportation to mass graves outside the camp perimeter. Where the permafrost reigned interment could not be very thorough: 'Sometimes a skeletal hand or a well-preserved foot protruded from the grave; it had been heaved to the surface by the thaw, for in winter it was impossible to break through the frozen earth to make a sufficiently deep grave.' In the winter of 1944–5 in Kotlas a Polish prisoner lived in a room overlooking the mortuary. 'This was by no means a pleasant sight, especially when the death-rate in the camp was so high that there was no room for the corpses in the shed and they had to be stacked outside against the wall in roughly-covered piles, from which a leg or a ghastly, grinning face would stick out.'[42]

A careful scholar, whose figures are 'based on conservative assumptions at every point', has arrived at a total death toll in Kolyma of three million. On the same cautious principle, he estimates that twelve million died throughout all GULAG: a figure which may be compared with the total of fourteen thousand executions which took place in the last fifty years of Tsarist government.[43]

The enormous scale of this mass murder is difficult to appreciate in human terms. A German prisoner in Vorkuta learned that it was 'calculated that on the railways every sleeper cost one dead man and that in the mines there were two dead men for every yard dug underground'. Within a few years an entire generation of prisoners would be wiped out, to be replaced by another.[44] In the sheer number of victims destroyed, the Soviet Union easily out-distanced its ally of 1939–41. Dr Julius Margolin, a Zionist leader who was released after seven years in the custody of GULAG, wrote that 'Hitlerism has been beaten, while the Soviet camps continue to exist . . . Since they came into being, the Soviet camps have swallowed more people, have exacted more victims, than all other camps – Hitler's and others – together, and this lethal engine continues to operate full-blast . . . An entire generation of Zionists has died in Soviet prisons, camps, and exile.'[45] A woman, who was unfortunate enough to have prolonged experience of both systems, found that at Ravensbrück Camp it was not until the latter days of their dying regime that the Nazis were able to catch up the Bolsheviks in brutality: 'Things were declining to a Siberian level, and by the end of 1944 there was not a great deal of difference left between Ravensbrueck and Karaganda.'[46]

Varlam Shalamov, a former prisoner in Kolyma, describes how climatic conditions caused an enormous mass grave to open up and begin to slide down a hillside. A GULAG bulldozer 'scraped up these stiffened bodies, thousands of bodies, thousands of skeletal corpses. All was preserved: twisted fingers, putrefying toes – frozen stumps, the dry skin scored with blood, and hungry blazing eyes'. It seems likely that Shalamov was present at the scene of a terrible incident, described by a Ukrainian named Dashchin, who had escaped miraculously and later related his story. A camp in Kolyma 'contained 7,000 prisoners from all parts of the Soviet Union, and upon completion of the work there it was evident that the means of transportation to another locality were not available. The prisoners were too weak from malnutrition to go elsewhere on foot, for the nearest work-camp was thousands of kilometers distant. The problem was solved very simply. The prisoners were driven to a cliff that had been mined, and were blown into oblivion.'

The Nazis could virtually destroy the whole of European Jewry. What the Soviets were capable of is illustrated in a brief exchange between a Polish prisoner and a Soviet magistrate: ' "There are thirty million of us Poles: you won't find it so easy as you think to destroy us!" The magistrate laughed: "What's thirty million?" he said; "we've more than that in our prisons and camps already." [47]

Comparison between the two totalitarian systems of mass extermination can have little meaning. For the individual victim, whether a Jew in Belsen or a Russian in Pechora, the bottommost pit of suffering and despair had been reached. There were young girls in their teens, snatched from their families and placed at the mercy of camp criminals. A former inmate of a camp at Vorkuta recalled an all too familiar scene:

. . . 'You dirty bitch, I'll make you beg for it' . . . he caught her by the hair again and dragged her to her feet, punching her in the face, then pushing her mouth down to his fly. All the time she was screaming . . . Spitting blood, her face bruised and discoloured, she was still screaming as he tore her trousers down. Then he couldn't wait any longer: he ejaculated. The others who had been with him began to laugh. 'Did you see that? You don't know how to fuck, you need some lessons.' This blow to his male pride made him even angrier. She was just a piece of dirt who had resisted him and must be punished. Systematically, he punched her in the face and kicked her in the belly. Now she had stopped struggling. Bleeding from the mouth and nose, she only moaned and tried to protect her abdomen . . . 'Stop that, you stupid bastard, someone else might want to use her.' [48]

There were men, women and children, dying in droves of typhus, pleurisy, syphilis, starvation; compelled by the lingering instinct of survival to eat rats, their own vomit . . . even their fellow-prisoners. A man dying of blood-poisoning in a Kolyma hospital had been driven twenty-five miles through a snow blizzard, with a temperature of 104°, pleurisy, and an NKVD guard behind him lashing with his club at a huge suppurating carbuncle on the prisoner's back. A precious moment of respite comes in the long day's toil; you light a home-made cigarette with trembling fingers . . .

The foreman rushed across the excavation, and with a blow of his hand shoved the burning cigarette into the man's mouth. The man crouched, covering his face with his hands, while blood showed through his fingers. With a stream of oaths the foreman continued beating the worker on the head, then hit him in the

chest. The man fell to the ground. Then the foreman began kick-
ing the man with his heavy iron-studded boots . . . [49]

In a myriad gaols, trains and camps, the length and breadth of
Russia, was hidden a population larger than that of Canada, as large
as Czechoslovakia or Yugoslavia separately, or Belgium and Austria
put together. Year after year Russia knew the continual crying of
babies, snatched from their mothers for ever, at the age of one or
two; the howls of a drunken NKVD torturer, 'followed by the sound
of blows and a young woman's screams, which went on hour after
hour until at last they turned to a demented howl'; the 'human
phantoms' of Kolyma: 'It was a procession not of human beings, but
of corpses and trunks. The majority had neither noses, lips, nor ears;
very many were armless and legless.'

The only comparison to be made was with Hell itself,[50] a Hell
whose existence was denied by many in the West, and a Hell to
which British and American politicians and diplomatic officials were
to dispatch more than two million further victims. The bright side of
the moon, with its Stalin Constitution and its 'unrelenting opposition' to the evil of Nazism, warmed with its pallid rays the upturned
moon-faces of admirers in the West. The dark side was a land whose
inhabitants fell into three categories: prisoners, former prisoners,
and future prisoners.[51] It was also a land whose guardians were busy
with telegrams containing instructions like this: 'To N.K.V.D.,
Frunze. You are charged with the task of exterminating 10,000
enemies of the people. Report results by signal. – Yezhov.'[52]

II
Stalin the Leader

Over all this empire of fear – over the dying millions in the coal-mines of Vorkuta and the gold-fields of Kolyma, over starving city workers, blue-capped frontier guards, homeless collectivized peasants, GULAG widows, professional torturers, passport forgers, professors of the Institute of Marxist-Leninism, executioners – lay the shadow of one diminutive man. Cities, towns, factories, institutes and mountains were named after him; every newspaper, book and scientific textbook exalted him as the summit of all that was true, noble and wise; and millions united in lavishing public adoration on a man who had scarcely left a family in the land untouched by tragedy.

Iosif Vissarionovich Dzhugashvili, alias Stalin, was known by sight to very few of his subjects. Not for him were the mass rallies of Western dictators, the contacts with the crowd, the torrents of eloquence which brought millions to their feet in an ecstasy of communal fervour. His ways were secret and his personality unknown. He was accorded heroic characteristics – kindness, omniscience, modesty, indefatigable industry – but these were more in the nature of conventional epithets borne by Pharaohs and kings of old than because of any known aptness. Even today, when much is known, there remains a central residue of motivation that is likely to be for ever mysterious.

Photographs and portraits invariably represented Stalin as calm and majestic, physically massive and unshakeable. The reality was so different that many attributed his distaste for public appearance to a consciousness of the deficiency.[1] The composer Shostakovich recalled that he

> didn't look anything like his numerous portraits. Stalin had several painters shot. They were called to the Kremlin to capture

the Leader and Teacher for eternity, but apparently they didn't
please him. Stalin wanted to be tall, with powerful hands. Nalban-
dian [a court painter] fooled them all. In *his* portrait Stalin is
walking straight at the viewer, his hands folded over his stomach.
The view is from below, an angle that would make a Lilliputian
look like a giant.

The reality was very different; in particular, 'his right hand was
noticeably thinner than his left. He kept hiding his right hand'.[2] A
precise description of him in Tsarist police records at the age of
twenty-two refers to the fact that the second and third toes of his left
foot were fused together. He was only five feet four inches high, and
was thin, swarthy and heavily pock-marked. An accident in youth had
caused chronic stiffness of his left elbow and a shortening of the arm.[3]

Despite his small stature and slight physique he remained
physically wiry and strong throughout the main part of his life. In
1930 he accorded an American reporter a rare interview. 'Though of
vigorous physique', wrote Eugene Lyons, 'he seemed to me older
than his fifty-one years; his face was large-featured and fleshy, darker
in tinge than I had expected and faintly pock-marked, his shock of
hair thick, unruly, and touched with gray.'[4] In later years the strain
of the Purges and, above all, the shock of the German invasion began
to take their toll on his strong constitution.

In November 1941, wrote a Soviet eye-witness, 'I had not seen him
since 1933. Since that time he had changed greatly; before me stood a
man of short height with a tired, sunken face. In eight years he had
aged, it seemed, about twenty years. In his eyes there was not the
former strength, in his voice confidence was not felt.' His confidence
returned with Allied successes a year or so later, but the physical
deterioration was not to be stayed. His hair greyed and thinned considerably and his belly began to hang within the loose-fitting
uniforms he affected. His pock-marked features appeared more lined
and pitted than hitherto, his moustache was scrawny and streaked,
and his teeth blackened and stained. In June 1942 the British Ambassador was surprised at 'the shape and the size of him. I had expected
something big and burly. But I saw . . . a little, slim, bent, grey man
with a large head and immense white hands . . . when he shook my
hand he looked, almost furtively, at my shoulder and not at my face.'
At times this little, unshapely, awkward fellow could appear 'ill at
ease' and 'a rather ridiculous figure', unable to look visitors directly

in the eye or make polite small-talk. At others he exuded charm and good manners, captivating foreigners with his seeming modesty and good sense. Glimpses of another Stalin came only from the wolves' heads he was incessantly doodling, and from the sudden flash of his yellow eyes as he glanced vindictively at an offending minion.[5]

The charm and politeness were normally reserved for those who were too powerful or remote to fall under his control, chiefly visiting foreign statesmen. In private life he was generally coarse, cruel and uncultured, characteristics that had marked him from an early date. As Khrushchev recalled, 'Stalin's character was brutish, and his temper was harsh; but his brutishness didn't always imply malice towards people to whom he acted so rudely. His was a sort of inborn brutishness. He was coarse and abusive with everyone. I often experienced his rudeness myself.'[6]

This appears to have been the real Stalin, whose coarseness was not even restrained by the presence of his young daughter. 'At home', wrote Svetlana, 'when at table with his usual circle of "companions in arms", he always spoke the language of working men, often using obscene words . . . At these all-male, round-the-table gatherings, I alone could have been a restraining element, but my presence never prevented him from cracking coarse peasant jokes and telling coarse peasant stories.' Little Svetlana would steal away, only to be summoned back to witness increasingly unpleasant and savage scenes.

Stalin's was not merely the rough-and-ready brutality of a man of impoverished background and rudimentary education; it was a calculated rudeness designed to wound – and perhaps test – the submissiveness of his acolytes. 'On days when he was out of sorts he would say rudely in front of everybody, "Now get out, I'm busy!"'[7]

In the 1920s, when Stalin was still consolidating his power, his secretary witnessed a characteristic exchange between the Leader and his secretary Mekhlis, who happened to be a Jew. Unaware that Mekhlis was in the room, Stalin snapped out: 'Who does he think he is, this dirty little yid?' Suddenly he realized that Mekhlis was within earshot. He turned, staring curiously at his fawning subordinate. 'Well, little Lev, so you swallowed that?'

Mekhlis affected to look astonished. 'What? What are you talking about?'

A secretary intervened. 'How do you mean, what? You are a Jew, aren't you?'

'No,' replied Mekhlis, 'I am not a Jew – I am a Communist.'[8] This tactful reply earned Mekhlis the lasting patronage of his master.

Stalin's malicious and offensive manner was noted at an early stage of his development. A friend of his youth noted that he saw 'everywhere and in everything only the negative, the bad side, and had no faith at all in the idealistic motives or attributes of mankind.' He reacted violently against the seminary where he was educated by proclaiming himself a convinced atheist, though in later life he displayed those deeply superstitious traits which often accompany an excessively exaggerated 'rationalist' attitude. All in all, his boorish manners earned him opprobrium from Tsarist and Bolshevik authorities alike, and caused deep offence to his closest colleagues.[9]

When his power became absolute and all around him displayed unstinting servility, Stalin remained discontented. He found it necessary time and again to humiliate his followers. 'His personal secretary Poskrebyshev was a frequent butt. On New Year's Eve Stalin rolled pieces of paper into little tubes and put them on Poskrebyshev's fingers. Then he lit them in place of New Year's candles. Poskrebyshev writhed in pain but did not dare take them off.' Stalin paid these little attentions to the highest dignitaries of the Soviet state; this frequently happened before foreign visitors, as if to emphasize the utter impotence of these lay figures whose master could raise and cast down at will. Stalin took pleasure in frightening the ageing President Kalinin so that cigarettes fell from the trembling fingers of the old man before a wondering Tito; 'Stalin laughed, and the expression on his face was like a satyr's'. At a public dinner he toasted Maisky, Soviet Ambassador to Britain, as 'our poet-diplomat'. The frightened Maisky explained to his British neighbour that 'our last poet-diplomat was murdered – that is the joke!'[10]

It was his pleasure to compel his followers to become incapably drunk at those barbaric feasts which formed the pinnacle of Soviet social life. He himself generally remained sober on these occasions – sometimes having water substituted for vodka in his glass – so that he could safely lure his followers into humiliating buffooneries or unguarded revelations. But away on his own at his villa near Sochi on the Black Sea he could on occasion indulge himself with a day-long stint of solitary inebriation. One disgusted visitor observed,

He drank glass after glass of wine, and after a while he began to dance. It was a gruesome sight, and the more he drank the more fearful he looked. The whole performance seemed like a bad dream. He bellowed with laughter, staggering and stamping round the cabin completely out of time with the lovely music. The general impression was not only coarse and vulgar, but so bizarre that it seemed like a kind of sinister threat. The most frightening thing of all was that despite his drunkenness, he still seemed sober enough to observe my reaction to his conduct. We spent the whole day . . . with the drunken dictator, who seemed to me more and more like some dreadful monster.[11]

The desire to humiliate and terrify extended even to his own family. There were stories that he actually murdered his wife Nadezhda Alliluyeva, though the weight of evidence suggests she was driven to suicide in 1932 by his cruelty to her personally, coupled with her belated discovery of the tyrannical nature of his rule over Russia.[12] His son by his first marriage, Yakov, lived a wretched life and succumbed to a tragic death – both directly caused by his father. The boy could do nothing right for his father, who referred to him in front of subordinates as 'my fool'. In 1928 or 1929 Yakov tried to commit suicide but, like poor Kostia Trepliov in *The Seagull*, only succeeded in wounding himself. Stalin 'used to make fun of him and sneer, "Ha! He couldn't even shoot straight!"' In 1941 Yakov, serving in the Red Army, was captured by the Germans. Attempts were made to exchange him for various German prisoners held by the Soviets, but each time these were blocked by Stalin himself. Abandoned by his father, the wretched Yakov died in his camp under tragic circumstances.[13]

Stalin's second son (by his second marriage) Vasily was born in 1920. In contrast to Yakov, he was accorded public recognition seemingly indicating parental favour. By his early twenties he had become a lieutenant-general; an unprecedented speed of promotion which could be based only on hereditary principles. There were signs that Vasily was proving an heir worthy of his father's affections: he was a malicious informer, arrogant and vindictive. Nicknamed 'the Tsarevich' by his service colleagues, he 'had a poor physique, a ramshackle bearing and the complexion of a debauchee . . . his vanity was colossal.' Introduced by his father to strong drink, he soon became an incorrigible inebriate and died an alcoholic at an early age. His father does not appear to have been desolated by the loss and, as Khrushchev heard, he 'used to whip him regularly and assigned Chekists to keep Vasya under surveillance'. (Yakov, too, is said to have suffered repeated beatings.)[14]

To his youngest child, the celebrated Svetlana, he could be gentle and affectionate. Yet he could also be extremely cruel, pulling her hair because she flagged in a dance he had compelled her to perform at one of the Kremlin drinking orgies. When she had the temerity later to fall in love with a *Jewish* film director, her father had him sent to Vorkuta. 'But I love him!' protested Svetlana in anguish.

> 'Love!' screamed my father, with a hatred of the very word I can scarcely convey. And for the first time in his life he slapped me across the face, twice. 'Just look, nurse, how low she's sunk!' He could no longer restrain himself. 'Such a war going on, and she's busy the whole time —— !' Unable to find any other expression, he used the coarse peasant word.

Stalin struck her again and again, ending with the jibe, 'Take a look at yourself. Who'd want you? You fool! He's got women all around him!'[15]

If this was Stalin's attitude to his own family, his treatment of his colleagues and subjects was scarcely likely to be better. Reposing no faith in human affections, he regarded fear as the only motive on which he could rely, and believed that 'every man has his price'. Caution and stealth personified, 'his every mood was deliberate and calculated. Every step he ever took, good or bad, was measured carefully'. The most trivial reactions of those around him were studied through narrowed eyes. In 1951 he was to declare in confidence: 'I trust no one, not even myself'. Small wonder that he could not bear to be alone, compelling his henchmen to keep him company at all hours.[16]

It is tempting to look to the circumstances of the dictator's childhood for some explanation of his warped and possibly paranoiac character.[17] Unfortunately the facts are too scanty to be able to form any satisfactory judgment, in large part because Stalin himself took elaborate measures to destroy the evidence. His parents were poor, but so were many others. His father had a savage temper, drank heavily and frequently beat his son – all faults which the son was himself one day to display. The boy was of small and unattractive appearance, and it seems likely that at an early age he acquired a deep sense of grievance and inferiority. It is not unusual for youths growing up in these circumstances to develop in much the same way as the young Stalin. He became increasingly bitter, cynical, authoritarian and atheistical – rejecting a parental God traditionally presented in the form of a father.[18]

In Lenin, Stalin found a man who could articulate with astonishing clarity the confused strivings and resentments that clouded his own spirit. Against unbelievers Lenin could unleash a flood of vituperative oratory which, in the confined world of the Bolsheviks, seemed unanswerable. The fragile shell of conviction of their own rectitude which protected the Party microcosm from external dangers was safe in the hands of such a Leader. Stalin's life task was firstly to make himself indispensable to his mentor, and secondly to prove worthy of continuing his life's work. Only in his latter years did he begin to show signs of chafing at his self-imposed discipleship.[19]

Stalin indeed owed everything to Lenin. It was his part in organizing (though not participating in) a violent bank robbery at Tiflis in 1907, during which numerous people were maimed and killed, that earned him the lasting approval of the Bolshevik leader. Stalin's ruthlessness was a quality Lenin relished, whilst also strongly approving the use of robberies ('expropriations') to increase Party funds. It is curious that Lenin seems to have been alone in liking and valuing Stalin; virtually all his other colleagues came to dislike him for the vicious, crude streak which they took to be the dominant factor in his character.

Latterly the working-class Stalin's brusque manners gave brief offence to the ailing Lenin who, like Trotsky, set great store by the middle-class etiquette of his upbringing. Stalin was 'rude' and 'ill-bred', he wrote; and Khrushchev in 1956 was to make much of these mild strictures, claiming that Lenin's 'acute mind . . . detected in Stalin in time those negative characteristics which resulted later in grave consequences'. It is difficult to take this view seriously, and the composer Shostakovich's sarcastic comment seems more to the point: ' . . . what kind of fault was rudeness? On the contrary, it was almost like valour.'[20]

Though Stalin's debt to Lenin was indeed immense, Stalin's recognition of that debt was almost exaggerated. To him Lenin remained the genius whose undying faith and brilliant intellect had enabled a tiny band of conspirators to overthrow the government of the largest country on earth and gain limitless power for themselves. Only Lenin had understood and mastered that historical cataclysm,

and Bolshevik power in Russia could be regarded as the personal
creation and inheritance of Lenin himself.[21] Throughout his rule
Stalin extolled Lenin as a giant of intellect and humanity, preserved
his widow and a few fortunate colleagues as relics,[22] and in short felt
that his own rough rule was legitimized by the *imprimatur* of
Lenin's creation and succession.

The ruthless streak in Stalin's character that had aroused Lenin's
admiration was dominant. Possibly his sadism stemmed from the
childhood beatings. To NKVD interrogators working on two fallen
rivals, Stalin, 'green with fury', yelled, 'Give them the works until
they come crawling to you on their bellies with confessions in their
teeth!' When he received reports of the efficacy of this approach,
'Stalin grinned and kept stroking his right moustache . . . he rose
from his chair and, rubbing his hands excitedly, said: "Bravo, boys!
Well done!"' During the war, when he learned of some officer's
mistake, 'Stalin used to ask, "Did you punch him in the snout? If he
does something like that again, punch him right in the snout!" As
for interrogations, his instructions were simple: "beat, beat and,
once again, beat!"'[23]

It was the thought that every day saw the world rid of more of his
enemies that eased Stalin's fears. In April 1943, a British visitor
remarked how 'he cracked his joke about the way he had disposed of
most of his fifth columnists. I have never seen Stalin in sunnier
temper.'

He prided himself on the guile with which he would lull a
victim's suspicions before striking the fatal blow. He would invite a
colleague to dinner, pay particular attention to him – and then order
him to be shot. As Bulganin once confessed to Khrushchev, 'it has
happened sometimes that a man goes to Stalin on his invitation as a
friend. And, when he sits with Stalin, he does not know where he
will be sent next – home or to jail.' This was precisely the feeling
Stalin wished to convey; only eternal vigilance could ensure survival. The normal links between individuals did not exist for him.
'Do you know what gratitude is?' a comrade once asked him. Stalin
took out his pipe and murmured reflectively, 'Oh yes, I know; I
know very well: it is a sickness suffered by dogs.'[24]

Clearly Stalin suffered in part from mental delusions, though
there was nothing irrational in imagining that the recurring and
increasing bloodbaths he authorized had earned him widespread
hatred. According to his daughter, by 1948 he 'was bitter, as bitter as

he could be against the whole world. He saw enemies everywhere. It had reached the point of being pathological, or persecution mania . . .' The more absurd the fantasy, the more real it seemed to him; and woe betide anyone who suggested otherwise.[25]

It was probably inevitable that Stalin would come to share his brother dictator in Berlin's fear and hatred of the 'universal Jew'. It was not so much a belief in the Jews' racial inferiority that agitated Stalin's breast, as a conviction that he was threatened by a vast conspiracy engineered by this strange and secretive people. Everywhere their hand was visible: they 'were trying to set up a Jewish state in the Crimea in order to wrest the Crimea from the Soviet Union and to establish an outpost of American imperialism'; they 'planted' a Jewish husband on his daughter Svetlana; they banded together under the guise of doctors for the purpose of poisoning the Leader of Peoples.

However, Stalin's antipathy to the Jews was not the all-absorbing obsession it was to Hitler. His anti-Semitism, which can be traced back to his early youth, was a reflection of his hatred for any group of people who remained unassimilated, unatomized under his rule. In Ronald Hingley's pithy apothegm, 'the mature Stalin was not narrowly biased against any specific section of humanity, for his sympathies were broadly and generously anti-human in general.' None the less his hatred lighted particularly heavily on this broken and persecuted people. The fact that he publicly condemned anti-Semitism as a crime indicates the more clearly that his own anti-Semitism stemmed from genuine prejudice, rather than an attempt to elicit popularity from anti-Semitic sections of the populace. Despite this, it was observed that popular anti-Semitism increased enormously during the period of Stalin's rule; partly in response to none too subtle indications of approval from above, and partly as an irrational reaction to the appalling tribulations of the age.[26]

On the official level persecution of the Jews ranged from the existence of a secret 'quota' in public (i.e. virtually all) employment, whereby strict limits were set on the number of Jews employable, and an outright purge of Jews from universities in 1953, to the imprisonment and torture of thousands of so-called Zionists in the notorious camps of GULAG. Eventually, Stalin prepared for a 'final solution' of the Jewish 'problem': every Jew in Russia was to be banished to the inhospitable wastes of North Kazakhstan. Only the Leader's death prevented this completion of Hitler's task. Perhaps

the most revolting aspect of this policy was the Soviet surrender of numerous anti-Nazi Jews to the Germans during the
period of Stalin's alliance with Hitler, described elsewhere in this
book.[27]

Stalin's obsessive belief in the presence of enemies, Jewish or
otherwise, all around him, sleeping or waking, strikingly recalls the
fears of our primitive ancestors, who believed themselves surrounded by persecuting demons.[28] Other delusions gathered thick and
fast in Stalin's cloudy conception. His vanity, leading him to
imagine himself the ultimate authority on subjects ranging from
grand strategy to musical composition, and from economics to philo-
logy, seems to indicate that a mind which was chillingly clear in its
central purpose contained less balanced facets.[29] Another weakness
was said to be a *penchant* for pornography; if true, this was yet
another taste shared with his friend and rival, Adolf Hitler.[30]

Many of Stalin's more morbid fancies may perhaps be seen as
stemming from a pronounced inferiority complex. His diminutive
and unattractive appearance has already been noted,[31] and also the
wretched circumstances of his childhood. One may doubt Roy
Medvedev's theory that Stalin felt out-distanced by his 'brilliant'
Bolshevik comrades;[32] they may have been able to recite impromptu
longer screeds from the Marxian scriptures, but their understanding
of men and affairs was greatly inferior. Nevertheless, his ferocious
jealousies, intellectual pretensions and obsessive vanity point to
deep-rooted if unconscious feelings of inadequacy.[33]

Long before the outbreak of the Second World War Stalin acquired
absolute power in Russia unparalleled in history. Unfettered by any
restrictions of religion, morality, law or custom, his total freedom of
manoeuvre made even Hitler's appear almost law-abiding.[34] The
Soviet Union possessed a legislative body, a constitution and a code
of laws, but these had literally no function whatever, serving merely
to bolster the self-deception of the ruler and his Marxist theocracy;
to persuade some members of the public that a substance of legality
existed in Russia; and, above all, to gull foreign observers into complacent acceptance of Soviet claims and aims.

The endless circular Politburo doctrinal discussions of Lenin's
time came to a swift close. A former official in the Politburo Secretariat has provided a pithy account of the improved fashion of conducting affairs under the Boss (*khozyain*):

The meetings of the Politbureau began by Stalin reading out the agenda. After that he often talked for hours with Beria in Georgian. Nobody understood what they were saying. Then he announced in Russian the resolutions to be adopted. Everyone agreed. End of meeting.[35]

Stalin took an equally succinct view of the importance of the Communist Party of the Soviet Union. In 1923, when an important issue was about to be put to their vote, a GPU report suggested that the majority would be opposed to the leadership. Kamenev ventured to ask Stalin his opinion. 'Do you know, comrades,' replied the Leader quietly, 'what I think about this business? I think this: who votes in the Party, and how, is of no importance; what is extremely important is who *counts* the votes, and how.'[36]

The only limitations on Stalin's power were natural restrictions of time and space; politically he could do as he pleased. The system was so centralized that, as a former NKVD officer explained in 1938,

. . . if you take the last worker in the Soviet Union, there are never more than three persons between him and Stalin, either through the Party or the administration. A worker usually knows the director of his works. The factory director knows the chairman of the Chief Administration and he knows the People's Commissar. And the Commissar is in direct touch with Stalin. It's the same in the Party. The ordinary rank and file Communist is in connexion with his district secretary, and all the district secretaries receive their orders from the Area Committee. And in many cases the area secretaries are in direct touch with Stalin. Others have to go via the Vice-Secretary of the Central Committee in Moscow. And so you see that there are never more than three people between the simplest people in the towns and Stalin.

The speaker, an NKVD lieutenant named Brande, went on to explain that

. . . at least once a week I saw the head of the Kharkov NKVD and he went to Moscow at least once every two months to see Yezhov [Head of the NKVD]. The heads of all the districts meet in Moscow to receive instructions from the Commissar, namely Yezhov. They were also in touch with him on a direct line if they wanted to speak to him about anything in between their meetings.

Yezhov, of course, was in constant touch with Stalin. Now you
see . . . that there were only two men between me and Stalin?

It was in this way that a hint from Stalin to Yezhov in the middle of
August had resulted in prisoners being beaten by their interrogators
in gaols throughout Russia.[37]

Stalin built up in his early years of power a personal secretariat,
distinct from the Secretariat of the Central Committee, by means of
which he could control and check all state organs, including the
political police.[38] This personal secretariat was headed by a little,
round-headed, bald flunkey named Poskrebyshev, whose fawning
manner and unscrupulous nature will be familiar to readers of *The
First Circle*.[39] No state department or official bore any authority
which was not immediately under Stalin's eye; even the working
timetable of officialdom was governed by the dictator's peculiar
working hours. A former high official of the *Sovnarkom* explained:

Stalin normally begins his day around eleven in the morning,
working steadily until four or five. He then usually knocks off
until ten or eleven in the evening, remaining at work until three,
four or even later in the morning; officialdom in the capital regulated its existence by the eccentric Stalin clock . . . The rest of the
country, being in continuous telephone contact with headquarters
and sensitive to its moods, also reflected this schedule.

Various theories circulated concerning the cause of this odd timetable. It seems most probable that it was his confessed fear of being
alone which made Stalin wish to keep his colleagues working
around him into the small hours.[40]

Stalin could tolerate not even the faintest semblance of independent thought in his subordinates. Life at his court was a continuing nightmare of fear and tedium, with its endless round of
surrealist discussions, drunken cavortings and infantile film shows.
Foreign visitors saw how all fell silent as the master spoke, and even
the bravest of his generals visibly cringed with fear in his presence.[41]
Small wonder, when no one could ever be certain that his invitation
to court was not a prelude to execution, torture or consignment to a
slave-camp. Usually the violence was restricted to crude horseplay,
but at others the tyrant could be heard shrieking out in harsh
Georgian accents that culprits should be bound in chains, beaten to a
pulp and ground to powder. Yet despite these terrifying scenes,

senior colleagues dared not absent themselves lest their fate be sealed behind their backs.[42]

Such, in outline, was the nature of Stalin's government in Russia, where preservation of the despot's powers had become the guiding purpose of the entire state apparatus.[43] It was the mantle of Marxism which gave it legitimacy in the eyes of Stalin and his (predominantly Western) admirers. Stripped of that threadbare covering it appears simply the vehicle of one man's unstable neuroses: lust for power, destructiveness, sadism, suspicion and material greed.

It was Bernard Shaw, whose admiration veered from one dictator to another, who observed that he found it hard to believe that Stalin was 'a vulgar gangster'.[44] In fact there are numerous indications that, but for opportunities offered to men of his type by the Revolution, he would have been restricted to the paths of ordinary crime. It was the Erivan bank robbery that raised Stalin so high in Lenin's estimation. Not long after that, the Tsarist authorities confined him in Bailov prison, overlooking the Caspian. A fellow-prisoner noted that 'Koba' ignored the unwritten rule that political prisoners should not associate with common criminals. He was instead 'always seen in the company of cutthroats, political blackmailers, robbers, and gun slingers'. His closest friends were two brothers named Sakvarelidze, sentenced for forging five-hundred rouble banknotes.[45]

In 1912 Stalin was exiled to Vologda. Later, he recalled fondly how he there 'hung around mostly with the criminals . . . These criminals were nice, salt-of-the-earth fellows. But there were lots of rats among the political convicts. They at once organized a comrades' court and put me on trial for drinking with the criminal convicts, which they charged was an offense.'[46] It may well be that the indiscriminate mixing of political and criminal prisoners in the camps of GULAG presided over by Stalin stemmed from a desire to avenge the insults of 1912. As the mixing formed a universal rule, it seems certain that it would have been authorized by the Leader himself. It was the persecutions the 'politicals' suffered at the hands of genuine criminals which, by common consent, formed the most unbearable aspect of an already tortured existence.[47]

Once in power, Stalin's predilection for gangsters remained as strong as ever. Boris Shumiatsky, pre-war head of the Soviet film industry, noted his fondness for Hollywood gangster films. He was also fond of playing with guns; occasionally to the peril of his companions. Discussing Molotov's visit to the United States in 1942, his thoughts at once flew to the legendary capital of violent crime; the Foreign Commissar, he jocularly remarked, had sneaked off 'to Chicago, where the other gangsters live'.[48]

Stalin's belief in the efficacy of 'expropriations' had not ceased when the Party gained power in Russia. In 1937 OGPU agents in Republican Spain arranged the theft of the entire Spanish gold reserves. The bullion was secretly shipped to Odessa, where special GPU units transported it to Moscow. Stalin held a magnificent banquet in the Kremlin to exult over this skilful seizure of some sixty million pounds sterling.[49]

An even more extraordinary example of straightforward crime perpetrated by the Soviet Government received worldwide press attention in the early 1930s. In 1928 Stalin launched the first Five Year Plan, which was designed to force through industrialization in order to make Soviet Russia a first-rate military power. However, the country was exhausted, poverty-stricken and bankrupt, and it was necessary to build up massive reserves of foreign currency and gold. Thousands of citizens were arrested on various pretexts and dispatched to work as slaves in the inhospitable gold-mining region of Kolyma,[50] though this was clearly insufficient as a short-term solution.

Sweeping measures were adopted by the OGPU to extort gold and jewellery from hoards, for the most part tiny, held by the population at large. Anyone suspected of concealing a gold watch or a wedding ring was dragged off to a GPU gaol and subjected to tortures until he disgorged (assuming he had anything to disgorge). Few were able to resist the horrors of the *parilka* ('sweat room') and the 'conveyor'. Those who did soon succumbed to the next stage in Soviet refinement: watching their own children being tortured before them. Jews in particular were suspected of concealing their wealth, and widespread anti-Semitism amongst GPU agents gave them especial pleasure in inflicting pain and humiliation on the *zhidovskaya morda*, 'Yid snouts'. An aged Jew was forced to drink his own urine before a circle of jeering louts. Others suffered hideous torments as an inducement to make them inform on their co-religionists.[51]

It was scarcely likely that Russia's economic problems would be solved by methods of extortion reminiscent of the reign of King John in England, and Stalin's thoughts soon turned to a new venture. In May 1928 hundred-dollar bills began flooding into banks all over the world, and it was not long before experts discovered them to be forgeries. For some time criminals in the West were suspected, though the notes' quality and bulk were such that it was difficult to see how even the largest criminal network could have sufficient resources for the operation at its disposal. The police forces of a dozen countries set to work, and it was not long before it was established that the bills came from Russia. A private bank, Sass and Martini, had been bought in Berlin by agents acting for the Soviets, through which millions of dollars' worth of forged notes were funnelled to the West. Western Communists and other criminals organized the distribution, but despite extreme skill used in printing the bills the whole scheme was detected and brought to a halt by the American, German, Polish and other police forces.

This wild endeavour to place the Soviet Union's finances on a sound footing was clearly doomed from the start. GRU (Military Intelligence) officers responsible for implementing it were highly sceptical of any prospect of success, but as the scheme clearly emanated from Stalin himself they had no choice but to try their luck. Perhaps the idea germinated from conversations recalled with the Sakvarelidze forgers, Stalin's companions in Bailov gaol sixteen years before. Of symbolic interest was the extensive employment of Chicago gangsters as intermediaries in this operation, thus opening indirect links between Joseph Stalin and his able contemporary, Al 'Scarface' Capone.[52]

It might be said, therefore, that Stalin was quite literally possessed of a criminal mentality, and that the distinction between himself and Capone essentially derived from the difference in opportunities offered by the respective societies in which they operated. That such a man as Stalin should gain power in Russia is not very surprising, given the atmosphere and circumstances of post-revolutionary society. The philosophy of terror and the means of its application had been bequeathed to him by Lenin,[53] and the parallel Brown Revolution in Germany had thrown up a similarly sadistic and unscrupulous leader.

What is extraordinary is that such a state led by such a man, whose crimes ranged from the sordid to the spectacular, could arouse enthusiastic admiration from large numbers of well-educated people living safely outside the aegis of his power, all of whom had extensive opportunity of understanding the realities of Soviet rule. Crude and palpably detectable efforts were made on occasion to conceal the truth from Western visitors,[54] but it was impossible that barbarism practised on such a scale over a quarter of a century should not have been easily recognized for what it was.

In fact it was for not a few the cruelty and violence that formed the attraction. Bolshevik ruthlessness suggested to many, as it did to Stephen Spender, that 'the destructive element' was 'the way'. In Europe and America Soviet Communism aroused a neo-religious fervour amongst Communists and fellow-travellers, and even their opponents frequently conceded that harsh and firm rule was a necessity *for Russians*. All this stemmed from a multiplicity of emotions: anti-capitalist nostalgia, the fears and guilt of middle-class intellectuals, the longing for one simple answer to the world's problems, the appeal of what was 'new' and 'young'. The existence of an idealized Soviet Union justified the chiliastic faith of young men and women who found themselves heirs to a vulnerable middle class.[55]

On one occasion Litvinov warned Stalin of the dangerous effect his more public cruelties might have on Western democratic opinion. 'Never mind, they'll swallow it', murmured the dictator sardonically.[56]

III
Life at the Top

To the world at large Stalin was assiduous to present the image of a tirelessly industrious leader, content with the barest of material goods. In 1931 an American journalist secured an interview. He was struck by the plain office where the dictator worked: 'quiet, orderly, unhurried but efficient'. His thoughts wandered on as he waited. 'Imagine what the ante-chambers of the former rulers were like, the pomp and grandeur, the courtiers and generals, and look how simple all this is! Stalin may be inaccessible to reporters and diplomats, but I should judge . . . that he is accessible enough to his own Party people.'[1]

Some of Stalin's tastes – his clothes and favourite films, for example – were simple enough in all conscience. But if Western admirers of Stalin could have peeped behind the scenes they might have been strangely surprised. In 1919 Mr and Mrs Stalin had moved into a spacious country house near Usovo, about twenty miles from Moscow.

> The house was remodelled in the twenties, and under Stalin's management the place was transformed into a thriving, well-kept estate with various outbuildings, gardens, orchards, a turkey run, and a duck pond. In order to remain active outside the home, Nadya [Stalin's wife] relied heavily on nursemaids and private tutors to care for her son, Vasily, and her daughter, Svetlana.[2]

These pickings represented a modest beginning. By the 1930s Stalin's wealth had swollen beyond recognition. Apart from the Zuvalovo *dacha* described above, Stalin acquired another at Kuntsevo, to which he moved in preference. There was yet another near Kuntsevo, built by the Soviet architect Miron Merzhanov. But three houses can seem constricted when one has a stepchild, servants, house-guests . . . so, as his daughter relates,

. . . my father had two other places outside Moscow . . . They
were Lipki, an ancient estate on the Dimitrov Highway with a
pond, a wonderful house and an enormous park lined with tall
lindens, and Semyonovskaya, a fine old estate that had a house
built just before the war, large, spring-fed ponds dug by serfs in
the old days, and extensive woods . . . My father seldom visited
either place, sometimes not for a year at a time, but the staff always
expected him at any moment and were in a perpetual state of
readiness. And if the motorcade actually did take off from
Kuntsevo in the direction of Lipki, pandemonium would break
loose there and everyone from the cook to the guard at the gate,
from the waitress to the commandant, would be seized by panic.

Five country houses and a suite in the Kremlin were very well, but
there were holidays to consider too. His favourite architect,
Merzhanov, built Stalin 'several *dachas* in the south' – it was hard to
remember how many. By 1937 there were at least four, and then
there was the luxury villa near Gagri, presented to the dictator by
Beria, much as Cardinal Wolsey gave Hampton Court to Henry VIII.
It is not clear whether this is identical with Stalin's magnificent
mountain residence at Abkhasia, which was suspected of being an
imitation of Hitler's 'Eagle's Nest' at Berchtesgaden.[3] Unlike foreign
statesmen, or his predecessors the Tsars, Stalin rarely entertained
foreign dignitaries, and all these mansions and villas were kept for
the private amusement of himself and his cronies. Later, after 1946,
another '*dacha* was built at Novy Afon, another not far from
Sukhumi, and a whole cluster were built on Lake Mitsa. Another
dacha was built in the Valdai Hills in Novgorod Province in the
north'.[4]

In 1935 a visitor to the *dacha* at Sochi noted the great park protected by GPU troops.

Dwelling houses for them, and for the servants, abutt on the
driveway just inside the gates. Next, as you ascend the hill, comes
the garage, with room for twenty-five or thirty cars. Higher up and
nearer the home of Stalin are three villas for the Dictator's guests,
equipped with tennis courts, squash courts, a special house for
billiards, etc.

Infinitely more luxurious was a great country house at Zelyony Myss
on the Black Sea. Stalin

. . . carved out a vast park area with a tremendous sea front, permanently closed it to the public, and there built another home. This estate with its landscaped parks and preserves is kept a careful secret from the Russian people. I cannot quote figures on the exact cost of landscaping, building, and the like, but from the expanse of the grounds I doubt if Hearst's San Simeon is much more costly than the palace of Zelyony Myss.

All these great homes were magnificently furnished and equipped, containing 'everything from billiard rooms to motion-picture halls and stables of thoroughbred horses'.[5]

Despite this apparent superfluity of space, Stalin's son Vasily found, like many growing youngsters, he needed a place of his own. This was easily arranged in 'the freest country on earth'. Vasily denounced Marshal Novikov, head of the Red Air Force, to the NKVD, and then moved into Novikov's manor as the Marshal departed for prison. The furnishings, however, did not come up to the expectations of the 'Tsarevich', and had later to be lavishly supplemented with looted property from East Germany.[6]

Stalin disposed of a fleet of foreign cars, Rolls-Royces, Packards, Cadillacs and Lincolns, with chauffeurs standing by, day and night. He lavished millions of roubles on the public staging of operas, concerts and films which took his fancy, appearing himself as a regular 'first-nighter' in the former Imperial box. In short, there was no whim, however extravagant or eccentric, which the state budget could not be brought to indulge.[7]

It should not be imagined that Stalin's wealth consisted of money in the bank. His salary was in fact quite modest. It was just that there was no limit to the facilities he could obtain *without* money. 'Everything he needed – his food, his clothing, his *dachas* and his servants – was paid for by the government. The secret police had a division that existed specially for this purpose and it had a bookkeeping department of its own. God only knows how much it cost and where the money all went,' writes Stalin's daughter Svetlana. 'My father certainly didn't know.' Stalin had no idea of the value of money he rarely saw, and continued to think in terms of the value of pre-Revolutionary coinage.[8] It was there if he needed it, however. Once he pulled open a drawer in his wife's room: it was literally stuffed with ten-, twenty- and thirty-rouble notes.[9] No one was ever able to calculate Stalin's effective income, but the annual account came to an 'astronomical' figure. 'Maintaining Stalin cost the state much more than the American people pay for their President, and it may not have been much more expensive to support Nicholas II,' writes Roy Medvedev.[10]

The fact is that Stalin virtually owned the Soviet Union in as absolute a sense as property can acquire. On holiday by the Black Sea, he expressed a desire for a certain type of Georgian fish-dish. The NKVD obtained what he needed by dropping their grenades into a lake where the fish bred, destroying the livelihood of a neighbouring village. When the villagers objected they were all deported to the care of the GULAG authorities in Kazakhstan. A blind man's dog awoke the despot with its barking; it and its master were instantly put to death.[11] It seems clear that he regarded Russia as a personal fief to dispose of as he wished. No real property rights existed in the Soviet Union except Stalin's; he could literally do as he chose with anything. When Hitler's invasion appeared to threaten this comfortable state of affairs, Stalin lamented in anguish that 'All which Lenin created we have lost forever.'[12] The inheritance was in danger of being stolen.

The Marxist belief that inequalities would be eradicated under a pure Communist government was rejected in Soviet practice soon after the Revolution, and did not survive very long in theory. 'Egalitarianism has nothing in common with Marxian socialism,' stated Stalin in 1931,[13] and the structure of Soviet society already revealed the accuracy of this view. Those who had sacrificed so much and so long saw no reason why they should not receive some material consideration for their services.

Trotsky had by 1922 installed his parents 'in a large yellow-painted *dacha* in the beautiful Neskuchny Park near the Moskva River. The house had belonged to a well-to-do Russian before the Revolution . . . ' Voroshilov, Commissar for War, owned a big, three-storeyed *dacha* near Moscow, with an immense library. In common with other Soviet leaders he received a free copy of every book published in the Soviet Union; not necessarily an enviable privilege. Either this or another of the Marshal's homes was a huge mansion modelled on the late Tsar's palace at Livadia. Kaganovich, Head of the Central Control Commission, had an equally palatial residence, but it was 'the home of a rich parvenu, full of ugly expensive objects and palm trees in buckets standing in various corners. Kaganovich himself was loud and coarse. He looked like a very fat landowner.'

The other luminaries of the Party hierarchy maintained a similarly high standard of living. Krylenko, the State Prosecutor who preceded Vyshinsky as the Fouquier-Tinville of the Russian Revolution, had taken over Prince Gagarin's splendid mansion, but his luxurious existence appeared modest in comparison with that of the Soviet writer Maxim Gorki. *He* possessed a fine Moscow home and two great villas in the country. 'At his country villas his favourite flowers, imported from abroad, were planted. He smoked special cigarettes which were ordered for him in Egypt. Any book from any country was delivered to him at his first request.'[14]

As Kamenev, Chairman of the People's Council for Control and Defence, sped past the street-long Moscow bread queues in his magnificent Rolls-Royce, the éclat of his life-style was eclipsed only by the patrician arrogance of Zinoviev, President of the Communist International. A foreign observer remembered 'an incident in the summer of 1921 when the departure of a train in which I was going from Petrograd to Moscow was delayed at the order of Zinovyev just because the schedule was inconvenient for him, and two coaches crammed full with passengers were disconnected because Zinovyev insisted that his heavy parlor car be attached to the train.' At Moscow the passengers' descent was further delayed as the Party satrap was in no hurry to rise from his couch. Later he could refresh himself in Karl Radek's luxurious suite in the Kremlin Palace, described by a former Kremlin official.[15]

Stalin's close friend Abel Yenukidze had become quite satiated with the grandeur of his existence. What is he interested in? his secretary was once asked. 'Oh, he loves to compare how he lives with the way the czars used to live.'[16] It would be unjust to suppose that the Communist leaders were slow in acquiring their elevated tastes. Before the Revolution Anastas Mikoyan led strikes and ran study groups for workers in oil refineries at Baku and Batoum owned by an industrialist named Zubalov. Immediately after the Revolution Mikoyan moved into Zubalov's recently vacated mansion. Svetlana Stalin recalled happy visits to the new owners.

The Mikoyans' house to this day is exactly as the exiled owners left it. On the porch is a marble statue of a dog, the former owner's favorite. Inside are marble statues imported from Italy. The walls are hung with Gobelins, and downstairs the windows are of stained glass. The garden, the park, the tennis court, the

orangery, stables and greenhouses are all exactly as they have
always been.[17]

The Commissars for State Security, whose vigilance protected all
this wealth and luxury, lived no less grandly. Yagoda's flat was
'beautifully . . . furnished in the Asiatic style, with carpets on the
walls, divans and thick rugs on the floor'. As for his successor Beria,
his mansion was 'sumptuous, immense. The big white house stood
among tall spruces. The furniture, the wallpaper, the lamps had all
been made to the architect's designs . . . '[18]

The wealth and privilege of this oligarchy were almost as limitless
as those of Stalin, with the grimly precarious proviso that they remained in the Boss's good graces. This indeed lent a bitter taste to
all the merry-making,[19] and may in part account for the grossness of
these parvenus' private pleasures, which resembled markedly the
life-style of successful gangsters, prevented by the nature of their
trade from enjoying the fruits of their expropriations too publicly. In
consequence, those who had so fortunately fallen into 'Lenin's
inheritance' displayed no reticence in enjoying the good life.

In the 1920s and 1930s details of this epicurean way of life were
kept reasonably secret from hostile critics, but with the wartime
alliance many foreign visitors were enabled to witness the new class
at its pleasures. The American General Deane arrived in Moscow in
October 1943. He came from a country relatively untouched by the
privations of a war economy, but nothing he had seen at home prepared him for the wonders of a Soviet luncheon.

I had never before seen such an elaborate table service. The center-
pieces were huge silver bowls containing fresh fruit specially procured from the Caucasus. It was only at such functions that one
saw fresh fruit in Moscow. Beautiful cut glass ran the gamut from
tall thin champagne glasses, through those for light and heavy red
and white wines, to the inevitable vodka glass, midway in size
between our liqueur and cocktail glasses, without which no
Russian table is set. There were bottles the entire length of the
table from which the glasses could be and were filled many times.
Interspersed among the bottles were silver platters of Russian
zakouska, including fresh large-grained dark caviar, very black
pressed caviar of the consistency of tar, huge cucumber pickles,
raw salmon and sturgeon, slices of not very well cooked ham,

salami, chocolates in bright-coloured tinfoil, and innumerable other delicacies that the Russians must have in order to work up an appetite for the meal to come. Knives, forks, and spoons were of gold, and service plates of the finest china heavily encrusted with gold. The whole spectacle was amazing and called to mind the banquet scene in Charles Laughton's movie *Henry VIII*.

Luncheon was an endless succession of courses, starting with a heavy borsch, progressing through a delicious fish in hollandaise sauce, a roast, and a salad, and ending with a huge architectural monstrosity made of ice cream which presented a series of interesting and different problems as it was attacked successively by the guests on its way around the table.[20]

'All very nice', as the English General Jacob commented on witnessing a similar display in 1942, 'except that one remembers that the vast majority of the population are practically starving'.[21] General Deane's gargantuan feast was in no way exceptional, as many similar accounts testify. From Stalin himself[22] downwards, members of the Soviet élite appear to have found these orgies of drinking and gorging the pinnacles of pleasure in their pampered existence.[23] Nor was their enjoyment tarnished by reflections on the source of all this conspicuous waste. The magnificent salmon, for example, that formed so splendid a feature of the Party leaders' dining-tables, could have told a tale. At Balagannoye Camp in the Kolyma complex of GULAG camps, women slaves dressed in sacks worked twelve to fourteen hours a day gutting salmon and extracting the red caviar. 'The hands of the women at the tables are red and swollen; the skin on the back of their hands is cracked and the salt burns in the cuts.' Yet they eagerly volunteered for this back-breaking work as, unlike fellow-prisoners starving in the nearby gold-mines, they were occasionally able to eat (illicitly of course) pieces of salmon heart or liver.[24]

If a commissar chose to dine out, he could satiate himself to exhaustion on a meal as splendid as any enjoyed by a Chicago millionaire, and infinitely more so than a duke dining in wartime Britain. At the Hotel Aragvi in Moscow, dinner 'cost forty-five dollars a plate in American money' in 1943. Some idea of relative standards can be gauged from the fact that a meal at the comparable Hotel Moskva cost 1,400 roubles – to those who could afford it: a hairdresser at the same time was earning 250 roubles a month.[25]

Life for the rich could be very sweet indeed. There was the GPU-
run Moscow Casino, where wealthy Party chiefs, scented and expensively dressed, could gamble away their surplus wealth. At the
theatre a Scottish visitor marvelled at the 'new proletarian aristocracy' in the auditorium, 'immaculate in uniforms and neat blue
suits, their wives resplendent in sable and redolent of Soviet scent'.
At the Hotel Metropole one could indulge every night in rich food,
dance to the music of 'a jazz band of symphony orchestra proportions', or sit back with a drink in the bar listening to one of
Russia's only surviving gypsy choruses. As couples moved rhythmic-
ally around the great ballroom there was occasionally a shout of
laughter as a man, drunker than ordinary, tumbled into the ornamental fish-pond in the centre.[26]

Immediately after the Revolution the privileged class of Bolsheviks found no difficulty in 'socializing' (as the popular expression
ran in the Soviet Union)[27] the property of the late Tsar and nobility.
Domestic servants of the old regime were pressed back into service.
The average Party bigwig 'was served by a parlour maid, a cook and,
if the children were still small enough, a governess'. Naturally this
list does not include the below-stairs servants who cleaned the rent-
free flats and houses. Outside, 'in the Moscow parks swarms of
children from the Kremlin's upper circles were to be seen accompanied by governesses who talked to them in French or English.'[28]

These trained domestics could be relied upon to maintain standards. In 1936, at a ball arranged by the NKVD,

> Men in dinner jackets and uniforms and women in long evening
> dresses and operetta costumes were dancing to the music of a jazz
> band. Many women wore masks and were dressed in wonderfully
> decorative costumes . . . borrowed from the wardrobe of the
> Moscow Grand Opera. The tables were covered with bottles of
> champagne, liquors and wine. Outcries, boisterous laughter and
> giggling drowned the strains of music. One colonel of the frontier
> guards shouted in drunken ecstasy: 'Oh boys that's real life!
> Thanks to Stalin for our happy childhood!'[29]

Not all the new class's pursuits were as refined as this. Bernard Shaw
pictured the leadership as bound 'by vows of poverty and chastity'.[30]
Their poverty-stricken existence has already been noted, and chastity
would have to be a very elastic term indeed if applied to the Soviet
leadership. A few excesses here and there were unlikely to disturb

Stalin, whose successive Commissars of State Security kept bulky files on such activities, just as Heydrich was doing in contemporary Germany. Yagoda himself, Head of the GPU political police, organized orgies at his Moscow home, whilst his successor Beria made a speciality of drugging young girls – many of them still at school – and raping them. In Khrushchev's words, he was 'a really awful man, a beast, to whom nothing was sacred.' Rudzutak, a member of the Politburo with similar tastes, 'in 1932 got the thirteen-year-old daughter of the second secretary of the Moscow Committee drunk and then raped her.' Kuibyshev, Stalin's friend, kidnapped the intoxicated wife of a Party colleague and disappeared with her for three days. Marshal Budenny, whose blunders cost untold Russian lives in 1941, murdered his wife by shooting her in the back, for which he was pardoned by Stalin a week later. The old Civil War hero kept numerous mistresses and raped a succession of secretaries. This type of higher morality was widespread in the Party, as scandals such as that at Smolensk in 1929, at Irkutsk, Artemovsk, Sochi and elsewhere sporadically revealed. Any political party or bureaucracy will have its rotten apples, but the Soviet Communist Party seems to have had a great deal more than its fair share. No organization in modern times enjoyed such absolute power, and none was so absolutely corrupted. The NKVD in particular attracted types destitute of any sort of morality or honour.[31]

Before the Bolshevik *coup d'état* in October 1917, Lenin had repeatedly stressed that one of the major advances of the future Communist state would be the 'withering away' of the bureaucracy characteristic of capitalist states. Administration could be performed by anyone, and citizens would in turn take on the tasks of government, receiving exactly the pay accorded to manual workers. Once in power, virtually all Lenin's promises and prognostications became dead letter,[32] but none so swiftly as the idea of equal pay for rulers and ruled. A decision of the Central Committee to award its members salaries twice as high as those of Petrograd master craftsmen actually occurred just *before* the Revolution, and from then on the new class never looked back.[33] Officially, salaries continued to be regulated at a level that could be considered relatively modest, but for the discrepancy with Marxist ideals and Lenin's promises. But by the end of the 1920s 'a thin layer of privileged people gradually came into being – with "packets" (cash payments secretly provided for officials to top up their salaries), country villas, and cars.' Living in increasing luxury in the midst of a population descending ever deeper from poverty to starvation, they 'justified themselves by saying that, as people engaged in building a new order, it would have been sheer hypocrisy for them to deny themselves their due as incumbents of power.'[34]

Commendably free from hypocrisy, the rush of the new élite to obtain their share of the good things of life became a stampede. Theirs was not only the natural greed of a parvenu middle class unfettered by moral or legal restraints, but also the knowledge that at any moment they could be snatched from their luxury flats and villas to find themselves in a cramped *sobachnik* cell in the Lubianka, at the mercy of a GPU interrogator. There was a desperate scramble for the best noblemen's country and town houses[35] and, a little lower down the scale, to obtain sinecure posts with comfortable salaries. A professional factory manager in charge of a printing works in 1926 found that he had to maintain eighty-four Party parasites who had there found a comfortable nook for themselves.[36]

Roy Medvedev suggests that 'the test of power' was especially hard 'at a time when the Party acquired almost unlimited power'.[37] Many people might wonder whether it was desirable to apply such a test where the result must be so predictable. Much the same characteristics were exhibited in Germany after the parallel Brown Revolution. National Socialism was quite as idealistic as Soviet Marxism, but there too the Party Comrades felt entitled to some reward for their services. Factories and businesses were inundated with ill-qualified Nazis demanding and receiving pleasant postings. Many were as incompetent as their Soviet counterparts, but it was difficult to turn down a man who laid a revolver on your desk. The harassment and expulsion of Jews from businesses conveniently left many a vacant post for a Party stalwart to fill. Like Lenin, Hitler complained loudly about the over-opulent life-style of many of his followers, and like Lenin he felt obliged to watch them become richer and fatter: 'how could I otherwise meet the justified desires of my party comrades for some recompense for their years of inhuman struggle?' Hitler and Stalin shared a shrewd perception that this newly-gained wealth and privilege bound the Party to its Leader by links of gratitude and guilt.[38] The Jews in Germany corresponded broadly to the Russian propertied classes in this paradigm; dogma and self-advancement became inextricably intermingled in the motivation of those who supplanted them. A German Jew dismissed a workman from his factory for Communist propaganda. Came the Revolution, the Communist joined the Nazis and triumphantly entered the factory at the head of a band of brown-shirted SA.[39]

The wealth of the new rich did not consist only of fine houses, furniture, cars, servants, special facilities for the theatre, special shops, Black Sea rest homes;[40] nor only in the satiety of untrammelled power – the power to take over an orphanage for private use, or 'expropriate' a non-Party member's dog, nor even the enjoyment of virtual immunity from prosecution for civil crime.[41] There was also the intangible but delightful pleasure of belonging to a chic élite, with its precisely-gauged hierarchy of ranks. There were uniforms, titles and the relative size of Stalin's portrait hanging in office or home to indicate valued status.[42] Gradually, too, this new bourgeoisie was transforming itself into an hereditary class.[43] Stalin's daughter Svetlana attended a school for privileged children where precautions to preserve her special position were so rigorous as to make her life a misery. Her brother Vasily attended School Number 19, in the same street as the British Embassy in Moscow. Only the children of the very privileged were entitled to attend this Soviet Eton. One of them was to recall later,

> I revelled in the society of those boys. Their manner was arrogant and swaggering and they showed the conviction of personal power as though they had been suckled to it . . . They were cruel and egocentric. But they were good company, for I was one of them . . . Every pupil considered himself immeasurably superior to his teachers by virtue of the fact that his father occupied a high rank in the service . . . We had a fine time. We danced, flirted with girls, went to the theatre, had parties and enjoyed ourselves tremendously. The difficulties, the miseries and the burden of the common people were no concern of ours. We were the heirs of the universe, and drank in all the best that life had to offer our senses and in the way of ever new pleasures.[44]

So great were the luxuries and privileges enjoyed by the Party chosen they might have seemed to belong to a different race from that 95 per cent of the population of the USSR which lived in conditions of unimaginable destitution and suffering. The Communist leadership in fact lived like an occupying power in a conquered land. When the central government moved to Kuibyshev after the German attack on Moscow, half the population of the city was simply driven out to provide room for the ruling few and their accompanying horde of relations, servants and police protectors. A Pole travelling in Russia that year encountered a group of Party officials on a train:

> They were wearing well-cut clothes of good-quality material as well as expensive furs. They had with them elegant travelling bags, colourful woollen blankets, costly jewellery, gold watches, silver cigarette-cases, up-to-date cameras, Thermos flasks and gramophones complete with excellent records. During the journey, they helped themselves to wine, chocolate and high-grade tinned goods.

They were accompanied by a posse of servants. The Pole's thoughts flew irresistibly to less fortunate, non-Party, Russians.

> The sight of a man lying under a wall in the street and starving to death is by no means uncommon in Russia. I drew the attention of a militiaman in Kotlas to one such case. 'Well, what of it? Let him die!' was the answer I got.

Occasionally the masters of the Russian soil could show glimmerings of sympathy for those doomed to a less fortunate social position. As Party Secretary Ivan Rumyantsev travelled in state through the Smolensk countryside he would amuse himself and his bored retainers by scattering kopecks to be scrambled for by children and peasants. During the war Victor Kravchenko found himself on a long train journey with Comrade Borodin, a Member of the Supreme Soviet. Travelling first class, the great man invited Kravchenko to join him for gourmet meals served by obsequious orderlies, at which the two men played cards, discussed the war, the scenery, and 'the relative virtues of various Caucasian wines and other such problems'. 'Only the occasional sight of hungry, half-naked homeless children at stations spoiled our journey. At one station Borodin tossed some well-gnawed chicken bones out of the window. Instantly hungry children pounced on these treasures, fighting furiously for every scrap.' There happened to be a delegation of British trade-unionists on the same train, and Kravchenko could not help wondering what was their impression of this interesting scene.[45]

When Trotsky was travelling into exile at Alma-Ata in 1928, his enormous baggage-train is said to have excited the attention of watching peasants, who cried out that a great lord must be passing by. The story may be a Stalinist fabrication, but there can be no doubt that the unprecedented contrast between wealth and poverty in the Soviet Union struck glaringly upon the consciousness of the oppressed millions. It was not just that the new rich proclaimed their rank and inaccessibility in a manner lacking all the normal palliatives of privilege: cultural refinement, pleasing manners, the customary acceptance of hereditary authority. There was, above all, the unremitting hypocrisy of a system which appeared to exist for no other purpose than the maintenance of this gilded crew, and yet at the same time daily thundered forth extreme doctrines of social equality.

In every field of life the discrepancy revealed itself uncompromisingly. A British general was startled to discover in Moscow that non-commissioned soldiers were not permitted to sit in the stalls at the theatre.[46] In the same year (1944), a Soviet admiral travelling in Britain was outraged to learn that private soldiers were allowed to sit in the same railway compartment as an officer.[47] Even shopping was conducted on a strictly hierarchical basis, as the wife of Comintern leader Otto Kuusinen found in the 1920s:

The average housewife could not buy as much as she liked by any means. All food was rationed, and only small quantities were available. For instance, a housewife could not generally buy more than a hundred grammes of butter – she might sometimes get 200 grammes if she queued for long enough. But the high-ranking officials, who had an unlimited number of ration books, could order as much of the available foodstuffs as they wished. Queues formed from early in the morning, and a policeman was on hand to keep order. As each customer came out of the shop with a couple of small packets, another was allowed in. Our cook didn't have to queue, however. As soon as she showed the policeman the book, he called out: 'Make way, make way!' As she came out of the shop laden with parcels, the women outside would shout at her angrily, not only because she had been let into the shop before them, but also because she had been allowed to buy so much. Alexandra [the Kuusinens' cook] herself had not fully grasped the magical power of our ration books: she thought we paid for the foods, since the books were always stamped 'paid' at the end of the month, but in fact we never paid a kopeck. Many lower-ranking Comintern officials also had ration books which allowed them unlimited purchase in the State shops, but they had to pay cash for their purchases; only we, the 'aristocrats', were paid for by the 'classless' society.[48]

In matters of life and death the distinction was even more marked. When the leaders of the state fell ill the astonishing advances of Soviet medical science were abruptly forgotten. Only German efficiency and cleanliness were suitable for men who had sacrificed so much for the world's suffering millions. 'Chicherin [Foreign Commissar] went to Rantzau's physician at Wiesbaden for treatment of his ailments; Trotsky went to a clinic in Berlin to find relief from his stomach troubles in the spring of 1926; . . . and in his last months Lenin, too, had been treated by many eminent German physicians and surgeons.'[49] Apart from other difficulties, Soviet medical men were perhaps inhibited by the knowledge that, if their cures failed, they were liable to be thrown in gaol without trial.[50]

For the natives there was socialized medicine, the admiration of streams of perceptive Western visitors. It is only necessary to describe the best treatment available in Soviet Russia to arrive at some conception of the worst. An American journalist living in Moscow suddenly found he had a sick wife on his hands. As a foreign Communist, he was privileged on both counts to be able to send her to the Botkinsky Hospital, second only in reputation to the Kremlin Hospital which was reserved for 'the most important strata of Moscow's hierarchy'. The doctors had diagnosed appendicitis, and after desperate hours of form-filling, telephoning, and pulling strings with high officials, a bed was found for her. Battered along the icy streets in an ancient ambulance, her first destination was a draughty office, where she was laid on the floor preparatory to filling in an immense questionnaire and being stripped for examination. Next she was dragged on an open sledge in sub-zero weather to the hospital proper, where she was to be immersed in a filthy communal bath. Eventually her husband's agitated remonstrations secured her a bed in a cacophonous general ward. There at least she was accorded 'special feeding': black soggy bread, thrown on to her bed by a grimy porter. Fortunately the three doctors' diagnosis proved wrong, and Mrs Lyons began to recover – as much from the treatment as the illness. 'Except under unusual circumstances, bed linens were changed once a week. The blankets were not washed but merely disinfected, so that they were crusted with the dirt and vomit of previous patients.'[51] It was all a far cry from Chicherin's spa sanatorium in Germany.

One may perhaps find parallels somewhere in history to the fantastic disparity in living conditions of rich and poor in Soviet Russia, but in making comparisons it should not be forgotten that the abject poverty and suffering of the Russian poor was almost entirely the result of mistaken or malicious policies pursued by the rich. That the rich in turn lived in justified fear of their master may have soured their pleasure somewhat, but it no more excuses their complicity than does the plea of obedience to orders when made by Nazi criminals. As Professor Leszek Kolakowski concludes, in his great study of Marxism, 'The whole party became an organisation of torturers and oppressors: no one was innocent, and all Communists were accomplices in the coercion of society. Thus the party acquired a new species of moral unity, and embarked on a course from which there was no turning back.'[52]

IV
Safeguarding the New Society

If there is a consistent thread to be traced in Stalin's policy it is fear, a fear so absolute and omnipresent that one can safely claim that it governed his waking and sleeping hours. Other rulers, more or less tyrannical, have had cause to fear assassination but continued to lead public lives. Stalin alone appears to have believed himself to be living in a country where every man's hand was against him. As his atrocities mounted year by year, so he surely knew that there was scarcely a person in the land, man, woman or child, who did not have cause for a bitter hatred against the architect of all their sufferings.

Everything in Stalin's life suggests that at any rate that was what *he* believed. His gruff, impassive appearance concealed – was perhaps intended to conceal – a highly nervous temperament. The evidence suggests he was not a brave man. In his revolutionary days he had been an arch-apostle of the use of violence against the authorities, but on no recorded occasion did he allow himself to be present where that violence was likely to take place.[1] His shortened left arm precluded him from conscription in 1916,[2] but he played no part in the brief fighting that placed the Bolsheviks in power in 1917. In the Second World War he never visited the front line, though an heroic painting of him standing in a bunker, apparently in full view of the enemy, was widely distributed. To Churchill, though (who had served on the Western Front in the previous war), he claimed twice that he was frequently at the various fronts.[3] In June 1942 he was visited by the new British Ambassador, Sir Archibald Clark Kerr. Kerr reported afterwards to the Foreign Office,

> Just as I reached him at the end of the interminable passages of the Kremlin, the airraid sirens began . . . He asked if I would like to go to the dugout. And here I made my first blunder by saying no. Both he and Molotov winced a bit and I had to change a clumsy no

into a clumsier yes. It was not a good start. Stalin said that it would be quieter in the dugout and he led the way, very quick-footed, I thought, to the lift, banging the door on us and remaining behind himself. It was a long way down – a sort of dogleg business. One lift, then a longish walk and then another lift. Great steel doors admitted us to a long, vaulted, almost floodlit room. Before I had wholly got over the dazzle there was Stalin standing mysteriously in our midst. I can only imagine that he came down by some special, extra speedy, oneman chute.[4]

The possibility of a German bomb landing on his office was slight, though frightening enough. What was really daunting, however, was the prospect of assassination. Rather than provide the faintest opportunity for the death he sensed stalking ever round him, he turned himself into a virtual prisoner within his own system. Otto Kuusinen, who was as close to him as anyone could be, observed that 'the more ruthless and cold-blooded he became, the more he lived in an almost insane fear of his life.' For years he shaved himself, being terrified of the prospect of being approached by a barber with an open razor.[5]

Stalin's precautions against poisoning were quite extraordinary, suggesting acute paranoia were it not perfectly rational to suppose his enemies to be legion. Before any food reached his kitchens, it was all chemically analysed by a team of doctors in a special laboratory. 'Formal written records saying, "No poisonous elements found", with official seals attached and signed by a responsible specialist in poisons, were attached to every loaf of bread, every package of meat or fruit.' All this food had come from special farms run by the political police. 'Planting, harvesting, transport, cooking and catering were done by special Ogpu agents immediately responsible to no other than Yagoda.' Stalin followed the Russian custom of drinking tea all day long, and this presented a special hazard. A woman was employed whose sole duty was to prepare and serve the tea.

The process was governed by the strictest rules: the sealed packets of tea were locked up in a special cupboard to which Olga held the key. She had to open it in the presence of a supervisor, whose duty was to scrutinise the packet and make sure that the stamp and seal were intact. The packet was then opened and the right quantity of tea taken out. The rest was thrown away by the supervisor – on no account was tea to be taken twice from the same packet.

Alas, one day the supervisor noticed that a label had been prematurely broken. No poison was discovered, but Olga was at once dispatched to the Lubianka Gaol. One might imagine that after all these precautions Stalin could sit down to dine free from worry. But no: he would invite his companions to try each dish before him. 'Look, here are the giblets, Nikita. Have you tried them yet?' The narrow, oriental eyes watched the food go down safely. As the waiters were also police bodyguards, the system really did seem foolproof.[6]

But how could one breathe safely when even the very air around might have been tampered with? After all, Yagoda had tried to murder his successor as Commissar of State Security with noxious vapours. Dr Dyakov from the NKVD laboratory would appear from time to time in the Kremlin to take away samples of the atmosphere in his test tubes.[7] The dictator could breathe again.

In the Kremlin Stalin lived as if continually under siege. Some fifteen thousand NKVD troops were permanently stationed in the area of Moscow surrounding the fortress. Preliminary screening before recruitment went to fantastic lengths, and continued throughout the guards' service. For what if an infiltrator were to penetrate the Guard itself? The Guard Directorate's Personnel Section employed officers permanently engaged in checking the background and behaviour of the remainder, whilst others spied on these in turn. But what if one of *these* were a traitor? Marxist ingenuity came up with a solution known as *shakhmati*, 'chessboard'.

This is how it worked: At irregular intervals, sometimes ten minutes, sometimes longer apart, the N.K.V.D. guards were shifted like pawns on a chessboard. They were moved without warning and according to an intricate pattern by signal from a central control point. No guard could therefore know precisely where he would be stationed at a given time. In that way the collusion of four or five guards to pass an unauthorized visitor was made impossible.

A visitor was liable to be searched fifteen times on the way to his destination by uniformed NKVD men placed the length of each corridor. As Stalin moved from his quarters to the Kremlin palace, guards would remove all officials in his way, regardless of rank. The procession was a very slow one; to cross over to the Kremlin cinema, he was accompanied by detachments of guards and even armoured cars. At sessions of the Supreme Soviet or Party congresses, an armed NKVD officer sat amongst every dozen or so deputies.[8]

Even Stalin could not live permanently cooped up in the Kremlin. In particular, he journeyed regularly to and from his *dachas* on the outskirts of Moscow, and less frequently to his palaces and homes on the Black Sea. Here was a moment of risk for which further elaborate precautions were required. Special broad avenues – the Vosdvizhenka and the Arbat – were built leading to the Mozhaisk Road, so that Stalin could travel unimpeded to and from the Kremlin. About ten in the morning on working days swarms of NKVD guards would assemble outside the Kuntsevo *dacha*. Stalin would emerge furtively and slip into his enormous armour-plated Packard, its dark-green windows three inches thick and bullet-proof even from machine-gun fire. Some four hundred NKVD men, equipped with every type of small-arm, sprang into a fleet of Lincolns, and the whole cavalcade, sirens screaming, flew out on to the highway and along the empty streets towards the Kremlin. Amber lights blinking at crossroads and street corners warned Muscovites to keep away, whilst thousands more NKVD men searched houses and guarded vulnerable points en route. Ordinary citizens, well aware of the danger, took care to avoid the area when the Boss was passing. In 1949 a pedestrian was knocked down and killed by an escort car. His body was dispatched at once to the mortuary, and no inquiry made as to his identity. The route was decided by Stalin himself, who only informed his bodyguards at the last moment. Later he made arrangements to avoid all these dangerous journeys in the open and conduct them in safety beneath the earth's surface. A special branch of the Moscow metro was extended to Kuntsevo, and underground tunnels were built connecting the Kremlin with important government buildings.[9]

The *dacha* itself appeared vulnerable in comparison with the walled Kremlin. Khrushchev noted,

> Every time we got to the Nearby Dacha, we used to whisper among ourselves about how there were more locks than the time before. All sorts of bolts were attached to the gate, and a barricade had been set up. In addition there were two walls around the dacha, and between the walls there were watchdogs. An electric alarm system and all sorts of other security devices were installed.[10]

A friend of the composer Shostakovich knew one of the bodyguards, who in a confidential moment confessed the hazards of the job:

> The work was well paid and, in the eyes of the bodyguard, was highly respectable and responsible. With his many co-workers, he patrolled Stalin's *dacha* outside Moscow. In winter on skis, in summer on bicycles. They circled the *dacha* without stopping, all day and all night, without a break. The guard complained that he got dizzy. The leader and teacher almost never went outside the *dacha* grounds, and when he did come outside behaved like a real paranoiac. According to the guard, he kept looking around, checking, peering. The bodyguard was in awe. 'He's looking for enemies. One look and he sees all', he explained delightedly over a bottle of vodka to my friend.[11]

Similarly elaborate precautions were adopted when Stalin travelled south to the Black Sea. As a senior NKVD officer explained:

> Each year before going on vacation to Sochi, in the Caucasus, Stalin would give orders to make ready simultaneously his train in Moscow and his steamer in the city of Gorky. Sometimes he would go by train from Moscow direct to Sochi, and sometimes he travelled by steamer along the Volga to Stalingrad and from there in his special train to Sochi. Nobody knew beforehand the route or the day of departure. His train and steamer were kept in readiness for several days. And only a few hours before departure would he reveal the itinerary. Before and behind his train of armoured steel two other trains moved with detachments of bodyguards. Stalin's train was adapted to withstand a two-week siege. In case of alarm the windows could be automatically closed with armoured shutters.[12]

Because 'he lived in an almost insane fear for his life', Stalin never dared pay visits to factories, art galleries or other public places where he might encounter his resentful subjects. He was particularly terrified of crowds, and was furious when on one occasion a crowd of loyal Georgians enthusiastically advanced on his train at Kutaisi station.[13] He never moved freely amongst his people, as did dictators and democratic leaders in the rest of Europe. But there were occasions when he had no choice but to brave the open streets. These virtually comprised a few military parades in Red Square, state funerals, and regular visits to the theatre. If the precautions adopted to protect his daily routine appear extraordinary, those requisite on these more 'public' occasions were quite fantastic.

At Teheran and Potsdam Western observers were amused by the extent of the precautions. For a five-minute stroll, Stalin required a screen of hundreds of 'thugs' armed with tommy-guns, even though the park in which he walked was ringed with thousands of troops.[14] This surprised onlookers, but they were little aware that what was visible was but the tip of the iceberg. On 1 May and 7 November, the two Bolshevik anniversaries, Stalin was obliged to appear before that Red Army he so feared and on which he was so dependent. In 1937 Fitzroy Maclean saw him emerge unobtrusively from a little side-door in the Kremlin wall, followed by trembling members of the Politburo, and ascend Lenin's Mausoleum. As vast hordes of disciplined troops thundered past, Maclean was amused to hear loud-speakers relaying amplified cheering to compensate for the absence of any spectators. Maclean and his Embassy were well aware that massive precautions were taking place to protect Stalin from the non-existent crowd. Two years later it was reported that

> As on previous occasions they [the troops] filed past Lenin's mausoleum between ranks of uniformed N.K.V.D. troops who divided the marching columns and separated them from the distinguished spectators. N.K.V.D. officials also patrolled houses near the Red Square and sealed up lofts and garrets leading to the roofs.

Every single window gazing on Red Square was occupied by an NKVD agent, but the real object of dread was the Red Army itself. A former officer of the Kremlin Guard recalls the precautions he and his fellow-officers undertook:

> At all these Moscow parades or demonstrations in Red Square, whatever their nature, every third person on the reviewing stands is a member of the State Security, heavily armed with concealed weapons. To keep the 'loyal troops of the Soviet Army' or the 'spontaneous demonstrators of the grateful working masses' from too close contact with the Soviet leaders in the reviewing stand, the right files in every column are composed of State Security officers or agents or, at the least, trusted Party members appointed by their local committees and given special clearance for their duties. There are times when as many as ten columns of eighteen

files apiece will march through Red Square. The far right file of
each column belongs to the KGB.

One of the Guard's principal responsibilities during military
parades is to see that none of the troops involved is carrying any
live ammunition. The penalty for an omission in this case is
twenty-five years at hard labor for the soldier carrying the ammunition, his officers, and all State Security officers involved in his
clearance. As further insurance against excessive demonstrations
of popular zeal the State Security unfailingly stations a full battalion of its own troops, armed with automatic weapons, in the
basement of the Lenin-Stalin mausoleum, with reserves of more
militia and KGB troops standing nearby, generally in other base-
ments along Vetoshny Lane. Machine-gun posts are set up on the
wall of the Kremlin and armed guards posted in the attics of the
Kremlin and on the roofs of some of the nearby buildings: St.
Basil's cathedral, the GUM department store, and the Museum of
History.

One might suppose that this colossal system of checks and counter-
checks would have enabled Stalin to retain his confidence even
under an open sky. Not so: 'he wore under his tunic a heavy bullet-
proof vest which was made especially for him in Germany.'[15]

At the state funerals of those few Soviet leaders who died of
natural causes or had otherwise retained favour, similarly elaborate
precautionary measures were taken.[16] At the theatre, which he enjoyed, Stalin invariably sat in shadow at the back of the former Imperial box. His companions sat in the front seats, while NKVD
troops in and out of uniform occupied all the neighbouring rows. On
14 October 1944 there was a gala performance at the Bolshoi Theatre
in honour of the visit of Winston Churchill. During the first interval
Stalin invited Churchill to go forward to accept the plaudits of the
audience. A storm of cheering broke out, which increased in volume
every time the Prime Minister delivered his famous Victory sign.
Stalin had quickly withdrawn as the lights went on, but when ten or
fifteen minutes passed with Churchill still standing unscathed in
full view of the audience, the Generalissimo returned to take his
own share of the applause. The assembled courtiers and policemen
cheered themselves hoarse. Stalin's departure and reappearance delighted the kindly General Ismay, himself as brave as a lion, who was
quite 'astonished that such a ruthless man of steel as Stalin should

be capable of such old-world courtesy'.[17]

The indications are strong that Stalin was a physical coward. 'He was unable to swim and feared the water', points out Roy Medvedev. He was also frightened of flying and travelled in an aeroplane only once, to attend the Teheran Conference in 1943. There was no rail line between Baku and Teheran, so he had no choice, but his apprehension was plain to all.[18] (Molotov, his companion in fear during the Kremlin air-raid, was likewise afraid of flight.)[19] Stalin feared even his own guards of the MVD, muttering once to a Soviet admiral 'in a tone of bitter hatred, "they stand there watching . . . but they themselves can shoot you in the back at any moment".'[20]

The question naturally arises as to whether Stalin suffered from a psychotic disorder. Was he paranoiac, or did he sustain a neurotic personality? Roy Medvedev argues that, despite pathological tendencies that came to the fore in his later years, '*Stalin was beyond doubt a responsible* (vmeniaemyi) *man, and in most cases was fully aware of what he was doing.*'[21] Much of what went on in Russia during his time must appear to have been 'institutionalized paranoia', but by the same token the dichotomy between reality and fantasy was on the whole carefully preserved and served a valid purpose in sustaining the totalitarian order. And that in turn Stalin 'inherited' from Marx's philosophy and Lenin's practice; with obvious limitations, it can be said that Stalin's political freedom of action in this respect was limited.[22] For example, it may be noted that Stalin was frequently irritated by the personality cult he had himself instigated, yet retained it as being politically essential. Though far from being the genius his admirers in Russia and abroad claimed him to be, he could display an underlying common sense and shrewdness in affairs superior to that of the more flashy Lenin and Trotsky.[23] It was this Stalin who so consistently impressed Churchill and other visiting foreigners with his solid good sense.

It seems therefore that the amazing precautions taken to preserve the dictator's life sprang, not from any paranoiac obsession, but from a realistic fear that his life lay in daily peril of an attempt by his enemies.[24] There is ample evidence to prove this. Clearly Stalin had reason to fear assassination. Lenin had escaped death by a hair's breadth in 1918, and Kirov had been murdered in 1934. Any ruler must take sensible precautions, dictators rather more so, and Stalin more than more. But it was not only assassination he feared, but some more regular and open attack. It did not require a division of MVD troops to repel a lone adversary with a grievance, nor would such a solitary figure be likely to besiege his accompanying trainload of armed escorts for a fortnight. However monolithic Bolshevik power might appear to foreigners and to the cowed Russian people, it is clear that Stalin himself held a more realistic appreciation of the vulnerability of his rule. This has been well put quite recently by Milovan Djilas:

> As far as the cabal around Stalin was concerned, their desperate search for wine and song (women were strictly not part of the fare) was an expression of the conspiratorial nature of Soviet leadership. Every time I was invited to Stalin's table and became involved in this unseemly game of sycophantic toasting, marathon drinking, and politicking, with the dwarflike, pock-marked despot sitting in judgment over the lives of his subjects in his enormous empire, I could not suppress a feeling that these men had no confidence at all in the legitimacy of their rule and needed reassurance from, wherever it could be obtained: drink, 99.9% election results, vast armed forces, international treaties recognising their legitimacy . . . even adulation from fraternal foreign visitors like myself . . . What my visit to Stalin taught me was that these men regarded themselves as appointed to rule over and against the will of the people. They acted like a group of conspirators scheming to suppress, squash, circumvent, or hoodwink the inhabitants of some conquered land, not their own. Power for Stalin was a plot, with himself as chief plotter as well as the one cast to be plotted against. It was an expression of the civil war which Communists have always waged, and *will* always wage, against society.[25]

The possibility that the Russian people might, given an opportunity, rise up in revolution against Soviet power seems to have been close to Stalin's mind from the very earliest moment of the Bolshevik seizure of power. In 1919 or 1920 his secretary saw records of a large cache of diamonds, secreted for the use of Lenin and his immediate entourage should they fall from power.[26] NKVD reports on popular discontent were extremely frank, as the Smolensk archive reveals, and increasingly harsh purges could only intensify the tendency. As an MVD officer recognized, 'every man is an enemy . . . Throw a lighted idea into that powder barrel and the whole lot would go up!'[27]

That Stalin feared the worst when the German invasion shook Soviet society to its foundations he was later to imply himself in frank moments. In 1942, 'he repeatedly said that he himself was astonished at the spirit and determination of his people. He didn't know them; he had never dreamt that they could show such unity or resolution.' And in his speech at the Kremlin to Red Army commanders on 24 May 1945 he plainly indicated what had passed through his mind during those panic-stricken days in late June and early July 1941. Referring to the dreadful military reverses of 1941–2, he continued:

A different people could have said to the Government: you have not fulfilled our expectations; go away, we shall install another government, which will conclude peace with Germany and bring us a quiet life. But the Russian people did not do this, because it believed in the policy of its government and it made sacrifices, in order to ensure the downfall of Germany. And this confidence of the Russian people in the Soviet Government proved to be the decisive force which ensured the historic victory over the enemies of mankind – over fascism.

The note of surprise that the people identified themselves with the regime is patent. Also significantly revealing is the distinction drawn between the *Russian* people and the *Soviet* Government; elsewhere Stalin invariably referred to 'Soviet people'. It is interesting, too, to note that Stalin's son Yakov, interrogated by his German captors in 1941, rejected any idea of a German conquest of Russia but was dismayed at the prospect of a National Russian Revolution. 'That would be dangerous', he admitted.[28]

That the Russian people was regarded by Stalin as a potential enemy much more dangerous than the British or the Germans is evidenced above all by the extraordinary resources the Soviet state deployed against it. In January 1946, George Kennan at the US Embassy in Moscow reported of the NKVD that 'their budget for purely administrative expenditures is two-thirds as large as total spent for these purposes by entire remainder of Soviet Govt apparatus'.[29]

The Cheka, as the political police was first known, was established a mere six weeks after the Bolshevik seizure of power. On 7 December 1917 the All-Russian Extraordinary Commission for the Struggle with Counterrevolution and Sabotage came into being. In view of the Soviet Union's perennial popularity with certain sections of the

British, French and Italian trade union and Socialist movements, it is interesting to note that the purpose of the Commission was to 'concentrate its attention upon the press, sabotage, etc., of the Right Social Revolutionaries, saboteurs, and strikers'. Specifically, Lenin had urged the setting up of the Committee to deal with a widespread strike of civil servants, office-cleaners, chauffeurs and other people in government employment. Under the leadership of an obsessive fanatic, Felix Dzerzhinsky, the Cheka swiftly gained a reputation for savagery that eclipsed anything known in Europe since the French Revolution. Floggings, beatings and burnings proliferated. The slaughter of hostages and other wholly innocent people as 'class representatives' was another speciality.[30]

Right up to the end of his career Lenin continued to advocate the maximum use of terror against all who were, or might be, opposed to his ideas. In 1922, as a new criminal code was being formulated, he urged that 'the paragraph on terror must be formulated as widely as possible, since only revolutionary consciousness of justice can determine the conditions of its application'. The ailing dictator continued to the last to display close interest in all activities of the secret police, being a frequent visitor at their Lubianka headquarters. It was he who bestowed terroristic powers on the Cheka, continually extended its authority and scope, and urged it on to ever harsher measures. It was this weapon, 'the Sword of the Revolution', which Stalin inherited, enabling him first to gain control of the Party, and then cement his grip on Russia.[31] Stalin was the creature of the Revolution, not its destroyer, and it would be impossible to understand his nature or that of his policy were one to presume his power sprang *ex nihilo*.

Stalin continued Lenin's policy until it reached its logical conclusion. There was no aspect of Soviet life that was not subject to police control, including the Party itself. As Soviet power had to be total in order to survive, it was inevitable that the arbitrarily constituted Party oligarchy should be dispensed with.

Lenin took steps to prevent opposition groups from arising in future within the party. Rules were adopted prohibiting the formation of intra-party factions, and empowering the Central Committee to expel from its midst members who had been elected at the party congress. In this way, by a natural progression, the dictatorship first exercised over society in the name of the party, was now applied to the party itself, creating the basis for a one-man tyranny.[32]

Stalin's great achievement was to place the entire population of nearly two hundred million people wholly in the power of the police, whilst himself retaining in turn absolute power over the police. As two successive police chiefs and thousands of inferior officers had been purged, the Commissar for State Security might be supposed to have more than ordinary motives for employing the awesome power at his control to overthrow the menacing figure of the Boss. That there never seems to have been any danger of such a threat developing is adequate testimony to Stalin's extreme skill in manipulating the instrument of oppression.

Stalin retained within his own grasp direct links with the NKVD in every *oblast* and *raion* to such an extent that a simple lieutenant could assert correctly that 'there were only two men between me and Stalin'; the two men being the head of the Kharkov NKVD and Commissar for State Security Yezhov (this was in 1938).[33] To Stalin's suspicious mind the dangerous link must have been that of the Commissar for State Security. An elementary precaution was the establishment of a palace guard independent of the Commissariat. This was commanded by a companion of Civil War days, 'General' Nikolai Vlasik. Vlasik was a crude, bullying, semi-literate lout, who combined doglike devotion to Stalin with absolute control over all his personal security.[34]

The successive Commissars for State Security were skilfully chosen for their personal characteristics, combining exceptional lack of scruple with deficiencies of character that facilitated their removal when necessary. Yezhov was so subservient to Stalin that a colleague could regard his words as 'practically a phonographic record of the boss himself'. It seems certain he would in any other country have been regarded as certifiably insane. 'In the middle of an important and confidential telephone call he would suddenly burst out in crazy laughter and tell stories of his own life in the most obscene language.' According to Stalin himself, Yezhov was a drunken sot. In 1938 he was replaced by Lavrenty Beria,[35] by the precautionary method of inviting him and his immediate colleagues to a conference. They left their arms outside and were told, 'you are under arrest'. The crazy dwarf departed to prison,[36] and was succeeded by the 'plump, greenish and pale . . . with soft damp hands' Beria, whose oily manner and ruthlessness endeared him to his Chief. He displayed his suitability for the role by arranging for his eighty-year-old stepfather to be sentenced to ten years' forced labour in the death camp at Karaganda. His unpleasant table manners, vulgarity and vicious private life proved he had not weakened in his revolutionary vigour.[37]

Stalin's identification with the political police extended even to his family. His brother-in-law, Stanislav Redens, a longstanding Chekist from Lenin's time, was himself a brutal interrogator and head of the Moscow NKVD until he too disappeared in 1938.[38] There could be no direct link, of course, between the Boss and the members of a police force whose strength ran to hundreds of thousands of men. Every factory and other institution in the land had its supervisory unit,[39] and the only effective way to recruit men who were in no danger of identifying themselves with the working class they were intended to control was by according them privileges, keeping them in continual fear of being purged themselves, and recruiting types unlikely to retain normal human responses.

When Lenin and Dzerzhinsky first established the Cheka they recruited widely among Poles, Letts, Jews and other non-Russians among the Soviet population. They lived as far as possible lives segregated from normal people, and received pay and plunder as the perquisites of their dangerous role.[40] Most of these 'foreigners' were purged in 1938 and after, and recruiting had to be conducted on a more regular basis. Officers were drawn from the offspring of the privileged classes where possible: their schooling tended to fit them for the career. Others had proved themselves by their loyalty to the Party or other promising indications.[41]

The tasks of the NKVD, such as guarding slave-camps in the far North, preventing Soviet citizens from flocking abroad, torturing and executing suspects, and so forth, were not generally such as to attract or retain men of intelligence and integrity. 'Their educational level was low', and many broke entirely with their families to stress their undivided loyalty. A high proportion were of subnormal intelligence. Khrushchev (who should have known) described a senior official – an investigative 'judge' – as 'a vile person, with the brain of a bird, and morally completely degenerate'. As General Vlasik, commander of Stalin's guard, explained, 'We don't need the rotten intelligentsia'.

The mass of other ranks had to be recruited by cruder methods.

After the purge of 1938, in which many veteran Chekists were eliminated, cadres were replenished by 'young Communists from factories and schools, with only a few months' training to prepare them for their new tasks'. Even before that, extreme youth had become a characteristic of those enlisted, and many of Lenin's earliest executioners had been teenage youths; later, young student torturers used to attend interrogations in order to acquire practical experience. In wartime many of the NKVD mass murderers were little more than children, being rumoured to be 'the sons of Chekists who had managed to fix them up with safe jobs as executioners to save them from service at the front'.[42] Gangster types proliferated in the NKVD,[43] and there was certainly something very weird about a system that could sentence a deaf mute for the crime of hostile propaganda, and dispatch a ten-year-old boy to the Lefortovo Prison as an American spy – particularly as 'the NKVD never makes mistakes!' Nevertheless the strain often became too great. It was not unknown for an NKVD man to reach commissioned rank despite clear evidence of insanity.[44]

What was much more frequent was that the commissar would take the logical step of becoming insane within the insane system. At the Lubianka, for example, strange shrieks (nothing unusual in itself) were heard coming from a cell. Two NKVD officers, looking in, were alarmed to find *the interrogator* 'in a state of frenzy, raving and accusing a prisoner by the name of Friedland, a professor at the Leningrad Institute of Marxism, of an attempt to swallow the inkstand which was on Kedrov's desk'. Poor Kedrov had indeed lapsed into insanity, but nevertheless continued in his work, at which he was in fact very conscientious. A colleague took to the bottle, and 'the following spectacle presented itself . . . The officer was sitting at his desk, crying and lamenting, "Today I am interrogating you, tomorrow they'll interrogate me. Alas, our life is worth but a kopeck!" The prisoner was standing near the interrogator and patted his shoulder trying to comfort him.' Many of these sorely-tried servants of the state were driven to drugs and alcoholism, and in the Crimea there was a special police sanatorium 'for treatment of the drug-addicts and impotents'.[45]

Exact statistics as to the numerical strength of the NKVD in Stalin's time do not appear to exist. It must have been formidable. Stalin's bodyguard and those of his colleagues ran into thousands. In every town, every university, every factory and every military unit there was a section of the NKVD. Along the Soviet Union's more than fifteen thousand miles of frontier, hundreds of thousands of blue-capped guards were deployed to arrest people trying to get in or out. On Soviet ships sailing the oceans there were contingents of agents to ensure the crews did not escape; every embassy, legation, consulate, military and trade delegation bore its accompanying group, part watch-dog, part spy; every national Communist Party had its Comintern supervisors. Roving squads of assassins crossed frontiers and seas to track down their victims: here a White Russian general, there a defecting NKVD officer, and there again Trotsky himself. A special section dealt with the infiltration of Russian émigré groups and another with the 'wet business' – murder. In Paris and Berlin the chance of war revealed in special sections of the Soviet embassies 'soundproof walls, heavy, electrically operated steel doors, hidden spyholes and slots for guns to be fired from one room into another, an electrical furnace, and a bathtub in which the corpses were cut up . . . in addition to housebreaking implements, poison capsules, and the like'.[46]

They were busy men in the NKVD. The task which absorbed the greatest single number was probably that of administering the myriad camps of GULAG. The chief of GULAG was General Nedosekin, 'a large, fleshy individual, wearing a uniform of superfine cloth'. On a wall in his office was a large map of Russia, covered from coast to coast with large and small stars. These represented greater and lesser camps from Magadan in the east to Solovetskiye in the west.[47] Just how many men were employed as guards (VOKhRA) or other officials of GULAG does not seem to be known, but some sort of estimate can be attempted. The total must have been huge. About two thousand people were employed at the Moscow Headquarters alone.[48] A cautious estimate of the prisoner population in 1941 would seem to indicate ten or twelve million people at any given moment.[49] Now, a Colonel Vladimir Andreyev, who had been commandant of all or part of the Karaganda complex from 1937 to 1941, testified in 1951 after defecting to the West that he had had 3,400 armed guards serving under him.[50] The prisoners at Karaganda are estimated to have amounted to some 150,000 souls.[51] Thus there was one guard to every forty-four prisoners. On this basis ten million prisoners would have required nearly a quarter of a million guards. This, however, is a conservative estimate. There were probably more than ten million prisoners at the time, it is not certain that Andreyev was in charge of all the camps at Karaganda, and there were many officials besides those guarding the camps. A trustworthy witness states that, with the outbreak of war in 1941, there were two guards for every twenty prisoners, and conjectured that there must have been altogether a million camp guards.[52] All in all it may be hazarded that the NKVD fielded an armed force of up to half-a-million men.

If a state's degree of liberty or oppression is to be measured by the extent of the coercive powers employed to sustain its government, then Soviet Russia must be the most oppressive power the world has ever seen. Nor were these powers exerted mildly. Mass executions and slave labour put millions out of harm's way, and for those who might still be thought to nurture rebellious thoughts there were worse threats. A Cossack officer, handed over by the British to the NKVD in 1945, exclaimed to his captor,

'I can't tell you anything! I don't understand all this preamble. Finish it at once. A bullet in the back of the neck and . . . ' 'Oh, no, "Mr." Krasnov!' Merkulov laughed mockingly, relaxing in his armchair. 'Things don't happen so simply. What are you thinking of? A bullet in the back of the neck, and that's all? Nonsense, Your Honour! . . . Ah, if it were only death!'[53]

Merkulov was People's Commissar for State Security, and knew what he was talking about. Torture had long been abolished in Imperial Russia, but the Soviet regime showed no lack of resource in making up for lost time. There were straightforward beatings, for instance, 'with rubber truncheons on the back, the thighs and, what is much more painful, on the head'. One might receive 'a number of violent blows on the carotid artery, given with the back of the hand', or the interrogators 'had a way of beating their victims with empty bottles'. A man's back would be turned into 'one huge open wound', or the same treatment inflicted on the soles of his feet.[54] These beatings were not confined to male prisoners.

Women and young girls were thrown into the cells, beaten to pulp. Their hair was torn out from their scalps, their fingers broken, their toes crushed, their teeth knocked in, temples crushed, skin broken open. They were beaten on their heels and kicked in the stomach: their kidneys were laid open by beating. Alanka, the Ukrainian girl in our cell, returned to us unconscious, after having been ill-treated in a special way during menstruation

. . . If I had not seen it with my own eyes, I would not have believed it possible for young girls to be beaten as they were . . . One of these girls after being raped was carried back to the cell and laid beside her mother. The mother herself told me this. One young girl was so beaten that she died. In Brygidki a second young girl died from the beatings she received.[55]

It was not hard for the NKVD interrogators to add to the horror even of a simple beating. Men had their hands and arms broken, with no medical treatment to follow. A man in the Butirki Gaol was beaten with 'rifle butts and a rubber hose. His hands were clamped down to a board and gramophone needles were hammered into the flesh of his fingers under the nails. Then someone kicked him in the groin and he lost his senses.' His condition was such that he had to be castrated in the prison hospital. But as the man still refused to confess to imaginary charges of 'Trotskyism', his pregnant wife was hauled in.

Four men now came into the room, two of whom held Gorodietsky fast so that he could not move, while the other two laid hold of his wife and threw her onto the floor. As Gorodietsky screamed his vain protests they kicked and beat her tirelessly. At last she set up a terrible screaming and the men held back, for something was happening. Her baby was delivered, stillborn, on the cold floor of the interrogation room, while Gorodietsky's helpless rage and hate and pity welled up and nearly choked him. His wife was removed insensate to hospital.

It was threats of this sort of treatment to wife or children that often helped to induce the amazing 'confessions' at show trials which so delighted Western fellow-travellers. One man whose 'confession' was unsatisfactory learned afterwards that 'his son was picked up by the feet and his head shattered against a wall'.[56]

Beatings of prisoners and their families were a regular form of interrogation. There were also many refinements. Men had their teeth kicked out. They were subjected to the *stoika*, standing for ten or twenty hours until their legs were so swollen that they collapsed. They were seated on hot pipes until their buttocks were burned through. There was 'the plank': 'd'you know what that means? They fasten a chap under a strip of wood, and then hack at it with an axe. The victim dies. The blows loosen his kidneys and all his innards'.

Or a man would be stripped naked, strapped to a table, and have his genitals lashed to a pulp with heavy, soaking towels ('think of the worst agony you can imagine, multiply it a million times, and you may approach what I went through'). If these punishments were not horrifying enough, you could be left in a barrel of urine for twenty-four hours, or have a needle repeatedly stabbed through the back of the neck until a thrust penetrated between the vertebrae, injuring the spinal cord and causing convulsions. There were also horrible things to be done with dentists' drills, and fish-hooks to be dragged slowly across a victim's hands and back.[57]

A 'little, weak, and hounded man' was Isaac Brevda, professor at the Military Medical Academy. His speciality was the reclamation of suffering humanity, and he was an expert in plastic surgery. He was subjected to the *stoika* for two days, until the veins in his feet burst open. His spectacles were confiscated, and he was compelled to gaze at a 2,000 watt light-bulb for hours on end. Then his burly captors, good-humoured men all, 'played ball' with him, hurling him about the room. He emerged to learn that his wife had been sent to a camp, and his daughter brutally raped by another interrogator.[58] In 1946 a laboratory was opened in the Lubianka known as 'The Chamber'. There scientists practised ghastly experiments on prisoners, employing drugs and poisons whose effects they wished to establish. The authorities may have borrowed the idea from what they had learned of SS practices in liberated Germany. 'The Chamber' itself was abolished in 1953,[59] but today torture in psychiatric hospitals remains a favoured Soviet penal measure.[60]

In short, there was scarcely a device for increasing and prolonging the agony of their victims that the NKVD did not fasten upon with eagerness.[61] In the number of people on whom these savageries were inflicted and the length of time over which they took place,[62] Soviet cruelty far outstripped that of National Socialism – if comparisons on such a scale can have any validity. Torture in the USSR was (and is) employed on a mass scale as an important punitive means of overawing a resentful population. Lenin's rejection of the notion of any morality independent of ideology resulted in a doctrine accepting that 'tortures represent the people's noble rage against the exploiters'.[63] The practice became general immediately after his seizure of power, fresh refinements being introduced every year.[64] Stalin in turn took a deep personal concern in the particular torments to be employed, providing the interrogators with detailed instructions. Beria and Malenkov went further, actually attending in the cells to torture selected victims.[65]

Western visitors paid their fleeting visits. In books, articles and conversations they gave glowing accounts of Soviet progress in education, health, labour conditions and social emancipation. They retained intact a faith they desperately needed, deliberately concealing flaws that were evident even on the surface. The Russians, they held, had scarcely known the meaning of freedom, and were clearly more than content with the more tangible benefits of socialism. 'Between mouthfuls of chicken *à la Kievsky*', as a disgusted observer in Moscow noted, 'they said, "what if it does mean the sacrifice of a generation, or two generations, if it helps the construction of socialism!"' The helpless Russians hated these smug, rich visitors, but were obliged to suffer in silence under the familiar sentence: 'But they are Russians, my dear man, and they've never known any better.' If these visitors guessed the truth (as surely they did),[66] they were not going to say so. Implicit in this liberal view 'was the patronizing satisfaction that the Great Experiment was being tried out in the Great Social Laboratory so safely far away from home: upon the teeming Russian coolies instead of the sentient citizens of the West'.[67]

But Russians are not coolies. Harried, dragooned, massacred and driven off into slavery as in the days of the Tartar conquest, their resentment burned low. Even the NKVD was sensitive enough to public opinion to avoid wearing uniforms in the streets,[68] and a defeat of the NKVD football team, 'Dynamo', could provide momentary jubilation;[69] more could not be done. But Stalin guessed how they felt, and he was taking no risks. As the Russian proverb says, 'Feed the wolf as you will, but he will always look to the forest.'

Part Two

V
Munich Manoeuvres

On 13 September 1938, the London *Evening Standard* published a cartoon by Low which graphically posed the question hanging over the European crisis. Before a map of doomed Czechoslovakia sit the four leading statesmen of Western Europe: Hitler, Chamberlain, Daladier and Mussolini. The two dictators, their arms folded on their chests, appear aggressive and unyielding, whilst the British and French premiers turn apprehensively towards a gigantic newcomer standing confidently in the doorway. 'What, no chair for me?' exclaims Joseph Stalin, a smile, half-sarcastic, half-benign, on his face.[1]

Low's implicit view, that the four-power pact and settlement of the Czech crisis demanded the participation of the remaining European great power, was shared by wide sections of Western public opinion outside the Nazi and Fascist dictatorships. The Soviet Union was, after all, bound to France in a Treaty of Mutual Assistance (2 May 1935), in which each country bound itself to come to the aid of the other if menaced by the aggression of a third party. Similar pacts bound the French to the Czechs (16 October 1925) and the USSR to the Czechs (16 May 1935),[2] and in view of these and other bonds linking the Soviet Union to western nations fearing German aggrandisement, it did indeed seem extraordinary that the largest military power on the Continent was to be excluded from the settlement.

Repeated Soviet utterances at the League of Nations and elsewhere stressed that the Soviet Union would go all the way with France and Britain in fulfilling treaty obligations to Czechoslovakia, and this forthrightness drew an eager response from many in the West. On 21 September 1937 Maxim Litvinov, Soviet Commissar for Foreign Affairs, declared roundly that

We intend to fulfil our obligations under the Pact, and together
with France to afford assistance to Czechoslovakia by the ways
open to us. Our War Department is ready immediately to participate in a conference with representatives of the French and
Czechoslovak War Departments, in order to discuss the measures
appropriate to the moment . . .

As Winston Churchill, horrified at the planned appeasement of
Germany, was to write later: 'It is indeed astonishing that this public
and unqualified declaration by one of the greatest Powers concerned
should not have played its part in Mr. Chamberlain's negotiations, or
in the French conduct of the crisis.'[3]

This sentiment was widespread, even among many who, like
Churchill, strongly disapproved of all that Soviet Russia stood for.
The reason was clear and simple enough, for, as another concerned
observer pointed out, 'every hour that we live demonstrates more
clearly that it is Germany, not Russia that threatens the physical
existence of every country and of its individual citizens.'[4]

To such people Soviet Russia and the Red Army seemed the
obvious card to play. Conscious of British and French military un-
preparedness and the pacifism and appeasement which gripped large
sections of their populations, they saw the balance being righted by
the vast armies of the Soviets, directed as they were by a ruthlessly
single-minded leadership. With some two million men under arms,
they could surely offer or bring such aid to the threatened Czechs as
would cause even the megalomaniac Führer to have second
thoughts.

True, Soviet good faith was never at a premium; but her representatives had displayed unusual consistency in urging preventive
action against the Nazi menace ever since Hitler's accession to power
in 1933.[5] When the Wehrmacht moved into Austria in March 1938, it
was Litvinov who urged most forcefully that 'all the States and the
Great Powers in particular take a firm and unambiguous stand', and
Ambassador Maisky in London presciently warned that the
Anschluss was 'a menace to Czechoslovakia'.[6] Nor was Soviet
opposition confined to words: non-aggression treaties were signed
with neighbouring states from the Baltic to the Carpathian Mountains; in 1934 the USSR entered the League of Nations, becoming a
leading proponent of collective security designed to keep Germany
in check; and repeated assurances were transmitted to London, Paris

and Prague of Soviet willingness to join any measures, including military intervention, to forestall a German partition or conquest of Czechoslovakia.[7]

In the event, of course, the whole miserable business was settled at Munich by the four Western leaders on 29 September 1938. The Soviet Union, sworn ally of the victim and of her principal ally, played no part whatever in the deliberations and indeed might have ceased to exist so far as they were concerned. An almost unanimous opinion was sustained by those concerned that the Soviet Union, despite her apparent power and attested good will, was not to be accepted as an ally or even a consultant.

Hitler naturally had every objection to the intrusion of Soviet Russia into the Czechoslovakian imbroglio, as it was his professed belief that it was through the Czech-Soviet Pact that the Soviet Union, herself geographically isolated in the East, might insinuate her power in the heart of Europe.[8] The Führer's objections were shared by British Prime Minister Neville Chamberlain on not dissimilar grounds:

> I must confess to the most profound distrust of Russia. I have no belief whatever in her ability to maintain an effective offensive, even if she wanted to. And I distrust her motives, which seem to me to have little connection with our ideas of liberty, and to be concerned with getting everyone else by the ears. Moreover, she is both hated and suspected by many of the smaller states, notably by Poland, Roumania and Finland.[9]

His best informed advisers shared this sceptical view;[10] and the French, who possessed within their gates a huge Communist Party, totally servile to Moscow, objected if anything more forcefully. 'The primary advantage of this assemblage is that Russia is evicted from it. Too much could not be done to remove her from Europe, to send her back to Asia, to her internal struggles,' wrote Léon Bailly a week after the gathering.[11]

More surprising were objections from widespread circles in Czechoslovakia itself. 'We shall fight the German,' claimed the Czech Inspector-General Jan Syrovy, 'either alone, or with [the British] . . . and the French, but we don't want the Russians in here. We should never get them out.' The Agrarian Party was strongly opposed to encouraging Soviet intervention, and President Beneš declined the unilateral Soviet offer of assistance.[12]

These objections arose in part from fears that Soviet participation in affairs so far from frontiers imposed on her by the suspicious Entente powers in 1921 might lend aid and comfort to home-grown Communists. In addition it was felt that, for all Litvinov's assurances, the Soviets wished to provoke a conflict from which they could readily hold back. Then again there was the question whether the Red Army, whatever Soviet leaders thought, was capable of making any worthwhile military contribution in the event of a conflict.

This brief recapitulation of well-known facts leads to the essential question: what was Soviet foreign policy in 1938–9? Was it pro-Entente and as honest and consistent as Mr Litvinov's course of conduct suggested? Was it cowardly and pragmatic, lacking the strength to intervene, yet desperate to influence events so as in some way to ensure the survival of the homeland of socialism? Or was it supremely cunning and skilful, seeking to play one adversary off against another, until all Western and Central Europe was a smoking mass of ruins, across which the Red Army could move at leisure?

Soviet policy was in all probability a compound of all these conceptions, though by no means in equal proportions. The Soviets had reason to hate and fear the Nazis, and hence to ensure that their course of expansion was checked in Bohemia. Everything about Nazi ideology indicated that a resurgent Germany would sooner or later prove a menace to Russia.[13] In ringing tones Maxim Litvinov denounced the German threat to European peace, calling tirelessly for an alliance of European states to check the danger before it proved too late.

In contrast to the bloody past of the Soviet regime, which might make even Hitler's denunciations seem inadequate, the portly, jolly, bustling Litvinov appeared a genuinely humane and civilized statesman. Amidst the shameful prevarications of British and French leaders, and the brutal pronouncements of the two dictators, his calls for firmness and plain dealing appeared to many the sole voice of sanity on a darkening continent. As a Jew he had scant reason to feel anything but disgust for National Socialism, and there seems to be no reason to doubt the sincerity of his crusade.

But was his policy also that of his government? Would Soviet Russia really have stood shoulder-to-shoulder with the British and French had they decided to cry 'ne plus ultra' to Hitler's ambitions in the Sudetenland? To many in the West, frustrated by the seeming bankruptcy of their own leadership, Soviet Russia alone seemed to offer the leadership lacking elsewhere. The view has persisted, and there are still those who think that the cold-shouldering of Litvinov's offers not only removed the one chance of checking Hitler, but also caused – even justified – the subsequent Nazi-Soviet Pact.[14]

Until that remote day when the Soviet archives are opened to historians, we will never know the full story. But enough evidence is available to show that, whatever Litvinov's personal inclinations, the policy of the Soviet Government itself was far from being particularly altruistic or benign. At the League of Nations, where he conducted his most energetic campaigns to ensure Germany was compelled to remain behind her frontiers, the Foreign Commissar clearly enjoyed considerable latitude in conducting debate or negotiation. 'Litvinov rarely asked for time to consult his government,' wrote an observer; 'he seemed always ready to decide on the spot when to press his argument, to propose a compromise, or to resign himself to accepting the majority view. It was clear that he had at least as free a hand as was generally given to the Foreign Ministers of the democratic powers.'[15]

This in itself should have aroused suspicion: at what other time since the Treaty of Brest-Litovsk has a Soviet representative been allowed such freedom of manoeuvre? The indications are strong that Litvinov was indeed allowed to express as forcefully as he chose his strongly-felt views. But his projects could be repudiated, modified or turned to unexpected Soviet advantage as occasion demanded. Litvinov's policies were not those of his masters: he was but one card in the hand, and that not the strongest.

He seems to have been perfectly aware of his anomalous position, and admitted as much in an unguarded moment. At the height of the Czech crisis, when he was publicly reiterating Soviet pledges to stand by her Czech ally,[16] Litvinov held an interview with Arnost Heidrich, Director General of the Czech Foreign Office, who later recorded what passed.

On instructions of President Dr. Benes I discussed, in January, May and September 1938 in Geneva, this problem with Mr. Litvinov, at that time the Soviet Foreign Minister. Litvinov looked upon the situation pessimistically being of the opinion that the war could not be avoided. After having expressed doubts about the will and the possibility of France to give military assistance to Czechoslovakia in her potential conflict with Germany, Litvinov, in our conversation on May 11th 1938, stated that Soviet Russia would not repeat the mistake of Czarist Russia of 1914. He elaborated in about the following sense: 'We know that the Western Powers would like to have Hitler liquidated by Stalin and Stalin by Hitler, but in that they will not succeed. While in 1914–1917 the Western Powers, sparing their forces, watched the bloody struggle between Germany and Russia, this time shall we observe the contest between Germany and the Western Powers and shall not intervene in the conflict until we ourselves feel it fit to do so in order to bring about the decision.'[17]

That Litvinov's campaign was designed for external consumption only was borne out by Soviet reticence at home. In July the highly perceptive Fitzroy Maclean, 2nd Secretary at the British Embassy in Moscow, reported that

> the Soviet Government was now firmly opportunist . . . The purges, amounting to 75% of the higher command in the army for instance and as high or higher a percentage in all other walks of life, had gravely shaken efficiency. During the Czech crisis the Soviet Government had remained absolutely silent and were terrified of being drawn in. Nobody's life was safe.[18]

The fact is that the Red Army, then the biggest in the world, was known to be disproportionately ineffective as a military force. In 1933 a Comintern lecturer, who informed Soviet troops that there would be no war that year, was greeted with audible sighs of relief,[19] and three years later Western military observers found the Red Army manoeuvres unimpressive. (It has been remarked that 'Stalin's determined efforts to appease Hitler until the very moment of the German attack in 1941 suggest that the Soviet leader's assessment of his country's military power was not so far different from that entertained in the West.')[20] Small wonder that in 1936 Marshal Tukhachevsky, the Deputy People's Commissar for Defence, had to confess that 'at the present moment the Soviet Union would be unable to bring any military aid to Czechoslovakia in case of German attack'.[21] And then, at the height of the European crisis, between June 1937 and October 1938, there occurred that murderous purge of the officers' corps of the Red Army which deprived it of 70 per cent of its most experienced leaders.[22] Not only was the army's effectiveness as a fighting arm brought seriously into question, but the purge's timing revealed that Soviet leaders were far too preoccupied with the suppression of real or fancied sedition at home to contemplate any adventures involving the Red Army in a war hundreds of miles beyond the frontier. In the words of Professor Lukacs, 'in 1938 Stalin was no more prepared for war with Germany than were Chamberlain or Daladier'.[23]

It is difficult to establish certainty in these matters in the absence of access to Soviet records. Only these would reveal the true intentions of the Soviet Government. But it is instructive to consider what measures could have been contemplated were the Soviet Union to have honoured its Pact with Czechoslovakia.

Even if Soviet professions were sincere, there were serious, if not insuperable, obstacles in the way of Soviet military assistance to the Czechs. Given the state of Red Army military preparation, it is inconceivable that troops or planes could have reached Bohemia in sufficient numbers to influence the outcome of a German invasion. Prague was, after all, much nearer to the French frontier than the Soviet. Much more of a consideration was the fact that the Soviet and Czech frontiers were nowhere contiguous, being separated by a hundred miles of Polish and Romanian territory. Clearly intervention was only possible with the consent of Poland and Romania.

Neither government felt over-enthusiastic at the thought of opening their frontiers to a power with whom relations were traditionally hostile, and the conduct of whose armies was a byword for barbaric savagery. There was the strongest possible suspicion that the Red Army, once in possession of foreign territory, would be extremely unlikely to depart. That this suspicion was justified was proved a bare year later, when the Soviets took advantage of the Pact with Germany to overrun large areas of both countries – conquests repeated when opportunity offered in 1945.

Poland, which in any case had signed a non-aggression pact with Germany in 1934,[24] categorically refused passage to Soviet troops across her soil. Romania's refusal, though more cautiously expressed and hedged about with qualifications, was equally certain. Litvinov, unabashed, continued to assert cheerfully that Romanian consent would be forthcoming, and that Soviet forces could be dispatched to Czechoslovakia in time of war.[25] These assurances cost the Soviet Union nothing, since even in the unlikely event they were put to the test it would not be the Soviet Union's fault if they could not be implemented. France and Britain were well aware of the unlikelihood of direct Soviet help to Czechoslovakia through the Carpatho-Ukraine.

Polish fears were seemingly confirmed on 23 September 1938, when Moscow informed Warsaw that, in the event of a Polish attack on Czechoslovakia, Soviet Russia would be obliged to take up a belligerent stance. This threat bore a certain appearance of legitimacy in Western eyes, since the Poles were indeed harbouring plans to seize the Czech province of Teschen under cover of a German invasion. Large bodies of Soviet troops were reported moving up to the Polish frontier.[26]

The USSR could hardly have been in a happier position. Undeniable logistical difficulties facing any Soviet military participation in action against Germany would enable her to gain as much or as little territory from her immediate neighbours as she could, at minimal risk to herself, and with a cloak of League of Nations respectability to boot. Had Germany invaded Czechoslovakia in 1938, Soviet Russia could offer a number of alternative moves. If the invasion met little opposition, and France remained inactive, the Soviets could loudly request passage for their troops across Poland or Romania. Poland would refuse and Romania request League guarantees. Further prevarications could be spun out whilst events unfolded. If German successes continued unopposed, the Soviets could deplore Polish and Romanian intransigence, wring their hands, and return home.

If, on the other hand, the French and Czechs appeared to be gaining the upper hand, or if war in the West were locked in stalemate, Soviet armies could march forward to their aid across intervening territory. Polish and Romanian protests would arouse little sympathy in the circumstances, and it would be strange if large parts of their eastern lands did not remain permanently in Soviet hands. This possibility is not so very different from what actually happened during the next two years, when the Soviet Union used German expansion eastwards as a pretext for seizing Romanian Bessarabia and huge areas of eastern Poland.

In the absence of Soviet documentation it is not possible to know how calculated were these considerations in Soviet eyes. But the policy was not one which required in its initiation great subtlety or contingency planning; merely caution and a resolve not to lose opportunities. As Stalin himself had said in 1925:

Our banner remains, as before, the banner of *peace*. But if war begins, we shall not be able to sit with folded hands – we shall have to make a move, but the move will come last. And we shall act so as to throw the decisive weight onto the scales, the weight that could be preponderant.[27]

From the Soviet point of view the ideal situation would be one where the Franco-British allies and the Germans became locked in such mutually destructive combat that all danger to the Soviet Union from either side would be reduced; and, if all went well, pretexts could readily be devised for advancing the Soviet frontiers as far into Eastern Europe as circumstances permitted. As the Germans clearly meant business whilst the Western powers vacillated, no opportunities were lost of prodding the latter to action.[28] There was in any case little danger involved in an Allied victory. The Soviets would enjoy the reputation of having been active in support of Czech sovereignty, and Britain and France were too far off to object over-strongly had some chunks of Poland or Romania disappeared in the meantime. But what if Germany were the victor, either over an abandoned Czechoslovakia, or over the dilatory French as well? No Soviet policy-maker could afford to disregard this possibility.

Until the summer of 1933 the Soviet foreign policy world-view had been satisfyingly uncomplicated. Soviet Russia, the world's only genuine socialist state, was surviving solitary and embattled in a hostile world. Despite minor rivalries, the encircling bourgeois states were united in desiring the overthrow of the young socialist state, which must always remain to them a threat and reproach. France, Japan, the United States and Great Britain were the leading members of this menacing capitalist clique; of these Britain, with her vast empire straddling the globe, was undoubtedly the most dangerous. Between 1925 and 1930 the USSR increasingly feared an imperialist onslaught, most probably headed by the dreaded British.[29] With the Nazi accession to power, however, the situation was radically changed. There were now *two* centres of imperialist power, headed respectively by Britain and Germany. Both were hostile to the Soviet Union, naturally, but they were also at daggers drawn with each other. The Soviets had to consider how to act in this more complicated world.

Germany, until the early 1930s, had been the beaten and dismembered victim of the Treaty of Versailles. With her tiny army, restricted by the Treaty to a mere 100,000 men, she could represent no threat to the Soviet Union. She possessed too a large and devoted Communist Party, whose ultimate success (prophesied by Lenin on frequent occasions) was regarded as the key to the eventual world revolution. From 1921 the two unloved powers, ostracized by the Versailles victors, found themselves drawn together, and at Rapallo in the following year signed a treaty of collaboration which surprised and alarmed the great powers. Soviet Russia and Germany shared many points of agreement: resentment of France and Britain; a desire to re-establish the powerful military forces of which their defeats in the World War had deprived them; and discontent at the disabilities imposed on them by the Versailles Treaty.

Above all they hated Poland, a new nation carved by the Versailles powers out of former German and Russian territory. It was necessary to tread cautiously, as Poland was fiercely independent and closely linked to France. But nevertheless, 'We have never been Poland's guarantors and never will be', Stalin remarked pointedly to a German visitor; and an important Red Army general, flushed with drink, expressed Soviet intentions very clearly in 1930: 'Will we not be ready now in two years to carry out frontier adjustments and to kill the Poles? After all, we must once again partition Poland.'[30]

As France and Britain were regarded as the principal threats to Soviet survival, Germany's attempts to regain ground at their expense could be regarded only with favour in Moscow.[31] Germany in turn looked to Soviet Russia to assist in crushing Poland, France's ally.[32] With Poland gone and a common frontier linking her to a sympathetic Russia, Germany would be in a strong position to confront her two mighty adversaries in the West.

Germany chafed too at the clause confining her army, the Reichswehr, to 100,000 light-armed men. A secret reserve had soon been created (the 'Black Reichswehr'), but secrecy greatly restricted training facilities. Now, with the vast hidden spaces of Russia open to them, German generals could find the opportunity for which they longed. In January 1920, General Hans von Seeckt first set out the view that Germany should abandon her wartime policy of attempting to divide or destroy the Russian Empire. 'Now we have to come to terms with Soviet Russia,' he wrote; 'we have no alternative'. Two years later he elaborated further:

Poland's existence is intolerable, incompatible with the survival of Germany. It must disappear and it will disappear through its own internal weakness and through Russia – with our assistance. For Russia Poland is even more intolerable than for us; no Russia can reach agreement with Poland. With Poland will disappear one of the strongest pillars of the Versailles settlement, the preponderance of France . . .

Contact was established with representatives of the Soviet government, who were all for an immediate combined invasion of Poland. This was regarded by the Germans as dangerously premature, but thenceforward secret military co-operation proceeded at an ever-increasing rate. Junkers set up a factory near Moscow for the production of warplanes and, as early as 1926, 300,000 shells were produced in Soviet factories and shipped to Germany.

Even more important to the war machines of both countries was the exchange of training facilities. The Germans, with their incomparable tradition of military skill, provided training officers, many of whom were later to attain high rank in Hitler's Wehrmacht. The Soviets in return provided facilities for training and experimentation in war *matériel*. Three secret training-grounds were established in Russia: a tank school near Kazan, a poison-gas school near Saratov, and a flying school at Lipetsk. As the Treaty of Versailles had prohibited any form of German air force, the latter proved particularly important in the development of the future Luftwaffe. A huge modern aerodrome was constructed at Lipetsk under German direction, where German pilots underwent annual training in Junkers and Fokker warplanes. Occasionally rumours reached the West of these transactions, but their nature and extent remained concealed in a country that had become as remote as 'the dark side of the moon'.

This alliance between the largely monarchist and nationalist Reichswehr, led until 1927 by that epitome of monocled Prussian militarism General Hans von Seeckt on the one hand, and the apostles of proletarian revolution on the other, openly bent on the destruction of the old German social order, was necessarily subject to continual strain. But the generals remained as confident that they could keep their home Bolsheviks in order as were the Russian Bolsheviks that in due course Germany would collapse before the devouring flames of world revolution. The bonds of common interest outweighed old fears and hatreds to the extent that Soviet-

German military co-operation continued through the increasingly
right-wing era of Brüning, von Papen, and von Schleicher into the
early months of Hitler's rule. It was not until the autumn of 1933 that
German establishments in Russia were finally closed. For the new
Chancellor, von Seeckt's vision of a divided Poland was now far too
modest an aim.[33]

One of the main tenets of National Socialism, and a recurring
theme in *Mein Kampf* and Hitler's speeches, was a ferocious anti-
communism. 'Marxism', had written the future Führer, 'represents
the most striking phase of the Jewish endeavour to eliminate the
dominant significance of personality in every sphere of human life
and replace it by the numerical power of the masses.'[34] Moreover, it
was an openly-declared aim of the Nazi movement to seize and
colonize those vast Russian spaces which had been briefly held by
the Reich after the Treaty of Brest-Litovsk in 1918. The Soviet
Union's course seemed clear: she must temporarily bury her dif-
ferences with the Entente powers and make every endeavour to stifle
Nazi aggression at its inception. This was the policy pursued by
Litvinov in the League of Nations and elsewhere.

But was this straightforward policy enough? With every month
that passed the new Reich displayed alarming evidence of the ruthless vigour with which it was to pursue its aims. Simultaneously the
weakness (or was it duplicity?) of British and French policy became
increasingly apparent. It seemed likely that sooner or later Germany
would reach a point where her interests would collide violently with
those of the Entente. But Hitler's moves were invariably sudden and
secret. Another prospect inevitably presented itself: one in which
Germany abandoned the risks inherent in challenging the democracies and turned eastwards. True, Russia and Germany shared no
common frontier; but within a year of his accession to power Hitler
had signed a non-aggression pact with the Poles, and thereafter
stressed publicly Germany's respect and friendship for Poland.[35] It
was not difficult to picture the equally anti-communist Poles joining
in a German crusade against Bolshevism. Soviet policy, always cautious and empirical, must take measures to guard against this eventuality. A shift in policy was developing in the Kremlin so novel and
secret that the unfortunate Litvinov at first had to be kept in ignorance
of it.

VI
The Pact of Blood

On the night of 30 June 1934 in Germany came the first overt large-scale indication of the ruthless violence permeating the Nazi system. Hundreds of people were murdered by Hitler's SS gunmen, several of them in his presence. An elderly gentleman who had opposed Hitler's *Putsch* in 1923 was hacked to pieces with axes and hurled into a swamp; a general and his wife were shot down in their dining-room, leaving the lady's fourteen-year-old daughter alone with the bodies; in cities and towns all over the Reich people were riddled with bullets in their beds, or dragged off to death before hastily-improvised firing-squads. The principal victims were Brownshirt leaders whom Hitler had come to find an encumbrance now that he was solidly in power. Then, when the death lists were being drawn up, other possible enemies of the Party were added, as were private individuals against whom one or other of the Nazi satraps had nourished a grievance.

By the time the rattle of small-arms had died away in the Berlin Lichterfelde Barracks and the blood been swabbed from the cell walls of the Stadelheim Prison in Munich, more than a thousand people lay dead. The German people remained silent and terrified, whilst the foreign press speculated as to the nature of the 'plot'. Hitler and Göring breathed again; the blow had fallen and there were no repercussions. Now the Führer was really master in his household.

Across the Alps Mussolini condemned the massacre as crude and badly executed. In the democracies the action itself was denounced as barbaric, and its necessity a sign of the regime's precarious nature. Only far to the east, in the Kremlin, was the purge regarded with undisguised admiration. An awed Stalin announced to his hastily-convened Politburo that 'The events in Germany do not at all indicate the collapse of the Nazi regime. On the contrary, they are bound to lead to the consolidation of that regime and the strengthening of Hitler himself.'

The Führer had exhibited qualities he was well capable of estimating. Henceforth Stalin was to regard him with an entirely new fear and respect. He was particularly impressed, it seems, by the impunity with which Hitler had been able to massacre large numbers of suspected adversaries in broad daylight. Within a few weeks Stalin began preparations for his own first bloody purge: that following the mysterious murder of his rival Kirov.[1]

Before January 1933, when Hitler became Chancellor, Stalin had regarded him through orthodox Marxist spectacles. The German Communist Party, millions strong, was destined to throw off the shackles of capitalism and usher in the endless age of proletarian freedom. Lenin himself had prophesied that 'the crisis in Germany . . . will infallibly end with the transference of political power into the hands of the proletariat', though 'final victory is impossible without a long, stubborn war of life and death'.[2]

But where did the Brown Revolution come in this scheme of things? Lenin had left no *obiter dicta* on Nazism, which was still in its infancy when he died. Here was a chance for Stalin to make his own Marxian analysis, one which was, however, faithful to the Leninist canon. 'German Fascism is the spearhead of world capitalism', Communist Party orators explained at meetings all over the Soviet Union and Germany:

> Capitalism finally has thrown off its mask – the workers of the world now face a clear choice between Fascism and Communism. Can we doubt which they will choose? The Soviet Union stands alone as the bulwark against Fascism, and the proletariat of all countries is with us. Mussolini in Italy, Hitler in Germany, comrades, are the precursors of our revolution. By revealing the true face of modern capitalism-fascism, they push the masses to an understanding of the truth. There is force in our slogan: *The worse the better!*[3]

Dialectical logic, according to this scheme of things, had seen no disadvantage in occasionally combining with the Nazis in efforts to topple the real enemy, social democracy (or 'social fascism', as the Communists confusingly termed it). There was much in any case to draw together the proponents of the two great chiliastic upheavals of

modern times. The psychological, philosophical and historical connections between Communism and National Socialism were so close
that their supporters were for the most part consciously or uncon-
sciously aware of this. The Marxists were more chary of making any
compromising admissions, but the consistent Soviet policy of referring incorrectly to National Socialists as 'German Fascists' surely
betrays a consciousness of the dangerous parallel likely to be drawn
between the two philosophies.

This similarity has sometimes been obscured in the popular mind
by the continuing suggestion that Nazism was 'right wing', a phrase
of very imprecise meaning. If, as seems generally accepted, the term
is held to imply 'reactionary' and 'conservative' in politics and
morals, then the misconception is deep indeed. For, as a distinguished scholar points out, 'no one has ever produced a single institution that Hitler and his circle wished to conserve . . . they
wished to conserve nothing, and therefore cannot be labelled conservatives.'[4] In fact it is clear that National Socialism, 'although the
reactionary aspects of its ideology and its opposition to the political
results of the revolution [of 1918 in Germany] conveniently dis-
guised the fact, was a revolutionary movement.'[5] The distinction to
be drawn is not that between 'left' and 'right', but between totalitarian and other concepts of government. All modern totalitarian
doctrines aim at an ideal: the 'left' towards a socialist millennium,
and the 'right' to the stirring of the masses to active participation in
some national purpose.[6]

From the earliest days of the Nazi Party many of its members had
entertained a respect, frequently reciprocated, for what they regarded
as the sincerity, vigour and ultimately similar aims of the Communists.[7] The Marxist philosopher Ernst Niekisch advocated a programme which combined the ideas of Marxism and Nazism, and a
'National Bolshevik' movement seeking to effect this union received
sympathetic approval from Goebbels and Karl Radek, the Soviet
ideologist.[8]

Early Nazi membership was frequently recruited from the Communist Party (KPD), and vice versa.[9] In particular a very high proportion of the SA (Brownshirts) came over in ever-increasing
numbers from the ranks of the Communists. Ernst Röhm, the SA
chief, welcomed them for their fanaticism and love of violence,
nicknaming them 'beefsteaks' (brown outside, red within).[10] The
flow worked the other way too, and in 1923 Hitler is reported to have

admitted that 'either we act now or our SA people will go over to the Communists'.[11] (Similarly many young Italian Fascists flocked to join the Communist Party after the fall of Mussolini.)[12]

Of William Joyce ('Lord Haw-Haw'), an observer noted, 'Had it not been for his hysteria about Jews, he might easily have become a successful Communist agitator.'[13] Theo Habicht, Hitler's agent in Austria, was a former Communist; Anton Drexler, a Nazi Party founder, thought ex-Marxists made the best Nazis; even the red background on the Swastika flag was adopted by Hitler from his Marxist rivals' banner, and the *'Horst Wessel Lied'* was provided by Goebbels with words to a popular Communist tune.[14] The more rabid the Nazi, frequently the closer his spiritual links to Soviet Marxism: Roland Freisler (the 'German Vishinsky', as Hitler proudly termed him) was an eager student of Soviet terror methods, and had in 1920 actually been a Bolshevik commissar in the Ukraine; whilst Vidkun Quisling had been 'originally very favourably disposed towards the Communist "experiment" in Russia . . .'[15]

The National Socialist leader whose sympathies were closest to Bolshevism was Goebbels. There is little doubt that he could as easily have become a Marxist as a National Socialist; from an early age he stressed the primacy of his socialism over nationalism, regarding as he did the former as 'a final rejection of the materialism and capitalist mammonism of the West'. In 1925 he recorded in his diary a longing to go to Russia, and believed it was better to 'go down with Bolshevism than live in eternal capitalist servitude'. Believing that Communists and Nazis were 'cut out of the same cloth', he expressed glowing admiration for Lenin. 'Lenin sacrificed Marx and in return gave Russia freedom', he explained; 'no tsar understood the Russian people in its depth, in its suffering, in its national instincts, as well as Lenin.'[16]

Hitler's attitude to Bolshevism was more ambivalent, but he was quite candid about the debt National Socialism owed to Marxism. From the earliest days of the Party's struggle he expressed a strong preference for ex-Marxists as suitable members. With pardonable confidence, he declaimed in 1934,

It is not Germany that will turn Bolshevist, but Bolshevism that will become a sort of National Socialism . . . Besides, there is more that binds us to Bolshevism than separates us from it. There is, above all, genuine revolutionary feeling, which is alive everywhere in Russia except where there are Jewish Marxists. I have always made allowance for this circumstance, and given orders that former Communists are to be admitted to the party at once. The *petit bourgeois* Social-Democrat and the trade-union boss will never make a National Socialist, but the Communist always will.

This was no idle claim: more than half of the fifty thousand Brown-shirts recruited in Berlin in the previous year had been Communists.[17] For Stalin himself, Hitler expressed respectful admiration, contrasting strongly with the contempt and hatred he felt for Roosevelt and Churchill. 'Stalin', he asserted in 1942, 'must command our unconditional respect. In his own way he is a hell of a fellow . . . [He] is half beast, half giant.'[18]

Nazi leanings towards their Marxist rivals or counterparts were willingly and unwittingly reciprocated. Apart from anti-Semitism, the German Communist Party (KPD) advanced policies not very different from those of the Nazis. Their programme was dictated by the Kremlin, via the Comintern. 'To the last the Communist Party beat the drum of nationalism and whipped up the masses against Versailles. They could hardly hope to outbid the Nazis, but they served as valuable pacemakers and helped to prepare the workers for the anti-Western foreign policy of Hitler.'[19]

Stalin was convinced that the Social Democrats were the most formidable obstacle to Soviet power in Germany, and thought the Nazis merely hired bully-boys of capitalism who would have no hope of retaining power if they ever gained it. At the Sixth Comintern Congress held at Moscow in 1928, he laid it down that the principal object of attack for the German Communist Party was to be the Social Democrats. This policy was loyally adhered to until Hitler became Chancellor. Time and again Nazis and Communists united in opposition votes in Landtag and Reichstag motions, and in November 1932 a crippling transport strike in Berlin was organized by both parties in union. A Communist deputy in the Prussian Landtag was accused of assisting in a Nazi victory. 'Colleague Diel,' replied Stalin's man exultantly, 'that is just what we want! Our strategy must be such that first of all the Right for once comes to power. The whole body of workers will unite in opposition to this government. Nazi rule will not last long. It will soon collapse, and the inheritors will be ourselves!'[20]

By 1934 Stalin became aware of the fact that his German policy had been based on a fantastic misconception. Hitler had triumphed, and the Blood Purge of 30 June revealed that the new Chancellor was not to be edged aside by the KPD or his supposed capitalist employers. The new Germany was bursting with energy and strength, and the need for a *rapprochement* was pressing.

Marxist opinion was no more likely than National Socialist to jib at the seeming volte-face of a German-Soviet alliance. Continuing purges inside Russia ensured that Soviet public opinion remained tractable to any decisions taken by the dictator, whilst Communist parties in foreign countries had proved themselves so subservient to Stalin's lightest whim that he rightly anticipated no difficulties there.

Cautious feelers, couched in appropriately convoluted Marxist phraseology, were extended, indicating that the USSR might in certain circumstances be wooed by 'Fascist' Germany, coupled with hints that the corpse of Poland would make a not unacceptable wedding gift. At the Seventeenth Party Congress in January 1934, Stalin explained that a new imperialist war was imminent, going on to declaim grimly: 'Let not Messrs. bourgeois blame us if, on the day after such a war, certain governments near and dear to them, now ruling safely "by the grace of God" turn up missing.' The 'imperialist war' could only be one between Germany and the Entente powers, and the 'missing' governments those client-states of the Entente, from Finland to Romania, bordering on the USSR.[21]

Karl Radek, Stalin's chief spokesman on German affairs, wrote on 15 July 1934 (a fortnight after Hitler's Blood Purge), 'There is no reason why Fascist Germany and Soviet Russia should not get on together, inasmuch as the Soviet Union and Fascist Italy are good friends.' Privately, Radek expressed his belief that one day the SA would prove to have been a wonderful 'reserve' of future Communists.[22] German strength and Nazi ruthlessness were factors more impressive to Stalin than any other considerations; as he said emphatically to his police chief, Yezhov, in 1937: 'We must come to terms with a superior power like Nazi Germany'.[23]

Stalin had long approved of secret military co-operation with Germany, his brother-in-law Pavel Alliluyev having been Soviet military representative at Berlin until the rupture of 1933.[24] Despite Hitler's total suppression of the German Communist Party after the Reichstag Fire, Soviet statesmen such as Krestinsky, Molotov and

Litvinov went out of their way to reassure German diplomats of Soviet good will.[25] Throughout the first five years of Hitler's rule in Germany this wooing continued, and in July 1935 Stalin's close confidant and fellow-Georgian David Kandelaki put forward in Berlin the first open suggestion that the two countries might draw closer together on a political basis. However, at this stage Hitler mistrusted Soviet intentions too greatly; the proposition received a cool reply,[26] and German policy continued on the anti-Communist course which culminated in the Anti-Comintern Pact with Italy and Japan in 1936. These threatening moves only served to increase Stalin's respect and fear for a swiftly-rearming and resurgent Germany. Violent outbursts of anti-Nazi propaganda alternated with further discreet feelers regarding some sort of pact or *rapprochement*.[27]

German strength and Nazi ruthlessness continued to attract and frighten Stalin. In the late 1930s Nazism and Fascism seemed to be moving on a tide of victory throughout the world. In Spain, Italian- and German-backed Nationalist forces began to throw back Stalin's Republican protégés; the Japanese penetrated ever further into Chinese territory; and Hitler's every daring new move left the appeasing Western powers in greater diplomatic disarray. Stalin too was anxious to appease Hitler, but the Führer's continuing intransigence left him no alternative but to take other precautionary measures.

The previous chapter showed how Soviet diplomacy sought to incite Britain and France to take resolute measures to contain German expansion. Soviet approaches to the Entente powers made vastly more noise in the world than parallel discreet feelers extended to Germany. The Soviet Union joined the largely Entente-dominated League of Nations in 1934, entered into diplomatic relations with the United States, and was loud in advocating any measures, not excluding military intervention, that would preserve the integrity of Czechoslovakia.[28] Foreign Commissar Litvinov toured European capitals issuing assurances whose militancy was exceeded only by their insincerity.

At the time of the Munich settlement, British and French statesmen had rejected these Soviet offers of assistance. The subsequent brief idyll, with both German and Entente leaders feeling (with very different justification) that matters had been settled to their satisfaction, left the Soviets more isolated and frightened than before. Since Hitler's rise to power in 1933 Stalin's diplomacy had been two-pronged, with Litvinov urging collective security on Britain, France,

Poland and other European powers, whilst secret contacts tried again and again to induce Germany to guarantee Soviet safety. The policy was subtle in its way, but there was in reality scant alternative if a frightened and enfeebled Soviet Union was to survive.

These apparently conflicting policies could each be pursued as vigorously as the other. After all, success in either approach would present enormous advantages, whilst the more energetically Litvinov wooed the British and French, the more Hitler would appreciate the value of Soviet friendship.[29] Behind this cautious and shrewd policy lay differing considerations in Stalin's mind: determination to keep the Soviet Union out of any major war until it was clear who was to be the victor; a modest ambition to profit by any opportunity the crisis offered, in particular to destroy or absorb his violently anti-Soviet immediate neighbours; admiration for Hitler the statesman; respect for the resources of the world-encircling British Empire; and, above all, an entirely realistic apprehension that the fabric of Bolshevik society was fragile in the extreme, with little likelihood of surviving a severe shock.

In April 1939 Litvinov made a formal offer of a triple alliance of mutual guarantee with Britain and France, an offer which Churchill, Eden and other critics of Chamberlain's policy argued, then and later, should have been accepted.[30] But this and further proffers were received unenthusiastically by the British Government and allowed to drop. Chamberlain continued to nurture profound mistrust for the Soviets, and the states of Eastern Europe who were to be 'rescued' from a possible German embrace by that of the bear to their rear were less than eager to accept. (All depends on one's viewpoint. The Czechs lamented Munich as a betrayal of their country. The Finns, on the other hand, saw the settlement as the saving of theirs from the Soviets, who would have been bound to take advantage of any clash between Germany and the Entente.)[31]

Nevertheless, negotiations continued throughout the summer. In May, a Foreign Office delegation led by William Strang, head of the Central Department, arrived in Moscow with hopes of achieving something tangible. Every week saw the Nazi menace increasing, and even Chamberlain could not throw away the Russian card altogether. But this mission was no more successful than its successor, a military deputation in August led by Admiral Drax and the French General Doumenc. By then the game was up, and the dreaded Soviet-German *rapprochement* had become a reality.

Winston Churchill and others have suggested that a fine opportunity of checking Hitler was in this way missed.

> There can . . . be no doubt, even in the after light, that Britain
> and France should have accepted the Russian offer . . . The
> alliance of Britain, France and Russia would have struck deep
> alarm into the heart of Germany in 1939, and no one can prove that
> war might not even then have been averted.[32]

This was certainly the view of the public at large: in April a Gallup
Poll found that 92 per cent of people in Britain favoured an alliance
with the Soviet Union.[33] Indeed, but for pressure of public opinion,
Britain might have presented a still more frigid front to the proposed
ally. As a Government summary sardonically noted in early 1940,

> A future historian may perhaps wonder at the persistence shown
> by the British and French Governments in carrying on these ill-
> fated negotiations for so many months and in the face of such
> obvious difficulties. In fairness to His Majesty's Government,
> therefore, this review would not be complete without allusion to
> the remarkable wave of pro-Russian enthusiasm which swept
> Great Britain during the whole period . . . from the very outset of
> the 1939 negotiations, under the influence of the credulous be-
> lievers in Stalin's selfless readiness to protect the weak, of the
> defeatists who saw in the Russian 'steam-roller' our only defence
> against the German danger, of the professional friends of the
> Soviet Union, press and public worked themselves into a veritable
> fever.[34]

Just how insincere were Soviet proposals and reactions is impossible
to assess fully. A sceptical view was expressed by the former chief of
the Soviet military intelligence (GRU) network in Western Europe,
who had defected in 1937. In 1939 he wrote,

> Stalin's whole international policy during the last six years has
> been a series of manoeuvres designed to place him in a favourable
> position for a deal with Hitler. When he joined the League of
> Nations, when he proposed the system of collective security,
> when he sought the hand of France, flirted with Poland, courted
> Great Britain, intervened in Spain, he was calculating every move
> with an eye upon Berlin. His hope was to get into such a position
> that Hitler would find it advantageous to meet his advances.[35]

The succession of events suggests, sometimes with remarkable clarity, that Krivitsky's interpretation (published before the Nazi-Soviet Pact) was well-informed. Stalin's decision to move from merely placating Hitler to a policy of full-blown alliance seems to have taken place in the early spring of 1939. On 10 March, at the Eighteenth Party Congress, Stalin made a speech in which he expounded Soviet policy with regard to the European crisis. After recapitulating the aggressions of the Anti-Comintern powers (Germany, Italy, Japan), he went on to indicate his own country's role for the future: the USSR was immensely strong, militarily and industrially, and was vigorously opposed to Fascist aggression; *but* she would pay no heed to provocative suggestions in the democracies that Hitler had designs on the Ukraine, would not allow herself to become embroiled with Germany, and above all was not so simple-minded as to engage in pulling other people's chestnuts out of the fire.[36]

Hitler's response was swift. Five days later German troops poured into Bohemia, extinguishing the vestiges of Czechoslovakia that had survived the Munich settlement. Britain and France stood still, and on 1 April Hitler issued a grim confirmation of the correctness of Stalin's cautious policy: 'Anyone who declares himself to be ready to pull the chestnuts out of the fire for the Great Powers [i.e. Britain and France] must be aware that he might burn his fingers in the process.'[37]

The warning was superfluous; Stalin had no intention of burning his fingers and well understood where power lay. At very long last the Entente had awoken to the dangers of appeasement, and in a flurry of firmness offered unilateral guarantees of military assistance in the event of invasion to Poland, Greece, Romania, Denmark, Holland and Switzerland.[38] On 17 April the Soviet Union made that offer of a Triple Alliance with Britain and France, which not unnaturally appeared to many the one chance of placing a firm *ne plus ultra* before Germany's advance.

However, it seems likely that the offer was merely a ploy in accord with the policy outlined by Krivitsky, whereby Germany was to be cajoled and frightened into turning to the Soviet Union for friendship. On the very same day that the Soviets offered the alliance to Britain and France, they secretly approached the Germans with clear indications of a similar offer. The Soviet Ambassador in Berlin, Merekalov, called on the German Foreign Office for the first time since his arrival ten months earlier. Clearly acting on instructions, Merekalov explained to Secretary of State Weizsäcker that Soviet policy was in no way anti-German and that there was no reason why relations should not progress from normal to better and better.[39]

The proposition had to be kept secret from the temperamental Litvinov,[40] who might not play his part so convincingly otherwise; above all, the British and French must be persuaded to take the suggested triple alliance seriously. The real purpose of the proposal was of course to prod the Germans into taking Merekalov's hints seriously. Had the boot been on the other foot, the Soviet Government presumably would have taken care to leak the approach to Berlin to the British and French.[41]

The effect on Hitler was immediate. He abandoned the policy of backing Poland against the USSR, and set out to woo the latter as his ally. A fortnight later Stalin significantly dismissed the Jew Litvinov and replaced him with the sullen and robot-like Molotov, thus persuading Hitler that Russia was no longer 'Jew-dominated' and that henceforth foreign policy would follow precisely whatever course Stalin chose. Between May and August the two dictators moved inexorably closer together. On 17 May a Soviet emissary conceded frankly in Berlin that the Anglo-Soviet negotiations were unlikely to succeed. For, as the Germans bluntly pointed out, what could Britain offer? Participation in a war of which no one could see the outcome, and the guaranteed hostility of Germany. Germany, on the other hand, could offer precisely what Stalin longed for: neutrality and, if some more concrete arrangement were to be arrived at, certain unspecified but material advantages.

Two such despots, each with a lifetime of treachery and violence behind him, could not fail to entertain deep mutual suspicions. But common interest and mutual respect triumphed, and on 15 August Ribbentrop conveyed to Molotov proposals designed to establish Soviet-German friendship and clear up certain 'territorial questions' in Eastern Europe. Molotov was more than responsive, and on 23 August Ribbentrop flew into Moscow to sign the agreement.[42]

The visit was a delirious triumph from start to finish. Swastika flags (released from a film studio making a hastily-discarded anti-Nazi film) fluttered alongside the hammer-and-sickle, whilst a band thundered forth the 'Horst Wessel Lied' and 'The Internationale'. Ribbentrop felt himself walking on air, as all went by without a hitch. 'Things are going splendidly with the Russians!' he kept

exclaiming, noting too with high glee that the Soviet leaders were
'strong-faced men', with whom he felt as much at home as with old
Nazi Party comrades in Germany.[43] That night in the Kremlin, the
Treaty of Non-Aggression was signed.

Afterwards Stalin arranged a cosy little party for his new friends.
The conversation ranged widely, though a continual theme was provided by numerous gibes at the expense of the 'stupid' English,
whom the present proceedings were designed to confound. There
were merry toasts, too, as the champagne flowed. 'I know how much
the German nation loves its Führer,' proclaimed Stalin; 'I should
therefore like to drink to his health.' Molotov drank to Stalin, confirming as he did so that it had indeed been Stalin's 'chestnuts'
speech of 10 March that initiated this diplomatic revolution. Finally,
as his distinguished visitors left, Stalin called out 'that the Soviet
Government takes the new Pact very seriously; he could confirm on
his word of honour that the Soviet Union would not betray her
partner'.[44]

The next day Ribbentrop and his party flew back to Berlin to report
to Hitler. The latter was as delighted as Stalin, for whom he felt an
increasing personal admiration. 'Now I have the world in my
pocket!', he had exclaimed on learning of Ribbentrop's invitation.[45]
It was the triumph of a policy which had been germinating for some
time in the Führer's mind.

> A German-Russian alliance means simply the confluence of two
> streams which run toward the same sea, the sea of world revolu-
> tion. National Socialism will submit to *Gleichschaltung* with the
> Bolshevik world Revolution, or will subject that revolution to
> *Gleichschaltung* with itself: it amounts either way to much the
> same thing. It will be no ordinary coalition between two Powers
> for normal practical purposes. Germany and Russia, if they come
> together, will radically transform the world. That alliance is
> Hitler's great coming stroke.

So foresaw a former colleague of Hitler some months previously.[46]

The Non-Aggression Pact bound the signatories to observe peaceful relations with each other for ten years and, unless denounced
earlier, was automatically to be extended another five years – until
1954. A Secret Additional Protocol arranged for the demarcation of
Eastern Europe into German and Soviet spheres of interest. Finland,
Estonia, Latvia and Bessarabia fell to the Soviet sphere, while

Lithuania was marked down for Germany. A line was drawn through Poland, though 'the maintenance of an independent Polish state and how such a state shall be bounded can only be definitely determined in the course of further political developments'.

A few days previously a trade agreement of great military and political value to both powers had been signed. Germany was to receive crucial raw materials (lumber, cotton, feed grain, oil cake, phosphate, platinum, petroleum, etc.) to the value of some 180 million Reichsmarks, whilst the Soviet Union gained German industrial and military manufactures. At one swoop Germany had at once protected herself against any combination of Britain and France with the Soviet Union, and ensured that she could defy a British naval blockade, which had wrought such havoc on Germany's economy in the previous war.[47] The way was open for the first blow against Entente encirclement: the destruction of Poland.

Exactly a week after the signing of the Secret Protocol in the Kremlin, the Wehrmacht gave the world its first taste of the new style of warfare. At early dawn on 1 September a million and a half German troops crossed the Polish frontier in massive pincer movements from north and south. Some two thousand warplanes hurtled overhead, dealing destruction amongst the hastily-assembled and ill-equipped Poles. Two great army groups, under Field Marshals von Bock and von Rundstedt, thrust far beyond the Polish forces, up the Vistula and towards Warsaw.

A flurry of diplomatic activity broke out in the West, and on 3 September Britain and France honoured their pledges to declare war on Germany. But the Allies were impotent to help collapsing Poland, by now inaccessible to aid. Hitler was less disturbed by this predictable event than by the failure of Soviet Russia to move in the east. That evening Ribbentrop telegraphed the German Ambassador in Moscow, ordering him to inform Molotov that Poland would be destroyed within weeks. It was intended to occupy the western section of Poland allocated to Germany on 23 August: might it not be in the Soviet interest to move forward at once into *their* section? Behind this plea probably lay less any doubts that Germany was capable of winning victory single-handed, than a desire to impress upon the British and French that Soviet Russia was an active ally of Germany, and not a mere passive onlooker.[48]

But Molotov declined to act, cautiously suggesting 'that through excessive haste we might injure our cause and promote unity among our opponents.' It was not that the Soviets disapproved of German successes; on the 9th Molotov had telephoned Ambassador von Schulenburg on receiving a premature report of the fall of Warsaw:[49] 'Please convey my congratulations and greetings to the German Reich Government.' Ribbentrop appealed again for Soviet intervention, but Molotov explained that events had moved too fast for the ponderous Soviet war machine. Preparations were however under way. Meanwhile he had thought of an ingenious pretext for the Soviet invasion: it could be announced that the Soviet Union was moving to protect Ukrainians and Byelorussians in eastern Poland from the effects of the war.

However, he had learned that a difficulty stood in the way. It was rumoured that Germany and Poland were about to sign an armistice, which if true would make the Soviet pretext look very foolish. What was to be done? The fears lying behind Molotov's words (and hence Stalin's, since Molotov was a mere mouthpiece) are very evident. Soviet policy had to steer its way through a number of dangerous shoals. Britain and France had been slow to act, but their resources were immense – almost limitless, if backed by the United States. What if an Allied victory were to follow, and the Soviets were caught holding the baby? Alternatively, if they were too cautious Germany might make peace, leaving an independent rump of Poland behind the Vistula or the Bug. On what pretext could Russia attack such a Poland, no longer at war with Germany but still (presumably) allied to Britain and France? Or might the Germans simply push right on to the Soviet frontier? Soviet Russia lay temporarily supine, a great, sprawling, cowardly giant; afraid to act and yet obliged to do so.

However, as a fortnight passed with continuing German successes and little evidence of any serious activity on the part of Britain or France, Stalin's courage rose. Molotov explained that the Red Army was awaiting news of the fall of Warsaw (still gallantly holding out) before acting. That event would provide justification for Soviet 'protection' of Polish Ukraine and Byelorussia. In the event the Soviets did not wait that long (Warsaw held out magnificently until the 27th), and at the characteristic hour of 2 a.m. on 17 September, Stalin received von Schulenburg and informed him that the Red Army would attack Poland at dawn.[50]

Molotov's representation of this invasion as an act of protection sprang from a need 'to justify abroad, in some way or other, its present intervention'. It caused considerable irritation to the German negotiators who, for parallel reasons, wished Russia to display herself openly as an ally. As Molotov's 'abroad' could refer only to the Western democracies, Stalin still clearly nurtured some fear lest he be brought to account for his actions to a victorious Entente.[51] The ploy was by no means ineffective, and British diplomats, daunted by the grim prospect of *force majeure*, were reluctantly inclined to accept it at face value.[52]

On the very first day of the German invasion Moscow had furnished military intelligence co-operation to her ally,[53] and now, two and a half weeks later, the Red Army itself was on the march. A vast horde of semi-motorized and ill-equipped divisions streamed over the frontier past a skeleton force of bewildered Polish frontier guards. Encountering little opposition at first, they pushed on swiftly to meet the Germans, who by now were well up to the agreed demarcation line. Many Soviet and Polish soldiers greeted each other in friendly fashion, under the mistaken impression that the Red Army had come to repulse the Wehrmacht. But leaflets distributed by General Timoshenko's staff betrayed the barbaric nature of this Asiatic invasion: 'Soldiers! Kill your officers and generals. Do not obey the orders of your officers. Drive them from your land . . . Believe us, your only friend is the Red Army of the Soviet Union.'

On 19 September the guns of the fortress of Brest-Litovsk fell silent after a combined bombardment by Nazi and Soviet troops. A victory parade in the surrendered citadel once again saw the Red Flag and the Swastika fluttering side by side. On the 27th heroic Warsaw fell, and Polish resistance collapsed. The Germans were punctilious in observing the agreed demarcation line, and the conquerors settled down to digest the feast.[54]

Despite this easy 'victory', Stalin was if anything more apprehensive than he had been before. The Red Army's contribution had been about as valuable and courageous as Mussolini's similar jackal-like attack on defeated France in the following year. It seems certain that Hitler would have attacked Poland whatever Soviet Russia's attitude had been,[55] and the devastating nature of the German war machine must have struck dread into Stalin's fearful heart. He had been consumed with suspicion that the Germans would advance beyond the demarcation line.[56] In the early days of the German attack the Soviets had actually urged on the Polish defence, presumably in a vain effort to 'bleed' the Wehrmacht and provide time for their own huge but primitive army to mobilize. On 10 September Molotov claimed that three million Russians had already been mobilized; as it would be ludicrous to suppose that such a vast number was required to mop up the stricken Poles, one can only suppose this to have been a pathetic attempt to impress the Germans with Soviet military might.[57]

Behind the delay there may well also have lain a real fear of the Polish Army, of whose prowess Stalin had had personal experience in the disastrous campaign of 1920. For Soviet diplomacy during the final settlement after the Polish defeat betrayed a deep-rooted fear of Poland, both as a fighting nation which had never lain quiet under alien rule, and as the ally of the British, whose awesome power and ruthlessness alternated with that of the Germans in Stalin's nightmares. Hitler had not intended the total disappearance of Poland, but envisaged a rump state centred on Warsaw.

This idea did not appeal to Stalin, and on 25 September he proposed a division of the whole of Polish territory, which would in effect place the Soviet frontier very near the Curzon line. This was the frontier very roughly marking the eastern march of ethnic Poland, which the British had suggested in 1919 and with which in consequence they might again be content in 1939 if trouble arose. As this gave Germany more territory than the Pact of 23 August envisaged, Stalin suggested that Lithuania should be allocated in exchange to the Soviet share. He added that in that case 'the Soviet Union would immediately take up the solution (Lösung) of the problem of the Baltic countries in accordance with the Protocol of August 23, and expected in this matter the unwavering aid of the German government.' These proposals, which were acceptable to the Germans, illustrate the cunning and cowardice of Stalin's policy at this time. He clearly still feared the possibility of an Anglo-French victory, whilst having to live with the fact of a German one. The lands he now held had formerly been part of the Russian Empire, and their retention was unlikely ever to be a serious *casus belli* with the Allies. Any odium incurred by the conquest would fall on the Germans, who ruled over 90 per cent of 'Polish' Poland. At the same time, behind the screen of German armed might, the Red Army could assemble its millions and (with due caution) fall upon those tiny states on the Baltic in whose fate the Germans disclaimed any interest.

The formal settlement took place in the Kremlin. On 27 September Ribbentrop again flew into Moscow, and talks lasted from the next afternoon into the early hours of the morning. At 5 a.m. on the

29th the formal Treaty was signed. A preamble stated the civilizing mission of the two great powers: the USSR and the Reich 'consider it as exclusively their task, after the collapse of the former Polish state [how on earth had that come about?], to establish peace and order in these territories and to assure to the peoples living there a peaceful life in keeping with their national character.' This beneficial purpose was to be effected in the manner already indicated, viz.: the partition of Poland; the Soviet seizure of Lithuania in compensation for the German acquisition of Lublin and Warsaw; and a grim warning that 'both parties will tolerate in their territories no Polish agitation which affects the territory of the other party. They will suppress in their territories all beginnings of such agitation and inform each other concerning suitable measures for this purpose.'

So much for the Poles; as for their Allies, the signatories appealed for Britain and France to make peace now that Hitler and Stalin had 'created a sure foundation for a lasting peace in Eastern Europe . . . ' If not, they continued sternly, 'the governments of Germany and of the U.S.S.R. shall engage in mutual consultations with regard to necessary measures'.

At a celebratory banquet in the afternoon everyone was in a sunny mood. Stalin drank little, but encouraged everyone else. Ribbentrop, as before, was in ecstasies. A few days later the Italian Foreign Minister reported sourly that 'he is all out for the Russians. And he expressed himself in favour of the Communists in such an imprudent and vulgar way as to perplex anyone who listens to him.' Also at the feast was a Soviet functionary who was to play a crucial role in the 're-establishment of peace and order' in Poland. A German official recounted the incident:

> Beria, who was sitting on my right, was trying to make me drink more than I wished. Stalin soon noticed that Beria and I were in dispute about something, and asked across the table: 'What's the argument about?' When I told him, he replied, 'Well, if you don't want to drink, no one can force you.'
> 'Not even the chief of the NKVD himself?' I joked.
> Whereupon he answered, 'Here, at this table, even the chief of the NKVD has no more to say than anyone else'.[58]

Such was the fate of Poland, a fate eagerly advocated by Engels in a letter to Marx nearly a century earlier:

Take away from the Poles in the West as much as possible; under
pretext of defence, garrison their fortresses with Germans, let
them make a mess of things for themselves, send them into the
fire, eat up their land . . . and if the Russians can be got to move,
form an alliance with them, and force the Poles to give in.[59]

The shade of Engels cannot have been disappointed; the Poles were
being 'sent into the fire' to an extent which must have satisfied even
his vengeful spirit. From the opening days of the invasion events
revealed the nature of the warfare practised by the new ideologies.
Indiscriminate bombing of civilian targets was practised with increasing ferocity by the Luftwaffe, and on 12 September the entire
foreign diplomatic corps was witness to a particularly savage attack
on the defenceless open village of Krzemieniec.[60]

This was as nothing, however, to what went on behind the fighting lines. Hitler had given instructions to Himmler that 'whatever
we can find in the shape of an upper class in Poland is to be liquidated: should anything take its place, it will be placed under guard
and done away with at an appropriate time.' By 8 September
Einsatzgruppen of the SS were able to boast that they were killing
two hundred Poles a day, and by the end of September tens of
thousands of Poles had been murdered. Their names had appeared
on special lists prepared by Heydrich, and chiefly included noblemen, priests and Jews. On 27 September, when Ribbentrop was
flying to meet Stalin, Heydrich stated that 'of the Polish upper
classes in the occupied territories only a maximum of 3 per cent is
still present'. In this way Hitler promised to 'ensure that the Polish
intelligentsia cannot throw up a new leader class', and ordered
'Jews, Poles and similar trash to be cleared from the old and new
Reich territories'.[61]

By that time the Red Army had plucked up courage to fall upon
the shattered Poles' rear. What followed was horrifyingly predictable. The Italian Ambassador in Warsaw summed up the situation:
'. . . the German Air Force is . . . absolutely pitiless and has con-
stantly dropped bombs on civil populations, but the German horror
is surpassed a thousand times by the unspeakable horrors of the
Bolshevik advance.'[62] Clearly the Ambassador knew nothing as yet
of the activities of the Einsatzgruppen, but it would be difficult to
exaggerate the nature of the Soviet invasion.

There was no need for the creation of Marxist Einsatzgruppen, since the NKVD and its predecessor the Cheka had been practising activities like theirs for twenty years. As the Red Army edged nervously up to the demarcation line, terrified lest the Wehrmacht change its mind and roll onwards, thousands of NKVD troops spread over the defenceless countryside behind. The Red Army had confined itself to rape (old women were the principal victims, owing to a belief that the rapist would live to the age of his victim; as a result ninety-year-old women were frequently raped over and over again), and pillage. Even the pillage was occasionally restricted by the invaders' blank terror when faced with astonishing devices like electric irons.

It was the NKVD, however, which struck real fear in the Poles. Arriving a few days after the 'regular' troops, they set up head-quarters in every town, working by preference at night-time. Like the Gestapo, they came equipped with lists of proscribed categories of citizen, ranging from aristocrats and priests to officials of the Red Cross, persons speaking Esperanto, philatelists, and the like. Hastily herded together into prisons, they were held until the long, dark lines of cattle-trucks came hissing and clunking into the local rail-way station. The journey that followed was a nightmare preparatory to the fate that awaited them at their destination. One such truck, for example, held thirty-six prisoners.

The train had taken six weeks to do the journey to Moscow and during this time bread and water had been given to the prisoners at only a few irregular intervals. Of the truck's thirty-six passen-gers, only three reached their destination alive. Their train had stood still for long periods at sidings and once a week the truck door had been opened just enough to enable the dead to be dropped out.

Corpses of children froze in the snow and their mothers, vainly striving to restore them to life, covered them with their own bodies and felt the same deathly chill creep up their limbs and touch their own hearts.

Surviving children, for whom the Soviet authorities seem to have entertained a particular hatred, screamed and cried continually from cold, hunger and fear. The trucks were smeared with excrement left by crack troops of the Red Army who had used the incoming trains as transport. Through holes in the sides Polish families caught a last glimpse of a well-loved farm, a favourite cow, or a doomed church. NKVD guards deliberately deprived prisoners of water, so that they were reduced to drinking their own urine; tongues turned black and stiff and protruded from ghastly mouths and throats. Babies were born during the seemingly endless journey, only to die in the arms of their dying mothers.

As one Pole who experienced the same hellish journey explained: 'Volumes could be filled with nothing but the story of the trains. And even then it would not have been told, for there are no words which can reproduce the emotions experienced and the sensations undergone. The reader can be given facts. He cannot share the *experience*.' These sufferings were not caused merely by neglect or lack of resources. Scarcely an occasion has been recorded where the accompanying NKVD guards exhibited any feeling except those of gratuitous cruelty and contempt.[63]

The destination of all these miserable people was of course the slave-camps of the GULAG administration and similar penal institutions, whose aim was to work real or supposed enemies of the regime to death. Their 'crimes' ranged from overt hostility to foreign occupation, to 'illegal crossing of the frontier' – i.e. waking up in the Soviet-occupied zone after the invasion.[64] The death-rate was fearful, causes ranging from whole working parties frozen to death and abandoned, to the 3,000 Poles who died of lead poisoning in the Chukhotsk lead-mines in August 1940.[65]

Altogether, it is estimated that between a million and a million and a half Poles (including prisoners-of-war) were deported to the Soviet Union between 1939 and 1941.[66] Within two years some 270,000 were dead from murder, malnutrition, disease and starvation.[67] The total population of the occupied territories was about twelve million;[68] which is to say that about a tenth of the population was abducted to slavery and imprisonment, of whom about a quarter were deliberately done to death.

It is interesting to compare these statistics with the then populations of Britain and the United States. Had the Red Army had occasion to liberate Britain in 1939 from her exploiting class of capitalists, the equivalent proportion of people removed to camps in Siberia and the Arctic Circle would have been about five million; that is to say, the entire population of Greater London, Yorkshire, Lancashire or Scotland. Of these about one and a quarter million men, women and children would have died; a proportion from a bullet in the back of the neck, and the rest from neglect or cruelty. In this way the entire population of Warwickshire, Middlesex or Staffordshire could have been liquidated down to the last inhabitant.

In the United States NKVD units would have dispatched about thirteen million people across the Pacific to Vladivostok and the Kolyma camp complex: the entire population of New York. Eighteen months later three and a quarter million would be no more, the wolves tearing at their corpses lying rigid in the permafrost; roughly speaking, the whole population of West Virginia, North Dakota, New Hampshire and Arizona.

Of course equally horrific scenes were taking place in the more densely populated region of Poland occupied by the Germans. As the Gestapo and NKVD set about their parallel task it was clear they shared a common objective, and opportunities of friendly co-operation were not lacking. Working relations were opened between the two security forces, in the course of which a Gestapo representative made regular consultative trips to NKVD General Ivan Serov, in Soviet-occupied L'vov.[69] Germany and Soviet Russia had agreed in the Treaty of 28 September to combine in suppressing Polish opposition to their joint rule, and effective measures were taken to implement this. Large numbers of Polish prisoners-of-war were exchanged at the border fortress of Brest-Litovsk.[70]

Even more symbolic of the determination of the two totalitarian states to bury their former hostility and act as friends was a secret agreement to surrender political refugees whom each had harboured before the volte-face of the Pact of 23 August. German Marxists living in Moscow were handed over to the Gestapo at Brest-Litovsk.[71] These unfortunate people were thus enabled to make a first-hand comparison between the penal systems of the two Socialist states; a comparison which tended to throw a poor light on the facilities of GULAG.[72]

The worst sufferers of all were the Jews of Poland. On the German side the full fury of SS *Einsatzkommandos* fell on these defenceless people. The campaign started with gratuitous bullying and cruelty. In Turck on 30 October 1939,

A number of Jews were herded into the synagogue and there were made to crawl along the pews singing, while being continually beaten with whips by SS men. They were then forced to take down their trousers so that they could be beaten on the bare buttocks.

One Jew who had fouled his trousers in fear was compelled to smear his excrement over the faces of other Jews.

Scenes like this formed the prelude to mass murder and expropriation, now too well known and documented to require elaboration.[73] Anti-Semitism had been widespread in certain quarters in pre-war Poland, but the Jews realized now that a menace worse than anything their unhappy race had experienced throughout centuries of persecution had fallen upon them.

Small wonder that many looked upon the Soviet invaders to the east as deliverers, or at least much the less of two evils. Soon after the invasions large numbers began to flee into the Soviet zone.[74] During the first confused weeks of the war many managed to cross over, but their treatment at the hands of the NKVD was such that they finished with an almost universal loathing of the USSR and all it stood for. As the Polish Ambassador in Moscow noted in 1942, 'Their attitude to Russia today is very much sharper and more inflexible than that of pureborn Poles, who had no illusions that Russia would give them friendly treatment.'[75] One such was Dr Julius Margolin, a distinguished Zionist. Before the war he held a view shared by many in Western Europe and the United States:

It is true that their system is no good for us in Europe. But it appears that it is a regime that suits the wishes of the Russian people. It's their business, they have asked for it. For us Europeans it is valuable as a great social experiment, and all of us can learn many important and valuable things from the Soviet Union.

However, Dr Margolin found himself undergoing the 'great social experiment'. He spent five years in GULAG camps, and after his return to civilization in 1946 published a full and honourable recantation:

Russia is indeed divided into two parts, the 'free' Russia [and] the other Russia – the second Russia, behind barbed wire – is the thousands, endless thousands of camps, places of compulsory labor, where millions of people are interned . . . Since they came into being, the Soviet camps have swallowed more people, have exacted more victims, than all other camps – Hitler's and others – together, and this lethal machine continues to operate full-blast . . . An entire generation of Zionists has died in Soviet prisons, camps, and exile.[76]

History is accordingly presented with the extraordinary fact that Jews resorted to bribery and other desperate measures in efforts to escape from Soviet territory to the tender mercies of the Nazis.[77] Many, however, were spared the disillusionment of this double flight. Over the winter of 1939–40 thousands of terrified Jews, fleeing from SS savagery, arrived in no-man's-land on the eastern bank of the river Bug. They had left behind them the whips and rifle-butts of Heydrich's bullies, but now they found themselves faced by a wall of NKVD frontier troops, who opened fire with machine-guns and released savage dogs on anyone attempting to cross over. During the bitter winter months great crowds of Jews slept under the open sky, wedged between the lands of the allied conquerors. Their numbers continued to dwindle as many died of exposure and privation, whilst others in despair returned to the German zone, and so ultimately to the slaughter-houses of Maidanek and Belsen.

Some of them, however, did not give up and remained on the banks of the river, waiting for an opportunity to cross. Sometimes, at night, one would break away from this shapeless human mass, run several hundred yards across the snowy plain, and then, caught in the beam of a Soviet searchlight, fall on his face, hit with a machine gun bullet. Then piercing wails mixed with outbreaks of spasmodic crying, hands were raised like the thin flames of the fires, angrily threatening the sky, then everything died down again into the silence of waiting.[78]

At the end of the year (1939), Stalin sent warm greetings to Hitler, remarking that the friendship between the peoples of the Soviet Union and Nazi Germany had every reason to be solid and lasting, cemented as it was by blood.[79] This was true enough: the blood was that of thousands of Poles and Jews.

VII
Digesting the Plunder

In Moscow, on the night of 15–16 August 1942, Churchill asked Stalin how he had come to sign the pact with Hitler in 1939.

> Stalin replied that he thought England must be bluffing; he knew we had only two divisions we could mobilise at once, and he thought we must know how bad the French Army was and what little reliance could be placed on it. He could not imagine we should enter the war with such weakness. On the other hand, he said he knew Germany was certain ultimately to attack Russia. He was not ready to withstand that attack; by attacking Poland with Germany he could make more ground, ground was equal to time, and he would consequently have a longer time to get ready.[1]

This account seemed convincing enough in the light of subsequent events to become received truth within the Soviet Union, and to have been accepted by numerous historians elsewhere.[2] In fact scarcely a word of it is true. Stalin did not appreciate Allied military weakness until the late spring of 1940; it seems certain that he did not believe that Germany would attack Russia within the foreseeable future; and, if ground did equal time, Stalin gained less than three weeks by his concessions: the time it took the Wehrmacht to cross Soviet-occupied Poland in June and July 1941. Khrushchev was to claim later that the Pact was a distasteful necessity;[3] it is questionable whether it was a necessity, and certain that it was not distasteful.

To Stalin himself and (to the extent that any independent public opinion existed in the USSR) most Party functionaries, the Pact was not a stern necessity but a highly congenial alliance. Indeed, it seems for a while to have been only fear (of the Allies, not the Germans) that prevented the Soviet Union joining Germany as a co-belligerent.

For Hitler, on the other hand, there is no question but that the Pact was indeed a breathing-space, and that war with the Soviet Union remained his ultimate aim. He cherished a personal admiration for Stalin and respected Bolshevism as an ideology comparable in many ways in its dynamic force to National Socialism. But ever since his declared intention of carving out German *Lebensraum* in the great spaces of the East, written in the pages of *Mein Kampf*, his purpose rarely wavered. It was all a question of timing.[4] However, the virtual certainty that the two great ideological powers would clash on the field of arms did not affect day-to-day relationships between the Nazi and Soviet leaderships, most of whose members thought the Alliance of permanent value and there to stay. As Ribbentrop explained to the Italians on 10 March 1940, the Soviet Union had become a respectable partner: she was now nationalistic, had dealt effectively with her own Jews, and was no longer interfering in German internal affairs.[5]

So far as the political and economic aspects of the Pact can be separated, it was the political advantages which interested Stalin, and primarily the economic ones that absorbed Hitler. Clearly the latter realized the force of Bismarck's dictum and Germany's mistake in 1914, and did not relish the idea of war on two fronts. But the likelihood of the Soviet Union's coming to Poland's aid was so slight as to be virtually discounted, and the indications are that Hitler would have attacked Poland, Pact or no Pact. As he declared privately in November 1939, the Pact would last as long as it suited Stalin and himself.[6]

The Pact continued to suit Stalin very well, and it was with a real sense of betrayal that he finally received the abrupt news of its rupture on 22 June 1941. The Secret Protocol, which was scrupulously honoured by Germany during the first year, accorded the Soviet Union a sphere of influence well to the west of her frontiers in Eastern Europe. Virtually all this region corresponded to the portion of Imperial Russia which had been dismembered at the time of the Revolution. For twenty years the Soviet leadership had contemplated the missing territories with jealous but fearful eyes. Finland, the Baltic States, eastern Poland and Bessarabia were all Russian by rights. The long-deferred spread of the Revolution must inevitably start with these rump states. Above all, as Stalin's suspicion and fear grew in the 1930s, they contained free and violently anti-Soviet segments of prominent national groups in the USSR. If Ukrainians or Byelorussians dreamed of counter-revolution, it would surely be at the instigation of their compatriots living safely beyond Stalin's rule, who could in turn tempt the intervention of one or other of the great powers.

Stalin could not breathe easily until all component races of the former Russian Empire were safely under NKVD control. Now the greatest military power on the continent had not only given him total freedom to absorb the desired territories, but it also stood on guard beyond the demarcation line, prepared to ward off any intervention by the meddling Entente powers. Even so, Stalin displayed a caution which revealed a marked lack of confidence in the capacity of the Red Army to take on any but the very smallest state. Poland was attacked only when her armies had virtually disintegrated, and the three little Baltic States were compelled under threats to accept Soviet military 'bases'. But their full absorption was postponed until the following summer as was confrontation with Romania, whilst massive preparations began for an attack on Finland, whose entire population was scarcely greater than the strength of the Red Army.

Hitler's gift was generous, but then so was the return he received. On 11 February 1940 Molotov and Ribbentrop signed a German-Soviet Commercial Agreement. The Soviets agreed to supply Germany, over the next eighteen months, with raw materials worth some 650 million Reichsmarks. Of almost equal value was a Soviet agreement to allow German imports to cross Soviet territory, and for the Soviet Union to act for Germany as a purchaser of metals and raw materials in the rest of the world, thus circumventing the British blockade. In return, Germany would, over the following twenty-seven months, transport to the USSR industrial products, processes and installations, and war *matériel*.[7]

The Soviets received a considerable amount of valuable armaments, but as events were to show they did not result in any substantial increase in Soviet military potential. For example, the German Navy transferred its unfinished battle-cruiser *Lützow* to the Red Navy. She was towed to Leningrad, but the German engineers' work was interrupted by events in 1941, and by the end of the war the useless hulk was still lying in harbour.[8]

The benefits of the agreement to Germany, on the other hand, were incalculable. Provision was made for the supply from Russia of a million tons of grain for cattle, 900,000 tons of mineral oil, 100,000 tons of cotton, 500,000 tons of phosphates, 100,000 tons of chrome ores, 500,000 tons of iron ore, 300,000 tons of scrap iron and pig iron, and numerous other commodities vital to the German war effort. In September 1940 Germany's own grain reserves, it was noted at the German Foreign Office, 'will be used up in the current crop year, so that we would enter the next crop year without such reserve.' Germany was totally dependent on Soviet supply of this essential commodity, and in May 1941 the same official noted with satisfaction that 'The quantities of raw materials now contracted for are being delivered punctually by the Russians, despite the heavy burden this imposes on them, which, especially with regard to grain, is a notable performance, since the total quantity of grain to be delivered under the Agreement of April 10 of this year . . . amounts to over 3 million tons up to August 1, 1942.'[9]

Russian oil and cotton were equally crucial to the effective maintenance of the German war machine during the campaigns of 1940 and 1941, as was rubber from the Far East imported by the Trans-Siberian Railway. Indeed, so vital was this last factor, that General Thomas (head of the Wehrmacht War Economy and Armaments Office) opposed war with Russia on the sole grounds that it would cut Germany's rubber lifeline.

Both countries were fully aware of Germany's dependence on Soviet raw materials and import facilities. 'The supplies from the Russians have heretofore been a very substantial prop to the German war economy', noted Dr Karl Schnurre of the Foreign Office in September 1940; whilst on 13 November Molotov emphasized to Hitler 'that the German-Russian agreement had not been without influence upon the great German victories'.[10]

How far German victories in 1940 were actually dependent on supplies deriving from Soviet Russia obviously cannot be accurately estimated. Certainly the extraordinary mobility and firepower of the Wehrmacht owed a very great deal to Soviet oil, guncotton and other raw materials. They drove a coach and four through the Allied policy of wearing down German aggression through the stranglehold of blockade – a weapon perfected at the end of the previous war, with disastrous effects on Germany's war economy, which had certainly shortened the war and was probably the major factor in Germany's defeat in 1918.[11]

In the autumn of 1939 Churchill informed Roosevelt that his 'accounts of Hitler's oil position make us feel he is up against time limits'.[12] He was not yet to know that thousands of tons were already

preparing to be moved westwards from the oilfields of Baku. As
Hitler told his generals on 22 August, 'We need not be afraid of a
blockade. The East will supply us with grain, cattle, coal, lead and
zinc.'[13] All in all, as a careful scholar has suggested, it is an 'open
. . . question . . . whether without Soviet aid, particularly in the
matter of oil supplies and rubber transit, the German attack in the
West in 1940 would have been successful as it was, and the attack
on the Soviet Union would have been possible at all.'[14]

Certainly, from the Soviet point of view, economic aid to Germany
was not merely a *quid pro quo* but a positive means of aiding the
German war effort. It was they who made the comparison with
Britain's receipt of lend-lease supplies from the United States,[15] and
Soviet co-operation with Germany displayed good will and an
anxiety to please unequalled since the Revolution. 'The Soviet
Union', said Stalin, 'was interested in having a strong Germany as a
neighbour and in the case of an armed conflict between Germany and
the Western democracies the interests of the Soviet Union and of
Germany would certainly run parallel to each other.'[16] Affectionate
Christmas greetings were exchanged by the dictators that December,[17] and Ambassador von Schulenberg was presented with a very
fine villa (*dacha*) by the Soviet Government.[18] German consular
offices in the Soviet Union closed since 1937 were re-opened;[19] a
privilege consistently denied to Soviet Russia's next allies, Britain
and the United States, after 1941.

Whilst the Soviet Union held back from joining Germany as a
belligerent, she furnished Germany with military co-operation far
beyond that the United States was giving Britain at the time. The
German Navy was allowed facilities at Murmansk on a scale which
contrasts favourably in many ways with restrictions placed on Allied
use of the same port between 1941 and 1945. The German liner
Bremen found refuge there, as did a succession of blockade-breaking
vessels; and measures violating international law were adopted by
the Soviet authorities to allow the Germans to escape with a captured
American merchant ship, *City of Flint*.[20] German auxiliary cruisers
were equipped at Murmansk for raids on British shipping.

More than this, the Soviets actually allowed Germany her own
naval base on Russian soil. In October 1939 the German and Soviet
navies combined to establish the base, known as 'Basis Nord', at
Zapadnaya Litza Bay, near Murmansk. It proved to be a valuable base
for U-Boats operating in the North Sea, and played an important role

helping supply the invasion of Norway. (After that the base proved unnecessary and was abandoned.) The Soviets helped a German raiding cruiser, *Schiff 45*, to make her way through the ice round Siberia to the Pacific, where she sank and captured 64,000 tons of Allied shipping. In this and many other ways the Soviet Government lent enormous assistance to the otherwise extremely vulnerable German Navy.[21]

It was not only in their external relations that the two totalitarian powers moved closer together. Anti-Soviet propaganda was muted in Germany,[22] whilst in Russia quite extraordinary measures were adopted to ensure that the population supported the new alliance with enthusiasm. Anti-German books, posters and films were removed from circulation, and the press adopted a highly partisan attitude in favour of the German war effort. Exhibitions were staged in Moscow exalting Nazi artistic, economic and military achievements, and special productions of Wagner's operas were staged in the capital's theatres. Even in the secret world of GULAG, Beria issued a decree forbidding the use of 'fascist' as a term of opprobrium. So entrenched did loyalty to the German alliance become that a Pole was actually imprisoned five weeks after the German invasion of Russia 'for anti-German activities', as was the former Soviet Counsellor at the Paris embassy a month after that![23]

It was not only inside Russia that Soviet loyalty to the Pact with Hitler was displayed. Throughout the world national Communist parties were affiliated to the Comintern, whose headquarters was at 6 Mokhavaya Ulitsa, opposite the Kremlin in Moscow. Theoretically the Comintern was an independent body, co-ordinating the struggle of the national parties to effect world revolution. On the fifth floor of the headquarters building was the office of OMS (*Otdyel Mezhdunarodnoi Svyazi*, 'International Liaison Section'), which was an inner body whose duty was to direct Communist Party tactics. In fact, the Comintern enjoyed no independence whatever and was simply an arm of the OGPU (afterwards NKVD), whose guards in plain clothing policed the building, treating high functionaries of the International with ill-disguised contempt.[24]

Abroad, however, the NKVD could play only a contributory part (in the form of bribes, blackmail, murder, etc.) in maintaining Communist unity under Soviet leadership. Genuine loyalty and devotion to the cause were tested as never before by the extraordinary news of the Nazi-Soviet Pact. For obvious reasons no foreign Communists were kept informed of developments, and the news came as a profound shock. In Britain John Strachey wept profusely, dreading that his whole political position was shattered. However, he was able to derive comfort from the undoubted fact that, 'if Russia were a socialist country, then everything it did was in the interests of socialism.'[25] Others went through similar emotional contortions, but large numbers swiftly sprang into line. On 2 February 1940 the German Communist Walter Ulbricht was permitted by the Nazi Government to publish an article in *Die Welt*, stating that 'Those who intrigue against the friendship of the German and Soviet people are enemies of the German people and are branded as accomplices of British imperialism.'

The British *Daily Worker* adopted a similar line up to the German invasion of Russia.[26] On 7 October 1939 Claud Cockburn greeted the Nazi alliance jubilantly: 'In this tremendous week there has burst suddenly into the view of the world the possibility of peace. By possibility I mean practical possibility. And I mean a genuine peace.' It was Hitler's appeal, made in the Reichstag the previous day, to which Cockburn was referring. Stalin had as yet made no approach to the Allies. This peace offensive was among many factors tending to sap Allied morale that winter.[27]

In the United States the American *Daily Worker* adopted an identical line. On 19 September, when war was raging in Poland, it published a declaration of the National Committee, proclaiming the war to be an imperialist one which should be opposed by the workers. Fellow-travellers such as Dashiell Hammett, Theodore Dreiser, Anna Louise Strong and Corliss Lamont adopted a similar pro-Soviet and pro-Axis line, though others withdrew in disgust.[28] Communist trade unionists set out to sabotage production in munitions factories, lest any aid reach Britain or France, and right up to the eve of Operation Barbarossa, Communist propaganda did everything possible to dissuade the United States from helping the beleaguered democracies.[29]

However, the British and American Communist Parties represented minorities with small popular appeal. In France the situation was very different. There the Communist Party enjoyed the support of large sections of the population and had a following running into millions. Like its British and American counterparts, it had no capacity for formulating individual policy and followed Stalin's directives unswervingly. One of its leading deputies, Jacques

Duclos, had been recognized by Trotsky as an 'old GPU agent'.[30] The Party worked so energetically to undermine the French war effort as to suggest in effect a fifth column. Its leader, Maurice Thorez, fled to Moscow within a month of France's declaration of war to direct resistance to his country's preparations against Germany.[31] In November 1940 Thorez and Duclos exulted openly over the fall of France,[32] and Thorez admitted 'that the struggle of the French people has the same aim as the struggle of German imperialism. It is a fact that in this sense there is a temporary alliance'.[33]

This alliance expressed itself in concrete terms. German propaganda leaflets dropped over the Maginot Line pointed out frighteningly that 'Germany, after her victory over Poland and since her pact with Russia, disposes of inexhaustible resources in men and materiel!'[34] whilst all the Communist deputies petitioned President Herriot to make peace in response to Hitler's appeal.[35] After Communist publications had been suppressed by decree in France, the Party continued to publish its propaganda on German presses, as an amused Ribbentrop informed Ciano.[36] These leaflets urged troops, dockers and others engaged in essential war work to resist and sabotage their country's effort. In March 1940 a Party leaflet claimed that the Allied failure to launch an offensive was due to the effectiveness of this defeatist propaganda, and there can be no doubt that this, coupled with serious cases of sabotage in munitions factories, played a major role in the catastrophic defeat of June 1940 – a defeat in which Thorez and Duclos rejoiced openly.[37]

On 18 June (the day General de Gaulle issued his appeal in London) Communist delegates called on the German censorship office to request permission to publish the Party journal *L'Humanité*. Arrested by the vigilant French police, they were liberated by the Gestapo on the 25th. Further negotiations with the Nazis followed, and on 1 July 1940 *L'Humanité* published an article pleasing alike to her Soviet masters and Nazi allies:

NOT FOR ENGLAND

General de Gaulle and other agents of British capital would like to compel Frenchmen to fight for the City [of London] . . . Frenchmen will give Cambronne's reply [*merde*] to these gentlemen . . .[38]

The Communists' anti-British propaganda was peculiarly vitriolic, and energetic attempts were made to inflame the French troops against their ally.[39] Astonishing as it may appear at first sight, it seems clear that the French Communist Party's anti-patriotic campaign was directed at one remove by Hitler himself.

Later Khrushchev was to recall that 'Stalin once told me that Hitler had sent a request for a favor through secret channels. Hitler wanted Stalin, as the man with the most authority and prestige in the Communist world, to persuade the French Communist Party not to lead the resistance against the German occupation of France.' Stalin claimed he had indignantly rejected 'such a degrading deal . . . Hitler had stooped to new depths of filth and vileness.'[40] But from the event it is abundantly clear that Stalin had been only too happy to join Hitler in those congenial depths. Thorez was a virtual prisoner in Moscow, and it is unthinkable that he should have issued his instructions to the French Party without Stalin's authorization.

French Communist support for Stalin's ally, then, played a significant and perhaps crucial role in the destruction of French will to resist. As France was the lynch-pin of Entente opposition to Hitler, this blow was of enormous strategic importance.[41] What is of particular significance in the present context is the fact that the French Communist Party had long distinguished itself by a subservience to Stalin so total as to make it virtually an arm of the GRU or NKVD.[42] Their devoted aid to Hitler in 1940 therefore provides further confirmation that Stalin saw his own interest coinciding with a Nazi victory. Had fear of German strength been his only consideration, he could readily have disowned the Comintern and the foreign Parties as independent bodies following policies of their own. But the strongest disciplinary measures were taken to ensure that all worked for the common cause. All over the world Communist Parties sabotaged or ignored anti-Nazi national movements. In Yugoslavia, where the Communist movement had directed all its energies to vilifying the British and French, Tito's first appeal for struggle against the German invader came . . . on 22 June 1941! It was not the conquest of Yugoslavia which aroused his ire, but the invasion of Russia.[43] Even in far-off Buenos Aires, Nicholas Cheetham at the British Embassy reported that Nazi diplomats 'are collaborating with local Communists in a very dangerous attempt to win over the masses with the cry of "away with British capitalism and commercial exploitation".'[44]

All in all, Stalin's attitude to Germany was that of an active and loyal ally, prepared to go to almost any lengths to oblige the Nazis, short of actually joining in the fighting. And so far as that went, the only inhibiting factor was an overriding fear of entering into warfare with any power larger than Finland or Latvia. As intelligent British diplomats remarked, it was not so much military defeat that Stalin dreaded, as the likelihood of consequent internal revolt against his savage regime.[45] But he went far beyond mere placating of his formidable ally, and the extent of his support for the Germans suggests surely that he was working for a German victory. Of course a bloody stalemate on the Maginot Line would have suited him better still, but as so delicate a balance could not be achieved he saw his chance of survival lie in the triumph of his powerful Nazi protector, rather than that of the Allies. For they were the friends of Poland and Finland, plunder he was determined not to disgorge.

Much of Stalin's appeasement of Germany can be put down to plain fear and a desire to please. But the energetic war of sedition and propaganda was superfluous on these grounds alone, and its secret aspects reveal the true direction of Soviet policy. He overestimated French and British military strength and, mistrusting the Red Army, felt that only the Wehrmacht could be relied upon to protect him.[46]

Probably Stalin's most successful propaganda coup of all was the propagation of the myth that Soviet territorial acquisitions in 1939 were designed to establish a forward strategic line in case of a German attack. This tale has received wide acceptance, but is manifestly untrue. Eighteen months later, when Hitler launched his invasion, virtually nothing had been accomplished in the way of fortifications, defensive lines or military airfields to exploit ground gained by the Nazi-Soviet Pact.[47] It is difficult to think of any plausible reason why Stalin should have declined to order these works for fear of distressing Hitler, and it seems clear that strategic considerations ranked very low in Stalin's priorities. Indeed, as George Kennan observed, the national armies of Finland, Romania and the Baltic States would have protected Russian's flanks infinitely better than as conquered and depressed satrapies.[48] As it was, Finland and Romania were turned into effective allies of the Germans and the Baltic States provided Hitler with excellent troops.

What Stalin gained in the East by the Pact of 1939 was control over neighbouring territories, whose independence, hostility to Bolshevism, and racial, religious or cultural affinity to bordering peoples

of the Soviet Union might be suspected of providing permanent
allure to many millions of Stalin's wretched subjects. His priority
is indicated by a series of elaborate purges and deportations, involving hundreds of thousands of people of suspect categories in
each of the conquered countries. These were meticulously planned
and effected, and phased over the whole period of Nazi-Soviet
co-operation.

All in all, Stalin's foreign policy between 1939 and 1941 closely
paralleled that of Mussolini. The Soviet Union and Italy acted as
jackals to Germany's lion, eager to join in the spoil and yet terrified
of the consequences. When opportunity offered, they ventured on
the conquest of countries on the scale of Albania or Estonia, but only
after agonized indecision and fearful anticipation. In October 1939
the Duce explained that 'as things stand Italy represents for Germany
an economic and moral reserve, but that later on she may also play a
military role'.[49] This could be taken as an exact summary of Stalin's
view: the only difference being that Mussolini did eventually pluck
up courage to join in the conflict.

In the Secret Protocol to the Pact of 28 September 1939, Germany
had allocated a sphere of influence to Soviet Russia comprising a
great belt of territory in Eastern Europe. This included Finland,
Estonia, Latvia, Lithuania, eastern Poland, and Bessarabia. Stalin
was anxious to absorb these into his empire, but despite his receipt
of express German permission to treat any or all of these countries as
his own, he set about their absorption with extreme caution. This
procedure makes a remarkable story; less perhaps as yet another
exemplar of Soviet aggression than as an indicator of Stalin's thinking during these vital months. In the virtual absence of Soviet documentation the historian must rely on deduction and inference from
other sources; nevertheless a surprisingly consistent and credible
pattern emerges.

The Secret Protocol to the Pact of 28 September allocated all three
Baltic States to the Soviet Union. This represented a major re-
adjustment to the original agreement made by Ribbentrop and
Molotov on 23 August. Then it had been stipulated that 'the
northern boundary of Lithuania shall represent the boundary of the
spheres of influence of Germany and the U.S.S.R. In this connexion
the interest of Lithuania in the Vilna area is recognized by each
party.' Vilna was the former capital of Lithuania, which had been
incorporated into Poland in 1920 during the confused period of the

establishment of the Polish Republic. Both Stalin and Hitler were desirous of dismembering Poland, and the detachment of Vilna seemed one effective way of doing this. Lithuania was presumably included in the German sphere because Hitler wished to extend Reich control along the Baltic coast northwards from East Prussia. For the same reason Stalin objected; besides, Lithuania had been part of the Russian Empire.

On 25 September Stalin proposed that the Soviet Union should take Lithuania, Germany receiving in exchange large areas of Poland formerly allocated to the Soviets. This proposal, as already noted, was accepted by the Germans (together with a bounty of 7,500,000 gold dollars) and included in the agreement of 28 September. The concession by Germany may have arisen from irritation at Lithuanian refusal of a German invitation to participate in the partition of Poland. From Stalin's point of view the bargain was an excellent one. His Polish frontier now roughly corresponded with the Curzon Line, which might make it acceptable even in the event of an Allied victory. Lithuania had no ties of alliance with the British and French, and there were virtually no Lithuanians outside Stalin's control who might agitate for assistance if the Allies defeated Germany and set about restoring national independence to countries despoiled by Germany. Stalin's characteristic caution and weighing up of all eventualities displayed themselves as clearly as ever.[50]

On the same day that Stalin broached this proposition to Ambassador von Schulenburg, he suggested also that, with German permission, he would set about solving the 'problem' of the Baltic States and expected the full support of Germany in the matter. The phraseology clearly betrays Stalin's fear and dependence upon German protection as he prepared for the destruction of these three small states. His subsequent moves revealed even more clearly how much he dreaded the consequences of a false move. The Pact signed and the three-million-strong Red Army mobilized, he had only to engulf the Baltic lands with their minuscule armies. Instead he proceeded very carefully, by stages spread over many months.

He started with Estonia, the smallest (population 1,130,000) and most remote from any of the warring powers. On 24 September the Soviets demanded the right to establish naval, military and air bases on Estonian territory. Foreign Minister Karl Selter was informed that Estonian neutrality constituted a danger to the Soviet Union, as the authorities had permitted a Polish submarine to escape from an

Estonian port and sink a Soviet steamer near Leningrad.

The true story was as follows. The submarine *Orzel* put into the Estonian port of Tallinn on 15 September to land her sick captain. As it was wartime the Estonians decided to intern the vessel, removing her charts and the breech-blocks of her guns. Despite this, the Polish sailors managed to overpower their guards and sail the *Orzel* into the open Baltic. After surmounting extraordinary hazards, the ship managed to gain the safety of British waters and later played a gallant part in the Norwegian campaign.[51] The Soviets claimed that the Polish submarine had sunk one of their steamers near Leningrad, but as the steamer in question put into an Estonian port some months later an air of doubt must hang over this claim. In fact, the only genuine infringement of Estonian neutrality had been a series of violations of her air-space by cruising Soviet bombers.

However, force and not truth was to be the arbiter of the conflict. At a meeting of the Estonian Cabinet on 26 September, Selter explained to his colleagues that they had little choice in the matter. Molotov, after requesting the conclusion of a 'Treaty of Mutual Assistance', had provided a sinister warning. If you refuse, he had added, 'the U.S.S.R. will achieve the aims mentioned in the Security Pact by resorting to different means.' In face of this threat, Selter was instructed to return to Moscow and conclude the best terms possible in the circumstances. As the Germans had expressed their complete disinterest in the matter, Estonia had no bargaining counters and was obliged in effect to sign away her independence. The Soviet Union was enabled to set up naval bases on Estonia's Baltic islands and in the port of Paldiski, and a number of aerodromes. Twenty-five thousand Red Army troops were to garrison these bases: the nucleus of a future invasion force.

As Stalin murmured to the delegation after all was signed and sealed, 'I can tell you that the Estonian Government did wisely . . . It could have happened to you what happened to Poland . . . Where is Poland now?' It was 28 September, and Ribbentrop was in Moscow to sign the German-Soviet Boundary and Friendship Treaty. Several days before that Estonia had already become the second country to see Red Army trucks and tanks pouring across her frontiers. An eye-witness noted,

The Russian soldiers were poorly dressed, many had wooden-soled boots on. Their faces were pallid, undernourished; one-third of them were marked with chicken-pox – young men, about twenty . . . Many of them had never seen butter, and did not know what cream was. Our shops were overrun by them. They brought their old shoes in order to show that they needed a new pair. They gazed in wonder when they heard that one could have more than one cake apiece in coffee-shops. And then they ate twenty . . . Officers were allowed to bring their families with them to Estonia. The women came in rags with the exception of some in fur coats. Those women were invading our shops for pretty clothes. At their first military ball in Tallinn, their women wore nightgowns, mistaken for ball-gowns in our shop-windows![52]

For the moment the Red Army behaved reasonably correctly. Before long, however, the unhappy Estonians were to learn that savagery lay not in their visitors' manners and appearance alone.[53]

No sooner had Stalin seen that the preliminary moves against Estonia had aroused no unpleasant repercussions, than he made similar demands upon her neighbour, Latvia (population 1,951,000). On the same day as the Estonian Treaty and the Nazi-Soviet Friendship Pact, 28 September, Stalin left his friend Ribbentrop watching the inevitable *Swan Lake* to deal with a Latvian delegation summoned to Moscow. Threats and hints similar to those accorded the Estonians produced their effect. On 5 October Foreign Minister Munters signed the second of the Pacts of Mutual Assistance. Terms were similar to those of the Estonian Pact, except that the number of Red Army troops to be installed was increased to thirty thousand. Stalin informed Munters candidly that Hitler had given him *carte blanche* to occupy the Baltic lands: 'With Germany we have established relations on a lasting basis, and also in regard to the Baltic States our views do not differ from those of Germany.'

The consequences also paralleled those in Estonia. Soviet troops promptly entered the country behaving correctly enough, but startled the inhabitants by their bedraggled and primitive appearance. *Politruks* were overheard accounting for the Latvians' obvious and embarrassing prosperity with an ingenious example of Marxist dialectic:

You see, capitalistic Latvia can afford an abundance of goods in its capitalist-owned shops, because the masses, the underpaid and exploited workers, are unable to buy them. On the other hand, the masses in the Soviet Union are so adequately paid that they can afford to go and buy up all available goods. This creates temporary shortages on the home market. Anyone can understand this.[54]

Last on Stalin's list was Lithuania (population 2,575,363). As that country bordered on the victorious Third Reich, he may well have felt he should tread a little more cautiously, despite the fact that Hitler had given him permission to proceed. On 2 October Lithuanian Foreign Minister Urbsys arrived in Moscow, to be greeted with demands similar to those inflicted on his two predecessors. The number of troops to be introduced to the bases was increased yet again, to fifty thousand. The Lithuanian delegation argued pertinaciously against the presence of Soviet troops, 'because it would reduce Lithuania to a vassal state'. Stalin listened at first with apparent patience, but at last broke in: '*Vy slishkom mnogo dokazyvaete*' [You're talking too much]. Soviet troops were massed ostentatiously on the frontier and by 10 October Molotov informed Urbsys that he would wait no longer. Stalin himself had struck out a clause safeguarding Lithuania's integrity when the war ended, and the Lithuanians must sign, like it or not.[55]

A feature of all three treaties was a clause expressly laying down that 'Realization of this Pact shall not affect to any extent the sovereign rights of the Contracting Parties, in particular their State organization, economic and social systems, military measures and, in general, the principle of non-intervention in internal affairs.' At the state dinner on 5 October to honour the signing of the Latvian Treaty, Stalin made a speech, giving 'his Bolshevik word of honour that the Soviet Union would adhere to its promises and obligations as specified in the accords just concluded.'

But an ominous indication as to the nature of this 'Bolshevik word of honour' made its appearance about this time. Maps of Lithuania printed for the Red Army General Staff were dated 'First edition *1939*' (my italics) and bore the caption 'Lithuanian S[oviet] S[ocialist] R[epublic]'.[56] And just what *that* would entail had also been decided. On the day after the signing of the last of the three treaties, 11 October 1939, Stalin gave a magnificent banquet in the Kremlin in honour of the Lithuanian delegation. He spoke jovially to his cowed visitors, assuring them repeatedly of his honest intentions. Occasionally, however, his thoughts must have flown to a different scene enacting itself not far away.

Just a few streets from the brightly-lit halls of the Kremlin lay the sombre outline of the Lubianka building at 2 Dzerzhinsky Square. A bas-relief of Karl Marx at the entrance was the last sight of the outside world for thousands of visitors, for it was here that political prisoners were brought from the Lefortovo and Butyrki gaols for interrogation and execution. In tiny cells known as *sobachniki*, or 'dog-kennels', they awaited their interrogators. In some cases the Judas hole in the door was surrounded by a painted, staring eye; in others the whole room was painted blood-red.

The interrogators were types to satisfy even Lenin's most blood-thirsty injunctions, and had no need of Stalin's reminder to 'beat, beat, and again beat'. A Finnish officer was questioned by a major in the NKVD:

> He was short and very broad-shouldered, almost square. Small, malevolent eyes glittered from under the low brow and the canine teeth of the lower jaw were long and protruding like a gorilla's. The bow legs and the large, hairy hands reaching to the knees further emphasized the impression of an ape.

As often as not women were the objects of these creatures' attentions, and the passages would echo to terrible, animal-like screams as they were beaten with rubber hoses or subjected to more refined tortures. The other prisoners would crouch terrified in their cramped hutches, whilst myriads of cockroaches seethed and swarmed on ceiling, walls and floor.

In the basement were the execution chambers. Prisoners were 'led down a long corridor . . . escorted by a member of the Prosecutor's staff, a doctor and the Governor of the gaol. Two men of the NKVD would hold him by the arms while a third shot him in the back of the neck at close range.' The corpses were thrown into a special crematorium, burning night and day. All that was left of the unfortunate inmates of the Lubianka, in many cases, was a great heap of spectacles and pince-nez. For these indeed a use was found: they were lent to shortsighted new arrivals who had difficulty in signing their 'confessions'.[57]

The Lubianka was a huge interrogation-centre, torture-chamber and crematorium. It also housed the headquarters offices of the NKVD, that potent organization whose prisons housed thousands of wretches, and whose camps throughout the Soviet Union disposed of millions upon millions of slaves. For twenty years the peoples of

Russia had suffered under this oppression; now, at Hitler's invitation, it was beginning to spill over the frontiers into the small and helpless Christian states to the West. The men who presided over Lenin's legacy worked in luxurious offices in a remote part of the building with deep-piled carpets, heavy furniture of the imperial era, and gilt-framed portraits, graded in size according to the rank of the official, of the beneficent Father of Peoples.[58]

In one of these that Wednesday, 11 October 1939, sat Ivan Alexandrovich Serov, a high-ranking Commissar of the NKVD. Thirty-four years old, he was short, thick-set, very attentive to the smartness of his impeccable uniform, and as utterly callous, cynical and cruel as his master Lavrenty Beria.[59] As Stalin exchanged toasts with his Lithuanian guests, Commissar Serov appended his signature to

ORDER NO. 001223

regarding the Procedure for carrying out the Deportation of Anti-Soviet Elements from Lithuania, Latvia, and Estonia.

STRICTLY SECRET

Written in cold quasi-legal language, the document began by explaining that 'the task of deportation of anti-Soviet elements from the Baltic Republics is a task of great political importance'. NKVD units enforcing the task were enjoined to keep their weapons 'in complete battle readiness', and to begin their operations at dawn. They were to break into designated houses, assembling families in single rooms. Locked doors were to be smashed in and protesting neighbours dispersed. Transported in carts or trucks to the nearest railway station, the prisoners' departure was to be rigorously guarded by NKVD troops. At the station the head of each family was to be skilfully separated from his wife and children, and loaded into a separate truck. (It is noteworthy that the 'anti-Soviet elements' were invariably assumed to consist of entire families, including small children.) The deportees' destination was not specified.

This document unexpectedly became accessible to historians when it fell into the hands of the Germans at Valka, as the NKVD fled in the summer of 1941.[60] It is clear that it could not have been issued without Stalin's express authorization, and the fact that he chose to have this done on the very day he entertained the Lithuanians is significant. Professor Ulam points out, 'in his youth the Georgian Mensheviks had branded Stalin a *kinto* – a tough, sardonic street urchin. And he retained to the end some characteristics of an impossible adolescent.' 'So they thought they could fool Stalin?' he would chuckle to himself; 'just look at them, it's Stalin they tried to fool!'[61] It seems that he gained almost as much pleasure from laughing at the gullibility of those he sought to delude as he did from the material gains of his duplicity. This was something that Churchill and, above all, Roosevelt might have gained from appreciating.

The historical outcome further demonstrates that the timing of Serov's Order No. 001223 was designed more in private derision of the Lithuanian leaders than for any immediate administrative purpose. For Stalin was not yet ready to launch his attack on the Baltic civilian population, and it was not until the following year that the terror erupted. In the autumn of 1939 he was far too apprehensive to try his luck further. Hitler might take offence if his partner appeared too greedy. And what if the dreaded British carried the war into the Baltic? Already, on 12 September, Churchill had circulated to Ministers and Chiefs of Staff 'Plan Catherine', which called for British naval domination of the Baltic. A fleet of five heavily-armed cruisers, accompanied by flotillas of destroyers, submarines, supply vessels and, possibly, an aircraft carrier, would sail under smokescreen through the Kattegat and wreak havoc on coastal installations. As Churchill noted, apart from confounding the Germans, 'the influence of this movement upon Russia would be far-reaching . . .'[62]

Given the poor state of British security at the time, it is likely that news of these plans was transmitted to NKVD or GRU headquarters in Moscow. Anthony Blunt had been recently recruited to Military Intelligence, and Kim Philby was in London, enjoying the confidence of many influential officials. Another possible source of information might have been Captain John Herbert King, a cypher clerk at the Foreign Office working for the NKVD. Identified by the defecting Soviet intelligence chief, Walter Krivitsky, he was arrested on 25 September 1939. It is clear that there were even more highly-placed traitors in the Foreign Office and elsewhere, and any one of these could easily have passed information to the NKVD resident at the London Embassy, Ernst Henry.[63]

Stalin's range of experience was limited, and he may well have recalled the dangerous days of 1918 and 1919, when the Royal Navy blockaded the Red Fleet in Kronstadt and the Baltic States originally established their independence under the protection of the guns of

Admiral Cowan's warships.[64] Whilst options remained open, the 'neutrality' of the Baltic States might for the moment prove a stronger safeguard than their absorption. Meanwhile, Soviet military presence was established in the new bases, Order No. 001223 lay accessible in the Lubianka archives and, the moment a safe opportunity offered, these excrescences on the edge of the Soviet empire would be rubbed out for ever.

So far as the Germans were concerned, they regarded these moves with equanimity. Stalin had stuck to his side of the bargain, and was entitled to his deserts. There was, however, one small matter to tidy up. For centuries Courland, the region in which the Baltic States were established, had been regarded as the furthest outpost of Teutonic, and indeed European, culture. German noblemen and knights had built castles and settled German farmers on their estates. As a result, each Baltic State now possessed a thriving minority of German inhabitants. Hitler was quite content to invite the onrush of Bolshevik barbarism into Eastern Europe, but drew the line at the idea that Germans might succumb to the advancing wave. In a Confidential Protocol to the Pact of 28 September, it was stipulated that Reich nationals and other persons of German descent should not be prevented from migrating to Reich territory. The transfer of population was to be organized 'by agents of the Government of the Reich in cooperation with the competent local authorities'. These proved to be Himmler and the SS on the one hand, and the NKVD (presumably headed by Serov, who signed Order No. 001223 and enjoyed a similar role in the Ukraine at this time) on the other. Within a few weeks thousands of Germans and Germanic Balts were being ferried across the Baltic to Reich soil. There they were settled on lands near Danzig from which the SS had recently ousted their Polish owners.[65]

The decks were cleared, potential bones of contention removed, and the two great allies could swallow and digest at leisure all that remained of civilization in their respective spheres of influence. For Hitler, the Pact afforded time and safety for his coming lightning strike against the West. To a grateful Stalin, the protective grey wall of the Wehrmacht allowed him to pursue what was in truth an extension of the internal policy of the USSR. The independence of the border states seemed a standing threat to his monolithic rule, but now Hitler would keep their Western protectors at bay while Beria, Abakumov, Merkulov and Serov prepared for the liquidation and deportation of all whose existence was believed to threaten NKVD rule. From the White Sea to the Black, a wall divided Europe. On the far side the Germans stood guard, suppressing anti-Soviet propaganda with an iron hand. On his side, Stalin could mop up what opposition remained. It was a perfect dovetailing of interests, or so Stalin believed. As he was to repeat nostalgically after the War, 'Ech, together with the Germans we would have been invincible!'[66]

VIII
David and Goliath

Negotiations with the three little Baltic States had proceeded without a hitch. By permitting the entry of Soviet troops on to their soil they had virtually signed away their independence. Germany had shown no signs of discontent at the Soviets thus claiming their side of the bargain, and by obtaining Estonian, Latvian and Lithuanian consent (however reluctant) to this skilful half-measure, the concern felt by the Allies and United States for the independence of small neutral states had been placated. As soon as the warring powers were sufficiently distracted, Baltic independence could be snuffed out.

All that remained on Stalin's shopping list were Finland and the northern Romanian province of Bessarabia. The latter had better be left until last, as it required careful handling. Germany had a strong interest in Romania on account of her oilfields and strategic position in the Balkans. The Pact had allocated Bessarabia to the Soviet Union, but one could not be too careful when dealing with a man like Hitler.

Finland, on the other hand, presented no real problems. Situated as she was in the remote wastes of the snowy north, she was separated by neutral Norway and Sweden from the hostile powers. Her tiny population (3,695,600) was no bigger than Soviet Russia's annual increase,[1] and her little army was poorly equipped, owing to her Social Democratic government's preference for social over national security.[2] There was no reason to suppose that the Finns could not be dealt with as easily as the Lithuanians, with their comparable population and resources. Finland had formerly been part of the Russian Empire, and would soon be so again.

Stalin had long cast acquisitive eyes on Finland. In 1920 he had suggested to Lenin that Finland should be federated with the Soviet Union along with other states, as a preliminary to total absorption within the future world Communist state.[3] Finland's geographical proximity to the former Russian capital Leningrad, and the fact that her southern coastline dominated the Gulf through which the Red Fleet must pass from its base at Kronstadt, made her appear a dangerous neighbour. Of course there was no fear that Finland herself might attack the mighty Soviet Union, but she might provide a platform whence a great power could intervene in northern Russia. In plain terms such a power must be either Germany or Britain.

Before the war Germany had appeared the more likely proposition. On 12 April 1938 ceremonies were held in Finland to celebrate the twentieth anniversary of the liberation of Helsinki from the Soviets. This had been accomplished with the aid of German troops led by the formidable Count Rüdiger von der Goltz, who himself arrived with a German delegation to take part in the commemoration. The implications were too clear to be ignored, and Stalin understandably became very alarmed. Two days later, on 14 April, Second Secretary Boris Yartsev of the Soviet Embassy in Helsinki telephoned the Foreign Minister, Rudolf Holsti, requesting a private interview. The Minister was startled, as such a request was quite contrary to diplomatic protocol, but agreed.

On his arrival, Yartsev explained that he had just arrived from Moscow, where his 'superiors' had expressed their anxiety to improve Soviet-Finnish relations. Yartsev went on to say that his country had strong reason to believe that Germany was planning an invasion of Russia, and that her General Staff must necessarily include in such a plan an attack through Finland. What would the Finns do in this event? From the Soviet point of view it was impossible to await the Germans' arrival politely on the Finnish-Soviet frontier. The Red Army would pour into Finland, attempting to encounter the Germans as far from the border as possible. This naturally did not present a very cheerful prospect to the Finns. But if they were prepared to resist a German landing, the Soviet Union bound itself to supply Finland with lavish military and economic aid, and guaranteed to evacuate all her forces after the war was finished. The danger from Germany was greater than Finland supposed, went on Yartsev, as plans had been laid that, in the event of a Finnish refusal to co-operate, a German-inspired Fascist *coup* would install a government prepared to do so. The Soviet envoy concluded with some very odd instructions: the Soviet Ambassador in Helsinki, Derevianski, must on no account learn of the present discussion, which had to be kept secret also from First Secretary

Austrin. As Finnish Intelligence had identified Yartsev as the NKVD representative in the Embassy, Holsti understood that through Yartsev he was dealing directly with Stalin.

But Holsti could offer no encouragement to these proposals. He denied that any threat from Germany endangered his country, nor was his government in so enfeebled a situation as to fear the triumph of the small Fascist party. Finland would remain neutral, closely linked to her Scandinavian neighbours. Yartsev jibbed at this. His Government required 'guarantees' that Finland would not support Germany in the event of a war. 'What do you mean by guarantees?' asked Holsti curiously. But here Yartsev suddenly dried up. This he could not reveal; no doubt subsequent negotiations would divulge their nature.

But this is just what did not happen. Negotiations continued for several months throughout the summer and autumn of 1938, culminating in a discussion in Moscow on 7 December. Just as Yartsev had explained that Ambassador Derevianski 'does a lot of talking, but his words have no importance', so now to their surprise the Finnish delegates found themselves meeting, not Foreign Commissar Litvinov, but Anastas Mikoyan, Commissar for Foreign Trade. It was explained coolly that Litvinov had no knowledge of the meeting. The Soviets wished to lease certain strategic islands in the Gulf of Finland for use as potential defensive fortifications should war break out. At the same time there was no question of militarizing these posts until the actual outbreak of hostilities. The Finns could not agree to any such infringement of national sovereignty, however, and subsequent negotiations with another of Stalin's secret emissaries foundered on the same rock. As the international situation worsened in the spring of 1939, discussions broke down altogether and matters rested in this unsatisfactory position when Ribbentrop and Molotov divided Eastern Europe between them in August.

Throughout these discussions the Soviet negotiators emphasized how vital it was that the conversations remain entirely confidential. The Finns remained puzzled by these strangely secretive and inconclusive exchanges, and even now it is impossible to assess Stalin's intentions satisfactorily. Clearly, in early 1938 he was frightened by what he mistakenly thought to be incipient Finnish-German military co-operation, coming as it did so soon after Hitler's triumphant absorption of Austria into the Reich. He wished the Finns could somehow convince him they would themselves fend off any German intervention, and that if war broke out the Soviets would have a legitimate foothold in the country.

But why conduct matters so secretively, keeping the whole affair from Litvinov, who was not brought in until nearly a year after Yartsev's first visit to Holsti? Obviously the Germans must not know, lest the Soviet probes provoke the very intervention they were intended to frustrate. Britain and France, too, would resent interference in neutral Scandinavia, and the legitimacy of Litvinov's calls for collective security against aggression would be called in question. It was not Litvinov's opposition that Stalin feared, but his indiscretion. Like Louis XV, Stalin often pursued two or more parallel foreign policies, unknown to his Foreign Office (*Narkomindel*). To the world at large Litvinov issued clarion calls for collective security against Nazi expansion. Privately, Stalin prepared to issue feelers for a Soviet-German *rapprochement*. Lest that fail, he made efforts, hamstrung by the need for secrecy, to bluff Finland and the Baltic States to accept Soviety military 'co-operation' when war came. The latter policy was dropped when Stalin found that an agreement with Hitler would hand the border states over to him anyway.

Perhaps the most important revelation emerging from these intrigues is the further confirmation they provide of the extent to which Litvinov and his policies represented a smoke-screen obscuring Stalin's real intentions.[4]

The Pact of 28 September 1939 signed, Stalin made haste to cash his cheques. As described in the previous chapter, the three Baltic States, Estonia, Latvia and Lithuania, succumbed to irresistible pressure. Stalin had to act swiftly, or events might arise to obstruct this unique opportunity. The day the Lithuanian delegates departed, 12 October, Finnish diplomats were summoned to the Kremlin. Foreign Commissar Molotov expected no nonsense; the Swedish, Norwegian and Danish ministers in Moscow had presented notes expressing the hope that nothing would be done to infringe Finland's independence and neutrality. Molotov refused to accept the notes, which were left in his ante-room.

The Finnish delegation, who were not warned what to expect, found Stalin himself present. After a brief preliminary discussion, Stalin outlined Soviet demands. The Soviet Union required extensive cession of island and coastal bases in the Gulf of Finland, together with other territorial adjustments designed to protect

Leningrad from a hostile naval force, and to remove the dangerous proximity of the frontier from that vulnerable city. The meeting then broke up, and the Finnish delegation telegraphed Stalin's proposals to Helsinki.

Stalin was in a hurry. Hitler's Reichstag speech of 6 October had offered 'peace' to the Entente, and if peace really did break out the subsequent settlement might prevent the Soviet Union acquiring her due share of the spoils.[5] Stalin's backing for Hitler's move suggests, however, that he was entirely confident that the seizure of Finland and Bessarabia would proceed smoothly and swiftly. But on 14 October, when Stalin resumed the talks, he was surprised to find the Finnish delegation firm in its declaration that the terms were unacceptable as they stood and would require consultation with the government at home.

Stalin accepted this with perfect good humour. Let the Finns go home to obtain the requisite authority, and come back within the week. 'We'll sign an agreement on October 20', cried out Molotov jovially, 'and the following evening, we'll throw a party for you.' Their merriment was perhaps increased by thoughts of the document People's Commissar Serov had drawn up during the similar party thrown two days earlier for the Lithuanians. No doubt a duplicate of Order No. 001223 could be got ready for these self-confident Finns! Of course they must naturally save face by delaying the negotiations for a few days – even the Lithuanians had pulled at the reins a little. These were amazing days: in the space of three weeks Stalin's brilliant diplomacy would regain all the territories lost to Russia during the Civil War! Not even the immortal Lenin could accomplish that, let alone the vain dilettante Trotsky.

The Finnish Council of State met on 21 October and discussed the proposals earnestly. Sweden showed little inclination to come to the aid of her close neighbour. Prime Minister Per Albin Hansson wished something could be done, but 'I have to deal with a complacent people which wants to be left in peace'. The Swedish public displayed the greatest sympathy, but there was no great eagerness to do anything that might cause a rupture with the bear in the East. Clearly the Finns would have to make some concessions, and a considerably watered-down alternative to Stalin's sweeping demands was drawn up. Meanwhile it would be best to be ready for any contingency, and the Council appealed to the Finnish public to subscribe to a 500-million-mark defence loan. Within a month it had been over-subscribed by 200 million marks.

On 23 October the delegation returned to Moscow. As the ensuing discussion proceeded it began to dawn on Stalin and Molotov that the Finns were taking the discussion quite literally, and believed that Soviet demands could really be whittled down! Indeed, after two hours negotiations ground to a halt. Neither side would give way, and the Finns decided there was no point in continuing. As Väinö Tanner, the Finnish Finance Minister recalled, 'Molotov seemed astounded at our departure. He said as though by the way, "Is it your intention to provoke a conflict?"' This was the point at which the Finns should have been recalled to reality, but the leading Finnish delegate replied quietly, 'We want no such thing, but you seem to.' Stalin smiled enigmatically as they filed out. Perhaps some blood-letting would be no bad thing after all. Little Finland must collapse even more quickly than Poland. As the Soviet press reported in a series of vivid articles, Finland was seething with discontent. The alienated proletariat, oppressed by its capitalist and White Guard masters, was on the point of widespread revolt. Desertions from the Finnish army increased daily, and virtually the whole country awaited only the arrival of the fraternal Red Army to take to the streets with tears in their eyes and flowers in their hands. After all, the Poles had received their Marxist liberators with 'great elation' (as Khrushchev recalled)[6], and Finland was not immune either to the Laws of History.

Whilst these reports were a little fanciful, there was no escaping the fact that Finland was in an even more hopeless position than Poland had been at the beginning of the previous month. Sweden had swiftly declared her intention to remain a bystander in the event of war. Britain saw a Soviet advance in the Baltic as essentially detrimental to Germany's hegemony, and so considerations of *Realpolitik* were likely to outweigh her natural sympathy for a small democracy in distress.

By the same token, the Finns felt that Germany might well support her stand. They were unaware of the Secret Protocol to the Pact, which had accorded Finland to the Soviet sphere. The Germans were already annoyed with the Finns, whose people expressed widespread distaste for the doctrines of National Socialism, and whose government had had the effrontery to decline a non-aggression pact proffered by Hitler. From early October the Finns were informed that Germany 'would hardly be in a position . . . to intervene in the

Russian-Finnish conversations'. The German Foreign Office ordered its diplomats abroad to stress that the Finns had brought all this trouble on their own heads, and their dislike of Nazism and admiration for British democracy placed them beyond the pale of German sympathy. 'England's guilt in the Russo-Finnish conflict should be especially emphasized. Germany is not involved in these events. In conversations, sympathy is to be expressed for the Russian point of view. Please refrain from expressing any sympathy for the Finnish point of view,' the note concluded.[7]

For a while Stalin and Molotov continued frustrated and a little baffled by the obstinate Finns. They seemed to imagine that negotiations involved genuine bargaining, whereas of course they were merely a brief formality acting as prologue to the swift disappearance of their country from the nations of the earth.

'Ach, Finland,' Molotov was to say later; 'that is a peanut.'[8] The negotiations could not be protracted much longer: time was passing, winter was coming on, Bessarabia still awaited liberation, and the dread thought that peace might descend on Europe provided sleepless nights for the selfless men of the Kremlin. On 3 November the fact that their patience was wearing thin was revealed by Molotov's grim remark: 'We civilians don't seem to be making progress; now it is the soldiers' turn to speak.' Yet even after this the Soviet leaders made a few fitful attempts to keep the discussion going. Some demands were modified, but by now public opinion in Finland was not prepared to see the Red Army or Fleet exercising any control over Finnish territory. They had lived too long next to the bear to believe he would be content with a mere paw in the door. The example of the Baltic States was to prove them right.

As it gradually dawned on Stalin that the Finns were not going to give way, he began to consider what he should do. His hand was being forced, and it was no longer possible to apply the technique of absorption by stages, which was working so well in the Baltic States. In any case, he believed that a great power might attack Leningrad through the Gulf of Finland. Before the Non-Aggression Pact it had been German intervention that he feared. Though his suspicions were not entirely lulled, that contingency now seemed improbable. The Red Fleet had its new bases on the Baltic coast, and that the Germany Navy should sail in procession all the way from Wilhelmshaven to Kronstadt, when she now enjoyed a common land frontier, seemed less than likely.

But there remained the older, inveterate enemy. Britain maintained the greatest navy in the world, and even now that long-standing adversary of Bolshevism, Winston Churchill, was planning to send a powerful force into the Baltic. It was suspected in London that Stalin's Baltic bases were intended for defence against Britain rather than Germany, and it may be that this view was correct.[9] Stalin's mind had flown back, as it often did, to the miraculous days of the Civil War, when Lenin and he had saved the infant Revolution when it was within an ace of destruction. *Then* the White Russian General Yudenich 'attacked through the Gulf of Finland and later the British did the same. This can happen again . . . England is pressuring Sweden for bases right now. Germany is doing likewise. When the war between these two is over, the victor's fleet will come into the Gulf.' So argued Stalin.

A Finnish military adviser had already pointed out the highly implausible nature of this kind of strategic thinking, but Stalin was so convinced of the amazing duplicity and cunning of the British that he believed them capable of anything. As Soviet Ambassador Ivan Maisky told Eden, 'where wild beasts are loose, every country has to take certain precautions for its own safety'.[10] The Finns could not possibly be so defiant without secret British encouragement.[11] The situation was in danger of getting out of hand and the moment of decision (something Stalin hated) had arrived.

As Molotov and *Pravda* had strongly hinted on 3 November, the time had come for the civilians to leave the stage. There was no alternative to war, and it would not be a war with limited objections. The bases demanded had been but a preliminary to the eventual absorption of the whole nation. Germany had made it abundantly clear she had no objection. There were the dreaded British, but how long would it take Allied aid to reach far-off Finland? The Germans had shown in Poland what a modern army, possessing overwhelming superiority in air power and armour, could accomplish. The disparity between Finland and the Soviet Union was infinitely greater; as Stalin liked to point out, Finland's population was just about equivalent to that of Leningrad.

All that remained was to concoct a legitimate pretext, a consideration of considerable significance in Soviet Marxist thinking. It may seem surprising, therefore, that Molotov on the eve of the invasion delivered a broadcast assuring his listeners that 'irrespective of the regime existing in Finland, we consider her an independent sove-

reign state in her external and internal policies . . . The peoples of
our country are ready also in the future to render the Finnish people
assistance in assuring its free and independent development.'[12]
Though the Soviet leadership had made it clear it did not intend to
respect its Non-Aggression Treaty with Finland, recognition of Finland's independence appeared to preclude any legitimate justification for conquest. In fact, though they were quite unaware of the
fact, the Finns were preparing a drastic change in their government.

Otto Kuusinen was a 58-year-old Finnish Communist, who had
sought asylum in the USSR after the collapse of the Bolshevik attempt to control Finland in 1918. His obsession with the more hair-
splitting niceties of Marxist theorizing attracted the admiration of
Lenin and subsequently that of Stalin. He rose to prominence in the
Comintern, the GPU-controlled organization destined to Bolshevize
the world, and became Stalin's principal adviser on foreign affairs.
The dictator had paid fleeting visits in his youth to England and
Poland, but remained in many ways astonishingly ignorant of the
world outside his office in the Kremlin. Kuusinen knew how to
make himself useful, and was skilful at feeding Stalin ideas in such a
way that he imagined he had concocted them himself.

As a result of his earlier frustrated ambitions he loathed his native
country, and longed for an opportunity to regain power there and
revenge himself on all who had slighted him. It seemed his opportunity had come. Prolonged discussions lasting deep into the night
took place in the Kremlin, in which Stalin, Molotov and Kuusinen
played the leading roles. Kuusinen had been known affectionately to
Lenin as the 'Finland-swallower', after an article he had written
describing Finland as a speck of dust that ought to be swept off the
map. He had long dreamed of ruling over a conquered and purged
Finland, and it was this prospect that was now offered him by Stalin.
A 'Democratic Government of Finland' would be set up with the aid
of Soviet arms, and Kuusinen would be at its head. In this way the
irruption of the Red Army across the frontier would not be an infringement of Finnish sovereignty, but a sustaining of it.

Stalin was greatly tickled by this sort of patently detectable casuis-
try. When the Finns objected to the presence of a Soviet base on the
peninsula of Hango, he offered to turn it into an island by cutting a
canal (he could always replace the slaves who had died on the White
Sea canal project); and Molotov jocosely countered the Finns' dislike
of Soviet bases on their territory by pointing out that it would no

longer *be* their territory. These lies and subterfuges had little practical impact, but it was amusing to see how eagerly they were swallowed by pompous liberals and fellow-travellers in the West.

The future Commissar of People's Finland was not a very savoury character; in fact he would come out badly even in a comparison with his fellow-Scandinavian Vidkun Quisling, who at this time was conducting exactly parallel negotiations with the Nazi leadership in Berlin. Kuusinen's wife, son and numerous close friends were dispatched to labour camps without any objections from him, and he even seized opportunities to deprive them of minor comforts they might otherwise have enjoyed. The fate of the son, who died of tuberculosis, attracted even the vile Beria's sympathy, but Kuusinen remained indifferent. His indifference to human suffering was remarkable even amongst the Soviet leadership, which is perhaps saying something.

Ambition and desire for power were leading factors in his character. It looked now as if they might be gratified; though, as he confessed privately, the overlordship of poor Finland would scarcely be enough. ' . . . he dreamed of controlling Finland and, eventually, being "proconsul" for the whole of Scandinavia; then, after the rest of Europe had surrendered to communism, he would return to Moscow and be the *eminence grise* of the Soviet empire.'

Even more dominant in his nature were longings for vengeance on those who had slighted him, and it was perhaps this characteristic that endeared him to Stalin, whose nature was so similar. Kuusinen's wife noted that 'After much thought, it seems to me that the true key to his personality was hatred . . . He wanted to return home under the banners of the Red Army and wreak revenge on the country which had rejected him.'[13]

As negotiations ground to their inevitable halt, Stalin pushed ahead with preparations for an assault on Finland by the Red Army, with Kuusinen travelling in the baggage train, ready to set up his puppet government. Khrushchev recalled the day of decision. He joined Stalin, Molotov and Kuusinen in the Kremlin. 'When I arrived at the apartment, Stalin was saying, "Let's get started today." ' Apparently it had already been decided that, if the Finns 'didn't yield to our ultimatum, we would take military action. This was Stalin's idea. Naturally I didn't oppose him. Besides, in this case I agreed that it was the right thing to do. All we had to do was raise our voice a little bit, and the Finns would obey. If that didn't work, we could fire one shot and the Finns would put up their hands and surrender.'

Stalin's battle-plan was scarcely original. Deeply impressed by the German success in Poland, he determined to copy that campaign (or the campaign as he understood it) to the letter. Firstly, it was necessary to show the world that the peace-loving Soviet Union was not the aggressor. Hitler's SS had staged an attack on a frontier radio station at Gleiwitz by concentration camp inmates dressed in Polish uniforms. Then, on 1 September 1939, Hitler informed the Reichstag of this 'attack', and announced that Germany was launching her counter-attack.[14]

Stalin arranged for a similar provocation on the part of the Finns. On the afternoon of 26 November Finnish border guards heard artillery fire near the village of Mainila, on the Soviet side of the frontier. The Finnish Government was at once informed by Molotov that their artillery had maliciously opened fire on Mainila, killing four men and wounding nine. The Finns were instructed to withdraw their forces twenty to twenty-five kilometres from the frontier. In fact there was no Finnish artillery within miles of Mainila, and it was established conclusively that the shots had come from the Soviet side of the border. Whether Beria had supplied corpses as evidence, in imitation of Heydrich's Gleiwitz theatricality, is unknown, and the incident appears to have been merely a ritual preliminary to the onslaught.[15]

The next stage was the gigantic *Blitzkrieg* attack, where vast numbers of bombers and tanks would unleash such devastation on Finnish troops and civilians as to overwhelm them within days. The Soviet leadership was supremely confident: the world would now see that Hitler was not the only leader to have mastered modern techniques of warfare! In Moscow Voroshilov and Potemkin (Molotov's deputy) proclaimed exultantly that the war would be over in four days, whilst an official at the Berlin Embassy thought three quite enough.[16]

The task of launching the initial attack on the Finnish lines was entrusted to one of Stalin's favourite commanders, artillery Marshal G. I. Kulik. Kulik was known to his subordinates as a loutish, ignorant bully, who owed his promotion to his having worked with Stalin in the defence of Tsaritsyn in 1918.[17] Kulik's subordinate, N. N. Voronov, recalled the military conference preceding the invasion. All present irradiated confidence, and in reply to his query Voronov was told to ensure a supply of shells lasting not more than ten or twelve days. There were shouts of mirth when Voronov announced that he would prefer to allow for two or three months.[18]

Three days after the Mainila incident the USSR broke off diplomatic relations with Finland. Next day, 30 November, Stalin gleefully picked up the ringing telephone at his office in the Kremlin. Kulik's guns had begun the bombardment![19] Four Soviet army groups were assembled on the frontiers from Petsamo to the Gulf of Finland. They totalled some 600,000 men, equipped with vast masses of tanks, artillery and machine-guns, supported by 3,000 warplanes. This huge mass began to surge forward on all four fronts. The lightly-armed Finnish frontier guards fell back slowly on to pre-arranged defence lines.

There had been no declaration of war – another good tip provided by the Führer. In Helsinki the Cabinet was hastily convened as soon as the news broke. The country was somewhat superfluously declared to be in state of war, and Marshal Mannerheim, the veteran saviour of Finland in 1918, was appointed Commander-in-Chief. As the meeting progressed, a sinister drone was heard amongst the grey clouds above. A fleet of Soviet bombers had appeared over the capital. A few showered leaflets urging workers to desert the 'White kulak army' and join the Red Army in overthrowing their capitalist and feudal overlords. To encourage them in this high-spirited venture thousands of incendiary and high-explosive bombs rained down upon the defenceless city.

The Cabinet meeting broke up, and ministers strolled off to their offices. Despite careful precautionary instructions issued earlier, crowds in the streets were seen for the most part going earnestly about their business as if nothing were happening. When the all clear was sounded the citizens of Helsinki set out to survey the damage. It was by no means so bad as might have been feared, considering the scale and ferocity of the attack, but inevitably numbers of people had been killed and buildings destroyed. The nature of the destruction suggested that, whilst Red Air Force pilots had found the city a large enough target not to miss altogether, any further degree of accuracy was beyond their skills. Prominent casualties were the Milk Central Building, which had apparently been hit in an unsuccessful attempt to destroy the parliament house, and the Soviet Embassy.[20]

Despite these slightly farcical touches, and the remarkable coolness with which the Finns faced the coming onslaught, it was clear that tragedy was in the offing. Finland had known the Red Terror in 1918, and had ever since received a steady trickle of fugitives, who had made their way through the snow-forests from the icy horrors of GULAG camps on the Belomorsk Canal or the coal-mines of Vorkuta. Everyone knew that a Soviet victory meant not merely the imposition of an alien government, culture and laws, but death, torture and slavery for thousands, and the extinguishing of all vestiges of civilized life for the remainder. In Soviet Karelia, just across the frontier, large sections of the Finnish-speaking population had been deported to Siberia each year since 1934.[21] Finland would fight, whatever the cost, regardless of the odds, with or without allies. 'I am proud of my people and what they are doing these days', proclaimed the aged Jean Sibelius from his home outside bombed Helsinki.

Meanwhile, a very different type of Finn was enjoying his brief hour of triumph. As the guns of the Red Army blazed along the frontier, and the Red Air Force bombed its own Embassy, Moscow Radio announced that it had picked up a broadcast from 'an unknown station somewhere in Finland'. This was a transmitter operating from within territory liberated by the risen proletariat, no longer on its knees. It announced that a 'Finnish Democratic Government' had now been established, with the virtuous Mr Kuusinen as its Prime Minister and Foreign Minister. This respectable administration, it was further announced in Moscow, had established itself at Terijoki, the first town to be freed by the Red Army.

A day later Moscow Radio reported that the new Prime Minister had arrived in Moscow, which had recognized his government. The statesman had come to negotiate a treaty with the Soviet Government. These negotiations moved with surprising swiftness, and within forty-eight hours of his state's coming into existence, Prime Minister Kuusinen had agreed to every single one of those reasonable Soviet demands the reactionary Finnish Government had wilfully obstructed for the past two months. In recognition of this exemplary co-operation the Soviet Government for its part offered a large barren area of Soviet Karelia to the Finnish Democratic Government. A number of renegade Finns with Russian accents held the remaining portfolios in the new Ministry; there was even a Minister for Literary Matters, named Paavo Prokkonen. Kuusinen, it was claimed, headed an army of fifty thousand men who were reputed to have been equipped with magnificent uniforms of Charles

XII's time, to be worn in the triumphal procession as the future Proconsul of Scandinavia entered conquered Helsinki. The accuracy of this rumour is unknown, as no one ever saw the army.

The truth is that Terijoki was a comfortable seaside resort just inside the frontier, which had been entirely deserted by its inhabitants on the arrival of the Red Army. The only 'Finns' in the place were a few-score ageing renegades who had somehow survived the terrible Comintern purge of 1937. As for Prime Minister Kuusinen, it seems very doubtful whether he troubled to move to Terijoki at all; certainly not until some time after signing the Treaty of 2 December.

The main effect of this move on the part of the Soviet Government was to convince the Finns that the total subjugation of their country has been on the Soviet agenda for weeks, and the demand for bases a mere smoke-screen. As early as 13 November, when the Finnish representatives had indicated their readiness to resume negotiations, Kuusinen had contacted a Finnish Communist living in Sweden, Arvo Tuominen. Kuusinen explained that negotiations were achieving nothing, that the Soviet Government had more forceful methods in prospect, and that Tuominen could expect to be offered 'a job he would like'. A week later he learned that this was the office of Prime Minister in the coming Finnish Democratic Republic. Tuominen was not prepared to become a traitor, and later revealed the whole intrigue. The fortnight or so's delay that intervened before the invasion was perhaps due to protracted military preparations and earnest discussions in the Kremlin as to the international implications. But Finland's policy of neutrality, her abandonment by Sweden, the terms of the Nazi-Soviet Pact and her geographical isolation made her appear easy meat.

The military events that followed are too well known to require detailed description, neither do they fall directly into the subject-matter of this book. The Soviet 7th and 13th Armies struck first along the narrow isthmus between Lake Ladoga and the Gulf of Finland. Great columns of tanks were followed by massed infantry units, whilst wave after wave of bombers passed overhead to strike terror into the defenceless civilian population. Kuusinen's victory parade into Helsinki seemed near, and it appeared the Red Army would gain the capital in less time than it had taken the Wehrmacht to seize Warsaw. The War's second great *Blitzkrieg* was under way.

Or so it seemed to Stalin and his advisers. Alas, matters did not quite turn out as they had anticipated. An elaborate system of booby-

traps held up the vanguard units before the panzers struck at the
Mannerheim Line. Soviet propaganda then and since has represented this defensive work as a massive replica of the Maginot Line.
It was 'impregnable', Khrushchev remembered.[22] In fact it was
largely an improvised obstruction of slit-trenches and tank-traps, in
part constructed by the holiday labour of schoolboys and students. A
mere sixty-three concrete defensive positions straddled the eighty-
eight-mile redoubt, of which two-thirds were too old to be of much
effect. To destroy the oncoming waves of armour, the Finnish Army
at the outbreak of war disposed of just two anti-tank guns for each
battalion – a hundred in all, to stretch across more than seven hundred miles of front. Pre-war insistence on improvement of living
standards as a priority over defence had left the Finnish Army extremely poorly equipped. To oppose 3,000 Red Air Force bombers
and fighters, the Finns possessed 162 antiquated aircraft.

Soviet strategy was simple. Whilst the main thrust smashed the
Mannerheim Line and followed the excellent communications linking Leningrad to Helsinki in the south, the 8th Army would crush
Finnish resistance in the outlying territory north of Lake Ladoga.
Further north still, the 9th Army would advance past Suomussalmi
to Oulu on the Gulf of Bothnia, splitting Finland in half at her
'waist-line'. Finally, in the extreme north, by the Barents Sea, the
14th Army, based on Murmansk, would seize Petsamo, Finland's
only Arctic port and centre of famous nickel-mines, so cutting communications with Norway and the outside world.

At first the world was convinced that Finland must simply be
swamped in face of such odds. But what the Finns lacked in numbers
and equipment, they made up in courage and resource. Finnish
sharpshooters passed round the tank columns' flanks, pouring
murderous fire into the massed infantry behind. The infantry destroyed or demoralized, the armour was routed in a number of
ingenious ways. There were mines made of old piping filled with
chloride resin, triggered by concealed trip-wires. There were non-
magnetic mines tucked into wooden boxes, whilst others were held
in water-tight containers, ready to discharge under the ice as Soviet
tanks trundled overhead. Even more primitive methods included
large holes sawn in the ice, strips of cellophane that resembled water
when photographed from the air, and dummy defences constructed
from cardboard. As the steel monsters blundered through this network of traps, Finnish troops (most of them conscripted civilian

reservists) sprang out of camouflaged hiding-holes and rammed branches and crowbars into the slow-moving tanks' tracks. As the crews emerged, blinking, to effect repairs, they were picked off mercilessly by snipers in the shadows of the surrounding forest. Most terrifying of all were the famous 'Molotov cocktails'. An empty vodka bottle, filled with a mixture of kerosene, tar and petrol, with a flaming petrol-soaked rag tied round the neck, was lobbed into an open hatch or gun-port, filling the interior with blazing fire.

This novel type of warfare brought the Soviet 7th and 13th Armies to a crumbling halt some twenty miles from their frontier. General Meretskov, the Red Army commander, decided to launch a feint attack on his right flank at Taipale on Lake Ladoga, whilst the real offensive was prepared for Viipuri, further west. Meanwhile the Red Air Force could wreak devastation at will, operating from its newly-gained base at Tallinn in Estonia. Two enormous battleships, the *October Revolution* and the *Marat*, slid out of Kronstadt, accompanied by a flotilla of destroyers.

The result was inglorious. By 17 December the 13th Army was in full retreat from Taipale, whilst three days later the 120,000 Red soldiers hurled against Viipuri were driven back with appalling slaughter. In the air Finnish pilots, in their tiny Dutch Fokkers and American Brewsters, set about the Red air armada. They proved as skilful as their infantry counterparts in the forests below, descending out of a grey, leaden sky on to massed squadrons of superbly-constructed and equipped Ilyushin and Tupolev bombers. Nearly a thousand Soviet aeroplanes had been destroyed by the end of the war, to sixty-two Finnish machines. Finnish air aces performed extraordinary feats, perhaps the most notable being that of Lieutenant Sarvanto, who on 6 January 1940 downed six out of seven Ilyushins in four minutes flat.

The Red Fleet blundered about the Gulf until a few well-placed shells from Finnish coastal batteries caused its withdrawal. Khrushchev relates the epic exploit of a Soviet submarine, which tried in vain to sink a Swedish merchantman under the impression it was a Finnish warship. German naval officers on a watching vessel observed the action with ill-disguised amusement.

Stalin's temper became vicious when he received the news of these disasters. He screamed abuse at his old crony, the buffoonish Voroshilov, People's Commissar for Defence. Stung beyond restraint, Voroshilov actually yelled back at his master: 'You have

yourself to blame for all this! You're the one who annihilated the
Old Guard of the army; you had our best generals killed!' This
wrangle took place at one of Stalin's late-night feasts; the dignified
scene ended with Voroshilov's overturning a large dish of roast
suckling pig.[23]

Voroshilov amazingly survived the outburst and stayed on as
Stalin's court fool. Some months later he was set aside from his post,
but long before that he had in effect been replaced by Semion
Timoshenko, a former barrel-maker and less incapable soldier, who
took over from Meretskov on the Finnish front.

Meanwhile the Finns themselves took the initiative with an offensive launched on 23 December. This beat back the Soviet forces some
distance, and threw the enemy into such confusion that no further
attack could be sent against the Mannerheim Line for six weeks. The
Finns dug in and prepared for the next attack. The daily bombardments proved an irritant but little more. Light relief was provided by
occasional loudspeaker broadcasts from the Soviet lines, containing
appeals from Prime Minister Kuusinen to his rebellious subjects. As
the firing was halted for these performances, the Finns took the
opportunity of snatching a leisured moment in the field latrine.

While the major battles had been raging on the Isthmus, the four
Soviet Army Groups to the north had surged forward across the
frontier. In those winter wastes there were no trenches or fortifications; only the endless snow plains and pine forests. Into this
wilderness wound long columns of hundreds of thousands of Soviet
troops. Great snowdrifts hampered their advance and made protection of their flanks virtually impossible. But not for the Finns: in the
long darkness of the winter night, Finnish soldiers on skis swept
silently across the drifts, circling through forest glades and over
frozen swamps, until they saw the dark mass trudging menacingly
westwards. Most Finns lived half their lives on skis; they were
tough as leather, hard as steel, and included several Olympic
athletes. (The Games had been due to take place in Helsinki in 1940.)
From out of the night came deadly accurate firing from rifles and
Suomi sub-machine-guns the Finns carried slung across their backs.
Before the helpless Russians could unsling their rifles the Finns had
long since glided swiftly away into the darkness. So deadly was this
type of warfare that the colossal disparity in size of the two armies
became largely meaningless. Simo Häyhä, a small farmer who had
won numerous trophies for marksmanship before the invasion,

would slip out each day 'to hunt Russians'. In the end he was wounded, but not before he had killed 500 Russian soldiers.

The Soviet advance was repulsed. North of Lake Ladoga a few Finnish battalions drove back 36,000 Soviet troops, equipped with 335 pieces of artillery. Soviet casualties included 4,000 killed, 600 taken prisoner, and the capture of 59 tanks, 31 guns, 342 machine-guns and 3,000 rifles: a boon to the ill-equipped Finnish Army. The Soviet drive to the sea at Oulu fared equally disastrously. After bitter fighting, two of the three divisions involved were virtually wiped out.

With the New Year, fighting became more bitter still. The Russians were desperately weary and dispirited, exhausted with a war seemingly pointless and of no advantage to Russia. Their sufferings were appalling, particularly those of the thousands of conscripts from the warm lands of Soviet Central Asia. In a typical regiment a hundred froze to death before the rest were ordered to the rear. In order to re-establish morale, large bodies of well-armed NKVD hung about the rear of the armies, ready to mow down individuals or units attempting to leave the battlefield. In January 1940 a Russian prisoner informed his captors that all retreating soldiers were being shot.[24] Fighting under these barbaric conditions, it is scarcely surprising that the Red Army once again confirmed its barbaric reputation. From the first days of the invasion Red Air Force planes made a regular practice of machine-gunning civilians on open roads or in their villages, and private houses were singled out for incendiary attacks. For the Red Army it seemed normal practice to burn prisoners alive, or put out an officer's eyes with a bayonet.[25] Plunder from Finnish homes was displayed temptingly in Moscow shops.[26]

Though terror greatly appealed to the Soviet leadership as an effective means of waging war, and was to be employed on a much greater scale in the coming struggle against Germany, it could not of itself solve the disgraceful débâcle in Finland. As Voroshilov had riposted to Stalin, the military purge of 1937 had left the Red Army virtually leaderless. Of the higher command, 3 of the 5 Marshals had been executed, 14 of the 16 Army Commanders, 8 of the 8 Admirals, 60 of the 67 Corps Commanders, 136 of the 199 Divisional Commanders, and 221 of the 397 Brigade Commanders; altogether half the officer corps, about 35,000 men, had been shot or imprisoned on Stalin's orders. As the Finnish War itself extorted a further heavy toll, virtually no regimental commander could be found who had graduated from the Frunze Military Academy.[27]

All this is irrefutable evidence that Stalin feared the Red Army infinitely more than he did the Germans or any other foreign power; but now something had to be done to restore a situation which had made the Soviet Union the world's laughing-stock. Sweeping measures were taken. A number of unsuccessful generals were shot out of hand. More constructively,

> the entire Soviet effort was reorganized. The mass infantry attacks, which had presented the Finnish machine-gunners with such persistent and generous targets, were to be discontinued. The aimless artillery fire was to be directed henceforth against enemy fire-points. Newly arrived divisions or reinforcements were not to be committed to action without some acquaintance of the conditions under which they would have to fight. The *Model 1939* rifle was issued to the infantry; the new KV tanks were brought into action. Armoured infantry sledges and electric digging machines were rushed to the front.[28]

In January 1940 these elaborate preparations were being hurried through at desperate speed. The Finns *had* to be crushed within the next few weeks. The frustration of Soviet plans to occupy the country, the shameful and revealing weakness of the Red Army's performance, and the ridicule these had aroused throughout the world, were bad enough. The comparison with Hitler's lightning conquest of Poland, so eagerly intended in November, was now a worse than hollow mockery. But there was a much more potent cause of apprehension than all these weighty factors. Clear indications were coming through that Britain and France intended to throw their enormous resources into the scale. How could the Finns be beaten then? And how could the Soviet Union avoid in that case being drawn into the war of the great powers? Stalin needed a swift victory, be the cost what it might.

IX
The Undeclared War

Not the least of Stalin's worries was world-wide attention focused on the increasingly protracted Winter War. Soviet Russia had attacked a small, free and peace-loving neighbour with no obvious motive save that of national aggrandizement. The unexpected Finnish military successes strongly appealed to chivalrous instincts. 'The Red Czar is now the executor of the traditional imperialism of Czarist Russia', declaimed a pamphlet published by the British Labour Party; 'Stalin's Men use the freedom which they enjoy to defend War and Tyranny, a war of conquest by an alien and powerful despot against a small outpost of republican democracy.'[1]

There was a feeling of moral liberation in the air: at last both variants of totalitarian despotism had removed their masks, and Hitler and Stalin had revealed themselves for what they were. Only Communists continued to defend Soviet aggression, and they had already made themselves as unpopular as could be by their support for Hitler's 'peace offer'. The Phoney War was pursuing its inglorious course. The Germans had shown no inclination to break their teeth against the Maginot Line, and the distant struggle under the Northern Lights became almost a welcome diversion.

The War Cabinets of Britain and France had of course to take a more prosaic view of events. How, if at all, did Finland's plight affect their conduct of the war against Hitler? At first glance it seemed absurd to suppose that any practical measures could be taken to antagonize the Soviet Union while it remained questionable whether defeat could be inflicted on Germany. But as Finnish resistance stiffened and Soviet weakness became more apparent, the temptation to fish in these troubled waters became greater.

The initiative came from the French. France's large Communist Party was working hard for the cause of the Nazi-Soviet settlement in Central and Eastern Europe, and by its spread of defeatist and subversive propaganda was clearly imperilling the Allied cause. The existence of this enormous fifth column in France had long polarized political viewpoints, and much influential public opinion favoured any measures that might strike at the fount of Comintern activity in Moscow. There was also a defeatist element on the Right, subsequently revealed in Vichy, which privately hoped for a German alliance in a crusade against Bolshevism.

Apart from these underlying considerations, coupled with genuinely altruistic sympathy for Finland's plight, there were realistic strategic factors connected with the prosecution of the war against Germany. These were threefold. Firstly, Germany was known to be dependent in great measure on supplies of iron ore from the Gällivare mines in northern Sweden. At the same time as aiding the Finns, an Allied expeditionary force could occupy the ore-fields, which lay on the direct line of communications from Narvik on the Norwegian coast to Finland. Secondly, Germany was if anything even more dependent on the oil, grain, cotton and other vital commodities she was known to be receiving from the Soviet Union. War against the Soviet Union, whether limited or general, must threaten those supplies. In any case, so long as Finnish resistance was sustained, much if not all Russia's resources would have to be diverted to her own war effort. Lastly, the French were reluctant to provoke a serious outbreak of hostilities on the home front, and welcomed a chance to prosecute the war vigorously on distant horizons. This prospect appealed to the Premier, Daladier, who was being accused of conducting an insufficiently energetic policy.

Britain, however, entertained these proposals with less enthusiasm. Neville Chamberlain's belief was that time lay on the side of the Allies (provided they continued to build up their economic and strategic superiority) and that major confrontations should be avoided if possible. The Foreign Office, too, felt that war with the USSR was a contingency to be avoided. The proponent of a more vigorous war policy, Winston Churchill (then First Lord of the Admiralty), greatly favoured action to deprive Germany of Swedish iron ore, but was at the same time generally anxious to avoid war with the USSR, which he had long regarded as a potential ally in the life-and-death struggle with Germany.

Eventually notes were passed to the Norwegian and Swedish governments explaining that a request for transit of Allied troops might come in due course. Both countries objected vigorously that they had no desire to become involved in the war, and that Allied guarantees of protection had proved to be of little value. There would be nothing the Allies could do to prevent a German occupation of Denmark and the devastation of southern Scandinavian cities by aerial bombing. This rebuff was registered in London with little concern, it being improbably held there that an appeal by the beleaguered Finns in due course would provide an irresistible appeal to Norwegian and Swedish chivalry.

On 5 February 1940 the Supreme War Council met in Paris. The French, ever anxious for real action on the Finnish front, had proposed to dispatch fifty thousand troops directly to Petsamo, Finland's port on the Barents Sea. If the Red Army could be driven out of all Karelia, Finland's front would be immeasurably shortened, with her left flank resting on the White Sea. But the British pointed out that this would frustrate the real point of the operation, the seizure of Gällivare, and their proposal was accepted. But events were now moving much faster than these dilatory Allied war plans.[2]

The prospect of British and French intervention in the North filled Stalin with trepidation. The war had now to be brought to an early and successful close, whatever happened. Fifty thousand crack British and French troops, equipped with the most up-to-date artillery and machine-guns presented a formidable prospect. And what might three hundred bombers from the RAF not do to Leningrad? The Finns with this aid might be able to fight the Red Army to a standstill; they had virtually done that already without any help. They had begun to negotiate for honourable peace terms, but it was unthinkable that Stalin could agree to a mere draw.

On 1 February massed hordes of Red Army tanks, artillery and troops, more than half a million strong, began a great offensive on the Mannerheim Line. The main attack fell on the town of Summa, a strongpoint on the Finns' right flank. The preliminary barrage exceeded anything seen in warfare since the worst fighting on the Western Front in 1918. In twenty-four hours, 300,000 shells rained down on Summa alone. Finnish observers counted 440 field-pieces drawn up in a single sector a mile and a third broad; they were almost touching, hub to hub.

Five days later came the final Soviet offensive. A hundred and fifty tanks rumbled forward before a sea of great-coated infantry. Overhead roared two hundred bombers, unleashing a hail of explosives on fortifications and rear communications. Great smoke-screens blanketed the oncoming flood from sight, broken by the lurid flash of hundreds of guns firing together in a rolling barrage that crept backwards and forwards over the thinly-held Finnish lines. The Finns were short of artillery, had virtually no air cover, and were fast running out of ammunition. But they would *not* give in. Their machine-gunners, almost fainting with exhaustion, fired until the barrels of their guns were smoking with heat. Thousands upon thousands of Russians fell, but with the grim ranks of NKVD battalions covering them from behind they had no choice but to fall on again.

The Russian dead lay in heaps as far as the eye could see, but new waves came on over the frozen corpses of their comrades. Inevitably the Finns were overrun at several points. A Soviet attack turned the Finnish right flank by launching assaults across frozen Viipuri Bay. Marshal Mannerheim ordered a withdrawal of the depleted garrisons to a second line. The exhausted Finns moved slowly back, fighting every inch of the way. Russian casualties were mounting by thousands (quantities fell under their own artillery fire), but the Finnish ranks were so thinned it seemed they must be swamped. Week followed week, however, and still the Finns fought on, and it was not until well into the following month, on 12 March, that Finland finally and reluctantly signed a peace treaty in Moscow.

For Stalin, there was no time to be lost. Daladier had announced to the sceptical Finns that the fifty thousand British and French troops were at long last on their way. The terms offered the Finns were relatively mild, considering their military exhaustion. The USSR acquired a belt of land north and west of Lake Ladoga, another near Salla in the north, a naval base at Hango, and ominous restrictions on Finnish sovereignty. In particular, Finland's association with a Scandinavian defence pact was prohibited. This action reveals the singular blindness of Stalin's foreign policy, as such a pact might well have inhibited German intervention in Norway, and Finland's subsequent resumption of the war in 1941. In fact the whole disgraceful Finnish adventure, which cost more than 200,000 Russian lives (Khrushchev put the figure at one million),[3] turned Finland from the Allied camp, where all her sympathies had lain in 1939, to become an unwilling but vigorous co-belligerent with Germany.[4]

Finnish casualties were small in comparison, but by any normal standard fell heavily on a nation poor in resources and population.

Nearly 25,000 soldiers had been killed,[5] and the ceded territories were abandoned by their entire populations, who trekked back into reconstituted Finland in the ten days allowed them by the Soviets.[6] Thus an eighth of the population of Finland were deprived of their homes. They were fortunate, perhaps. Soviet hatred and fear vented themselves on people of Finnish blood living in Leningrad and Soviet Karelia. They were swept up by the NKVD and dispatched to GULAG camps in the Arctic Circle.[7]

Despite this, there can be no doubt that Finnish heroism paid dividends. Soviet support for the Kuusinen 'government' revealed unequivocally that total absorption of Finland into the Soviet system was Stalin's ultimate war aim.[8] By the time of the peace negotiations early in 1940, Kuusinen had been forgotten. (He was not purged, but continued to eke out the shameful existence of a pensioned traitor.) By March Stalin had reconciled himself to the imposition of terms which, though harsh, provided for the survival of Finland as a nation. And that, after all, had been what the Finns had been fighting for.[9] Fear of Allied intervention was undoubtedly the cause of Stalin's haste in concluding a treaty very different from his original war aims,[10] but the prospect of prolonging a war so costly in men and material must also have daunted him. Ultimate responsibility for the worst military blunders rested on Stalin, as Soviet sources have accepted since.[11] Whether he was prepared to admit as much to himself is questionable, but he must have been aware of the terrible strain the war was exacting on Soviet resources and morale. In a hundred days of war against a country with the population of Leningrad, the Red Army had already suffered losses equivalent to an eighth of those lost fighting the combined armies of Germany, Austria-Hungary and Turkey during the whole of the Great War.

The disparity between Soviet hopes and realities had never been so clearly displayed. Documents captured by the Finns listed garrison roles assigned to Soviet troops in a future occupied Finland, and the standard of the Red Army 18th Division operating north of Lake Ladoga had borne as emblem an embroidered map of Europe with a Soviet dagger reaching into its heart.[12] Now the Soviet authorities had to reckon with the intangible effects of Finnish propaganda, extolling in moderate and reasonable terms the benefits of democratic freedoms, on a depressed, poverty-stricken and mismanaged soldiery. One problem at least could be solved, though. Several thousand Russians had fallen prisoner to the Finns. Well treated in accordance with the provisions of the Geneva Convention on Prisoners-of-War (signed by Finland, but not by the USSR), they had glimpsed the realities of life in the non-Communist West. The dangers of this virus infecting the Soviet population at large were obvious, and prisoners returned after the war were conveyed at once to labour camps and for the most part never seen again.[13]

These Russian prisoners constituted a subject of great interest to the Finns and the Allies. Numbers of Russians had succeeded, despite draconian penalties, in escaping from the Soviet Union ever since the Revolution. Their stories were consistent and credible, but it could be argued that they were in some respects untypical of the population at large in that they had, by braving the dangers of emigration, revealed themselves to be exceptionally obdurate opponents of the regime. Now the Finns held sizeable numbers of Russians of all ranks and classes, taken by the random chance of war out of their homes[14] and held in temporary quarantine from alien influence. British Intelligence, contemplating the possibility of war with the Soviet Union, could not miss this unique chance of assessing Russian national morale.

In February 1940 two Russian-speaking British Intelligence officers, Major Gatehouse and Captain Tamplin, travelled to Finland and visited the camps. They conducted intensive interrogations among two thousand prisoners held in four camps. Their lengthy report provides a fascinating and perhaps unique glimpse of Soviet realities in 1940, so heavily cloaked from the outside world, and so soon to be dramatically changed beyond recognition (and to some extent beyond the recall of memory) by the German invasion of 1941.

The report began by explaining, on the testimony of the prisoners themselves, that they were men who

had undergone, in most cases, undescribable hardship and privation, who had been warned that they would be shot or tortured to death if captured, who mostly had never seen a Finnish soldier until the moment of surrender or capture, who had blindly obeyed orders, who were disillusioned about their home country by what they saw after capture, who were appreciative of the humanity and kindness extended to them, who possibly were inclined to give the answer they thought would please, who wanted an end to the war and a safe return home, who were still in terror of their own 'command personnel' Politruks and any O.[ther] R.[ank] communists, who, in fact, had been browbeaten, bullied, starved, frozen, half-killed and mutilated, and some of them still did not believe they were not going to be shot. Some had been shot and left for dead by their own commanders, or seen their friends shot; others had 'liquidated their superiors'.

Throughout the report it was stressed that the prisoners' 'ignorance was abysmal – a large number hardly literate'. Twenty years of propaganda and censorship had left them totally ignorant of the outside world. Many believed the USSR had liberated Poland, and few had even heard of the partial take-over of the Baltic States. Those whose units had served in Poland explained that they had been held in barracks isolated from the population. Nevertheless they had been astounded by their glimpses of Polish standards of living and absence of bread queues. They had reacted similarly to what they saw of Finland on their way to the camps.

Conditions in the Soviet Union were described in detail: the universal terror imposed by the NKVD, which arrived stealthily in the night to remove its victims without trace; the unending propaganda, which had stupefied all individuality of thought; the deplorably low standard of education among the barely-literate masses; the wretched physical condition of people starved for twenty years; all these formed a familiar tale of woe. It was not surprising that, among the peasants, there was widespread nostalgia for the days of the Tsar, when there was 'good food in plenty, and the special dishes for holiday occasions'.

After the NKVD, the collective farm (*kolkhoz*) was the most hated institution in the land.

The normal method for the creation of the Kolkhoz was for the idlest and least capable peasant in any community to turn violently communist, and thereby obtain the local authorities' sanction to collectivize his neighbours. By this means he is appointed director at a fixed fat salary as compared with the coppers paid to the other peasant farmers, whose larger and better holdings and stock have gone into the pool to create the farm.

The peasant loathed the exploitation which kept him and his family permanently at starvation level, and regarded 'the whole proceeding as a form of legalized robbery and swindle'.

The troops of the Red Army were kept in such professional ignorance 'that few men know the numbers of the other Regiments in their division, a number do not know the names of the larger cities in the Soviet Union outside their own locality, and some do not know who is Voroshilov.' One may contrast this real-life sample with the bland assertions of contemporary Western fellow-travellers that Soviet education had virtually eradicated illiteracy and ignorance throughout the Union.[15]

A particularly sinister fear, in the light of coming events, was expressed by the prisoners.

All ranks, with a few communist exceptions, are genuinely terri-fied of any notification being made of their capture, as they had been warned that, should they surrender, dire retribution would fall on their families. The most humane treatment they expected for their families was that they would be deprived of food and home, and consequently starve or freeze to death. With only a few exceptions, all ranks refuse to return to the Soviet as exchanged Prisoners of War. They are confident of being instantly shot.

Higher ranks were composed of Party members, and were largely loyal to the regime. But the ordinary privates

. . . hate and distrust their Commanders and Commissars. They realize their military inefficiency and ignorance, and blame them freely for the enormous losses they have sustained. They quail under the iron discipline and fear the unsparing use of the re-volver for driving men on into the attack. In a number of cases met with, men had been shot by their commanders and left for dead, and in others men claimed to have shot their own commanders. Reports were so general, and feeling among Prisoners of War so strong, as to leave no doubt of these shootings being almost daily occurrences. Patriotism, as such, is dead. The Russian marches to war with a revolver at his back, and prefers the chance of death at the hands of the enemy to the certainty of death if he refuses.

Almost all the prisoners displayed a lively interest in religion, particularly those of the Orthodox faith. Persecution of religion was still intense, and the open practice of a religious faith dangerous and difficult, but there were indications of a slight relaxation of official hostility since 1937. The thirst for instruction was extraordinary, and bibles, prayer-books and crosses distributed by the Finns were ac-cepted with eager gratitude. Services held in the prisoners' camps were crowded out, and crucifixes widely worn (many appeared from concealed recesses of the prisoners' clothing or knapsacks). All in all, religion seemed to provide the only real source of hope and meaning in the degraded and poverty-stricken lives of the Russian masses. The interrogating officers concluded: 'The suppression of faith appears to be deeply resented by the peasants. They cannot understand why it should be considered harmful or contemptible. Religion to the Russian is primarily emotional, and it is possible that its severe suppression may have been the cause of keeping it alive.'

The report concluded this review of public feeling in the USSR by reasserting Major Gatehouse and Captain Tamplin's gloomy impression of the average Russian's outlook.

> Among the prisoners of war there was an obvious fatalism. They accept the persecution in civil life and the brutal discipline of military life, the permanent shortage of food and clothes, and the ordering, herding and hectoring by the Soviet Government as being the dictate of an unkind fate. They do not seem to think that they can themselves improve their lot. They give an impression of people who feel that it is a miracle they survive from day to day, not only at war, but even at home . . .
>
> (a) There is a permanent state of fear of everything Soviet.
> (b) The war is unpopular, and any peace movement would be welcomed.
> (c) The peasant hates the Kolhoz and longs for the restoration of his land.
> (d) The mass still clings to religion in spite of its outward suppression.

Finally, the report moved from a factual assessment of the Russian outlook to a specific, speculative question that was clearly implicit in the purpose of their mission. Was there any chance of an uprising or counter-revolution from amongst the oppressed masses against the Soviet regime? If war broke out between the Allies and the USSR, could the former hope to engineer an upheaval such as that which had overthrown the Provisional Government in 1917 and destroyed Russia's capacity for military resistance? To this the Intelligence team could only, on the evidence of what they had seen, return a pessimistic reply.

An appeal to the average citizen of the Soviet Union to take active measures against the present regime can be ruled out for the following reasons:

  (i) Fear of the N.K.V.D.
 (ii) Fear of agents-provocateurs.
(iii) Fear of reprisals on dependents.
 (iv) Lack of leadership.
  (v) Political apathy.

. . . the political value of prisoners of war can be assessed as zero . . . The military value of the prisoners of war is nil. It is most unlikely that any reliable military force, or even formation, could be raised from among these men. They have lived through terrible experiences in the present war, and do not mean to risk a repetition. This risk they would most certainly not take voluntarily. Any possibility of using them as a military force can be ruled out. Their greatest hope is for an end to the war, so that they might creep home to their families.

Only amongst the sizeable Ukrainian contingent were there faint indications of more positive aspirations. 'They were more strictly religious as a body', and displayed stirrings of interest in the possibility of nationalist opposition. But 'No man would admit any actual knowledge, and no man was ready to take part in any secret agitation. Having created a friendly atmosphere, a party of thirty Ukrainians were asked if all, or any, would be prepared to march, armed against the present regime. After considerable hesitation, one man said – "I might go".'[16]

Valuable as this report must have been to British military authorities, its interest for historians is infinitely greater. With all the limitations and reservations that must necessarily accrue to an assessment made under such circumstances, this random analysis probably represents the nearest approximation to a Gallup Poll taken in Soviet history. There is much corroborative material to confirm the accuracy of this image of the Russian people in 1940: crushed, beaten, deprived of hope; sullenly resentful, yet fatalistically resigned to acceptance of an oppression seemingly too pervasive and ruthless to counter.

But though this Intelligence report presents a scrupulously accurate impression of the prisoners' psychology, other evidence indicated that some of its conclusions might require modification in the swiftly-changing circumstances of the time. Firstly, despite all the blunders and horrors inflicted on the Soviet soldiery, there were signs that the innate patriotism and military qualities of the Russian people had not been totally extinguished. The unparalleled humiliation the Finns had inflicted on Russia had aroused the ridicule of the whole world, a ridicule which was hard to bear, however unjust the cause for which they were fighting. As a divisional commander observed indignantly, 'All this is insulting and degrading for us. Here we are – a great people. Russians learned how to fight long ago. But what sort of devilry is involved here? There aren't so many Finns, but still we can't cope with them properly. It's insulting!'

This feeling became widespread amongst the troops as the war drew to a close. 'Soldiers and officers suddenly felt that this situation could not be tolerated any longer – that somehow there was something shameful about our situation.' A new military attitude began to display itself. Volunteers sacrificed their lives in an unordered attack on a Finnish bunker; Russians took to roaming the woods in search of the formerly invulnerable Finnish snipers. A new spirit was in the air, intangible, fragile, and yet real. It had nothing to do with hatred of the Finns, but sprang from roots much older than those of the Bolshevik regime.[17] Of course, the Soviet victory was almost entirely due to overwhelming superiority of numbers and equipment, together with improved tactics and leadership, but the moral factor was not negligible.

If this latent upsurge of patriotic feeling was undetectable to the British Intelligence team, so too was another significant factor. They had totally discounted the possibility of recruiting any anti-Soviet military force from amongst the prisoners, whose apathy under irresistible oppression seemingly far outweighed the universal resentment. The report had noted that 'The overthrow of the Government can only be achieved by foreign military intervention, such intervention to be presented to the Russian as a crusade for the restoration of his rights and liberty, i.e. restoration of peasant private ownership of the land and return of religious freedom.' Such a crusade was of course far beyond the Finns' capacity or intentions, but nevertheless an attempt was briefly made to enlist the Russian prisoners in their struggle against the common enemy.

Boris Bajanov had been Stalin's personal secretary until 1928, when, disgusted with the crimes of the still infant Soviet regime, he fled across the frontier to Persia. After many adventures, he found

himself living in France in 1940. Urged and authorized by Russian
émigré organizations, and assisted by the French military authorities, he travelled to Finland to see if anything could be made of the
Russian prisoners as a political force. On 15 January he was received
by Marshal Mannerheim at Finnish GHQ. Mannerheim was sympathetic but sceptical. Authorizing Bajanov to visit a camp containing five hundred prisoners, he observed: 'If they follow you, organize your army. But I am an old soldier, and I doubt that these
men, who have escaped from hell and been saved virtually by a
miracle, will be willing of their own accord to return to that hell.'

But Bajanov persisted, and set about recruiting amongst the inmates of the designated camp. His plan was not to form an anti-
Bolshevik military unit to fight alongside the Finns, but to employ
his people in appealing to their comrades fighting on the other side.
The success which followed was unexpected by everyone save
Bajanov. Of five hundred men, four hundred and fifty answered their
compatriot's appeal. The remaining fifty expressed sympathy, but
were too fearful to act. With the officers, however, there was no
success. Menaced by an NKVD cell in their midst, they were far too
frightened of the inevitable reprisals on their families at home to
volunteer.

Bajanov instead employed White Russian émigré officers, and
began training his little force. But increasing chaos caused by Soviet
aerial devastation delayed preparations so far that two weeks' work
became two months'. It was not until March that the first section
appeared on the front. The effect was instantaneous: about three
hundred Red Army men were induced to desert in a few days. But
Finland was on the point of calling for terms; on 12 March peace was
agreed, and on the 14th Bajanov had to beat a hasty retreat from
Finland before the inevitable Soviet request for extradition was delivered to the helpless Finns.[18]

These divergent modifications, together with the verdict expressed in the British Intelligence report, surely provide a singularly
accurate estimate of the state of Russian public opinion, so far as
such a thing can be said to exist or be estimated at all. The battered,
cowed and resigned population, scarcely one of whom did not possess a close relative murdered by the state or vanished into slavery,
was too crushed under the weight of NKVD power to contemplate
change, let alone resistance. Only foreign intervention or war could
stir those sluggish waters, and the Finnish conflict, during its brief

course, indicated the likely outcome of such a crisis. Given a real opportunity to revolt and restore basic human rights and decencies, Russians would flock to overthrow their government. As a powerful counterbalance lay instincts of national pride which, if channelled with reasonable intelligence, could arouse Russians to defend their Motherland, whatever the government. Which of these two factors would prove the stronger depended in large part on the nature of the foreign intervention and the Soviet response. Within fifteen months these issues would be put to the test.

As Finnish resistance began to crumble in February and March 1940, so French and British plans for intervention began tardily to get under way. The unexpected tenacity of the Finnish defence had led Allied statesmen to contemplate the formerly uncontemplatable. To add Soviet Russia to an undefeated Germany as a further enemy might seem with hindsight to have been midsummer madness. In the end the proponents of intervention were themselves to abandon the plan as impractical. The lightning collapse of France herself was after all, at the time of the Finnish armistice, a bare three months away. How could Britain and France, therefore, have considered fighting the USSR as well as Germany?

Military intervention against the Soviet Union was considered as a serious proposition by the Allied governments for four months after mid-December 1939. As has already been noted, the aim was not the ridiculous one of conquering Russia, or even the scarcely less fantastic one of defeating her armies in the field. It was, by the exercise of a skilful strategy, to deny Germany supplies on which her war production depended. Swedish iron ore deliveries alone were, as the Germans themselves confessed, 'decisive for the German conduct of the war',[19] and it has been seen that Russian oil, grain, cotton and other raw materials were of equally critical importance.

Just before the close of the Finnish War, the British Chiefs of Staff drew up a report for the Cabinet on 'Military Implications of Hostilities with Russia in 1940'. This surveyed Soviet internal weakness, with its intense political discontent, poor communications already stretched to capacity, almost total dependence on Caucasian oil, and military exhaustion after the débâcle in Finland. Against this had to be weighed Soviet capacity to cause damage and dislocation to important neighbouring British Imperial interests and communications, principally in the Middle East and Afghanistan. The Soviet capacity to strike far beyond her frontiers appeared, however, not to be so formidable as to be beyond the resources of the Empire to counter. It was possible that powers traditionally hostile to Russia, such as Turkey, Japan and possibly Italy, might take the opportunity of striking at Soviet power.

Turning from defensive tactics to offensive possibilities, the Chiefs of Staff pointed out that blockade of Soviet shipping in her Northern and Black Sea ports was feasible. From this they passed swiftly to examination of the focal purpose of the whole project: the destruction of the Caucasian oilfields. These lay at Baku, Grozni and Batum, very close to the Turkish and Persian frontiers. The Soviets were clearly aware of their importance and vulnerability, but ground and air defences were unlikely to be of high quality. It was possible Germany might rush in reinforcements of anti-aircraft batteries and fighters to her ally's aid, and for this reason alone it was essential to strike swiftly and hard. RAF bombers already operational on Middle Eastern airfields would be unsuitable for such an operation, and a minimum of three squadrons of Mark IV Blenheims would have to be provided from Britain. These 'should be ready to operate from bases in Northern Iraq or Syria by the end of April'. The destruction of the oilfields could be devastating, but would require 'sustained operations over a period of several weeks'.

The deployment of these aeroplanes, together with reserves and troops to protect the airfields and Britain's own oil interests in Iran, would cause serious depletion of British home defence forces; but, as the Report noted, the 'importance of early and effective operations against the oil installations in the Caucasus in the event of war with Russia might well be so great as to justify the inevitable risks involved elsewhere'. If in addition naval forces could, with Turkish connivance, enter and dominate the Black Sea, they could effectively throttle the oil supply routes to Germany.

The Chiefs of Staff had been asked to provide a full résumé of the effects of war with the USSR on Britain's strategic position, and they had done so, making the most of the various options available. But the tone of the Report was on the whole guarded and pessimistic, stressing that the destruction of Russia's oil sources could have little immediate effect on the war, and that Britain's resources would in the process be stretched even beyond their existing dangerous limits. It ended with the significant observation that 'Without Turkish or Iranian co-operation, we cannot attack the Caucasian oilfields at all except by infringing territorial rights'.[20]

This dampening estimate accorded generally with the views of Chamberlain's government. The Cabinet agreed to disperse forces it was no longer possible to send to Finland. Chamberlain and Halifax preferred to concentrate on diplomatic measures designed to secure Norwegian and Swedish co-operation in obstructing the iron-ore exports to Germany. Only Churchill continued to press for a more forward military policy, including a descent on Narvik and some sort of armed intervention in Scandinavia.

Once again the real impetus for action came from Paris. Premier Daladier was obliged to resign from office after the failure of his scheme to aid the Finns, and his successor, Paul Reynaud, was even more disposed towards energetic measures. On 25 March he proposed to the British Cabinet that action in Norwegian waters and assaults on the sources of Russian oil were essential to destroy the Soviet economic base of the German war machine. Churchill was strongly sympathetic, but Chamberlain continued sceptical and obstructive.[21] On 8 April Lord Halifax presided over a meeting of British ambassadors from the Soviet Union, Turkey and other concerned states. At the end of a long discussion he summed up by stating that 'it seemed to be generally agreed by the meeting that on the whole it would be better to postpone the Baku project for the moment and to reconsider it in the autumn . . . ' This heralded the end of British interest in the scheme, though, as Lord Hankey significantly pointed out, 'preparations for its execution should, nevertheless, be proceeded with, in order that we should be in a position to take advantage of any unforeseen alteration in the situation'.[22]

Preparations did indeed continue throughout March and April, and were wide-ranging in their scope. Intelligence reports suggested that the Chiefs of Staff Report might have been unduly pessimistic in some significant respects. From Washington the British Ambassador, Lord Lothian, passed to the Foreign Office an account of conditions inside the Soviet Union provided by three engineers from the Asiatic Petroleum Company, who had returned home only a few weeks earlier. They were 'skilled technical people with no political bias and very objective'.

They all said that labour conditions in Russia were bad. There was a continual shortage of labour, the population was undernourished and work output was unbelievably low. The soldiers they saw were badly equipped and unimpressive. Only efficient service was OGPU [political police]. The engineer who worked in Baku district said that there were no real defences against any serious attack. There were no anti-aircraft guns and refineries at Baku would be easily occupied or destroyed even though they were in three totally independent units. Equally Baku-Batoum pipe lines could not be defended against a determined attack . . . General conclusion was that it was difficult to over-emphasize the disorganisation in Russia.

Another American expert estimate considered that 'as the whole district [of Baku] was simply saturated with oil there would be a blaze unequalled in the history of the world and probably the damage would take a great many years to repair.'[23]

Meanwhile more direct methods of intelligence-gathering were implemented, ones which came near to providing the preliminaries for war itself. At the main RAF base at Habbaniyah in Iraq, orders were issued on 30 March 1940 for 'No. 84 Squadron to supply photographs required by G.H.Q. Middle East, as early as possible.' From England arrived a twin-engined Lockheed civil aeroplane, camouflaged duck-egg green and skilfully converted to take photographs covering a wide area. Landed at Habbaniyah, the Lockheed had its markings painted out. Then, on 30 March, pilot Hugh Macphail took off with two RAF photographers. They sped over the deserts towards the north-east and crossed high above the mountains of neutral Iran until they saw ahead of them the hazy blue expanse of the Caspian. Soon they were passing over the sea, leaving the coastline of Soviet Azerbaijan comfortably to their left. Ahead lay the cape whose southern shore guarded the ramshackle town of Baku and its surrounding sprawl of unsightly oil installations. The inadequacy of the Baku defences was made tellingly clear as the British plane cruised overhead, photographing the town, port and environs at leisure. During the space of an hour, it made six runs across the port. Then, the mission accomplished, the Lockheed winged out high above the sea and dwindled from sight into the southern sky. Macphail and his companions returned to Habbaniyah just nine hours after their departure.

On 5 April the daredevil Macphail took off again from Habbaniyah for the north. This time his mission took him far above the savage terrain of eastern Turkey. Emerging over the Black Sea, he began a similar reconnaissance over the terminus of the oil pipeline at the port of Batoum. This time, however, he was driven off by anti-aircraft fire, but not before he had compiled a satisfactory pictorial record of Batoum as well. Macphail had experienced the only shots fired in the simmering 'war' between the Anglo-French and Germany's Soviet ally.

The Air Ministry now had a bulky dossier providing detailed plans enabling General Wavell's Middle East Command to launch the most crippling single blow it was possible for the Soviet Union to sustain.[24] Meanwhile, as if this were not enough, ominous plans were on foot for the photographing of Murmansk, a port crucial to the Red Fleet's operations in northern waters, and palpably vulnerable to any Allied action in conjunction with the Finns.[25]

The French, as ever, were eager for the action to begin. On 30 April German Intelligence intercepted a telephone conversation between Reynaud and Chamberlain. The French Prime Minister assured the British that French Middle East Command would be ready for the Baku assault by 15 May. Chamberlain replied with characteristic reservations, but gave no indication that the plans were not intended ultimately to be put into effect.[26] There can be little doubt that the Gestapo passed this piece of information on to their counterparts in the NKVD, through the usual channels.

In the end these ambitious projects were overtaken by events and permanently shelved. The principal factors in this abortive outcome were, firstly, British reluctance to enter whole-heartedly into the venture; and, secondly, the continued refusal of the intervening neutral countries (Sweden, Norway, Turkey and Iran) to allow the passage of Allied troops or aeroplanes.[27] (It may be noted, on the other hand, that the RAF reconnaissance of Baku and Batoum suggests that Iranian and Turkish air space at least could be violated with impunity in certain circumstances.) Given the nature of Allied – particularly British – dilatoriness at the time, the project seems unlikely ever to have had much chance of success. It was most seriously under consideration in April, and in May and June the Germans were to launch their devastating attacks on Norway and France. How could the Allies have even contemplated such a scheme? It has been accorded universal ridicule by historians ever since, culminating in Professor Lukacs's suggestion that 'Melting the polar icecap and putting Russia under water would have been a comparable idea.'[28]

There is no doubt that the prospect of war between Britain and

France on the one hand and the Soviet Union on the other was a daring and decidedly risky venture. In the spring of 1940 the odds were so strongly in favour of Germany that almost any Allied policy must appear hopeless. But it may be argued that a risky forward strategy would have been preferable to a passively complacent one.[29]

X
Forest Murmurs

The likely outcome of a British and French attack on the USSR in 1940 must remain a matter for speculation. What is not, however, is Stalin's reaction to the threat of that attack. Soviet archives remain closed, but enough is now known to suggest that those who feared to provoke the somnolent Russian giant were perhaps being overly cautious.

Throughout the period of threatened Anglo-French intervention in Finland, the Soviet Union became extremely polite and eager to come to satisfactory terms with the Allies. On 30 January Ambassador Ivan Maisky told R. A. Butler at the Foreign Office that his Government was very anxious to co-operate with the British, and hinted strongly that the Pact with Germany was merely an arrangement of temporary convenience. In February and March similar approaches were made to Sir Stafford Cripps and Lord Halifax, the Foreign Secretary. There was talk of a trade agreement; all these negotiations seemed impressive enough to act as a factor in inducing the British to abandon the Baku project.[1] Only Fitzroy Maclean, of the Foreign Office Northern Department, seems to have appreciated that Soviet approaches were not so much a reason for abandoning plans for action against the USSR, as a direct result of those plans. 'After all', he was to write in August, 'the temporary improvement in the Soviet attitude towards Great Britain, which occurred in March, was entirely due to the fear of the Soviet Government that we were preparing to bomb the oilfields.'[2]

Stalin might well feel he had much to fear. The destruction of 90 per cent of the Soviet Union's oil resources would undoubtedly cause immense disruption and even chaos throughout the country, with incalculable results. And the cunning British were making other equally alarming plans. Preparing for every eventuality in the case of armed conflict with the Soviet Union, the Foreign Office and officials of Military Intelligence were opening up contacts which appealed to the John Buchan in the 'lean, brown men' whose versatility, courage and resource continued to maintain the far-flung British Empire. In the previous war T. E. Lawrence had raised desert tribes against the Turk with devastating results. What if the same game were to be played with the oppressed nations of the Caucasus and Soviet Central Asia? Their resistance to Bolshevik rule had been suppressed only after years of unspeakable savagery, and it was most likely that discontent, racial, religious and ideological, still simmered amongst hardy tribesmen of mountain and desert.

Unknown to the public at large, much official thought was being given to 'possible subversive action in Transcaucasia and Soviet Central Asia', and Maclean himself, who had travelled in both areas, was being considered as a likely infiltrator. Contacts were opened with various émigré groups, notably *Prometheus*, an organization based at Paris and Constantinople, representing Turkoman resistance movements in Soviet Azerbaijan, Crimea, Turkestan and Kazan. How much support the *Prometheus* movement enjoyed inside the USSR cannot be determined. It should not be underestimated, however;[3] who would have suspected the strength of Ukrainian nationalism had the German invasion not provided it with an opportunity for overt action?[4]

The grandson of the Caucasian hero Shamyl (immortalized by Leo Tolstoy), Said Shamyl, visited the French Commander-in-chief in the Middle East, General Weygand, at Headquarters in Beirut.[5] Said Shamyl represented the interests of fighting mountain tribes in North Caucasus, and the purpose of his visit was to effect liaison with the army of Weygand, which formed the potential nucleus of an expeditionary force to the Caucasus. Weygand had been ordered to prepare his force for this eventuality, but the sixty thousand troops under his command were hopelessly inadequate for such an expedition unless Turkey were also to intervene.[6]

All these intrigues and preparations have a faintly fantastic ring about them, coming as they did just before the German military machine irrupted north and west into Norway and France. They need not be dismissed as wholly impractical, however. Within three years the Germans were to enjoy astounding success in recruiting allies from amongst these very Soviet peoples under circumstances much less favourable. 'What might have been' is nevertheless only of passing interest: what is important is the effect these threats made on Stalin, and what this in turn reveals of his policy-making.

There is no doubt that Stalin was very frightened indeed. In the first week of March there was such a panic in Moscow at the prospect of the destruction of Baku that Soviet officials inquired at the American Embassy as to the likely extent of the damage. They were not comforted by the response: Baku would become one sheet of flame, and the refineries would be out of action for years.[7] Weygand's ramshackle army assumed a menacing significance grossly out of proportion to its real capacities. Its existence and the possibility that it might be used to intervene in the Balkans or the Caucasus were well-established topics of public speculation. In view of poor security at the time and the influx of expensively educated traitors into British government services, it is likely that Stalin knew more than most about the bold projects being hatched. It is intriguing to note that his predilection for intelligence material gathered by clandestine methods may have led him to over-react to a never very serious threat.

Konni Zilliacus was a well-known British left-wing socialist publicist. Though sometimes tinged by personal idiosyncrasies, his beliefs generally accorded closely with Stalin's. He supported the Soviet invasion of Poland in 1939, and was to be a defender of the dictator's policies in post-war Eastern Europe. In 1947 he was gratified to be received by Stalin himself in the Kremlin, and was expelled from the Labour Party two years later for his excessively fulsome support of Communist activities.[8] British Intelligence had reason to believe that his support for the Soviet system went further than merely writing turgid screeds for the *New Statesman*: he was an important agent of the Comintern, and hence of Stalin's NKVD.[9]

In early 1940 he found himself temporarily in uniform and managed to visit General Weygand's Headquarters in Beirut. As an Allied officer he enjoyed a certain amount of latitude and saw, or claimed to have seen, staff maps prepared to facilitate the passage of Allied troops across Turkish Armenia to attack the Caucasus, also aerial photographs of Baku and Batoum.[10]

The idea that Weygand's makeshift force should march seven hundred miles across the mountains of Syria and Turkey to the Caucasus was too absurd ever to have been seriously contemplated.[11] But it may well be that Stalin received and accepted Zilliacus's grotesquely inflated estimate and reacted accordingly. Clearly acting as usual under Comintern direction, the French Communist Party launched a strident campaign against the 'menace' of Weygand's army. Propaganda was launched amongst French troops for its recall, and an anxious appeal urged: 'Soldiers, if they send you against the Soviet workers, refuse to fight the Red Army, which is the international army of workers and peasants'. The Communist newspaper *L'Humanité* estimated that Weygand disposed of up to half a million men and, 'thousands of tanks, hundreds of aeroplanes'![12] Behind these inflated claims one can detect the very real fears of Joseph Stalin.

The Caucasus and Central Asia seemed the USSR's weak fronts. The populations were both restive and warlike,[13] the terrain ideal for guerrilla warfare, and the proximity of the major oil-sources to the frontier might turn any invasion swiftly into a disaster. The British, with their long tradition of frontier service in India, were masters of the skills needed to stir up primitive peoples, and Lawrence of Arabia and his Intelligence mentors loomed large in Communist demonology.[14] In the 1938 trial of Bukharin, the doomed Soviet leader had been accused, *inter alia*, of wishing to assist in a British plot to annex Soviet Central Asia to their Empire. The charge was of course entirely trumped-up but, as Professor Ulam remarks, 'the trial still reveals a fairly accurate chart of his [Stalin's] nightmares. It is clear that he was concerned that Soviet border regions would gravitate toward the neighboring states . . . What more natural than that traitors among the Uzbeks should look towards the British in India?'[15] That Stalin believed hatred of the Soviet regime to be so widespread in those regions as to imply a desire for secession from the USSR was to be confirmed by the dreadful post-war purges in the Caucasus and regions to the east, which resulted in the deportation of sizeable proportions of entire nations to GULAG camps or exile in inhospitable remote regions. There was no attempt to establish individual guilt or innocence; the authorities were convinced that entire peoples were disloyal.[16]

Soviet intentions were ably summarized by Fitzroy Maclean on 1 April 1940. Pointing out the regrettable effectiveness in many quarters of Soviet propaganda (Lord Beaverbrook and his cartoonist Low were among the most readily deluded), he explained:

It is at present the aim of the Soviet Government, while continuing their co-operation with Germany and thus diminishing the effectiveness of the Allied blockade, to avoid becoming involved in hostilities with the Allies. In particular, both the Germans and the Russians wish to avert an Allied attack on the Caucasus, at any rate until they have had time to strengthen their defences. They are, therefore, endeavouring to convey, both to the Allied Government and to French and British public opinion, the impression that the Berlin-Moscow Axis is not particularly solid, and that if we only play our cards carefully and avoid offending Soviet susceptibilities we may yet succeed in detaching the Soviet Union from Germany. After their experience of last summer, they doubtless hope to be able to keep us in play by such means for an almost indefinite period. [17]

Such appears to have been the state of Soviet hopes and fears at the beginning of April. At any moment the attack might begin in the Caucasus. In the North it was clear that similar danger menaced Leningrad and Murmansk, both cities vulnerably susceptible to foreign attack. During March the British Government had steadily increased pressure on Norway to allow the mining of her coastal waters. The belligerent powers appeared to be concentrating their strategies on the question of control of the Swedish iron-fields. So far from being deterred by the collapse of Finnish resistance, British determination to establish military supremacy in northern Scandinavia seemed to increase as each week went by. True, the aim now was to close the ore-fields to the Germans, but once British troops were landed in Norway, how was it possible not to believe either that they would wish once more to play the Finnish card, or that Finland herself might not provoke a resumption of the conflict? And this time Allied troops could be poised on the frontier!

On 8 April the British Admiralty announced that minefields had been laid in Norwegian territorial waters. Early that morning four British destroyers had sown mines in the approaches to Narvik. Clearly Britain's long-standing inhibition against violating Norwegian neutrality had been dispelled, though the famous raid on the *Altmark* on 16 February had already revealed that British forces were capable of a bold forward policy, regardless of the consequences. As a subsidiary to the mine-laying, the British 'Operation Wilfred' also envisaged the landing of French and British forces, which would garrison Narvik and other vital ports, and advance to the Swedish frontier.

Hitler, however, was not the man to watch these developments at leisure. Allied intentions to intervene in the North had been public

knowledge since the beginning of the year, and the German naval
and military staffs had not let the grass grow under their feet. Even
as British mines splashed into the sea in the Vestfjorden, a German
invasion fleet was on its way. The same evening, as the long dark
Northern night drew on, the Admiralty learned that, with astonishing skill and daring, Admiral Raeder's warships had landed German
troops simultaneously at points circumscribing the entire coast of
Norway, from the capital, Oslo, in the south, to Narvik in the icy
North. The Luftwaffe droned menacingly over the capital, the
Norwegian Royal Family and Government fled inland, and at 7.30 on
the evening of the next day (9 April) the Nazi counterpart of Stalin's
Otto Kuusinen, Vidkun Quisling, was broadcasting triumphantly on
the national radio. The blow to Allied prestige was devastating, and
the world watched spellbound.

The news was broken to the British in most unpalatable form. All
their elaborate plans turned out to have been anticipated with breath-
taking speed and decision. Almost the first inkling of the blow that
was falling came in signals from the destroyer *Glowworm*, minutes
before she plunged to the bottom of the North Sea. A few hours later
Moscow learned of events, though in much more congenial fashion.
At dawn on 9 April German Ambassador von Schulenburg requested
an interview with Molotov, and by 10.30 he was closeted with the
Commissar for Foreign Affairs. Von Schulenburg explained that
Germany had been obliged to intervene in Denmark and Norway, as
'we had absolutely reliable reports regarding an imminent thrust of
Anglo-French military forces against the Norwegian and Danish
coasts and therefore had to act without delay'. This of course was
true (a rare event in Nazi diplomacy), as was the Ambassador's telling comment. He pointed out that 'the Reich Government is of the
opinion that our actions are also in the interest of the Soviet Union,
for execution of the Anglo-French plan which is known to us would
have caused Scandinavia to become a theatre of war, and that in all
probability, would have led to a re-opening of the Finnish question.'

The normally impassive Molotov was clearly elated at the news:
'The Soviet Government quite understood the measures which were
forced upon Germany. The English had certainly gone much too far;
they had disregarded completely the rights of neutral nations. In
conclusion, Molotov said literally: "*We wish Germany complete success in her defensive measures*"' (my italics).

This enthusiastic sympathy came in striking contrast to Soviet attitudes in recent weeks, which had cooled perceptibly towards her ally in important respects. The reasons for this abrupt switch were abundantly clear to the well-informed von Schulenburg. In a memorandum drawn up two days later, he recapitulated the symptoms of Soviet discontent.

In all fields we suddenly came up against obstacles which were, in many cases, completely unnecessary; even in little things like visas they started to create difficulties; the release of the *Volksdeutsche* imprisoned by the Poles, which was promised by treaty, could not be achieved; the deportation of the German prisoners long imprisoned in Soviet jails suddenly stopped; the Soviet Government suddenly withdrew its promises already given with regard to Basis Nord in which our Navy is interested, etc. These obstacles, which were apparent everywhere, reached their climax in the suspension of petroleum and grain shipments to us. On the 5th of this month I had a long talk with Herr Mikoyan, during which the attitude of the People's Commissar was very negative.

Then, only four days later, came the breaking of the news of the invasion of Norway.

During this talk it became apparent that the Soviet Government had again made a complete volte-face. Suddenly the suspension of the petroleum and grain shipments was termed 'excessive zeal of subordinate agencies' which would be immediately remedied. (Herr Mikoyan is Assistant Chairman of the Council of People's Commissars, i.e. highest Soviet personality after Herr Molotov!). Herr Molotov was affability itself, willingly received all our complaints and promised relief. Of his own accord he touched upon a number of issues of interest to us and announced their settlement in a positive sense. I must honestly say that I was completely amazed at the change.

The explanation was not far to seek.

In my opinion there is only one explanation for this volte-face: our Scandinavian operations must have relieved the Soviet Government enormously – removed a great burden of anxiety, so to speak. What their apprehension consisted of, can again not be determined with certainty. I suspect the following: The Soviet Government is always extraordinarily well informed. If the

English and French intended to occupy Norway and Sweden it may be assumed with certainty that the Soviet Government knew of these plans and was apparently terrified by them. The Soviet Government saw the English and French appearing on the shores of the Baltic Sea, and they saw the Finnish question reopened, as Lord Halifax had announced; finally they dreaded most of all the danger of becoming involved in a war with two Great Powers. Apparently this fear was relieved by us. Only in this way can the completely changed attitude of Herr Molotov be understood. Today's long and conspicuous article in *Izvestia* on our Scandinavian campaign . . . sounds like one big sigh of relief.

The '*generous* help' which Stalin had promised Hitler in the German-Soviet Commercial Agreement of 11 February 1940 was to be resumed.[18]

There can be no doubt that von Schulenburg's analysis was correct. With the defeat of Finland Stalin must momentarily have hoped that he had checked the Allies' scheming; but their bellicose plans for intervention in Southern Russia had continued unabated, and latterly it had become very clear that the long-deferred landings in Norway were imminent.[19] The Soviet Union had been powerless to do anything but lie uncomfortably awaiting the attack. Now Germany had intervened, and the Wehrmacht was fighting Stalin's battle for him. If ever he felt gratitude in his life, this must have been the moment.

But this gush of relief had to be qualified. German pre-emptive action had been astonishingly bold. It was also very risky, given Britain's supremacy on the seas and her evident determination to cut off and destroy German forces in Norway. Within four days of the landings a British flotilla had sunk or disabled the ten German destroyers bottled up in Narvik.[20] By the middle of the month sizeable Anglo-French forces had landed at Narvik and besieged the garrison, and 'Mauriceforce' had occupied Namsos and pushed on across Central Norway down the Gudbrandsdalen towards Lillehammer. In the event, all these valiant attempts were to be more than countered by superior German vigour, training and equipment, but such was by no means clear to those living through the hectic April of 1940. At the Supreme War Council on 22 April the French still contemplated pouring in enough men to liberate all Scandinavia; and as late as 2 May, when the tide was turning fast, Churchill stressed that 'it is far too soon to strike the Norwegian balance-sheet yet, for the campaign has merely concluded a single phase'.[21]

Thus both sides proclaimed faith in their coming victory until the beginning of May, and Stalin watching from the sidelines was no more able to predict the outcome than the protagonists. For the Soviet dictator a German victory was as vital as if it had been the Red Army which was battling for Namsos and striving to retain Narvik. The situation which had so terrified him in prospect in March had now come to pass in April. Then he had hastily patched up a compromise peace with the Finns at the mere prospect of Allied intervention on their side. But now French and British troops were landing on the Norwegian coast in ever-increasing numbers. The Scots and Irish Guards in Narvik were a mere hundred miles from the Finnish frontier, and only three hundred and fifty from the Soviet Union itself! The War Office even proposed to send a battalion to Kirkenes, facing Petsamo. Whether GRU Intelligence was aware of this is unknown, but a general Allied advance eastwards must clearly have appeared on the cards. And all this while plans for the destruction of Baku and the subversion of the Caucasus and Central Asia continued unabated. Stalin's fears can be readily inferred, and it will be shown shortly that we possess horrific evidence that he actually panicked.

Would Germany pull through? Stalin's 'loyal attitude'[22] to Hitler was once again being 'cemented with blood'; in its modest way the Soviet Union even played a direct part in the ultimate German victory. During the planning of their invasion of Norway, great concern was expressed by Admiral Raeder over the question of supplying forces under General Dietl intended for the seizure of Narvik, the focal point of the entire operation. To obviate the dangers of sending a slow-travelling supply vessel the whole length of the exposed Norwegian coast, the tanker *Jan Wellem* sailed from Germany's port on Soviet soil, 'Basis Nord' near Murmansk. The *Jan Wellem* arrived safely at Narvik, and played a crucial part in supplying the destroyers which inflicted heavy damage on the British flotilla immediately after the invasion. More important, it provided vital supplies for General Dietl's troops, enabling them to hold out until communications were opened through neutral Sweden.[23]

Through the Comintern network, directed by NKVD and GRU channels, the Soviet Union set out to circumvent the Allied war effort more effectively from within. The French and British Communist Parties launched an insidious campaign designed to show that the German landings were merely a legitimate response to the prior Allied plans. 'Everyone knew that if Britain invaded Norwegian territorial waters with minefields, the Germans would respond with counter-action. Nobody is fool enough to suppose that they would not', wrote Claud Cockburn in the *Daily Worker* on 13 April.[24] Even as he wrote, British sailors were dying under a rain of bombs and torpedoes in the freezing waters of the Ofotfjord. The French Communist Party likewise obediently launched a ferocious propaganda campaign against the Allied action, declaring that the purpose of the intervention was a plot to effect British capitalists' control of the Swedish iron-ore-fields.[25]

More covert aid was also extended by Stalin to Hitler, the effects of which can as yet be only glimpsed as they momentarily break the surface. Nazi and Soviet intelligence agencies were correctly believed to co-operate where, as was frequently the case, national interests coincided. As Walter Krivitsky, the defecting GRU chief, testified, 'Inasmuch as Stalin's pact with Hitler is really an alliance of the two armies, operating in specified zones, I have no doubt that such exchange of military secrets and information . . . is indispensable to both Hitler and Stalin'.[26] It even seemed likely, as a Foreign Office official minuted on 9 February, that 'the Communists & Mosleyites are now working together'.[27]

Ten days later, when British troops were fighting their way towards Lillehammer, two brothers named Fyrth were charged with supplying naval secrets to the *Daily Worker*.[28] Whilst the Red Navy could certainly have benefited from British technology, there can be no doubt that at that moment German warships were more surely fighting Stalin's battle than was his own inactive fleet.

Stalin's fears can be readily understood. There was much to suggest to a suspicious mind that an Allied victory would seriously menace Soviet interests. There were trivial but upsetting details acting as pointers. To someone as imbued as Stalin was with the events of the Civil War, which had so miraculously preserved Bolshevik power, the very name of the Chief of the Imperial General Staff conjured up memories of British troops operating on Russian soil in conjunction with anti-Soviet Russians. In 1919 Sir Edmund Ironside had commanded the British expeditionary force at Archangel. By what might appear a sinister coincidence, the commander of Allied forces operating in the extreme North of Norway, General

Mackesy, had also served with the White Armies in South Russia in 1919–20.[29]

Whether these factors affected Stalin's attitude remains speculation, but there existed a much more material consideration to exercise his mind. On 19 September 1939, after the Soviet invasion of Poland, the British Government had condemned the attack as unjustified and stressed that it was intended to fulfil British obligations to Poland and prosecute the war until that object had been achieved.[30] It was left unclear whether Poland would be restored to her frontiers of 1938, but there could be no question but that, in the event of an Allied victory, an independent Poland would be resurrected. The Soviets would undoubtedly be required to evacuate all or part of their occupation zone, presumably under threat of war should they decline. All this recalled uncomfortably events twenty years earlier, when Allied victory in the West led to a resurgent Poland driving Bolshevik armies back from Warsaw, whilst British and French expeditionary forces co-operated with anti-Soviet Russian armies at Murmansk and Baku.

The Poles remained a potent threat in Stalin's mind. It was their armies which had inflicted on him the greatest humiliation of his career, when his blundering refusal, in August 1920, to come to the aid of Tukhachevsky's advance on Warsaw led to the Poles' crushing rout of the Red Army. Tukhachevsky had paid for this with his life in 1937, but the formidable national and martial spirit of the Poles burned as fiercely as ever. Unlike the Russians, who could be battered, crushed, beaten and tortured into submission, the Poles possessed an unpleasantly durable quality which had caused their nation time and again to rise up after disaster. This resilience and courage aroused grudging respect in Stalin.

> He said . . . on one occasion that nations which had been ruled by powerful aristocracies, like the Hungarians and the Poles, were strong nations. Stalin was a great admirer of powerful states and powerful institutions even when he was opposed to them; and his fear of the Hungarians and the Poles was a revealing back-handed recognition of Polish and Hungarian stamina.[31]

It was probably for this reason that Stalin 'considered it wrong to leave an independent Polish rump state', at the time of the partition with Germany.[32]

Despite their subjugation in the previous autumn, the Poles were in many ways in a stronger position than they had been on the eve of achieving national independence in 1919. Britain and France recognized their exiled government, which was established at Angers. They still possessed sizeable military units, warships and aircraft fighting alongside the Allies. In the event of any external shock to the Soviet Union, a plausible scenario of likely events must include an uprising of the Poles against their oppressors, with the Polish armed forces in the West attacking across the frontier.

The latter event was certainly on the cards. When the French were contemplating sending aid to the Finns earlier in the year, one project seriously under review was that of dispatching a Polish expeditionary force to Petsamo. The Poles disposed of three destroyers and two submarines, but this small force could always be supplemented by seconding ships from the Royal Navy. The scheme was shelved,[33] but Polish army units were earmarked for the planned campaign. These were not diverted when Finland surrendered, and remained ready for a new Northern expedition. They were finally embarked on 21 April at Brest under the command of General Bohusz, their destination being (significantly, one may suppose, from the Soviet point of view) Narvik and the extreme North of Norway. There they played a gallant part in the fierce fighting which ensued.[34]

These operations cannot have escaped Stalin's notice. Others, more covert, would if known have appeared in a yet more sinister light. Fitzroy Maclean learned on 15 April from the Polish Embassy in London that their Government was financing the Caucasian separatist organization, based in Turkey and known as *Prometheus*. The possibility of assisting this group in subversion and sabotage within the Soviet Union was under contemplation by the British, and Maclean suggested that contact be established with Colonel Colin Gubbins, a specialist in irregular warfare and afterwards head of the Special Operations Executive (SOE).[35]

An even more potent source of disruption and disaffection lay in the 200,000 or so Polish prisoners-of-war held in Soviet camps. It would be surprising if no one envisaged calling on their assistance in the event of an open rupture between Anglo-French-Polish forces and the Red Army. In the late summer of 1941, when it seemed the Soviet army and state system might collapse under the weight of the German attack, the British contemplated taking emergency action to destroy the Baku oilfields, with or without Soviet consent, if the

Germans seemed in danger of drawing near. Even in this desperate moment Stalin appeared as frightened of the British as of the Germans, and could not be drawn on the subject. What if he made peace and resumed his alliance with Hitler? The possibility was mooted of asking the Poles to contact their compatriots in Soviet camps, and induce them to take military action in the Soviet rear. One camp, at Temir-Khan-Shura, was conveniently near Baku. The scheme was a desperate one, but it is unlikely to have been only the British who were reminded of the exploits of the former Czech prisoners-of-war in Russia in 1918, who seized control of the Trans-Siberian Railway and joined anti-Communist Russians and the Allies in driving the Bolsheviks back across the Urals.[36]

Whether or not similar schemes were under discussion in April 1940, Stalin must certainly have felt the Poles rated high on the list of dangers threatening him and his regime. He could do nothing about the Polish armed forces abroad, except pray for a German victory in Norway. But what of the millions of Poles in Soviet-occupied Poland, and the thousands of captured soldiers held in camps? Of all the powerful enemies that menaced him, they at least were within his power. Five days after the Allied Supreme War Council had agreed its plans for sending an expedition to Finland, on 10 February, NKVD troops had raided thousands of Polish homes, dispatching 'whole villages of small farmers and farm labourers, forestry workers, ex-soldiers from the last war who had received grants of land, civil servants, local government officials and members of the police forces'.

This might seem to have lopped off what popular leadership in Poland had survived the massive deportations that followed the Soviet invasion in September 1939. But in April, with Allied troops crossing the North Sea in increasing force, the Soviet Government felt sufficiently fearful to unleash yet another mass purge. Once again Polish towns and villages heard the muffled rattle of trucks moving surreptitiously through darkened streets, the whispered commands and foot-falls, and the dreaded sharp knock at the door. Those removed this time in their thousands 'included the families of persons previously arrested, the families of men with the Polish Army, persons in trade (of whom the majority were Jews), farm labourers from sequestered estates and more groups of Polish, White Ruthenian and Ukrainian small farmers and farm labourers'. Operations on this scale, involving the movement of tens of

thousands of people in appalling climatic conditions, were clearly
meticulously planned at a central source and reflected central policy
decisions made by Stalin himself.[37]

These two mass deportations should have left the Polish masses
cowed and subdued. But what of their natural leaders? In three large
camps the Soviets held some fifteen thousand Polish officers. Many
were regular soldiers, but large numbers had been called to the
colours on the eve of war. All in all, they represented the cream of
the educated classes in pre-war Poland, or at least as many as Stalin
had been able to lay hands on. They were held in three widely-
separated camps, far from the Polish frontier, at Ostashkov, Kozielsk
and Starobielsk.[38] What if these men, taking advantage of the
enormous disruption a war must cause in the interior, were in some
way able to escape and incite their compatriots to revolt? It was this
spectre of counter-revolution that haunted Stalin's waking and sleeping. War was terrifying enough, but an uprising of the millions of
GULAG slaves, the Poles, Balts, Caucasians, Ukrainian peasants . . .
the list was endless. The collective hatred of millions of injured
people was a fearful vision to contemplate.[39]

In the camps themselves there was little thought of resistance or
escape. On the contrary, a mood of optimism prevailed amongst the
Polish officers. Spring was late that year, after the terrible winter of
1939–40, and with it came an upsurge of hope. Unwise words (had
they known) were exchanged openly between the Poles: the Allied
offensive in the West must very soon begin that would destroy Hitler
and leave his ally the Soviet Union friendless and vulnerable. And in
the south General Weygand was assembling his huge army, with an
air force that could within hours bomb the vital oil installations at
Baku. To the ubiquitous NKVD spies these must have seemed significant threats.[40]

At the beginning of April Poles in the three camps were overjoyed
to be told they were being dispatched to distribution centres from
which, it seemed, they would be returned home to occupied Poland.
The evacuations started on three successive days: on 3 April from
Kozielsk, on 5 April from Starobielsk, and 6 April from Ostashkov.
Every morning at 10 a.m. the camp commandant would receive a
telephone call from Moscow, from NKVD headquarters in the
Lubianka building. Long lists were read out of the prisoners to be
moved that day. Then those named were conducted to lorries which
conveyed them to a nearby railway station. Throughout the whole of

April and early days of May trainloads holding a hundred to two hundred prisoners at a time departed to unknown destinations. No news reached the Poles left behind, who for the most part continued optimistic. The worst prospect most could envisage was to be handed over to the Germans.

Today of course we know very well the fate that overtook these unhappy men. Three years later the Germans were occupying the area around Katyn village and wood, and uncovered ghastly evidence of the crime which had taken place. Katyn lies near Smolensk, where the railway line to Vitebsk stops at the little station of Gniezdovo. Not far off, in a clearing on the edge of the forest, lay one of those NKVD execution grounds that had dotted the map of Russia since the Revolution. As even the efficient Germans were shortly to find, the continued massacre of millions of people is a cumbersome business, requiring enormous and efficient allocation of men and resources. Transport must be arranged, hundreds of trained executioners kept continually in readiness, and some method found of disposing of the ever-mounting heap of the slain. And all this had to be accomplished in secrecy! It was not however a task beyond the skills of Lenin and his heirs.

One of these execution grounds and graveyards had been established at Katyn in 1918, and there year after year thousands of Russian men and women ended their unhappy lives. In 1931 a fence with warning signs was erected round the area, and in 1940 these were reinforced by NKVD guards and wolf-dogs.[41]

Hard by the slaughter-ground was a pleasant two-storey brick and timber building. Some idea of the mentality of these guardians of the Revolution may be gained from the fact that the NKVD had chosen this spot to maintain a club-house for the recreation of their hard-worked members. Returning after a long day's toil at the nearby enclosure in the forest, tired Chekists could relax with a drink as one of their number played a gentle nocturne on the club piano – a cultured rarity in post-revolutionary Russia. The music echoed faintly through the now-silent glades of the forest, and the only irritant was the swarming of millions of flies that gathered at this particular spot. Evidently there was an attraction about the place that overcame this nuisance.[42]

On 3 April the first detachment of Poles left Kozielsk Camp. Packed into 'Stolypin' wagons, the sixty-two men travelled all that night until at dawn they glimpsed through cracks the gilded cupolas

of the churches of Smolensk glinting in the dawn sun. Not long
after, the train stopped at a small station. The trucks were unbolted
and the prisoners descended into the pallid glare of the early morning. There was a drab station yard with a few squat huts nearby, but
no sign of inhabitants. A squad of NKVD guards was drawn up,
armed with rifles equipped with the long four-edged bayonet peculiar to the Red Army and police. An NKVD colonel supervised the
detrainment, and with few words spoken directed the transfer of the
prisoners into a bus with whitewashed windows, which backed up to
the first truck. Half the prisoners got in and the bus moved off,
leaving the remainder locked in their truck. The bus drove swiftly
along a road from the station into the nearby forest. It drew up by an
enormous freshly-excavated pit. Beyond great heaps of earth at the
sides snow lay on the ground; it was dark and still in the surrounding forest.

A body of NKVD troops was waiting at the halting-point. As the
prisoners emerged one by one from the bus, each was seized by
guards, had his hands tied expertly behind his back, and was brought
to the edge of the pit. Each of the guards held a pistol whose muzzle,
at a sign from the NKVD colonel, he placed at the nape of a Pole's
neck. A signal was given, and a 7.65mm bullet was fired through the
victim's skull, the missile smashing its way out of his forehead. The
bodies toppled neatly over into the pit.

Next day a larger party, three hundred and two in all, arrived and
was slaughtered in the same way. For more than four weeks parties
arrived almost daily. Occasionally, in the brief moment when the
prisoners first gazed down into the bloodstained horror of the pit, a
man screamed. At once his coat was thrown over his head and the
shot fired through the cloth. Others, braver or more desperate, made
a gesture as if intending to struggle. The executioners were trained
and experienced in their craft: a guard lashed out with his rifle at the
bound man, smashing his jaw with the butt. Others, whose screams
seemed likely to persist, had sawdust rammed into their mouths.
Gradually the pit filled, with hundreds and then with thousands of
men. It was necessary for the guards to climb down and drag the
bodies about so that the heap should be more evenly distributed.
The pile of corpses grew and grew, until it was a dozen deep. The
place was awash with blood, and the twisted mass began to coagulate
as the murderers stumbled across the stacked corpses. Sometimes a
body stirred: at once a guard clambered over and stabbed deep into

the trunk with his bayonet. At other times men were pushed in alive and shot in the customary way, so that the bullet passed through the man's head into the body of a comrade beneath.

The whole business was arranged with great speed and skill. Twenty-two years' experience (the life-time of the world's first Marxist state) lay behind the organization. When the last convoy arrived, on 11 May, well over four thousand corpses lay in a twisted, broken heap, a dozen or fifteen men deep, the lowest layers already beginning to putrefy under gouts of blood seeping down from the distant daylight overhead. Finally, their task fulfilled, the NKVD detachment shovelled earth back in a thick layer, and planted rows of young pine saplings over the mound. It was fortunately still the planting season. Then, at last, we may presume, the guards trudged thankfully up to their club-house. Forty years on, many of them have no doubt achieved high rank and enjoy honourable retirement in Moscow and Leningrad. The Soviet Union endures.

The fate of the Polish officers at Kozielsk came to light by the chance of war. In 1943 German occupying forces excavated the burial-ground at Katyn, and broadcast its discovery to an embarrassed world. 'The less said about that the better', grunted Winston Churchill,[43] whilst Roosevelt declared it all to be 'German propaganda and a German plot'.[44] Just over four thousand Polish corpses were found at Katyn, but the resting-place of more than ten thousand others at Ostashkov and Starobielsk is uncertain.

Nearly four thousand at Starobielsk were transported to Kharkov, after which all trace of them disappeared. A document has been published in the West purporting to be a final report on the massacres from the Head of the Minsk NKVD to his superiors in Moscow, in which it is stated that the inmates of Starobielsk camp were liquidated at Dergachi, near Kharkov. But the document is of unknown provenance, and without corroborative evidence must remain a suspect source.[45] The city of Kharkov itself ranked high in the annals of the NKVD as a place of doom for the enemies of the Revolution. In 1919 the head of the Kharkov Cheka (the former name of the NKVD in Lenin's time) was a sadist named Saenko, exceptionally cruel even by Soviet standards. On the night of 22 June 1919 he and some of his aides massacred a hundred and fourteen prisoners in the manner to become regular practice: the victims were shot through the back of the neck on the edge of the pit in which they were to be buried. Before their deaths the prisoners had suffered such hideous tortures that only twenty-four of the bodies were in a sufficient state of preservation to allow identification.[46] It may be that liquidations continued in Kharkov, as they had done at Katyn.

Finally, more than six thousand Polish officers at Ostashkov were spirited away to certain death. Once again doubt remains over the whereabouts of their final resting-place, but a credible story (resting on the testimony of two Russian witnesses) relates how they were taken north, to the edge of the White Sea. There they were placed on board two barges, drawn by a steamer, and towed away from land. After a time the barges were deliberately sunk, and all their passengers drowned.[47] Such a procedure would certainly have appealed to Stalin, who had disposed of people of whom he disapproved in similar fashion at Tsaritsyn in 1918.[48] Such *noyades* are reported to have become regular NKVD practice.[49]

The disposal of the Polish officers was a highly-organized, synchronized operation. It was organized by Commissar for State Security Raichman, Head of the Operational Administration of the NKVD, under the direct supervision of Lavrenty Beria. It is certain, too, that the whole affair was closely supervised by Stalin himself; partly because of its size and importance, but much more on account of the danger of possible international repercussions.[50]

The timing of the disposal of the Polish officers is highly significant, and it is surprising that apparently no historian has remarked on the fact. The month of April 1940 was exceptionally critical for the Soviet Union. The first real clash of the great powers in Norway, a country bordering on Finland and very close to Soviet frontiers and concerns, must inevitably have been a subject of intense interest to the Soviet leadership. It is likely, too, that important troop movements were taking place throughout April and May, to counter any unexpected development in the war. In addition, the Soviet Union had resumed large-scale shipments of raw materials to Germany, almost abandoned in the previous month. The highly deficient Soviet transport system must already have been under great strain, without undertaking the month-long shifting of thousands of Poles across the Russian countryside.

Then again, the massacre must have appeared at the time as an operation fraught with risk. No one knew that the Allies might not crush Germany, or at least compel her to accept their peace terms. The very first condition would undoubtedly be the restoration of Poland, in which case the missing Polish officers would become a subject of international attention. Stalin could scarcely have ignored this risk, but clearly he felt that the danger of the Poles somehow organizing resistance amongst their compatriots in the USSR was even greater. It has been suggested on many occasions that Stalin's aim was to wipe out the natural leadership of Poland at one blow, so preventing the resurgence of Poland as a nation. But this view ignores the fact that the majority of the Polish officer corps was in German hands, and so beyond Stalin's reach. Of course, Stalin's dearest wish was indeed to see Poland destroyed as a nation, but the evidence suggests that the massacre of the officer prisoners-of-war in April 1940 was in pursuance of a specific policy aim: the prevention of an internal upheaval within the Soviet Union, in which the Poles might be expected to play a leading part.[51]

After the crisis passed in May with the repulse of the Allied forces in Norway and the invasion of the Low Countries, German strength was revealed in all its terrifying might. On 18 June Molotov summoned the German Ambassador 'and expressed the warmest congratulations of the Soviet Government on the splendid success of the German Wehrmacht'.[52] Once again one may detect the 'one big sigh of relief' von Schulenburg had sensed when informing Molotov of the German intervention in Norway. But with hindsight Stalin's fears in March and April that the Allies might seize Norway, deny Germany the Swedish ore-fields, revive the Finnish menace, destroy the oil refineries in the South, spread dissension and revolt in Turkestan, the Caucasus and elsewhere, and spark off a Polish revolt, must have seemed grotesquely exaggerated.

And when the whole balance of forces altered in 1941 with the German invasion of Russia, the slaughter of a large section of the officer corps of a country now an ally became a serious embarrassment. Britain was demanding the release of the imprisoned Polish soldiers to join in the common war effort . . . and there, all the time, was the Wehrmacht, pressing nearer to Smolensk and Katyn Forest.[53] Small wonder that Soviet officials, including Beria's second-in-command Merkulov, confessed under pressure that there had been a *rokovaya oshibka*, a fatal mistake.[54] The risks must have been apparent from the first; only the wished-for German victory could have made the murders safe, and that was far from predictable in March and April 1940. That Stalin, so very cautious and procrastinating a tyrant, was nevertheless induced to take the risk is revealing of his intense fears as war approached his frontiers in

April. Something like the panic he displayed on the next occasion such a danger menaced, in June 1941, seems to have gripped him. And it is significant that the prime factor in both cases was fear of revolt at home. More than this, he must surely have feared an almost instantaneous break-up of the Soviet Union in the event of hostilities – so swift that there might not then be time to dispose of the Poles.

In view of all this, the timing is of crucial importance. Trainloads first left from Kozielsk on 3 April, but prisoners were notified of the coming transfer at the end of March. That was clearly the time when the original decision was made, since it was also the date when the prisoners' families abruptly stopped receiving their mail.[55] The latter part of March was also the period when the Allies finally concerted plans for pre-emptive action in Norway and South Russia. On 25 March Reynaud passed an important communication on strategy to the British Cabinet. Action was urged in Norwegian waters, and also in the Black Sea and the Caspian: 'not only to cut off German oil supplies, but above all to paralyse the whole economy of the USSR before the Reich can succeed in organizing it for its own benefit'. At the War Cabinet meeting two days later, Churchill, normally cautious over measures likely to provoke the Soviet Union, pressed equally vigorously for an assault in the Black Sea and against Baku. In fact British reservations were to prevent anything of the sort, but this was so little apparent that the meeting of the Supreme War Council on 28 March appeared concerted in its advocacy of action on both fronts.[56]

Rumours of these Allied proposals abounded throughout March, but it seems extremely unlikely that Stalin would have decided on the drastic and highly risky step of eliminating the Polish officers on the basis of mere rumour or general possibility of conflict. Given his reaction to the German threat in June 1941, his likely reaction would have been one of agonized indecision. His actions followed so closely the calendar of Allied strategic planning as to suggest strongly that he possessed more or less accurate knowledge of their deliberations. As von Schulenburg observed on 11 April: 'I suspect the following: *The Soviet Government is always extraordinarily well informed* [my italics]. If the English and French intended to occupy Norway and Sweden it may be assumed with certainty that the Soviet Government knew of these plans and was apparently terrified of them.'

The implication is strong that Stalin's intelligence services had illicit access to the deliberations of Allied leaders. Either of the two notorious British traitors, Burgess and Maclean, might easily have had access to Anglo-French military plans. Maclean was attached to the British Embassy in Paris from 1938 to the fall of France,[57] whilst Burgess maintained a liaison with Daladier's *chef du cabinet*, a Communist homosexual named Edouard Pfeiffer.[58] Neither traitor is likely to have known that information passed to NKVD head-quarters might result in the wholesale massacre of fifteen thousand defenceless people, but there is little about their characters to sug-gest they would have held back had they known. 'He that toucheth pitch shall be defiled therewith.'

XI
Friends and Neighbours

By the spring of 1940 Stalin had every reason to regard his ally Hitler with undiluted admiration and gratitude. In just eight months the Führer had showered gifts on to the astonished *Vozhd* which even in the optimistic days of 1920 would have seemed inconceivable to Russia's leaders. Whilst Hitler kept Britain and France at bay, Stalin was granted *carte blanche* to absorb the *cordon sanitaire* of anti-Communist states on which the Soviet Union had cast jealous and fearful eyes for two decades. As if this were not enough, Hitler had solemnly bound himself to suppress all anti-Bolshevik propaganda on *his* side of occupied Eastern Europe.

At first all had gone swimmingly. Half of Poland was devoured and the Baltic States placed in thrall. Then came the Finnish reverse. As 1939 drew to a close, and the Red Army met increasingly bloody reverses, the Soviet Union appeared to be in greater danger than at any moment since 1919. Indignant at Soviet aggression and brutality the world arose, shook off its torpor, and appeared to be preparing for a global crusade against Bolshevism. Britain and France, their armies as yet unscathed by war, began massive preparations for intervention in Karelia. Negotiations opened for attacks in the Black Sea, the Caucasus and Turkestan with the connivance and perhaps assistance of Turkey and Persia.

This was bad enough. Now other threats began to pile Ossa on Pelion. In Scandinavia public sympathy for the Finns was vociferous. Volunteers, particularly from Sweden, began to pour across the frontier. They came, too, from Hungary, whose people felt racial and religious kinship with Finland. Italy, Germany's partner in the Pact of Steel, cried loudly for military action to defend this gallant outpost of Christian European civilization. 'In reality, the whole of Italy is indignant about Russian aggression against Finland', wrote Foreign Minister Ciano on 2 December, and preparations began for massive shipments of men, aeroplanes, artillery and ammunition. Old antagonisms became temporarily dissolved when Britain agreed to allow Italian volunteers to pass through her ports on their way to the front.[1]

By 13 December the original war between the Anglo-French and the Germans seemed forgotten as the world's representative body, the League of Nations, condemned Soviet aggression and urged member-states to come to Finland's aid. Next day the USSR was solemnly expelled from the League.[2] Countries as various as Bolivia and Belgium declared their support for the move, but nowhere was enthusiasm for Finland's cause greater than in the dormant giant across the Atlantic. The United States provided a ten-million-dollar loan to enable Finland to buy foreign arms, and a 'moral embargo' began to slow supplies of military raw materials to the Soviet Union. Public outrage was great, and President Roosevelt himself, who at this stage was realistic enough to fear a Nazi-Soviet attempt at combined world domination, declared on 10 February that

> The Soviet Union, as everybody who has the courage to face the facts knows, is run by a dictatorship as absolute as any other dictatorship in the world. It has allied itself with another dictatorship, and it has invaded a neighbor so infinitesimally small that it could do no conceivable possible harm to the Soviet Union, a neighbor which seeks only to live at peace as a democracy, and a liberal, forward-looking democracy at that.[3]

The Soviet Union, whose armed forces were struggling with increasing difficulty to overcome this 'infinitesimally small' victim, must, but for one factor, have regarded the hostile world-wide combination with extreme dread. The one factor, however, was decisive. Throughout the crisis Hitler stood loyally by his ally. The German Foreign Office made it clear from the outset that the Secret Protocol to the Pact of 23 August would be honoured, and that Finland had been awarded to the Soviet Union. German diplomats abroad were instructed to support the Soviet viewpoint. On a more active level, Germany prevented the transit of Belgian and Italian war material across her territory, informed the Swedish government that any major intervention on the Finnish side would be regarded as a *casus belli*, and instructed German warships to assist the Soviet naval offensive in the Baltic.[4] As an ally, Germany could scarcely have done more without actually going to war with the Finns. On 11 December Ribbentrop assured the Soviet Ambassador in Berlin that he regarded Finland's resistance as bound up with British war plans.[5] Even the reports of foreign journalists sympathetic to Finland were refused transmission by the German telephone system.[6]

Protected by his German shield, Stalin had been able to impose terms on the Finns. No sooner had he done so, however, than Anglo-French war plans became more menacing than ever. Poised to strike in Scandinavia and the Caucasus, their aggressive designs were checked still more effectively by the brilliantly daring German intervention in Norway. The Wehrmacht guarded Soviet frontiers from the Arctic Ocean to the Balkans. Only a defeat of Germany herself could now endanger Soviet security, and that was about to become a very remote eventuality.

On 10 May the German war machine struck at Holland, and a few days later burst into Belgium and France. By the end of the month the main Allied resistance had been shattered, and on 22 June Marshal Pétain accepted German terms. In just over a month Germany had utterly defeated one partner in the hostile coalition, and had driven the other back across the sea. So long as the issue appeared to hang in the balance, Stalin had displayed his customary caution by slowing up supplies of raw materials to Germany. On 22 May the Germans noted that 'deliveries are still far from satisfactory, especially in the case of petroleum, in view of the present consumption in the west . . . in these circumstances it is especially important to the Reich Government to obtain a maximum of airplane gasoline, automobile gasoline, and other petroleum products in the coming weeks'. A week later, when Belgium had surrendered and Boulogne and Calais fallen, Deputy People's Commissar Krutikov assured Berlin that he had just received instructions to deliver all the copper, nickel and tin stipulated 'in the next few days', because the Soviet Government 'assumed that because of increased military activity in the west these metals were now needed urgently'.[7]

Soviet relief and gratitude at Germany's action were once again made evident. Early on the morning of the invasion of the Low Countries, Ambassador von Schulenburg called on Molotov to inform him that the day of reckoning had at long last arrived. Molotov expressed his delight, adding that he understood perfectly that Germany had to protect herself against the Anglo-French threat, and stressing his confidence in Germany's victory. His faith was rewarded, and on 17 June, the day Pétain sued for an armistice, the Foreign Commissar summoned von Schulenburg to his office 'and expressed the warmest congratulations of the Soviet Government on the splendid success of the German Armed Forces'.[8]

There can be no doubt of the sincerity of Stalin's expressions of gratitude. A German defeat in the Low Countries would have been disastrous for Soviet Russia. In a moment of panic he had ordered the massacre of the Polish officers; now, during agonized days in mid-May, he had been forced to contemplate the possibility of a victory by Poland's allies. Recognizing this, Stalin had not remained entirely a spectator of the conflict. Under his direction, the French Communist Party had struggled fiercely to ensure a German (or, to be fairer, a German-Soviet) victory. A massive propaganda operation had striven to denounce the war, discredit France's leaders, and disseminate suspicion of her British ally. Widespread sabotage took place in French factories, and defeatist literature spread among the troops. How decisive a part all this played in France's defeat is impossible to estimate. Certainly the French Communist Party itself took a great deal of credit for its achievement, and proclaimed immediately after the collapse:

> French imperialism has just suffered its greatest defeat in history . . . The French and World working class should look on this event as a victory and understand that one should see in it one enemy the less . . . It is evident, for the proof of this state of affairs, that the struggle of the French people has had the same aim as the struggle of German imperialism against French imperialism. It is correct that in this sense we had a temporary ally. Lenin taught us that one should not hesitate, when the moment dictates and it is in the people's interest, to ally one's self temporarily even with the devil . . . Whoever does not understand this is not a revolutionary.[9]

Communist subversion of the French war effort was a two-pronged weapon, simultaneously sapping the general will to resist whilst it frightened weaker and more unscrupulous members of the Right into preferring a German-dictated peace to a Communist France. That this would be the likely outcome was recognized by Stalin in a speech made in the following year. Disingenuously and improbably attributing the subversion to the Germans, he declared,

The Germans knew that their policy of playing up contradictions
between classes in separate states . . . provided its results in
France, whose rulers, allowing themselves to be frightened by the
spectre of revolution, in fear laid their country at Hitler's feet,
giving up all resistance.[10]

Stalin was shrewd enough to have anticipated that this was what
would happen.

So it was that the German Army won the most spectacular victory
of the twentieth century. Stalin's part in it has been obscured, yet it
should not be forgotten that Guderian's tanks operated largely on
Soviet petrol as they dashed for the sea at Abbeville, the bombs that
levelled Rotterdam contained Soviet guncotton, and the bullets that
strafed British Tommies wading to the boats at Dunkirk were
sheathed in Soviet cupro-nickel. A handful of British soldiers were
later to suffer first-hand experience of the extent to which the Soviet
Union regarded herself as Nazi Germany's ally. Taken prisoner at
Calais, Dunkirk, and elsewhere, British prisoners-of-war were
transported to camps in Germany. Some succeeded in escaping to
Poland, where they were helped on their way by the Resistance. At
great peril to their lives they succeeded in crossing over to the USSR.
There, no doubt, they expected to be shipped home, or at worst
interned. But their reception provided no doubt that they were in a
hostile country. They were shot at, wounded, beaten up, and thrown
into gaol. Rifleman John Yeowell, for example, was sentenced to
twenty-five years in a forced-labour camp, and James Allan was near
to death by starvation in prison before he succeeded in escaping a
year later to the British Embassy in Moscow.[11]

Stalin must have grinned to himself as he reflected on the success
of a policy which saw the Wehrmacht fighting his war for him, as he
moved forward in the rear to collect the plunder. In the previous
autumn Hitler had consented to his absorption of the eastern European border states. At the time Stalin had proceeded with great caution. Fearful of Anglo-French intervention in the Baltic, he had
restricted his initiative to compelling the three little countries to
accept Soviet garrisons. These were confined to their bases, behaved
in a generally disciplined manner, and did not interfere directly with
the states' internal affairs. Now Stalin saw his opportunity had come,
though he was still very careful not to burn his fingers.

On 14 May von Kleist and Guderian established their first bridgeheads west of the Meuse, outflanking the Maginot Line. Two days later the Soviet newspaper *Izvestia* noted with sinister significance,

> The recent war events once more proved that the neutrality of small states, which do not have power to support it, is a mere fantasy. Therefore, there are very few chances for small countries to survive and to maintain their independence. All considerations of small countries on the question of justice and injustice in relations with the Big Powers, which are at war 'to determine if they are to be or not to be', are at the least, naïve.[12]

Two days after this warning shot, Red Army units began a large-scale transfer of troops, tanks, artillery and aeroplanes to their base at Gaizunai in the centre of Lithuania. These continued for a week; the Red Army was not equipped to move more speedily, and Stalin was exceedingly anxious to take no unnecessary risks.[13] By 25 May the German 15th, 19th and 41st Corps had broken the French lines, poured through to the Channel, and begun to invest the retreating British Expeditionary Force in Boulogne, Calais and Dunkirk.

The Soviet serpent began to raise its head. A note was presented to the Lithuanian authorities, accusing them of kidnapping two Soviet soldiers. The Lithuanians promised Molotov they would investigate the matter. It was discovered that the soldiers had taken up very comfortable quarters of their own with some fair Lithuanians, and that no governmental coercion had been employed to bring about this state of affairs. Despite this the Soviets pressed forward with their complaints. The Allies were suffering increasing reverses in the West and on 28 May, the day Belgium surrendered, Commissar Loktionov arrived in Kaunas to press Soviet charges. The Lithuanian government, only too aware of the danger threatening them, offered to undertake any measures the Soviet Government required to obtain satisfaction. The Foreign Minister offered to fly to Moscow, but a stern reply demanded the presence of Prime Minister Merkys. Merkys obediently repaired to the Soviet capital, where from 7 June onwards he was subjected by Molotov to a series of virulent and entirely false accusations of anti-Soviet scheming.

However, on 12 June, Merkys returned home without having received any concrete demands from Molotov. The Kremlin still cast nervous glances at the rapidly unfolding drama in the West. German successes continued unabated, with their armies pushing forward to the Seine. But the miracle of Dunkirk had saved nearly 340,000

British and French troops, who were making preparations to land in Brittany and re-enter the campaign. On 4 June Churchill made his pugnacious speech in the Commons, in which he vowed that Britain would 'go on to the end, we shall fight in France . . . we shall never surrender . . . until, in God's good time, the New World, with all its power and might, steps forth to the rescue and the liberation of the Old'. British stubbornness had surprised the world again and again throughout history. What if the tables were yet turned? But on 14 June Paris fell to General von Küchler's 18th Army, and the swastika floated from the Eiffel Tower. Now was Stalin's moment to act; the meddling Allies were clearly on the run, and it would be as well to settle matters swiftly before Hitler's terrible 143 divisions began to return home.

That day an ultimatum was handed to the Lithuanian Foreign Minister demanding the trial of two high officers of state whose actions had offended the Soviets, the reconstruction of the government in a form acceptable to the USSR, and the free movement and unlimited increase of Red Army troops within the country. Somehow the Soviets have never been able to describe conquest and absorption of neighbouring states in round terms – there is always the lingering fear that they might one day be called to account for their actions. The Soviet-Lithuanian Peace Treaty of 1920, the Non-Aggression Pact of 1926, and the Mutual-Assistance Pact of 1939 were forgotten as if they had never been. As the President hastily fled the country into East Prussia, 300,000 Red Army troops poured across the frontier: one soldier to every eight Lithuanians in the country. As Stalin noted, 'the bravery of Red Army warriors is unexampled'.[14] Lithuania, for centuries an eastern bastion of European civilization, had passed into the darkness.[15]

Latvia likewise had signed a Peace Treaty (1920) with the USSR, and a Non-Aggression Treaty (1932). The day after Soviet troops flooded into Lithuania (16 June), Latvia received a similarly threatening ultimatum to that of her southern neighbour. One day *before* this, Red Army (or NKVD) troops had stormed a Latvian frontier-post. They managed to burn down the building and departed with a dozen or so prisoners, leaving behind as mementoes of their visit the corpses of two men and a woman, together with another woman and child both dangerously wounded. This exploit was probably originally intended as an 'incident' to justify the coming invasion. But even Molotov seems to have appreciated that the murder and abduction of a number of peaceful Latvians might not appear altogether convincing before world opinion as a proof of *Latvian* aggression, and the delicate operation played no part in subsequent negotiations. The day after the ultimatum, columns of Soviet tanks crossed the frontier at two points; by teatime they were trundling through the nation's capital, Riga.[16]

On 16 June, too, the Estonians received their ultimatum. All three independent states were accused by the Soviets of various failings, all of which by a coincidence came to a head on the same day. The charge against Estonia is of particular interest. On 28 May *Pravda* complained that

> A certain part of the Estonian intelligentsia regards the occupation of Norway and Denmark by the Germans as an aggression, as an enslavement of small nations. This part of the intelligentsia preaches a loyal attitude towards England and expresses its hatred of Germany and everything German . . . The ruling circles of Estonia are trying to remain neutral with regard to the events in the west . . . The Estonian Press likewise tries to avoid awkward problems and emphasizes its loyalty towards England.

On 15 June an Estonian passenger aeroplane was shot down at sea – presumably another unsuccessful attempt to create an 'incident' affording proof of Estonia's intention to invade and conquer the Soviet Union. On 17 and 18 June the Red Army overran the country.[17]

A recent Soviet history describes what followed. Forgetting to mention the invasion of 17 June, the authors pass directly to dramatic scenes on the 21st, when a massive popular revolution against the bourgeois government broke out in Estonia's capital.

> On the same day tens of thousands of people came out into the streets of Tallinn. Work was stopped everywhere. Before the government had any time to take measures, it found itself standing quite alone, eye to eye with the majority of the people who hated the government for its betrayal of the national interests.[18]

In reality, a few hundred imported revolutionaries from the Soviet Union joined a handful of native Estonian Communists in a demonstration in Freedom Square. The 'revolution' was orderly enough: tanks of the Red Army were present at every street corner to ensure it remained so. Despite every effort, however, representatives of the risen masses remained very meagre in number, and Estonians were amused to see in the Soviet-controlled press photographs of dense crowds, waving, laughing and cheering. In such a small country it was not difficult to recognize many of the faces: the photographs were those of the crowd at a recent national singing festival.[19]

For a few days the Revolution and the bourgeois Baltic governments co-existed. President Smetona of Lithuania had fled to East Prussia on 16 June, preferring not to entrust himself and his family to Soviet chivalry.[20] His foresight was rewarded: the unfortunate Presidents of Latvia and Estonia were shortly afterwards removed by the NKVD to an unknown destination. The fate of President Päts of Estonia was particularly tragic. Like millions of less well-known people, he disappeared into the darkness of the USSR, his people remaining in ignorance of his fate. Then, in 1974, the International Red Cross learned from Soviet sources that the President had died on 18 January 1956. Three years after that, messages were smuggled out of the Soviet Union bearing Päts's signature and finger-prints. Preserved for nearly thirty years, they contained greetings to Estonians all over the world and a prayer that 'our homes should remain free in our free homeland'. He described the appalling conditions under which he had been held ever since the conquest of his country. Kept in 'a hospital for the Jewish poor', his plight was as wretched as those of his persecuted fellow-inmates. Deprived of all personal possessions, even the use of his own name ('here I am only No. 12'), and fed with revolting rations, 'I have become weak, my hearing and eyesight have weakened . . . I will be soon 80 years old, there are few days of life left for me. Having been born free, I would also want to die in freedom'.[21]

It was not long before the peoples of the Baltic States were to undergo like sufferings and worse. Three of Stalin's most ruthless henchmen were sent to impose NKVD rule on the conquered countries. To Lithuania came Vladimir Dekanozov, a Georgian colleague of Beria's, whose energetic work in the purges from 1937 onwards had earned him promotion within the NKVD, and clearly qualified him to settle matters with the Lithuanians.[22] Latvia was accorded Andrei Vyshinsky, the Public Prosecutor in the same purges, who could recognize a class enemy when he saw one. Finally, the liberated proletarians of Estonia saw Andrei Zhdanov, Stalin's satrap in Leningrad, slink furtively into his new capital 'in an armoured car accompanied by two tanks'.[23]

What followed was grimly predictable. Between 14 and 17 July elections were held in Estonia, Latvia and Lithuania, Communist majorities proving to be 92.8, 97.8 and 99.19 per cent respectively. So many Baltic Communists had been slaughtered by Stalin himself in 1936 and 1937 that there was difficulty in raking up enough candidates, but somehow the difficulty was overcome. In Estonia 'one of the highest posts went to a man of Estonian origin who had hitherto been an assistant station-master in the North Caucasus'.[24] Finally, on 5 August, the Supreme Soviet very generously agreed to admit the three republics as constituent members of the USSR. The emotions of the time were well caught by a Latvian poet who, with the assistance of colleagues, composed this beautiful effusion:

We raised our heads
And caught a glimpse of Stalin
Standing in a simple gray suit.
Nodding his head, he greeted the Letts:
'Now your sad past has vanished beyond seven hills,
Now there is a place for you in the free Soviet family.
Rear yourselves so that you would rise higher
in the almighty Soviet State.'
And on his affectionate face something else could be read:
'We are as strong as a rock, as a cliff,
We are an unbreakable force,
We are the embodiment of liberty, humanism, beauty.'[25]

In this way three independent, prosperous and civilized countries vanished from the map of Europe. Almost at once there arose an acute shortage of goods in the shops of Tallinn, Riga, Kaunas and elsewhere.[26] In Moscow, on the other hand, the special shops open only to the rich who were not restricted to ration-books,

. . . were suddenly lush with unfamiliar foreign items; with suits, dresses, shoes, cigarettes, chocolate, crackers, cheese, canned goods, a hundred other items obviously of non-Soviet origin. This was the overflow of goods from the frontier areas taken over by the Red Army . . . loot seized in the Baltic countries . . . Muscovites were thrilled to be able to buy these wonders of capitalist production, in the 'socialist' capital. Thousands of Soviet officials sported looted elegance and amazing stories, sometimes no doubt exaggerated, about the good things to which the Soviet liberators helped themselves in the conquered areas spread through the capital.[27]

However, it can safely be said that the Balts would have been reasonably content had it been only material goods that the NKVD dispatched in trainloads to the interior of the USSR.

No sooner had the independence of the three countries been overthrown, than the whole apparatus of Soviet civilization began to be imported.

> People began disappearing at night and were never seen again. There was never a court procedure, people just vanished . . . Aino Kallas . . . lost her two children during this year. Her daughter was killed by a Russian marksman in her friend's garden where she was picking berries. She died instantly, falling at the feet of her three-year-old daughter.[28]

So wrote an Estonian woman. In Latvia,

> night after night, the dreaded black vans of the secret police raced through the streets of its cities and over the highways of its remotest districts. Hundreds upon hundreds of men, women, and children were spirited away into the vastnesses of the Soviet Union, never to be heard from again.

In the first year of Soviet occupation, 34,250 Latvians vanished without trace − more than 2 per cent of the population. Equivalent purges would have accounted for nearly three million Americans, nearly a million Britons, or 840,000 Frenchmen. Not all had left the country: 1,355 people, including 109 women, 25 schoolchildren, *and 4 children under the age of six*, died in the torture chambers of the NKVD in Latvia itself.[29]

Evidence of these atrocities became unexpectedly available when the Red Army was driven out by the Germans in 1941. In Lithuania a document was captured, containing the NKVD plan of 7 July 1940, 'preparatory to liquidation. Active abolition of the leading influence of parties hostile to the State: Nationalists, Voldemarists, Populists, Christian Democrats, Young Lithuanians, Trotskyists, Social Democrats, National Guardsmen and others. The action must be carried out simultaneously through all Lithuania on the night of July 11/12, 1940.' What this involved, some examples will show. Juozas Viktoravicius, a 32-year-old workman, was interrogated in Kaunas Gaol.

Here my hands were put into iron chains and wrenched. They beat me with the edge of the hand on my neck, and with a ruler they rapped the knuckles of my hands. With their thumbs they squeezed my abdomen, with a press they repeatedly struck my shoulders and tore at the injured places. Finally they noosed my sex organs with a piece of cord and pulled at them. In the course of the torture I collapsed and fainted twice. I was questioned thus for 45 hours without stopping. The inquest having finished they bound my hands and feet and put me into cold water in the basement of the NKVD building. In the water I collapsed again. Having come back to prison I was not recognized by my friends.

Others had their testicles kicked to pulp, were seated on red-hot stoves, had needles rammed under their fingernails, were scalped, had their jaws ripped down to their necks, and had their eyes gouged and their tongues torn out. Executions took place in specially equipped death cells. Elsewhere, at Kretinga, victims were bound to trees with iron hoops before being burned alive. Others there had been buried alive, some after having had their scalps and hands skinned.

Four miles outside the capital, Kaunas, the NKVD fenced off an area hidden in the forest of Petrošiunai. It was strictly forbidden to approach the site, and passers-by felt little inclination to do so, as occasional screams and shots were heard from within. After the German invasion the inhabitants were able to examine the spot. It proved to be a miniature Katyn. Prisoners in the main Kaunas Gaol who were sentenced to death were brought there. Mass graves containing a total of four hundred and fifty corpses were uncovered. In order to avoid the sound of shots in Kaunas itself, the commandant of the gaol had instructed his executioners to slaughter each victim by battering in his temples with a hammer. The bodies were terribly distorted, many of them still bound in chains, as numerous horrifying photographs testify.[30]

What, if any, was the purpose of all this cruelty? There was not the slightest chance of any serious Baltic resistance in the face of overwhelming Soviet might, the Soviets in their turn being protected from outside interference by the alliance with Germany. It seems that Stalin could never rid himself of the fear that a popular uprising might one day endanger his power. The Estonians, Latvians and Lithuanians must receive their first taste of the whip as a warning

not to be ignored. And, in case unsettled times gave others dangerous ideas, he unleashed the NKVD yet again on unhappy Poland.

> In June, refugees from all other parts of Poland who were in
> Eastern Poland on the 17th of September 1939 were carried off.
> The registration of these people had been made particularly easy
> by an announcement some months previously that all refugees
> wishing to return to the German Occupation would be allowed to
> do so upon submitting their names. With them were also
> members of the learned and professional classes and 'speculators'.

Other victims included thousands of Jews from Polish villages
(many of them Communists), who were sent to some of the worst
forced-labour camps north of the 70th parallel. They 'died rapidly in
the severe climate of the north with Biblical curses on their lips and
the angry look of cheated prophets in their eyes.'[31]

The Secret Protocol to the Nazi-Soviet Pact had taken note of
Soviet Russia's 'interest in Bessarabia', which Germany declared
herself ready to concede.[32] The province of Bessarabia had belonged
to Imperial Russia for over a century, but had fallen to Romania at
the time of the Revolution. There were several reasons why Stalin
was anxious to restore the region to Russia. A sort of natural justice
seemed to require that he should own at least all that Nicholas II had
ruled, and he had long-term ambitions of meddling among the Slav
nations of the Balkans. Above all, Bessarabia contained a large
Ukrainian population, and the existence beyond his control of segments of the subject peoples of the USSR appeared very dangerous
indeed. Their freedom and prosperity gave them an unfair advantage
when competing for the loyalty of Soviet Ukrainians, and they
presented a temptation to any power seeking to inflame nationalist
sentiment within the USSR. Nevertheless, it was necessary to proceed very cautiously. On 13 April 1939, just over a year previously,
Romania had been the recipient of unilateral guarantees of military
aid in case of attack by both Britain and France. It were best to see
how the war went, without risking any action which might draw the
Soviet Union into a major conflict.

Soon after the surrender of Holland and the German advance into
Belgium, it became clear that the tide was running against the
Allies. The huge and clumsy Soviet military machine began to
gather itself together, clogging most of Southern Russia's transport
system. News of these movements soon reached the Romanians,

who appealed to Germany if possible to restrain her ally. German interest in Romanian oil was considerable, nor could the Reich be anxious to see war break out in the Balkans whilst they still faced Anglo-French armies in the West. The Germans expressed strong reservations over the question of help, but in any case the Red Army as yet showed no signs of crossing into Bessarabia. The Allies were not yet beaten, and the NKVD may have got wind of Romanian threats that they would resist an invasion. The Romanian Military Attaché in Berlin informed the Germans on 23 May 'officially that Rumania would accept battle with the Russians; there were sufficient troops as well as fortifications'.[33]

Whatever the cause, the weeks rolled by without any overt signs of Soviet action. On 17 June, with Paris taken, the British driven into the sea, and the Wehrmacht at the Swiss frontier, Molotov congratulated the Germans on their victory, and informed them of the annexation of the Baltic States, which 'had become necessary to put an end to all the intrigues by which England and France had tried to sow discord between Germany and the Soviet Union in the Baltic States'. Then, on the 22nd, the French signed the Armistice at Compiègne. The Allies were beaten, and next day Molotov announced to German Ambassador von Schulenburg that the USSR was about to lay claim to Bessarabia. This was covered by the Secret Protocol, but von Schulenburg was startled to learn that the Soviets wanted the province of Bukovina as well. He asked Molotov to wait while he consulted his government: Germany had a considerable interest in Romania. In order to reassure their powerful ally, the Soviet press published an announcement that 'the good neighbourly relations, arising from the conclusion of the Nonaggression Pact between the USSR and Germany, cannot be shaken by any rumours or petty poisonous propaganda, because these relations are not based on motives of opportunism but on the fundamental interests of the USSR and Germany'. Molotov drew the Ambassador's attention to these friendly words; the latter believed the article from its style to be the work of Stalin himself.

Ribbentrop replied with an assurance that Germany intended to abide by the Pact, and 'takes, therefore, no interest in the Bessarabian question'. Bukovina was another matter, and it was hoped all could be settled without war. Molotov hastily replied that Soviet demands would be restricted to part of Bukovina, and suggested that the Germans should follow up the Soviet ultimatum with a hint to

EASTERN EUROPE SUMMER 1940

NORWEGIAN SEA

SWEDEN

FINLAND

Helsinki

Leningrad

NORWAY

Oslo

Stockholm

ESTONIA

LATVIA

LITHUANIA

BALTIC SEA

DENMARK

Smolensk

Berlin

POLAND

Warsaw

USSR

GERMANY

CZECHOSLOVAKIA

L'vov

N BUKOVINA

BESSARABIA

Budapest

Grosswarden

HUNGARY

ROMANIA

BLACK SEA

The bold line marks the division
of spheres agreed by the U S S R and Germany in 1939

Territory occupied by the U S S R in 1939-40

Territory occupied by Germany in 1939-40

BULGARIA

Romania that she should comply. All went as planned. On 27 June Ribbentrop instructed the German Minister in Bucharest to advise the Romanians to accept the Soviet demand. The same day Molotov delivered his ultimatum, and the helpless Romanians were obliged to withdraw as the Red Army poured into the last of the territories offered Stalin by Hitler the previous August.[34]

Bessarabia and occupied Bukovina were immediately sealed off from the world as the grim procedure of 'Sovietization' began. It was not until December that any outsider managed to enter the region; one of the first was John Russell, of the British Embassy in Moscow. At Czernowitz in the Bukovina he saw distressing scenes in a once pleasant little Romanian town, soon to 'be one with the gloomy settlements of Russia – I had almost said, with the cities of the plain'.

> The . . . impression which the town gives is one of profound gloom. This is largely caused by the rows of shuttered windows on all the main streets; to judge by Poland and the Baltic States, this is one of the unavoidable accessories of Soviet occupation. Commerce is nationalised, capital confiscated, private enterprise liquidated; individual traders go out of business and put up their shutters; State shops are then instituted – on paper; and on paper they remain for some months, whilst the population queues up outside the few stores that are still open.

Prices were trebling, quadrupling, and rising fast. Only the NKVD operated with ostentatious efficiency, looting without disguise and turning families into the street where a house took their fancy. Not that there were not very many houses already empty:

> Dr. Koppelman, a charming Jewish advocate, formerly legal adviser to our consulate, told me that he did not dare to begin to count the number of his friends who had disappeared. In Russia proper it is rare to see a daylight arrest, such things always happened at night, but in Czernowitz, every day that I was there I saw little groups being escorted under armed guard to the railway station.[35]

Many of the small shopkeepers whom Dr Koppelman missed were already in far-off Siberia. At malaria-ridden Kolpashev, 'beggars were squatting in front of the polyclinic. They were destitute Bessarabians. It was horrible to see how they sat there, removing their rags, searching them for lice. If a passerby tossed them a piece of bread, they fought for it among themselves fiercely.' At least they had survived: at the nearby settlement at Bilin, Soviet working conditions had killed fifty in sixteen weeks.[36] The usual methods were employed in abducting them: night-time raids; separation of husbands from wives, and both from their children; all transported in cattle cars on a journey lasting weeks, until the greatly depleted survivors began a lingering death in the cruel embrace of GULAG. Between two and three hundred thousand people (out of two million) were removed in this way. (The same proportion of Frenchmen would have amounted to about four and a half million – the population of greater Paris.)[37]

The timing of the Soviet invasions of the Baltic States and Romania is of considerable interest and significance. At the time and since it has been widely concluded that 'Stalin did not trust the Germans and wanted to close down the bargain while they were busy and before they could have second thoughts'.[38] This view is surely not borne out by the events themselves. True, Molotov came cap in hand to remind the Germans of the agreement, and request permission to go ahead in Romania. But this was merely deference to be expected from the junior partner in the alliance. At no time did the Germans cavil at Soviet claims, except in the case of the extended Soviet claim to all Bukovina, when Molotov readily stepped into line. As Ribbentrop stated at the time of the annexation of the Baltic States: 'Our attitude toward the Soviet Union in this question was finally and irrevocably established by the definite Moscow Agreement.' A day later Secretary of State Weizsäcker confirmed that 'in view of our unaltered friendship with the Soviet Union, there is no reason for nervousness on our part, which some of the foreign press has tried to impute to us in only too transparent a manner.'[39]

Had Stalin's aim been to take advantage of Germany's embroilment in the West, he would presumably have acted in the mid-days of May, when the Wehrmacht was inextricably engaged in Belgium. He was capable of swift timing: the Baltic and Bessarabian invasions took place within twenty-four hours of ultimatums being delivered. Instead Stalin waited patiently until Paris fell before attacking the Balts, and not until the Armistice itself did he settle accounts with Romania. It was German *victory*, not German involvement, that Stalin needed to act in safety. As Molotov confessed on 30 June to his puppet Foreign Minister of Lithuania, 'It would be unpardonable if the Soviet Union did not seize this opportunity which may never recur'.[40] Stalin's timing was perfect; with his ally occupying France's capital, he could swallow up the more vulnerable Baltic States, and with France's defeat he could afford to ignore the Franco-British guarantee to Romania.

The Soviets themselves did not disguise the fact that it was an Allied victory which they feared, and that they regarded the British and French as their enemies. If there was anywhere the Soviets had just cause to anticipate Nazi machinations it was in Romania, which the Reich was clearly moving towards making a German protectorate. Yet in December 1940 a visitor found the NKVD and Party in occupied Bukovina conducting a frantic campaign against the fancied plots of British Intelligence.[41] This view continued right up to the eve of the German invasion of Russia. In June 1941 the Latvian journal *Karogs* published a hair-raising story of Anglo-French plotting at the time of the annexation, and inquired triumphantly, 'Do you think that the mighty Soviet Union will watch calmly how our own Latvian capitalists are flirting with others like themselves beyond our borders, across the Baltic Sea?' It was the Western Imperialists who were being alluded to,[42] even as Germany's one hundred and forty-eight divisions lay poised on the frontier.

Until the fall of France Stalin lived in fear of an Allied victory, which would endanger all his hard-won acquisitions. After June 1940 the danger seemed past, and Stalin could breathe again. As he pointed out crushingly to the British Ambassador, who had ventured a warning note, Stalin

did not see any danger of the hegemony of any one country in Europe and still less any danger that Europe might be engulfed by Germany. Stalin observed the policy of Germany, and knew several leading German statesmen well. He had not discovered any desire on their part to engulf European countries. Stalin was not of the opinion that German military successes menaced the Soviet Union and her friendly relations with Germany. These relations were not based on transient circumstances, but on the basic national interests of both countries.[43]

XII
Clearing the Decks

Winston Churchill once described Soviet policy methods in these pithy terms: 'They will try every door in the house, enter all the rooms which are not locked and when they come to one that is barred, if they are unsuccessful in breaking through, they will withdraw and invite you to dine that evening'.[1] This analogue was particularly apposite in 1940 and 1941. A rap on the knuckles from Hitler was not to be ignored, but anything was worth trying once.

The defeat of Britain and France had repercussions not only in Europe, but wherever their world-wide imperial connections ran. To east and west of the Soviet Union loomed the formidable power of Japan and Germany, but southwards lay possibilities extremely attractive to the Soviet rulers. In Iran the British stake in the oilfields, represented by the Anglo-Iranian Oil Company, had led Britain to watch over Iran's territorial integrity. But now the Germans had brought Britain to bay in her own island, and Stalin could contemplate the resuscitation of certain long-term Soviet aims. A long report from the German Minister in Teheran dated 19 May 1940 makes curiously topical reading forty years later. Erwin Ettel noted that the Soviet Government appeared to be deliberately fostering poor relations between the two countries, very likely in order to preserve pretexts for intervention should that become opportune. Pointing out Russia's inaccessibility to the open seas, Ettel encapsulated Soviet Russia's ambition in a few words: 'It is the attainment of the old Russian goal to have access to the warm waters . . . A glance at the map shows that the shortest route from the Soviet Union to the warm waters would be through Iran.' The Minister felt strongly that

Germany must in her foreign policy take seriously into account this Soviet Russian expansionist drive to the Persian Gulf . . .

The Shah and the members of his Government are, without a doubt, clearly aware of the dangers which threaten Iran from the Soviet Union . . . Should Iran become part of the Soviet Union, the latter would gain a predominant place in the sphere of petroleum which would, in practice, be tantamount to a position of monopoly. The picture would not be very different if, through the concession forced upon Iran by the Soviet Union to maintain military bases on the Persian Gulf, Iran was to become a state dependent upon the Soviet Union . . . No one will, in the long run, be able to ignore the understandable aspiration of the Soviet Union to obtain such success.[2]

For the moment only covetous glances could be directed at Iran. Stalin cast his eyes around the map and came to rest once again on little Finland. That at least he had German permission to absorb. How maddening to think that, a bare two months earlier, he had called off the conquest and allowed Finland mild peace terms – and all through fear of the British and French! And where were they now? Might it not be possible to have another try? From the end of May Soviet newspaper attacks and other pressures increased against the Finns. In September Stalin grew apprehensive at news of German troop movements across Finland, but was informed that all that was involved was the transport of troops and guns to northern Norway. Nevertheless, the Germans were now clearly more interested in Finland's integrity than they had been at the time of the Pact, and with the German Army in force in Kirkenes it were best to tread warily. The Germans, too, were aroused by Soviet threats to absorb the Petsamo nickel concession.[3] Stalin made no move, and bided his time. Finland could wait. That route led nowhere, and was in any case blocked from outside interference by the German occupation of Norway.

No, the most likely opening for intrigue and expansion seemed to lie in the Balkans. There Stalin could count on the twin weapons of Communism and Pan-Slav sympathy to prepare the ground. True, the Germans had slapped down his claim to the whole of Bukovina, but the entire region was clearly in a state of flux. Besides, the British too were starting to poke their snouts around those parts, so it was clearly free to all comers. One can detect a new, ebullient mood in the Kremlin.

Stalin's enemies in Europe were well taken care of, and his agents were able also to strike far beyond the seas against opponents of the regime. On 24 May 1940 NKVD assassins burst into Trotsky's fortified retreat in Mexico and sprayed the former War Commissar's bedroom with bullets. Trotsky escaped, but the hunt was closing in for the kill, and on 20 August Ramon Mercader drove his icepick into the exile's brain. Stalin and Trotsky shared a delusion that the latter was popular with dissident elements in the USSR, and the dictator must once again have felt 1940 was his fortunate year.

Things could hardly be going more smoothly, and the temptation to fish in Balkan waters increased. Stalin, too, grew more assured in his dealings with Hitler. After all, the Soviet Union was now a great power too, was it not? An obscure strip of Lithuanian territory was due under the terms of the Pact to revert to Germany. Stalin could not bear to part with it, and begged the Führer 'to consider whether, in conformity with the extraordinarily friendly relations between Germany and the Soviet Union, a way cannot be found which would leave this strip of territory permanently with Lithuania'. The Germans, a little taken aback, agreed to the concession in return for financial compensation.[4] Next Molotov complained that Germany had violated a clause of the Pact by not consulting her ally over the Vienna Award, a disturbing result of which was that Germany and Italy had guaranteed Romania's new frontiers. Ribbentrop tactfully explained that the guarantee was directed primarily against Bulgaria and Hungary, but Molotov was unlikely to overlook the fact that a door had been effectively slammed in the face of Soviet designs on the remainder of the Bukovina. His protest, however, received a smart rebuff. This protracted wrangle betrayed a certain amount of irritation on both sides.[5]

There were other causes of perturbation. Increasingly large bodies of German troops were moving into Romania (for 'training purposes', the Germans claimed). Germany, Italy and Japan signed a Three-Power Pact, not directed against the Soviet Union, but nevertheless not including her. There were German troops moving across Finland; true, they were on their way to Norway, but Finland was definitely the Soviet Union's plum. Finally, the Soviets had responded to a slowing-up of German economic supplies by cutting drastically her own shipments of raw materials. The latter was a very important consideration indeed. Germany's war economy owed an enormous debt to Soviet petroleum and grain. As a senior German Foreign Office official pointed out, the Soviet Union had received

150 million Reichsmarks' worth of goods from Germany. In ex-change, she had supplied exactly *twice* the value in raw materials. In addition, Germany's 'sole economic connexion with Iran, Af-ghanistan, Manchukuo, Japan and, beyond that, with South America, is the route across Russia . . . ' All in all, Stalin was beginning to feel a little discontented with his once-trusty ally.[6]

Much of this friction might have been avoided had Germany acted with some tact and caution. These were not Hitler's strongest quali-ties, however, and he felt increasing justification in disregarding Soviet sensibilities. For it was about this time that he began to contemplate seriously the prospect of going to war with the Soviet Union. Britain had declined his offer of peace on 19 July, and pros-pects of a successful cross-Channel invasion were fading. War with Russia began to present an enticing alternative. Expansion into the Ukraine had always been the fundamental base of his plans for the German people. Then again, if Britain could not be tackled head-on, he could isolate her by destroying her only prospective ally on the Continent. He felt frustrated and restless; here he was with an army capable of anything, but time was passing, and if he waited much longer the initiative might pass from him. Nascent signs of Soviet truculence and independence irritated the Führer and justified him in regarding an attack eastwards as a pre-emptive strike.[7]

Ribbentrop, whose vanity impelled him to sustain his 'brilliant' achievement in Moscow the previous August, was distressed by these evident signs of Soviet discontent. There seemed to be no reason why it could not all be smoothed over. Germany had no intention of interfering in Finland, and the guarantee to Romania did not impinge on the terms of the Moscow Pact. On 13 October he wrote a long letter to 'Herr Stalin'. Recapitulating with genuine enthusiasm the close co-operation that had subsisted between the two 'authoritarian regimes', the German Foreign Minister pointed out the considerable advantages that had accrued since to both parties. Britain, time and again, had tried to spread the war the length and breadth of Europe, only to be foiled on each occasion by force of German arms. In Scandinavia Germany had prevented the extension of the combat area to a region very dangerous to the Soviet Union, and with the capture of the files of the French General Staff in Paris the extent of the Anglo-French plans for the destruction of the Caucasian oil centres had been uncovered. Passing on to explain, plausibly enough, German moves in Finland and Romania, and the

Three-Power Pact, as being in no way directed against the Soviet Union, Ribbentrop urged that the Soviet Union, Italy, Japan and Germany ought 'to adopt a long-range policy and to direct the future development of their peoples into the right channels by delimitation of their interests on a world-wide scale'. To further this purpose, he proposed that Molotov visit Berlin for discussion.

Stalin replied, agreeing cordially 'that a further improvement in the relations between our two countries is entirely possible on the permanent basis of a long-term delimitation of mutual interests', and consenting to Molotov's visit. On 12 November 1940 the Foreign Commissar arrived by train in Berlin. This was his first visit abroad, and despite his spaniel-like devotion to Stalin, the Leader clearly felt distrustful. A team of NKVD watchdogs ('good gangster types for a film', noted a senior German official) accompanied him, led by Dekanozov, the *Gauleiter* of Lithuania, and Merkulov, Beria's deputy. The Germans avoided playing 'The Internationale' at the station, and the cortège drove through streets filled with curious but silent spectators. However much Ribbentrop delighted in the 'hard-faced men' from the Kremlin, Berliners sensed there was something strained in the alliance of the two totalitarian powers.

The first discussion began that morning. Ribbentrop recapitulated details of German strength and Allied weakness. (England, the former champagne salesman explained, 'was led by a political and military dilettante by the name of Churchill, who throughout his previous career had completely failed at all decisive moments and who would fail again'.) The United States, whatever its plans might be, would never be allowed to interfere, and the downfall of Britain was imminent. What remained was to delineate future areas of expansion for the Three-Power Pact countries (Germany, Italy and Japan) and the Soviet Union. Leaving the United States aside for the moment, could not all four powers expand southwards into the vast spaces of Africa and Asia, agreeing on spheres of influence and so avoiding a clash of interests? Just over a year previously the USSR and Germany had agreed to carve up Eastern Europe; now it was the world that was to be apportioned between them and their partners.

Molotov was agreeable to the general idea of a totalitarian world, but displayed much of the attitude of suspicion and haggling over points of detail that were to frustrate and mystify Soviet Russia's next allies, Britain and the United States. Where precisely was the USSR's sphere of influence to lie? What exactly was the purpose of the Tripartite Pact? Talks were resumed after breakfast, when the Führer himself made his appearance. After a preliminary survey, in which he and Molotov cordially agreed that 'the two greatest peoples of Europe' should be able to come to a profitable agreement, Hitler asserted that the Russian empire (*das russische Reich*) could develop perfectly in accord with German interests. Molotov quite agreed, but inquired again about German activities in Finland. Moreover, the USSR had interests in the Balkans, a region whose future required clarification. He perfectly agreed with the planned destruction of Britain and exclusion of the United States from Europe and Asia. But the nature of the proposed Four-Party Pact had to be examined in detail. When Hitler stressed Germany's record of co-operation, Molotov grumbled about German interest in Finland and Romania.

Hitler began to feel irritable. As he rambled on grandiloquently about undefined 'spheres of interest', Molotov returned again and again to the Finnish and Romanian questions. Behind these restrained exchanges clearly lay a Soviet desire to finish the reckoning she owed Finland, and a German determination *not* to see Red Army troops in Petsamo. Relations stiffened further when Molotov displayed a pertinacious interest in Bulgaria, Russia's traditional ally to the south, and then went on to express Soviet Russia's direct concern with the affairs of Turkey, Greece, Hungary, Yugoslavia, Romania, and even the Baltic Sea up to the sound between Norway and Denmark; these regions 'could not be immaterial to her under any circumstances'. When Molotov travelled back to Moscow, he left behind an atmosphere of indignation and suspicion. On 26 November this was confirmed when Molotov received Ambassador von Schulenburg. With the NKVD watchdog Dekanozov checking his every word, the Foreign Commissar confirmed that the Soviet Union was prepared to join the Tripartite Pact *provided* very specific assurances were received regarding the USSR's rights in regions as farflung as Sakhalin Island, Finland and Bulgaria. The German Foreign Office made no reply to these impudent demands, and draft versions of the proposed new Pact gathered dust in von Schulenburg's safe at the Embassy.[8]

Hitler retired to the Berghof, furious at this revelation of Bolshevik greed and aggression. Stalin's demands confirmed everything he had suspected about the Soviets. They were thoroughly untrustworthy allies, who would seize the first opportunity of profiting by a German reverse to move forward into Europe. This was what he had always known and prophesied; he conveniently forgot that Soviet conquests and ambitions in Europe owed infinitely more to himself than to Stalin. Uninvited and unaided, the Red Army would not have dared attack Estonia, let alone Poland. It was now that the Führer finally resolved upon the destruction of the Soviet Union before it became an uncontrollable menace to German plans. On 18 December he issued the notorious *Weisung Nr. 21: Fall Barbarossa*. The Soviet Union was to be obliterated as an effective military agent on the Continent by overwhelming onslaught of German armed forces. Preparations were to be completed by 15 May 1941, and the concentration of forces would be ordered eight weeks before the attack took place. Victory seemed certain; as Himmler pointed out in a secret speech to Party officials, 'Russia is militarily quite harmless. Her officer corps is so poor that they do not even bear comparison with our NCOs; her army is as badly equipped as trained. They cannot possibly be any danger to us'.[9]

Totally unaware of the fearful forces about to be unleashed against her, the Soviet Union continued over the winter of 1940–41 to conduct a forward foreign policy, particularly in the Balkans. When British troops landed in Greece to assist in repelling the Italian invasion of 28 October, the Wehrmacht began massive preparations for a counter-stroke. There was a great build-up of troops in Romania, and arrangements were made for transit through Bulgaria. All this in addition provided a pretext for explaining Germany's crucial interest in the whole Balkan region and those two countries in particular. Dekanozov, who had become Ambassador in Berlin, protested that his government 'considered the appearance of foreign military forces on Bulgarian territory as a violation of its security interests'. This view was summarily rejected by the German Foreign Office, and the German Embassy in Moscow was instructed on 22 February 1941 to release the ominous information that Germany now had 680,000 superbly-equipped troops in Romania, which were 'more than enough to meet any eventuality in the Balkans from any quarter whatever'.

This and other German rebuffs did not prevent the Soviets from continually reasserting their claims in the Balkans, particularly Bulgaria. On 25 March the Soviet Foreign Ministry declared that Turkey could count on Soviet neutrality if anyone attacked her – the aggressor envisaged being clearly Germany. Finally, on the night of 26–7 March an internal coup in Yugoslavia overthrew the Regency, which had been ready to collaborate with the Germans. The new government was preparing to resist German demands, and looked to the USSR as an ally. Now the Soviets pressed boldly forward, and just after midnight on the morning of 6 April a Yugoslav-Soviet Treaty was signed, to a fanfare of publicity in the Soviet press. Though the Treaty in no way bound the Soviet Union to military intervention, the commitment was clear, and was intended as an incitement to Yugoslav resistance.

Hitler's response was swifter even than usual: within six hours of the signature of the Yugoslav-Soviet Treaty thirty-three German divisions irrupted across the Yugoslav frontier, while Stukas dropped out of the sky on to helpless Belgrade. A prophetic prelude to an infinitely vaster operation under preparation was the almost total destruction of the Yugoslav Air Force on the ground. While Hungarian and Italian forces struck from north, west and south, German troops based in Austria, Romania and Bulgaria drove deep into the country. Yugoslavia fell to pieces under these hammer-blows; within a week Belgrade had surrendered, and just eight days after the invasion the Royal Government sued for peace.

The attack had been characteristically launched on a Sunday. Molotov did not return to Moscow until that afternoon, to be greeted with the news by von Schulenburg. The Foreign Commissar thought Germany's action 'extremely deplorable', but did not mention the Soviet-Yugoslav Pact, which was forgotten as swiftly as it had been conceived. Stalin had deceived himself very badly. His subsequent actions betray bitter regret at the rash policy he had recently adopted, and a desperate anxiety to restore the Nazi-Soviet Alliance to its former equable course. As for the German invasion of Yugoslavia, that was relegated to an article on the back page of *Pravda*.

Stalin's seemingly forward policy did not derive from any access of resolution or feeling of increased strength. He had been simply following his usual policy of fishing in troubled waters, and was taken utterly by surprise at the degree of German resentment – to say nothing of this fresh evidence of the ferocious vigour of German arms. For nearly a year Germany had scrupulously observed their Non-Aggression Pact. She had been most obliging over the Soviet request to retain the strip of Lithuanian territory due to be handed over to Germany. For once Stalin's habitual caution had begun to desert him. Hitler had treated him as an equal, and he began to feel like one. Many of his enemies, external and internal, had been laid low during this extraordinary year. With the passage of time he almost forgot that the division of labour had been scarcely equitable. It was the Germans who had defeated the armies of Poland, Denmark, Norway, Holland, Belgium, France and Britain. Apart from the inglorious Finnish campaign, Soviet arms had been stained only with the blood of thousands of Polish, Baltic and Bessarabian civilians and prisoners-of-war.

Boldness unchallenged can prove an intoxicating draught. A year before, Stalin would no more have thought of interfering directly in the affairs of Bulgaria or Yugoslavia than with those of Paraguay. True, his various demands were firmly rebuffed by the Germans. But their replies had been polite, and no harm could come of asking. When Molotov visited Berlin, he was sarcastic and aggressive in his demands. Despite this, the dreaded Führer (Molotov had been openly apprehensive before their first encounter)[10] had been politely moderate in his replies. Molotov was not to know of the hidden rage and contempt seething beneath the surface, and became quite cocksure. His confidence increased with every hour, and on his return to Moscow he invented his famous *réponse d'escalier* to Ribbentrop: 'if the British have lost the war, why are we in this air-raid shelter and who is dropping those bombs?'[11] Soviet forthrightness did not appear to have aroused any resentment, and Ribbentrop in particular had oozed charm previously reserved for purchasers of his employers' champagne.[12]

The Soviet tactic (well-nigh universally employed) of demanding twice what they wanted and being content with half, had for once gone seriously astray. Hitler had no intention of conceding anything to an ally whom he rated many degrees lower than Mussolini, and was angered by what he saw as an emerging Soviet threat. In reality there was no threat, only a rather pathetic hope of setting everyone by the ears and picking something out of the confusion. Stalin's own racial theories had led him to believe that the Serbs would put up a more effective resistance than the French,[13] and that Hitler's armies would become bogged down in a prolonged Balkan conflict, of which Britain would doubtless take advantage. It is not true that Stalin hoped in this way to delay or destroy the coming German invasion of Russia, for as yet he had no idea that any such event was pending.

Nothing had happened as he had prognosticated. Not only was

Yugoslavia's army utterly routed, with 340,000 prisoners taken to 151 German dead, but the Wehrmacht had simultaneously invaded Greece. By the end of April the gallant Greeks had surrendered, whilst their British ally evacuated what troops she could to Crete. There was no more Balkan imbroglio for Stalin to meddle in; from the Peloponnese to the North Cape, Germany bestrode Europe in triumph.

The Soviet dictator hastened with undignified speed to mend his bridges. On 13 April the USSR signed a Treaty of Neutrality with Japan, thus securing her eastern flank. Strange scenes took place when Stalin and Molotov went to bid the Japanese Foreign Minister farewell. They reveal very clearly the extent of Stalin's fear and respect for the two great military powers hemming in his country from east and west. The scene at the Moscow railway station was described in an unpublished report by Jack Scott, reporter for the London *News Chronicle*:

The departure of the Japanese Minister, Matsuoka, from Moscow was one of the most astonishing performances I ever saw in almost ten years in Russia . . . At 5.50, when the train should have left, the cars began to arrive. First Count von der Schulenburg, German Ambassador, then Italian Ambassador Rosso, then numerous Japs with suitcases and handbags. The number of plainclothes men on the platform multiplied several times, there were about fifty diplomats, and as many plainclothes men. Matsuoka arrived at 5.55 and walked up the platform flanked by his Ambassador and Minister. They shook hands in a rather dazed fashion with Schulenburg and Rosso . . . I was getting cold . . . so I turned to go . . . and started down the platform. I went about five steps and almost bumped into someone. It was Stalin, dressed in his military coat, in leather boots and overshoes, and his brown vizored cap. Molotov was two steps behind him . . .

The Japs came to life with a bang when Stalin and Molotov made their appearance. They surrounded the Soviet leaders, and began shaking their heads slapping their backs and talking in several languages and in very awkward voices. Then we realized why the Japs had seemed dazed. They were all very definitely in their cups, even some of the Russians. So, as the foreign diplomats and we newspapermen gathered around craning our necks, Molotov and Stalin began embracing the Japs, patting them on the shoulders and exchanging expressions of intimate friendship. As few of the Japs or Russians could speak each other's language, the most frequently heard remark was 'ah . . . ah'. Stalin went up to the aged and diminutive Japanese Ambassador-General, punched him on the shoulder rather hard, with a grin and an 'ah . . . ah', so that the General, who has a bald and freckled pate, and is not more than four feet ten in height, staggered back three or four steps, which caused Matsuoka to laugh in glee.

I was wedged in between half a dozen towering German military men dressed up like Christmas trees, trying my best to see what was going on. Stalin's plainclothes personal guards looked very worried because they could not keep their eyes on Russia's bull-necked and grey-haired 'vozhd'. The Japanese Military Attaché staggered up to the very dapper and fastidious Barkov, chief of Protocol, and began slapping him on the back.

Just then Stalin detached himself from the crowd of Japanese, and came over toward me. Stalin is a small man, about five feet five or six in height, and has a very distinctive bear-like walk. He swings his arms very low, and puts his right arm forward at the same time as the right foot, instead of vice-versa like most people. The sixty-one year old Stalin swung up to Colonel Krebs, Assistant German Military Attaché, who was standing right in front of me, tapped him on the chest and looked up at his face searchingly for a few seconds. 'German?' he said, not sure of the uniform. The six foot German stood at attention and mumbled out an embarrassed affirmative in bad Russian. 'Ah ha', said Stalin, slapping him on the back and shaking his hand, 'Budyem s vami druzyami', 'We will be friends with you.' The Colonel said nothing and Stalin laughed, and patted and shook for a dozen seconds.

This incident impressed me tremendously. He made this declaration of friendship, for a German soldier he did not know, with sincere conviction. He would like very much to be friends with Germany . . . I am convinced that Stalin really wants to get along peacefully with Germany. If there are hostilities between Germany and Russia, I am convinced that it will be Germany that fires the first shot.

The crowd surged along down the platform. Everyone was craning their necks, trying to understand what Stalin was saying. Molotov was exchanging 'ah ha's' with Tatekawa. For the third time Stalin shook Matsuoka's hand, and then embraced him. 'We will organise Europe, and Asia,' he said in a somewhat cracked voice, in his imperfect Russian. 'We will even organize the Americas', he added, and burst into a guffaw, which Matsuoka echoed.

Then Stalin and Matsuoka got into the special car which was to take the Japanese across the Trans-Siberian. I did not get in the car, but one of my Japanese colleagues who did told me that Stalin said to Matsuoka – 'You are an Asiatic, so am I. Out there, outside the windows', he said, waving his hand toward the platform where the diplomats were standing asking each other what they had heard, 'are all those Europeans.' Again raucous laughter from both the Asiatics.

Finally, after Stalin and Molotov had spent nearly twenty minutes on the station platform, the train whistled and pulled out, an hour and twenty-five minutes late. Stalin ambled down the platform, got into his huge Packard armour-plated car with its three-inch thick machine-gun bullet proof dark green windows, and his squad of guards, and drove off.

We went to the press department and spent the evening trying to get the story through the censorship. We did not succeed. Stalin and Molotov had come to the station, and the atmosphere had been friendly; that was all we could say.[14]

Others present witnessed further effusive demonstrations of friendship. Stalin swore to Matsuoka that he was a loyal supporter of the Axis powers and an opponent of England and the United States. Then, in case that were not duly reported to the right quarter, he took the first opportunity of hugging the surprised aristocrat, von Schulenburg; 'We must remain friends, and you must now do everything towards that end!' he pleaded.[15]

Two days later the Commissariat for Foreign Affairs suddenly informed the German Embassy that a long-standing dispute over the German-Soviet frontier in Lithuania would be settled exactly in accordance with German wishes.[16] Finland had recently been a prime bone of contention between the Nazi and Soviet Governments. Now Stalin rushed to patch up good relations with the Finns, settling the border question and that of the Petsamo nickel concession, ending hostile propaganda, and dispatching a large wheat consignment, hitherto delayed.

In every aspect of his relations with Germany, Stalin took ostentatious care to demonstrate that Molotov's seeming intransigence and rapacity over the previous winter had all been a laughable misunderstanding. On 6 May Stalin became Chairman of the Council of People's Commissars, i.e. Prime Minister. Though he had been dictator for comfortably more than a decade, he had up to this point been content with a nominally subordinate role. As von Schulenburg noted, this move was intended to indicate a replacing of Molotov's hard-bargaining attitude with one much more conciliatory to Germany. At the May Day parade Stalin had taken the unusual step of standing next to Dekanozov, Ambassador to Berlin. On 18 April a new Commercial Agreement had been ratified, and the flow of vital raw materials to Germany continued as in the earlier heyday of good relations. Dr Schnurre at the Wilhelmstrasse noted with pleasure,

> I am under the impression that we could make economic demands on Moscow which would even go beyond the scope of the treaty of January 10, 1941, demands designed to secure German food and raw-material requirements beyond the extent now contracted for. The quantities of raw materials now contracted for are being delivered punctually by the Russians, despite the heavy burden this imposes on them, which, especially with regard to grain, is a notable performance, since the total quantity of grain to be delivered under the agreement of April 10 of this year . . . amounts to over 3 million tons up to August 1, 1942.

Finally, Stalin took ostentatious steps to display his contempt and dislike for Britain and her allies. The Soviet Government had maintained diplomatic relations with Vichy ever since the fall of France. Now, on 6 May, recognition was withdrawn in Moscow from the legations of the exiled governments of Belgium, Norway and Yugoslavia. Some weeks before, the pro-Nazi Rashid Ali had staged an anti-British coup in Iraq, and on 12 May the Soviet Government opened diplomatic relations with his short-lived regime. The British Ambassador, Sir Stafford Cripps (formerly a rather uncritical admirer of the Soviet Union, now thoroughly disillusioned), was virtually ignored by the Soviet Foreign Office (*Narkomindel*) and lived an isolated existence within his Embassy compound.[17] When, on 11 June, Cripps was recalled to London, an authoritative Soviet press statement took the opportunity of denouncing British provocation and extolling the unbreakable unity binding Germany and the USSR: ' . . . according to the information at the disposal of the U.S.S.R.,

Germany is abiding by the provisions of the Soviet-German pact of non-aggression as steadfastly as is the Soviet Union, in view of which, in the opinion of Soviet quarters, rumours about Germany's intentions to disrupt the pact and to undertake an attack upon the U.S.S.R. are devoid of any foundation . . .'[18]

Molotov deferentially handed a copy of this reassuring farrago of self-deception to von Schulenburg on 14 June. By that date Stalin had been well-nigh swamped by reports from all sides warning him of the imminent danger. In March 1940, acting on intelligence received from the Berlin Embassy, United States Secretary of State Cordell Hull informed the Soviet Ambassador of German invasion plans. Ambassador Oumansky turned very pale and promised to inform his government.[19] In April Churchill warned Stalin of British Intelligence reports of threatening German military preparations.[20]

Soviet GRU, NKVD and diplomatic sources dispatched accurate information increasing to a flood in the weeks before Operation Barbarossa. On 15 April a German reconnaissance aeroplane made a forced landing near Rovno. On board were found a camera and exposed film.[21] On 6 May the Soviet military attaché in Berlin reported that the attack would take place on the 14th (Hitler's 'Directive' of 18 December had envisaged 15 May as the day), and his deputy updated this estimate to 15 June.[22] Between April and June the famous spy Richard Sorge dispatched a series of warnings from Japan, containing accurate information culled from the German Embassy in Tokyo.[23] The Soviet military attaché in Vichy France sent a succession of similar reports over a period of months.[24] On 11 June Stalin was informed that the German Embassy in Moscow had received orders to prepare to close down.[25] Military intelligence from units stationed in frontier areas reported the ever-increasing access of military strength opposite, and intensification of German aerial reconnaissance.[26]

Ambassador von Schulenburg himself, who was strongly opposed to war with the USSR, approached Dekanozov (who happened to be in Moscow) and in a long interview tried desperately to persuade him to induce his masters to begin negotiations with Hitler. Short of actually revealing the invasion plans, he did everything he could, but Dekanozov mulishly refused to be drawn.[27] Finally, in the last days before the attack, NKVD frontier guards repeatedly intercepted heavily-armed infiltrators who had crossed the borders preparatory to destroying bridges and other communications.[28] Marshal F. I.

Golikov, who was chief of Military Intelligence from July 1940, has confirmed that an enormous amount of information on the German preparations was received: quite enough to draw the correct conclusion.[29] Stalin possessed more than enough information to form a correct assessment of the situation, but declined to act on it.[30]

Stalin had, for whatever reason, succeeded in deluding himself that relations with Germany would proceed on the same comradely path as before. This is not to say, however, that he was unaware of the atmosphere of crisis that hung over Eastern Europe. Security was what he longed for. Hitler had provided that in the outside world, but what of the Soviet peoples themselves? It was precisely at a period of international tension like this that cracks might be expected to appear in the structure of Soviet society.

The most dangerous regions were those border areas recently absorbed. In the Baltic States and Poland there must still be many prepared to intrigue with neighbouring states for a restoration of their independence. That was only the beginning of the danger. In 1917 a disproportionate number of Bolshevik leaders, Stalin included, had been drawn from the 'national minorities', where nationalist sentiment had combined with social resentment to form an explosive mixture.

From the moment that Hitler had presented Stalin with the Baltic States, NKVD agents had set to work there drawing up lengthy lists of suspect persons. These were people whose social origins or political and religious affiliations made them a potential danger. There was no question of restricting the purge to those who opposed Soviet power. The wording was precise; people appeared on the swiftly-growing lists 'regardless of concrete data concerning their anti-Soviet activities'. By August 1940 the three countries had been wholly absorbed into the Soviet Union, and preparations got fully under way. In November the NKVD drew up a list of classifications of persons to be 'registered for later arrest or deportation to Russia'. There were no less than twenty-nine such categories.

Socially dangerous categories included members of every non-Soviet political party from Trotskyists and anarchists to Social Democrats and Liberals. Active members of Jewish organizations such as the Bund, Zionists, etc., were of course especially suspect, as were freemasons, 'mystics', and anyone who had occupied any sort of noteworthy office in government or public administration from policemen to prison warders. Anyone who escaped that net would also have to ensure that he had never taken part in a strike since the Soviet invasion, was not of aristocratic descent, was not a member of the diplomatic service, did not represent a foreign firm, had not been an official of the Red Cross, was not a *relative* of someone who had fled the country, a *relative* of someone the Soviet authorities had convicted on some other pretext, or a *relative* of someone who had engaged in anti-Soviet propaganda.

For six months the NKVD worked under great pressure to draw up their lists, and on 31 May People's Commissar Merkulov ordered that 'Persons of anti-Soviet leanings engaged in active counter-revolutionary agitation are to be prepared for deportation into remote areas of the USSR'. On 4 June, Serov, Merkulov's deputy, issued detailed instructions as to the conduct of operations. Stringent measures were expounded, ensuring that disturbances were avoided as the prisoners were taken to entraining points. Especial attention was drawn to the instructions for separating husbands and wives, who were destined never to see each other again:

. . . it is essential that the operation of removal of both the members of the deportee's family and its head should be carried out simultaneously, without notifying them of the separation confronting them . . . The convoy of the entire family to the station shall, however, be effected in one vehicle and only at the station of departure shall the head of the family be placed separately from his family in a car specially intended for heads of families. During the assembling of the family in the home of the deportee, the head of the family shall be warned that personal male effects must be packed in a separate suitcase, as a sanitary inspection of the deported men will be made separately from the women and children.

In the middle of June, as the Wehrmacht moved up into its final jumping-off positions at the frontier, the NKVD launched the operation. It followed the cruel pattern of its myriad predecessors and successors, and need not be described in detail here. In the early hours of the morning hundreds of trucks drew up outside marked households. White-faced families descended with what luggage they could take, and were transported at speed to nearby railway stations. A lorry-driver later recalled his journey.

A family was taken in its home in Kadriorg: husband, his pregnant wife and their one year old child. The women and the child

were put beside me in the driver's cabin and I was told to drive
slowly. The woman cried all the time and was on the verge of
collapse from tiredness. In the harbour she begged that her
husband should be allowed to come to her in order that she could
leave the child in his care, but this was not permitted . . .

Husbands, wives and generally children were all separated and
placed in cattle-trucks, fifty or sixty to a truck, without room to sit or
even crouch, without food, water or sanitary facilities, and with a
journey lasting weeks lying ahead. Very many died of thirst in the
appalling June heat. Babies were born whose brief existence on earth
consisted of a few hours or days in the heat and stench of a swaying
truck. Their tiny corpses accompanied their mothers until the trainload of living and dead reached its Siberian destination. There, as an
eye-witness related,

When we arrived, a pole was struck into the ground and we were
told: 'Now you can live here'. First of all we had to make dug-outs
for ourselves but the ground was frozen and work terribly hard.
The guards had a canvas tent which was covered with moss and
snow. We built a house for the guards, an office, a kitchen, and a
bathhouse. We had to sleep in the mud of our dug-outs. In the
morning we were glued to the frozen ground. Men died like flies
but new prisoners were brought to replace them.

At least they were spared the sight of their suffering wives and
children, who naturally succumbed much more swiftly. The overall
death-rate was reported to be in the region of 25 to 30 per cent, for
which the NKVD had to compensate by regular fresh deliveries.

It was not only the victims themselves who endured suffering
impossible to describe effectively, but all those who were left behind. An Estonian woman described how she 'walked the street next
day, and met everywhere people with tear-stained faces. Fathers,
mothers, sons, daughters, friends, acquaintances – everybody had
someone to mourn after'. The nightly terror had just begun. Who
knew that he or his family was yet safe? At the same time as the terror
struck in the Baltic States, a similarly massive operation swung into
action in Soviet-occupied Poland – the fourth since the Soviet invasion in September 1939. There too no family was exempt. Thousands more disappeared for ever. A large proportion of those abducted consisted of 'children from summer camps and orphanages'.[31]

An enormous swathe of Europe's population, stretching from the Gulf of Finland to the Carpathians, had been devasted by this man-made destruction. It resembled nothing so much as the ravages of the medieval plague, vividly described by Boccaccio at the beginning of the *Decameron*, or the aftermath of a major war. Latvia lost 14,693 of her citizens; 8,436 males and 6,257 females. Of these, no less than 3,065 were children, half of them under six years old. But age weighed less than nothing in the eyes of the rulers of Soviet Russia. It was the same regime which had conducted a 'Children's Purge' in 1935; which had in the same year publicly imposed the death penalty on children over the age of twelve,[32] and could cheerfully impose a three-year sentence on a small schoolboy – no trial, he was just whisked uncomprehending off to gaol, tears streaming down his face and his satchel still on his back.[33]

34,260 Lithuanians were engulfed by the same fate, 12,000 Estonians, and unknown thousands of Poles. Those who had vanished without trace were in the hands of GULAG, whence few returned alive. Those who stayed at home were by no means sure of a safer existence. They too were in the hands of the NKVD. When Riga Gaol was opened after the German invasion, Latvians discovered amongst the day-to-day equipment of the Soviet state, 'instruments to break the bones of shins and arms, to squeeze testicles, to pierce the soles of feet and to pull off the nails and skin from hands, to squeeze the main nose ligament until the victim bleeds profusely, electrical appliances, etc.' Recovered corpses resembled cuts of meat displayed on a butcher's slab. What prisoners had undergone was indescribable, even by the survivors. As a Pole in an NKVD prison recalled, 'The cries which we heard were not always even recognizably human. Once, when a man was being tortured, he cried out not like a man but like a slaughtered pig.'[34]

For a whole week the Soviet transport system from the western frontier regions to the interior was crowded with slow-moving railway convoys shifting slave shipments east, through Leningrad, Minsk, Moscow, Kiev.[35] This was the week of 14 June to 22 June 1941, and such were Soviet priorities. Just across the frontier, more than three million men in field-grey, backed by 3,350 tanks, 7,184 pieces of artillery, 600,000 lorries and 2,000 warplanes, were making last-minute preparations as they awaited code-word 'Dortmund' – the signal for the invasion of Russia.[36] At 3.30 on the morning of Sunday 22nd the western sky was lit up by the flashes of thousands of

German guns. Half an hour later the German Ambassador broke the
news to Molotov in the Kremlin. 'Surely we have not deserved that!'
exclaimed the frightened Foreign Commissar.[37]

XIII
Friends Fall Out

For weeks before Hitler's dawn attack on Russia on 22 June 1941 colossal preparations had been in progress making ready for the greatest single operation in the history of warfare. For six months thousands of trains had been rolling into concentration areas in Poland, East Prussia and Romania. By mid-June huge accumulations of infantry, tanks, artillery, transport vehicles, horses and ammunition had been brought up within striking range of the frontier. Before the first pallid light stirred in the eastern sky on the 22nd, some 3,200,000 men were gathered, their every move in the coming strike planned meticulously down to the last round of ammunition. Every precaution had been taken to ensure that Red Army intelligence was kept in ignorance of these preparations, as a major factor in the success of Operation Barbarossa lay in the element of total surprise. It was vital to cause maximum confusion and panic among the unwieldy masses of the Red Army, and to wipe out advanced units of the Red Air Force before their warplanes could take to the air. Only in this way could Soviet armies be cut up piecemeal and swallowed up behind swiftly-moving armoured thrusts. If the Red Army were merely rolled back, it would not be long before Russian distances, climate and manpower began to slow a German advance to a halt. The event proved successful beyond all expectation.

Despite intelligence warnings at all levels which had poured in over recent weeks, most Soviet units were utterly unprepared for the stunning blow which fell upon them. Strict orders had been received not to fire on German aircraft (an officer who disobeyed was nearly shot himself), trench-digging and mine-laying had been abruptly cancelled on 21 June, and Soviet warplanes were openly massed on aerodromes where they presented a marvellous target for the Luftwaffe. Officers of varying ranks had at considerable risk to their lives issued orders to guard against surprise attack, but overall the atmosphere was summed up in Timoshenko's and Zhukov's order issued three hours before the onslaught: 'The assignment of our forces – not to give way to provocative actions of any kind which might produce major complications'.

When the attack came, confusion became infinitely worse confounded. The blazing Upper Inkerman lighthouse generously guided German bombers and mine-layers sweeping out of the darkness on to Sevastopol, where ships of the Black Sea Fleet lay moored. At a vital bridge across the Bug, German troops invited NKVD frontier guards to discuss 'important business' with them, and then machine-gunned them as they crossed over. The unmined bridge fell at once into German hands, and trucks, tanks and guns began rolling across towards the sleeping Soviet 4th Army. At the key fortress of Brest-Litovsk there were Rifle Regiments with no rifles, and artillery with no shells. A devastating German barrage began to open on the unprepared defences, causing extensive casualties and chaos. (The last time Brest had come under fire, Soviet and Nazi troops had been besieging it as comrades-in-arms.) As for the Red Air Force, by noon that Sunday it had lost 1,200 machines, most of them obliterated on the ground. Perhaps the heaviest casualties in those first days of war came from NKVD frontier guards, who found the German infantry rather harder to stop than the unarmed Jewish refugees they had been machine-gunning the previous year.[1]

Soviet lack of military preparation for the attack is too notorious to require retelling here. That an attack might come suddenly and without declaration of war was clear, if only from the circumstances of the Nazi invasion of Poland and the Soviet attack on Finland. After the Finnish débâcle considerable improvements had been effected: hundreds of officers were returned to service from the camps and gaols in which they had been languishing since 1937 and 1938; equipment and training were overhauled and improved; and disciplinary measures were increased to improve officers' authority. But, as Professor Erickson suggests, 'there were, in effect, many debates but few decisions, and even those were questionable'.[2] The weaknesses remained much more remarkable than the improvements. The huge territorial gains provided by the agreement with Hitler proved to be a military liability, contrary to what Stalin and much Soviet historiography was to claim later. Politically, the Pact had supplied Germany with two allies, Finland and Romania, and removed the 'trip-wire' of the armies of Poland and the Baltic States.

Then the shifting of the frontiers hundreds of miles to the west led to a situation where the old border defences had been largely dismantled before the new ones were properly equipped. There had been ample time to construct a new defensive line, but Stalin's indecision, coupled with the reluctance of officials to take responsibility within the socialist bureaucracy, and the wasteful and clumsy exploitation of slave labour on construction work, all combined to leave defences in a state of grotesque disarray. In all other fields, armaments, communications, location of strategic industries and supply-dumps, and military discipline and skills, the Soviet Union lagged ludicrously behind Germany, despite her immense superiority in manpower and resources. As Khrushchev was to complain, 'Even the tsar, when he went to war against Germany in 1914, had a larger supply of rifles than we had the day after Hitler invaded'.[3]

Overall, the Soviet Union was quite unprepared to defend itself against a major attack. But what is still very striking is the total surprise with which Stalin greeted the invasion, and his refusal to adopt even minimal precautionary measures. On 18 June the Japanese General Yamashita travelled by train from Berlin to Moscow. Gazing impassively from his slowly-moving carriage, Yamashita noted in the German countryside and towns the ceaseless activity of Wehrmacht units moving up towards the frontier. But after Brest-Litovsk, on the Soviet side, he saw no military preparations whatever. The fields slept empty under the summer sun as the remaining hours ticked by towards Barbarossa.[4] Then, four days later, when the same fields were shadowed by the passage of thousands of Luftwaffe bombers droning eastwards towards Riga, Minsk, Kiev and Vinnitsa, the helplessness of the malicious but hamstrung giant became apparent. Some half-hearted precautions had been authorized: Luftwaffe reconnaissance planes infringing Soviet space could be requested to land; black-out measures were ordered to be prepared (but not implemented); and, with three hours to go, an order placed troops in western military districts on combat readiness. This did not provide overmuch time for units to get ready, particularly those which received the order only *after* the attack was launched. There was in fact no battle-plan; only Stalin could issue instructions when the time came. Matters did not look propitious, particularly when recent Red Army manoeuvres and war-games had invariably resulted in German victories.[5]

From beleaguered command-posts, field telephone centres and

bomb-ravaged aerodromes, messages poured into Moscow: 'We are under fire. What are we meant to do?' Back came the reply, 'You must be feeling unwell. And why isn't your message in code?' The Commander of the Black Sea Fleet, Admiral Oktyabrsky, was informed in reply to his urgent appeal for instructions that Sevastopol was not under attack. He was not reassured: bomb explosions were rattling his headquarters' windows even as he spoke. The future Marshal Malinovsky was told, on asking whether he could return fire if the enemy attacked, 'Do not give in to provocation, and do not open fire!'[6]

The cause of this well-known surprise and confusion remains in part a mystery. There is no doubt that Stalin was taken entirely off his guard, and panicked. But why, when the whole world and many of his own military men held their breath in anticipation of such a blow, was Stalin alone seemingly impervious to warnings? What was he doing during the days of silence which followed the opening of Russia's agony? The Soviet dictator was, after all, probably the most suspicious and cautious despot in history. He trusted neither family, friends nor colleagues, and his idea of countering a threat was to liquidate it even before hostility became a potentiality. Why did he fail to react to the most dangerous and in many ways the most obvious menace of his whole career?

It fell to Molotov to broadcast the startling news on 22 June, and it was not until 4 July that Stalin himself mumbled out his own rambling radio appeal to the Soviet people. What he was doing in the interval remains obscure. According to Khrushchev, he collapsed into panic-stricken immobility, blurting out that 'all which Lenin created we have lost forever', and waiting prostrated with fear until members of the Politburo came to demand that he take action to organize resistance. At this time he was 'paralysed by his fear of Hitler, like a rabbit in front of a boa constrictor'.[7] Since then senior Soviet military men have published memoirs indicating that Stalin was not wholly removed from the conduct of the war, and that he took part in some discussions. It is difficult to know what value to place on testimony necessarily loaded with later political implications. As Roy Medvedev has recently written, 'Most testimony of this kind, however, was simply part of the renewed campaign to rehabilitate Stalin in the second half of the 1960s'.[8]

The answer seems to be that he was in Moscow at the time and most likely played some part in discussions, if only because of his extreme terror of being left alone. But he was almost stunned with terror then and for some time after. To his sister-in-law he cried out frantically in August: 'Things are very, very bad! Get yourself evacuated. One can't stay in Moscow.' Later the poor woman received a ten-year sentence for having witnessed this pathetic spectacle.[9] According to a senior NKVD officer, the terrified tyrant closeted himself with his predecessor's mummy in the Red Square mausoleum; perhaps he was inquiring of that great man how to preserve 'all which Lenin created'.[10] Just outside in the barricaded square, aeroplanes were drawn up by the Cathedral in case there was need for a hurried departure.[11]

For some time the armies fought, collapsed and surrendered without any direction from central authority. Between 24 June and 2 July he signed no documents.[12] Khrushchev suggested that he did not wish to incur responsibility for disasters at the front, but it is scarcely likely that that would have been his first consideration at such a time. He was gripped by blind terror, greater even than that which led to the massacre of the Polish officers at Katyn. As on that occasion, he feared that the whole structure of 'Lenin's inheritance' was crumbling away. In 1946, secure after victory, he wrote,

> As is well known, in the foreign press one often finds statements that the Soviet system is a 'risky experiment' doomed to downfall; that the Soviet system is a 'house of cards', having no roots in real life, and is only linked to the people by means of the Cheka; that it would only need one little push from outside for this 'house of cards' to be shattered in pieces.[13]

As Professor Ulam notes, Stalin 'was reliving his own fears and humiliations of the first years of the war', when he had indeed believed Soviet rule to be dangerously fragile.[14]

This well-grounded fear explains much of Stalin's reaction to the invasion. He dreaded the invader greatly, but his prime fear was reserved for the Russian people itself. The country seemed to be disintegrating precisely in the manner his worst nightmares had foretold. But there is one aspect that remains mysterious. Stalin had felt the Pact with Germany to be the safest and most profitable course for his country to take, and from his point of view the decision was probably wise. His grovelling appeasement of Nazism, particularly after April 1941, was based on a realistic consciousness of weakness. Soviet military feebleness and lack of effective preparation for war was merely a reflection of the barbarity and backwardness of the regime.[15] Given these factors, it was inevitable that the superbly led, equipped and trained Wehrmacht should drive the Red Army before it. This fully explains Stalin's panic during the early days of the invasion, but still leaves two other questions unresolved. Why did Stalin refuse to believe the increasing stream of warnings that Hitler was preparing his attack, and why did he refuse to issue effective orders for his troops to retaliate should the attack take place? As Robert Conquest points out, this is 'one of the most peculiar things about his entire career. The man who had never attached the slightest value to verbal assurances or paper promises does really seem to have thought, or hoped, that Hitler would not attack Russia'.[16] Hitler had attacked Bohemia, Poland, Holland, Belgium, Yugoslavia and Greece; all without any declaration of war, and with the use of overwhelming force from the first moment. Even if he thought an attack highly improbable, he must surely under any normal circumstances have thought it possible.

It has been suggested in explanation of Stalin's indecision on the night of 21–2 June 1941 that he had hitched the USSR so firmly to the Nazi wagon that he had left himself no leeway for manoeuvre, and he feared that any sort of unusual mobilization or military activity might provoke the war of which he was so terrified. There is clearly a great deal of truth in this, but it is surely insufficient as an explanation. It is difficult to see how Stalin could under any circumstances have thought that taking elementary precautions (such as dispersing and camouflaging air force units) would provoke a war; nor why he was so adamant in the early hours of the invasion that troops should not return fire. Stalin himself instructed them 'not to give way to provocative actions of any kind which might produce major complications'; at 3.30 a.m. on the 22nd, as news of the attack began coming in, he grudgingly instructed units to defend themselves, but not to advance across the frontier. It was not until 9.15 that evening that he came to grips with reality and ordered a general counter-attack.[17]

Stalin's words provide a tantalizing hint of his conception of the crisis. Clearly, he believed that a dissident element in the German High Command was attempting to provoke a war, contrary to the policy of the German Government. If the Soviet response were to be restrained, the Germans would be able to check their 'wild men'. For all his realism, Stalin viewed the outside world in large part through

Marxist spectacles, from which just such a distorted picture could emerge. But it is still not sufficient as an explanation. Hitler, despite similarities between the rival ideologies, was a rabid anti-Communist, and had provided a succession of proofs of his ruthlessness and lack of scruple. How did Stalin, the most suspicious of men, come to abandon even the most elementary precautions, and indeed become persuaded that war with Germany was *impossible*?

It is highly unlikely that we shall ever know the answer to this question, but it is tempting to speculate a little. I think it will be conceded that it is improbable that Stalin merely selected one hypothetical projection of Soviet-German relations, and then cheerfully abandoned any precautionary anticipation of alternatives. Stalin's instructions carry the implication that he possessed information denied to his generals which made his interpretation correct. If so, it must have been very authoritative evidence indeed, outweighing as it did all the reports he had received concerning the Barbarossa preparations. This is confirmed by Stalin's reaction to the attack. He behaved not as one receiving news of a contingency long dreaded as a possibility, but with total astonishment and disbelief. Counterbalancing evidence for a time seemingly outweighed even the fact of the invasion itself. What was that evidence? It is possible that Stalin was the victim of a bold Nazi deception operation. There was only one person who could halt a German invasion should anti-Bolshevik generals form a conspiracy to launch one unauthorized, and that was Hitler himself. Roy Medvedev suggests that Stalin never trusted Hitler, and was 'playing a very dangerous, complicated, and in his own view cunning, game with Germany . . . '[18] This seems to be nonsense. Within a month of the invasion it was Stalin himself who confessed bitterly to Harry Hopkins that 'he trusted that man',[19] and in a speech on 6 November 1941 he implied that it was only the attack which converted the USSR from friend into enemy.[20]

It sounds as if Stalin may have received a personal assurance from Hitler that he would never go to war with the Soviet Union, together with warnings of a possible generals' plot to provoke a conflict against the Führer's wishes. If so, there were reasons why he should choose to believe in Hitler's good faith. As long before as 1935 Hitler had indicated that Germany and the Soviet Union could become friends only if the latter were to abandon her policy of international subversion and become a respectable military despotism no longer threatening her neighbour's stability.[21] The ferocious purges of the

next few years afforded proof that this was coming to pass, and
Stalin's dismissal of prominent Jews in April 1941, and assumption
of the titular as well as real headship of government in May, was
probably intended to convey the message to Hitler that he was indeed master in his own house.

Well before that, Hitler had provided convincing marks of his
tender regard for Stalin's safety. Marshal Tukhachevsky, Deputy
Commissar for Defence, had long excited feelings of hatred and fear
in Stalin's breast. He was everything that Stalin detested: he came of
noble blood, was handsome and immensely strong, and possessed a
formidable military talent.[22] When he was first appointed to command in 1925, Stalin expressed fear that here was material for a
potential Bonaparte.[23] Nevertheless it was not until twelve years
later that Stalin felt able to strike, and in 1937 Tukhachevsky was
charged with conspiring with Nazis to overthrow the state, and executed. Though no open trial took place (possibly because Tukhachevsky was too tough to be brought to 'confess'), Stalin possessed a
remarkable dossier documenting the Marshal's negotiations with
Nazi representatives.

This had been procured by Reinhard Heydrich, sinister chief of
Germany's security service, the *Sicherheitsdienst* (SD). He had been
approached by a Russian émigré, General Skobline, who claimed to
possess documentary evidence of the conspiracy to overthrow Stalin.
Heydrich was delighted with the information, which would enable
him to strike at the German General Staff, whom he felt to be obstructing Nazification of the armed forces. Heydrich passed the
dossier to Hitler, adding doctored evidence further incriminating the
German generals. Hitler at once saw that he held Stalin's fate in his
hands. Should he allow the conspiracy to proceed or not? He decided
a Stalin-dominated Russia was of more value to Nazi Germany than a
powerful military dictatorship. Fearful that his generals might warn
Tukhachevsky, Hitler ordered the whole business to be withheld
from them. Heydrich cleverly leaked the documents to Stalin via
President Beneš of Czechoslovakia in the middle of May. Next
month Tukhachevsky was dead, and Stalin followed up with the
notorious purge of most of his officer corps.[24] Meanwhile Heydrich
proceeded with measures for the removal of General von Blomberg,
Minister for War, and General von Fritsch, Commander-in-Chief of
the Wehrmacht. Within a few months they had been forced into
retirement.[25]

It is still unclear whether Tukhachevsky was really planning a *coup*, or whether the whole plan originated in the imagination of the NKVD or SD, who had differing motives for concocting it. What matters is that Hitler and Stalin believed in it, and that they had narrowly escaped a very serious conspiracy by the General Staffs of both nations, directed against their respective political leaderships. Not for the last time, the Gestapo and NKVD found themselves working in harness. There was nothing essentially surprising in the idea of conspiratorial links between the German and Soviet generals, as up to 1933 they had co-operated closely in secret training and arms production. A German report noted that Tukhachevsky had expressed admiration for the German Army as the foremost fighter against world Jewry, and that the Wehrmacht in turn strongly sympathized with his plan to replace Stalin's rule with a military dictatorship.[26]

If, in 1941, Hitler had warned Stalin that conspiratorial elements in the German High Command were planning some sort of provocation on the frontier, it can be seen that even the mistrustful Stalin had strong reasons for accepting the good faith of his fellow-dictator. Had he not saved him from an identical threat only four years earlier? Hitler was, after all, a realist who must see that Stalin, who had dismissed Litvinov and other Jews from office and who had most loyally sustained the Pact in face of much internal opposition, was an ally worth preserving. The German generals had opposed Ribbentrop's peace policy (so Stalin believed),[27] but Hitler was as determined as he was to preserve the alliance 'cemented by blood'. All in all, there were many good reasons for Stalin to repose faith in his friend's assurances.[28]

For the parallel with Hitler's warning over the Tukhachevsky 'plot' to be exact, one would expect to hear that rebellious elements in the Red Army were believed to be conspiring with their German counterparts. This in fact seems to have been the case, at least in Stalin's heated imagination, as in the days immediately preceding and following the invasion he launched sweeping arrests and executions within the upper echelons of the Red Army and Air Force.

The suggestion (it is no more) that Hitler sent personal assurances to lull Stalin's suspicions as Barbarossa got under way would clarify many points otherwise obscure. It would explain Stalin's insistent belief that the attack was a military provocation, not to be responded to. It would explain the ferocious military purges within the Red

Army at the time, and the fact that the NKVD kept a very strict and suspicious eye on the movements of Red Army units near the frontiers.[29] The German Foreign Office was bombarded by telegrams from a frantic Stalin, desperate to know what was going wrong.[30] Then again, Stalin's *only* positive response to insistent warnings on the eve of the invasion was to order Moscow's anti-aircraft defences to be placed on alert![31] Clearly, he believed that the real danger menaced the Kremlin, not the frontiers. Above all, the suggestion that Hitler himself provided Stalin with the story of the coming 'provocation' explains why Stalin continued so confident in his belief even after German guns began firing. He had the best authority for doing so!

There were several channels by which Hitler could have passed on his reassurances to Stalin. The incrimination of Tukhachevsky had been handled in total secrecy by a senior NKVD officer dispatched by Yezhov to Berlin, who negotiated directly with Heydrich at SD Headquarters.[32] Contacts between the two security services increased after the signature of the Pact. A Gestapo representative travelled regularly to L'vov in 1940 to consult with People's Commissar Ivan Serov on the question of repatriation of Poles. In spring of the same year, as Khrushchev relates, 'I remember Stalin once told me that Hitler had sent a request for a favor through secret channels.'[33]

It might be questioned why, if Stalin was really deceived in this way, no record of the exchange came to light later. But there is no reason to suppose more than a handful of people were involved. Any subordinate Gestapo officials who fell into Soviet hands in 1945 would have received short shrift at the hands of the NKVD. Heydrich himself was assassinated in 1942, and Stalin and Hitler had extremely strong motives for *not* revealing what had happened. Stalin could have no desire for the world to see how easily he had been duped, nor the extent to which he had lain under Hitler's influence. For his part, Hitler maintained that the attack on Russia had occurred in response to a Soviet military threat, and he could not afford to leak a story proving the falsehood of this claim.[34]

All in all, Stalin regarded himself as Hitler's junior partner, and was prepared to believe anything his Führer told him.[35] Whether Hitler lent a personal hand in deceiving Stalin over the coming invasion may never be known, but seems more likely than other explanations of Stalin's delusion.

One thing seems certain. Initially, at least, Stalin was convinced that he had a great deal more to fear from the Russians than the Germans. With Hitler he might yet be able to patch up a compromise peace; but if the Russian people took this opportunity to rise from their knees, it required little imagination to guess what the consequences would be for him. If the Germans had any sense at all, this would be the first weapon they would surely look to as they penetrated deeper into the country. To most outsiders the country appeared monolithic, a nation irrefrangible save in the unlikely event of a foreign conquest. To those on the inside the picture was less comfortable.

The whole country was indeed saturated with Marxist terminology and Leninist institutions, so that no one at any moment could forget that he was living in the world's first socialist state. After the ending of Lenin's compromise NEP policy, Soviet rule became so extraordinarily oppressive as to lose any appeal save to those who increasingly gained personal profit from the system. By 1941 the nation had known man-made tribulations unexampled in history, and it would be incredible to suppose that the regime rested on any popular basis.

At the same time there is no way of assessing precisely what the population felt. There must always be a residue of acceptance of the *status quo*, however abominable, and a cowed people had come in a strange way to live with the all-pervading lie. The state apparatus appeared so omnipotent as to make opposition pointless, and the continuing destruction of millions of people, together with the savage repression of the remainder, seemed much like an inexplicable natural disaster such as a plague, an earthquake, or a particularly atrocious winter. It were idle to live out one's life repining against the natural order of things, and one had to be thankful that life was tolerable at all. The generation is still living that underwent this experience, but the survivors are hard put to it to recall what precisely were their overall feelings towards a system which there was then no safe means of criticizing, even in one's thoughts. Today in the Soviet Union older people prefer to forget their time of troubles, and the younger generation knows much less about conditions in their country in the 1930s and 1940s than does educated opinion in the West.

Nevertheless, with all these reservations, common sense dictates that very few could have wished for the return of such a system were its power to be temporarily removed or dissolved; and that, given opportunity and time to shake off deeply-ingrained instincts of fear and passivity, most citizens of the USSR would have welcomed the overthrow of their slave-masters and torturers. Concrete evidence pointing in this direction is provided by the dawning self-confidence of Red Army prisoners held by the Finns in 1940, and by the reaction of millions more prisoners-of-war taken by the Germans. But for day-to-day purposes there is no doubt that a black and helpless apathy lay upon the Russian people. To some this is indicative of a gaping flaw in the Russian national character. They should perhaps ask themselves how long Americans, British, French or Germans would hold out against the weaponry of oppression described in an earlier chapter.

Whatever illusions of the altruism of Soviet socialism lingered amongst the people at large were not shared by their rulers. On 15 December 1941 Vyshinsky spoke frankly to the Polish Ambassador. Warmed by copious libations of vodka, he remarked jovially,

'You people laugh. That was a great inspiration to me. I love cheerfulness and laughter.'

The Pole was surprised. 'But surely the Russians laugh and make merry too?'

'You're wrong, Ambassador. You don't know the Russians.' Vyshinsky's face flushed heavily; he leaned across to me, and said in a strained tone: 'I assure you the Russians are a gloomy people; sluggish, lazy, dull, dirty, without initiative, hostile to any form of cultural progress.'

'But you're exaggerating, Commissar', I interrupted, suspecting that he was trying to provoke me into some indiscretion.

'Never! Nothing can be got out of this people by ordinary means. It can be raised to a higher level only by such a form of government as Stalin applies. Only by force and compulsion! And that's why I'm such a fervent adherent of Stalin and defend his system.'[36]

Vyshinsky's openness may have owed as much to the political situation as to the liquor he had imbibed. By the time he was speaking to Ambassador Kot, the Wehrmacht had taken 3,800,000 prisoners: a greater number than the entire German army of invasion itself. Ill-equipped, poorly led, and deprived of intelligible orders from above, the Russians had been encircled and generally provided with no alternative to surrender.

Large numbers, however, had welcomed capture. They knew nothing of Nazism except what official propaganda had told them. For six years Germany had been reviled almost as much as British imperialism or American capitalism. Then, for nearly two years, the Germans had become honourable allies, battling against the British and French plutocracies. Now, while the Soviet Government boasted that relations had never been better between the two countries, German troops suddenly appeared, declaring their intention of liberating the country from Bolshevism.

As tattered columns of retreating Russians trudged away from the battlefield through the yellow dusty roads of Byelorussia, Luftwaffe planes passing low overhead rained down thousands of leaflets on the bewildered throng. After more than twenty years of Soviet power, thousands of Russians saw openly published expositions of what all knew but none dared say. German propaganda leaflets put their case with telling force:

STALIN – THE BRAZEN CHEAT!

What an outcry was raised in its time about the so-called Great Stalin Constitution! And what in fact was achieved? All constitutional guarantees remained on paper. Try to talk in the Soviet Union about 'freedom of speech' (Article 125), risk taking advantage of 'freedom of conscience' (Article 124) – the NKVD will swiftly demonstrate what is meant by 'inviolability of the individual' (Article 127). All Stalin's other promises are proved to be equal swindles! The peasants were promised the land they tilled, but instead they were enslaved in collective farms. For the workers, instead of freedom of labour and raising of living standards, they prepared Stakhanovite slavery . . .

STALIN – THE PITIFUL COWARD!

Why does Stalin hide himself within the Kremlin walls behind the broad backs of his bodyguards? He is terrified of his own colleagues, thirsting to avenge their slaughtered friends and comrades. He is fearful of the people's rage, awaiting the hour of reckoning . . .

STALIN – THE FAILED GENERAL!

Considering it the propitious moment, Stalin at the peak of the conflict between Germany and England began to concentrate his forces on the German frontier. However, the devilish plan was discerned at the right moment by Germany, which was ready to anticipate the stab in the back. Stalin boasted that he would 'destroy the enemy on his own territory'. But things turned out otherwise! The German forces, convinced of the justice of their actions, proceeded to defeat the Red Army and to seize one Soviet region after another. All the Baltic States, Byelorussia, the town of Smolensk, and most of the Ukraine up to Nikolaev and Krivoi Rog have been taken by German forces. Leningrad, Moscow and Kiev are threatened next.

FURTHER RESISTANCE IS USELESS![37]

Except for the allegation that Stalin had been preparing aggression against Germany, every charge made in this broadsheet was entirely true. Indeed, as the most important weapon in the Soviet arsenal of oppression – slavery – was omitted, it may even be said to have erred on the mild side. Never in the history of warfare had a government furnished an invader with such a potent indictment. It can scarcely be wondered at that thousands of Russian troops, encircled in the forests of Byelorussia or trudging hopelessly eastwards, took advantage of the attached pass which urged them to surrender under promise of good treatment. There are doubtless those who would term them traitors, but men like Kuzma Belogrudov, standard-bearer of the 436th Rifle Regiment, might have found this lofty moralizing a little less than adequate to the situation. At fifty, he had spent twelve years in a GULAG camp, where he had had all his teeth smashed out and two ribs broken. He had lost four sons and two brothers, done to death in the cellars of the NKVD. At Mogilev, on 19 September 1941, he joined the rest of his regiment in marching out to join the Germans. Precisely what he was betraying he might have found hard to answer.[38]

On surrendering, Russian soldiers were generally received by sympathetic German officers, often native Russian-speakers from the Baltic States. Either unaware of, or reluctant to confront, the realities of Nazi policy, these encouraged their prisoners to believe that a German victory would result in a free, national Russia. The ghastly fate of Russian prisoners in German camps was as yet unknown, as of course was Hitler's larger plan for the destruction of Russia and the Russian people on a scale rivalling Stalin's.[39]

Those Russians who, ignorant of the nature of National Socialism, looked to Germany as an ally might perhaps have claimed a consistency denied to some of their critics. In 1919 Winston Churchill had declared roundly,

> Of all the tyrannies in history, the Bolshevist tyranny is the worst, the most destructive, the most degrading . . . A way of atonement is open to Germany. By combatting Bolshevism, by being the bulwark against it, Germany may take the first step toward ultimate reunion with the civilised world.[40]

That National Socialism was Bolshevism's blood-brother could not as yet be known to Russians. A dreadful awakening was imminent.

XIV
War on Two Fronts

After eleven days' silence Stalin emerged and summoned up courage to address the Soviet people. Only once before had he ever spoken on the radio,[1] and listeners were startled to hear the harsh Georgian accent which he had never been able to shake off. His tone was monotonous, weary, punctuated by staccato pauses, and by the clink of a glass and gulp of water as he steadied his nerves with a drink. The ungainly, frightened dictator was no orator. His speech was couched in the form of a pathetic, almost grovelling appeal for help, together with large doses of Soviet and personal clichés, lists of towns and peoples, and impotent threats against the 'German fascists'.

'Comrades! Citizens! Brothers and sisters! Warriors of our army and fleet! I am addressing you, my friends!' he began, with unprecedented camaraderie. Much of the speech was concerned with explaining away the Nazi-Soviet Pact and prognosticating the German downfall. But the most significant threats were clearly directed against his own countrymen. In the same plodding tones, with an undercurrent of menace, he warned that 'in our ranks there must be no moaners and cowards, panic-mongers and deserters; our people must know no fear in fight and must selflessly join our patriotic fight for liberation against the fascist enslavers.' He went on to urge strengthening the Red Army's rear, and emphasized that 'We must organize a ruthless fight against all disorganizers of the rear, deserters, panic-mongers, rumour-spreaders; liquidating spies, diversionists, enemy parachutists, and providing swift aid in all this to our destroyer battalions.' The last was a clear, if oblique, reference to the work of the NKVD, whose activities will be examined shortly. 'We must swiftly drag before the Military Tribunal all those whose panic-spreading and cowardice hinder defence work, no matter who they are.'[2]

The quavering notes of self-pity, cowardice and impotent hatred permeating this speech aroused widespread disgust and ridicule amongst its listeners. To millions it conveyed an unintended message of leaping hope. Over primitive loudspeakers in factories, collective farms and slave-labour camps boomed the minatory message. As an inmate of Vorkuta recalled,

> We stood in silence, our eyes on the ground, but I knew that every prisoner there was suddenly thrilled by a spasm of hope, with that bewildered blindness of slaves for whom any hand which opens the prison gates is the hand of Providence itself.

'They are coming!' whispered a myriad voices, driven by despair to welcome aid, whoever brought it.[3]

During those first days of Russia's agony, her leader had remained closeted from the outside world. Terrified that the NKVD network which held the state together might snap under the weight of the invasion, he could yet think of no alternative policy to tightening those bonds more harshly than ever. 'Beat, beat, and again beat' was all the statecraft he knew. Passively, even fearfully, he watched Beria apply the clamp.[4] Massive recruitment to increase the enormous NKVD army at once began throughout the countryside.[5] Moscow was placed directly under the control of NKVD General Silinov, 'and every district, urban and rural, had its own NKVD headquarters, although public order could have been adequately safeguarded by militia units alone'.[6] The United States Embassy noted the exceptional activity of the political police in questioning and arresting citizens during the first days of the invasion, and Party functionaries were issued with guns to defend themselves against the people.[7]

The Red Army was a prime object of suspicion. In 1927, at a meeting of the Central Committee, Stalin had proposed the expulsion of Trotsky from the Party. The defiant tribune sprang to his feet, crying out at Stalin's faction:

> You are a group of talentless bureaucrats! If one day the fate of the Soviets lies in the balance, if war breaks out, you would be totally incapable of defending the country and achieving victory. Then, when the enemy is a hundred kilometres from Moscow, we will do what Clemenceau did in his time: we will overthrow this useless government; but with this difference, that Clemenceau was

content to gain power, whereas we would in addition shoot this
band of despicable bureaucrats which has betrayed the Revolution.
Yes, we will do it![8]

It is unlikely that Stalin forgot this threat. Trotsky himself, whom
he seems to have feared much more than Hitler,[9] had been liquidated
a year before; but as the Germans pressed closer to Moscow he felt
his apprehension grow. (Here one can at least say for Stalin that the
Soviet Union would very likely have fared even worse under
Trotsky, who in 1934 was still advocating the primacy of cavalry in
modern warfare: 'one horse is needed for three soldiers'.)[10]

The military purge of 1937 revealed the extent to which Stalin
mistrusted and feared his own army, and in June 1938 appeared
confirmation that the fears had seemingly been justified. In that
month General Lyushkov, head of the NKVD in the Far Eastern
provinces, defected to the Japanese. He took with him invaluable
knowledge of the disposition of Red Army forces all over the Soviet
Union. More than this, he claimed that a wide-ranging conspiracy
existed among senior Red Army officers, with the aim of overthrowing Stalin. Details of Lyushkov's revelations were passed back
to Moscow by the famous spy, Richard Sorge. The Moscow Centre
showed signs of great excitement, urging Sorge to obtain further
details.[11] (It may not be without significance that details of
Lyushkov's revelations have disappeared from a Foreign Office file
on the subject.)[12]

As the Germans drove the Red Army headlong before them and
neared the gates of Moscow and Leningrad, Stalin began wholesale
purging and killings of officers up to the rank of general. This was
the only incentive known to him when dealing with failure; but a
strong additional motive must have sprung from apprehension of the
conspiracy Trotsky had prophesied, and which his own fears pictured all too clearly. Why else would he have ordered numbers still
held in NKVD camps and gaols to be executed?[13]

More effective and realistic measures for keeping the soldiers
firmly under control included the reintroduction of political commissars. As Professor Ulam has remarked, the varying fortunes of
this set of functionaries provide an accurate barometer of Stalin's
alternating periods of fear and confidence. Introduced by Trotsky in
the Civil War to check the loyalty of former officers of the Imperial
Army recruited to lead the Red Army, they acted as spies, checking

continually on the loyalty of all ranks, and possessing authority superior to that of the regular officers.[14] They were abolished after the Civil War as being no longer necessary, but were reintroduced at the time of the Army purge in 1937.[15] The disastrous course of the Finnish War secured their further abolition in 1940; but with Stalin's frantic renewal of fear and suspicion in the following year, commissars were reintroduced on 16 July 1941.[16]

The commissars were headed by a peculiarly repulsive creature of Beria's, L. Z. Mekhlis, whose spies penetrated every mess-room and field headquarters. Even the bravest and most devoted officers were subjected to continual harassment, insults and interrogation. When General Gorbatov returned wounded from the front in July 1941, he unwittingly infringed NKVD etiquette by not reporting at once to Mekhlis. 'Evidently he did not learn enough in Kolyma', murmured the Commissar sourly to a colleague – a reference to Gorbatov's recent emergence from the notorious gold-mining slave-labour complex.[17] Though there were exceptions, who behaved gallantly under fire and loyally assisted their fighting colleagues, the majority were loathed and despised for their arrogant ways and suspected cowardice.[18] Nor was resentment confined to private grumblings: soldiers frequently killed their political watchdogs and deserted to the enemy.[19]

Despite these measures, Stalin's obsessive conviction that Red Army men of whatever rank would seize any safe opportunity to join the enemy impelled him to take further precautions. NKVD border guards had the primary duty of insulating the Soviet Union from the outside world. For this reason they maintained no direct contact with advanced military units, and vital information of enemy incursions often reached the latter only by way of Moscow.[20] But regular NKVD supervision began to appear inadequate to Stalin as the War went on, and a year later an important subdivision was created. This was the Main Administration of Counter-Intelligence, better known under the ominous acronym accorded it by Stalin himself: SMERSH (from the words *smert shpionam*, 'death to spies'). 'But', explained a former NKVD officer, 'its real task was not the apprehension and punishment of foreign spies; it was the detection of the slightest sign of disaffection, or even the expression of discontent, among the Soviet soldiers, sailors and airmen.' And a former SMERSH officer has elaborated further:

Their job was to prevent, or in the last resort to root out any elements in the army hostile to Soviet power. They kept an eye on everything and everybody, from commanders of fronts and marshals to the most humble soldier in a transport convoy. They also controlled all the political bodies in the armed forces. No one was above suspicion. A permanent network of informers was secretly recruited and maintained throughout the army.

A battalion watched behind every front, with its own arms, prisons and executioners. A frequent duty was to supply 'blocking detachments' – units whose job was to drive prisoners forward over minefields, or others dressed in white to attract enemy fire, and to shoot retreating troops.[21]

In September 1941 a Secret Military Order was issued (the first of many), ordering soldiers to kill themselves rather than surrender. Those who voluntarily surrendered would be punished if recaptured; in the meantime their families would suffer retribution. As a military doctor reflected, who was himself taken prisoner, such an order was easier to give than to obey. And who would benefit by such suicides?[22] Many have imagined that the purpose of this absurdly savage order was to compel Russians to fight on to the death. This, however, was only a subsidiary aim. Where it is not possible to escape, a prisoner-of-war is of course more trouble to the enemy than a suicide's corpse. The chief purpose was to prevent Russians defecting to the enemy, as it was presumed that anyone escaping Soviet power must necessarily wish to work against it. For the same reason the USSR had refused to accede to the 1929 Geneva Convention on Prisoners-of-War, and denied prisoners any comforts from home or from the International Red Cross. Nazi cruelty to Russian prisoners resulted in millions of deaths – a result greatly to the satisfaction of the Soviet Government, which had also done its bit to bring about so convenient a solution.[23] On 6 November 1941 Stalin announced that the Soviet Union had '350,000 killed, 378,000 *missing*, and have 1,020,000 wounded men. In the same period the enemy lost in killed, wounded and *prisoners* more than 4,500,000 men' (my italics).[24] It will be noticed that Germans became prisoners, whilst Russians just disappeared.

Stalin went on to deride the German idea that 'the precarious state of the Soviet system and the Soviet rear' would result in nationalist and peasant uprisings, enabling the Wehrmacht to advance to the

Urals, and claimed that the peoples of the USSR formed 'a single unbreakable camp'.[25] But he was far from being as confident as he claimed. In the tense weeks preceding his speech, his 'lieutenant Poskrebyshev spent hour after hour at the telephone, getting information from every member of the Central Party Committee and from every Party Secretary as to what the mood of the people was and whether the masses were loyal to Stalin'.[26]

It was evident to all that that loyalty was a highly questionable factor. Three days after war broke out, observers in Moscow noted that there was none of the enthusiasm one would expect in the capital of a country facing the greatest war in its history. There were no patriotic demonstrations, whether organized or spontaneous – only fictitious reports of such in the press.[27] As the Germans drew nearer, a regular panic set in. Thousands of Government and Party officials either fled eastwards or dispatched their families there together with trucks and cars overflowing with all the household treasures they had accumulated during twenty years of the rule of the proletariat. (Starving peasants stopped and looted many of these in the countryside beyond.) The NKVD panicked, having no inclination to renew contacts with their brethren of the Gestapo. Files in the Lubianka were burned, and for three remarkable days (16–18 October) Moscow was virtually unpoliced. Shops, warehouses, the homes of the rich, even the deserted British Embassy, were broken into and looted. Frightened crowds thronged the streets and packed the railway station. In luxury restaurants, officials who had not been able to escape liquidated their fears with vodka, assisted by prostitutes who already no doubt anticipated new customers. The Mikoyan meat-combine was stripped of its last sausage, and a pallid, starving crowd surged into the Mayakovsky sweet factory. The Marxist apparatus vanished in a trice, as if it had never been. Party cards were discreetly burned, and slogans scrubbed from walls. Then, on 18 October, the military position stabilized, and the NKVD reappeared in town. Following a special decree from Stalin, thousands of people were summarily shot, and Leninist norms were restored. For a brief moment Stalin and his aides had been given a real glimpse of what would happen if the NKVD apparatus were dismantled. As many said at the time, five hundred German parachutists could have seized the whole city.[28]

On every side the Party and police appeared momentarily isolated. Public reaction was sullenly hostile to the regime, discontent rang-

ing from cynical remarks about the Leader to open prayers for a
German victory. Opinion in the countryside was particularly strong,
where peasants angrily criticized Poles released from GULAG camps,
because they wished to renew the struggle against Germany. An
observant Polish officer, who travelled widely in Russia at that time,
was struck by the way

> the lower strata of the Russian population . . . were all impressed
> by the spirit of revolt, by the hatred of the regime and the un-
> popularity of the war, which were everywhere in evidence during
> those first few months when, as a result of the chaos caused by the
> German offensive, the iron grip of the NKVD was relaxed.[29]

To this general hatred of the Marxist regime was added strong
nationalist sentiment among the various minority peoples, who
identified Marxist savagery with Russian rule. In the Baltic States
and the Ukraine hundreds of thousands of people flocked to welcome the Germans, and volunteer for the various legions and mili-
tias recruited by the Wehrmacht and SS.[30] Even far-off Kazakhs,
Kirghiz and Turkomans prayed for the arrival of the German deliverers, and Poles held in camps there contemplated joining local
nationalist opposition and fighting their way out to Persia.[31]

All this was no more than Stalin had expected for many years.
Special military tribunals were set up by the NKVD in every town
and village remaining under Soviet control, and thousands of people
suspected of disloyal views were shot or transported to camps. A
mere mention of the Molotov-Ribbentrop Pact, or even of the
blundering Marshal Voroshilov, could earn the rash speaker a ten-
year sentence. Dragooning of the population was greatly increased in
order to keep the masses disciplined. Pointless ditch-digging and
other 'defensive' tasks were allotted to large numbers not already
engaged in war work.[32]

On the Volga lived a colony of Germans, whose ancestors had
settled there in the time of Catherine the Great. An obvious focus of
fear in this panic-stricken atmosphere, they were ordered to be
banished to Siberia. It was claimed that 'thousands and tens of
thousands of diversionists and spies' among them were planning an
uprising in favour of the Germans. This might have seemed odd,
since 99.7 per cent of them had voted for Party candidates in the last
election, so the NKVD satisfied themselves by providing a primitive
pretext. A training aeroplane with its marking painted out was flown

over the capital of the Volga-German Republic, Engelsstadt. It was then claimed to have contained the first load of German agents. There were more than 400,000 of these Germans, and they were transported to concentration camps in Kazakhstan and other desolate regions. There they were joined by about the same number again of people of German descent from other parts of Russia. Their treatment on the journey and at their destination was savage; at one camp two or three men were taken out to be shot almost every night for a year and a half. In 1943 many of the survivors were dispatched to the front for work in labour battalions, and after that to slave-labour in Vorkuta or Karaganda – the wives, in the usual spiteful manner, being separated from their husbands.[33]

During those early months until the German attack was checked before Moscow, the police regime lashed out in its bewildered state at all sections of the subject population. Nowhere did the flail fall more heavily than on the hidden slave-population, and it was clearly on them that the main focus of Stalin's terror was directed. As a former Soviet official, then in Moscow close to the Government, wrote: 'Perhaps, in their nightmares, they saw twenty million slaves suddenly crashing through prison walls and barbed-wire enclosures in a multitudinous stampede of hatred and vengeance, in a flood-tide of destruction . . . '[34]

Most of the camps were in areas remote not merely from the Germans but from all human habitation. But a massive supply of slave-labour was engaged in work on the new frontier-defences, as well as on other projects in the Ukraine, Byelorussia and the Baltic States. Orders were passed from NKVD Headquarters to the GULAG Administration that all camps threatened by the German advance were to be evacuated eastwards. If that proved impossible, all the inmates were to be massacred.[35] The German attack had been so swift and unexpected that evacuation proved difficult in many cases. A German officer met a tattered column of five or six thousand of them on the road from Minsk to Smolensk. They had been working on the military aerodrome at Minsk when the Germans arrived and released them.[36]

They were luckier than many. In prisons and camps all over western Russia, nervous NKVD men set about fulfilling Beria's instructions before fleeing the inexorable advance of the German Army. Thousands of political prisoners of the Left were shot, lest they offer leadership to the uprisen masses (Trotsky's parting threat had not

been forgotten). In Minsk, Smolensk, Kiev, Kharkov, Dneprope-
trovsk and Zaporozhye virtually all prison inmates were slaughtered.
In the Kabardino-Balkar Republic hundreds of slaves working in a
molybdenum *combinat* were machine-gunned, by orders of the local
commissar, 'to the last man and woman'.[37] In the Ukraine a train was
evacuating a party of some five hundred slaves to the east. Suddenly
the NKVD guards heard the sound of artillery fire further up the
line. Suspecting they were cut off, they halted the train, surrounded
it, and ordered 'everybody out of the train!' A survivor recalled what
followed.

> Our door was opened and we received the same orders. People
> began to step down onto the railroad bed. Suddenly at some signal
> the guards opened up with submachine guns and machine guns
> which were mounted on the car platforms. The prisoners began to
> rush around. Some fell and were covered with blood. Some tried
> to hide under the wheels; others climbed back into the cars. The
> firing continued. When the shouts outside had subsided, the
> guards came to the doors of the cars and began to shoot inside.
> The walls were pierced with hundreds of bullet holes. Sometimes
> they simply threw grenades through the open doors.

Eventually the guards departed, believing they had fulfilled their
orders. In fact fourteen wounded men had survived amongst the
heaps of dead.[38]

Where there was no immediate danger of the Germans intercept-
ing the slave-cargoes, columns often moved on foot. A young Polish
lieutenant has given a description of a dreadful journey, in which
two thousand prisoners were driven by savage dogs (human and
canine) of the 207th Convoy Regiment, from Artemovsk in the
Ukraine for weeks eastwards into the steppes. A senior officer of the
NKVD guard made it clear that his task would be held satisfactory if
5 per cent of the captives survived the journey. This estimate proved
more or less accurate: after a few weeks of the journey only 550 men
of the 2,000 were still living. They were then crammed for a time
into two huts, in one of which the death-rate ran at ten to fifteen
every day. One half of the column had been halted in a great open
animal pen on the empty wastes between the Don and the Volga;
there for five days and nights they lay on the open ground in a
temperature that fell to 20° below, during which time they received
no food. At the end of this journey through the Valley of the Shadow

of Death, Lieutenant Solczynski was addressed by a Russian woman as 'daddy'. He asked her how old she thought him. 'Fifty', she answered. Before they set out he had been a youthful-looking thirty-one.[39]

In most cases, as in Kharkov, Uman, Rovno, and Tallinn prisons, the inmates were massacred hurriedly before the NKVD swiftly betook itself to a safer climate (those terrible Germans were drawing nearer). At Tartu 192 prisoners were shot, and their bodies thrown down a well. At Kharkov matters were simplified by tossing grenades into each crowded cell. On 28 June German soldiers in Dubno found the mutilated corpses of five hundred women and children.[40] On 26 June at Praveniškiai, near Kaunas in Lithuania, guards drove five hundred prisoners into the middle of the camp yard and machine-gunned them. At Tcherwene in White Ruthenia thousands upon thousands of Poles, Ruthenians, Ukrainians, Russians and Lithuanians were similarly mown down.

Occasionally the NKVD had time to pause in their retreat and conduct matters in a more leisurely and congenial fashion. In Lithuania, at the town of Telsiai, seventy-three prisoners were taken to a nearby forest at Rainiai. They were tied to trees, and there the guards experimented with various Soviet methods of prolonging death. Some had their eyes slowly gouged out. Others were scalped and had their brains squeezed out of their skulls. Men had their tongues torn out, their sides and legs slowly cut open, or had bayonets thrust into their mouths and down their throats. In most cases the bodies were covered with so many wounds that it was impossible to determine the precise cause or moment of death.[41]

Perhaps the worst – certainly the most notorious – massacre took place at the city of L'vov in the Ukraine. Several thousand prisoners of various nationalities had been gathered in the three main gaols. When news of the invasion arrived, large numbers were evacuated eastwards in train-loads of sealed cattle-trucks. At the same time it became clear to the authorities that the Germans might arrive at any moment, and Beria's order was instructed to be brought into effect. When the Germans did enter L'vov, on 29 June, they encountered a hideous spectacle. The whole city stank of putrefying flesh, and the prisons were surrounded by agonized relatives of those suspected of being held within. Next day a German Field Police Group began an investigation. What they found was described in a report drawn up a week later.

Very soon, in advancing into the cellars, we found a layer, composed of a viscous mass, into which the corpses had congealed. In the first prison, bodies were stacked four or five deep on the cellar floor. Some of the cellar doors had already been bricked up by the Russians. A large number of the bodies must have been buried in this way already sometime before war broke out, since putrefaction – as stated – had made great progress then. The number of people killed in the whole town of L'vov may be estimated at about 3,500.

In the second of the prisons . . . the impression gained on the first day after entering the city was: From the service wings of the prison, which were situated on the ground floor looking out on a courtyard surrounded by a wooden fence, one body after the other was carried into the yard. In this case, there was no doubt that the victims had been murdered only a few days before our capturing L'vov. The cellars in question had ceilings that were splashed with blood, and in a room which had apparently served for interrogations the floor was covered with a layer of dried blood that was 20 centimetres (about 8 inches) deep. The bolshevik hangmen had literally waded in blood.

Though most of the prisoners had clearly been massacred in haste (the NKVD Commissar fled so quickly he forgot to take his wife), others had suffered at length before having their lives mercifully extinguished. Men had had their sexual organs, and women their breasts, ripped or cut off. Eyes had been gouged out, bodies were beaten or crushed into unrecognizable masses of bones and flesh, and many of those still identifiable as human bore on their faces distorted expressions of unimaginable agony. A Polish lady, who visited the prison on 30 June,

> saw a table in a room covered with many corpses that had been slaughtered. The bodies gave the impression that the persons on and by the table had been beaten to a pulp. One dead man was seated in a chair, with a Russian bayonet sticking out of his mouth, that must have been pushed in by force. Hands and arms hung down in queer positions, as if they had been broken several times . . . I saw the dead body of a small girl, aged about eight years, hanging from the ceiling lamp. The body was unclothed, and the child had been hanged by a towel. The view was so terrible that I nearly fainted. Some people had to take me home. I have not

yet been able to this day to calm myself from the impression made by these terrible views.

Another woman saw yet more horrific sights.

Among other bodies, I saw that of a woman, whose one breast had been cut off, whilst the other one was deeply lacerated. Another woman's abdomen had been cut open, she had been pregnant. From the open wound the head of an unborn child stuck out. All the teeth had been broken from the mouth of a male corpse. A small girl was dressed on the upper part of her body, whilst the lower part was naked and smeared all over with blood, especially near her private parts, so that I had no doubt that a sexual crime had been committed against her.

Many cells contained corpses piled to the ceilings. Elsewhere the guards had partially incinerated them with petrol. One of the prisons was itself set on fire in order to destroy any survivors concealed under the 'mountains of male and female corpses'.

A remarkable specimen of Bolshevik ingenuity only came to light later. When searching out their victims before assembling them in the gaols, the NKVD had ostentatiously employed numbers of local Jews as informers and guides. This caused a ferocious outburst of anti-Semitism among elements of the great crowds afterwards thronging round the prisons, many of whom had lost relatives in those Soviet abattoirs. But in fact the Jewish informers had themselves been slaughtered by the NKVD after their work was completed, along with a number of Zionists already in their hands.[42] As an observant inhabitant of L'vov remarked, 'the Soviets made a special point of inciting one nationality against the other . . .'[43]

These revolting details are not printed here out of any desire for sensationalism, though in the writer's view we owe it to the poor victims that we understand something of what they suffered. Above all, it is crucial to an understanding of the war in the East to appreciate that Soviet forces were waging a war on two fronts. While the Red Army, appallingly badly equipped and led, struggled against the German invader, a bloody civil war was being waged by the NKVD against the unarmed population immediately in its rear. And of the two wars, it was undoubtedly that waged against the subject populations that represented the main priority in Stalin's eyes. NKVD and SMERSH troops of all ranks received up to twenty-five times the pay of regular soldiers, a commensurately superior food-ration, uniforms and equipment, and tended to be recruited from among the more reliable type of Red Army conscript.[44] In Chapter IV it was estimated that before the war the NKVD fielded some half-a-million troops, guarding the frontiers and GULAG camps, maintaining prisons and communications, and so forth. After the outbreak of war the numbers were immensely increased. A prisoner in one of the northern camps found 'something incredible in the arrival at Yercevo of fresh contingents of young and healthy N.K.V.D. soldiers to strengthen the garrisons of camps on the shore of the White Sea . . . ' This was within a fortnight of the Barbarossa attack, when the Red Army was reeling back in bloody confusion. The prisoner calculated that, as there were now two guards to every twenty prisoners, there could easily have been a million guards disseminated throughout all GULAG. Extraordinary though this estimate may seem, it need not be wildly out. Not only is there the observed increase in guards to take into account, but the fact that thousands of political prisoners were now regarded with too much mistrust to continue in various responsible, if lowly, posts in camps. These included Volga and other Soviet Germans, some Poles, and political offenders generally. They were sent out to work in the labour-gangs, and were replaced at their posts by 'free' officials, no longer available for other war work. Again, the GULAG working day was increased from eleven to twelve hours, which must have involved a corresponding increase in guard duties, and hence the number of guards.[45]

The GULAG authorities were not concerned merely with those camps which lay in the path of the German advance. In remote Kolyma, on the other side of the world, a prisoner listening to Molotov's plaintive broadcast on 22 June turned round to see a machine-gun being hauled up into one of the perimeter towers.[46] Far in the darkness of the North, beyond the endless tundra and on the edge of the ice-bound Arctic itself, lay the forced-labour camps of Vorkuta. Whilst the aurora borealis flickered out its eerie effects on a dark, frozen and silent world, thousands of slaves toiled in the coal-mines underground. Such a place was not likely to be high on the Wehrmacht's list of immediate objectives, yet it was felt an example should be made. A group of a hundred prisoners was chosen apparently at random, marched out into the tundra, and mown down with machine-gun fire. Thousands more perished in this way throughout the camps.[47] All these 'preventive' activities inevitably required very large numbers of extra guards, and replacements for the slaughtered slaves.

Here, then, were up to a million well-armed and trained troops busily engaged in fighting Stalin's secret war against the Russian people, who might otherwise have been thrown into the desperate conflict with the Germans. It should not be forgotten that it was at this very time that Stalin was frantically begging for British aid to stabilize the front. On 3 September he appealed in anguished tones to Churchill, urging that Britain launch a second front in occupied Europe within the next month or so. Ten days later he was even more desperate, begging for twenty-five or thirty British divisions to be sent to fight *on the Russian front*, arriving either at Archangel, or across the Caucasus from Persia. He continued pressing for this improbable expedition throughout the rest of the year.[48] That he dared not raise a comparable number of divisions from the enormous pool of trained and armed manpower maintained by the NKVD suggests that he considered *their* task at least as important as that of sustaining the disintegrating front line.[49]

It is worth recalling, too, that this war on two fronts was inextricably interlocked. The dual strategy frequently caused a clash of interests, one which seems almost invariably to have been settled in favour of the campaign against the internal 'enemy'. As the Soviet 4th Army battled against all odds to save L'vov, the city's NKVD was working for a whole week with machine-guns, grenades and high explosives in its frantic effort to liquidate thousands of Ukrainian prisoners. Thousands more were being transported east under heavy armed guard, and all NKVD forces were successfully evacuated immediately after completing the slaughter. The 4th Army was less lucky; repeatedly encircled, only a shattered remnant managed to cut its way out.[50]

During the first days of the invasion, Colonel-General Kuznetsov's troops on the north-western front put up unexpectedly tough resistance to the German Army Group North's irruption into Lithuania. Giant Soviet KV-1 and KV-2 tanks in particular took the Germans by surprise. In 'a fantastic exchange of fire' German anti-tank shells simply bounced off these armoured monsters. But as the battle raged with increasing intensity, von Manstein's panzers broke their way through and then raced for the Dvina bridges. Soviet forces broke up in increasing disorder, and by 25 June were no longer operating as a cohesive whole. German superiority in training and tactics had taken their customary toll, but major supportive factors in the disaster were the almost total breakdown of communications on the Soviet side and exhaustion of fuel and ammunition within two days of fighting.[51] Yet at the very moment of this life-and-death struggle, the NKVD had free use of the main railway lines linking the Baltic States with the interior. The mass purge which they had launched on the night of 13–14 June continued as if no invasion had taken place, and truckloads of kidnapped Balts took up much of the scanty railway system at a time when Kuznetsov's troops desperately needed every shell and gallon of petrol they could lay hands on. Documents detailing these rail shipments later fell into the hands of the Germans. In Latvia the picture is as follows. On 22 June, the day of the invasion, German bombs rained down on military aerodromes from Riga to Kronstadt and Panzer Group 3 slid over the Niemen, whilst a desperate General Kuznetsov was still awaiting a response from Moscow. On that day six trainloads of Latvian prisoners, heavily guarded by men of the 155th Special Battalion of the NKVD, moved slowly out of Skirotava Shunting Station and steamed eastwards through meadows and forests. At the old Soviet frontier the difference in track gauge compelled a day's delay while the prisoners were being transferred to a Soviet train. Two days later, as the Soviet 8th Army poured back in disarray to the Latvian capital, Riga, at least six more trains carrying prisoners moved out of Riga itself and Skirotava. On the 27th, with the Luftwaffe in control of the skies and the sound of guns very clear in Riga, prison trains again left Riga for Pskov.[52]

It is only necessary to extend this picture from the Baltic to the Black Sea, and to imagine the number of troops, trains and trucks involved in these bloody but unmilitary tasks, to envisage the appalling waste of manpower and *matériel*, and misuse of communications, it involved. In Solzhenitsyn's short story, 'An Incident at Krechetovka Station', Lieutenant Zotov, the deputy station commander at a railway junction just behind the front line, is represented as witnessing the continual passage eastwards of trainloads of ' "returnees" – troops who had been surrounded, had capitulated to the Germans and after being retaken by Soviet forces were being shipped off to the detention camps.' A typical cargo was a thirty-truck trainload of such prisoners, guarded by armed NKVD 'bluecaps'.

Altogether, it may be no exaggeration to suggest that the NKVD's 'internal war' during the first weeks after the invasion resulted in

Russian casualties comparable to those sustained at the same time by the Red Army. And of course the German Army never captured a tithe of the prisoners held by the NKVD. The wholesale massacres stemmed from a carefully-considered central policy. Beria was the immediate instigator, but he can scarcely have acted without Stalin's authority. Again, it is significant that important and intricate decisions were being made with regard to this problem at a time when Stalin could still think of no orders to give his embattled regular troops.

Massacres at L'vov and elsewhere were no improvised response to the German attack, but represented long-standing Soviet policy. As early as 1929 two thousand political prisoners (mostly Poles) were shot on the Solovetskiye Islands in the White Sea, following a rumour that a British ship was coming to rescue them.[53] This would appear to confirm the suggestion that it was the immediate fear of war which brought about the massacre of the Poles at Katyn and elsewhere in 1940.

Russians are often criticized by foreigners for their supposed sheep-like docility in face of oppression, and anyone who has studied the literature of Soviet slave-labour may with some justice find it incredible that an uprising of the unarmed, starving and debilitated mass of slaves could ever have been contemplated as a likely eventuality, let alone have constituted a real threat to 'Lenin's inheritance'. But, despite the obvious difficulties and disadvantages, the threat implicit in the existence of between ten and twenty million embittered enemies of Soviet power cannot be entirely dismissed. Despite the enormous resources of the Soviet state, whose *raison d'être* was in large part the continued suppression of the slave and helot population, revolt simmered endemically in the camps of GULAG. A mutiny in Kemerovo Camp in 1938, where prisoners refused to work until rotten food was replaced, was suppressed by firing-squads.[54] An uprising of Latvians at Kotlas in 1941, though easily and bloodily put down, may well have disturbed Stalin by its implications.[55] As an NKVD political officer remarked in Kolyma at that time, 'Counterrevolution is not asleep in the camp.'[56] In 1942 a much more serious revolt broke out at Ust-Usa, in the Pechora complex. Enterprising prisoners donned uniforms captured from NKVD men locked in a bath-house, seized arms, and set about spreading the revolt. Eventually all the rebels were killed, but only after prolonged fighting, involving the use of military aircraft.[57]

There was never the slightest hope of a general uprising on a par with those of ancient Rome. The camps were isolated in remote regions; the only route to Kolyma, for instance, was by sea. Above all, the prisoners were in such debilitated physical condition as to be incapable of sustained action. There was only one possible hope for liberation, and that lay in assistance from abroad. As an engineer in Yertsevo explained, 'War in Russia is the only possibility for the downfall of the present system . . . The Government and the Party cannot be overthrown without outside help.'

Prisoners in Vologda in 1942 put it more bluntly. 'When are these Germans coming?' was the question, repeated again and again. News of the German invasion had sent a *frisson* of hope throughout the camps.[58] A few years later hopes rose again; this time for the arrival of a British and American liberation army.[59] To many in the West, then and since, this eternal restlessness of Russian workers and slaves was troublesome and distasteful. These men (and women and children) were acting in opposition to their lawful government; *ergo*, they were traitors, who could quite legitimately be beaten senseless with rifle-butts and pickaxe-helves, thrown into cattle-trucks, and handed back to the NKVD for disposal. A Polish prisoner in Vorkuta saw things differently:

> I think with horror and shame of a Europe divided into two parts by the line of the Bug, on one side of which millions of Soviet slaves prayed for liberation by the armies of Hitler, and on the other millions of victims of German concentration camps awaited deliverance by the Red Army as their last hope.[60]

Fugitives from GULAG living in the West had for many years been pointing out that, given an opportunity, millions of Russian slaves would rise to assist a foreign invader.[61] It seems odd that nothing on these lines was attempted by the Germans. A plan was drawn up at one point to parachute 'battalions of specially trained Russians, commanded by Baltic German SS Leaders, in several of the large and more isolated Russian labour camps. The guards were to be over-powered and the inmates, in some cases numbering more than 20,000 or more, liberated and helped to make their way back to the settled areas'. Contact was actually made with one of the camps, but the scheme had to be shelved in face of Luftwaffe claims that they lacked sufficient resources.[62] Even armed, the slaves could not have been of great military value. But they were desperate men, millions strong, and could have caused chaos and devastation far in excess of their fighting capacity. Much of Soviet Russia's economy depended on slave-labour, and this would have been seriously disrupted.[63] Above all, the evidence suggests that such an uprising would have struck terror into Stalin and his aides more than any other measure. It is worth noting that Hitler also came to employ millions of Russian slaves, and was so nervous of a rebellion on their part that in 1942 military emergency plans were devised (Operation *Walküre*) to counter the threat.[64] But then the Allies, too, curiously made no attempt to enlist their aid, or that of the millions in German concentration and extermination camps.[65]

For Hitler, liberation of the slaves of GULAG held no great attraction. His aim, after all, was to enslave all Russians; a measure in which he was entirely successful, though not in the way he had intended. Stalin had believed the triumph of Nazism was worth assisting, as this would speed the ultimate downfall of the Western capitalist parliamentary regimes. In the long term he too may be proved right, though at a fearful cost to the Russians and other Soviet subject peoples. This was not a contingency likely to daunt him.

XV
A Pyrrhic Victory

Stalin and his advisers entertained deep fears in the autumn of 1941 that Soviet Russia was a house of cards, held together only by the bonds of the NKVD, which would require only one determined push to collapse as suddenly as had Imperial Russia in 1917. Propaganda appeals and military directives urging the carrying of the war on to enemy territory stemmed not from ignorant bombast, but from acute fear that the population waited only to link arms with the enemy.[1] Risings there were indeed, on a large scale. Within forty-eight hours of the invasion, Ukrainian nationalists flocked to arms. Elsewhere, the Lithuanians and Chechens did not even await the arrival of the Germans before rising in revolt.[2] A tremor ran through the country and its leader.[3] Could a blanket be somehow drawn over events after October 1941, it would surely be a rash historian who prognosticated from the then state of affairs a Soviet revival and ultimate victory. Foreign military and political observers were pessimistic in their assessments, allowing the USSR only a few weeks of resistance, culminating either in total defeat or the arrangement of a humiliating 'Vichy-style' peace.[4] Even those who, like former US Ambassador to Moscow Joseph E. Davies, professed a belief that the Red Army 'would amaze and surprise the world'[5] probably did so more out of ideological loyalty than realistic appreciation – and, in some cases, fear of what the Germans might uncover in NKVD archives.

What was the secret of Russia's stiffening resistance and ultimate recovery? To this type of unanswerable question the historian can reply only with indications of numerous converging factors, avoiding at the same time any notion that the recovery was inevitable or built into circumstances prevailing in June 1941. A succession of monthly Soviet Gallup Polls would provide a very imprecise guide; in the absence of anything remotely approaching such a gauge one can turn only to general trends of a political, military and psycho-

logical nature which provide some illumination, however inadequate.

Firstly, of course, there was the ever-ready Bolshevik instrument
of coercion. Stalin feared lest the bonds of NKVD rule be loosened,
but this did not mean that he would not continue to tighten the
clamps as far as they would go. NKVD and SMERSH control of the
armed forces extended from the widespread use of penal battalions[6]
to the deployment of NKVD battalions in the rear of the line and
continuing purges of all ranks.[7] The civil population, 'free' and
slave, was also subjected to greatly increased repression and polic-
ing.[8] Soldiers and civilians who fell into the hands of the enemy
were treated as real or potential traitors, and in the Crimea and
Caucasus entire nations held to have sympathized with the Germans
were subjected to slaughter and deportation.[9]

But the whip and the bludgeon alone could not beat the Nazis.
That was a lesson learned, however clumsily and belatedly, in the
Finnish War, where the old methods barely gained a patched-up
victory over that diminutive adversary. Vyshinsky had admitted to
the Polish Ambassador that Marxist doctrine was merely an outward
cloak legitimating the machinery of despotism. Stalin's first wartime
appeals to the Soviet people revealed clearly that he too was well
aware of the disparity between propaganda and reality. In his notorious radio speech on 3 July he addressed his listeners with unprecedented warmth as 'brothers and sisters . . . my friends!' Apart
from a passing reference to the great Lenin, he made virtually no
allusion to Marxist dogma or socialist practice. Instead he urged his
fellow-citizens to rise up and 'defend their freedom, their honour,
their country'. No reference was made to the invincible Red Army's
victories in Finland and Poland. He reminded Russians how their
forefathers, serving in the armies of the Tsars, had triumphed over
Napoleon and Kaiser Wilhelm. There was much talk of freedom,
independence, democratic liberties, and reminders that the gallant
peoples of Europe and America were their allies. Winston Churchill,
the man who had done his best to destroy the Bolshevik litter at
birth, received markedly greater praise than Lenin.

On 6 November, listening nervously for the approaching drone of
Luftwaffe bombers, the Father of Peoples gave his address on the
twenty-fourth Anniversary of the Revolution. With obvious relief,
he pointed out that the Soviet Union had not cracked up under
German hammer-blows, and that the people were presenting a solid

front to the enemy. Amidst repeated boasts that the German Army
was all but defeated, came plaintive hints that a Second Front in
Western Europe might yet save the situation. With some embarrassment, too (remembering a recent friendship, 'cemented in blood'),
he complained that National Socialism was not really socialism at
all. No, it was in Britain and the United States that one found
'elementary democratic liberties', with trade unions, Labour parties
and parliaments (what would Lenin and Trotsky have thought of this
admission?). Then followed one of those hortatory lists, which with
Stalin passed as flights of eloquence. He conjured up the spirits of
the Russian great, of revolutionary figures from the past, and also of
Pushkin and Tchaikovsky, of Glinka (composer of *A Life for the
Tsar*), of Count Leo Tolstoy, of generals Suvorov and Kutuzov, who
had led the Tsars' armies to victory. 'Long live the unbreakable
friendship of the peoples of the Soviet Union!' concluded the
trembling tyrant hopefully. Next day, in Red Square, Stalin
addressed in similar terms serried ranks of NKVD men guarding
absent crowds. Again he passed swiftly over the revolutionary tradition, concentrating on the pious hope that the Russian people
might be inspired by 'the manly images of our great ancestors –
Alexander Nevsky, Dmitri Donskoi, Kusma Minin, Dmitri Po-
zharsky, Alexander Suvorov and Mikhail Kutuzov'; a distinguished
group indeed, including two grand dukes and three princes![10]

This exaltation of the Russian Imperial past and of the political
and legal benefits of Western parliamentary institutions greatly
startled Stalin's listeners and those millions who subsequently read
the texts of the speeches in *Pravda*. Could the shock of military
defeat be compelling the Government to adopt a policy of genuine
reform? This had happened before in Russian history, after reverses
in the Crimea and the war with Japan. Roy Medvedev quotes an
unnamed 'well-informed person working in the Party *apparat* in
those years', who told how Stalin composed his text in the flat of an
old female Bolshevik, Elena Stasova. The woman, a doctrinaire
Marxist, was horrified at the Tsarist allusions and generally non-
Marxist tone of the speech. But Stalin was gloomily adamant, reply-
ing, 'We will never rouse the people to war with Marxism-Leninism
alone.'[11]

Cynical realism had always been a distinguishing trait of Stalin's
character. He lived in many respects in a world of illusion, but when
it came to an emergency he recognized well enough the distinction

between dreams and reality. It was these qualities of native cunning and pragmatism that had endeared him to Lenin, and enabled him to outwit the unworldly Trotsky. Like his servant Vyshinsky, he was perfectly aware that the cant of Marxism-Leninism was an effective cloak for dictatorship in the modern era, and if to save Lenin's inheritance it was necessary temporarily to wear another cloak, then what effective Russian ruler would hesitate? Since 1934 there had been a tentative effort to play the patriotic card.[12] Now the moment had come to persuade Russians that they were fighting, not for 'Lenin's inheritance', in which they held such a scanty share, but for the old, historic Russia – even, if some preferred it, for Holy Russia. In that anguished September of 1941, when the Wehrmacht appeared to be carrying all before it, Stalin confessed to Averell Harriman (the US Ambassador in Moscow) that 'he was under no illusions, the Russian people were fighting as they always had "for their homeland, not for us", meaning the Communist Party'.[13]

In virtually every aspect of Soviet life the historic glories of Russia's Imperial and Orthodox past replaced Socialist Internationalism as the symbolism for which Russians could be expected to fight and die. Specially painted portraits of Suvorov and Kutuzov replaced the forgotten favourites Marx and Engels on the walls of Stalin's study.[14] The High Command of the Red Army was renamed the *Stavka*, as under Tsar Nicholas II.[15] Other revivals of the past followed: the restoration of Military Academies (modelled on those of the pre-Revolutionary past), of Guards Regiments, and even of those epaulettes which had been *par excellence* the mark of the arrogant White Guardist. The Orders of Lenin and the Red Banner were replaced by those of (Prince) Suvorov, (Prince) Kutuzov and (Grand Duke) Alexander Nevski.[16] Some idea of the extent of the change may be gained from the reaction of Russian prisoners taken by the Germans in 1941 and 1942, before epaulettes and other archaic marks of rank had been reintroduced. Liberated by the British, their first glimpse of the gloriously clad Soviet repatriation officers led them to believe they must be former Tsarist officers, come to lead them once again against the Red foe![17]

Soviet literature, painting, theatre and cinema extolled the greatness of many of Russia's rulers in the past, such as Alexander Nevski and Peter the Great. Most remarkable of these was Eisenstein's apotheosis of Ivan the Terrible, whose character and conduct bore marked resemblances to those of the Leader.[18] Of course this switch

in propaganda came in response to popular sentiment, and many of
the symptoms of revived patriotism sprang spontaneously from
below. Soldiers broke impromptu into choruses never heard since
1917: Lermontov's 'Borodino', and the rousing *'Soldatushki, bravi
rebyatushki'*, with its echoed response from the marching ranks.[19]

But it was in the field of religion that Soviet Russia made its
greatest volte-face. The Metropolitan Sergei called upon all believers
to rise in defence of Holy Russia. The NKVD was well aware that
the deeply religious instincts of the Russian people had survived
the persecution of the Church instigated by Lenin and carried to
ferocious conclusions by Stalin. Now churches were gradually re-
opened, services openly conducted, seminaries revived, and anti-
religious newspapers closed on grounds of 'economy of paper'. In
September 1943 Stalin received the Metropolitan Sergei and other
Church dignitaries in the Kremlin, and a few days later Sergei was
crowned Patriarch of Moscow in the Cathedral.[20] Needless to say, the
whole exercise was entirely cynical in its intention and further con-
firms the fact that the Party leadership had for some time abandoned
any real belief in Marxist ideology.[21] Whilst a few church dignitaries
were liberated from labour-camps in the Far North, thousands upon
thousands of other believers died for their faith in Christ or
Muhammad.[22]

Appealing as it did to deepest national instincts, the Party's beating of the patriotic drum aroused a response amongst the Russian
people that surprised Stalin. By December 1941 the front had been
stabilized and the Germans held after some very bloody engage-
ments. The Polish Ambassador, who had earlier noted widespread
apathy and support for the Germans throughout the countryside,
now remarked on 'a greatly increased feeling of strength'. Russian
troops were proud of their increasingly determined resistance, and
wounded men in field hospitals were begging to be returned swiftly
to the front. (Through the hundreds of thousands of his compatriots
spread all over the USSR, Dr Kot was uniquely placed to assess
Russian opinion.)[23] During the war with Finland a resurgent spirit
of patriotism and martial pride had become evident, and now that
Russia's historic capitals were menaced by the enemy the old fighting spirit animated itself once more. Then, as the Red Army began
to achieve its own triumphs and glorious battle-honours, men felt the
exhilaration of approaching victory, the consummation of a common
purpose bravely earned. All the sordid frustrations, misery and

wickedness of the previous twenty-five years seemed to dissolve before the one shining purpose: to drive the arrogant enemy out of the Russian land his legions had defiled. A long and glorious history was repeating itself; the Teutonic Knights, the Tartars, the Poles, the Swedes and the French had all dreamed of planting their banners on the Kremlin, and each in turn had been driven headlong back over the frontiers.

Military life itself provided an emancipated sense of freedom and fulfilment that contrasted with the insecurity, fear and purposelessness of recent years. Soldiers, despite their hardships, were on the whole better fed and clothed than had been peacetime workers. The NKVD, SMERSH and Party *politruks* exercised full control over the armed forces, but the prestige of gallantry in action, promotion, decoration and the camaraderie of men sharing a common danger provided an exaltation that enabled them to raise their aspirations above these grim reminders of another Russia. Above all, a man could for the first time in twenty years enjoy pride and self-respect in his achievements. Reward and recognition on the whole were based for the first time on genuine merit, and it was impossible not to share in the irrational but almost universal feeling that a better world must emerge at the end of this superhuman struggle. As a young engineer officer explained to a puzzled German prisoner:

When I speak of our ideal, I don't of course mean the rubbish our Party members talk. I mean that which we fought for in our advance from the Volga to the Elbe. Or perhaps you think we bled and starved for the collective farms, Stalin, the *Cheka* and the Party bosses? Of course not. We fought for Russia and the prospects of a new life. You must realise one thing: on the ruins of the old world – and there is nothing left but the ruins, even where the old façade still stands – a new world is arising everywhere today, and with it a new man.

Alas for the new man – these brave words were uttered in a forced-labour camp, ten years after the war's end.[24]

This resurgence of patriotism was a response to Russia's danger. After initial glowing hopes that the Germans were coming to free Russia from her nightmare of two decades, came a terrible disillusionment. Despite strong pressures from within the Wehrmacht and elsewhere Hitler's intention was to reduce Russia to a German-dominated population of slaves. Russian émigrés, including the

Grand Duke Vladimir, were prohibited from issuing propaganda appeals to the Russian people, nationalist aspirations in the Baltic States and Ukraine were firmly repressed, and a policy of systematic brutality leading to virtual extermination was accorded to Russian prisoners-of-war.[25] On 22 August 1941 orders were given to preserve the hated collective farms in order to guarantee the harvest.[26] As for the most cruel institution of all, the camps of GULAG attracted Himmler's attention as a useful repository for *his* slaves![27]

In his speech of 6 November 1941, Stalin was able to quote chapter and verse documenting the Nazi policy of deliberate brutality, and it was not long before even the most sceptical disbeliever in Soviet propaganda had learned of deeds of Nazi barbarism equal in vileness to anything perpetrated by the NKVD. German savagery lacked the secrecy and pseudo-legality of homegrown brutality, and resentment grew proportionately. Much of it undoubtedly stemmed from an acute sense of betrayal. A wave of relief had passed over much of the country at the thought of deliverance coming from the only source possible, a foreign invasion. Now the invaders were slaughtering Jews, kidnapping Ukrainians to work in German slave-camps and factories, and arranging for thousands of Russians to die terribly in prisoner-of-war camps. Perhaps Mother Russia would teach them a lesson after all![28]

Altogether, as many perceptive Germans realized, Nazi brutality was a godsend to Stalin and the NKVD state. In May 1942, leading anti-Soviet Russians working with the Germans complained bitterly that Nazi attitudes were fighting a hopelessly losing battle against Stalin's much-trumpeted restoration of the churches and other seemingly nationalistic reforms. If Russians had to choose between tyrannies, then on the whole they preferred the familiar variety.[29]

Violence and cruelty as instruments of compulsion were understood very well by Stalin, and he frankly recognized the change this had brought in popular attitudes towards the war. On 1 May 1942 he admitted,

A change has taken place in the ranks of the Red Army. Complacency and frivolity towards the enemy, which was apparent among troops in the first months of the patriotic war, have disappeared. The atrocities, looting and violence committed by the German fascist invaders against the peaceful population and Soviet prisoners-of-war have cured our soldiers of this disease.

Our troops have become more bitter and ruthless. They have really learned to hate the German fascist invaders. They understand that it is impossible to conquer the enemy without learning to hate him with every fibre of one's soul.[30]

Accordingly he urged the extermination of every German remaining on Russian soil – a theme taken up by Soviet propagandists generally.[31]

There are indications that Nazi cruelties were not merely exploited by Stalin, but actually initiated and provoked as part of a Soviet policy designed to prevent German fraternization with the Russian people. In 1940 there is said to have been a discussion in the Kremlin on the matter, at which the crucial importance of Nazi inhumanity was urged as a deterrent to Russian defections.[32] It appears likely that it became a matter of policy to provoke the Germans into committing atrocities on a scale sufficient to deter the much-feared defection of large sections of the population to the enemy.

On 14 June 1941, the German 1st Armoured Group War Diary noted that 'The Russian method of warfare will be ruthless. Use of gas and bacteria must be reckoned with'.[33] From the earliest days of the invasion this ruthlessness became apparent. Among the slaughtered heaps found in the L'vov massacre on 30 June were the uniformed corpses of four Luftwaffe pilots.[34] Of course it is impossible to distinguish cause and effect when analysing the barbarities of warfare in the Eastern Campaign. The Germans bore with them a pre-arranged programme of unprecedented savagery,[35] whilst on the other hand the Red Army has never at any time precisely distinguished itself for chivalry in war. Evidence of NKVD massacres at L'vov, Vinnitsa, Katyn and elsewhere confirmed the German view that Bolshevik Russia was irredeemably savage and backward.

It is possible, however, to disentangle one aspect of this cruellest of all wars. Stalin went out of his way to invite Nazi ill-treatment and later extermination of Russian prisoners-of-war. He absolutely refused to permit the provisions of the Geneva Convention to apply to them, ignored International Red Cross efforts to intervene on their behalf, and even declined to allow the British to send them comforts. He was fully aware of the appalling mortality that resulted from this policy, and referred to it repeatedly in his speeches as evidence of Nazi cruelty. It is quite clear, therefore, that the deaths of over three million Russians in German custody was a piece of deliberate Soviet policy, the aim of which was to cause the liquidation of men regarded automatically as potential traitors, whilst arousing the anger of the Soviet people against the perpetrators of the crime.[36]

There can be little doubt that Russian resistance to the Germans had hardened from the end of 1941 into strongly patriotic determination to achieve victory. There were many converging factors determining this revolution in public opinion which, in the first weeks of the invasion, had for the most part been at least passively content to accept the overthrow of Soviet power.[37] There were long dormant feelings of patriotism aroused by Stalin's skilful propaganda measures, increasingly bitter resentment of German atrocities, and military *amour propre* stimulated first by successful resistance and later by the continuing succession of victories. Then again there were the physical and moral benefits of British and American aid, with its constant reminder that Soviet Russia was no longer an outcast, but one of the United Nations dedicated to the overthrow of Fascism and the triumph of principles of freedom enshrined in the Atlantic Charter.[38] Despite a series of appalling strategic blunders,[39] Stalin was eventually perceptive enough to reject Timoshenko's doctrine of massed head-on attacks,[40] and to arrange the promotion of some very able generals indeed.[41] Though many fine officers continued to languish in slave-camps, others were released and returned to duty.[42]

Given the stabilization of the front and the barbarity of the enemy, it is not surprising that most soldiers, whatever their feelings before, came to throw themselves into the task of defeating the invader. At last an honourable course offered itself, one which absorbed mental and physical energies in a way which nothing before the war had done, and which seemed, if successful, to promise better things when it was achieved. There was nothing political in this, and it would be wrong to regard it as proving widespread support for the regime. The security of an army depends on an ascending hierarchy of loyalties, and no soldier can fight effectively without accepting the legitimacy of the order behind him. The heroic struggle of the Red Army and Russian people in the Second World War is frequently interpreted as evidence of the strength, and even the virtue, of the Soviet Government. This is surely absurd. The Russian war effort was neither more nor less admirable and heroic than that of the Germans in 1944–5. Both peoples fought with incredible bravery and tenacity, largely because they had little choice in the matter. They accepted their pernicious governmental authorities and political systems, again, because this was not the occasion, nor was there the opportunity, even to contemplate doing otherwise. Their thoughts were occupied to the full with the task in hand.[43] Finally, it is worth noting that thousands of Russian soldiers serving in the German Army fought as bravely against Stalin as did their former comrades of the Red Army for him. As a perceptive Red Army officer put it,

> I was haunted by the idea of gladiators. It was many years before the thought crystallized in my mind, and even now I find it very difficult to put it into words. Roughly, it was this: All of us Soviet men and women were dominated, not by a sense of duty, not by our own will or desires, but by inexorable compulsion. Just as compulsion from without, not love of the arena, placed the Roman gladiator in his unfair fight, so, too, did an iron compulsion decide the fate of a man in a concentration camp – the fate of some brilliant Soviet general – and decided it with the same ruthlessness. Every one of us was doing something that he couldn't help doing. An unseen force had destined us to be the gladiators of the twentieth century, and we became gladiators.[44]

Alexander Gorbatov was the best type of Soviet general, who served with distinction throughout the war. He had seen the very worst side of the system as a prisoner in Kolyma, was horrified and baffled by the purges, but nevertheless accepted the authority and legitimacy of the Party leadership.[45] But he had served with equal gallantry and unquestioning obedience to orders in the Army of Nicholas II,[46] and clearly would have done his duty under any government that maintained authority in Russia. The oath and chain of command form a soldier's politics, until the system itself breaks down. Only then do all these multifarious links dissolve and make it possible for a man to face the system as it is.

In January 1942 a French newspaper reporter was allowed to visit the front west of Moscow. At Volokolamsk she met the commander of the 20th Army, who was leading the spearhead of Zhukov's massive counter-attack against the German 9th and 3rd Panzer Armies.[47] The General was only forty years old, tall, strong, active and plainly dressed. He showed his visitor piles of German trophies, and ex-

plained the tactics by which the Germans had already been hurled
back eighteen miles. Speaking with professional confidence, he
asserted that enemy morale and strength were weakening and that
the Wehrmacht 'is now a wounded beast – although still very
strong'. He vigorously urged the opening of a Second Front to ease
pressure on the Red Army, but was calmly confident of ultimate
success. He frequently invoked the name of Stalin, 'as if the man in
the Kremlin were his commander-in-chief, his direct superior', and
concluded by muttering: 'We must annihilate the enemy . . . Everybody, *everybody* must fight the fascists . . . My blood belongs to my
Fatherland.' The reporter departed, feeling that 'here was a man who
waged war with something more than determination, something
more than courage: he waged it with passion.'[48]

Yet who can know a man's secret thoughts? Six months later
General Andrei Vlasov was a prisoner of the Germans, his forces
encircled as a result of Stalin's mishandling of the offensive. Within
weeks he was touring prisoner-of-war camps in Germany, urging
Russians to join the anti-Bolshevik crusade and fight against the evil
of Stalinism.[49] By the end of the war he commanded an 'army' of
800,000 Russians, many of whom fought long and hard against
Stalin's system. Who can doubt that, but for the chance of his capture, Vlasov would have continued to serve in the Red Army as
devotedly as General Gorbatov? By the same token, how many
Gorbatovs would have turned against Stalin, were a real choice
placed before them?

By 1945 the hurly-burly of war might have momentarily driven
resentment into the recesses of men's consciousness, but Stalin was
taking no chances. With victory there must follow a dangerous
euphoria. It was then that Russians would expect some reward after
all the sacrifice. The years of war had added both to Stalin's confidence and to his fears. There was the wholly unexpected victory
over Germany on the one hand, and the transformation of the USSR
from a backward oriental state, whose armies were scarcely a match
for the Finns, into the second of the two military powers dominating
the earth. On the other there was the increased self-confidence of
Soviet Man (particularly Red Army Man), who must undoubtedly
have been poisoned by contact with Western prosperity and liberal
ideas, picked up in Eastern Europe and through contact with the
Allies. All sorts of rash promises and concessions granted in the
darkest days of danger had now to be carefully withdrawn. Worst of

all, Stalin's deepest fears had been confirmed, when up to a million Russians had volunteered to help the Germans, and thousands of anti-Soviet nationalist troops and partisans, in the Baltic States, Byelorussia, the Ukraine, the Crimea and the Caucasus, had taken up arms against the Soviet state. For years after the war Bandera's Ukrainians and Baltic partisans fought on in the forests – something Stalin in 1940 must have thought eliminated for good. Red Army orders issued to troops on first re-entering the Western Ukraine in January 1944 read as if referring to entry into a hostile foreign country. No one was to leave camp alone, or travel unarmed; arms, camps and units were to be carefully guarded; 'acceptance of al-coholic drinks from the civil population is to be strictly forbidden'; and all new recruits were to be checked lest the ubiquitous OUN (Ukrainian Nationalist Movement) had infiltrated the ranks.[50]

Perhaps the greatest fear was that the Soviet armies, millions strong, who had advanced on the wings of glory into the heart of old Europe, might become unpleasantly infected by what they saw. For the two and a half decades of their power, Soviet rulers had con-sistently displayed inordinate fear of the effect 'abroad' might have on their brainwashed but still susceptible subjects. Frontiers had been mined, ploughed up to reveal footprints, and guarded by bat-talions of NKVD cavalry and infantry, whilst punishments of in-creasing ferocity, culminating in the law of 1934 visiting fearsome penalties on the relatives of fugitives, menaced those few citizens bold enough to attempt flight. During the war it was as much as any citizen's life was worth to make contact with Allied diplomatic or military representatives, whom Stalin was willy-nilly obliged to admit in stringently restricted numbers into the country. Embassies and military missions were treated like medieval lazarettos, which few dared approach.

But now, with the invasion of Poland, the Balkans and Germany, millions of Soviet citizens were visiting the dreaded 'abroad'. They could for the first time compare conditions in their own country with those of people living in capitalist or semi-feudal lands to the west. The comparison was unlikely to emerge in favour of the Planned Economy and bound to upset those who could not grasp the *poli-truks'* ingenious explanations of the discrepancy. Stalin's method of solving this problem was simple and direct. The Red Army, which had never enjoyed a reputation for old-world chivalry, was en-couraged to behave in occupied territories in so barbaric a fashion as, firstly, to destroy or loot as much of the damning evidence of capitalist comforts as possible, and secondly to create an irredeemable rift between the conquerors and their victims.

No distinction was made as to whether 'liberated' countries had fought for the Allies or the Axis. In Poland, recounts a former NKVD officer, 'to be a Pole at all was virtually a sufficient ground for suspicion'. In L'vov gaol, scene of the dreadful massacre in June 1941, the torture-chambers came back into employment. Thousands set off once again on the dreary and corpse-littered route to Siberia.[51] In 1942 an NKVD officer had told a Polish general, 'It will take us twenty years to efface the impression of your passage through our country.'[52] With the entry of Soviet troops into Poland itself, the problem had increased a hundredfold and required drastic measures for its solution. The reoccupied Baltic States suffered their third major Soviet purge in five years. Up to half a million inhabitants are estimated to have been removed from an already depleted population in the year of victory. They were accompanied by scenes of gratuitous cruelty too sickening, and, alas, repetitive, to set down here.[53]

As 1944 drew on, Soviet armies moved beyond the recovered territories awarded them by Hitler in 1939 into south-eastern and central Europe. On 23 August Romania surrendered after a pro-Allied *coup d'état* nominally headed by young King Michael. Despite the fact that the Romanian Army was now fighting for the Allies, Romania was treated as a conquered country. About 320,000 Romanian soldiers had been taken prisoner (about 130,000 of whom were captured after hostilities ceased). In addition to these were 100,000 more who had been recruited into the Hungarian Army. Of this total of 420,000, less than half (190,000) ever returned home. In February 1945 Soviet authorities admitted that 50,000 had already died of undefined causes. The remaining 180,000 had been swallowed up into the ever-hungry belly of GULAG. They were joined by a quarter of a million civilians, taken on racial grounds (e.g., they were of German origin) or those of 'political unreliability'. Few are likely to have survived, in view of the fact that in one camp alone well over 50 per cent of the inmates died within the first year. Those Romanians who remained behind in their homeland were not always much luckier. About 100,000 were held in gaols and camps. Outside, the 'free' population was reduced to such straits that there were frequent cases of cannibalism in the devastated countryside.[54]

Hungary's turn came next. Some 600,000 people were abducted by the NKVD and disappeared eastwards. They included many of the prisoners 'liberated' from Auschwitz, Buchenwald and Ravensbrück, and almost the entire Hungarian population of Ruthenia, which province was intended in name as well as fact to join the other free republics of the USSR.[55] NKVD activities were as ruthlessly conducted in Czechoslovakia, though on a rather smaller scale. Three years were to pass before the country became completely Bolshevized and passed into the darkness.[56]

All this catalogue of rape, pillage, murder and slave-raiding must of course in large part be put down to the generally barbaric character of the Red Army, which acquired most of its day-to-day supplies 'at the expense of the enemy or of the local population . . . We were witnessing a return to the administrative methods of Attila and Genghis Khan', as a not unsympathetic eye-witness recorded.[57] But in Yugoslavia it was made clear that high policy played its part too. There the Soviets occupied only the north-eastern corner of the country, and in any case must have wished to provide a favourable impression in the one country in Europe likely to fall willingly into their lap. Even so, there were reported 1,204 cases of looting with assault, and 121 cases of rape – 111 of these involving murder, a combination apparently much in favour with Soviet Man.[58] When a Yugoslav partisan leader took an opportunity of complaining about this to Stalin himself, the jovial Leader explained that the Red Army, which after all included large numbers of criminals, had earned its pleasures. He then recounted with pride an incident in which he extended his protection to a major who had raped a woman and murdered a fellow-officer who remonstrated with him.[59]

It was the final advance into Germany itself in which Stalin showed his hand openly. Hatred of Germany and all things German was understandable after all Russia had suffered, even if barbarity on both sides was to be reckoned in roughly equal measure. To Ilya Ehrenburg, the Soviet Streicher, race hatred became an obsessive, vitriolic mania. In his much-printed book *Voina* ('The War'), published in 1943, his words became frantic with openly sadistic gloatings:

We shall not speak any more. We shall not get excited. We shall kill. If you have not killed at least one German a day, you have wasted that day . . . If you kill one German, kill another – there is nothing funnier for us than a pile of German corpses. Do not count days, do not count versts. Count only the number of Germans killed by you . . . Do not miss. Do not let through. Kill.

This passage and many others like it were printed as leaflet guides to conduct for Soviet troops entering East Prussia. Everything that followed lived up to Ehrenburg's most frenzied fancies. Scarcely a German woman, from grandmothers to four-year-old children, survived unraped east of the Elbe. A Russian officer encountered a girl who had been raped by at least two hundred and fifty men in a week. Regular sexual congress might satisfy some of the conquerors, but as often as not they needed more to make pleasure exquisite. Afterwards one could stab a woman in the breast and stomach with a blunt dagger made of plexiglass, or ram a telephone or a broken bottle into her vagina. Small children made more sporting targets than adults for revolver practice ('let them kill the little Fritzes in the heat of the moment until they get sick of it themselves'). Then it was always amusing to rape, abuse and mutilate children of either sex in front of their parents . . . they could be finished off afterwards; they hadn't much to live for, after all. One did not even need to check too thoroughly whether they were German; it was all 'in the heat of the moment'. A Russian girl, kidnapped by the Nazis, was cycling down a street. She was exceptionally attractive, too attractive to miss . . . 'Hey, you bitch!' shouts a merry Red Army man, unhitching his machine-gun and firing a burst into her back. She took an hour to die, whimpering: 'what for?'

At Nemmersdorf in East Prussia, one of the first German villages to be captured, the Red Army staged its German 'Katyn'. Forty-eight hours later the Wehrmacht recaptured Nemmersdorf, and discovered what the Eastern liberators of Europe were bringing with them. Eye-witness accounts provide some idea of what had happened, though it is hard enough to imagine. Peasants had been nailed on barn doors, tortured, or shot. Fifty French prisoners of war were massacred out of hand. A military doctor

 . . . saw where a whole column of refugees had been rolled over by Russian tanks; not only the wagons and teams, but also a goodly number of civilians, mostly women and children, had been squashed flat by the tanks . . . On the edge of a street an old woman sat hunched up, killed by a bullet in the back of the neck. Not far away lay a baby of only a few months, killed by a shot at close range through the forehead . . . a number of men, with no other marks of fatal wounds, had been killed by blows with shovels or gun butts; their faces were completely smashed. At least one man was nailed to a barn door.

Scarcely a single inhabitant, man, woman or child, had survived the Soviet presence.[60] All in all hundreds of thousands of defenceless people died, as many more were deported to slave-labour,[61] and millions were driven for ever from their homes.

A number of Red Army officers and men were shocked and shamed by this incontrovertible evidence of the bestial nature of their soldiery. After all, when the Russian Imperial Army overran East Prussia in 1914, there were *two* cases of rape recorded and some damage to fruit trees.[62] But protests were unavailing. An officer attempting to prevent individual crimes was accused of bourgeois humanism and expelled from the Party.[63] It was clear that the destruction of civilized life in occupied Germany was a matter of high policy. When reports were brought to Stalin of Soviet tanks regularly shelling civilian refugees, women and children, Stalin replied in high good humour: 'We lecture our soldiers too much; let them have some initiative!'[64] Eventually Marshal Koniev issued orders requiring the restoration of orderly behaviour, but this was only when the goodly work was near completion, and indiscipline was starting to endanger military efficiency.

The purposes of this licensed savagery were several. It was necessary to cow conquered populations into total submission. Millions of people were murdered, imprisoned or dragged off to GULAG. Eastern Europe was plundered, and its civilization set back a thousand years.[65] This was the era foreseen by a prominent Soviet military theoretician, an era when Soviet Russia would 'throw against the oppressors such masses as the world has known only in the era of the great invasions, as in the time of Attila and Alaric, when the Roman legions were torn apart and destroyed by millions of "barbarians".'[66] There was perhaps the further need to allow the Red Army a period of blood-letting and raping, in order to let off steam after their unheard-of sacrifices in achieving victory.

Above all, there was the necessity of linking the Army and political leadership in a bond of crime and guilt – a consideration probably also to the fore in the increasing barbarism of Hitler's Reich as its end drew near.[67] The conquests of 1945 had drawn within Soviet power for the first time foreign nations such as Poland, Hungary and eastern Germany. These were nations possessed of martial spirit and national pride celebrated in history. Stalin confessed once that he had a healthy respect for 'nations which had once been ruled by powerful aristocracies, like the Hungarians and the Poles'. He believed this made them 'strong nations', possessed of racial stamina.[68] As for the Germans, his respect verged on awe at their indomitable unity, strength and courage. In retrospect it may seem extraordinary that Stalin could apparently have feared that a conquered Germany could rise up again, in the face of modern techniques of maintaining control over subject populations. But German resurgence after 1918 dominated most people's thinking in 1945, however different in fact had been the circumstances. Stalin's suggestion to the sympathetic Roosevelt that fifty thousand German officers and technicians should be shot after the war revealed his way of thinking, as did his massacre of the Polish officers in 1940. Above all, Stalin was essentially an insecure tyrant, as his need for 99.98 per cent favourable election results and universal adulation, however ridiculously expressed, reveals. Possibly this stemmed from feelings of personal inadequacy, confirmed by the astonishing overnight collapse of the Tsar's Empire.

Stalin had always trembled at the vision of revolution in the cities.[69] Events in 1944–5 had done nothing to diminish that fear. The nationalist Home Army had risen in Warsaw and fought for two months against the best units the Wehrmacht and SS could throw against them. A sinister-seeming pointer to subsidiary danger was the presence in the skies over Warsaw of American bombers dropping arms to the Poles, despite Soviet disapproval.[70] A month after the collapse of Polish resistance in Warsaw, Stalin ordered his armies to take Budapest 'literally in a matter of days', following intelligence reports that the Hungarian Army was totally demoralized. On 29 October 1944 the attack was launched, but the Hungarian and German defenders fought with such unexpected tenacity that the city held out behind the Soviet lines until 13 February 1945.[71] Prague fell into Soviet hands without a struggle, but in circumstances potentially even more alarming than those in hard-fought Warsaw or Budapest. Soviet historiography maintains that the Czech capital was liberated on 9 May 1945 by units of the First Ukrainian Front Army.[72] In fact the city was saved from possible devastation at the hands of the Germans by the intervention of thousands of anti-Soviet

Russian troops of General Vlasov's 'Liberation Army'. General Patton's tanks also pushed forward to the outskirts; a combination that might well have taken on sinister import in Stalin's suspicious mind.[73]

It is characteristic of Stalin's outlook that his European conquests aroused as many fears as they allayed. Internal security remained his priority, and the NKVD now had new nations, warlike and hostile, to control. Much of the Red Army was posted outside the frontiers of the Soviet Union, and hence dangerously exposed to subversive foreign influences for the first time in Soviet history. Now a river of blood separated the conquerors from their subject peoples. In Germany above all there was reason to fear a resurgence of national spirit. As Stalin himself admitted, 'one can expect Germany to start a new war after about twenty-five years.' Naturally all the usual means would be employed to convert the Germans to Communism, but 'Communism on a German is like a saddle on a cow'.[74] German Communists were accordingly treated with ill-disguised contempt by their masters, despite their excessive servility.[75] NKVD and SMERSH control over the Red Army in occupied territories was total, but extraordinary precautions had nevertheless to be taken to prevent any fraternization with the local population.[76]

A major reason for Russian wartime solidarity was the widespread feeling, not confined to Russians, that something better must come out of all this suffering. By a tragic paradox, it was precisely this emotional response which helped to ensure that no improvement could take place. The indications were plain that a dangerous mood of post-war euphoria was abroad, coupled with widespread hopes that life could become easier and the USSR emerge from her attitude of permanent antagonism to the rest of the world. On 14 October 1944 Winston Churchill attended a performance at the Bolshoi Theatre, at the end of which he received a standing ovation which lasted fifteen minutes.[77] Much more unnerving were events in central Moscow as the capital celebrated Victory in Europe. On 9 May 1945 extraordinary scenes took place, unprecedented since the Revolution. Thousands upon thousands of Muscovites poured into the square before the United States Embassy, and began to cheer any and every sign of American life. Frantic cries of enthusiasm hailed the Stars and Stripes, and every American the crowd could lay hands on was hoisted aloft and passed joyfully over their heads to the outer fringes. It was a cold day, but for over twelve hours, well on into the night, thousands of Muscovites continued their rapturous vigil outside the Embassy. Signs of official embarrassment became plain. Police tried to move the crowd on, and a brass band was set up as a rival attraction. But astonishingly all their efforts were in vain, and the people did not disperse until their enthusiasm was temporarily spent. Similar scenes were repeated during Eisenhower's visit in August. The Soviet press had made the barest announcement of his trip, yet he was cheered and followed everywhere by admiring crowds.[78]

All this was in stark contrast to Stalin's own Victory Parade in June. Never, even in Moscow, had such elaborate precautions against mishap been taken. The entire city swarmed with NKVD patrols.

> To get to the centre of Moscow one had to pass through several cordoned-off zones. The first one was manned by NCOs of NKVD Internal Troops, the next by Chekist officers. The nearer one got to the Kremlin and the Lenin Mausoleum, the higher were the ranks of the officers manning the cordon. In front of the guests' stands, shoulder to shoulder in an unbroken line, stood officers of the Main Operational Administration of the NKGB. A second line of officers of the same administration, none below the rank of major, stretched the whole length of the façade of the Mausoleum. Behind and beside the Mausoleum stood officers of the Special Operational Group which formed Stalin's personal bodyguard.

Chekists in plain clothes even swarmed among the dignitaries and Allied visitors on the stands.[79] A fresh breeze had momentarily stirred the stifling atmosphere, and Stalin was taking no chances. As a Red Army officer reflected on the morning of 9 May,

> What were we hoping for? The past would not return and the dead would not live again. Perhaps we were glad that we would be returning to the peaceful existence of the pre-war years? Hardly! Our great joy that day arose from the fact that we stood at a frontier, a frontier that marked the end of the darkest period of our life, and the beginning of a new, still unknown period. And every one of us was hoping that this new period would fulfil the promise of the rainbow after the storm, would be bright, sunny, happy. If anybody had asked us what we really expected, the

majority would have expressed our common feeling very simply: 'To hell with all that was before the war!' And every one of us knew exactly what had been before the war.[80]

No one was more aware of this mood than Stalin, and it struck a chill into his heart.[81] The alliance with the Anglo-Americans had spread the infection he had so long dreaded into the heart of his domains. A succession of new and violent precautionary measures was undertaken to tilt Russia safely back to the atmosphere of the 1930s. The NKVD launched a campaign to prepare the people for the coming war against the British and Americans ('The real war, to bring about the final destruction of the capitalist world, was only just beginning').[82] Sharper measures, of a more direct nature, warned Soviet citizens, high and low, who was master in the USSR. A military *coup* following a Bonapartist precedent seemed the most likely contingency, and cunning steps were taken to downgrade Marshal Zhukov.[83] At SMERSH Headquarters at Baden-bei-Wien a colossal screening operation took place with the aim of uncovering NCOs and officers with 'unreliable' class connections, whilst a top-level SMERSH commission in Moscow decided the fate of generals and marshals. Thousands of soldiers of all ranks were demobilized and allotted fates varying from return home to compulsory labour in Central Asia.[84] Similar purges swept through all levels of Soviet life. Anyone who had for whatever reason been outside the borders of the Soviet Union, or otherwise come in contact with foreigners or foreign ways, was particularly suspect. Millions of former prisoners-of-war and slave-labourers working in Germany were consigned to an even harsher life in Siberian camps, whilst within GULAG itself new precautionary measures were put into effect to overawe the slaves.[85]

All these measures indicate the extent of Stalin's fear that unseemly ideas of personal and political freedom might be brought back to Russia from Europe by returning soldiers, prisoners, slaves and refugees. An exactly parallel situation had existed after the Napoleonic Wars, when Russian officers brought back the intoxicating ideas of the French Revolution and Napoleonic *Zeitgeist*. This infection culminated ten years later in the Decembrist attempt to overthrow the autocracy and establish a parliamentary constitution. The democracies by their very nature represented a mortal threat to the Soviet order.[86] It mattered not a bit how well Stalin managed affairs with the impressionable Churchill and the gullible Roosevelt.

Under their anarchic system reactionary politicians and newspapers could run the most scurrilous campaigns against the USSR. Polish and even Russian émigrés could engage freely in anti-Soviet propaganda. Above all, there was the sheer vulgar affluence of capitalism, apparent in the wrist-watch and camera of the humblest GI. Stalin had been so fearful of the effects of foreign propaganda that he had ordered the confiscation of all private radios in the Soviet Union the day war broke out.[87] Now millions of Russians had actually seen the wealth and ease of Europe for themselves. As Churchill shrewdly put it, 'They fear our friendship more than our enmity.'

This terror (it scarcely amounted to less) of the insidiously infectious nature of European and American liberties is surely the key to Stalin's changes of policy between 1939 and 1941. Until August of 1939 the USSR was a fragile, intensely vulnerable state, isolated from the outside world and able to survive only through a sort of juggling act, playing off the Entente powers and Nazi Germany against each other. But what Stalin needed was security, and after 1934 he recognized that only Germany could offer that. The Nazi-Soviet Pact protected Stalin against British or French military attack; much more significant, it preserved Soviet Russia's ideological quarantine. As early as July 1933 Goebbels had shown what could be hoped for, when he temporarily ordered the German press not to print attacks on the Soviet Union.[88] In Germany such an order was obeyed, and after the Pact all anti-Soviet propaganda was effectively prohibited both in Germany and occupied Poland.[89] In addition, though National Socialism owed much to and in many ways closely resembled Marxism, it differed in one material aspect. With its accent on the racial superiority of the Germans it could have no appeal to foreign peoples whom its doctrines condemned to perpetual inferiority. Much more than Fascism, National Socialism was not for export, and indeed Hitler evinced little desire to make it so.[90] Even Stalin, in his franker moments, could contrast Western European and American freedom with Nazi oppression.[91]

The genial co-operation accorded to Germany at the time of the Pact was without precedent, and stands in striking contrast to the attitude displayed towards her next Allies, Britain and the United States. Even at the most desperate moments of the war, the Soviet Union feared to let in more than a handful of British or American personnel, however vital their presence to the war effort. Those that were admitted were continually subjected to harassment, restrictions, blackmail and insult. As the Foreign Office reported in February 1945, 'Russian attitude to our [Military] Mission in Moscow has been throughout deliberately unco-operative, and both before and after D Day there has been no attempt to work on basis of reciprocity.'[92] The same attitude applied in every field where co-operation might have been expected. No greater contrast could be made with the earlier policy of allowing the Germans to establish consulates, and even a naval base, on Soviet soil.

Stalin was never at ease with the Anglo-American alliance, as his peace feelers to Hitler during the war betrayed. With the initial terrible reverses of 1941–2 he may in desperation have hoped to save something out of the carnage by a 'Vichy-style' peace, similar to that which he had supported at Brest-Litovsk in 1918. After Stalingrad, when German might was checked but still formidable, a compromise settlement between the two totalitarian giants appeared enticing. And further attempts to inveigle the retreating Germans into terms in 1944 may well have been in part due to the anticipated fear of enjoying a common frontier with the Anglo-Americans.[93] These attempts proved fruitless, partly because Hitler continued to reject them, and partly, as Allied intelligence estimates pointed out, no feasible basis for peace existed which did not leave the USSR open to another German attack.[94] Stalin had to fight on, whether he liked it or not.

With the defeat of Germany, Stalin had no choice but to live in a world where the Soviet Union would live cheek by jowl with the victorious democracies. The Anglo-Americans, brimming with hope of international co-operation towards peace, had with the best intentions entangled the Soviets in a whole web of ventures intended to draw the powers indissolubly closer: the United Nations, the European Advisory Commission, the German Control Commission, and so forth. At the same time the exuberant democracies were even more vociferous in extolling all those legal and political protections Lenin had swept away in Russia in 1917, even institutionalizing them in the Atlantic Charter, the Four Freedoms, the Declaration of Human Rights. Superficially the contrast between the 'free world' and the totalitarian power was immensely more pronounced than before the war. Then the picture had been much more confused, with two or three rival forms of totalitarianism competing and quarrelling, and a whole series of intermediary authoritarian states of archaic flavour.

This surely answers the leading question: why, if Stalin could enjoy a friendly and seemingly stable alliance with Hitler, could he not do the same with the British and Americans? The answer appears to be that he simply could not afford such a relationship. The only way to preserve 'Lenin's inheritance' was to tighten the clamps on what he held, and repel dangerous external influences by drumming up an atmosphere of hostility and suspicion. The Cold War in part arose through clashes of interest, but a much more important factor was simply the Soviet need for a Cold War.

Maxim Litvinov, the superseded pre-war Foreign Commissar, opposed this policy of permanently provoked tension. At the Dumbarton Oaks Conference in 1944 he unavailingly urged a realistic great-power alliance designed to preserve world peace, but tactfully avoiding contentious discussion of the powers' internal affairs.[95] On 21 November 1945 he bumped into Averell Harriman at a Moscow theatre performance. He expressed pessimistic views on the situation, and Harriman (as he reported next day to the State Department)

> . . . suggested that time might cool the strong feelings that had been aroused. [Litvinov] replied that in the meantime, however, other issues were developing. I again suggested that if we came to an understanding about Japan it might clear the atmosphere. He replied that we would then be confronted with other issues. I asked him what we, for our part, could do about it. He replied 'Nothing' . . . I then said, 'You are extremely pessimistic', to which he replied, 'Frankly, between us, yes'.[96]

Litvinov felt so strongly about what he regarded as a misguided and dangerous policy that he opened his mind again to an astonished American journalist. He believed that good relations might have been possible once, but now hostility between the two ideologies was too great. The reporter, Richard C. Hottelet, then asked him the central question: would Soviet policy be mitigated if the West were suddenly to give in and grant all Russian demands? Litvinov 'said it would lead to west being faced after period of time with next series of demands'.[97]

The policy advocated by Litvinov approximated to old-fashioned great-power politics. The Soviet Union should hold on firmly to its gains, at the same time making every effort to preserve her good wartime relationship with the Allies.[98] Stalin rejected this view in characteristic fashion, making arrangements – later unaccountably cancelled – for Litvinov's murder.[99] Friendship with the democracies was far too dangerous a game. Open the hothouse windows, and how long would that frail plant, Marxism, survive?[100]

XVI
Western Attitudes

In the democratic West during the war years, millions of people came to elevate Stalin's Russia as a model to be admired and emulated. From the moment that the German invasion compelled the Soviet Union to fight on the same side as the Allies, an extraordinary quasi-religious emotion swept over people of all classes. It was for the most part wholly uncritical and irrational, and frequently resulted in the press, radio and cinema representing Soviet society as actually superior to that in the democracies.[1] In 1942 Harold Nicolson remarked 'how sad it is that the British public are wholly unaware of the true state of Russia, and imagine that it is some workers' Utopia. Anyone who makes even the slightest critical remark . . . is branded as "an enemy of the Soviet".'[2] Such was the atmosphere in Britain, where what George Orwell was to castigate as the 'Russian mythos' reigned almost unchallenged. The same delusions were widespread in the United States. A Soviet official, who had just arrived from home, was startled to be informed on every side of the near-perfection of the society in which he lived. Gentle efforts to enlighten his hosts proved hopeless. 'The slightest effort to scrape off a little of the tinsel, to expose the squalor and moral ugliness underneath, was resented by most Americans as if their deepest religious convictions were at stake.' He felt acutely that this attitude stemmed from 'a remarkable callousness to the tragedy of the Russian people. It was based in large part on ignorance, which was excusable, but also in large part on indifference, which was plainly insulting.'[3]

Of course the reason for this near-unanimity of opinion, shared by the most unlikely people, was the intense feeling of relief, firstly when the Nazi threat was deflected eastwards, and secondly when it became clear that Russia was bearing the brunt of the fighting and was doing most to bring Hitler to his knees. Nevertheless these feelings of gratitude and admiration were ludicrously misplaced. The Soviet Union had not entered the war voluntarily and, but for Hitler's treacherous attack, would in all probability have continued as his loyal ally. Within and without the Soviet Union Communists everywhere had worked hard for nearly two years to assist the Nazi war effort, and had played a major part in the downfall of France. Yet in Britain and America people beat their breasts in shame at not being able to provide the Second Front the USSR had declined to supply in 1939 and 1940. They forgot also that it was Soviet brutality and aggression which had transformed Finland and Romania from a pro-British attitude into becoming allies of Germany.

Stalin's political and strategic blunders accounted for much of Russia's distress, yet the suffering so caused generally redounded to his credit. It should not be forgotten, either, that Soviet cruelty greatly prolonged the conflict, costing all belligerent nations millions of lives. In the USSR the Germans found (and emulated) evidence of barbarism horrifying even by their standards. At L'vov, Katyn, Vinnitsa[4] and elsewhere they discovered the mass graves of Bolshevism's victims. This evidence of how the Soviets treated their own people, coupled with the harsh treatment they visited on prisoners-of-war, was the major cause of Germany's obstinate determination to fight on to the end, long after it had become clear her cause was doomed. Allied efforts to induce captured Germans to appeal to their countrymen to surrender were met with the un-answerable reply that 'most Germans would rather die in battle than face . . . a prospect' of being sent to die slowly in Siberia.[5] And military intelligence reports told of German and Italian units fight-ing desperately on 'because of a universal fear among the personnel of "Bolshevism"'.[6] It was difficult to exaggerate this fear. An example may suffice here. Among a group of German soldiers from the Russian front on leave in a French village was 'a very young soldier with completely white hair and an expression of extreme suffering'. A Frenchman, M. Charles Sellier, spoke to him and learned 'that he had seen eleven of his comrades passed under a circular saw. He was to have been the twelfth, but a bombardment dispersed the Soviet troops, enabling him to escape and rejoin his unit'.

Possibly the most extraordinary example of the 'Russian mythos' is one which survives largely intact today, even among some repu-table historians. This is to the effect that much is owed to the Soviet regime because the Russians lost an estimated twenty million war dead. These enormous figures inflicted feelings of acute guilt on Allied leaders and public then and since, and are still used by Soviet spokesmen as credit when attempting to extract concessions from the West.[7] The origin of the specific figure usually cited appears obscure. In 1947 pro-Soviet writers in the West were accepting a figure of seven million Soviet war dead.[8] In 1945 Mikoyan boasted that victory had been achieved with 'the least possible losses'. Later, when more precise figures became available – or when it was appreciated that more, not less, blood was advantageous – M. Suslov claimed (in 1965) that twenty million had perished.[9] But even this figure appears to have been an underestimate. A careful analysis of the first post-war census, that of 1959, revealed that something like twenty-five million more people died in the war years than normally would have been expected. In addition the projected birth-rate was down by twenty million; a figure to be accounted for by a possible wartime decline, and greatly inflated infant mortality.[10] It seems that, in all, a staggering total of not less than thirty million Russians died in the war years, if we make the modest assumption that at least a quarter of expected births took place.

This figure may be compared with the numbers dead from all causes as a result of the First World War. That war lasted about the same length of time and involved roughly the same number of Russian soldiers. The total death-rate was 1,660,000.[11] How can one account for this amazing discrepancy? Fire-power was much greater in the Second World War, but despite this, casualties in most theatres tended to be considerably lower than in the previous conflict, with its bloody struggles fought often at very close quarters. The British Empire, for example, lost nearly a million men in the First War, and less than a quarter of that number in the Second. But the best comparison must surely be that with the Wehrmacht, which needless to say fought the same battles over the same period of time and with much the same numbers. By 30 November 1944 the German Army in Russia had lost 1,419,000 men killed, and another 907,000 missing. It seems probable that about two and a half million Germans in all were killed in battle on the Eastern Front.[12]

The number of Russian troops killed on the Front is not known with any degree of precision. The Soviet authorities were little concerned with the fate of the individual soldier, and no record appears to have been preserved of losses incurred. During the war Stalin quoted obviously doctored statistics designed to minimize Soviet casualties, and afterwards only informed guesses could be made. A Soviet demographer has estimated that about 7,500,000 soldiers were killed in battle or died of wounds, which is perhaps as close to the truth as we can hope to get.[13] This leaves 22,500,000 civilian deaths unaccounted for, but it will be best to examine the military casualties separately.

How can it be explained that three Russians died for every German soldier killed? Firstly, there were the prisoners-of-war. Of five and a half million Russians taken by the Germans, more than three million had by 1945 been murdered or died through neglect and ill-treatment.[14] Though the major blame must clearly fall on the Nazi butchers responsible, not much less should be accorded to the Soviet regime which collaborated in the crime. By refusing to accede to the Geneva Convention on Prisoners-of-War or to collaborate with the International Red Cross, the Soviet Government (as it well knew) effectively sentenced its citizens to death.[15] German ill-treatment of Russian prisoners did not come about as a response to Soviet brutality, as it was a policy already decided upon before the invasion.[16] Nevertheless, had Soviet Russia accepted the provisions of international law in this matter, it may be fairly questioned whether Hitler would have been able to continue with his policy of extermination of Russian prisoners. He was not unduly concerned with legal procedures, still less with humanitarian considerations. But had the Soviet authorities treated German prisoners in a civilized manner, pressure for Germany to respond in kind must (the evidence suggests) have had considerable, if not irresistible, effect.

If the three million Russians who died in captivity are deducted from the the estimated total of 7,500,000 total military war dead, the USSR still lost around two of her soldiers for each German. This can only be attributed to the Red Army's barbarous manner of waging war, in which lives counted as nothing in the succession of blundering offensives conducted by Stalin's General Staff in 1941–2. These tactics included the use of penal battalions. Like virtually everything else in the Soviet state, this was a concept originated by the resourceful Lenin. On 20 October 1919 he ordered ten thousand of the Petrograd 'bourgeoisie' to be dispatched to the front ('machine-guns to the rear of them, a few hundred shot') and driven against the White lines.[17]

The NKVD collected droves of 'enemies of the people' from their prisons and camps, and sent them off, untrained and frequently unarmed, to the battlefield. There, with NKVD machine-gunners crouching safely behind them, they were hurled in waves against German defensive positions. On occasion they were deprived of camouflaged uniforms, so as to draw enemy fire. Their most useful task was the clearance of minefields: driven on in extended ranks, they moved slowly forward until they had blown up every mine. The head of the Soviet Military Mission in Britain, General Ratov, actually declined an offer of British mine-detectors, explaining blandly that 'in the Soviet Union we use people'.[18] In a typical attack on a German position one penal battalion lost 500 of its 1,500 men. They had one rifle to every three men; the well-armed NKVD men behind them confined their role in the battle to killing all their own wounded. It is impossible to know how many 'soldiers' were killed in this way, but the number must run into hundreds of thousands. A particularly unpleasant aspect was the frequent inclusion of women in punitive units.[19]

Apart from losses incurred by this and other wasteful forms of fighting, where losses were considered immaterial provided objectives were attained, there were other unusual causes of casualties. Svetlana Stalin tells how Beria

carried out the abominable liquidation of whole army units, at times very large ones, who, during the swift German advance into the Ukraine and Byelorussia, had found themselves cut off from their own lines, and who later, against frightful odds, had found their way back.[20]

Actions like this, frequently resulting in minor battles between NKVD and regular troops, continued until the end of the war.[21]

Thus the disproportionate scale of Soviet military casualties can readily be accounted for, but what of civilian losses, totalling as they did some 22,500,000 lives? Large numbers perished as a direct or indirect result of German actions. Possibly a quarter of a million civilians were killed during operations against Soviet partisans, and some 750,000 Russian Jews were massacred at Babi Yar and elsewhere. A further million people may have died in the Ukraine in 1941–2, when the Germans made no attempt to feed the urban population. Yet another million civilians could have perished during the siege of Leningrad and other cities. Finally, up to half a million Russians died working as slave-labour in the Reich.[22] Thus about four million Russian civilian deaths may be laid at the door of the Germans. A further death toll must have resulted from the 'scorched earth' policy pursued by both sides when retreating.

However generously these figures are interpreted, there is still a residue of some ten to fifteen million Russian corpses to account for. Any calculation remotely approaching exactitude is clearly impossible, but it is not difficult in general terms to account for this fantastic mortality.

Firstly, there were the losses incurred during Stalin's invasions of Poland and Finland in 1939–40. The first campaign resulted in minuscule casualties,[23] but in Finland they were enormous. Khrushchev believed that a million men died there, though the true figure may be about a quarter of that number.

Secondly, Soviet policy in compelling the evacuation of large sections of the population suspected of sympathy for the invaders resulted in widespread epidemics throughout the countryside.[24]

Thirdly, the NKVD conducted widespread purges behind the lines throughout the war, particularly in reoccupied territories, their victims being counted in unknown thousands or, very likely, millions. This culminated in a regular war against Ukrainian nationalists and other opponents of the regime.[25] About 1,600,000 people were deported from among the Crimean Tartars, Caucasian Republics and Volga Germans. Perhaps another million Germans from elsewhere in the Soviet Union underwent the same fate, and a similar number of Ukrainians.[26] Finns from Soviet Karelia had already been deported *en masse* in 1939.

Fourthly came unprecedented mortality in the greatly swollen camps of GULAG. The normal death-rate, terrible as it was, increased enormously through difficulties caused by the expanded prison population and other wartime aggravations of conditions.[27] To this must be added the myriads exterminated in prison massacres such as that at L'vov, when being evacuated eastwards to escape the German advance, and in the camps themselves.[28] A former prisoner, who with his comrades conducted a rough-and-ready estimate, reckoned that seven million GULAG inmates were slaughtered in the first year of the war.[29] There is no means of checking such figures, but nothing in the history of GULAG suggests it need be exaggerated. Fifthly comes the category of Russians who, as prisoners-of-war, deported slave-labour or refugees, fell into German hands and were subsequently repatriated. A total of some 5,500,000 were recovered, of whom 2,272,000 were obligingly handed back by the British and Americans.[30] Thousands were massacred on arrival, whilst the overwhelmingly majority of the remainder disappeared and died in forced-labour camps.[31]

It will readily be seen that all this mortality accounts without difficulty for the missing statistic of Russian losses. However one assesses the proportion, it is clear that casualties directly attributable to the Germans account for only a third, or at most half, of Soviet overall losses in manpower in the years 1939–45, even if we discount the heavy responsibility that must rest on the Soviet Government for the military and political blunders of 1941–2, and the fate of the prisoners-of-war in Germany. Most Russians killed at that time died in the invasion of Finland and in the subsequent war of the NKVD against the civil and military population of the USSR.

It was this government and the political system it enforced which aroused the enthusiastic loyalty of so many in the West. Though much of what was going on in Soviet Russia was hidden from view, more than enough information was accessible to those who wished to know. The truth was available in countless books and articles written by fugitives from the USSR, from thousands of Soviet citizens and (after 1941) Poles in the West, from Western visitors such as Malcolm Muggeridge, Eugene Lyons and Andrew Smith, and even from published Soviet sources. What was glaringly obvious to Arthur Koestler and George Orwell might have been equally so to Louis Aragon, J. D. Bernal or Lillian Hellman.[32] How did it happen that thousands of intelligent people inveigled or encouraged millions less intellectually endowed into blind admiration of mass murder, torture and slavery?

At the time, support for the Soviet Union often took the form of neo-religious adulation, in which truth and Stalin's communism were identified and hostile criticism simply heresy. The continually accruing mass of evidence revealing it for what it really was had to be exorcized as an unscrupulous challenge to faith, and its opponents excoriated in a shrill vein of heavy-handed sarcasm which owed much, in appearance at least, to Lenin's inimitable style of polemics. With hindsight, apologists for the generation of Marxists and fellow-travellers claim that their faith was the inevitable reaction to an era of triumphant Fascism, faced in the West by bankrupt politicians bent on appeasement or betrayal. Only the Soviet Union and the international Communist movement stood firm against the

rising tide of reaction. In these circumstances it was perfectly understandable that allegiances should become polarized, and criticism of
the Party be equivalent to defeatism in face of the enemy.

It is necessary only to state this argument for its absurdity to
become patent. For every man who became a Communist in order to
counter Fascism, another became a Fascist in order to counter
Communism. As Communism formed the prior totalitarian threat,
this argument is surely more exculpatory of Fascism and Nazism
than the reverse. Recently a distinguished scientist, Professor Eric
Burhop, wrote to defend the intellectuals' swing to the Left, pointing out that

> The great depression of the 1930s had eaten deep into the whole
> social fabric. Huge unemployment, malnutrition, the dole, means
> test, hunger marchers – these were the realities of the time.
> Clearly the conventional capitalist market had failed and it is not
> surprising that the brightest spirits in our universities were look-
> ing toward alternative social systems . . . [33]

Translate this interpretation into a contemporary German context,
and the argument becomes a rationale of the appeal of National
Socialism. It was totalitarian politics that appealed, and the label
depended on local circumstances.[34]

The motives that drove people, in particular the young and the
intellectuals, to seek totalitarian solutions were multifarious.
Bertrand Russell once asked John Strachey why he had adopted
extreme left-wing views: 'Did you hate your father, your childhood,
or your public school?' Strachey replied light-heartedly, 'a bit of all
three'.[35] The exchange was jocular, but contained the germ of
reality. The shattering of old authorities, religious, political, moral
and social, left millions with an unpleasant sensation of abandonment in a hostile world. Traditional wisdom had inevitably been
replaced by an anarchy of ideas, and the newly-risen class of intellectuals sought power in this spiritual vacuum. Soviet Marxism
seemed to legitimize the intellectuals' desire for a society ruled by
them in virtue of their superior knowledge.[36]

This may explain the attraction of an authoritarian ideal, but not
the concomitant appeal of cruelty and violence which made Stalin
the lodestar of so much of the Left. For cruelty was surely the most
striking common characteristic of the radical Left in the 1930s and
1940s. One Communist, it is true, abandoned his faith when he read

Professor Vladimir Tchernavin's memoir of life in GPU prisons and GULAG camps, *I Speak for the Silent* (1935). 'About me', he recalled later, 'had closed a separating silence – the deathly silence of those for whom Tchernavin spoke – and in that silence I heard their screams . . . I did not know what had happened to me. I denied the very existence of a soul. But I said: "This is evil, absolute evil. Of this evil I am a part." '[37]

But such a reaction, shared by Orwell, Koestler and a handful more, was rare indeed. Few Western Marxists and their sympathizers suffered sleepless nights over the revelations of Tchernavin and his like. If anything, their faith grew stronger at this evidence of Bolshevik determination to continue the fight whatever the cost. They visited Moscow, flaunting their wealth in the face of starving Russia. There were women like Jane, encountered in Moscow by Eugene Lyons,

> . . . a thin, high-strung New York liberal who quivered visibly at the sight of a new man. In Bolshevism she found not only a job but escape from the restraints of an unsatisfactory husband and the supervision of a middle-class family. Sitting on an unmade bed in her hotel room she could talk for hours about freedom for women under the Red flag. 'Starvation, forced labor, the extermination of the intelligentsia,' she said, 'bah! It's worth it, I tell you, because Russia has liquidated sex bugaboos. Equality of men and women, the single standard . . . It's worth it!'

All kinds of personal and social inadequacies drove a troubled generation into projecting its neuroses on to a perfected proletarian Utopia.[38] The cataclysms of the Great War and the Russian Revolution, the loosening of traditional social and familial ties,[39] and the assault on man's most cherished instinctive beliefs, resulting from the discoveries of Darwin, Marx, Freud and Frazer – all these had a profound effect on the generation that survived the Great War. In a world of vanishing landmarks people suffered feelings of deprivation and abandonment. It was inevitable that many, particularly among the young and the middle class, were impelled by this alienation into ill-suppressed sadistic courses. Michael Grant has noted how a similar state of affairs developed in the Roman Empire. As the old city-states and principalities were broken up and absorbed,

> the resultant lonely defencelessness of the individual had created a widespread 'collapse of nerve'. In the vast Roman world these

symptoms became accentuated, permanent and ubiquitous. Millions of people felt shiftless, unsupported, un-looked after, lost – and above all bored. The plunge into religion was one compensatory reaction. But another was immersion in sanguinary sadism.

From this arose the horrors of gladiatorial combats and other savage spectacles.[40]

This combination of mass 'religious' enthusiasm with extreme cruelty has been characteristic of the mid-twentieth century. Sadism orginates in feelings of weakness and inadequacy for which it is necessary to compensate by humiliating and inflicting suffering on others. The Christian tradition has made cruelty *per se* discreditable, but 'holier than thou' causes, when indulged from an exclusive standpoint, can represent a circuitous form of the desire to degrade.[41] As Jung observed, 'Hate had found respectable motives, and had emerged from the state of more secret and personal idio-syncrasy. And all the time the highly respectable public had not the slightest inkling that they themselves were thus living in the immediate neighbourhood of evil.'[42]

The apparent docility of the Russian masses in face of oppression merely increased the hatred and contempt of Western admirers of Stalin. 'It is impossible to avoid the conclusion that, in human beings, a show of weakness on the part of the defeated is as likely to increase hatred as to restrain it. Perhaps our most unpleasant characteristic as a species is our proclivity for bullying the helpless', as Anthony Storr has noted.[43]

It was Jean-Paul Sartre who believed that 'To keep hope alive one must, in spite of all mistakes, horrors, and crimes, recognise the obvious superiority of the socialist [i.e. Soviet] camp.'[44] Setting aside his unfortunate closing phrase, this declaration can only imply that it is better for millions of Russians to suffer 'horrors and crimes' than that he, Sartre, and his friends should have to abandon their illusions. News of these and similar views expressed in the West occasionally percolated through to Russian intellectuals, who were obliged to digest their contempt in secret.[45] By a paradox, it was only in the forgotten world of GULAG that Russians could talk with relative freedom, and mark with sarcastic relish the Western intel-lectuals' moral contortions.[46]

By 1945 the Soviet Union had achieved a remarkable conquest over much of Western public opinion. The intellectuals of the Left, caught up in the turmoil of their inner contradictions, saw Stalin's Russia as an ideal society run by meritocrats like themselves.[47] Amongst the masses, millions believed the USSR had humbled monocled aristocrats and generals, booted out frock-coated bosses, and exalted the 'workers' into a proletarian *Herrenvolk*. They contentedly swallowed the pro-Soviet propaganda of Lord Beaverbrook and Claud Cockburn, and were in any case robustly indifferent to Russian realities.[48] To these natural sympathizers the War had added the great mass of remaining public opinion which, with great emotion and scant logic, believed the Red Army had poured out its blood on behalf of the Anglo-Americans in order to sustain democracy.[49]

There was in addition a widespread feeling in Europe that old institutions and classes would not survive the war, and that for better or worse the Soviet Union represented the wave of the future. This feeling extended to many who were strongly attached to the old order. Winston Churchill, offered the use of Walmer Castle in 1941, doubted 'very much . . . whether anybody will be able to live in such fine houses after the war.'[50] Oliver Harvey noted in his diary in 1943 that 'under the stimulus of Russia and of a strong Leftward trend in England, Europe is moving Leftwards. The "comfortable" capitalist regimes of pre-war are doomed. Unless it is to be communist, it must at least be Beveridge.'[51] Faced by what they saw as inexorable reality, some hoped to preserve their own positions amidst the rising tide of socialism. Harold Nicolson had indulged a faint hope that whilst Chatsworth and other grand palaces of the aristocracy would have to be sacrificed, his own more modest Sissinghurst might be preserved. He congratulated himself that in any case he had not 'the slightest objection to Russian communism'.[52]

These widespread fears led to the anomalous state of affairs where Labour Party leaders such as Attlee, Bevin and Greenwood remained strongly hostile to Communism and suspicious of Soviet Russia,[53] whilst prominent Conservatives made unconvincing efforts to re-insure with the future. Lord Beaverbrook patronized left-wing politicians such as Bevan and Michael Foot, and hoped by his all-out championship of unrestricted aid to Russia in 1941–2 that he would gain the leadership of the Left.[54] Perhaps the supreme exemplar of this mode of thought was Britain's Foreign Secretary, Anthony Eden. 'He hates the old Tories and would rather join the Labour

Party if they remained dominant', his private secretary noted in 1941. Essentially a vain, shallow and humourless character, he believed his strength lay 'among the people', referred to himself as 'the Red Eden', and was immensely flattered when in 1943 he learned that a secret meeting of trade union leaders had nominated him as successor to Churchill.[55] Like Beaverbrook, he believed that wholehearted support for the Soviet Union would win him the public support he needed.[56] He had always admired and liked Stalin, and nurtured long-lasting delusions concerning his benevolence and moderation. Regarding Churchill as 'dangerously anti-Russian',[57] he advocated a policy which, with rare lapses or misgivings, amounted to generous acquiescence in Stalin's aims, in matters ranging in importance from Stalin's claim to territories awarded him by Hitler, to declining to demand hospital facilities for British sailors at Archangel. In April 1943 the Head of the Northern Department of the Foreign Office summed up policy towards the USSR as having been governed by 'the sort of rule of thumb under which we . . . never say anything unpleasant to the Russians if we can possibly help it however much we disapprove of their doings . . . '[58] Even the Soviet betrayal of Warsaw did not shake Eden's faith, and on 20 December 1944 he told a friend he had 'a real liking for Stalin', who had 'never broken his word'.[59] As late as December 1946 Eden explained to a now sceptical Foreign Office 'that there was disagreement in the Politburo and that we should concentrate on arriving at an understanding with Stalin who alone had moderate ideas'.[60]

It was under this leadership that British policy towards the Soviet Union was formulated, and which made it possible for Stalin to receive vital British help in his post-war campaign to reassert totalitarian powers over the Russian people. Before Eden became Foreign Secretary in December 1940, the Northern Department of the Foreign Office (which deals, *inter alia*, with the Soviet Union) contained men such as Fitzroy Maclean who were in the highest degree aware of Soviet realities. But as the war continued, and officials were promoted or seconded elsewhere, a new breed of young men took their place. Educated at Oxford and Cambridge during the turbulent years of the rise of Hitler, the Italian invasion of Abyssinia, and the Spanish Civil War, they were not immune to strong currents of left-wing opinion flowing through the universities. To them Soviet Russia was not the ramshackle tyranny analysed by their predecessors, Oliphant, Vereker or Maclean, but the shining hope of the coming generation and the first bastion against Nazism. They made no attempt to disguise their views, which upset the old guard of the Conservative Party and resulted in accusations that Eden was 'only promoting Left-wing people in the F.O.'[61] They tended to be critical of the Poles[62] and were convinced of Soviet goodwill.

Geoffrey Wilson, for example, was a thirty-year-old barrister who had been Chairman of the Oxford University Labour Club in 1930 and who became personal secretary to Sir Stafford Cripps, accompanying him to Moscow when he became Ambassador there in 1940. (The NKVD was naturally very anxious to penetrate this mission, and unsuccessfully attempted to infiltrate Guy Burgess as an attendant official.)[63] After Cripps's departure in 1942, Wilson stayed on as First Secretary at the Embassy. With Molotov's special permission he toured extensively in the Urals and elsewhere.[64] Though most travellers in the USSR at that time came away intensely depressed by the unmistakable evidence of unheard-of suffering and oppression, together with the open use of slave-labour,[65] Geoffrey Wilson's faith in Soviet integrity remained undimmed. Back in London in 1943-4, he wrote urgently to the British Ambassador in Moscow, seeking a pretext to return. 'I want to get to Moscow again for a bit,' he wrote. 'My faith grows weak here and I find that it revives in Moscow and when I can wander about in Russia.'[66]

As the autumn of 1944 drew on Stalin was preparing increasingly for the day when the USSR and the Anglo-Americans would meet in the heart of Europe. At the top of the list of his priorities would be the pressing need for re-imposition of Party control over the Soviet people and the neighbouring lands of the Molotov-Ribbentrop Award, which were on the point of being recovered. In practical terms this meant blocking any outside attempt to interfere with the suppression of the Polish Home Army, and Allied co-operation in recovering the millions of Russians known to have been absorbed by the Germans into Central and Western Europe. If they remained outside NKVD control, they could represent a potent focus of Russian opposition to the regime. The concept of exiled governments heading internal resistance movements had been a major innovation in the war and, with Stalin's obsessive concern with security, loomed high in his fearful imaginings.

Geoffrey Wilson seems to have sensed this with exceptional clarity and exerted himself to influence his country's policy in a way that accommodated Stalin's two principal aims. He was forthright in his advocacy of Britain's abandonment of King Peter in Yugoslavia, and of the Polish Government-in-exile in London. In the New Year of 1944 the Soviets had organized a puppet Communist 'government' on Polish soil, and Wilson urged that Britain should recognize this group and abandon 'people that they [the Soviets] regard as fascists'. Neither the Katyn massacre nor the declared Soviet intention to recover the territory awarded them by Hitler had disillusioned him.

In April 1944 Wilson circulated within the Foreign Office an in-fluential paper, urging in essence that Soviet intentions in Eastern Europe and elsewhere were honourable and reasonable, and that the British Government should abandon lingering suspicions of Stalin's motives it might still be harbouring.[67] Scornful of any notion that the dictator might revert to oppressive or expansionist policies,[68] he strongly urged censorship of newspapers making even the mildest criticisms of Soviet life, following an approach from an NKVD agent, Constantin Zinchenko, attached to the Soviet Embassy.[69] Above all, he was anxious that Britain should abandon support for the Polish Government-in-exile, and come to terms with Stalin's puppet Lublin Committee.[70] His great fear was that Churchill would obstruct smooth relations with the Soviet Government. 'Russian matters are pretty tricky at the moment', he wrote in August 1943, 'B—— B—— face [Churchill] is the real snag . . . now that he can see the end of the war in sight my impression is that he does not care two hoots about the Russians.' To the eccentric British Ambassador in Moscow, Sir Archibald Clark Kerr, Wilson lamented further that 'It's too sad that Stalin & Mol [otov] were not at Eton & Harrow. What can we do about it?'[71] Wilson was clearly referring to Eden and Churchill's public-school background, but it is unlikely that Sir Archibald relished the implications of this coy innuendo. Though he too had not been to a public school, he was inclined to view these things *de haut en bas*. Class undoubtedly represented an important factor in Wilson's thinking. On another occasion he rejected a suggestion by the Polish General Anders that a victorious Red Army might prove a menace to European civilization, on the grounds that a person of his (upper) class background would be bound to think like that.

Another question important to Stalin in which Geoffrey Wilson interested himself was that of the British Military Mission to

Moscow. The Foreign Office had advised its successive Heads to accept without protest any restrictions the Soviet authorities cared to impose on them. Neither General Martel nor his successor, General Brocas Burrows, was the kind of man to stomach this sort of treatment indefinitely.[72] Both were anxious, for obvious professional reasons, to visit the front line. This desire was continually obstructed for reasons which appeared merely obscurantist to the generals, but which were important enough to Stalin. There was much going on behind Red Army lines which it was not healthy for inquisitive Englishmen to observe. Widespread indiscipline and poor organization of rear areas and supply systems might provide the West with a less daunting picture of the invincible Red Army than Stalin's post-war aims required. Still more vital was the necessity to prevent the Western powers from finding out what the NKVD was up to as the Red Army began to overrun Polish territory. In midsummer 1944 a major Soviet offensive brought their troops into eastern Poland, and orders were at once issued for the liquidation of Polish Home Army units: an operation that once again saw the NKVD co-operating on occasion with their former colleagues of the Gestapo.[73] The anticipated liberation of British and American prisoners-of-war would provide an additional pretext for the presence of British officers from the Military Mission in ravaged Poland, and Stalin decided it was time to get rid of the pertinacious General Burrows.

This did not at first appear a straightforward task. Where Burrows's predecessor Martel had been (often with successful results) blunt and outspoken in his attitude, Brocas Burrows was careful not to affront Soviet susceptibilities. He spoke fluent Russian, rejected Martel's declared policy of 'open reprisals'; and it was admitted even by Christopher Warner at the Foreign Office's Russian desk 'that General Burrows . . . has tackled his difficult job very sensibly, has been patient and has kept a balanced view'.[74] What could be done to get rid of him? He had managed at last to arrange a brief visit to the front in early July 1944, and by September the Red Army was at the gates of Warsaw. Stalin's dilemma rested on the fact that he liked to have *some* evidence, however tenuous or spurious, when concocting a case. It was moreover necessary to overcome British objections to Burrows's recall. The NKVD was set to work and soon came up with incriminating material. On 24 September Stalin informed Ambassador Clark Kerr that General Burrows had

described Red Army officers as 'savages', which had greatly offended
Marshal Vassilievsky and other senior commanders. Reporting on
this conversation to Eden, Kerr declared the charge to be 'baffling',
as in fact Vassilievsky was on the best of terms with Burrows and had
clearly not been primed with the accusation issued in his name.
Nevertheless, Stalin appeared to be convinced of the truth of the
allegation, and the War Office was reluctantly obliged to withdraw
Burrows.[75] Burrows was equally hard put to understand what had
brought about the accusation, and it was from an unexpected source
that Clark Kerr received confirmation of Stalin's charges.

Geoffrey Wilson had long cast a critical eye on the Military
Mission in Moscow. He had objected to Martel's forthrightness, and
about this time urged investigation of an officer at Murmansk who
had seen too much of Soviet treatment of repatriated Russian
prisoners-of-war.[76] On 3 October he wrote to Kerr from London,
'There's one thing I ought to warn you of. That stuff about savages,
etc. that Burrows was accused of – there's more in that than meets
the eye . . . I will tell you more about it when I see you next'.[77]
What had in fact happened was that the NKVD had planted micro-
phones in General Burrows's office, and so had been able to overhear
private criticisms not intended for Soviet ears. Thus there was
certainly 'more than met the eye' in Stalin's complaint, but the
British authorities did not discover that the 'bugging' had taken
place until the following summer.[78] Wilson was in close contact
with men in a position to know what was going on, as he knew
Zinchenko and other officials at the Soviet Embassy, and was in
touch with Colonel Ivan Chichaev, Head of the NKVD Mission in
London.[79] But they could scarcely have revealed the secret of the
bugging of Burrows's office to him, as in that case Wilson would
naturally have informed the Military Mission in Moscow.

Eventually Wilson came to fear that his 'peculiar views' would
land him in 'difficulties', even with his none too shrewd superiors,[80]
and that he might have to retire from the Foreign Office to accept
'some very tempting offers from outside which I can't afford to
ignore indefinitely'.[81] His fears proved groundless, and he was sent
to assist in the negotiations at the Yalta Conference in February
1945, where the fate of Poland and the Russian prisoners-of-war
were, *inter alia*, decided.

He appears to have been the first British official to suggest (on 28
April 1944) that Russians liberated in the West should be repatriated

by force. After the Normandy landings in June, thousands of these
Russians were brought to Britain and held in camps. When they
learned that they might indeed be compelled to return to the USSR,
several committed suicide. Geoffrey Wilson hastily approached the
News Department to ensure (successfully) that no news of this
leaked to the public. As he explained later, it was vital 'to avoid the
risk of a serious public scandal'. When the International Red Cross
pressed an inquiry as to whether the Russians were being treated in
accordance with the Geneva Convention on Prisoners-of-War,
Wilson claimed inaccurately that all the prisoners had been forced
into German uniform, and therefore did not come under the category
of prisoners-of-war.[82]

Neither horrifying descriptions filed by the Foreign Office of
atrocities committed on the returned prisoners, nor the Soviet
extinction of independence and freedom in Eastern European
countries served to disillusion Geoffrey Wilson from his 'peculiar
views'. In September 1946, when Poland, the Baltic States, Romania,
Bulgaria, Hungary, eastern Austria and Germany had been drastically
purged and pillaged, Wilson told a Fabian Society meeting that in
most of these countries a social revolution had come about. 'It seems
to me that, as Socialists, we can do nothing but rejoice that these
revolutions have taken place.'[83] Wilson had retired from his temporary posting at the Foreign Office, and not long after assisted in
drafting the International Bill of Human Rights.[84]

These optimistic views were shared by a close colleague in the
Foreign Office, who had been with Wilson at the Moscow Embassy,
and played an even more significant part in the secret hand-over of
Russian prisoners to the NKVD. At the end of June 1945 Thomas
Brimelow, another socialist, expressed his confidence that Soviet
conquests would ensure a more equitable distribution of property.[85]
It was not until 1946, with Ernest Bevin firmly in the saddle as
Foreign Secretary, and a new Head of the Northern Department
(Robin Hankey), that the Foreign Office began to adopt a more real-
istic attitude towards Soviet Russia.

This jungle of illusion and self-deception was of the greatest
importance to Stalin when consolidating his aggrandized empire.
But whilst he doubtless appreciated the assistance he received so
generously, he had no intention of watching the meal prepared without joining in the cooking himself.

XVII
Close Designs and Crooked Counsels

Anthony: These many then shall die; their names are prick'd.
Octavius: Your brother too must die; Consent you, Lepidus?
Lepidus: I do consent.

(Julius Caesar, IV, i, 1–3)

Forced repatriation of Soviet citizens was certainly the most remarkable example of Western appeasement in 1945. But there is one particular operation which in turn stands out from the rest, whose details have remained concealed up to now. Even today the full story cannot be told, though there are men living who could undoubtedly reveal the truth should they agree to speak. But new evidence recently uncovered has at last made it possible to give a clear outline of the story.

On 17 January a brief notice in *Pravda* announced the trial and execution of six men, all condemned for heading White Guard detachments co-operating with the Germans against the Soviet Union during the Great Fatherland War. They were listed as Ataman (Cossack leader) P. N. Krasnov, Lieutenant-General A. G. Shkuro, Major-General Prince Sultan-Ghirey, Major-General S. N. Krasnov, Major-General T. I. Domanov (all described as commanders of the White Army), and a German General, Helmuth von Pannwitz. To a Russian readership the list of names required no commentary. It comprised six of the most dangerous and inveterate opponents of Soviet power, whose activities spanned the thirty years of the Bolshevik regime's existence. With the aid of foreign arms, these men had on successive occasions been within an ace of overthrowing the dictatorship.

Peter Nikolaevich Krasnov had led the troops which in September 1917 marched on Petrograd in an unsuccessful attempt to pre-empt the forthcoming Bolshevik *coup*. A year later he led his Don Cossacks against Tsaritsyn (later Stalingrad), whose Red Army defenders were headed by Stalin himself. Krasnov retired to exile, where he wrote polemical novels and articles violently hostile to the Soviet Union. In the Second World War he worked with anti-Soviet Russian military units raised by the Germans. By this time he was largely a figurehead of resistance, and at his death in 1947 he was nearly eighty years old.

Next in fame was Andrei Shkuro, another veteran Cossack leader. A daring guerrilla leader in the First World War, his Kuban Cossacks wrought havoc on Red Army units in southern Russia during the Civil War. Shkuro's 'Wolves', as they were known, had a reputation for plunder and banditry as well as daring, and Shkuro himself spent his years of exile carousing with White Russian comrades and performing astonishing horseback feats in a travelling circus. When the Germans raised Cossack units in 1943, the veteran Shkuro found himself much in demand wherever vodka and Cossack choruses flowed around the camp fire.

Prince Ghirey, another veteran of Civil War days, had similarly joined Caucasian volunteers in German service. Of the remainder, Semeon Krasnov was the old Ataman's son and Timofey Domanov was a captured Red Army Major appointed by the Germans to command a fugitive Cossack settlement known as the *Kazachi Stan*. General von Pannwitz was the sole non-Russian among them. A distinguished German cavalry officer, he had been appointed to command the 15th Cossack Cavalry Corps, which fought against Tito's partisans in Yugoslavia.

No indication was provided as to how the dead White leaders had fallen into Soviet hands, beyond the fact that they had been 'arrested'. The *Great Soviet Encyclopaedia* later stated that Peter Krasnov had been captured by Soviet forces in 1945. This was untrue, as in fact all six men had been handed over by British military authorities in Austria, to whom the generals and their followers had surrendered in 1945. Since the publication of *Victims of Yalta* in 1978 the public has become familiar with the story of Allied forced repatriation at the end of the last war, and it might well be assumed that the six generals were surrendered to the Soviets under the now notorious agreement signed on 11 February 1945 at Yalta.

In fact this was not so. The Yalta Agreement, both in its wording and its interpretation, exclusively concerned the repatriation of Soviet citizens: that is, people who on or after the outbreak of war had been citizens of the Soviet Union. The distinction was regarded as highly significant from the start, since the Soviet authorities claimed thousands of Balts, Poles and Romanians whose territories had been granted to them by Hitler in 1939. Neither Britain nor the United States was prepared to recognize those conquests, and they declined to hand over citizens of the occupied regions who were unwilling to go. A further category was the millions of White Russians who had emigrated at the time of the Revolution, and who now enjoyed foreign citizenship or were categorized as stateless. They too had never lived in the USSR, and could not be regarded as its citizens.

Of the six generals slaughtered in the courtyard of Lefortovo Prison in 1947, only one (Domanov) was liable to return under the Yalta Agreement. Of the remainder, four were White Russians and one a German. To this day the Foreign Office is adamant that such men should not have been knowingly handed over, and professes ignorance as to how such a tragedy came about. Everywhere else that Russians fell into British hands careful screening took place to ensure that only Soviet citizens were liable to forcible repatriation. If occasionally there were tragic errors, they were due to the confused circumstances of the time. However, my research indicates that the return of Krasnov and his companions was no blunder, but a carefully organized plan.

After the German surrender on 9 May 1945 British-occupied Austria was administered by 5 Corps of the 8th Army, commanded by Lieutenant-General Charles Keightley. He established his headquarters at Klagenfurt and began to restore order amongst the chaotic debris of war. One of the most urgent issues was to establish a *modus vivendi* with the neighbouring Soviet authorities, and on 12 May Keightley travelled to Wolfsberg inside the British zone to confer with a deputation from Marshal Tolbukhin's staff. During the discussion a Soviet officer present raised a question that was giving much concern to his Government. It was known that some forty or fifty thousand Cossacks serving on the enemy side had surrendered to the British in Austria over the past few days.

No minutes of this exchange survive in the relevant British archives, though the meeting itself is recorded in a film now preserved in the Imperial War Museum. Further details can be reconstructed, however, from the autobiography of the then Deputy Chief of the General Staff of the Red Army, General Semeon Shtemenko. In the second volume of his memoirs, which treats of the final defeat of

Germany, he describes the capture of the Cossack leaders. After an account of the anti-Soviet background of Generals Peter Krasnov, Andrei Shkuro and Sultan Ghirey, and their surrender to the British in Austria, the following significant passage appears:

> The Soviet Government then made a firm representation to our allies over the matter of Krasnov, Shkuro, Sultan-Ghirey, and other war criminals. The British stalled briefly; but since neither the old White Guard generals nor their troops were worth much, they put all of them into trucks and delivered them into the hands of the Soviet authorities.[1]

Shtemenko was in an exceptionally strong position to know the facts and his wording is significant.[2] 'The Soviet Government then made a firm representation to our allies over the matter of Krasnov . . . *The British stalled briefly* . . . ' This can only mean that the British at first refused the request. Only after some consideration did they accede. It will be seen shortly that Shtemenko's version is borne out by British documents to which he could have had no access. But why did Keightley turn down the demand at Wolfsberg on 12 May, as Shtemenko's account implies? After all, consistent British policy since the previous September had provided for the return of all captured Soviet citizens to the Soviet Union. In the previous October Allied Force Headquarters had been informed by the Foreign Office that Soviet nationals captured or liberated in Italy were to be sent home regardless of their wishes.[3] Thereafter they were shipped to camps in Egypt and transported to the Soviet Union by the Middle East route. On 22 March 1945 1,657 men of the 162nd Turkoman Division, a hard-fighting Wehrmacht unit recruited from captured Soviet Central Asians, were dispatched by sea from Taranto to Odessa.

If the Turkomans could be sent home under the Foreign Office ruling, why did Keightley not regard the Cossacks as similarly affected? During the three weeks that their fate was being decided, thousands of other Soviet citizens – liberated prisoners-of-war, captured personnel serving with the Germans, refugees – continued to be handed over to the Soviets. They were allowed no choice in the matter, force being frequently applied, and no authority beyond pre-existing British policy, effected throughout the previous seven months, was required to empower Allied commanders in the field.[4]

The reason seems clear. The Cossack units captured in Austria included a very large proportion of what 5 Corps's 36 Infantry Brigade War Diary termed 'Tsarist exiles', i.e. Russians who had emigrated at the time of the Revolution. Under no circumstances could existing British policy on forced repatriation be held to apply to them.

Keightley's initial refusal to agree to hand over the three White Russian generals suggests that he had already been briefed as to the significance of their non-Soviet citizenship. If not he must in any case on his return to HQ at Klagenfurt have called for a full report in order to give the Soviet request proper consideration. Brigadier C. E. Tryon-Wilson, then serving on Keightley's staff, clearly recalls the list of names presented by the Soviets, and the embarrassment caused by the fact that none of the three was covered by the Yalta Agreement. For if Keightley did not already know the identity of the listed Russians, Tolbukhin's request obliged him to investigate it at once. There was no difficulty here. Krasnov and his companions were held by 36 Infantry Brigade, commanded by Brigadier Geoffrey Musson, in the valley of the Drau around Lienz and Oberdrauburg. Their surrender had been negotiated on 7 May, when a Cossack deputation crossed the mountains to confer with Musson and his divisional commander, Major-General Robert Arbuthnott. The Cossack representatives were General Vasiliev, a former officer of the Tsar's Imperial Guard; Nikolai Krasnov, grandson of General Peter; and Olga Rotova, an English-speaking Yugoslav citizen who had worked for the Standard Oil Company. None was a Soviet citizen, and the two British generals heard a detailed account of their origins and status. Next day Musson motored to the Cossack HQ, where he met General Krasnov himself and negotiated the surrender of the Caucasians with Prince Ghirey. Shortly afterwards, on 10 May, General Shkuro fell into the hands of the British, who were intrigued to note that he 'had fought under Denikine', the commander of the anti-Bolshevik White Armies in 1918.

Thus, when General Keightley came to check the names listed by Tolbukhin, he found that the principal Cossack and Caucasian commanders, together with sizeable numbers of their followers, were (as the 36 Infantry Brigade War Diary put it) 'displaced persons of nationalities other than Soviet'. On 6 May Allied Force Headquarters at Caserta (AFHQ) had sent a precise definition as to what constituted a Soviet citizen to 8th Army HQ.[5] The Cossack generals could not be more clearly excluded from this category.

There was a further embarrassment. At the time of the Cossacks'

surrender to Keightley's forces, old General Krasnov had written a
letter to Field-Marshal Alexander, who, as Supreme Allied Commander in the Mediterranean (SACMED), held final responsibility for
everything that took place in Allied-occupied Italy and Austria. In his
appeal Krasnov drew 'attention to the special position of the Cossack
host' and 'reminded him how they had fought together against the
Communists during the Russian Civil War and requested that the
British troops under his command protect the Cossack Land from the
Soviets and transmit to his government the request that all of them be
accorded political asylum as stateless refugees'.[6]

This letter was passed up from the local Battalion Headquarters to
36 Infantry Brigade, and thence via 78 Infantry Division to 5 Corps
HQ. Its passage and reception were recalled by Brigadier Tryon-
Wilson and General Sir Geoffrey Musson. Subsequent letters written
by the Cossack general never reached their destinations, and it seems
certain that this and a further appeal to Alexander at the end of the
month were suppressed *en route*. It is not difficult to see why.

As Krasnov's letter intimated, there was good reason for the Field-
Marshal to feel sympathy for the Cossacks' plight. This stemmed not
only from his intensely chivalrous outlook but also from old association with their cause. As a young Major in the Irish Guards he had
been seconded in 1919 to command forces raised by the infant Baltic
States to resist a Bolshevik invasion. The White Russian General
Yudenitch awarded him a high decoration which he continued to wear
with pride. The Cossacks represented the last fighting units of those
White Armies whose cause Alexander had once shared. It must have
appeared inconceivable that Alexander could be induced to accede to
the Soviet demand, given this close sentimental association and the
fact that as an old émigré Krasnov and the two other Cossacks named
in the Soviet list were not in any case liable for return. What was
Keightley to do? He felt strongly inclined to comply with the Soviet
request. But he had not the authority to do so, and to go beyond his
powers required a political decision.

To cope with exigencies of just this type the British Government
had in December 1942 appointed a Minister Resident at AFHQ, whose
duty was to provide a political presence at Headquarters. This was
Harold Macmillan, who worked in close co-operation with Field-
Marshal Alexander at Caserta, and was at the same time in regular
communication with the Prime Minister (Winston Churchill) and
Foreign Secretary (Anthony Eden). If Keightley had reasons for not

seeking instruction from Alexander, Macmillan was the person to whom he should turn.

The day after Keightley's receipt of the Soviet demand, 13 May, Macmillan flew in to his HQ at Klagenfurt. The two men talked together about the situation facing British forces in Austria. The problem of the Cossacks was discussed, Keightley explaining that they were an encumbrance to the already overstretched Allied supply system and might prove a bone of contention between the British and Soviet authorities. The obvious solution was to hand them over to Tolbukhin's forces, but a serious obstacle had arisen.

Beyond this we possess no further direct account of what transpired in the discussion, and efforts to elucidate the matter have been unsuccessful. General Keightley unfortunately died shortly before I could contact him. I wrote three times to Mr Macmillan, in 1974, 1975 and 1981, the first time with a general inquiry and afterwards with more specific questions. He stated firmly that he was unable to assist me.

Fortunately, however, a fairly full picture can be reconstructed from related evidence. Firstly, it is important to note that no one was more aware of the relevant British policy than Harold Macmillan. Immediately after the signing of the Agreement at Yalta, he received from the Foreign Office a lengthy telegram dictating the policy to be established in the area administered by AFHQ. He was informed that

> The line which we have taken and which you should follow is that all persons who are Soviet citizens under British law must be repatriated and that any person who is not (repeat not) a Soviet citizen under British law must not (repeat not) be sent back to the Soviet Union unless he expressly desires to be so.[7]

Despite his knowledge of British Government policy, it is difficult to avoid the conclusion that it was Macmillan who persuaded or encouraged Keightley to surrender the people demanded by Tolbukhin. Keightley's initial rejection of the request indicates that he knew he lacked the power of himself to consent, and was seeking higher authority. That authority can only have been the Minister Resident. Keightley's subordinates were on several occasions informed that what followed was based on a 'political decision'.

In his memoirs, drawing on a diary kept at the time, Macmillan wrote:

Among the surrendering Germans there were about 40,000 Cossacks and White Russians, with their wives and children. These were naturally claimed by the Russian commander, and we had no alternative but to surrender them. Nor indeed had we any means of dealing with them had we refused to do so. But it was a great grief to me that there was no other course open.

Possibly inadvertently, he thus made it clear that he knew of the presence of the White émigrés among the Cossacks of Soviet origin; also, as his concluding sentence implies, that all the Cossacks had the strongest objection to returning. The reference, too, to the claim by the Russian commander shows that he knew about Tolbukhin's demand. It was this that contained the specific request for Krasnov, Shkuro and Ghirey.

The only alternative to Macmillan's involvement would be that Keightley, for motives unknown and at great risk to himself, decided to deceive Alexander and set up the operation on his own initiative. This is not only highly improbable *per se*, but invites the question why in that case he did not accede to Tolbukhin's request when he first received it.

Before passing on to describe the remarkable subterfuges which followed, it is necessary to note that the political decision which sent Krasnov and his comrades to their doom did not stand in isolation. Besides the two large bodies of Cossacks, those under Krasnov and the former Red Army major Domanov at Lienz, and the Cossack Corps under von Pannwitz (nearly 50,000 people in all) further east, there were two other large bodies of 'Russians' held by 5 Corps. At Klein St Veit there were 4,500 men of the *Schutzkorps*, a unit largely comprising White Russians resident in Yugoslavia. Led by a Colonel Rogozhin, they had withdrawn before Tito's advance and surrendered to the British. And around Spittal, near Lienz, was the Ukrainian nationalist SS Division known as Galicia. Its 10,000 men had fought against the Red Army, and contained a high proportion of men who were, in British eyes, Soviet citizens.

Both these units were reprieved, and not handed over to the Soviets. Unfortunately all documents relating to this important decision have disappeared from the archive, so one can only guess at the reason. A Colonel Walton Ling of the Red Cross, who had formerly served with the White Army in south Russia, took up the cause of the *Schutzkorps* with great enthusiasm at 5 Corps HQ. It may well have been felt that he would have raised a dangerous outcry should Rogozhin's men be threatened with surrender to the Soviets. Similarly, the Ukrainians included very many Polish citizens who were in touch with General Anders and 2 Polish Corps in Italy – awkwardly vociferous friends.

Whatever the reasons, a decision was definitely arrived at not to repatriate the *Schutzkorps* and the Galicia Division. This was a major political decision. It is hard to believe that Tolbukhin did not claim at least the Ukrainians; Stalin himself was to do so at Potsdam two months later. It seems inconceivable that General Keightley could have taken it upon himself to make a whole series of far-reaching political decisions of this sort. It was precisely to settle this sort of contingency that Macmillan had been sent to AFHQ.

One thing is certain, and that is that within twenty-four hours of Macmillan's visit to Klagenfurt, General Keightley adopted the astonishing decision to suppress Krasnov's letter and withhold from his superiors the fact that the Soviets had demanded the three White Russian generals. For the next day, 14 May, he dispatched this telegram to Field-Marshal Alexander:

On advice Macmillan have today suggested to Soviet General on Tolbukhin's HQ that Cossacks should be returned to SOVIETS at once. Explained that I had no power to do this without your authority but would be glad to know Tolbukhin's views and that if they coincided with mine I would ask you officially. Cannot see any point in keeping this large number Soviet nationals who are clearly great source contention between Soviets and ourselves.

Keightley's telegram deliberately concealed the fact that a request had already been received from the Soviets, and that the names of those most prominently listed in it were those of men who were *not* Soviet citizens. That this was no 'slip up'[8] is clearly borne out by events which followed in quick succession.

Alexander's reply (presumably there must have been one) is absent from the files. One can therefore only guess at what it contained: possibly a reiteration of the familiar ruling that Soviet citizens were to be summarily returned to their own authorities. What it could not have included was any specific authority to hand over the Cossacks. For on 17 May Alexander dispatched an inquiry of his own to the Combined Chiefs of Staff in Washington.

To assist us in clearing congestion in Southern Austria we urgently require direction regarding final disposal . . . Approximately

50,000 Cossacks including 11,000 women, children and old men. They have been part of German armed forces and fighting against Allies . . . to return them to their countries of origin immediately might be fatal to their health. Request decision as early as possible as to final disposal.

The decision taken at Klagenfurt to conceal the presence of White Russians among the Cossacks was clearly not an idle precaution. Even though he had reason to believe that only Soviet citizens were involved, the high-minded Field-Marshal expressed the strongest distaste to sending them to a barbaric fate. And despite his instructions to return all Soviet citizens, he was playing for time with this appeal to the Combined Chiefs. At the same time he suggested to Eisenhower that the Cossacks be shifted to Germany, as AFHQ forces in Austria faced a possibly imminent clash with the Communist Yugoslavs. This telegram in turn aroused the interest of Winston Churchill, who as Secretary of State for War in 1919 had been deeply committed to British intervention on behalf of the White cause in the Russian Civil War, and whose sympathies were similar to Alexander's. 'How did they come into their present plight?' he inquired, calling for a further report; 'Did they fight against us?'[9]

Churchill did not receive his report until 5 June, while it was only on the 20th that the Combined Chiefs (in a reply to Alexander's inquiry) approved the handover of those Cossacks who were Soviet citizens. However, the great bulk of Cossacks had already been surrendered to the Soviets between 29 May and 2 June, under conditions of great brutality. Around 28 May Colonel Phillimore of the War Office in London learned that the Cossacks were being 'exchanged under the Yalta Agreement' by 5 Corps, and recommended that their action be approved. About the same time officials of the Foreign Office agreed that all Cossacks 'who are Soviet citizens' should be delivered to the Soviets, in a communication to the Cabinet Offices.

As will be shown shortly, the decision to repatriate the Cossacks in Austria, by force if necessary, had been made at 5 Corps HQ no later than 20 May. The deliberations on high had been anticipated by the event itself. How had this come about? The answer seems to be that Churchill for some reason did not wait for an answer to his questions of 20 May, but issued instructions to Alexander to proceed with the extradition.

For on 26 May Geoffrey McDermott of the Foreign Office wrote to

Colonel C. R. Price, Military Assistant Secretary at the War Cabinet Offices, confirming 'that the Cossacks are covered by the Yalta Agreement . . . and accordingly [we] consider it essential that all of them who are Soviet citizens should be handed over to the Soviet authorities in pursuance of our general policy'. As this recommendation postdated arrangements for repatriation already in effect in Austria, it is clear that this could not have been the ruling which empowered Keightley to act. But what was the point of a ruling given after the event? This has been plausibly explained by Mr McDermott himself:

> My best guess is that F-M Alexander had been told, orally perhaps, by someone very important, such as Winston, to make the necessary arrangements for the repatriation . . . and in due course to go ahead. Then the conscientious Cabinet Offices asked for something on paper from the FO . . . Even a letter from a junior official, such as myself, would suffice for their records.

This supplies the missing piece in the jigsaw. On 25 May 5 Corps finally received a directive to repatriate all Soviet citizens in Austria. As late as the 22nd AFHQ had continued to forbid the use of force in returning Soviet citizens, so it seems that some time between 22 and 25 May Churchill instructed Alexander to hand over the Cossacks. Equally, it is certain that the Prime Minister had only Soviet citizens in mind, since it was they who were specified in the Foreign Office note and the AFHQ order.

What induced Churchill to act in this way before receiving a reply to his inquiry, and before Alexander heard from the Chiefs of Staff, is not known. It is possible that he received a report from Harold Macmillan in person, stressing the urgency of the operation. Macmillan flew to England to confer with the Prime Minister on 19 May. Next day Churchill sent off his inquiry about the Cossacks. With the man most empowered to know about them at his elbow, it would be surprising if he had not discussed the matter with the Minister Resident. Equally, Macmillan is unlikely to have missed the opportunity of repeating to the Prime Minister the urgently felt view he expressed to Keightley a week earlier: that the Cossacks must go back. If so, he certainly did not mention the presence of White émigrés among them. The names of Krasnov and Shkuro would have undoubtedly aroused sympathetic memories. For it was Churchill who, as Secretary of State for War, had been the most ardent advocate in 1918–19 of support for their White Armies in the war against the Bolsheviks.

On 22 May Macmillan returned to AFHQ at Caserta, and the following day negotiations opened at Wolfsberg for the return of the Cossacks. In face of the Prime Minister's directive to return the Cossacks as Soviet citizens liable under the Yalta Agreement, Alexander could only issue the order. The deceit had passed without a hitch. But the Prime Minister and the Supreme Allied Commander were not the only people it was necessary to hoodwink, and as the end of May approached an atmosphere of crisis gripped Keightley and his confidants at 5 Corps HQ.

The tone and implication of General Shtemenko's account quoted earlier suggested that the émigré leaders were the prime objects of Soviet interest. Naturally they wanted the rest of the Cossack officers and men, but that was subsidiary to the main purpose. To their British collaborators it was clear that the fate of Krasnov and his fellow-generals was in any case inextricably linked to that of their followers. Clearly there was no way in which all three could be spirited away from the Cossack camp without making it dangerously clear, before or after the event, that a secret agreement had been made for their abduction.

The majority of Cossack and Caucasian officers at Lienz and Oberdrauburg were drawn from the emigration of 1917–21, as well as a substantial minority of other ranks and their families. They could not be screened off from their Soviet comrades, as AFHQ instructions required, because that would of course preserve the three officers the Soviets were most anxious to obtain. To Keightley – and presumably to Macmillan – this presented a very serious dilemma.

They were determined, for motives as yet unknown, to fall in with the Soviet request. But how could they acquire the necessary authorization from AFHQ that would cover the men most wanted by the Soviet authorities? Alexander would certainly reject any suggestion that men not covered by the Yalta Agreement should be abandoned to the Soviets. Under what authority, in that case, could Keightley act?

A skilful scheme was devised to steer the business through this and other pitfalls. An application could be made to Alexander, drawing no inconvenient attention to the fact that White Russians were involved. To this he would presumably be obliged to reply, however reluctantly, that the provisions of the Yalta Agreement must hold good. Soviet citizens had to be delivered to the Soviet authorities. Meanwhile, all that was required was to conduct a speedy and secretive operation, in which *all* Cossacks, regardless of citizenship, were delivered to the Soviets. Once in the hands of their enemies there was no reason to fear that any White émigré would live to tell the tale.

This part of the plan appeared virtually foolproof, the only impediment to its success lying in the possibility that the Field-Marshal might learn independently of the presence of his former White Russian comrades in the area held by 5 Corps. This was a danger readily obviated. It has been mentioned that Krasnov wrote to Alexander some time in the first fortnight of May, but significantly received no reply. At the end of the month, immediately before the handovers, Krasnov wrote again to Alexander, and also to King George VI, King Peter of Yugoslavia (many of the Cossacks were his subjects) and the Pope. None of these petitions reached its destination.

Shkuro also wrote to explain the Cossack situation to the British. On or about 23 and 24 May he set out a detailed exposition of his 'part in the organisation in particular'. His was an especially embarrassing case, as he had actually been created a Companion of the Bath by King George V in 1919, for gallantry performed alongside British troops in south Russia. The existence of these letters is proved by a reference to them in 36 Brigade War Diary, which records that they were forwarded to divisional headquarters. But the letters themselves have disappeared from the files, and there can be no doubt that they too failed to get beyond 5 Corps HQ. Three days after the delivery of his second letter, Shkuro was seized at early dawn and removed to solitary confinement until he was handed over on 29 May.

A great deal of thought had to go into the way orders were worded. Unfortunately nothing is recorded of the discussions which must have been held at 5 Corps HQ. Lord Aldington, who as Toby Low was then Brigadier General Staff at Klagenfurt, informs me that he can recall nothing of the whole business. This is disappointing, as the post he held was central to all the planning.

The danger was pressing. By 20 May commanders in the field were made aware that large-scale handovers were intended, and inquiries were arriving as to which Russians were liable. On the 21st a very curious document entitled 'Definition of RUSSIAN NATIONALS' was sent by 5 Corps to Brigadier Musson at 36 Infantry Brigade HQ. It explained that

1. Various cases have been referred to this HQ in which doubt has been raised as to whether certain fmns [formations] and groups

should be treated as SOVIET NATIONALS in so far as their return to the
SOVIET UNION direct from 5 Corps is concerned. Rulings in these
cases are given below.

RUSSIAN SCHÜTZKORPS . . . will NOT be treated as SOVIET NATION-
ALS until further orders.

Following will be treated as SOVIET NATIONALS:

   ATAMAN Group

   15 COSSACK CAV CORPS . . .

   Res units of Lt-Gen CHKOURO

   CAUCASIANS . . .

2. Individual cases will NOT be considered unless particularly
pressed. In those cases and in the case of appeals by further units or
fmns, the following directive will apply:-

(a) Any individual now in our hands who, at the time of joining
the GERMAN forces . . . , was living within the 1938 bdy of USSR,
will be treated as a SOVIET NATIONAL for the purposes of transfer.

(b) Any individual although of Russian blood who, prior to
joining the GERMAN forces, had not been in USSR since 1930, will
NOT until further orders be treated as a SOVIET NATIONAL.

(c) In all cases of doubt, the individual will be treated as a SOVIET
NATIONAL.

'Ataman Group' was, as General Musson informed me in 1974, a guide
name for General Krasnov and his group of senior generals at Lienz.
Only one of these (Domanov) was a Soviet citizen, as Musson and his
superior, Arbuthnott, knew well. The 15 Cossack Cavalry Corps was
largely officered by Germans and White Russians – not Soviet citizens. 'Reserve units of Lt-Gen CHKOURO' is a skilfully ambiguous
phrase which may be read or not as including Shkuro himself. The
Caucasians, like the other units, were for the most part led by old
émigrés.

Thus the list of units repatriable in section 1 included a prominent
proportion whom section 2 declared non-repatriable. And where was
the main body of 22,000 Cossacks at Lienz? They were inexplicably
not mentioned at all! We might expect Musson and recipients of this
mélange of contradictions to have scratched their heads and picked up
the telephone for Brigadier Toby Low at Klagenfurt.

In fact the 'Definition' of 21 May was the product of very careful
thought indeed, and had been devised with great skill. If anyone
at Army HQ or AFHQ got wind of the affair, the 'Definition'

provided evidence that every effort was being made to screen and hold back non-Soviet citizens.

That the 21 May 'Definition' was purely a smokescreen to conceal the fact that Krasnov, Shkuro and the White émigrés were to be included in the impending handover is proved by what ensued. If General Arbuthnott or Brigadier Musson felt any inclination to question the self-contradictory document, this was swiftly dispelled. As General Musson emphasized recently, ' . . . it was made very clear to me by General Arbuthnott and by General Keightley and his senior staff officer [Toby Low] that all [Cossack] officers had to be returned and that the orders came from Field Marshal Alexander's headquarters.'

General Arbuthnott, as Brigadier Tryon-Wilson (a staff officer at 5 Corps HQ) recalls, did indeed raise strong objections, but received a similar flat order to obey. Keightley told him a political decision had been made, which they had no choice but to accept. The day after the issue of the 'Definition' of 21 May, AFHQ issued the following order:

1. all who are SOVIET citizens and who can be handed over to RUSSIANS without use of force should [be] returned by EIGHTH ARMY.
2. any others should be evacuated to 12 ARMY GROUP.
3. definition of SOVIET citizen is given in AFHQ letter . . . of 6 May addressed to . . . MAIN EIGHTH ARMY. ref your A 4073 of 21 May asking for policy re COSSACKS.[10]

This instruction makes it clear, so far as AFHQ was concerned, that as yet not even the use of force was contemplated, still less the unwilling return of White Russians. It was not until 25 May that the order came through on which the repatriation operations were based:

Ruling now received 15 Army Gp. all SOVIET CITIZENS including arrestable categories will be treated as surrendered personnel and will therefore be handed over to RUSSIANS. For 5 CORPS, please take action accordingly.[11]

White Russians were still implicitly excluded from return in this order, but the instruction that 'all Soviet citizens . . . will . . . be handed over to Russians' could be taken to imply the employment of force in the case of recalcitrants. ('Arrestable categories' presumably refers to people charged with war crimes.)

However, it would be wrong to suppose that this order of 25 May represented any conscious alteration in attitude on the part of AFHQ. It was the outcome of negotiations conducted with the Soviets at Wolfsberg on 23 and 24 May, where logistical questions were settled, as to how, where and when the Cossacks were to be delivered to the Red Army. The implication seems to be that AFHQ hoped that the vast majority of Soviet refugees held in Austria could be handed over with the minimum of trouble. Already in Germany some 20,000 Soviet citizens had been dispatched to the Soviet zone.

As AFHQ could have learned from SHAEF, these operations took place without incident, though it was not hard to conjecture that amongst those returned were many who would rather not have gone. No doubt it was hoped that the operations in Austria would pass off equally smoothly.

The astonishing discrepancy between the operation envisaged by AFHQ and plans effected by 5 Corps is clearly revealed. No later than 15 May General Horatius Murray of 6 Armoured Division became aware during his visits to Keightley's Headquarters that plans were on foot to hand over all Cossacks, regardless of their wishes or citizenship. Contrary to the Geneva Convention this was to include the German officers of the Cossack Corps, to whom General Murray issued a clear warning. Then, on or just before 20 May, Brigadier Musson of 36 Infantry Brigade was informed that he was to prepare for the handover of all Cossacks and Caucasians held by his troops in the Drau Valley.

These measures to ensure the safe delivery of Krasnov, Shkuro and Ghirey took place *before* any reply was received to 5 Corps' inquiry as to what was AFHQ's 'policy re Cossacks'. By the time the order came from 15 Army Group to hand over all Soviet citizens, 5 Corps had *already* issued detailed instructions for the handover. The facts are indisputable, and there appears to be only one possible explanation. General Keightley must have received prior instructions through a secret channel independent of AFHQ.

On 24 May (the day *before* 15 Army Group instructions arrived, authorizing the handover of Soviet citizens!), 5 Corps issued elaborate orders arranging the transfer of the Cossacks to Soviet hands. Like all documentary orders connected with the handover it contained a preamble restricting those liable for return to Soviet citizens. This was however intended only for purposes of deception, for a significant paragraph emphasized that

It is of the utmost importance that all the officers and particularly senior commanders are rounded up and that none are allowed to escape. The Soviet forces consider this as being of the highest importance and will probably regard the safe delivery of the officers as a test of British good faith.

It is implicit in this that it was particularly Krasnov and his comrades who were to be rounded up. In 6 Armoured Divisional area General Murray deliberately allowed scores of German and Cossack officers to evade return, without any repercussions from Corps HQ.

Concealment of the fact that this gross infringement of international law was being effected, in all orders, reports and war diaries before and after the event, indicates that people higher up the chain of command were being kept in ignorance of the plan. Above all, Field-Marshal Alexander was seen to represent a potent danger, who had to be prevented from knowing what was being done by his subordinates.

As great a fear lay in the possibility that someone among the many officers and men involved in implementing the handover, realizing what was going on, might begin to ask awkward questions and, if sufficiently incensed, raise an outcry not easily stilled. This was unlikely to happen, given the fact that most troops would not be made aware of the impending operation until the latest moment possible. Even then, the speed and efficiency of the operation, the language barrier and the Cossacks' ignorance of the terms of the Yalta Agreement all militated against the likelihood of effective protest.

Still, such *might* happen, and an effective precaution had to be taken. Should a British officer protest against the legality or morality of handing White Russians to the Soviets, it could be explained hastily that there had been an administrative error. As every written order contained the stipulation that only Soviet citizens were to go back, the explanation would appear probable enough. In fact, just such an incident did take place among officers of 6 Armoured Division. A French-speaking Cossack officer from Paris asked Major Henry Howard how the British could contemplate handing over a former officer of the Tsar. Howard saw the anomaly and protested to a sympathetic Brigadier Usher. A telephone call to Klagenfurt resulted in interpreters and documentary material for screening being rushed to the spot.[12] A handful of émigrés had to be withheld: a small price for the avoidance of scandal in surrendering the remaining hundreds.

Shkuro having been removed to close guard away from the Cossack camp, Krasnov and the others still had to be secured, and it was this obstacle which engendered the 'tactic of deception' which aroused so much indignation then and since. On 27 May the Cossacks around Lienz and the neighbouring Caucasians at Oberdrauburg were informed that they were invited to a conference with Field-Marshal Alexander at a point east of Oberdrauburg. The Cossacks fell for the ruse, entered the trucks provided . . . and were driven at once to a wired cage at Spittal. Next day they were in the hands of the Soviets at Judenburg, who slaughtered many on the spot and dispatched the remainder to lingering deaths in the camps of GULAG. Only Krasnov, Shkuro, Ghirey and a handful of the leaders were preserved for a special fate.

The lying and trickery used in this way to lure men to a dreadful death have been regarded as uncharacteristic of British military honour. This view appears to be correct. Though the deception plan was transmitted by 5 Corps to Brigadier Musson at Oberdrauburg, it seems that it did not originate with the British military authorities, but was suggested to them by their Soviet colleagues.

When General Keightley's staff officer negotiated the handover of Cossacks at Wolfsberg on 23 and 24 May, he was officially dealing with the Chief of Staff of the 57th Soviet Army. However, the Red Army had no authority to interfere in the matter of repatriation of Soviet citizens. This lay entirely in the hands of SMERSH. With the German collapse in 1945, SMERSH received a new task. As a former officer of the organisation has explained,

> Smersh had clear instructions from Stalin. We were to bring back the maximum possible number of Soviet citizens into the Soviet Union, if possible all of them, regardless of whether they wanted to come or not. It was not a good idea to have such a large number of our citizens outside Soviet frontiers. Including women and children there were between five and six million. In the first place they were undesirable witnesses against communism and the Soviet system. Secondly, the Soviet Union had suffered colossal human losses in the war and was short of manpower.[13]

SMERSH headquarters in Austria was established at the pleasant spa of Baden-bei-Wien. A number of large houses in a secluded quarter were occupied and the cellars converted into interrogation and torture chambers.[14] It was from this centre that negotiations with 5 Corps over the surrender of the Cossacks were conducted.

It is clear that co-operation between SMERSH and the British command was extremely close. Armed SMERSH guards were admitted to 78 Infantry Division area in order to check that no Cossacks escaped, and they joined British troops in firing on fugitives seeking refuge in the mountains. The main body of Cossacks at Lienz was first informed of the coming repatriation by an officer from Corps or Divisional HQ. He prefaced the order with these remarks:

Cossacks! Your officers have betrayed you and led you on a false path. They have been arrested and will not return. You can now, no longer fearing or guided by their influence or pressure, discuss their lies and speak out about your wishes and beliefs.[15]

This phraseology bears a strongly Marxist tinge thoroughly uncharacteristic of British military procedure. It is likely that it originated with SMERSH as part of their collaborative advice. Not surprisingly the order itself has not been preserved in the Corps or Divisional War Diaries.

The ruse whereby the Cossack officers were deceived into going peacefully to their deaths appears also to have been adopted at 5 Corps HQ from a suggestion obligingly provided by SMERSH. It was a standard Soviet security precaution to separate groups destined for destruction by the issuance of false invitations of this type. Only a few weeks earlier the NKVD had invited sixteen of the most active Polish resistance leaders to peaceful discussions with Marshal Zhukov, and then flown them at once to Moscow and the Lubianka Gaol.[16] Even the details of the operations were identical. In both cases the name of a respected Allied commander-in-chief had been invoked. The NKVD had been particularly solicitous that the Polish General Okulicki, commander of the underground army, should attend. Similarly, the British took particular precautions to ensure the safe delivery of General Krasnov. On 28 May a staff officer from Corps or Divisional HQ called at the Cossack headquarters in Lienz to request the officers' presence at the 'conference', adding, 'Please do not forget to convey my request to old Krasnov. I beg this of you most urgently'.[17]

Close co-operation between SMERSH and 5 Corps staff ensured that matters ran smoothly. Krasnov, Shkuro, Ghirey and the remaining Cossack and Caucasian officers were delivered to SMERSH at Judenburg. Much later, when the embarrassing fact of the betrayal of Russians not covered by the Yalta Agreement became public knowledge, apologists for the British action claimed that there had been a

tragic misunderstanding. In the House of Lords it was announced
that there had been 'some mistakes . . . in the heat and utter turmoil
of the summer of 1945 . . . it was impossible . . . to weed out all
individual cases'. In 1975 General Musson, whose 36 Infantry Brigade
effected the deception, wrote to me to say he could 'see little reason
for any sweeping suggestion that "someone on high saw to it that
Krasnov and Shkuro were sent back come what may". It sounds quite
ridiculous to me.'

That was not how it appeared in 1945. Colonel Pulford, whose
Lancashire Fusiliers provided the Cossack officers' escort *en route*,
recorded his impression after receiving the orders from Brigadier
Musson: 'The Russians were particularly keen on the return of the
officers, many of whom were Tsarist émigrés', he wrote in his War
Diary.[18] And a Russian girl outside Lienz on 26 May overheard British
officers discussing the coming operation – a conversation in which
the names of Krasnov and Shkuro received significant emphasis.[19]

About 1,600 Cossack officers were presented to SMERSH at Judenburg, of whom well over a thousand were old émigrés bearing
French, German, Yugoslav or League of Nations passports. The night
before, General Krasnov had drawn up a third petition to Field-
Marshal Alexander, protesting at this gross infringement of international law. Signed by all the Cossack officers, it was given to the local
British commander.[20] But, like its predecessors, it appears never to
have reached its destination and has vanished from the British archive. Thanks to the ingenious deception apparently suggested by
SMERSH, the Cossack officers were handed over without untoward
incident beyond a regrettable series of suicides *en route*.

Far worse scenes were soon to follow. No official screening of
non-Soviet citizens could be permitted among the Cossacks and
Caucasians in the Drau Valley, as this would have alerted British
troops to the existence of the crucial distinction. And that in turn
could have endangered the central purpose of the operation. The two
battalion commanders on the spot, Colonels Malcolm and Odling-
Smee, were never informed by Brigadier Musson that it was only Soviet
citizens who were liable for return. They were not permitted a
glimpse of that clause which accompanied every single written order
relating to the operation, with its precise definition as to what constituted a Soviet citizen. On the contrary, they were told emphatically
that every Russian man, woman and child in the valley must be
dispatched to the Soviet Union. Acknowledging that 'as there are so

many women and children, some of you will feel sympathetic towards these people', Brigade orders of 27 May nevertheless stressed that the operation must be carried through as efficiently and thoroughly as possible. In particular, as an accompanying order laid down, 'any attempt whatsoever at resistance will be dealt with firmly by shooting to kill'.

The women and children did indeed represent a serious problem. The fugitive Russians were accompanied by their families, consisting of some five thousand women and three thousand children.[21] The British soldiers, hardened veterans of campaigns stretching from North Africa to the River Po, were sickened by the task before them. What followed is too well known to need retelling here. The mental anguish of young Major 'Rusty' Davies, who was compelled to lie to and deceive the Cossacks with whom he had become friends; the ghastly scenes in the barracks square at Peggetz, when weeping soldiers of the 8th Argylls broke up a religious service attended by thousands of Cossacks, beating men, women and children senseless with rifle-butts and pick-handles, and forcing them into cattle-wagons destined for the charnel-houses of GULAG; the dozens of suicides, men even shooting their wives and children rather than let them suffer mass rape by camp criminals in Vorkuta, or starvation in the 'crèche' at Kolyma. In the panic babies were trampled to death, men were separated for ever from their wives, and wives from their children. Blood was spattered over the priests, their ikons and crucifixes. Those few people who escaped to the forests and mountains were hunted down by patrols accompanied by SMERSH executioners, and shot or rounded up for the next handover.

These scenes are fortunately unique in British military history, and amidst the terrible sufferings of the Cossacks one should not forget the agonies of remorse many British soldiers underwent then and since. Battle-hardened men broke down and wept, many of them coming to their Chaplain, Kenneth Tyson, in bewilderment to ask for counsel. 'This is not what we fought the war for!' was a continuing refrain. Decades have passed, and Rusty Davies still suffers nightmares when his reluctant role in 1945 returns in unguarded moments. With rare exceptions,[22] all troops involved in this disgraceful undertaking were revolted by what their orders compelled them to do.

Of the hundreds of White Russians delivered at Judenburg, *thirty-one* were released to the West in 1955–6, to be followed by a swiftly-dwindling trickle. Their foreign passports saved them: the same passports which the British had ignored in Austria in 1945.

There can be little doubt that the scenes of treachery and cruelty in the Drau Valley arose from the nature of the deception required to lure Krasnov, Shkuro and Ghirey into Soviet hands. But for this it would have been possible, firstly, to screen all the old émigrés. Their precise number is not known, but there must certainly have been at least three thousand in the camp. (Many of the babies were simply too young to have been born in the Soviet Union.) The NKVD at Judenburg expressed surprise at receiving them, and their subsequent ordeal (culminating in death for the majority) was directly the responsibility of those who authorized the deed.

Apart from this it is quite clear that the violence committed on the defenceless refugees who bore Soviet citizenship also arose in large degree from the necessity to extend the order for handover to *all* Cossacks at Lienz. Even a hint to Colonel Malcolm that certain categories were exempt could have brought the situation of General Krasnov and the others into dangerous consideration. What might otherwise have occurred is readily ascertained by a comparison with parallel events to the east.

There a large body of Cossacks from the 15 Cossack Cavalry Corps was held by 6 Armoured Division, under Major-General Horatius Murray. General Murray greatly objected to the dispatch of men who had surrendered in good faith to certain death. He and his subordinates conveyed clear warnings to their prisoners, with the result that thousands escaped from their unwired camps. When it was belatedly brought to his notice that there were old émigrés among those held, measures were promptly taken to screen them. No SMERSH executioners were permitted to enter the divisional area.

5 Corps HQ at Klagenfurt made no objection to any of these actions and no ill results followed, whether in the form of Soviet protests or an excess of Russian refugees in the British zone of Austria. It was to entrap the émigré generals that the whole operation was designed, and if numbers escaped elsewhere it mattered little. Any attempt to coerce General Murray into more rigorous action risked discussions that could throw light in awkward places. But for the secret agreement to comply with the SMERSH request, Keightley might have turned a blind eye to similar leniency practised in 78 Infantry Divisional area.

The Soviet authorities were undoubtedly delighted with the sacrificial offering though, as SMERSH men at Judenburg confessed, it was much more than they had expected. The secret agreement to hand over three old gentlemen had swelled by an inevitable process into death, torture and unbelievable privation for thousands.

Of course it was impossible that a crime of this magnitude could be perpetrated without some of the instruments sensing that something was wrong. Brigadier Musson recalled thirty years later that after 1 June 'people began asking questions and saying people should not have gone back'. One such question came on 29 May, when 8 Argylls HQ at Lienz notified Musson at Brigate HQ that

> GERMAGEN RODIONOFF was evacuated yesterday with the Cossack officers. He is not a Russian [i.e. Soviet] subject and has been living in PARIS for 15 years. Apparently, he is a teacher. His family is in France, and it would appear that he has been put in the Cossack camp by mistake. May we have your advice. It seems highly probable that there are a large number of persons at present in the Cossack camp who are not of RUSSIAN [i.e. Soviet] origin. What is the position regarding these people?

Brigadier Musson did not reply until the majority of Rodionoff's fellow-émigrés had been handed over in the bloody days of 1 and 2 June. In the meantime Major Davies, horrified by the patent injustice, unofficially and contrary to orders began himself to 'screen' numbers of White Russian men and women. It was clear that some conscience-stricken officer might begin to put two and two together, with potentially explosive results. 5 Corps HQ evidently became aware of the danger, for on or about 3 June a 'new order' to screen non-Soviet citizens came down the line. As by then the great majority of Cossacks, in particular the three 'wanted' generals, were already safely in the hands of SMERSH, it was a simple matter to cut losses and lay to rest continuing suspicions.

This screening order is, like so much else, not to be found in the relevant War Diaries. It is easy to see why. All orders connected with the handovers contained a clause excluding non-Soviet citizens from return. The existence of a subsequent instruction to *commence* screening would make it clear that earlier instructions had been dead letter, and inserted for a purpose that can only have been fraudulent. A month later a detailed report of the operation from 36 Infantry Brigade HQ claimed that

> . . . such measures as were possible under the conditions prevailing at the time, were taken within 36 Inf Bde to ensure that non-

SOVIET nationals were not included amongst those evacuated to the SOVIET authorities.

This would have aroused ridicule from officers of the 8 Argylls or 6 Royal West Kents, who had just handed over émigrés who wore Tsarist uniforms, came from Paris and Belgrade, and in some cases spoke fluent English and wore British decorations. Needless to say the report was not intended for them, but to present a false picture in the event of awkward inquiries from above. That this was no illusory fear is borne out by a tantalizingly incomplete but suggestive piece of evidence.

The Rev. C. W. H. Story was at the time Acting Deputy Assistant Chaplain-General to 5 Corps. Recently he explained how he learned of the tragic events in Austria at that time.

> . . . one day I received a phone call from the Rev. John Vaughan, Chaplain to the Hampshire Brigade, stationed at Graz, asking if I could help. His men were nearer mutiny than anyone had known before. They had come to him to ask if Chaplains Branch could do something. They were being ordered to force White Russian p.o.w. at bayonet point into transport bound for Russia . . . I rang the Deputy Chaplain-General . . . at GHQ, CMF, Caserta. He became very angry at the news & immediately rang the Chaplain-General, Canon Ll. [Lloyd] Hughes at the War Office. What happened after that I cannot be certain. The Chaplain-General would not have direct access to the Prime Minister but to the Adjutant General who would have that access.
>
> My memory is that the following day I was told that the telephone wires had been humming & that Churchill himself had given instructions that no man must be repatriated against his will.

Mr Story was unable to confirm whether it was indeed the Prime Minister who intervened, but his information may have been correct. At Potsdam Churchill was to urge forcefully that the policy of compulsory repatriation be abandoned. What had aroused his intervention there was a Soviet request to have the 10,000-strong Ukrainian Division in Italy handed over. Many officers of units guarding them had put in strong objections to any repetition of the brutal scenes at Lienz. It seems likely that knowledge of this and shared concern led Churchill into making his stand, which he abandoned only on learning that the Ukrainians were not in fact liable for repatriation.

Further confirmation of intervention from above was provided by Alexander's then Chief of Staff. In 1974 General Sir William Morgan informed me that the Field-Marshal's reaction to the news of the violence employed at Lienz was one of outrage and shock, and that he made it plain that similar scenes would not recur so long as he remained Supreme Allied Commander – a vow he kept. One can only speculate as to whether Alexander forbade further brutalities independently, or in response to Churchill's intervention. Equally it is not established whether 5 Corps's belated hasty instruction to institute screening on 3 June resulted from Alexander's reaction, or was a precaution designed to anticipate it. What seems fairly certain is that it was the brutality which aroused Churchill's and Alexander's anger; they remained ignorant of the 'inner plot' to surrender White émigrés.

Is it possible, then, on the evidence available, to establish precisely what occurred during those three weeks in May 1945? Much of course is missing, possibly beyond recovery. Many documents are absent from the archive, most likely abstracted by someone determined that the story should continue a secret. These include all documentation relating to the Soviet *démarche* requesting the surrender of Krasnov, Shkuro and Ghirey; Alexander's reply to Keightley's telegram of 14 May; all documents dealing with the decision to grant asylum to the *Schutzkorps* and the Ukrainian Division; Shkuro's two letters and Krasnov's petitions; the SMERSH-inspired announcement read to the Cossacks on 29 May; and Divisional orders of 3 June (or thereabout) to screen White Russians. A powerful hand, it seems, has sifted very carefully through the voluminous documentation – an interesting indication in itself.

There is no question but that the Soviet authorities requested Krasnov, Shkuro and Ghirey by name, and that 5 Corps was fully aware that these men were not covered by the Yalta Agreement. In addition to the weight of circumstantial evidence recapitulated in Chapter Eleven of my *Victims of Yalta* there is now the account provided by General Shtemenko, and the extremely frank admission given by Brigadier Tryon-Wilson, who was then Brigadier AQ on 5 Corps staff. The evidence is overwhelming that General Keightley, with the aid or connivance of some of his subordinates, arranged that the White Russians were handed over to SMERSH. The operation had to be cloaked in secrecy. Firstly, it was necessary to conceal what was happening from Field-Marshal Alexander, who would certainly have prevented the action. Secondly, it was considered essential to mislead officers in the field, lest anyone with an over-tender conscience raise an outcry that reached higher quarters. As there was no safe means of singling out the three intended victims, it became necessary to include thousands who might have escaped the net.

This then appears to be a plausible reconstruction of events, or at least as much of the story as the available evidence allows:

12 May 1945. General Keightley visited a Red Army delegation at Wolfsberg. A senior officer from SMERSH requested the handover of Cossacks held by the British in Austria, demanding particularly forcefully Generals Krasnov, Shkuro and Ghirey.

Keightley explained that he had no power to hand over Russians who were not Soviet citizens, but agreed to follow up the inquiry. He then returned to Klagenfurt. There he asked his divisional commanders to account for the Cossacks and other dissident 'Russian' units held in their areas. In particular he asked (if he did not know already) for details of the three generals whose names he had been given. From 78 Infantry Division he would have learned that Krasnov, Shkuro and Ghirey were held by units of 36 Infantry Brigade, and that they were all three Tsarist émigrés.

13 May. Harold Macmillan flew in to Klagenfurt from Caserta to discuss the Soviet proposals. Keightley explained the request he had received, and the fact that the White Russian generals were indeed held by his forces. The discussion must inevitably have touched on the extremely embarrassing petition addressed by Krasnov to Field-Marshal Alexander.

Macmillan was very anxious to comply with the Soviet request, and urged Keightley to accede. The general replied that he could do nothing without Alexander's agreement, and asked how that was to be obtained without revealing that Krasnov and his fellows were to be included. Macmillan's own instructions forbade him to allow the surrender of non-Soviet citizens, but it was nevertheless decided to withhold from Alexander the information that the Soviets were after his old White Russian comrades. Most of the Cossacks were probably Soviet citizens, and it should not be difficult to include the old émigrés among them when they came to be returned. On the other hand, a decision was made not to hand over the *Schutzkorps* or the Ukrainian Division. These and other matters settled, Macmillan flew back to Caserta.

14 May. Keightley telegraphed Alexander to explain that Macmillan recommended the surrender of the Cossacks in response to Soviet pressure. Adding his own support for Macmillan's suggestion, he was careful to refer to the Cossacks as 'this large number Soviet nationals'.

This necessarily implies that Keightley was a liar, since he well knew that many of the Cossacks were not 'Soviet nationals'. It was a lie he was to repeat in more elaborate form two months later. Disturbed by reports of barbaric scenes at Lienz, Lady Limerick of the British Red Cross asked him personally what had occurred. He denied flatly that any violence at all had been employed in returning the Cossacks. There had been a mild protest, but his troops 'only had to "shoot twice" and in neither case hit anybody. They [the Cossacks] . . . agreed to return to Soviet Territory together with their wives and children'. As for accusations that many White Russians had been included, Keightley '[said] that he did not know and it was impossible to find out – he thought some might be, but that the only evidence they had, was that they had been fighting in the German Army, and none to prove that they were White Russians'.

17 May. Alexander, though unaware of the presence of White Russians, was sufficiently disturbed to raise the matter with the Chiefs of Staff.

19 May. Macmillan flew to England to confer with Churchill.

20 May. Unknown to Alexander, Keightley had all but completed preparations for returning all Cossacks, regardless of their citizenship.

21 May. Keightley telegraphed AFHQ, requesting information on 'policy re Cossacks'.

22 May. AFHQ replied, laying down that Soviet citizens only could be returned, but even they were not to be compelled. Macmillan returned from England to Caserta.

23 May. 5 Corps began negotiations with Soviet representatives at Wolfsberg for the handover of all Cossacks.

24 May. These negotiations were brought to a successful conclusion. 5 Corps issued instructions for the handover of Cossacks.

25 May. 5 Corps was instructed by AFHQ to hand over 'all Soviet citizens' in Austria.

26 May. Brigadier Musson of 36 Infantry Brigade ordered his battalion commanders holding Cossacks in the Drau Valley to send *all* Cossacks back, without regard to citizenship.

27 May. General Shkuro was removed from Lienz at dawn and held in isolation at Spittal.

28–9 May. The Cossack officers were invited to the 'conference' with Field-Marshal Alexander, and conveyed to SMERSH at Judenburg.

1–2 June. The majority of rank-and-file Cossacks, with their women and children, were entrained at Lienz for repatriation.

3 June. 5 Corps for the first time enforced screening of non-Soviet citizens.

Churchill and Alexander had been duped into consenting to the surrender of the Cossacks and Soviet citizens. The crucial fact that many were White Russians was carefully withheld from them. General Keightley of course ran grave risks in deceiving the Supreme Allied Commander in this way, but presumably allowed himself to be overruled by Macmillan's arguments. Macmillan in his memoirs claims that his motive in advocating the return of 'Cossacks and White Russians' was to ensure the safe return of liberated British prisoners-of-war from the Soviet zone of Austria. It is true that on 3 June Tolbukhin first allowed the use of this overland route. Before that prisoners had been obliged to travel all the way to Odessa and return home by sea.

No doubt this 'concession' arose in part as a mark of gratitude for the surrender of the Cossacks. But that the opening of the zonal frontier would have continued obstructed as a result of the retention of three old White generals must have seemed incredible. Neither Anglo-Soviet treaties nor international law could have countenanced such an agreement. If the agreement was so shameful that it had to be concealed from the Prime Minister and SACMED, and even from the very soldiers obliged to implement it, what pressures could the Soviet Government have applied had Macmillan and Keightley declined to countenance it? The Americans never at any time contemplated the return of White Russians in their hands, and none of their troops liberated by the Red Army were delayed in their return as a result.

The speedy return of British prisoners-of-war must certainly have been a consideration in the minds of the men who plotted Krasnov's death. But the secret pact made between 5 Corps and SMERSH at Wolfsberg reflects too much the background of the larger agreement made by Eden and Molotov in Moscow in October 1944 not to have been governed by similar considerations. In August 1944 Foreign

Secretary Anthony Eden had set out the arguments in favour of forced repatriation as persuasively as he and his advisers could argue. The major consideration was claimed to be that 'To refuse the Soviet Government's request for the return of their own men would lead to serious trouble with them.' By this he seems to have meant unseemly wrangles over points of order at conferences, and tart exchanges of notes between the two foreign ministries.

Last and least weighty of Eden's points was that any attempt to frustrate Soviet desires in this direction could mean that British prisoners-of-war might not 'be well cared for and returned as soon as possible'. Neither then nor at any other time did Eden or his advisers express a fear that Stalin might actually *prevent* the return of Englishmen in German camps.

Eden's policy towards the Soviet Union rested on the belief that any concession to Soviet demands, however base or cruel, that did not in his view affect British strategic or political interests was necessary to the furtherance of good relations between the powers. This leads one to wonder whether Macmillan, contrary to all his instructions and at considerable risk to his political career, urged the return of the émigré generals on his own initiative. Or was his action not merely a reflection of Eden's overall policy, but actually a part of it? Did Macmillan consult Eden? It would seem to be a possibility, and it is certainly hard to imagine the impatient Eden wasting much sympathy on the ageing remnants of the beaten White Army.

One of the émigrés handed over at Judenburg by 5 Corps was young Nikolai Krasnov, grandson of the General. He had left Russia when only four months old, and spoke Russian with an accent. He accompanied his grandfather to the Lubianka. There he was taken with his father to the luxurious office of Vsevolod Nikolaevich Merkulov, People's Commissar for State Security and first deputy to Beria himself. Merkulov had been an early associate of Beria in the Caucasus. He had clambered the ladder of power with Beria in 1939, and now was one of the three men who controlled the enormous Soviet weaponry of oppression. He had played a key part in the massacre of Polish officers at Katyn in 1940, and controlled the savage deportations of civilians from the Baltic States in 1941.[23] In 1940 he had travelled to Berlin to supervise Molotov's negotiations with Ribbentrop and Hitler,[24] and he brought appropriate experience to the exchanges his subordinates were conducting with Eden and Macmillan.

In Lubianka on 4 June 1945, Merkulov extended a lengthy in-

terview to Nikolai Krasnov and his father before dispatching them to
the northern camps of GULAG, from which few ever returned.
Astonishingly, young Nikolai survived that nightmare world north of
the seventieth parallel. His father died there, but Nikolai was
amnestied in 1955 as a Yugoslav citizen (a fact to which he had
personally drawn the attention of Generals Arbuthnott and Musson
on 8 May 1945). He came to Sweden, where he wrote a vivid account of
unbelievable sufferings. His persecutor Merkulov was already dead,
executed along with others of Beria's associates in 1954.

In 1945 it must have appeared incredible beyond belief that Nikolai
Krasnov would one day repeat to the world words uttered to him in
the house of the dead. But so it was, and Nikolai Krasnov's book
provides a unique glimpse of the views of the man who, under Beria,
knew more of Soviet intelligence dealings than any man alive. 'For
twenty-five years we've been waiting for this happy meeting with
you!' he gloated; 'victory is with us, with the Reds. As it was in 1920,
so it is now . . .'

Merkulov dwelt lovingly on the suffering awaiting the prisoners in
the Arctic Circle. Death would seize them before long, but first they
could work for the Motherland:

> A spell of timber felling, a spell in a mine-shaft with water up to
> your belt . . . You will feel your legs turn to macaroni – but you'll
> work! Hunger will make you!

Merkulov roared with laughter, and turned to a new theme:

> But the fact that you trusted the English – that was real stupidity!
> Now there are history's shopkeepers! They will cheerfully sell
> anything or anyone and never bat an eyelid. Their politics are those
> of the prostitute. Their Foreign Office is a brothel, in which sits its
> head – a great diplomatic 'madam'. They trade in foreigners' lives
> and in their own conscience. As for us, we don't trust them,
> Colonel. That is why we took the reins into our own hands. They
> don't appreciate that we have checkmated them, and now they are
> forced to dance to our tune, like the last pawn on the board.

Merkulov was not inhibited in his boasting. His oldest enemies had
fallen miraculously into his power, and he could allow the victims a
candid glimpse of the chasm into which they had fallen. 'Do you know
where you are and with whom you are speaking? In the Lubianka!
With Merkulov! I am boss here. I say what I like!'[25]

Merkulov's reference to the Foreign Office is significant. Neither at the time of the interview nor when he came to write his account of it had Nikolai Krasnov any reason to believe that the Foreign Office had been responsible for his fate. He had been handed over by British military authorities in Austria. Like most other Cossacks, he visited most blame on the head of the unfortunate Major Davies. If his thoughts ran higher up the chain of command, they passed from Colonel Malcolm up to Alexander – and presumably above him there was Winston Churchill.[26]

Merkulov, on the other hand, certainly *did* know precisely who was responsible for the surrender of the old émigrés. He knew, of course, that their handover was an entirely separate matter from the agreement made at Yalta; and as it was officers working for him who had negotiated the secret arrangement made at Wolfsberg, he must have been familiar with every circumstance of the transaction. He too had no reason to drag in the Foreign Office unless the allusion was relevant.

Is it possible to go further into Merkulov's revelations? The imagery he employed in describing the Foreign Office may be significant. He knew, as we do not and probably never shall, the full extent of Soviet penetration of the Foreign Office at that time. He was the ultimate control directing links with traitors such as Burgess and Maclean, and without doubt maintained others of whom we know nothing. All that remains dark to us was clear to him. He knew all about Burgess and Maclean's homosexual activities, the 'vice den' in Bentinck Street, the still more highly-placed homosexuals whose activities Burgess carefully recorded.[27]

Could Merkulov's contemptuous reference to Anthony Eden as the 'madam' presiding over this 'brothel' bear a pertinent significance? It seems an odd phrase to use, if Merkulov merely regarded Eden as a gullible statesman, unable to detect what was going on before his eyes. Certainly the strong implication of Merkulov's words is that the Krasnovs' fate had been decided by the Foreign Office, presided over by its 'madam'.

What might have induced Eden to take part can only be conjectured. Never a very humane man, he may have felt the sacrifice would help to sweeten the atmosphere in post-war dealings with Stalin. If so, he was mistaken.

Alternatively the possibility cannot be ruled out that Merkulov's agents in Britain (at the 'Trade Delegation' in Highgate, or the official

NKVD Mission in Kensington) possessed means of their own of applying pressure on the unstable Foreign Secretary. There is much that is unexplained.

*   *   *

When Harold Macmillan flew back to Britain on 26 May 1945, all thought of the émigré Cossacks must soon have passed from his mind as he prepared for the hurly-burly of the General Election. While they vanished to Siberia, he began that brilliant ascent which led him ultimately to the highest position his country could bestow. Yet by an odd irony of history their paths were to cross again for a brief and forgotten moment.

Some twelve years later Khrushchev allowed a tiny trickle of Cossacks who had managed to survive the camps of the Arctic Circle and Siberia to leave Russia. A few score at most, of the thousands handed over in 1945, emerged in this way. All of these were holders of foreign passports, and it was for this reason that they were allowed to leave the country. This meant also that they were without exception men who should not, under the terms of the Yalta Agreement, have been handed over. Completely broken in health by the unspeakable sufferings they had undergone, they could find no work in the West and were forced to subsist on miserable pittances doled out to them by charitable folk. Eventually they began to nurture a hope that the British Government might assist them. Appeals were drawn up, setting out in detail their non-Soviet citizenship, their surrender to the NKVD in 1945 by the British Army, the dreadful sufferings they had undergone in camps like Vorkuta and Potma, and their present helpless state. As one of them, Captain Anatol Petrovsky, put it,

> The long years of suffering and separation from my relatives, being held as a criminal in the mines of Siberia, Vorkuta, and other places, I have lost my strength and health. As a result I am unable to undertake any real work and am forced to live as a displaced person, receiving only token support from the town hall.
>
> Taking into consideration the fact that I was handed over to the Soviets, an illegal action, as the British Military Command knew I was not a Soviet citizen . . . [Petrovsky requested that the British Government] grant me material aid to compensate for the years of Soviet imprisonment, 1945–1956 and so recompense me for loss of

health and allow me to live out my remaining years without facing starvation.

The British writer, Peter Huxley-Blythe, who forwarded these appeals to the Prime Minister on 4 September 1958, pointed out 'that compensation to these officers need not come from public funds but the money appropriated from the Cossack Bank [at Peggetz] on May 26, 1945 . . .' As that money consisted largely of the Cossacks' savings from their pay, such confiscation is expressly prohibited by Articles 6 and 24 of the Geneva Convention.

On 17 October Huxley-Blythe received a reply to the Cossacks' petition, which had been passed to the Foreign Office.

Sir,

I am directed . . . to refer to your letter of the 4th of September to the Prime Minister . . . about persons of Russian origin who are now domiciled in Germany and Austria.

The case submitted by these officers was carefully considered . . . A thorough examination of the facts led to the conclusion that no action could be taken to assist the persons named in your letter.[28]

The Prime Minister to whom the appeal had been directed was the Right Honourable Harold Macmillan, former Minister Resident with AFHQ in 1945.

XVIII
Hands Across the Sea

However favourably the British and Americans came to regard the wartime Soviet Union, Stalin did not feel he could afford to allow the grass to grow under his feet. He did not trust his Allies, Churchill in particular, and must in any case have been well aware that his post-war ambitions would arouse Western antagonism when their extent became clear. Left-wing sympathy was very useful. Indeed, in some ways a crypto-Communist or fellow-traveller could be more valuable than a card-carrying Party member.[1] But the Communist fifth column in the West was far too important a weapon in Beria's arsenal to be left idle, nor did Stalin ever wholly trust foreign Communists living freely outside his domain.

In 1943 Stalin announced the dissolution of the Comintern, the Moscow-based organization which provided a clearing-house for direction and co-operation within the world Communist movement. This was widely interpreted in the West as an indication that the Soviet Union had now become 'a national state, run on Communist lines, rather than a centre of world revolution'. In Britain some cynics believed the move to be a devious scheme intended to allow the British Party to apply for affiliation to the Labour Party, but Stalin is scarcely likely to have acted for so trifling a purpose.[2] The truth is that the Comintern was not abolished at all, save in name, and it and the Parties under its direction continued as if nothing had happened. It had been entirely financed and controlled by the NKVD, and amounted merely to a subsidiary of that formidable organization – one rated fairly low in Stalin's estimation.[3]

The NKVD itself retained all its powers, and the Red Army's victory over Germany had enormously increased the loyalty and prestige of the international Communist movement which still operated loyally under its control. But the overthrow of the Hitlerite Fascists left the Sword of the Revolution with an even more daunting confrontation. The Soviet Union had now to collect its strength for the final struggle, achieve its own atomic bomb, and maintain iron discipline among its population. As Beria's deputy, Minister of State Security Victor Abakumov, explained to an audience of SMERSH officers at NKVD Headquarters in occupied Europe near Vienna in the summer of 1945,

> Comrade Stalin once said that if we don't manage to do all these things very quickly the British and Americans will crush us. After all they have the atom bomb, and an enormous technical and industrial advantage over us. They are rich countries, which have not been destroyed by the war. But we will rebuild everything, with our army and our industry, regardless of the cost. We Chekists are not to be frightened by problems and sacrifices. It is our good fortune . . . that the British and Americans in their attitudes towards us, have still not emerged from the post-war state of calf-love. They dream of lasting peace and building a democratic world for all men. They don't seem to realise that we are the ones who are going to build a new world, and that we shall do it without their liberal-democratic recipes. All their slobber plays right into our hands, and we shall thank them for this, in the next world, with coals of fire. We shall drive them into such dead ends as they've never dreamed of. We shall disrupt them and corrupt them from within. We shall lull them to sleep, sap their will to fight. The whole 'free western' world will burst apart like a fat squashed toad. This won't happen tomorrow. To achieve it will require great efforts on our part, great sacrifices, and total renunciation of all that is trivial and personal. Our aim justifies all this. Our aim is a grand one, the destruction of the old, vile world.[4]

Massive funds were disbursed to achieve this grand aim. Throughout the non-Communist world, and particularly in Britain and the United States, the NKVD deployed almost limitless resources, human and financial. Foreign Communists were for the most part willing to act as unpaid agents of the Soviet Union,[5] but it was Soviet policy generally to induce its servants to accept remuneration.[6] The aims generally were to undermine Western morale and will to resist, to obtain military and industrial information, and to subvert high-ranking or key governmental personnel. So far as the latter were concerned, the first purpose was to induce them to pass on secret information of interest to the Soviets. The second, and most

important of all, was to impel them to obstruct, influence or direct
their countries' policies in ways calculated to advance the interests of
the Soviet Union. This last was the most difficult, if most rewarding,
operation; but if successful could be of incalculable benefit to Soviet
aims.

It is essential to note the importance which espionage played in
Stalin's scheme of things. His early life had been entirely conspiratorial in nature, and he retained to the end a love of hoodwinking his
enemies and laughing at their gullibility behind their backs. Beria
was his closest confidant, and the bank-robber turned statesman took
deep personal interest in activities which, on a smaller scale, would
have been of a purely criminal nature. Stalin himself on occasion
dictated the messages that were transmitted to agents abroad. It was
he who concocted the acronym SMERSH for the Soviet counter-
espionage force. Above all, he took personal charge of important
operations, particularly those relating to murders conducted on
foreign soil.[7]

The Soviet spy-network was capable of extreme subtlety as well as
blundering incompetence. Its consistency lay in the enormous
extent of its activities. Many people are surprised by the continuing
exposure of highly-placed traitors in wartime and early post-war
Britain and the United States. What should be remembered, however, is that the temptation to defect was no mere baited hook swung
temptingly over the pond, but a finely-meshed net which dredged it
continually from end to end. Many became Beria's men from natural
conviction. Where this was lacking, the NKVD and GRU searched
patiently for personal weaknesses offering an opening. Much of their
training was directed towards exploiting these deficiencies.

Whilst some of those who collaborated with the Soviet apparatus
were, to all appearances, able and balanced, the great majority seem
to have suffered from personality defects making them potentially
resentful of the societies in which they lived. Hitler had understood
the use that can be made of these people. 'We shall find such men,
we shall find them in every country', he said. 'We shall not need to
bribe them. They will come of their own accord. Ambition and
delusion, party squabbles and self-seeking arrogance will drive
them . . . Mental confusion, contradiction of feeling, indecisive-
ness, panic: these are our weapons . . . I have learnt from the
Bolsheviks.'[8] His policy paid dividends, especially among intellectuals, artists, actors, journalists and the like.[9] Just so the Soviet

espionage service was instructed to exploit to the full 'stupidity, greed, failure to grasp the real situation, thirst for respect or the outward appearance of power'.[10] Some Western traitors possessed attractive personality traits, and many more exhibited extreme courage and skill in advancing the cause of their adopted country. Alger Hiss and Bruno Pontecorvo,[11] for example, had achieved brilliant success and led normally moral lives outside their services to Beria.

These were, however, the exceptions. A far greater number exhibited weaknesses that must in part explain their betrayal. Burgess, Maclean and Sorge were socially awkward drunkards.[12] Burgess, like Philby, seems to have been motivated by a desire to feel cleverer than the colleagues he was deceiving, a need perhaps resulting from a failure of adolescent promise to materialize.[13] In this, as in much else, they resembled their patron in the Kremlin. Their female equivalents were often equally neurotic, being frequently unhappy, pitiable people clearly deprived of affection in youth.[14] Many were depressed individuals leading humdrum lives who welcomed the glamour, excitement and sense of importance which spying brought into their existence.[15] Virtually all justified their course of conduct by claiming that they owed a higher loyalty than that of mere patriotism: they served the international proletariat, personified at present by the embattled Soviet Union. This was naturally the approach adopted by NKVD agents when inviting prospective customers to join them.[16]

The NKVD was not content to rely on loyalty, however. A highly suspicious organization, serving a morbidly suspicious master, it was also aware that the very deficiencies which so often turned people to Communism made their reliability suspect. Pressures were held in reserve or brought into play when required. In particular, it was considered very important to induce recruits to work for money, even when they had no need of it or sincerely wished to work from idealistic motives alone. Money placed the recipient in a dependent position and bound him to the service. Either he would come to need the money more than he anticipated, or he would be susceptible to blackmail. Few resisted tempting offers for long, again no doubt justifying the process on the grounds that there were necessary expenses incurred in preparing for the day of liberation. In the NKVD card index on informants an important sub-heading related to 'FINANCIAL CONDITIONS', and a typical entry read,

'Financially secure, but takes money. It is necessary occasionally to
help.' As an NKVD paymaster in New York explained, 'who pays is
boss, and who takes money must also give something.' Enormous
sums were disbursed in this way, exciting sarcastic comment from
Stalin himself ('they are nothing but hirelings on our Soviet pay-
roll').[17]

With the advent of the wartime alliance, incentives and opportunities for the recruitment of foreigners greatly increased. Lend-
lease and military co-operation required the presence of large
numbers of Soviet personnel in Britain and the United States;
naturally these included a high proportion of NKVD officers, from
the respective Ambassadors (Gousev and Oumansky) downwards. In
order to co-ordinate anti-Axis subversive activities on the Continent
there was even an agreement for collaboration between the NKVD
on the one hand, and SOE and OSS on the other. An official NKVD
Mission appeared in London, but President Roosevelt refused a
similar presence in Washington, fearing political repercussions.[18]
The proposed exchange of intelligence information proved however
to be a one-way flow, as the NKVD had no intention of supplying its
Anglo-American counterparts with secrets of any value. The London
NKVD Mission's only major contribution was the obstruction of an
SOE plan to subvert Russian slave-labourers working in the Reich;
they did not want the British meddling in the sensitive question of
the expatriates.[19]

Unexpected confirmation that the Soviet intelligence services
were as actively concerned in espionage on the British as the
Germans came to the attention of the Foreign Office in January 1944.
A lengthy document fell into the hands of the British naval authorities at Archangel, which turned out to be a set of instructions
issued to the Liaison Department of the Soviet Northern Fleet. The
official purpose of the Liaison Department was to supervise relations
between the Soviet authorities and British and other Allied visiting
personnel. However, as the instructions revealed, the Department's
major function was to spy on visitors, the sort of information required and its potential sources being specified in minute detail.
The Liaison Department was not part of the NKVD, but was instructed to work in the closest harmony with that organization. Apart
from collecting general information of a technical or strategic
nature, officers were required to make a very close study of all
visiting personnel, 'paying special attention to officers, writers,

signalmen, cypherers as follows: (i) Autobiography, promotion; (ii) Study of personal character, separating weak and strong sides (courage, determination, weaknesses, vanity, susceptibility to material advantages, wine, women, etc.) . . . ' To preserve an efficient record, a card index was to be maintained.

To Geoffrey Wilson at the Foreign Office this was merely 'in keeping with what we should expect', and made 'it all the more necessary to select our personnel with the utmost care, & to tell them how to behave.' As for the card index, he noted in the margin, 'I'd like to see my dossier!'[20] Doubtless he recognized at once the significance of the card index, as in 1940, when at the Moscow Embassy, he had been closely involved in extricating a junior British official from the clutches of the NKVD. They had asked the young man to supply confidential information from the Embassy archives. He had refused, but was urged to 'think carefully. You love your mother and father; it would not be pleasant for them to be sent to a labour camp.'[21]

'Susceptibility to material advantages, wine, women, etc.' had long been recognized by the NKVD as the chink in the enemy's armour. Visiting diplomats, military personnel, journalists and others were all appraised for possible exploitation. Life in Moscow for foreigners was generally so isolated and boring that temptations were more than ordinarily inviting. The first weapon, probably the most effective, was that of the *'mozhno'* (permitted) girls, who clustered then and now round any important visitor likely to be susceptible to their charms. Not all were on the regular NKVD pay-roll, but (as a former officer has explained) were 'obtained through the militia from a pool of available talent, mostly persons who are picked up off the streets for prostitution'.[22] Others, however, were girls whose social origins compromised them politically. Occasionally they fell in love with their victims and attempted to escape the country with them. But more often than not such weakness saw them shipped off to the death-camps at Kolyma.[23]

Journalists were a prime target of the NKVD. In 1942, the *Daily Telegraph* correspondent in Moscow complained, an NKVD agent 'made an obvious attempt to plant a Young Beauty on me. He had once brought her to see me, pretexting it was her 16th birthday . . . I kicked this young caller out rather brutally, accusing her of "hooliganism" & frightening her by saying I would complain of her racket in high quarters.'[24] Ralph Parker, of *The Times*, unfortunately succumbed to a similar attempt, the result being that his newspaper acted during the war virtually as British apologist for the worst excesses and most brutal aims of the Soviet regime.[25] The *mozhno* girls were expected to worm secrets out of their prey by the usual methods of persuasion. A further weapon was that of blackmail. Photographs, of a high technical quality, were secretly taken which recorded couples in compromising poses.[26] This was sufficiently well-known abroad, or should have been, but some diplomats at the British Embassy in Moscow may not have been as careful as they might. In August 1942 the Ambassador noted that ' . . . members of the staff, less hard-pressed, claim to have debauched some quite pretty girls'.[27] Clark Kerr was too much a man of the world to trouble himself over such escapades, but there may well have been relations or colleagues at home who would not feel so tolerant about what snapshots revealed.

Glimpses of this underworld of intrigue occasionally obtrude themselves. Brigadier George Hill was the representative of SOE in Moscow. A fluent Russian-speaker, he became deeply involved with an NKVD *mozhno* girl. Extraordinarily, he managed to persuade the Northern Department of the Foreign Office to authorize him to receive £20,000 worth of diamonds from Hatton Garden. These he passed to the girl, apparently believing that he would prise secrets from her.[28] Not surprisingly, the boot proved to be on the other foot. No less an authority than Kim Philby records that Hill was a welcome source of leaked information.[29] Later, Hill promised Colonel Ivan Chichaev, Head of the NKVD Mission in London, that he would provide him with details of SOE's 'toys': secret and deadly instruments developed for assassination and sabotage. But an SOE liaison officer, Major Manderstam, managed to obstruct both this move and another for Chichaev to lay hands on four liberated Russians who had agreed to aid the British in subverting Russians still in German captivity. 'I doubt if Col. Chichaev has a very high opinion of Major Manderstam', was Geoffrey Wilson's comment at the Foreign Office.[30] This looks like an allusion to the notorious anti-Semitism of the NKVD,[31] though despite his name Major Manderstam was not of Jewish origin.

Still more vulnerable to blackmail at the hands of the NKVD were homosexuals. In Britain sodomy was illegal and rendered the practitioners liable to a prison sentence. No one convicted of such an offence could have survived in public life. At the same time there was in the Foreign Office an extraordinarily tolerant attitude to the vice amongst many well-placed officials who themselves displayed no overt inclinations in that direction.[32] Guy Burgess preserved indiscreet letters and photographs incriminating fellow-diplomats; as he confessed with a grin, 'one day they will come in very useful'.[33]

Though blackmail could be, and was, used with deadly effect, it was far from being the only or even the prime cause of so many homosexuals' agreeing to work for the Soviet Union against their own country. There was a remarkable symbiosis between Communism and homosexuality which is not altogether susceptible to explanation. The combination was a frequent occurrence at the major British universities, and pre-war residents in Moscow noted how the city exerted a curious attraction for homosexuals – particularly British. They included Guy Burgess and his Oxford friend Derek Blaikie.[34] Clearly the motivation was in part less to do with the virtues of Marxism than with their predicament at home. Ostracized and menaced with punishment in their own community, it was natural that many reacted by hating the oppressively bourgeois ethos which still governed much of British life, and responded favourably to the movement which *par excellence* threatened the overthrow of that self-satisfied class. Then again, the same consideration required homosexuals to lead a double life, accustoming them to conspiratorial behaviour. To step from that to service to the Comintern was merely moving from the twilight to the dark. As John Vassall, convicted for treachery at a later date, remarked recently, 'in those days we didn't understand about the spy world. Not like now. It was never mentioned. Rather like homosexuality. They rather went together in that sort of way.'[35]

This can be only part of the explanation, however. The extreme commitment of many homosexuals to Stalin's brand of communism suggests in many cases more than a mere reaction to circumstances elsewhere. A certain type of homosexual seems attracted to symbols of masculine power, domination and sadism. Sartre and others noted how French homosexuals were drawn towards their Nazi conquerors, driven seemingly by a desire to submit to ruthless, disciplined force.[36] It was Hitler himself who pointed out that the effect of his speeches was the seduction and sexual ravishing of the crowds,[37] and a former confidant of the Führer who 'noticed that Hitler made the strongest impression on such people as were highly suggestible or somewhat effeminate . . .'[38] Much of the more militant and active element of Nazi membership, particularly the SA, comprised an aggressively homosexual practice and ethic,[39] complacently tolerated by Hitler. After the Röhm *Putsch* he hypocritically adopted measures to counter sexual perversion, but the Nazi spirit continued to the end imbued with a strong strain of sado-masochistic and homosexual themes.[40] It seems likely, therefore, that it was similarly the much-vaunted ruthlessness and bloody record of Soviet Communism that attracted this type of pervert, and made a man like Donald Maclean 'mad on Stalin'.[41]

Blackmail, persuasion, various forms of deception: any weakness was exploited by the NKVD to gain its ends. Essentially the aims were twofold. Firstly, it was important to acquire at all levels the sort of information any self-respecting intelligence service requires: details of troop movements, new weaponry, political moves, etc.[42] The second step was more difficult to accomplish, but vastly more rewarding than the mere acquisition of facts. This was the gaining of control over prominent decision-making figures in a foreign governmental machine. Once secured, such figures were usually turned into a 'sleeper apparatus'. Their task was to do nothing at all, possibly for years. Then, when they were activated, they might perform some signal service, betraying a crucial secret or, most valuable of all, actually using their power to influence policies in such a way as to advance the interests of the Soviet Union. 'The primary purpose', a former Soviet agent confessed, 'was not to acquire . . . information, but to move up rapidly within the government.'[43]

Significant glimpses of this process are caught from time to time, and there can be no doubt that many decisions taken in the West that ultimately served to advantage Stalin were activated by the Georgian puppet-master's strings. How often must he have smiled inwardly when at conference with Anglo-American statesmen he reflected how blissfully ignorant Churchill and Roosevelt were of what *he* knew. As he gazed around at the American delegation at the Yalta Conference, did his glance light for a moment on the dapper figure of Alger Hiss? Were there any others, whose faces still stare out at us from the photographs, whom the dictator knew to be '*nash*' – 'ours'? Hiss was a prominent State Department official, close to Secretary of State Stettinius, who played an important part both in Washington and internationally, as at the Dumbarton Oaks, Yalta and San Francisco Conferences. The Soviet Ambassador to the United Nations,

Andrei Gromyko, urged that Hiss should become its first Secretary-General. He was found to have passed secret documents to the Soviets, and in February 1945 was pertinacious in obtaining important OSS reports irrelevant to his own work, but without question of great interest to Soviet intelligence.[44] Hiss has consistently denied his guilt, but the incriminating evidence appears overwhelming.

(There is not space here to recapitulate the story in full, for which reference should be made to Professor Allen Weinstein's book and subsequent commentaries by Sidney Hook and others. Briefly, Professor Weinstein's meticulous investigation among the released FBI and Hiss defence files has shown clearly that Whittaker Chambers's account of the Communist underground in which he and Hiss operated is accurate; that Hiss lied over his association with Chambers, and over the whereabouts of the typewriter on which the purloined State Department documents were copied; that there is no evidence – as Hiss's partisans claimed – that Hiss's conviction resulted from a conspiracy in high places; and that Chambers's possession of the inculpatory 'pumpkin papers' cannot be explained other than by their having been passed to him by Hiss. As Melvin J. Lasky writes, 'now the guilt of Alger Hiss . . . may be taken as proven'.)[45]

What cannot be known now, or perhaps ever, is the extent that Hiss was able to direct United States policy into channels agreeable to Stalin. At the Yalta Conference it was noted that he 'had Mr. Stettinius' ear', Stettinius being the honest but inexperienced Secretary of State.[46] But there is no evidence of decisions being swayed in a subversive sense,[47] and if such took place it was necessarily undertaken with extreme caution and when safe opportunity offered. Stalin was certainly receiving copies of United States secret telegrams about this time,[48] and it may be that the major benefit to Stalin of highly-placed traitors in the West lay in the immense superiority of his well-informed diplomacy over that of the Americans.[49]

Another highly-placed traitor in Washington was Harry Dexter White, Assistant Secretary to the Treasury. White was in a strong position to influence United States policies, and his energetic character frequently enabled him to sway important decisions. Many policies forcefully advocated by him were favourable to Soviet interests, in particular his support for the notorious Morgenthau Plan, which would have reduced post-war Germany to a starving pastoral economy, ripe for Soviet absorption.[50] Like Hiss, White used his influence to place other Soviet sympathizers in key posts,[51] and supplied Beria with information.

Men like Alger Hiss and Harry Dexter White were well placed to lend aid to Stalin's determined efforts to out-manoeuvre the Western Allies in the confrontation that developed with the downfall of Germany. But government policies are rarely dictated by the influence or decision of a single man, and the role of these men was to lend weight to existing trends in official opinion favouring submission to Soviet requirements, rather than the making of key decisions in Soviet favour. But their influence was considerable, and the odds are clearly strong that they had other highly-placed collaborators whose identity remains secret. Under President Roosevelt's leadership, American policy towards the Soviet Union was inevitably ill-advised in many fields, and a ready prey to mischievous influences.

Apart from the 'big fish' like Hiss and White, who consistently but unconvincingly denied their guilt,[52] there were hosts of lesser agents and traitors in the field, many of whom were convicted of their crimes.[53] The ones who rendered greatest aid to the enemy were perhaps those who betrayed the secrets of the atomic bomb to Beria, thus advancing Soviet possession of this deadly weapon by several years.[54] Their story is too well-documented to require elaboration. Here it is more interesting to consider the conduct of greater men, whose actions perhaps fell short of actual treachery but who nevertheless allowed base motives to influence them into using their power to assist Stalin's oppressive and expansionist policy.

The Soviet Union from the moment of its inception dedicated all the resources of that vast country to the promotion of one aim: the preservation of Bolshevik power and privileges. Though the Soviet economy has remained throughout its history in a very poor condition, the resources of the state for any immediate and particular purpose are almost limitless. Bribery and corruption have long been potent weapons for the penetration and softening-up of capitalist states, and millionaires have succumbed to temptation as readily (or more so) than an indigent Admiralty clerk.

At the time of the Revolution there occurred massive expropriation of the wealth of the Imperial family, the aristocracy and other rich. Many art treasures were acquired by the new Bolshevik ruling class, but most were retained by them collectively as property of the 'state'. Almost at once a number of rich and unscrupulous foreign entrepreneurs descended on Petrograd and Moscow like kites on a rotting carcase.[55] Very soon they came to profitable arrangements with the Soviet authorities, whereby they exported shipments of art treasures at prices which in the West were knock-down, but in Soviet Russia provided valuable foreign currency at a time when the economy was suffering from ever worse difficulties. The competition to obtain these lucrative concessions was great, and the OGPU (later the NKVD) was not slow to extract further ancillary tribute. Andrew Mellon, Secretary to the Treasury, obstructed or deflected United States anti-dumping embargoes directed against the USSR after he had negotiated a personal multi-million-dollar art purchase with Soviet authorities in 1930.[56] Much more intimately involved in the Soviet art trade were the Hammers. Themselves of Russian origin, they discovered at an early date the profitable conjunction of 'socialism' and secret art deals with the Soviets. A singularly unpleasant clan, the father Julius had served time in Sing Sing for a sordid crime and his son Armand had been connected with bootleggers; whilst both were strongly suspected of being NKVD agents.[57] In 1932 they threw themselves and their money behind the presidential candidature of Franklin D. Roosevelt, the diplomatic recognition of Soviet Russia being their declared aim. The recognition duly took place on 17 November 1933. Immediately afterwards Julius Hammer, in salubrious conjunction with an ex-convict whom Roosevelt had pardoned on a manslaughter conviction, presented FDR with a small memento of the occasion. This was one of the most exquisite possessions of the late Tsar: 'a 1913 Fabergé model of a Volga River steamboat done in gold, silver, and platinum with a music box that played "God Save the Tsar"'.[58] Recognition of the Soviet Union was an event brought about as a result of many converging factors,[59] and it would be ridiculous to suppose that it was secured by bribery, direct or indirect. But the timing, conditions and other attendant circumstances are unlikely to have been totally uninfluenced by the Hammers' gold.

A much more dubious example of this type of exchange is afforded by that of Joseph E. Davies, a wealthy Washington lawyer whom Roosevelt appointed as Ambassador in Moscow from 1937 to 1938. A sweetener of $17,500 to the Roosevelt campaign fund in 1936 had done nothing to queer his chances, though his general qualifications for the post comprised virtually total ignorance of Russian history, politics and language. What he was interested in, however, was Russian antiques and art treasures. His wife, Marjorie Merriweather Post, was the heiress of a fortune built up on Grape Nuts, Post Toasties, Jell-O and the like, and felt with equal enthusiasm that Russian aristocratic heirlooms contributed polish to Grape Nuts money. The embassy to Moscow proved to be one long spending spree, with crates of antiques relaying monthly across the ocean to Mrs Davies's elegant home at Rock Creek Park.

The Davieses spent a great deal of money in the Soviet Union, at a time when the failures of the Five Year Plan left the country in dire need of dollars. But it was not only dollars that Stalin bought with this sizeable chunk of Russia's heritage. Ambassador Davies was given very special treatment: prices were frequently slashed, much was simply given him, and famous galleries like the Tretiakov were stripped of priceless treasures for his benefit. In commission shops (where ruined families sold their last possessions in an effort to survive) Davies watched delightedly as his NKVD guides knocked down a painting from five thousand to eight hundred roubles. In return for all this generosity Stalin doubtless expected, and certainly received, services in return. It was the critical period of the purges, when Stalin felt his regime to be hanging by a hair, when only rivers of blood could preserve the dictatorship. Davies threw himself energetically into a self-appointed campaign to justify the most improbable distortions of evidence and the most sanguinary sentences. His celebrated book, *Mission to Moscow*, consisted of a sustained apologia for all Stalin's excesses. All criticism was stifled even to the extent of deleting mild censures confided to his diary.

Joe Davies remained a staunch friend of the Soviet Union through the Nazi-Soviet Pact, and came into his own with the German invasion of Russia. His claim that the purges had eradicated a potential fifth column received wide acceptance, though this now sits oddly with the historical fact that nearly a million Russians joined the German Army. *Mission to Moscow* was made into a film, even more bizarre than the book, by Warner Brothers. Davies was dispatched by Roosevelt on numerous further missions to Moscow, and continued to extol Soviet policies in the peacetime period and the Cold War. In 1946 he defended the motives of those who had been caught betraying atomic secrets to Beria.[60] Stalin may well have thought Davies's one-man propaganda band worth the money. At the same time, the exchange does not of itself prove Davies to have been consciously serving Soviet interests to the detriment of his own country. He was an ignorant, conceited and arrogant man, perfectly capable of rationalizing his own interests into being also those of his country. No form of words was necessary to cement the unspoken contract.

Less easily explained away, however, was a particular service rendered soon after Davies's appointment as Ambassador. Under unidentified pressures from the White House, the Russian Division in the State Department was abolished, and its unique collection of material on the Soviet Union ordered to be broken up or destroyed. No reason was given for taking this seemingly contrary action at a time when the USA and USSR were becoming much more closely involved in each other's affairs. But it seems that the Russian Division under its scholarly director, Robert F. Kelley, knew more than was good for it, and tended to recommend firmer attitudes in face of Soviet truculence than seemed wise to certain people. As George F. Kennan wrote,

> I was surprised, in later years, that the McCarthyites and the other right-wingers of the early Fifties never got hold of the incident and made capital of it; for here, if ever, was a point at which there was indeed the smell of Soviet influence, or strongly pro-Soviet influence, somewhere in the higher reaches of the government.[61]

It cannot be emphasized too strongly that Communist or crypto-Communist influences at work in the wartime American and British administrations were but one factor among many in the decision-making process. It must have been rare for even the highest-placed traitor to have been able of himself to deflect or reverse his country's policy. Indeed, when Soviet Russia became an ally after June 1941, there was as often as not little cause for clashes of interest. An irresponsible and opinionated leader like Roosevelt could pursue policies and advocate views in all sincerity, which if pressed by a subordinate figure might in retrospect appear sinister rather than merely misguided. As Gibbon wrote of the Emperor Honorius's feeble response to the menace of the Goths,

> The incapacity of a weak and dispirited government may often assume the appearance, and produce the effects, of a treasonable correspondence with the public enemy. If Alaric himself had been introduced into the council of Ravenna, he would probably have advised the same measures which were actually pursued by the ministers of Honorius.

Despite this, the most cautious historian is obliged to recognize that treacheries occurred of whose influence he can be only dimly aware. In the United States the subversive careers of Alger Hiss and Harry Dexter White came to light only as a result of the revelations of their former co-conspirators Whittaker Chambers and Elizabeth Bentley. No similar defections from the Party took place in Britain, and the question remains whether Beria did not also possess men high in British governing circles labelled in the Lubianka records as 'nash'. The continuing spate of revelations about the Burgess, Maclean and Philby affair do indeed indicate that almost any misbehaviour and expression of suspect views could pass undetected or tolerated in the lax atmosphere of the time.

Recently Mr David Martin, in an important study of General Mihailovich's Chetnik movement in Yugoslavia, has brought forward disturbing evidence that British support was deflected from the General to Tito's Communist partisans in large part as a result of the machinations of Soviet sympathizers in key posts. SOE reports of Mihailovich's increasing successes over the Germans were apparently withheld from the British authorities, whilst Tito's activities were correspondingly extolled and exaggerated. Similarly, BBC broadcasts on the subject were mysteriously slanted in favour of Tito. At SOE in Cairo a Major James Klugman did not neglect opportunities to injure Mihailovich's cause and boost Tito's.[62] Klugman was a fanatical Communist who played a large part in the 1930s in recruiting youths at Cambridge and other universities to the Soviet cause. A rigid Stalinist, he may have come to regret his aid to Tito when the latter broke with Moscow in 1948.[63] By the end of the war British attitudes had so hardened that the Foreign Office legal adviser, Patrick Dean, accepted that Mihailovich should be handed over to Tito as a war criminal, should he fall into the hands of his British allies.[64]

A close collaborator of Klugman's was Douglas Springhall, who had also worked for the NKVD at universities in the 1930s, recruiting Kim Philby amongst others. In 1943 Springhall was caught stealing secret material from the Air Ministry, for which he received seven years' penal servitude. About the same time a Captain Uren, Springhall's colleague, received an identical sentence for a similar activity. The Soviet authorities retaliated by refusing the veteran Soviet correspondent of the *Daily Telegraph*, Alfred Cholerton, re-entry to the USSR. Next Cholerton heard that his secretary in

Moscow had been arrested. In view of Cholerton's exceptional understanding of the Soviet Union, it is interesting to note that he was convinced that this retaliation had been instigated by 'NKVD boys who run the intell.[igence] clearing house in [BBC/HQ at] Bush House'.[65]

The story of the forced repatriation of Soviet citizens and others at the end of the war is now well-known. Some six million Russian prisoners-of-war, slave-labourers and refugees had been drawn into German-occupied Europe. By the end of the war about half their number were in British and American custody. The agreement signed by both governments at Yalta provided for the return of all Soviet citizens to the USSR. The agreement ignored the question of those who did not wish to return, but the British had already decided that all should be compelled to do so, whatever their wishes. Under British pressure, and with strong reservations, the United States also agreed for a time to employ force on unwilling repatriates.

No sooner had the first shiploads of Russians arrived home than appalling reports reached the Foreign Office of arbitrary massacres, imprisonment and other savage ill-treatment of the prisoners. Subsequent revelations served to confirm this gloomy picture, and of more than two and a quarter million prisoners returned, the overwhelming majority perished horribly: either massacred on arrival, or dying slowly in forced-labour camps.

The policy rested on a Cabinet decision, swayed by the advocacy of Foreign Secretary Anthony Eden. But it was the permanent officials of the Foreign Office Northern Department who exerted themselves to implement the policy with maximum harshness, long after Eden had retired from office. Geoffrey Wilson and Patrick Dean had advocated forced repatriation before Eden took it up, and they and their colleagues went to extraordinary lengths to resist pressures from the military and others to mitigate or end so inhumane a practice. British laws were broken, the International Red Cross was misled, Foreign Secretary Bevin was lied to, and the British public deliberately kept in ignorance of what was being done in its name. The motive for all this diligence remains a mystery. As late as 1948 Patrick Dean was urging revival of the policy,[66] but neither he nor his colleagues today can be induced to explain their motives.[67]

It is the treatment of these Russians temporarily escaped from Stalin's control which most effectively illustrates the extent to which Western fellow-travellers were prepared, when it came to the point, to assist in preserving the rule of the NKVD over that unhappy people. They were in effect allies in his secret war. John Strachey was a well-known ex-Communist who happened to be living near a camp for the Russians in southern England. He 'was quite merciless. He said that they were quislings because they had been found in German uniform and that they deserved everything that was coming to them.'[68]

To Stalin the recapture of the fugitive Russians was of paramount importance. Their reluctance to return was striking evidence of the inhuman nature of the Soviet regime. Worse than this was the likelihood that they would form a powerful anti-Soviet Russian grouping beyond the reach of the NKVD.[69] The Germans had raised an 800,000-strong 'Russian Liberation Army', and the Anglo-Americans were suspected of wishing to do likewise.[70] Other reasons for the intense Soviet interest in its fugitive citizens are provided by a former SMERSH officer: 'In the first place they were undesirable witnesses against communism and the Soviet system. Secondly, the Soviet Union had suffered colossal human losses in the war and was short of manpower.'[71]

As a Cossack officer learned after being handed over to the NKVD in Austria, the policy represented 'an effort to frighten all who still carried in their hearts the hope of liberation – the reactionaries in the Soviet Union and abroad. It was also to prove that the Soviet Union could dredge up its enemies from the bottom of the sea and punish them with death, and that the free world, like Pontius Pilate, would wash its hands.' And a former officer of Vlasov's army confessed morosely that the Allies' betrayal would effectively prevent future desertions.[72] A SMERSH officer involved in their return stresses the internal propaganda value to Stalin: 'Of course, amongst Soviet troops and the population, the NKGB and the Soviet propaganda machine exploited to the full the fact that these extraditions had taken place.' Former Russian soldiers returned by the British and Americans were 'beaten to a pulp' and paraded before Red Army units as a warning. The resultant impression was one of the irresistible nature of Soviet power, coupled with the abject weakness of the West.[73]

For a brief but bloody moment Stalin's secret war against the Russian people had received direct assistance from highly-placed sympathizers in the West. If their motives remain a closely-guarded secret, their actions are plain enough. The Russian people had been shepherded back into the darkness, the weasel assisting the wolf. Such, as Bertram Wolfe pointed out, is

. . . the essence of totalitarianism: its two-fold war – an unending war on its own people to remake them in the image of its blueprint for the spirit of man; and on the rest of the world to conquer it for the inevitable and infallible Communist system. Indeed the two wars are inseparably interlinked: a regime which gives its own people no peace will give the world no peace either.[74]

Soviet policy has alternated extreme caution – even cowardice – with far-reaching schemes of aggression. But so long as that policy is conducted with uniform malevolence and lack of scruple, the civilized world has no alternative but to assume and guard against the worst.

Epilogue

Historians' assessments of Soviet intentions in the post-war period have been handicapped by the paucity of available documentary material and, inevitably, by contemporary political attitudes to a conflict which still continues. Hopes that the Soviet Union might co-operate in reconstructing a stable world order faded in 1946–7, and attitudes became polarized as the Cold War set in. To most historians and publicists in the West at the time, the USSR had become – probably always had been – a 'world bully', nurturing far-reaching schemes of aggrandizement extending possibly to eventual world conquest. Either the Soviets were acting according to a pre-scribed plan for world domination (consistently advocated, in the form of 'world revolution', by all Soviet theorists since the time of Lenin); or they were unscrupulous adventurers, seeking to advance their power whenever opportunity offered.

But when strict limits were afforded to Soviet potential expansion by the system of alliances stretching from NATO to SEATO, and these in turn were followed by drastic American military reverses in Vietnam, a new school of 'revisionist' historians arose. The re-visionists tended to advocate the view that it was over-pushing United States policies that had provoked a suspicious Soviet Union into adopting hostile and obstructive attitudes. In particular, the absorption of formerly independent states in Eastern Europe was seen as a natural defensive response, intended as a bastion blocking the traditional invasion route of Russia's enemies.

The revisionists' view was in part a healthy reaction against simplistic interpretations of the preceding period of tension. Soviet military and economic power had undoubtedly been exaggerated, and America's preponderant strength insufficiently appreciated. Furthermore, it was scarcely likely that the 'free world' had been solely motivated by altruistic hopes of extending democratic benefits to all peoples.

However, the 'revisionist' phase in historiography appears even
less likely to hold the field than the naïve 'crusading' version of the
Cold War itself. Its limitations have come under increasingly strong
fire from scholars well qualified to judge. It has been pointed out, for
example, that the 'revisionists' are, almost to a man, Americans
relying primarily on American sources. The implication is strong
that their line of inquiry tells us more of American attitudes at the
time of the Vietnam War and President Nixon's peccadilloes than of
events in the 1950s. Then again, they tend to ignore the Soviet side
of the struggle, discussing Western responses as if they existed in a
sort of limbo. Thirdly, it is too frequently presumed that Soviet
behaviour consisted in the main of traditional 'Great Power politics'
similar to, and inherited from, those of Imperial Russia.[1]

The last view is flawed by a basic misunderstanding of the role
played by ideology. As Arthur Schlesinger succinctly puts it:

> . . . the great omission of the revisionists – and also the funda-
> mental explanation of the speed with which the Cold War escalated
> – lies precisely in the fact that the Soviet Union was *not* a tradi-
> tional national state. This is where the 'mirror image', invoked
> by some psychologists, falls down. For the Soviet Union was a
> phenomenon very different from America or Britain: it was a
> totalitarian state, endowed with an all-explanatory, all-consuming
> ideology, committed to the infallibility of government and party,
> still in a somewhat messianic mood, equating dissent with
> treason, and ruled by a dictator who, for all his quite extraordinary
> abilities, had his paranoid moments.
>
> Marxism-Leninism gave the Russian leaders a view of the world
> according to which all societies were inexorably destined to
> proceed along appointed roads by appointed stages until they
> achieved the classless nirvana. Moreover, given the resistance of
> the capitalists to this development, the existence of any
> non-communist state was *by definition* a threat to the Soviet
> Union. 'As long as capitalism and socialism exist,' Lenin wrote,
> 'we cannot live in peace: in the end, one or the other will
> triumph – a funeral dirge will be sung over the Soviet Republic or
> over world capitalism'.[2]

A similar error, not confined to the 'revisionists', is a simple matter
of misused phraseology. Historians write of 'Russia . . . replacing

our own earlier idea of a "cordon sanitaire" with a ring of "friendly" neigbours on her western frontier',[3] and even George Kennan could suggest that 'behind Russia's stubborn expansion lies only the age-old sense of insecurity of a sedentary people reared on an exposed plain in the neighbourhood of fierce nomadic peoples', etc.[4]

But, in the total absence of anything approaching public opinion in the USSR, concepts of 'Russia' and 'the Russians' can have very little meaning in this context. It was Stalin himself who made all policy decisions. His concern was not with traditional national ambitions, but solely with the preservation of his authority and person. A ploy he frequently used was to portray himself as a moderate, resisting 'hard-line' elements in the Politburo or elsewhere.[5] In fact, of course, his colleagues and subordinates possessed no independent powers of decision whatever, beyond what they timorously hoped might anticipate the Boss's directives.

'I trust no one,' he ruminated aloud bitterly in 1951, 'not even myself.' As far as foreign affairs went, he scarcely bothered to inform or consult those around him. 'The rest of us in the leadership', related Khrushchev, 'were careful not to poke our noses into Eastern Europe unless Stalin himself pushed our noses in that direction. He jealously guarded foreign policy in general and our policy toward other Socialist [i.e. occupied] countries in particular as his own special province. Stalin had never gone out of his way to take other people's advice into account, but this was especially true after the war.'[6] Most foreign observers had long been aware of this state of affairs, and realized that men like Molotov and Litvinov 'have no policy of their own but are simply the mouthpieces of M. Stalin'.[7] The Foreign Commissar could scarcely interview a visiting ambassador without Stalin creeping about the next room to overhear the conversation.[8]

Within the natural limitations which restrict even the most absolute dictator, Soviet policy reflected the personal hopes and fears of Stalin himself. Of course he too was aware of and influenced by historical considerations, but any tendency to write in impersonal terms of 'Russia' or 'the Russians' seeking this or that aim is delusive.

On one level Stalin's statecraft was remarkably crude, simplistic – and practical. He envisaged power in very material terms: 'Do you know how much our state weighs, with all the factories, machines, the army, with all the armaments and the navy?' he demanded once.

'Well, and can one man withstand the pressure of that astronomical weight?'[9] As far as the question of the Soviet Union's post-war frontiers went, Stalin did not believe anything to be his which he did not actually hold. 'This war is not as in the past', he told Djilas in April 1945; 'whoever occupies a territory also imposes on it his own social system. Everyone imposes his own system as far as his army has power to do so. It cannot be otherwise'.[10]

Stalin's aim remained what it had been in 1940: to seize as much territory as possible in Eastern Europe as a defensive glacis against the outside world. This was the belt of territory presented to him by Hitler, but which had had to be regained from him by force. Efforts to persuade the British and Americans to recognize the Führer's award had failed,[11] and the only hope was to ensure he was there first.

Stalin's *Drang nach Westen* was a curious mixture of recklessness and caution. Enormous losses were incurred in the race to secure Budapest and Berlin. The war itself was even prolonged for a day on a pretext, in order that Soviet tanks might enter Prague in time; and a frantic race to seize Denmark (and hence control the Baltic) was forestalled by the arrival of Montgomery's forces in Lübeck only hours before.[12]

In September 1944 Stalin had granted an armistice on favourable terms to Finland. This unusual clemency was due to a desire not to antagonize at this early stage the Anglo-Americans who had shown such sympathy for the Finns in 1940, and to induce Germany's other allies (Hungary, Romania, Bulgaria) to look east rather than west for terms.[13] As the race neared its victorious climax, Stalin's actions continued to betray fear and respect for the enormous military strength of the Western Allies. He urged Tito's partisans in 1944 not to proclaim their Communist conviction too overtly, lest they 'frighten' the British; he abandoned any idea of annexing Greece when he saw the British must get there first; and he similarly cast aside any lingering ideas of attempting to absorb Denmark after the last days of the war.[14]

Marxist-Leninist doctrine and his own suspicious nature combined to cement Stalin's conviction that Western capitalists, aware of his hostile intentions, must be longing for the opportunity to unleash all-out war against the Soviet Union, with or without German assistance. 'They will never accept the idea that so great a space should be red, never, never!' he exclaimed.[15] He was soon to learn of

America's possession of the atomic bomb, if his agents had not already informed him.

In the West, Russian heroism and wartime propaganda had combined to exaggerate the formidable strength of the Red Army. A prescient few already saw it as a potent threat to Western Europe. To Stalin matters appeared in a rather different light. True, his armies had, with unheard-of gallantry and sacrifices, hunted down 'the Nazi beast in his lair'. But he also knew better than most how very near at times they had been to defeat, and also how much his conquests had owed to lend-lease supplies and American and British strategic bombing. Now the United States, with an industrial capacity and military resources dwarfing those of Germany at the height of her power, faced him in the heart of Europe.

It is salutary here to remind ourselves in parenthesis that Stalin was conscious of dangers of which historians are still barely aware. To provide but one example, hitherto unnoticed, it is necessary to cast back to the early days of the German invasion. A pre-war Soviet film, depicting the crushing defeat of a German invasion, had laid considerable emphasis on the widespread use of poison gas in the coming war. Clearly the deployment of this terrible weapon was anticipated with considerable apprehension, as it was in Britain and France at the same period. Unlike Britain and France, though, the Soviet Government was able to provide only the most limited precautions against such an attack. When war came the War Engineering Department had a totally inadequate supply of gas masks. Worse still, 65 per cent produced during the war were constructed from *ersatz* materials, quite useless for protection.

Small wonder that on 8 August 1941 the Soviet Union hastened to offer to observe the 1925 Geneva Convention on poison-gas warfare! The Germans did indeed possess ample supplies of different types of toxic gas. Given their air superiority on the Eastern Front, one can imagine what would have been the effect on the war's outcome had sustained gas bombardments been directed at the densely-packed populations of Moscow, Leningrad and Stalingrad in 1942. What undoubtedly saved Russia from such a blow was a firm promise made by Churchill (in response to Stalin's agitated plea) that the RAF would launch massive retaliation in kind on German cities.[16] This was a threat to which Hitler was likely to be personally responsive, as he had himself suffered terribly during a mustard-gas attack on the Western Front in 1918.[17]

In 1945 the USSR still possessed no strategic air force, and there can be no doubt that Stalin regarded the awesome striking power under Eisenhower's command with apprehension. In April 1944 he had warned his Chiefs of Staff against any idea that the defeat of Germany would be the end of their problems. There would be other dangers, equally great; notably the exposure of the Red Army to populations hostile to Communism, and stiffening relations with the Allies in the West.[18] Meanwhile, in the Ukraine, Byelorussia and the Baltic States, nationalist partisans were fighting Red Army and NKVD units on a scale recalling the bitterest days of the Civil War. Stalin was clearly fearful that the Western Allies would have the wit to play that card the purblind Germans had thrown away: the opposition of the Russian people to the regime. The extent of his fear may be gauged by his absolute refusal to consent to British arming of Russian sentries in prisoner-of-war camps or even enrolling them in a purely nominal 'armed Allied unit'. He feared this might provide cover for the levying of a new 'Vlasov' army.[19]

Fear of military confrontation with the Anglo-Americans, revolt inside the Soviet Union, or contamination of the Red Army in occupied Europe effectively inhibited Stalin from any rash ventures in 1945. There were points on which he would not give way, but they were points on which the Anglo-Americans had no effective means of bringing pressure to bear. The new Soviet-Polish frontier, the annexation of the Baltic States, the refusal to implement Churchill's illusory 'percentages' agreement: all these moves took place safely behind Red Army lines, and the worst the democracies could do was affect not to recognize their legitimacy.

Caution was everything. It was still hard to believe that the West was sincere in its belief in the possibility of genuine post-war co-operation between the two irreconcilable systems. The results of the Teheran Conference had seemed almost too good to be true (Stalin returned to the Kremlin 'in a particularly good frame of mind') and after Potsdam a Soviet official noted that 'the Soviet diplomats won concessions from the Western Allies to an extent that the diplomats themselves had not expected'. After the defeat of Germany Stalin had been fearful that the Americans might not pull back to the demarcation line, and remained convinced that Eisenhower could, had he chosen, have taken Berlin. Still, the Allies were co-operating, for whatever reason, and as Roosevelt had irresponsibly announced at Yalta that United States forces would withdraw from Europe within two years of victory, there was every incentive for a policy of 'softly, softly, catchee monkey'.[20]

Despite the overwhelming Soviet military presence in Eastern Europe, Stalin was careful for some time to maintain the pretence and even, to a limited, fast diminishing extent, the reality of tolerating non-Communist institutions and political parties. In Romania it was announced that there was no intention of altering the country's frontiers or social system.[21] It was more than two years before King Michael was obliged to leave the country. Similarly, in Poland, Bulgaria and Hungary the shades of independent institutions were permitted to linger on until election results proved that the most extreme efforts of intimidation and propaganda could not induce populations voluntarily to accept Communist domination. Czecho-slovak 'independence' survived a little longer, as a result of Stalin's confidence in the pliability of Dr Beneš and his colleagues.[22]

Postponement of the full establishment of the Soviet 'New Order' in Eastern Europe was clearly due to several factors. If the new regimes could gain power by constitutional and legal means, this would facilitate the task of Communist Parties in Western Europe, and it was essential, too, not to jettison chances of securing a settlement in Germany favourable to Soviet expansion.

In any case, Stalin was by no means so confident as hindsight might suggest. In Poland the carefully-planned abduction and trial of sixteen leaders of the Home Army resistance movement in March 1945 suggest that in his view effective Polish armed resistance to the imposition of Soviet rule posed sufficient threat to make it worth risking the inevitable outcry that would arise in the West.

All over Eastern Europe and the Soviet Union, the NKVD and SMERSH stretched their enormous resources to cauterize resistance. Soviet propaganda had tended for ideological reasons to exaggerate the role played by partisan and 'people's' armies in defeating Nazism, and they clearly were now taking no chances. Suspect elements of occupied countries were dispatched in an unceasing shuttle of trainloads to the GULAG camps, which continued to under-pin Soviet economic production until after Stalin's death.[23]

About five and a quarter million Soviet citizens were recovered from Western and Central Europe. All had to be elaborately screened, after which the majority were assigned to forced labour in GULAG camps and elsewhere.[24] At the same time deportations from the Caucasus, the Crimea, the Ukraine, the Baltic States and other regions of the USSR continued unabated.[25] As if this were not enough, the hard-pressed NKVD apparatus had to absorb millions of German, Japanese, Romanian and Hungarian prisoners-of-war.

Civil war smouldered and flared for years in regions evacuated by the Germans. A Soviet historian estimated that Lithuanian partisans killed about twenty thousand Soviet troops during the years 1944–8, and Khrushchev himself admitted that 'after the war, we lost thousands of men in a bitter struggle between the Ukrainian nationalists and the forces of Soviet power.'[26]

The eight years between VE Day and Stalin's death saw the dictator become increasingly jealous, vengeful and vindictive. Fear of the Soviet and Soviet-dominated peoples, mistrust of the power of the United States, apprehension at the onset of old age with all its dangerous frailties, and recurring bouts of paranoiac suspicion concurred to cause him to double and redouble precautions deemed necessary for his survival and that of the regime.

Danger loomed everywhere. The USSR was sealed in a quarantine more hermetic even than before the war. The tentacles of the NKVD uncoiled to crush incipient dissent even before its practitioners were aware of their own intentions. Jews, heretical biologists, bourgeois composers, critics of Lysenko's eccentric genetic theories, supporters of Marr's still odder philological speculations . . . all, all were engaged in conspiracies so dark that only the Leader could penetrate the arcanum. Like the thirteenth-century Cistercian Abbot Richalm, he saw agencies skulking behind every cause of disquiet.

> If he felt squeamish, he was sure that the feeling was wrought in him by demoniacal agency. If puckers appeared on his nose, if his lower lip drooped, the devils had again to answer for it; a cough, a cold in the head, a hawking and spitting, could have none but a supernatural and devilish origin.[27]

But Stalin was not mad, not even at the end when death interrupted the unfolding of the notorious 'doctors' plot'. As Adam Ulam writes, 'the madness lay in the system that gave absolute power to one man and allowed him to appease every suspicion and whim with blood.'[28] His formative years had been spent in an entirely conspiratorial atmosphere. Roman Malinovsky, one of Lenin's ablest colleagues, had proved to be a Tsarist spy. And now NKVD records contained the names of innumerable highly-placed men and women in capitalist countries who had outwitted the formidable British and American security services in order to betray their class and country. As Stalin chuckled at the blindness of his enemies, the uncomfortable corollary must have recurred as frequently: how many of *his* people were secretely leagued with 'the gentlemen from the Thames'? What if one of his closest cronies – Molotov, Mikoyan or Voroshilov, for example – were an English spy . . . or assassin?[29]

It is clear that 'the Soviet Union for internal reasons sought to put a distance between itself and the West'.[30] The absurd and cruel policy of refusing to allow Soviet war brides of US and British servicemen to leave the country betrayed the extent of Stalin's fears. War had stretched the resources of the police state to their limits – limits now being tested further by the herculean task of reimposing totalitarian controls within the USSR, and extending them to the conquered territories beyond. The military power of the Western Allies was daunting enough, but the danger to Soviet morale seemed still greater.

Hostility to the West was a prerequisite of survival. Illusions fostered by the 'abolition' of the Comintern began to be dispelled even before the war had ended. In November 1944 the French Communist leader Jacques Duclos was commissioned to write an article, published in April the next year, reasserting the duty of Communists everywhere to work for the Party's seizure of power.[31]

Duclos's article was the first clear call to generate a war atmosphere in the Soviet Union towards her Western Allies. In the Red Army speculation was tolerated or encouraged that the defeat of Germany heralded a new conflict with the remaining bastions of capitalism in the West;[32] and on 9 February 1946 Stalin himself, in a radio broadcast, warned that war with the capitalist powers, according to Marxist-Leninist dialectic, was a strong possibility. Privately, however, he had expressed caution over the timing. 'We shall recover in fifteen or twenty years, and then we'll have another go at it.' His colleagues had little doubt that the reckoning would come, though only the Great Strategist could decide when the time would be ripe.[33]

How realistic were these plans? Everything about Stalin's career suggests caution and even cowardice as the predominating factors in his make-up. Only once under his leadership had the Soviet Union risked launching unprovoked war (if one excludes the largely unopposed parade through eastern Poland in 1939), and the Finnish

War did not provide a very propitious precedent. Of course, the Red
Army of 1945 was not to be compared with its enfeebled predecessor
of 1940, but neither was the military might of the United States
comparable to that of the Finns. The Red Army was the most powerful instrument of war on the Continent, but the United States
possessed overwhelming superiority in the air and on the seas.
Above all, she had the atomic bomb.[34]

American government and public opinion were slow to respond to
the new threat, but Churchill's Fulton 'iron curtain' speech in March
1946 heralded a new era of awareness. It apparently received the tacit
approval of President Truman, and within weeks the Soviet Union
unexpectedly succumbed to pressure and withdrew her troops from
northern Persia. Any attempt to force Greece into the Soviet orbit
was similarly eschewed, through fear of provoking conflict with the
West. A very firm warning came in September 1946, when Secretary
of State Byrnes in a speech at Stuttgart promised that US 'Security
forces will probably have to remain in Germany for a long period. I
want no misunderstanding. We will not shirk our duty. We are not
withdrawing.'[35]

Stalin's creation of a war psychology was primarily intended to
facilitate the isolation of the USSR from the outside world, though it
was clearly also designed to prepare the public for war itself should it
come.

For Stalin found himself in a cleft stick. War entailed tremendous
risks; the stresses it imposed could cause dangerous rifts within the
regime, and in war an intelligent enemy could be expected to exploit
internal discontent. About half a million Soviet citizens had escaped
forced repatriation in 1945, and the democracies might well make
more effective use of them than had the Germans.

A special department of the state security system (Spetsburo)
operated against the émigrés on a scale which revealed the extent of
Stalin's apprehensions.[36] As for the interior of the Soviet Union,
there were serious indications of the extent to which revolt
simmered below the sullen silence of the Russian people.

In the forced-labour camps there were increasing signs of a new
spirit at large. The GULAG administration had to control a slave
population which had recently been augmented by many millions.
These included tens of thousands of former troops of the German-
raised 'Vlasov army'. These 'naturally looked upon themselves as a
kind of elite among political prisoners.' They were proud of the 1944

Prague Manifesto of democratic rights, and banded together against criminal elements in the camps.[37] Through them and other prisoners who had breathed the air of the capitalist West a new spirit of defiance was abroad in the camps.

It expressed itself in alarming ways. In 1946 Baltic nationalists managed to blow up the slave-transport ship *Dalstroi* at Bukhta Nakhodka, the port for Kolyma. The explosion devastated a large area of the harbour. About this time ex-Vlasov soldiers in Kolyma itself broke out into open rebellion, which was suppressed only with considerable losses on the part of guards and prisoners. The most unnerving aspect of these revolts was their connection with external threats to the Soviet Union. In 1948, when Stalin was testing the resolution of the West with the Berlin blockade, very serious disorders broke out in the coal-mining camps of Vorkuta. Led by ex-officers of Vlasov's and Krasnov's units, thousands of prisoners broke out, armed themselves with their guards' weapons, and marched towards the Urals. Their intention was to begin partisan warfare in the forests, but they were caught by Red Air Force planes on the open tundra and shot to pieces. Most of the rebels were executed, whilst thousands of prisoners all over the Soviet Union were shunted to special isolation camps, where they could be liquidated if the international crisis grew more dangerous.

Next year, in the Nizhni Aturyakh division of Berlag, another violent outbreak occurred, which was similarly suppressed with the use of large-scale military force. Then, in 1950, came the first postwar defeats of Communist armies in Korea. Elaborate preparatory precautions were taken throughout the Far Eastern camp complex of Kolyma to liquidate as many prisoners as possible (there were about a million), should United Nations forces attempt to liberate them. At the same time an uprising broke out in Vorkuta, headed by a Colonel Antonov. As the slave population comprised about one tenth of the population, the threat of revolt, if directed in collusion with an invading power, must have appeared daunting enough. To the end of his reign Stalin was troubled with reports of worsening unrest in the camps, and immediately after his death the most serious of all erupted at Vorkuta.[38]

Increasing insecurity contributed to lead Stalin to contemplate much more dangerous courses. As his spirit became further clouded with paranoiac suspicions and fears, the prospect of lashing out at the external enemy (without whose aid and encouragement the in-

ternal foe would have to abandon hope) began to appeal as a way out
of the impasse. During the war, hopes of an ultimately Soviet-
dominated Europe had arisen, to subside after Allied successes
following the Normandy landings.[39] Now the plans were dusted
down and updated.

There were favourable indications, despite Soviet weaknesses. In
June 1950, with Stalin's permission, North Korean troops invaded
South Korea. Initial hopes of a swift *Blitzkrieg* victory were dashed
by the intervention of United States and Allied forces. MacArthur's
forces cut off and destroyed most of the North Korean army and
advanced with astonishing rapidity into North Korean territory. By
October United Nations forces were approaching Chongjin. They
were now a mere seventy miles from the Soviet frontier, and a
hundred and fifty miles from Vladivostok. Apart from other major
strategic considerations, the seizure or blockade of Vladivostok
would have cut and controlled the only route to Magadan and the
gold-fields of Kolyma, with its million-strong slave population. It
was presumably at this moment that NKVD contingency plans for a
massacre of the slaves were prepared.

Hesitantly, and fearful of the consequences, Stalin consented to
allow the Chinese to intervene in the war. In November 1950
enormous numbers of Chinese Communist troops poured over the
frontier, and the tide turned as swiftly again. Fighting every inch of
the way, the United Nations troops were driven back to the 38th
parallel and beyond, and on 4 January 1951 Seoul, the South Korean
capital, fell once more into Communist hands. It was not until 24
January that United Nations counter-attacks caused the front to be
stabilized.

It was in this tense atmosphere that an extraordinary meeting is
said to have taken place in the Kremlin. In 1976 a Czech official,
Karel Kaplan, defected to the West, bringing with him an astonishing dossier. In 1968, during the 'Prague Spring', Kaplan had been
commissioned by Premier Dubček to examine Party archives in an
investigation of the 'treason trials' instituted by the Communist
government after the *coup* of 1948. For four months Kaplan toiled
among the archives, making voluminous notes. Then came the
Soviet invasion, and many of Kaplan's notes were confiscated. But
he had taken steps to conceal others, and by some means smuggled
some six thousand pages to the West. Many fascinating revelations
have come to light from this unique source, of which the most

extraordinary is the account of a meeting held in the Kremlin in January 1951.

According to the Kaplan papers, Stalin summoned to the Kremlin fifty leading Red Army generals, and the Minister of Defence and Party Secretary of each of the six satellite countries. The topic of discussion was the possibility of launching an invasion of Western Europe up to the shores of the Atlantic. Lounging in an armchair, Stalin dominated the proceedings like some medieval Mongol *ilkhan*. On the second day he explained to his satraps why he felt the time had come for the final onslaught. Contrary to hopes previously indulged, Western Europe had survived the post-war economic crisis and, thanks largely to the Marshall Aid Plan and the establishment of the NATO pact in April 1949, appeared to be increasing in stability and strength. The United States was beginning a massive increase in defence spending, and the Soviet Union had to act swiftly before the Americans established air force bases capable of launching nuclear strikes against Moscow.

All present concurred with Stalin's analysis, and it was agreed that the attack must be made within three, or at most four, years. There was much to encourage a mood of optimism. The masses would rise to assist their Red Army liberators. Deprived of her Western European markets, the United States would be isolated, impotent and poverty-stricken, to the far confines of the Atlantic. It will perhaps never be known how close the world was then to war. Mr Kaplan believes that the Soviet Union's parlous economic state, together with Stalin's death two years later, combined to cause the shelving of the decision.[40]

Mr Kaplan's account is fully credible. Stalin's daughter Svetlana reports that her father was at this time 'embittered against the whole world', and that an intense war atmosphere was prevalent in military circles. A leading Soviet aeronautics scientist has reported that Stalin had three years earlier aimed to be ready for war by 1951, instructing his scientists to press ahead with the design of long-range rockets. Much other evidence had already led the shrewd observer Boris Nicolaevsky to posit 1951 as the year when Stalin moved from general preparations for war to frenzied haste. Marshal Koniev was believed to be the intended commander of Soviet invasion forces.[41]

It seems certain that a third World War was never closer than in 1951, and that the survival of civilization hung on the whim of a morbidly suspicious and bitter old man, whose whole career testified how small a consideration was the death of millions if they stood in the way of the establishment of his Marxist nirvana. Fortunately his habitual caution predominated, though only after much indecision and perturbation of mind.

It may seem strange that the leader who had reluctantly discarded the idea of using military force against little Yugoslavia in 1948[42] should three years later have contemplated attacking the newly-formed NATO alliance. But it is the exception that proves the rule. Yugoslavia was isolated and poor, but her wartime struggle had proved her to be possessed of martial prowess and geographical advantages comparable to those of the redoubtable Finns in 1940. It would be a war of a whole people against the external aggressor, and who knew what international complications might not arise should the Red Army become bogged down amongst the mountains of Bosnia?

Western Europe, on the other hand, Stalin believed to be racked with internal conflict. The enormous Communist Parties of France and Italy represented a sizeable Trojan horse within the citadel. Their vociferous claims, together with those of fellow-travellers and pacifists everywhere, suggested to the *Vozhd* that the masses would prefer Soviet domination to that of the United States. On 7 August 1946 a British Labour Party delegation, opposed to what they saw as Foreign Secretary Bevin's anti-Soviet policy, had had an audience with Stalin in the Kremlin. Whilst the excited delegates were watching a film of life on a collective farm, Stalin left the darkened hall with the noted socialist ideologue, Harold Laski. A conspiratorial discussion followed, with Stalin explaining that a Soviet-dominated Continent could still allow (within limitations) Britain to pursue her own brand of socialism. Before this, Laski expressed his conviction that in the event of a quarrel between the USSR and the USA, Britain would support the former.[43]

The fact that war was eventually averted is no mitigation of the conduct of Laski and other fellow-travellers in Western Europe and America. There has been much complacent condemnation of the motives of the guilty 'Men of Munich'. But Chamberlain and his colleagues, however naïve their expectations and misguided their policies, were repelled by Nazi totalitarianism and desperately anxious to check its expansion. Laski and the majority of fellow-travellers and Communists, on the other hand, not only ardently supported Stalin's worst excesses,[44] but acted in a way calculated to bring the world to the brink of war. That Stalin drew back from the brink was no thanks to them. And what that war would have brought about was summed up pithily in a conversation between two Red Army generals:

'Of course we're not greatly interested in Western Europe as such,' the general answered after a moment's thought. 'It'll probably be more difficult to plant communism in the Europeans than in any other peoples. They're too spoilt economically and culturally.' 'There you are! You yourself admit it's very difficult to make Europe communist,' Klykov expressed his thoughts aloud. 'If we intend to build communism seriously there we'll have to send half the population to Siberia and feed the other half at our expense.'[45]

Europe was for the time being spared experiences Russians had undergone for more than thirty years. Stalin died on 5 March 1953, his project unfulfilled. It was his death that for a moment opened a terrifying vision of reality to his successors. An announcement of the event in *Pravda* two days later urged, in wheedling tones reminiscent of Stalin's own plea to the Russian people on 3 July 1941, 'the inadmissibility of any sort of disorder or panic'. However, NKVD precautions proved effective, and the 'disorders' were . . . postponed.[46]

Notes

Abbreviations

AIR   Air Ministry
CAB   Cabinet Offices
 FO   Foreign Office
NA   National Archives, Washington
OSS   Organization of Strategic Services
WO   War Office

Epigraph

1 Robin Kemball (ed.), *The Demesne of the Swans: Лебединый Стан (Марина Цветаева)* (Ann Arbor, 1980), p. 70.

Introduction

1 Stanislaw Mikolajczyk, *The Pattern of Soviet Domination* (London, 1948), p. 144.
2 Heinz Höhne, *The Order of the Death's Head: The Story of Hitler's S.S.* (London, 1969), p. 297. On 27 September 1939 Heydrich could report that 'Of the Polish upper classes only a maximum of 3 per cent is still present' (p. 299).
3 Alexander I. Solzhenitsyn, *The Mortal Danger: How Misconceptions about Russia Imperil the West* (London, 1980), pp. 70–1.

I The New Society

1 Cf. Leszek Kolakowski, *Main Currents of Marxism: Its Rise, Growth, and Dissolution* (Oxford, 1978), I, p. 363.
2 Quoted by A. Walicki, *The Controversy over Capitalism: Studies in the Social Philosophy of the Russian Populists* (Oxford, 1969), p. 51. Cf. Trotsky's fantastic vision of the coming communist universal art-form: Jean van Heijenoort, *With Trotsky in Exile* (Harvard, 1978), p. 128; Kolakowski, op. cit., III, pp. 51–2.

3 Rodney Barfield, 'Lenin's Utopianism: State and Revolution', *Slavic Review* (Urbana, 1971), XXX, pp. 45–56.

4 Kolakowski, op. cit., II, pp. 499–502; III, pp. 160–4.

5 Ibid., II, pp. 489–90, 498; III, pp. 50–1, 54–6. Trotsky's rejection of legal restraints was if anything even more violent and extreme (ibid., II, pp. 509–12).

6 Leonard Schapiro and Peter Reddaway (eds), *Lenin: The Man, the Theorist, the Leader; A Reappraisal* (New York, 1967), p. 137; van Heijenoort, op. cit., p. 84. Cf. Bertram D. Wolfe, *Khrushchev and Stalin's Ghost* (New York, 1957), pp. 288–94.

7 Kolakowski, op. cit., III, pp. 84–7. Aristotle described Soviet-style rule in its minutest particulars more than two millennia before it came into existence, stressing the need for ceaseless repression of potential enemies if a tyranny is to be preserved. See Benjamin Jowett (tr.), *Aristotle's Politics* (Oxford, 1905), pp. 225–31.

8 George Urban, 'A Conversation with Milovan Djilas', *Encounter* (December 1979), LIII, p. 30.

9 Merle Fainsod, *How Russia is Ruled* (Harvard, 1953), pp. 294–8, 309–11, 313–22.

10 Kolakowski, op. cit., II, p. 506.

11 Fainsod, op. cit., p. 311.

12 Merle Fainsod, *Smolensk under Soviet Rule* (London, 1958), pp. 93–6; and her *How Russia is Ruled*, pp. 325–6; Peter Deriabin and Frank Gibney, *The Secret World* (London, 1960), p. 116.

13 Fainsod, *How Russia is Ruled*, pp. 292, 314, 323–4; David Caute, *The Fellow-Travellers: A Postscript to the Enlightenment* (London, 1973), pp. 83–5.

14 Kolakowski, op. cit., III, pp. 87–8, 95–7; cf. Adam B. Ulam, *Stalin: The Man and his Era* (London, 1974), p. 387.

15 Boris Bajanov, *Bajanov révèle Staline: Souvenirs d'un ancien secrétaire de Staline* (Paris, 1979), p. 107; Werner Maser, *Hitler* (London, 1973), pp. 260–1; Hermann Rauschning, *Hitler Speaks: A Series of Political Conversations with Adolf Hitler on his Real Aims* (London, 1939), p. 236. For examples of Soviet constitutional realities, compare Vladimir Petrov, *My Retreat from Russia* (Yale, 1950), pp. 62–3; and his *Escape from the Future: The Incredible Adventures of a Young Russian* (Indiana, 1973), pp. 168–9.

16 A point stressed frequently by Solzhenitsyn. See *Архипелаг Гулаг 1918–1956: Опыт Художественного Исследования* (Paris, 1973–5), II, pp. 150, 196–8. Workers in a Leningrad shoe factory grumbled in 1934 that they had lost, not gained, by the Revolution (Petrov, *Escape from the Future*, p. 73); compare also the views of a poor peasant in a village near the Kama: Victor Kravchenko, *I Chose Freedom* (London, 1947),

pp. 382–5. For the hugely inflated prison population the contrast seemed even greater. Cf. Vladimir Brunovsky, *The Methods of the Ogpu* (London, 1931), pp. 138–9; Petrov, *Escape from the Future*, pp. 49, 220; Robert Conquest, *The Great Terror: Stalin's Purge of the Thirties* (London, 1968), pp. 292, 348; Antoni Ekart, *Vanished without trace: The story of seven years in Soviet Russia* (London, 1954), pp. 85–6. At Almahata Gaol, a cell which housed 24 people in Nicholas II's time contained 136 prisoners under Stalin (*Le Procès Kravchenko contre Les Lettres Françaises* (Paris, 1949), p. 207); and General Gorbatov found himself among 70 prisoners in a Butyrki cell designed for 25 in the Tsar's time (A. V. Gorbatov, 'Годы и войны', *Новый Мир* (April 1964), XL, p. 122).

17 Fainsod, *Smolensk under Soviet Rule*, p. 60. Stalin's childhood home at Gori, the home of a poor cobbler in Imperial times, ironically excited envy among Soviet visitors after its transformation into a museum. See Edward Ellis Smith, *The Young Stalin: the early years of an elusive revolutionary* (London, 1967), p. 18; Eugene Lyons, *Assignment in Utopia* (London, 1937), pp. 87–9. Shostakovich noted that a flat 'could hold ten or fifteen families' (S. Volkov, ed., *Testimony: The Memoirs of Dimitri Shostakovich* (London 1979), p. 68). For a well-informed war-time assessment of the Moscow housing situation, see CAB 66/54, 128.

18 Kravchenko, op. cit., pp. 324–5. See also the testimony of Prof. Lagovsky of the Kharkov Institute, in *Le Procès Kravchenko*, op. cit., p. 383; and the further account in Ekart, op. cit., p. 64.

19 Lyons, op. cit., pp. 361, 413–14; NA 861.00/11855, RG 165, box 3438. Compare the wretched condition of factory-workers seen by a Pole in a Central Asian town in 1942: Joseph Czapski, *The Inhuman Land* (London, 1951), p. 228.

20 Fainsod, *How Russia is Ruled*, pp. 80–90, 513–14; Kolakowski, op. cit., III, p. 21. Bukharin also believed in the mobilization of labour (ibid., p. 29).

21 Fainsod, op. cit., p. 107. Workers at an electrical plant in Moscow who were more than twenty-one minutes late had their salaries docked by 25 per cent for the next six months. If they repeated it within a week, they were dispatched to the forced-labour camp at Rebisk for six months (*Le Procès Kravchenko*, op. cit., pp. 199, 235–6). For the derisory purchasing power of a workman's wage in the USSR, see ibid., pp. 213–14. Cf. Unto Parvilahti, *Beria's Gardens: Ten Years' Captivity in Russia and Siberia* (London, 1959), p. 172.

22 Andrew Smith, *I Was a Soviet Worker* (London, 1937). For another English sojourner's frank account, see FO 371/29498. Compare the *Daily Herald* Moscow correspondent's account in CAB 6, 127–8; the impressions of Generals Jacob (Arthur Bryant, *The Turn of the Tide*

1939–1943 (London, 1957), pp. 468–9) and Ismay (*The Memoirs of General the Lord Ismay* (London, 1960), p. 231); Lyons, op. cit., p. 413; and the memories of Leonid Plyushch: *History's Carnival* (London, 1979), pp. 3, 9.

23 Lyons, op. cit., p. 580. Compare the views of Vice-President Wallace (Caute, op. cit., p. 270) and the British progressive headmaster, A. S. Neill (ibid., p. 4). Truth for Walter Duranty was a purely relative concept; see the amusing eye-witness account of his method of faking news in John Murray, *A Spy called Swallow* (London, 1978), p. 22; and, for comparable attitudes, Caute, op. cit., pp. 24, 73–4, 113, 125, 203–9; Lyons, op. cit., pp. 326–7, 428–31.

24 A British socialist MP, A. W. Haycock, rejected all the fugitives' accounts as 'necessarily biased statements' (*Forced Labour in Russia?* (London, 1931), pp. 42–3), an argument since employed by those anxious to explain away Nazi extermination camps. For specimens of the literature available to Western readers, compare the bibliography supplied by David J. Dallin and Boris I. Nicolaevsky in *Forced Labor in Soviet Russia* (London, 1948), pp. 309–19. The original establishment of what later flowered as GULAG is documented by Lennard D. Gerson, *The Secret Police in Lenin's Russia* (Philadelphia, 1976), pp. 147–9, 256–7.

25 Solzhenitsyn, op. cit., I, pp. 39–40.

26 Roy A. Medvedev, *Let History Judge: The Origins and Consequences of Stalinism* (London, 1971), p. 394. Solzhenitsyn suggests that the idea of the economic use of slavery was provided to Stalin in 1929 by Naphtali Frenkel, a sadistic GULAG official (Solzhenitsyn, op. cit., II, pp. 75–7). Medvedev's unidentified originator could be the same man.

27 Conquest, op. cit., pp. 356–9; Dallin and Nicolaevsky, op. cit., pp. 88–92, 105–7; Kravchenko, op. cit., pp. 198–9, 279, 284–5, 295–7, 315–24, 328, 336–41, 404–8, 414–16; Parvilahti, op. cit., pp. 111–12; Josef Scholmer, *Vorkuta* (London, 1954), p. 212; *Le Procès Kravchenko*, op. cit., p. 408; Nikolai Krasnov, *The Hidden Russia* (New York, 1960), p. 70. The NKVD was informed how many slaves the government required, and then kidnapped the requisite quotas from the 'free' population; cf. *Le Procès Kravchenko*, pp. 527–30.

28 Fainsod, op. cit., pp. 385–7; Free Trade Union Committee, American Federation of Labor, *Slave Labor in the Soviet World* (New York, 1951), pp. 5, 18–19. These figures were confirmed by a former GOSPLAN official, who testified before a United Nations Commission of Enquiry into Forced Labour in 1950 (Albert Konrad Herling, *The Soviet Slave Empire* New York, 1951), pp. 13–18); S. Swianiewicz, *Forced Labour and Economic Development* (Oxford, 1965), pp. 23, 42–4; Elma Dangerfield, *Beyond the Urals* (London, 1946), pp. 52–3, 72.

29 Stanislaw Kot, *Conversations with the Kremlin and Dispatches from Russia* (London, 1963), p. 86.

30 Alex Weissberg, *Conspiracy of Silence* (London, 1952), pp. 314–15, 319–20. These figures tally roughly with Ivanov-Razumnik's observation that the population of the Moscow Butirki Prison increased tenfold between 1933 and 1939 (*The Memoirs of Ivanov-Razumnik* (London, 1965), p. 224; cf. ibid., pp. 70–2). Robert Conquest makes the 1937 total about eight million (*The Great Terror*, pp. 335, 529–33). Another statistical source available to prisoners came from the officials who had to deliver their bread ration (Hans Becker, *Devil on my Shoulder* (London, 1955), p. 176). From Soviet informants Eugene Lyons deduced a pre-war total of five to ten million (*Stalin: Czar of All the Russias* (London, 1940), pp. 169–70; cf. Fainsod, op. cit., pp. 385–6).

31 Ivan Solonevich, *Russia in Chains: A Record of Unspeakable Suffering* (London, 1938), p. 21.

32 Zoltan Toth, *Prisoner of the Soviet Union* (London, 1978), pp. 34, 58; Gustav Herling, *A World Apart* (London, 1951), p. 9. A former prisoner, who had experienced camps and gaols the length and breadth of the Soviet Union between 1923 and 1946 stated that public opinion estimated that the concentration camp population formed from 10 to 12 per cent of the whole: i.e. between nineteen and twenty-three million souls. 'In his own opinion, there are more prisoners than this' (NA Decimal Files, 861.00/10–246). Figures supplied to Joseph Czapski varied from sixteen to thirty-five million (*The Inhuman Land*, p. 53). Cf. Krasnov, op. cit., pp. 107, 131, 202, 220. Victor Kravchenko believed there were between fifteen and twenty million (*I Chose Freedom*, p. 302); a former prisoner, Joseph Scholmer, put it at fifteen million (*Vorkuta*, p. 191), as does Solzhenitsyn (*Архипелаг Гулаг*, II, p. 201).

33 Elinor Lipper, *Eleven Years in Soviet Prison Camps* (London, 1951), p. 280; Vladimir and Evdokia Petrov, *Empire of Fear* (London, 1956), pp. 100–1. Dr Julius Margolin put the figure at '10 to 15 million people' (Dallin and Nicolaevsky, op. cit., p. 31).

34 Cf. Mikhail Rozanov, *Завоеватели белых пятен* (Limburg, 1951), p. 234; Bernhard Roeder, *Katorga: An Aspect of Modern Slavery* (London, 1958), p. 197; Parvilahti, op. cit., p. 62; Robert Conquest, *Kolyma: The Arctic Death Camps* (London, 1978), p. 23. Roy Medvedev utters a wise caution on the over-enthusiastic acceptance of exaggerated statistics in general: *On Stalin and Stalinism* (Oxford, 1979), pp. 140–1.

35 Conquest, op. cit., pp. 214–17; Lipper, op. cit., p. 158. Dallin and Nicolaevsky stress the varied factors influencing estimates (*Forced Labor in Soviet Russia*, pp. 84–7), and cautiously estimate that 16 per

cent of the adult population were slaves (ibid., p. 87). Soviet sources accepted a figure of eighteen million, but baulked at twenty million: (Arthur Koestler, *The Yogi and the Commissar and other Essays* (London, 1945), pp. 181–2, 185–6). Dimitri Panin lists some of the sources from which prisoners could formulate estimates, and concludes that in 1939–41 there were forty million slaves, reduced by 1943 to fourteen million (*The Notebooks of Sologdin* (London, 1976), pp. 90–3).

36 Ekart, op. cit., p. 44; Czapski, op. cit., pp. 34, 55. Cf. Petrov, *Escape from the Future*, pp. 97–117; Toth, op. cit., pp. 28–9; Margarete Buber, *Under Two Dictators* (London, 1949), pp. 58–66; Conquest, op. cit., pp. 19–35; Nikolai Tolstoy, *Victims of Yalta* (London, 1978), pp. 406–8; Lipper, op. cit., pp. 76–85, 291–3. In 1933 a ship carrying three thousand slaves to Kolyma foundered. The guards machine-gunned would-be escapers in droves (*Le Procès Kravchenko*, op. cit., p. 566).

37 Ibid., pp. 92–5; Dallin and Nicolaevsky, op. cit., pp. 127–9, 136–7. Similar losses took place on the voyage to the Northern Pechora camps (Rozanov, op. cit., p. 247).

38 Lipper, op. cit., pp. 40, 88–9.

39 Herling, op. cit., pp. 41, 150. Another Polish inmate estimated that 'during the first year about one-third of the prisoners die' (Ekart, op. cit., p. 11). In southern camps the tropical climate resulted in a 50 per cent annual death-rate (ibid., p. 85).

40 Petrov, op. cit., pp. 188–9, 191. Elinor Lipper reckoned the pre-1941 Kolyma death-rate at 30 per cent (*Eleven Years in Soviet Prison Camps*, p. 108), but noted that it was 50 per cent at the aptly-named Maxim Gorki camp in 1945 (ibid., pp. 169–70). Cf. ibid., pp. 231–2; *The Dark Side of the Moon* (London, 1946), p. 121; Czapski, op. cit., pp. 42–3. Dr Toth states that from 85 to 95 per cent of foreigners in GULAG died between 1945 and 1955 (*Prisoner of the Soviet Union*, p. 34). In 1928, on one of the Solovetskiye Islands, only 2,500 of 14,000 prisoners survived the winter (NA Decimal Files, 861.00/10–246). On another, 50,000 were reduced to 10,000 in a similar period (ibid.).

41 Aino Kuusinen, *Before and After Stalin: A Personal Account of Soviet Russia from the 1920s to the 1960s* (London, 1974), p. 141.

42 Roeder, op. cit., pp. 100–1; Lipper, op. cit., pp. 188–9; Ekart, op. cit., pp. 207–8.

43 Conquest, op. cit., pp. 217–31; compare his *The Great Terror*, pp. 533–5. A senior GULAG official claimed that thirty million people had been imprisoned and massacred *by 1936* (Toth, op. cit., p. 142). In the two years following, an NKVD official states there were two million executions (Vladimir and Evdokia Petrov, *Empire of Fear*, p. 72).

44 Roeder, op. cit., pp. 15–16; Raphael Rupert, *A Hidden World* (London, 1963), p. 86; Rozanov, op. cit., p. 273.

45 Quoted in Dallin and Nicolaevsky, op. cit., pp. 32–5; cf. Ekart, op. cit., p. 61.

46 Buber, op. cit., p. 298.

47 Czapski, op. cit., p. 53; *Колымские Рассказы* (London, 1978), pp. 876–9; M. Seleshko, 'Vinnytsia – The Katyn of Ukraine (A Report by an Eyewitness)', *The Journal of Historical Review* (Torrance, Ca, 1980), I, p. 344.

48 Edward Buca, *Vorkuta* (London, 1976), pp. 142–4.

49 Ibid., pp. 124–7; Toth, op. cit., pp. 48, 144; Lipper, op. cit., pp. 241–3; Petrov, *Escape from the Future*, p. 194; Shalamov, op. cit., pp. 495–6.

50 Anita Priess, *Verbannung nach Sibirien* (Manitoba, 1972), pp. 50, 55; Lipper, op. cit., pp. 120–2; *The Dark Side of the Moon*, op. cit., pp. 99, 107, 114. The heart-rending scene when the babies were dragged from their mothers is described by an eye-witness in *Le Procès Kravchenko*, p. 208; Parvilahti, op. cit., p. 57; Kuusinen, op. cit., p. 135.

51 So ran a cynical Russian saying (Petrov, op. cit., p. 159; Lipper, op. cit., p. 162). A Polish girl in a Siberian village in 1940 learned that 'almost every house in the village had, or had had, some member of the family either in prison or in a labour camp' (Maria Hadow, *Paying Guest in Siberia* (London, 1978), p. 70).

52 Vladimir and Evdokia Petrov, *Empire of Fear*, p. 73. In this context it is superfluous to note that, according to an Amnesty International Report, 'there has never been an acquittal of a political defendant in the USSR' (*Prisoners of Conscience of the USSR: Their Treatment and Conditions* (London, 1975), p. 32). This is very nearly true (three Poles were acquitted in 1945 in face of exceptional British and American concern: Z. Stypulkowski, *Invitation to Moscow* (London, 1951), p. 333). But even more effective testimony to the efficiency of Soviet justice was the claim of State Prosecutor Rudenko that no defendant before 1945 had yet pleaded 'not guilty' (ibid., p. 306).

II   Stalin the Leader

1 Victor Kravchenko, *I Chose Freedom* (London, 1947), p. 430.

2 S. Volkov (ed.), *Testimony: The Memoirs of Dmitri Shostakovich* (London, 1979), p. 198.

3 Edward Ellis Smith, *The Young Stalin: the early years of an elusive revolutionary* (London, 1967), p. 102; Robert C. Tucker, *Stalin as Revolutionary* (London, 1974), pp. 70–1.

4 Eugene Lyons, *Assignment in Utopia* (London, 1937), pp. 385–6.

5 Quoted by Otto Preston Chaney, Jr, *Zhukov* (Newton Abbot, 1972), p.

156; Kravchenko, op. cit., p. 430; George F. Kennan, *Memoirs 1925–1950* (Boston, 1967), pp. 279; Charles E. Bohlen, *Witness to History 1929–1969* (London, 1973), p. 131; Milovan Djilas, *Wartime* (New York, 1977), p. 386; FO 800/300, 22; Clark Kerr, 21 October 1943 (FO 800/301, 151); cf. David Dilks (ed.), *The Diaries of Sir Alexander Cadogan* (London, 1971), pp. 422, 580; John R. Deane, *The Strange Alliance: The Story of American Efforts at Wartime Co-operation with Russia* (London, 1947), p. 24; Stanislaw Kot, *Conversations with the Kremlin and Dispatches from Russia* (London, 1963), p. 116. Adam Ulam aptly contrasts Stalin's and Lenin's manner in this respect (*Stalin: The Man and his Era* (London, 1974), p. 358); Bohlen, op. cit., p. 263; Ronald Hingley, *Joseph Stalin: Man and Legend* (London, 1974), p. 420; Alexander Orlov, *The Secret History of Stalin's Crimes* (London, 1954), p. 288.

6 Strobe Talbott (ed.), *Khrushchev Remembers* (Boston, 1970), p. 289. For the authentic provenance of these 'memoirs', compare the penetrating commentary of Zeev Ben-Shlomo, 'The Khrushchev Apocrypha', *Soviet Jewish Affairs* (London, 1971), I, pp. 52–75.

7 Svetlana Alliluyeva, *Only One Year* (London, 1969), pp. 361–2; Roy A. Medvedev, *On Stalin and Stalinism* (Oxford, 1979), pp. 156–7.

8 Boris Bajanov, *Bajanov révèle Staline: Souvenirs d'un ancien secrétaire de Staline* (Paris, 1979), pp. 76–7.

9 Edward Ellis Smith, op. cit., pp. 43, 47, 344–9; Ulam, op. cit., pp. 26–7; Volkov (ed.), op. cit., pp. 143–7.

10 Roy A. Medvedev, *Let History Judge: The Origins and Consequences of Stalinism* (London, 1972), p. 331; Milovan Djilas, *Conversations with Stalin* (London, 1962), p. 97. Compare Stalin's spiteful jibes at Tito's expense (ibid., pp. 103–4), and his contemptuous treatment of Molotov at Teheran (Bohlen, op. cit., p. 340); Arthur Bryant (ed.), *Triumph in the West 1943–1946* (London, 1959), p. 305.

11 Talbott (ed.), op. cit., p. 264; Arthur Bryant (ed.), *The Turn of the Tide 1939–1943* (London, 1957), pp. 465–6 (Voroshilov was a favourite and not unreceptive butt: cf. *Witness to History*, p. 47, where Bohlen refers to him as 'obviously boot-licking'); General S. M. Shtemenko, *The Last Six Months* (London, 1978), p. 77; Aino Kuusinen, *Before and After Stalin* (London, 1974), p. 30. Alexander Orlov heard of such scenes (*The Secret History of Stalin's Crimes*, p. 322): interesting confirmation of the accuracy of this occasionally underrated source. Compare also Medvedev, op. cit., p. 329.

12 Kuusinen, op. cit., pp. 91–3. There is stronger evidence that Nadezhda's brother Pavel was murdered at Stalin's instigation (Medvedev, *On Stalin and Stalinism*, pp. 85–6). Authorities who provide in varying degrees a verdict of suicide on Stalin's wife are:

Bajanov, op. cit., p. 264; Svetlana Alliluyeva, *Twenty Letters to a Friend* (New York, 1967), pp. 108–15, 168–9, and her *Only One Year*, pp. 343–4; Alexander Barmine, *One Who Survived: The Life Story of a Russian under the Soviets* (New York, 1945), p. 264; Ulam, op. cit., pp. 354–5; Hingley, op. cit., pp. 226–8. Alexander Orlov refers to Yakov's being followed by Chekists: further confirmation of the accuracy of this source (*The Secret History of Stalin's Crimes*, p. 342).

13 Alliluyeva, *Twenty Letters to a Friend*, pp. 100–1; Barmine, op. cit., p. 262. Svetlana's confirmation of Barmine's account again provides interesting evidence of the general reliability of Barmine's memoir. Cf. Nikolai Tolstoy, *Victims of Yalta* (London, 1978), pp. 397–8. The Germans made much of their noteworthy captive in propaganda directed at the Red Army, even to reproducing the pathetic letter (19 July 1941) Yakov sent to his father (Ortwin Buchbender, *Das tönende Erz* (Stuttgart, 1978), pp. 68–70). The letter of course remained unanswered. The Americans in 1945 captured documents detailing the circumstances of Yakov's death, but sensitively kept them from Stalin as 'background of incident is unpleasant' (NA, RG 84, box 7, 72). A brief Soviet account was published by Mikhail I. Semiryaga, *Советские люди в европейском сопротивлении* (Moscow, 1970). The full story was finally published in the *Sunday Times* on 24 February 1980, providing a detailed account of Yakov's tragically sordid end.

14 For Vasily Stalin's unedifying career, cf. Barmine, op. cit., pp. 262–3; Talbott (ed.), op. cit., pp. 252, 290–1; Alliluyeva, op. cit., p. 107; Ulam, op. cit., pp. 676–7; G. A. Tokaev, *Comrade X* (London, 1956), pp. 332–3 (for Tokaev, cf. FO 181/1046).

15 Talbott (ed.), op. cit., p. 290; Alliluyeva, op. cit., pp. 179–81. Kapler was encountered in Vorkuta by a Polish prisoner, Antoni Ekart (*Vanished without trace: The story of seven years in Soviet Russia* (London, 1954), pp. 214–15) – valuable confirmation of the accuracy of this interesting source.

16 Talbott (ed.), op. cit., pp. 133, 167, 170, 303, 307, 481; Shtemenko, op. cit., p. 77; W. G. Krivitsky, *I Was Stalin's Agent* (London, 1939), pp. 94–5; Orlov, op. cit., p. 271; Preston Chaney, op. cit., p. 220.

17 Compare, however, *Let History Judge*, pp. 305–6, where Medvedev concludes that Stalin, whatever the state of his psyche, was for most of his life a responsible agent and conscious of the implications of his actions.

18 Robert C. Tucker, *Stalin as Revolutionary* (London, 1974), pp. 70–81.

19 Ibid., pp. 127–31, 424–61.

20 Ellis Smith, op. cit., pp. 193–211, 250–1, 344–6; Ronald Grigor Suny, 'A Journeyman for the Revolution: Stalin and the Labour Movement in Baku, June 1907–May 1908', *Soviet Studies* (1971–2), XXIII, pp. 373–94; Hingley, op. cit., pp. 47–8, 50, 62–4, 109, 144–5; Ulam, op. cit., pp.

16–17, 71; Bertram D. Wolfe, *Khrushchev and Stalin's Ghost* (New York, 1957), pp. 94–100; Volkov (ed.), op. cit., p. 16. Djilas makes the same point (George Urban, 'A Conversation with Milovan Djilas', *Encounter* (December 1979), p. 12).

21 Compare Khrushchev's words in Wolfe, op. cit., p. 176; Ulam, op. cit., pp. 261–2.

22 Medvedev, op. cit., p. 457.

23 Orlov, op. cit., pp. 129, 137–8; Talbott (ed.), op. cit., p. 170; Wolfe, op. cit., p. 204.

24 FO 800/301, 26. Compare his hidden presence at the treason trials (Fitzroy Maclean, *Eastern Approaches* (London, 1949), pp. 119–20) and the disgusting scene of his triumph over the dead Zinoviev (Orlov, op. cit., p. 350); Talbott (ed.), op. cit., pp. 99–100, 257–8; Medvedev, op. cit., p. 333; Wolfe, op. cit., pp. 158, 240; Bajanov, op. cit., p. 99. Compare Hitler's similar hatred for almost everybody (David L. Schoenbaum, *Hitler's Social Revolution: Class and Status in Nazi Germany 1933–1939* (London, 1967), pp. 20–1). The most famous utterance on the subject of revenge attributed to Stalin is of uncertain provenance: 'To choose one's victim, to prepare one's plans minutely, to slake an implacable vengeance, and then go to bed – there is nothing sweeter in the world' (Eugene Lyons, *Stalin: Czar of all the Russias* (London, 1940), pp. 33, 157). Bukharin seems to have been alluding to it in his famous talk with Kamenev in 1928 (ibid., p. 158). Extreme mistrust of all around must have been greatly exacerbated by the discovery that so many police informers had passed unnoticed in the ranks of the Bolsheviks (ibid., pp. 78–9).

25 Alliluyeva, op. cit., pp. 196–7; Talbott (ed.), op. cit., pp. 248–9, 260, 281.

26 Vladimir Petrov, *My Retreat from Russia* (Yale, 1950), pp. 42–3; Unto Parvilahti, *Beria's Gardens: Ten Years' Captivity in Russia and Siberia* (London, 1959), pp. 85–6; Lev Kopelev, *No Jail for Thought* (London, 1979), pp. 233–5, 237, 240. A British observer noted how much anti-Semitism had increased by the spring of 1944 (FO 371/43406). Cf. Menachem Begin, *White Nights: The Story of a Prisoner in Russia* (London, 1978), p. 233.

27 Joseph Czapski, *The Inhuman Land* (London, 1951), pp. 182–3; Gregory Klimov, *The Terror Machine: The inside story of the Soviet Administration in Germany* (London, 1953), pp. 40–1; Varlam Shalamov, *Колымские Рассказы* (London, 1978), pp. 103–4; Nadezhda Mandelstam, *Воспоминания* (New York, 1970), p. 333; Medvedev, *On Stalin and Stalinism*, pp. 147–8; David J. Dallin and Boris I. Nicolaevsky, *Forced Labor in Soviet Russia* (London, 1948), pp. 5, 32, 33–4, 38; Parvilahti, op. cit., p. 237. The persecution of Zionists was

started under Lenin in 1918 (Lennard D. Gerson, *The Secret Police in Lenin's Russia* (Philadelphia, 1976), p. 167); Stalin's anti-Semitism is too notorious to require exhaustive documentation. Reference may be made to the following: Ellis Smith, op. cit., pp. 135–6, 188–9; Orlov, op. cit., pp. 114, 341, 350; Kot, op. cit., pp. 153, 154; Alliluyeva, op. cit., pp. 181, 186, 196, and her *Only One Year*, pp. 148–50, 162, 383; Talbott (ed.), op. cit., pp. 258–69, 292–3; Medvedev, *Let History Judge*, pp. 493–9; Djilas, op. cit., pp. 139–40; Hingley, op. cit., p. 49; Robert Conquest, *The Great Terror: Stalin's Purge of the Thirties* (London, 1968), pp. 76–7.

28 Cf. Sir James Frazer, *The Scapegoat* (London, 1913), pp. 72–223, and his *Aftermath: A Supplement to the Golden Bough* (London, 1936), pp. 425–32. Adam Ulam draws a similar analogy (op. cit., pp. 301–3).

29 For Stalin's delusions of intellectual grandeur, see Wolfe, op. cit., pp. 214–26; Talbott (ed.), op. cit., pp. 269–75, 278–9; Volkov (ed.), op. cit., pp. 197–8. Solzhenitsyn's brilliantly-sustained reconstruction of the dictator's soliloquy seems almost as near the truth as we can get; see Gary Kern, 'Solzhenitsyn's Portrait of Stalin', *Slavic Review* (1974), XXXIII, pp. 1–22.

30 Cf. Hermann Rauschning, *Hitler Speaks: A Series of Political Conversations with Adolf Hitler on his Real Aims* (London, 1939), p. 257. Orlov, op. cit., p. 343. A colleague informed Orlov that Stalin had a homosexual relationship with his chief of the Kremlin guard (ibid., p. 350), but there is no means of verifying this allegation. Stalin reacted angrily to Eisenstein's intimations of homosexual elements in Ivan the Terrible's nature (Ulam, op. cit., p. 436).

31 Further reference may be made to the following authorities: Deane, op. cit., p. 291; Djilas, op. cit., p. 59; Barmine, op. cit., p. 257.

32 Medvedev, op. cit., pp. 326–8.

33 Cf. Orlov, op. cit., p. 341; A. H. Birse, *Memoirs of an Interpreter* (London, 1967), p. 160.

34 In theory Hitler's power was virtually absolute, and it is not necessary to emphasize how terribly that power was used. But in general there remained far-reaching spheres of German public and private life in varying degrees unaffected by the Nazi accession to power. See Edward N. Peterson's study, *The Limits of Hitler's Power* (Princeton, 1969).

35 Bernhard Roeder, *Katorga: An Aspect of Modern Slavery* (London, 1958), p. 402. Compare the dignified sessions of the Central Committee described by Krivitsky (op. cit., pp. 226–9).

36 Bajanov, op. cit., p. 74. For examples of Stalin's and Khrushchev's cavalier attitude to the rights of majorities, see Ulam, op. cit., p. 88.

37 Alex Weissberg, *Conspiracy of Silence* (London, 1952), pp. 402–5.

38 Hingley, op. cit., p. 234; A. Avtorkhanov, *Загадка смерти Сталина*, (Frankfurt, 1976), pp. 26—8, 35—7.

39 Cf. Bajanov, op. cit., pp. 78—9; Bohlen, op. cit., p. 131; Avtorkhanov, op. cit., pp. 24—6.

40 Winston Churchill, who may well have gained the information from Stalin himself, explained the dictator's nocturnal existence as 'a relic of the days when it was safer for him to lie low during the day' (Lord Moran, *Winston Churchill: The Struggle for Survival 1940—1965* (London, 1966), p. 204). Cf. Wolfe, op. cit., pp. 228—32; Talbott (ed.), op. cit., pp. 133, 167, 299, 303; Kravchenko, op. cit., pp. 398—400. Not a promotion in the country took place before a candidate had been vetted by the 7th Department of the NKVD (ibid., p. 391), and every safe in the country (except Stalin's) had a spare key in the hands of the same vigilant organization (ibid., p. 395). Stalin's power was total (Wolfe, op. cit., pp. 126—8; cf. ibid., p. 200).

41 Kot, op. cit., p. XXIII; *The Memoirs of General the Lord Ismay* (London, 1960), pp. 233—4.

42 Talbott (ed.), op. cit., pp. 246, 286—7, 296—315; Wolfe, op. cit., p. 158; Alliluyeva, *Only One Year*, p. 362; Volkov (ed.), op. cit., pp. 194—5.

43 George F. Kennan, *Russia and the West under Lenin and Stalin* (Boston, 1961), pp. 252—6.

44 Conquest, op. cit., p. 508.

45 Ellis Smith, op. cit., p. 221.

46 Talbott (ed.), op. cit., p. 301. It is a curious fact that Alger Hiss, during his spell in gaol, found his most congenial companions amongst Mafia mobsters and other criminals (Allen Weinstein, *Perjury: The Hiss-Chambers Case* (London, 1978), p. 526).

47 Cf. Parvilahti, op. cit., p. 87; Conquest, op. cit., pp. 337—9; and his *Kolyma: The Arctic Death Camps* (London, 1978), pp. 30, 79—87; Elinor Lipper, *Eleven Years in Soviet Prison Camps* (London, 1951), pp. 147—8; Medvedev, op. cit., pp. 278, 280—1.

48 Barmine, op. cit., p. 304; Volkov (ed.), op. cit., pp. 64—6. (Because of their dangerous implications, plays such as *Hamlet* and *Macbeth* were banned: ibid.); Talbott (ed.), op. cit., p. 303; the British Ambassador was surprised to receive a presentation tommy-gun as a parting gift (FO 800/301, 68); Winston S. Churchill, *The Hinge of Fate* (London, 1951), p. 447.

49 Krivitsky, op. cit., pp. 128—32; Gordon Brook-Shepherd, *The Storm Petrels: The First Soviet Defectors, 1928—1938* (London, 1977), pp. 196—202.

50 Cf. Vladimir Petrov, *Escape from the Future* (Indiana, 1973), pp. 163—4.

51 Lyons, op. cit., pp. 447—64.

52 For Stalin's venture into the forgery business, see Krivitsky, op. cit.,

pp. 135–58; Elisabeth K. Poretsky, *Our Own People: A Memoir of 'Ignace Reiss' and His Friends* (Oxford, 1969), pp. 123–4; Arnold Krammer, 'Russian Counterfeit Dollars: A Case of Early Soviet Espionage', *Slavic Review* (1971), xxx, pp. 762–73; Brook-Shepherd, op. cit., pp. 230–2.

53 Gerson, op. cit., pp. 134, 208–9, 247–8, 271–2.

54 In particular, the workings of the slave-labour, prison and *kolkhoz* systems. Cf. Parvilahti, op. cit., pp. 122–4; Albert Konrad Herling, *The Soviet Slave Empire* (New York, 1951), pp. 22–3; Dallin and Nicolaevsky, op. cit., pp. 224–8, 278–9; Lipper, op. cit, pp. 154, 288; Lyons, op. cit., pp. 424–5, 429; Andrew Smith, *I Was a Soviet Worker* (London, 1937), pp. 70–4, 131–84.

55 Cf. Arthur Koestler, *The Yogi and the Commissar* (London, 1945), pp. 19–20, 78–9, 80–2, 127–8; Mandelstam, op. cit., p. 273; Whittaker Chambers, *Witness* (London, 1953), pp. 9–12; Melvin J. Lasky, *Utopia and Revolution* (London, 1976), pp. 151–5. 'There is one side to the nature of intellectuals which finds fascination in power and even cruelty. Nazism attracted men of this type, but Stalinism did infinitely better because *it* could draw on the benefits of socialist phraseology' (George Urban, 'A Conversation with Leszek Kolakowski: The Devil in History', *Encounter* (January 1981), LVI, p. 25).

56 Boris Nicolaevsky, *Power and the Soviet Elite* (New York, 1965), p. 64; Volkov (ed.), op. cit., p. 111; Krivitsky, op. cit., p. 209; Bohlen, op. cit., p. 147; Barmine, op. cit., p. 251.

III Life at the Top

1 Eugene Lyons, *Assignment in Utopia* (London, 1937), pp. 383–4; cf. Winston S. Churchill, *The Hinge of Fate* (London, 1951), p. 446.

2 Robert C. Tucker, *Stalin as Revolutionary* (London, 1974), p. 223. It would be churlish to deny the new leaders any perquisites of power; what is noteworthy is the speed with which they were absorbed and their extent. As early as 1922 Soviet leaders began to name towns after themselves: Russia was becoming their personal fief (see Adam B. Ulam, *Stalin: The Man and his Era* (London, 1974), pp. 211–12).

3 In 1939 Stalin displayed great interest in Speer's architectural plans for the new Reich (Albert Speer, *Inside the Third Reich* (London, 1970), p. 168).

4 Svetlana Alliluyeva, *Twenty Letters to a Friend* (New York, 1967), pp. 15, 18–22, 24–5, 127–8, 190, 200; Alexander Orlov, *The Secret History of Stalin's Crimes* (London, 1954), p. 347; Alexander Barmine, *One Who Survived: The Life Story of a Russian under the Soviets* (New York, 1945), p. 268.

5 Ibid., pp. 268–9.

6 Svetlana Alliluyeva, *Only One Year* (London, 1969), p. 350, and her *Twenty Letters to a Friend*, p. 216; Strobe Talbott (ed.), *Khrushchev Remembers* (Boston, 1970), p. 253.

7 Barmine, op. cit., pp. 214–15, 268, 301–4; cf. Roy A. Medvedev, *Let History Judge: The Origins and Consequences of Stalinism* (London, 1972), p. 291.

8 Alliluyeva, *Twenty Letters to a Friend*, pp. 209–10, and her *Only One Year*, pp. 365–6.

9 Roy A. Medvedev, *On Stalin and Stalinism* (Oxford, 1979), p. 86.

10 Medvedev, *Let History Judge*, pp. 540–1.

11 Orlov, op. cit., pp. 347–9.

12 Bertram D. Wolfe, *Khrushchev and Stalin's Ghost* (New York, 1957), p. 176.

13 Elliot R. Goodman, *The Soviet Design for a World State* (New York, 1960), pp. 457–8.

14 Aino Kuusinen, *Before and After Stalin: A Personal Account of Soviet Russia from the 1920s to the 1960s* (London, 1974), pp. 23–4; Talbott (ed.), op. cit., p. 304; Alliluyeva, *Only One Year*, pp. 378–80, 385–6. By Soviet standards Voroshilov's fellow-Marshal Budienny 'lived very simply' (ibid., p. 378), but at least one eye-witness provides an extremely sumptuous description of his quarters. See Mikhail Soloviev, *My Nine Lives in the Red Army* (New York, 1955), p. 75; Orlov, op. cit., pp. 272–334.

15 Boris Bajanov, *Bajanov révèle Staline: Souvenirs d'un ancien secrétaire de Staline* (Paris, 1979), p. 137; Gustav Hilger and Alfred G. Meyer, *The Incompatible Allies: A Memoir-History of German-Soviet Relations 1918–1941* (New York, 1953), pp. 73, 117–18.

16 Orlov, op. cit., p. 304.

17 Alliluyeva, *Twenty Letters to a Friend*, p. 27, and her *Only One Year*, p. 381. Mikoyan's skilful adjustment of fortune recalls a sardonic joke in Nazi Germany to the effect that 'a "reactionary" was the occupant of a lucrative post coveted by a Nazi' (Richard Grunberger, *A Social History of the Third Reich* (London, 1971), p. 336).

18 Margarete Buber, *Under Two Dictators* (London, 1949), p. 42; Alliluyeva, *Only One Year*, pp. 388–9, and her *Twenty Letters to a Friend*, p. 203. Yagoda's magnificent Moscow home was in Spiridonovka Street, where he was reported in ruling circles to hold orgies, lasting several days and centred on his swimming pool (Anatoli Granovsky, *All Pity Choked: The Memoirs of a Soviet Secret Agent* (London, 1955), p. 32).

19 Cf. Leonid Plyushch, *History's Carnival: A Dissident's Autobiography* (London, 1979), p. 149.

20 John R. Deane, *The Strange Alliance: The Story of American Efforts at Wartime Co-operation with Russia* (London, 1947), pp. 14–15.

21 Arthur Bryant, *The Turn of the Tide 1939–1943* (London, 1957), p. 462. 'With the exception of the bureaucratic elite, the entire country lived in various degrees of famine' (Plyushch, op. cit., p. 149).

22 For Stalin's revels, see Talbott (ed.), op. cit., pp. 300–1, 304–5; Milovan Djilas, *Conversations with Stalin* (London, 1962), pp. 73–4, 94–106, 136. 'To his table fish was brought from special nurseries; there would be Georgian wines of special vintage, and fresh fruit flown from the south by plane. He did not know how many transports at government expense were needed in order to supply his table, nor did he know where the food came from' (Alliluyeva, *Only One Year*, p. 364).

23 Cf. Djilas, op. cit., pp. 50–1, 86; Bryant, op. cit., pp. 464–6; and his *Triumph in the West 1943–1946* (London, 1959), pp. 301, 311; David Dilks (ed.), *The Diaries of Sir Alexander Cadogan* (London, 1971), p. 423; Charles E. Bohlen, *Witness to History 1929–1969* (London, 1973), p. 147. Robert E. Sherwood, *Roosevelt and Hopkins* (New York, 1948), pp. 323–6; Robert Huhn Jones, *The Roads to Russia: United States Lend-Lease to the Soviet Union* (Oklahoma, 1969), pp. 48, 62 ·3; The Earl of Avon, *The Eden Memoirs: The Reckoning* (London, 1965), p. 302; James F. Byrnes, *Speaking Frankly* (New York, 1947), p. 44; Joseph Czapski, *The Inhuman Land* (London, 1951), p. 46.

24 Elinor Lipper, *Eleven Years in Soviet Prison Camps* (London, 1951), pp. 136–7.

25 Deane, op. cit., p. 58; Z. Stypulkowski, *Invitation to Moscow* (London, 1951), pp. 344–5.

26 Lyons, op. cit., pp. 85, 451–3; Fitzroy Maclean, *Eastern Approaches* (London, 1949), pp. 80–1; Barmine, op. cit., pp. 273–4. Two unfortunate Negroes – probably from the Hotel Metropole jazz-band – later ended up in the Arctic forced-labour camp at Vorkuta (Mikhail Rozanov, *Завоеватели белых пятен* (Limburg, 1951), p. 242).

27 For the expression, see Unto Parvilahti, *Beria's Gardens: Ten Years' Captivity in Russia and Siberia* (London, 1959), p. 89, and for the practice, Bernhard Roeder, *Katorga: An Aspect of Modern Slavery* (London, 1958), p. 58.

28 Granovsky, op. cit., pp. 26–7, 30–1; Hilger and Meyer, op. cit., p. 58; Ulam, op. cit., p. 449; Nadezhda Mandelstam, *Воспоминания* (New York, 1970), p. 110; Gregory Klimov, *The Terror Machine: The Inside Story of the Soviet Administration in Germany* (London, 1953), p. 36.

29 Orlov, op. cit., pp. 146–8.

30 David Caute, *The Fellow-Travellers: A Postscript to the Enlightenment* (London, 1973), p. 78.

31 Orlov, op. cit., pp. 245, 257; Talbott (ed.), op. cit., p. 338; Granovsky,

op. cit., p. 32; Medvedev, *On Stalin and Stalinism*, p. 83; Soloviev, op. cit., p. 79; Barmine, op. cit., p. 264; Lyons, op. cit., pp. 193–4; Merle Fainsod, *Smolensk under Soviet Rule* (London, 1958), pp. 206–7; Vladimir and Evdokia Petrov, *Empire of Fear* (London, 1956), p. 130; Thaddeus Wittlin, *Commissar: The Life and Death of Lavrenty Pavlovich Beria* (London, 1973), pp. 87–8, 178, 246, 250–3, 408; Medvedev, *Let History Judge*, p. 368; Oleg Penkovskiy, *The Penkovskiy Papers* (New York, 1965), p. 321; Peter Deriabin and Frank Gibney, *The Secret World* (London, 1960), pp. 230–9.

32 Leszek Kolakowski, *Main Currents of Marxism: Its Rise, Growth, and Dissolution* (Oxford, 1978), II, pp. 458–86, 500; Ernst Fischer (ed.), *Lenin in His Own Words* (London, 1972), p. 74.

33 Edward Ellis Smith, *The Young Stalin: the early years of an elusive revolutionary* (London, 1967), p. 358.

34 Mandelstam, op. cit., pp. 117, 249; Medvedev, *Let History Judge*, pp. 414–15, 538–43; Alex Weissberg, *Conspiracy of Silence* (London, 1952), pp. 279–80, 388–9, 475–8. Professor Kolakowski concludes that 'The Soviet exploiting class is a new social formation which in some ways resembles the bureaucracy of Oriental despotisms, in others the class of feudal barons, and in others again the capitalist colonizers of backward countries. Its position is determined by the absolute concentration of political, economic, and military power, to an extent never before seen in Europe, and by the need for an ideology to legitimize that power. The privileges its members enjoy in the field of consumption are a natural consequence of its role in society. Marxism is the charismatic aura with which it invests itself in order to justify its rule' (Kolakowski, op. cit., III, pp. 165–6).

35 Victor Kravchenko, *I Chose Freedom* (London, 1947), p. 71.

36 Bajanov, op. cit., pp. 219–20.

37 Medvedev, op. cit., p. 415.

38 Hermann Rauschning, *Hitler Speaks: A Series of Political Conversations with Adolf Hitler on his Real Aims* (London, 1939), pp. 96–104; H. Powys Greenwood, *The German Revolution* (London, 1934), pp. 153–4; Hermann Rauschning, *Germany's Revolution of Destruction* (London, 1939), p. 177; W. S. Allen, *The Nazi Seizure of Power: The Experience of a Single German Town 1930–1935* (London, 1966), p. 168; Louis P. Lochner (ed.), *The Goebbels Diaries 1942–1943* (New York, 1948), pp. 97, 101–2.

39 Rauschning, *Germany's Revolution of Destruction*, pp. 97–9; Greenwood, op. cit., p. 151. The *Kristalnacht* plunder doubtless stemmed from similarly altruistic motives (Grunberger, op. cit., p. 459).

40 Cf. Kravchenko, op. cit., pp. 285, 323, 345, 393–7, 412–13; Barmine, op. cit., p. 317; Elisabeth K. Poretsky, *Our Own People: A Memoir of*

'*Ignace Reiss*' *and His Friends* (Oxford, 1969), p. 163. The same scramble for material goods and privileges took place when the Communist Party seized control in Yugoslavia (Milovan Djilas, *Wartime* (New York, 1977), pp. 423, 430–1).

41 Fainsod, op. cit., pp. 402, 404; Parvilahti, op. cit., pp. 199–200.

42 Kravchenko, op. cit., p. 391.

43 Compare Arthur Koestler's telling survey, culled almost entirely from official Soviet sources: *The Yogi and the Commissar* (London, 1945), pp. 153–66.

44 Alliluyeva, *Twenty Letters to a Friend*, pp. 133–4; see also Granovsky, op. cit., pp. 31–4. For a particularly repellent and self-satisfied school memoir, see 'A. I. Romanov', *Nights Are Longest There: Smersh from the Inside* (London, 1972), pp. 12–26. Cf. Vladimir Petrov, *Escape from the Future: The Incredible Adventures of a Young Russian* (Bloomington, Indiana, 1973), p. 187.

45 Cf. Andrew Smith, *I Was a Soviet Worker* (London, 1937), pp. 43–7, 125, 169, 170–2; Alliluyeva, op. cit., pp. 165–7; Tadeusz Wittlin, *A Reluctant Traveller in Russia* (London, 1952), p. 179. Cf. Joseph Czapski, *The Inhuman Land* (London, 1951), p. 134; Fainsod, op. cit., p. 60; Kravchenko, op. cit., pp. 450–1.

46 *The Memoirs of General the Lord Ismay* (London, 1960), p. 377.

47 Incident related to me by the late Brigadier R. C. Firebrace. Admiral Kharlanov was head of the Soviet Military Mission in Britain.

48 Kuusinen, op. cit., pp. 26–7; cf. *Le Procès Kravchenko contre Les Lettres Françaises* (Paris, 1949), pp. 170–1; Menachem Begin, *White Nights: The Story of a Prisoner in Russia* (London, 1978), pp. 221–4.

49 Hilger and Meyer, op. cit., p. 151. Lenin shrewdly declined to be examined by a Soviet doctor, 'for who ever heard of a good Communist being a good doctor?' (Kuusinen, op. cit., p. 31). Chicherin and Bela Kuhn's wife also sought German medical treatment (Herbert von Dirksen, *Moskau Tokio London: Erinnerungen und Betrachtungen zu 20 Jahren deutscher Aussenpolitik 1919–1939* (Stuttgart, 1949), pp. 93–4, 140), as did Finance Commissar Krestinksy (*Daily Telegraph*, 12 July 1921).

50 *The Memoirs of Ivanov-Razumnik* (London, 1965), p. 343.

51 Lyons, op. cit., pp. 436–40; cf. CAB 66/54, 128.

52 Kolakowski, op. cit., III, p. 43.

IV   Safeguarding the New Society

1 Eugene Lyons, *Stalin: Czar of all the Russias* (London, 1940), p. 64.

2 Edward Ellis Smith, *The Young Stalin: the early years of an elusive revolutionary* (London, 1968), p. 321.

3 Ronald Hingley, *Joseph Stalin: Man and Legend* (London, 1974), p. 345. For an amusing eye-witness account of Stalin's visit to a stage-prop front-line command post – far behind the battle-ground – see General N. N. Voronov, *На службе военной* (Moscow, 1963), pp. 384–5.

4 FO 800/300, 22. Cf. Svetlana Alliluyeva, *Twenty Letters to a Friend* (New York, 1967), p. 166.

5 Aino Kuusinen, *Before and After Stalin: A Personal Account of Soviet Russia from the 1920s to the 1960s* (London, 1974), p. 30; Alexander Orlov, *The Secret History of Stalin's Crimes* (London, 1954), p. 341.

6 Ibid., p. 342; Kuusinen, op. cit., p. 143; Svetlana Alliluyeva, *Only One Year* (London, 1969), p. 365; Strobe Talbott (ed.), *Khrushchev Remembers* (Boston, 1970), pp. 299–300; W. G. Krivitsky, *I Was Stalin's Agent* (London, 1939), p. 177; Charles E. Bohlen, *Witness to History 1929–1969* (London, 1973), pp. 147–8.

7 Krivitsky, op. cit., p. 177; Alliluyeva, *Only One Year*, p. 365.

8 Orlov, op. cit., pp. 20–1; Victor Kravchenko, *I Chose Freedom* (London, 1947), pp. 394–5; Solomon Volkov (ed.), *Testimony: The Memoirs of Dmitri Shostakovich* (London, 1979), p. 195; John R. Deane, *The Strange Alliance: The Story of American Efforts at Wartime Co-operation with Russia* (London, 1947), pp. 7–8; Peter Deriabin and Frank Gibney, *The Secret World* (London, 1959), pp. 111–34 (Deriabin served as an officer of the Kremlin Guard from 1947); Alliluyeva, *Twenty Letters to a Friend*, p. 144; Väinö Tanner, *The Winter War: Finland Against Russia 1939–1940* (Stanford, 1950), pp. 38–9; Vladimir and Evdokia Petrov, *Empire of Fear* (London, 1956), p. 90; G. A. Tokaev, *Comrade X* (London, 1956), pp. 311–12; Talbott (ed.), op. cit., p. 336, Walter Bedell Smith, *Moscow Mission 1946–1949* (London, 1950), p. 37. Stalin's acute fear of assassination is attested by his daughter (Alliluyeva, op. cit., p. 134).

9 Ibid., p. 36. Orlov, op. cit., pp. 20, 339–40; Kravchenko, op. cit., p. 399; Deriabin and Gibney, op. cit., p. 119; Talbott, op. cit., pp. 298–9. For details of Stalin's and Molotov's cars, see Milovan Djilas, *Conversations with Stalin* (London, 1962), p. 65; FO 371/29480, 28. The metro and tunnels are described by Roy A. Medvedev, *On Stalin and Stalinism* (Oxford, 1979), p. 151.

10 Talbott (ed.), op. cit., p. 299. For the *dacha*'s defensive outworks, see Lord Moran, *Winston Churchill: The Struggle for Survival 1940–1965* (London, 1966), p. 57: 'They are plainly prepared for trouble with their own people'.

11 Volkov (ed.), op. cit., p. 148.

12 Orlov, op. cit., p. 21; cf. Kuusinen, op. cit., pp. 30–1; Alliluyeva, op. cit., p. 195.

13 Ibid., pp. 195, 201; Orlov, op. cit., p. 21. Cf. Deane, op. cit., p. 290.

14 Winston S. Churchill, *Closing the Ring* (London, 1952), p. 339; David Dilks (ed.), *The Diaries of Sir Alexander Cadogan* (London, 1971), p. 769. A whole division of Central Asian MVD protected Stalin from the Red Army at Potsdam (Bohlen, op. cit., p. 227).

15 FO 371/23685, 184; Fitzroy Maclean, *Eastern Approaches* (London, 1949), pp. 28-9; Deriabin and Gibney, op. cit., pp. 116-17; Vladimir and Evdokia Petrov, op. cit., pp. 132-3; Krivitsky, op. cit., pp. 249-50; Vladimir Petrov, *Escape from the Future: The Incredible Adventures of a Young Russian* (Bloomington, Indiana, 1973), p. 43. Always revelatory of Stalin's hidden fears, trumped-up charges at the 1936 purge trials included a supposed attempt to assassinate him at a May Day parade (Orlov, op. cit., pp. 20, 76-7, 98).

16 Andrew Smith, *I Was a Soviet Worker* (London, 1937), pp. 257-8 (Kirov's funeral); NA Decimal Files, 861.001/6-1646 (US Embassy report of Kalinin's funeral).

17 Tanner, op. cit., p. 69; Alliluyeva, op. cit., p. 144; Alexander Barmine, *One Who Survived: The Life Story of a Russian under the Soviets* (New York, 1945), p. 301. For the scene at the Bolshoi, compare *The Memoirs of General the Lord Ismay* (London, 1960), p. 377; Deane, op. cit., p. 155; Lord Moran, op. cit., p. 201. The well-informed Barmine had heard of only one occasion when Stalin appeared openly in the streets of Moscow – a nine days' wonder (op. cit., p. 258).

18 Medvedev, op. cit., p. 150. Svetlana's testimony (*Twenty Letters to a Friend*, p. 33) seemingly contradicts Barmine's statement that Stalin 'used to bathe in the Black Sea after the beach had been cleared for fully a mile around' (op. cit., p. 269). But the dictator did frequent warm baths near Sochi in about 1930, as a cure for his rheumatism (Alliluyeva, op. cit., p. 33), and in any case it is possible to bathe without swimming. At one time he possessed a small motor-boat (Kuusinen, op. cit., p. 30). Space prevents a detailed analysis of Barmine's memoir, but in general its reliability is patent. To give but one small instance: he notes Stalin's fondness for playing skittles (*gorodki*) (op. cit., p. 269); this has since been confirmed by the loyal General Shtemenko (S. M. Shtemenko, *The Last Six Months: Russia's Final Battles with Hitler's Armies in World War II* (London, 1978), pp. 37-8) and by Svetlana (op. cit., p. 33). See also Adam B. Ulam, *Stalin: The Man and his Era* (London, 1974), p. 587.

19 Alfred Seidl (ed.), *Die Beziehungen zwischen Deutschland und der Sowjetunion 1939-1941* (Tübingen, 1949), p. 171; Ulam, op. cit., p. 570.

20 Medvedev, op. cit., p. 151. Stalin's celebrated clash with Dmitri Schmidt in 1927 also suggests physical cowardice (Barmine, op. cit., p. 90).

21 Medvedev, *Let History Judge: The Origins and Consequences of Stalinism* (London, 1971), p. 306.

22 Leszek Kolakowski, *Main Currents of Marxism: Its Origin, Growth, and Dissolution* (Oxford, 1978), III, pp. 95–7; Ulam, op. cit., p. 387.

23 Hingley, op. cit., pp. 201, 280; cf. Ulam, op. cit., pp. 105, 186, 385–60.

24 Hingley, op. cit., pp. 286–8.

25 George Urban, 'A Conversation with Milovan Djilas', *Encounter* (London, 1979), LIII (no. 6), p. 30; compare Molotov's precautions at Chequers in 1942: Winston S. Churchill, *The Hinge of Fate* (London, 1951), p. 301.

26 Boris Bajanov, *Bajanov révèle Staline: Souvenirs d'un ancien secrétaire de Staline* (Paris, 1979), pp. 89–90. In 1922 it was widely believed that gold being stolen from churches in Smolensk *gubernia* by the Bolsheviks was intended as a resource should they be compelled to flee abroad (Merle Fainsod, *Smolensk under Soviet Rule* (London, 1958), p. 157).

27 Gregory Klimov, *The Terror Machine: The inside story of the Soviet Administration in Germany* (London, 1953), p. 266. The NKVD was desperately eager to anticipate and arrest people who *might* rebel (Vladimir and Evdokia Petrov, op. cit., pp. 140–1). In 1936, Krivitsky related, the 'western world does not realize how tenuous at that time was Stalin's hold on power, and how essential it was to his survival as dictator that he should be defended in those bloody acts by foreign communists and eminent international idealists' (Krivitsky, op. cit., p. 99).

28 Dilks (ed.), op. cit., p. 474; I. V. Stalin, *Сочинения* (Stanford, 1967), III [xv], pp. 203–4; Wilfried Strik-Strikfeldt, *Against Stalin and Hitler: Memoir of the Russian Liberation Movement 1941–5* (London, 1970), pp. 32–3.

29 NA 861. 00/1–1546.

30 Lennard D. Gerson, *The Secret Police in Lenin's Russia* (Philadelphia, 1976), pp. 19–25, 145, 151–4.

31 Gerson, op. cit., pp. 247–8, 271–2, 279–80.

32 Kolakowski, op. cit., II, p. 489.

33 Alex Weissberg, *Conspiracy of Silence* (London, 1952), pp. 402–5. The Smolensk Archive makes it clear that the Western *Oblast* NKVD came directly under Stalin's control (Merle Fainsod, *Smolensk under Soviet Rule* (London, 1958), pp. 84, 172).

34 Alliluyeva, op. cit., pp. 126–7; Deriabin and Gibney, op. cit., pp. 120, 126, 232; Thaddeus Wittlin, *Commissar: The Life and Death of Lavrenty Pavlovich Beria* (London, 1973), p. 358; A. Avtorkhanov, *Загадка смерти Сталина, заговор Берия* (Frankfurt, 1976), pp. 37–8.

35 Ulam, op. cit., p. 487; Krivitsky, op. cit., pp. 38–9; Elisabeth K. Poretsky, *Our Own People: A Memoir of 'Ignace Reiss' and His Friends*

(Oxford, 1969), p. 219. In view of the mystery surrounding Yezhov's end (Robert Conquest, *The Great Terror: Stalin's Purge of the Thirties* (London, 1968), p. 464), it is worth noting the testimony of a Pole who was in a Moscow prison with him in 1940–1 (NA 861.131/33).

36 So an official of the Secretariat of the Politburo described the scene (Bernhard Roeder, *Katorga: An Aspect of Modern Slavery* (London, 1958), pp. 205–6).

37 Alliluyeva, *Only One Year*, pp. 387–90; Talbott (ed.), op. cit., p. 300; Djilas, op. cit., pp. 100, 143, 144; Margarete Buber, *Under Two Dictators* (London, 1949), pp. 97–8.

38 Alliluyeva, *Twenty Letters to a Friend*, pp. 35–6, 55–60; *The Memoirs of Ivanov-Razumnik* (London, 1965), pp. 266–8.

39 Smith, op. cit., p. 89; Petrov, *Escape from the Future*, p. 18.

40 Gerson, op. cit., pp. 59–62, 128.

41 'A. I. Romanov', *Nights Are Longest There* (London, 1972), pp. 13–27; Anatoli Granovsky, *All Pity Choked: The Memoirs of a Soviet Secret Agent* (London, 1955), pp. 85–7; Vladimir and Evdokia Petrov, *Empire of Fear*, pp. 54–6, 122–7; Deriabin and Gibney, op. cit., pp. 55–7, 61–3.

42 Weissberg, op. cit., p. 456; Fainsod, op. cit., pp. 160–2; Bertram D. Wolfe, *Khrushchev and Stalin's Ghost* (New York, 1957), p. 162; Deriabin and Gibney, p. 126; Medvedev, op. cit., pp. 285–6, 303–4; Dimitri Panin, *The Notebooks of Sologdin* (London, 1956), p. 230; Nikolai Tolstoy, *Victims of Yalta* (London, 1977), p. 140; Gerson, op. cit., p. 195; S. A. Malsagoff, *An Island Hell: A Soviet Prison in the Far North* (London, 1926), p. 20. Vlasik's robust view was echoed by GULAG guards: 'this intelligentsia . . . is just a pain' (Varlam Shalamov, *Колымские Рассказы* (London, 1978), p. 30).

43 Cf. Whittaker Chambers, *Witness* (London, 1953), p. 310; Unto Parvilahti, *Beria's Gardens: Ten Years' Captivity in Russia and Siberia* (London, 1959), p. 43.

44 Ibid., p. 114; Kuusinen, op. cit., pp. 195–6; *The Memoirs of Ivanov-Razumnik*, p. 260; Ruta U., *Dear God, I Wanted to Live* (New York, 1978), p. 96.

45 Orlov, op. cit., pp. 90–2, 97–8; Klimov, op. cit., pp. 228–9.

46 Deriabin and Gibney, op. cit., pp. 184–5, 187; Vladimir and Evdokia Petrov, op. cit., pp. 80–2, 257, 263; Barmine, op. cit., pp. 16, 18; David Irving, *Hitler's War* (London, 1977), pp. 209–10, 842.

47 Joseph Czapski, *The Inhuman Land* (London, 1951), pp. 81–5, 87–9 (Czapski calls him 'Nasiedkine', the name of an NKVD interrogator (Alexander Solzhenitsyn, *Архипелаг Гулаг 1918–1956: Опыт Художественного Исследования* (Paris, 1973–5), I, p. 405; Medvedev, op. cit., pp. 128–9). Compare also Kravchenko, op. cit., p. 405; 'A. I. Romanov', op. cit., p. 138.

48 Vladimir and Evdokia Petrov, op. cit., pp. 100–1.
49 Cf. David J. Dallin and Boris I. Nicolaevsky, *Forced Labor in Soviet Russia* (London, 1948), p. 87.
50 *Slave Labor in the Soviet World*, publication of the Free Trade Union Committee of The American Federation of Labor (New York, 1951), p. 4.
51 Dallin and Nicolaevsky, op. cit., p. 72.
52 Gustav Herling, *A World Apart* (London, 1951), p. 176; cf. *Moscow Mission 1946–1949*, p. 115; *Le Procès Kravchenko contre Les Lettres Françaises* (Paris, 1949), p. 557. In 1943–5 the Gestapo numbered some forty thousand men – an interesting comparison (Hans Rothfels, *The German Opposition to Hitler: An Assessment* (London, 1970), p. 15).
53 General V. G. Naumenko, *Великое Предательство: Выдача Казаков в Лиенце и Других Местах 1945–1947* (New York, 1962–70), II, pp. 291–2.
54 Czapski, op. cit., pp. 219–21; *The Memoirs of Ivanov-Razumnik*, pp. 238–9; *Le Procès Kravchenko*, pp. 205.
55 *The Dark Side of the Moon* (London, 1946), pp. 87, 89–90. Torture of women and children was a widespread feature of Soviet gaols (*Le Procès Kravchenko*, p. 208).
56 Granovsky, op. cit., pp. 59, 62–3, 69. Cf. Krivitsky, op. cit., pp. 198–201; for the 'children's purge' of 1938, see Orlov, op. cit., pp. 53–4, 88.
57 Petrov, op. cit., p. 73; Krivitsky, op. cit., pp. 217–19; Klimov, op. cit., p. 265; Buber, op. cit., p. 61; Czapski, op. cit., pp. 255–6; Kravchenko, op. cit., pp. 447–8; *The Memoirs of Ivanov-Razumnik*, p. 350; Parvilahti, op. cit., pp. 160, 237; Tadeusz Wittlin, *A Reluctant Traveller in Russia* (London, 1952), p. 121.
58 Petrov, *Escape from the Future*, pp. 186–7.
59 Deriabin and Gibney, op. cit., pp. 137–9.
60 Vladimir Bukovsky, *To Build a Castle: My life as a dissenter* (London, 1978), pp. 155–76, 209–10, 281–4, 285–90, 301–3; Leonid Plyushch, *History's Carnival* (London, 1979), pp. 305–6, 309, 339, 345, 347, 355, 358.
61 Rats formed a favourite and not inappropriate instrument (Frank Gibney, ed., *The Penkovskiy Papers* (New York, 1965), p. 280.
62 Cf. Medvedev, *Let History Judge*, pp. 264–72; Conquest, op. cit., pp. 136–8. For a horrific eye-witness description of an NKVD torture-chamber, see Zoltan Toth, *Prisoner of the Soviet Union* (London, 1978), pp. 20–1.
63 Kolakowski, op. cit., II, p. 516.
64 Gerson, op. cit., pp. 143–4.
65 Medvedev, op. cit., pp. 296, 348; Deriabin and Gibney, op. cit., pp. 171–2.

66 British lawyers like D. N. Pritt and Dudley Collard *cannot* have believed, as they claimed they did, in the 1936 purge trials: cf. Henry Pelling, *The British Communist Party: A Historical Profile* (London, 1958), p. 102.

67 Eugene Lyons, *Assignment in Utopia* (London, 1937), pp. 93–5, 268. John Strachey, in his 1930 pamphlet *What we saw in Russia*, deliberately withheld any mention of 'seeing the most ghastly food shortages in the Russian towns' (Hugh Thomas, *John Strachey* (London, 1973), p. 86).

68 Poretsky, op. cit., p. 164; Vladimir and Evdokia Petrov, op. cit., p. 54. By the same token, care was taken to see that released prisoners were not too shabbily dressed on emerging into the Moscow streets (A. V. Gorbatov, '*Годы и Войны*', *Новый Мир* (April 1964), XL, pp. 136–7).

69 Compare the description of the match on 4 November 1949 in Moscow (NA 861. 00/11–949).

V Munich Manoeuvres

1 Reprinted by Sir John Wheeler-Bennett, in his *Munich: Prologue to Tragedy* (London, 1948), p. 366; cf. pp. 278–9.

2 The texts are printed in ibid., pp. 441–8.

3 Winston S. Churchill, *The Gathering Storm* (London, 1948), p. 239.

4 Norman Rose, *Vansittart: Study of a Diplomat* (London, 1978), p. 229. For French proponents of this view, see Wheeler-Bennett, op. cit., p. 102.

5 Cf. Telford Taylor, *Munich: The Price of Peace* (London, 1979), pp. 176–82.

6 Ibid., p. 621.

7 Wheeler-Bennett, op. cit., pp. 57, 86, 150, 273–8.

8 Taylor, op. cit., pp. 101–2; cf. Chamberlain's remark to Masaryk (Wheeler-Bennett, op. cit., p. 171).

9 Taylor, op. cit., p. 961.

10 The Secret Service believed the Soviet aim was to provoke war between Britain and Germany (David Dilks, ed., *The Diaries of Sir Alexander Cadogan* (London, 1971), p. 65). A parallel fear (perhaps a not unreasonable one, statesmen being unable to exercise the hindsight of historians) was that any Entente intervention in Germany 'would not bring Stresemann out of his grave, nor anybody remotely resembling him . . . Germany would then be fighting for her life with the powerful weapon of Bolshevism' (H. Powys Greenwood, *The German Revolution* (London, 1934), p. 271). For the cogent reasoning behind British and French doubts of the value of the 'Soviet card', cf. Simon Newman, *March 1939: The British Guarantee to Poland* (Oxford, 1976), pp. 120,

138–43; Gerhard L. Weinberg, *The Foreign Policy of Hitler's Germany: Starting World War II 1937–1939* (Chicago, 1980), pp. 86–9.

11 Wheeler-Bennett, op. cit., p. 301. Georges Bonnet, French Foreign Minister, doubted the Red Army's capacity to wage successful war (ibid., pp. 99–100).

12 Ibid., pp. 81–2, 89, 127–8, 175.

13 Cf. *Mein Kampf* (London, n.d.), pp. 557, 562.

14 Cf. Wheeler-Bennett, op. cit., pp. 106, 273–81; Golo Mann, 'Rapallo: The Vanishing Dream', *Survey* (London, 1962), XLIV–V, pp. 78–81.

15 Taylor, op. cit., p. 441.

16 Wheeler-Bennett, op. cit., p. 57.

17 NA Decimal Files, 861.00/2–1849. There is no reason to doubt the authenticity of this account; Litvinov was to commit several similar indiscretions in the future (Cf. Vojtech Mastny, 'The Cassandra in the Foreign Commissariat', *Foreign Affairs* (1976), LIV, pp. 366–76).

18 John Harvey (ed.), *The Diplomatic Diaries of Oliver Harvey 1937–1940* (New York, 1970), p. 158. In reality 'it is as a period of renewed Soviet isolation that the years 1936–38 should be regarded' (Max Beloff, *The Foreign Policy of Soviet Russia 1929–1941* (Oxford, 1949), II, p. 26). Compare the skilful reservation implicit in the important *Pravda* article of 17 September (ibid., pp. 148–50). The significantly muted Soviet internal reaction to Munich was also noted by Eugene Lyons: *Stalin: Czar of all the Russias* (London, 1940), p. 237.

19 'Interview with an Ex-Insider, IV: Moscow–Berlin 1933', *Survey*, XLIV–V, pp. 160–1.

20 Lt-Gen. Sir Giffard Martel, *The Russian Outlook* (London, 1947), pp. 13–26; Weinberg, op. cit., p. 549.

21 Taylor, op. cit., p. 453.

22 Robert Conquest, *The Great Terror: Stalin's Purge of the Thirties* (London, 1968), pp. 201–35, 459–63.

23 John Lukacs, *The Last European War: September 1939/December 1941* (London, 1976), p. 16; cf. Adam B. Ulam, *Stalin: The Man and his Era* (London, 1974), pp. 495–6. The Red Army was not even partially mobilized during the crisis (Weinberg, op. cit., pp. 417–18).

24 Text in *Documents concerning German-Polish Relations and the Outbreak of Hostilities between Great Britain and Germany on September 3, 1939* (London, 1939), pp. 1–2.

25 Cf. Beloff, op. cit., II, pp. 146–7; Wheeler-Bennett, op. cit., pp. 57, 100, 106; Taylor, op. cit., pp. 449–52, 526; Weinberg, op. cit., pp. 352–4, 414–17. The highly pro-Soviet US Military Attaché in Moscow estimated that the total Soviet military contribution possible would be two squadrons of bombers! (Charles E. Bohlen, *Witness to History* (London, 1973), p. 59).

26 Taylor, op. cit., pp. 428, 452–6, 843.
27 Robert C. Tucker, 'The Emergence of Stalin's Foreign Policy', *Slavic Review* (Illinois, 1977), XXXVI, p. 575. In 1920 Lenin was advocating a similar policy (Leszek Kolakowski, *Main Currents of Marxism: Its Rise, Growth, and Dissolution* (Oxford, 1978), II, p. 497).
28 Cf. Maisky's taunts (Wheeler-Bennett, op. cit., p. 393). Wheeler-Bennett was inclined to accept Soviet professions at face value (cf. ibid., pp. 278–81); Taylor, op. cit., p. 621.
29 *Slavic Review*, XXXVI, pp. 566–8; Gabriel Gorodetsky, *The Precarious Truce: Anglo-Soviet Relations 1924–27* (Cambridge, 1977), pp. 231–40.
30 *Slavic Review*, XXXVI, pp. 576, 580; F. L. Carsten, 'The Reichswehr and the Red Army, 1920–1933', *Survey* (London, 1962), XLIV–V, p. 130. In 1938 Assistant Commissar for Foreign Affairs Potemkin told the French Ambassador that they contemplated a Polish partition (Ulam, op. cit., p. 499).
31 *Slavic Review*, XXXVI, pp. 575–80; In 1938 an authoritative Soviet source declared that 'the "democratic" states are of course stronger than the fascist states' (Beloff, op. cit., II, p. 164).
32 ' . . . One might say that a common sharp hostility to the new Polish state was one of the most potent bonds between Berlin and Moscow, and another partition of Poland the silent maximal aim of both governments throughout the interwar period' (Gustav Hilger and Alfred G. Meyer, *The Incompatible Allies: A Memoir-History of German-Soviet Relations 1918–1941* (New York, 1953), p. 154).
33 For detailed accounts of German-Soviet military co-operation in the inter-war years, see ibid., pp. 187–208, 227–42, 250–1; *Survey*, XLIV–V, pp. 76, 114–32; Louis Hagen (ed.), *The Schellenberg Memoirs* (London, 1956), pp. 40–5; E. M. Robertson, *Hitler's Pre-War Policy and Military Plans 1933–1939* (London, 1963), pp. 12–13; W. G. Krivitsky, *I Was Stalin's Agent* (London, 1939), pp. 20–2; 'Geoffrey Bailey', *The Conspirators* (London, 1961), pp. 193–7; Lionel Kochan, *Russia and the Weimar Republic* (London, 1954), pp. 60–4.
34 *Mein Kampf*, p. 388.
35 *Documents Concerning German-Polish Relations*, pp. 1–5.

VI   The Pact of Blood

1 Nikolai Tolstoy, *Night of the Long Knives* (New York, 1972), pp. 123–45; Robert Conquest, *The Great Terror: Stalin's Purge of the Thirties* (London, 1968), p. 45; W. G. Krivitsky, *I Was Stalin's Agent* (London, 1939), pp. 17–18, 29, 204–5, 249; Alexander Barmine, *One Who Survived: The Life Story of a Russian under the Soviets* (New York, 1945), p. 251.

2 F. A. Voigt, *Unto Caesar* (London, 1939), pp. 107–8. In 1918 Lenin poured forth as many vaticinatory pledges as the prophet Merlin (Leszek Kolakowski, *Main Currents of Marxism: Its Rise, Growth, and Dissolution* (Oxford, 1978), II, pp. 476–7).

3 Victor Kravchenko, *I Chose Freedom* (London, 1947), p. 109; Kurt G. W. Lüdecke, *I Knew Hitler: The Story of a Nazi Who Escaped the Blood Purge* (London, 1938), p. 357. Cf. Golo Mann, 'Rapallo: The Vanishing Dream', *Survey* (London, 1962), XLIV–V, p. 77; Teddy J. Ulricks, 'Stalin and Nazi Germany', *Slavic Review* (1977), XXXVI, pp. 600–1. For evidence that the KPD attack on the Social Democrats was ordered by the Comintern in Moscow, see Arthur Spencer, 'National-Bolshevism', ibid., pp. 148–9. As a more practical corollary to this view, Stalin also hoped that Hitler's implacably anti-Versailles policy would embroil him inextricably with Britain and France, leaving the USSR a further breathing space (Margarete Buber, *Under Two Dictators* (London, 1949), p. xi; Robert C. Tucker, 'The Emergence of Stalin's Foreign Policy', *Slavic Review* (1977), XXVI, pp. 582–4). This convincing dialectical formula found favour with Party zealots even in the chill confines of Kolyma (A. V. Gorbatov, 'Годы и Войны', Новый Мир (April 1964), XL, p. 126: 'Чем хуже, тем лучше – скорее все разъяснится' – 'the worse it is, the better: the sooner will all become clear'.

4 Harold J. Gordon, Jr, *Hitler and the Beer Hall Putsch* (Princeton, 1972), pp. 5–6. For Nazism as a classless movement, see ibid., p. 7.

5 Jeremy Noakes, *The Nazi Party in Lower Saxony 1921–1933* (Oxford, 1971), pp. 249–50; cf. David L. Schoenbaum, *Hitler's Social Revolution: Class and Status in Nazi Germany 1933–1939* (London, 1967), pp. xxi–iii; Richard Grunberger, *A Social History of the Third Reich* (London, 1971), pp. 49–53.

6 Cf. J. L. Talmon, *The Origins of Totalitarian Democracy* (London, 1955), pp. 263–5.

7 Robert G. L. Waite, *Vanguard of Nazism: the Free Corps Movement in Postwar Germany 1918–1923* (Cambridge, Mass., 1952), pp. 272–6; Brigitte Granzow, *A Mirror of Nazism: British Opinion and the Emergence of Hitler* (London, 1964), pp. 196–7; Gordon, op. cit., pp. 19–20. Cf. the anti-capitalist programme of the Nazi *Niedersächsischer Beobachter* in 1927 (Noakes, op. cit., p. 103); the nationalist content of National Socialism arose from Germany's particular post-war predicament (Gordon, op. cit., pp. 11–13).

8 Noakes, op. cit., pp. 73–84; Herman Lebovics, *Social Conservatism and the Middle Classes in Germany, 1914–1933* (Princeton, 1969), pp. 145–7; Arthur Spencer, 'National-Bolshevism', *Survey* (1962), XLIV–V, pp. 133–52. Compare the view of Kurt Lüdecke, op. cit., p. 420.

9 Godfrey Scheele, *The Weimar Republic: Overture to the Third Reich* (London, 1946), p. 152; Max H. Kele, *Nazis and Workers: National Socialist Appeals to German Labor, 1919–1933* (North Carolina, 1972), pp. 47–8, 143, 187.

10 Konrad Heiden, *Hitler: A Biography* (London, 1936), p. 264; Lüdecke, op. cit., p. 597; Jean François, *L'Affaire Röhm-Hitler* (Paris, 1939), p. 30. Röhm's friend, Hermann Esser, had turned Nazi from rabid Social Democrat (Richard Hanser, *Prelude to Terror: The Rise of Hitler 1919–1923* (London, 1971), pp. 290–1); the head of Nazi radio had been a revolutionary sailor in 1918 (Grunberger, op. cit., p. 409).

11 Alastair Hamilton, *The Appeal of Fascism* (London, 1971), p. 139; Schoenbaum, op. cit., p. 19.

12 Hamilton, op. cit., p. 89.

13 William L. Shirer, *Berlin Diary: The Journal of a Foreign Correspondent 1934–41* (London, 1941), pp. 411–12.

14 Hans Rogger and Eugen Weber, *The European Right: A Historical Profile* (California, 1965), p. 340; Kele, op. cit., p. 47; Hanser, op. cit., p. 279; Roger Manvell and Heinrich Fraenkel, *Doctor Goebbels: His Life and Death* (London, 1960), p. 88.

15 Eliot B. Wheaton, *Prelude to Calamity: The Nazi Revolution 1933–35* (London, 1969), p. 313; Gustav Hilger and Alfred G. Meyer, *The Incompatible Allies: A Memoir-History of German-Soviet Relations 1918–1941* (New York, 1973), p. 42; *Brockhaus Enzyklopädie* (Wiesbaden, 1968), VI, p. 577 (reference kindly supplied by Dr Alfred de Zayas).

16 Helmut Heiber (ed.), *The Early Goebbels Diaries: The Journal of Joseph Goebbels from 1925–1926* (London, 1962), pp. 24, 34, 43, 44, 51, 62; Dietrich Orlow, *The History of the Nazi Party* (Newton Abbot, 1971–3), I, pp. 87–9; Kele, op. cit., pp. 92–3, 111, 131–2; Schoenbaum, op. cit., p. 24; Noakes, op. cit., p. 72; Manvell and Fraenkel, op. cit., p. 126; Louis P. Lochner (ed.), *The Goebbels Diaries 1942–1943* (New York, 1948), pp. 10–11.

17 Wheaton, op. cit., p. 436.

18 Waite, op. cit., pp. 272–6; E. M. Robertson, *Hitler's Pre-War Policy and Military Plans 1933–1939* (London, 1963), pp. 86–7; Noakes, op. cit., pp. 25–6; Lochner (ed.), op. cit., pp. 355–9; Percy Ernst Schramm, *Hitler: The Man and the Military Leader* (London, 1972), pp. 53, 162; Paul Schmidt, *Hitler's Interpreter* (London, 1951), p. 134; *Hitler's Table Talk 1941–1944* (London, 1953), pp. 587, 624; Hermann Rauschning, *Hitler Speaks: A Series of Political Conversations with Adolf Hitler on his Real Aims* (London, 1939), pp. 19, 134. At the outset of his political career Hitler was by no means so opposed to Bolshevism as is commonly supposed (Walter Laqueur, 'Hitler and

Russia 1919–1923', *Survey* (1962), MLIV–V, pp. 93–5). Compare his guarded acceptance of Bolshevism as appropriate for Russia in September 1938 (Max Beloff, *The Foreign Policy of Soviet Russia 1929–41* (Oxford, 1949), II, p. 145). Even in the camps of GULAG, Nazi Germans and Marxist Russians were drawn together by the bonds of ideological kinship (Raphael Rupert, *A Hidden World* (London, 1963), p. 89).

19 Scheele, op. cit., pp. 153–4; Eugene Lyons, *Stalin: Czar of all the Russias* (London, 1940), p. 225.

20 Lionel Kochan, *Russia and the Weimar Republic* (London, 1954), pp. 174–7; Wheaton, op. cit., pp. 132, 156–8; Roy. A. Medvedev, *Let History Judge: The Origins and Consequences of Stalinism* (London, 1972), pp. 438–40. Trotsky condemned the policy of concentrating hostility against the Social Democrats (Jean van Heijenoort, *With Trotsky in Exile* (Harvard, 1978), p. 2), but shared Stalin's delusion that 'Fascism . . . is a razor in the hands of the class enemy' (quoted by M. R. Werner, ed., *Stalin's Kampf* (London, 1940), p. 292).

21 Zhdanov specified Finland as one of these 'little countries' in a speech on 29 November 1936 (Max Jakobson, *The Diplomacy of the Winter War* (Cambridge, Mass., 1961), p. 18).

22 So Radek told the English writer Frederick Voigt in 1932 (Voigt, op. cit., pp. 277–8); in August 1934 he was as confident as ever of the value of the Brownshirts (Hilger and Meyer, op. cit., pp. 267–8).

23 Krivitsky, op. cit., pp. 38–9.

24 Svetlana Alliluyeva, *Twenty Letters to a Friend* (New York, 1967), p. 53; cf. Krivitsky, op. cit., p. 22.

25 Hilger and Meyer, op. cit., pp. 255–6.

26 Ibid., pp. 269–70; Krivitsky, op. cit., pp. 37–8, 248–9; Barmine, op. cit., p. 25. A cryptic note in the dossier of the murdered GPU agent 'Ignace Reiss' recorded that 'Conversations continue avec Adolphe, par Kandil' (Victor Serge, A. Rosmer, Maurice Wullens, *L'assassinat d'Ignace Reiss* (Paris, 1938), p. 22). This may be confirmation of Krivitsky's claim that Kandelaki was received by Hitler himself (Krivitsky, op. cit., p. 248). Marshal Tukhachevsky's warnings of German intentions and the inadequacies of Soviet military defence may have spurred the Kandelaki mission (cf. John Erickson, *The Road to Stalingrad: Stalin's War with Germany* (London, 1975), pp. 1–3).

27 Barmine, op. cit., pp. 24, 25–7, 29–31; Hilger and Meyer, op. cit., pp. 267–71, 278, 278–9; Beloff, op. cit., II, p. 67. Very strong hints of the desirability of a Soviet-German *rapprochement* were dropped in Berlin by a Soviet diplomat, Yevgeni Gnedin, on 11 December 1935, and again on 12 October 1936 ('Moscow and the Nazis', *Survey* (1963), XLLX, pp. 129–32). Cf. *Slavonic and East European Review*, XL, pp. 518–20.

28 Adam B. Ulam, *Stalin: The Man and his Era* (London, 1974), pp. 364–8, 399–407, 466–9.
29 For striking evidence that Molotov, unknown to Litvinov, had begun negotiations with Nazi Germany as early as September 1933, see Robert C. Tucker, 'On Matters Evidential: A Reply', *Slavic Review*, XXXVI, p. 606. In January 1937 the USSR abandoned a highly favourable trade agreement with Greece for fear it might upset Hitler (Barmine, op. cit., pp. 306–9), and by 1938 information reached the US Embassy in Moscow that a Nazi-Soviet pact was probably in the offing (Charles E. Bohlen, *Witness to History* (London, 1973), p. 58). Andrei Zhdanov is said to have been a strong believer in coming to terms with Hitler (G. A. Tokaev, *Comrade X* (London, 1956), p. 158).
30 Winston S. Churchill, *The Gathering Storm* (London, 1948), pp. 284, 286–7; the Earl of Avon, *The Eden Memoirs: The Reckoning* (London, 1965), pp. 54–5; John Harvey (ed.), *The Diplomatic Diaries of Oliver Harvey 1937–1940* (New York, 1970), p. 290; Harold Macmillan, *Winds of Change 1914–1939* (London, 1966), pp. 595–6.
31 Cf. David Dilks (ed.), *The Diaries of Sir Alexander Cadogan* (London, 1971), pp. 175, 180–2, 189–90, 191. Lascelles at the FO Northern Department, assessing Soviet weakness in face of Germany, estimated that the USSR 'will act empirically and solely with an eye to its own interests' (5 January 1939): FO 371/23677, 251–2. F. A. Gwatkin prophetically observed on the 14th that 'Russia is no friend of ours, though in certain circs. she might be an ally' (ibid., 254). For Finland, see Max Jakobson, *The Diplomacy of the Finnish War* (Cambridge, Mass., 1961), pp. 47–8.
32 Churchill, op. cit., p. 284. Cf. Telford Taylor, *Munich: The Price of Peace* (London, 1979), pp. 974–6.
33 John W. Wheeler-Bennett, *Munich: Prologue to Tragedy* (London, 1948), p. 394.
34 FO 371/24850, 125. For an able restatement of the Foreign Office case, compare Professor W. N. Medlicott's letter to *The Times*, 17 March 1964, and for contemporary views, Simon Newman, *March 1939: The British Guarantee to Poland* (Oxford, 1976), pp. 153–4, 215–16, 220. 'To whatever extent it was relevant, public opinion generally favoured Russia' (F. R. Gannon, *The British Press and Germany 1936–1939* (Oxford, 1971), pp. 27–8, 209, 250–1, 255, 257, 258).
35 Krivitsky, op. cit., pp. 19–20. Hitler sensed that Stalin was at heart uninterested in an English alliance (F. H. Hinsley, *Hitler's Strategy* (Cambridge, 1951), p. 15).
36 I. V. Stalin, *Сочинения* (Stanford, 1967), XIV, pp. 327–45. For earlier Soviet indications of this direction of policy over the winter of 1938–9, see Beloff, op. cit., II, pp. 211, 227. Isaac Deutscher provides a likely

explanation for this oblique approach (*Stalin: A Political Biography* (Oxford, 1949), p. 428); also why the German alliance appeared preferable to one with the Entente (ibid., pp. 434–5).

37 Cf. John Lukacs, *The Last European War: September 1939/December 1941* (London, 1976), p. 41. The British Ambassador in Moscow (Seeds) correctly interpreted Stalin's Aesopian allusions (Newman, op. cit., p. 130).

38 Wheeler-Bennett, op. cit., pp. 376–7. Quixotic though the gesture was, it alone decisively disposes of the perennial Soviet claim that British and French diplomacy aimed at directing Hitler's aggression eastwards (e.g. A. A. Gromyko *et al.*, eds, История Дипломатия(Moscow, 1965), III, p. 751). A guarantee to Poland was in effect a guarantee to the USSR, involving no obligations in return, and this was how events transpired. Compare the absurd farrago in ibid., p. 769. The facts are fully set out in Newman, op. cit., pp. 6–7, 64, 78–9, 130. As Professor Ulam points out, the soviets were 'terribly eager' that the British should issue their pledge to Poland, being well aware of the advantage to themselves (op. cit., p. 507).

39 Alfred Seidl (ed.), *Die Beziehungen zwischen Deutschland und der Sowjetunion 1939–1941* (Tübingen, 1949), pp. 1–2. The Soviet Union was the only non-Axis state to grant *de jure* recognition to the Nazi-created state of Slovakia (Gerhard L. Weinberg, *The Foreign Policy of Hitler's Germany: Starting World War II 1937–1939* (Chicago, 1980), p. 552).

40 Cf. *Slavic Review*, XXXVI, p. 606. In February Litvinov was uttering taunts clearly intended to provoke war in the West (Dilks, ed., op. cit., p. 152).

41 Cf. Professor Vojtech Mastny's perceptive summary: *Russia's Road to the Cold War: Diplomacy, Welfare, and the Politics of Communism, 1941–1945* (New York, 1979), pp. 24–8. Of course the picture is not black and white. Stalin's prime concern was to avoid war, and for this it was still necessary to insure with the Entente, or anyone else offering a modicum of security. Deputy Commissar Potemkin's tour of Eastern capitals soon after must have been similarly intended. Cf. Gerhard L. Weinberg, *Germany and the Soviet Union 1939–1941* (Leiden, 1954), pp. 6–20. But Potemkin's repeated assurances that the USSR would in no circumstances 'come to an understanding with Germany' suggest a strong measure of duplicity on Stalin's part, if not Potemkin's (cf. Beloff, op. cit., II, pp. 241–2).

42 Ibid., pp. 20–46; Seidl (ed.), op. cit., pp. 2–3, 5–6, 17, 39, 51, 56–83. On 14 June a surprisingly frank leak conveyed Stalin's real hopes and fears to the Germans (ibid., pp. 23–4). For the significance of Litvinov's replacement by Molotov, cf. Weinberg, *The Foreign Policy of Hitler's Germany*, pp. 570–2.

43 Schmidt, op. cit., pp. 135, 137, 164; Bohlen, op. cit., p. 82; Albert Speer, *Inside the Third Reich* (London, 1970), p. 168.

44 Seidl (ed.), op. cit., pp. 84–8; Bohlen, op. cit., p. 83; Schmidt, op. cit., pp. 137–8; Hilger and Meyer, op. cit., pp. 304–5. 'The speed with which they reached agreement impresses me because I spent fifteen months trying to get Soviet agreement to five treaties of lesser importance' (James F. Byrnes, *Speaking Frankly* (New York, 1947), p. 286). The intention of Stalin's 'chestnuts' invitation to Hitler to invade Bohemia is also confirmed in the Большая Советская Энциклопедия, 1940, vol. 46 (Beloff, op. cit., II, p. 285).

45 Ibid., p. 300; Schmidt, op. cit., p. 134. The next day, 24 August, Eden was asked about the Pact's implications. 'I had to say it meant war', was his blunt retort (The Earl of Avon, *The Eden Memoirs: The Reckoning* (London, 1965), p. 60).

46 Hermann Rauschning, *Germany's Revolution of Destruction* (London, 1939), p. 275.

47 Seidl (ed.), op. cit., pp. 89–91, 97–9.

48 The Germans believed (falsely) that 'Britain would be obliged to declare war on Russia too' (David Irving, *Hitler's War* (London, 1977), p. 9).

49 This canard had been launched by the Germans themselves (Nicholas Bethell, *The War Hitler Won* (London, 1972), pp. 113–14).

50 Ibid., pp. 101–13; Weinberg, *Germany and the Soviet Union*, pp. 52–4; Lukacs, op. cit., pp. 56–7.

51 Cf. Hilger and Meyer, op. cit., p. 312; Ulam, op. cit., pp. 514–15. Molotov's justification of the Soviet invasion was printed by Jane Degras (ed.), *Soviet Documents on Foreign Policy* (Oxford, 1953), III, pp. 374–6.

52 Bethell, op. cit., pp. 379–81.

53 Ibid., p. 303.

54 Ibid., pp. 320, 326–7. Amazing blunders characterized the Soviet advance, despite the lack of any serious opposition (Erickson, op. cit., p. 44).

55 Hinsley, op. cit., pp. 16–20.

56 Weinberg, op. cit., pp. 54–6.

57 Seidl (ed.), op. cit., p. 107; Bethell, op. cit., p. 168. At the end of August Voroshilov had pressed the Poles to apply to the USSR for military supplies (T. Jankowski and E. Weese, eds, *Documents on Polish-Soviet Relations 1939–1945* (London, 1961), I, pp. 40–1). The offer was renewed on 2 September (ibid., p. 42), but abruptly dropped on the 8th (ibid., p. 43).

58 Weinberg, op. cit., pp. 58–60; Seidl (ed.), op. cit., pp. 120–7; Hilger and Meyer, op. cit., pp. 313–14; Malcolm Muggeridge (ed.), *Ciano's Diary 1939–1943* (London, 1947), p. 162.

59 Letter of 23 May 1851, quoted by Sir Lewis Namier, *1848: The Revolution of the Intellectuals* (London, 1946), pp. 52–3.

60 Bethell, op. cit., pp. 62, 124–7, 130–1.

61 Irving, op. cit., pp. 12–13; Heinz Höhne, *The Order of the Death's Head* (London, 1969), pp. 296–307.

62 Muggeridge (ed.), op. cit., p. 160.

63 Eye-witness account of Mrs Lucy Roberts in a typescript kindly loaned to me; *The Dark Side of the Moon* (London, 1946), pp. 50–73; Albert Konrad Herling, *The Soviet Slave Empire* (New York, 1951), pp. 43–51; Unto Parvilahti, *Beria's Gardens: Ten Years' Captivity in Russia and Siberia* (London, 1959), p. 81; Thaddeus Wittlin, *Commissar: The Life and Death of Lavrenty Pavlovich Beria* (London, 1973), pp. 265–7. Before the invasion, Beria had ordered NKVD units in Minsk and other border cities to be ready to follow the Red Army into Poland (Vladimir and Evdokia Petrov, *Empire of Fear* (London, 1956), p. 94). On 30 September the NKVD kidnapped a Polish diplomat in Kiev and removed him to an unknown destination (*Documents on Polish-Soviet Relations 1939–1945*, I, pp. 89–90).

64 Cf. C. A. Smith (ed.), *Escape from Paradise* (London, 1954), p. 78.

65 Zoltan Toth, *Prisoner of the Soviet Union* (Woking, 1978), pp. 93–4; Robert Conquest, *Kolyma: The Arctic Death Camps* (London, 1978), p. 110 (cf. ibid., p. 96).

66 David J. Dallin and Boris I. Nicolaevsky, *Forced Labor in Soviet Russia* (London, 1948), pp. 263–4 (cf. ibid., pp. 27–9, 34–9); George F. Kennan, *Memoirs 1925–1950* (Boston, 1967), p. 200; Bethell, op. cit., p. 346; Harold Nicolson, *Diaries and Letters 1939–1945* (London, 1967), p. 434. A later detailed examination found that 'the total number of displaced persons should be a figure between 1,442,000 and 1,660,000' (*Documents on Polish-Soviet Relations*, I, pp. 573–4; cf. ibid., pp. 167–8).

67 Conquest, op. cit., pp. 218–19.

68 Free Europe Pamphlet, *The Soviet Occupation of Poland* (London, 1940), pp. 11–12. *Whitaker's Almanac* for 1946 gives a figure of thirteen million (p. 947).

69 Strobe Talbott (ed.), *Khrushchev Remembers* (Boston, 1970), p. 141.

70 Z. Stypulkowski, *Invitation to Moscow* (London, 1951), p. 26.

71 Conquest, op. cit., pp. 95–6; and his *The Great Terror*, pp. 118, 430–1; Dallin and Nicolaevsky, op. cit., p. 25; Alex Weissberg, *Conspiracy of Silence* (London, 1952), pp. 493–7. Margarete Buber, *Under Two Dictators* (London, 1949), p. 167; *Le Procès Kravchenko contre Les Lettres Françaises* (Paris, 1949), p. 557.

72 Buber, op. cit., p. 298. One might compare the German Communist girl encountered by Elinor Lipper in Kolyma, whose brother had died in an equivalent Nazi death-camp (*Eleven Years in Soviet Prison Camps* (London, 1951), p. 185). A Polish Jew in GULAG in 1941: 'At times I think that if I had to choose between *Pechor-lag* and the Dachau concentration camp, I would choose Dachau' (Menachem Begin, *White Nights: The Story of a Prisoner in Russia* (London, 1978), p. 204).

73 Höhne, op. cit., p. 307.

74 Bethell, op. cit., pp. 145–7.

75 Stanislaw Kot, *Conversations with the Kremlin and Dispatches from Russia* (London, 1963), p. 185; cf. Talbott (ed.), op. cit., pp. 144–5; *Documents on Polish-Soviet Relations*, I, p. 607. About 400,000 Jews escaped to Soviet-occupied Poland, of whom something over 15,000 were later permitted to leave the Soviet Union (Malcolm J. Proudfoot, *European Refugees: 1939–52* (London, 1959), p. 59). Another source estimates the total at 600,000, of whom 450,000 'just vanished' in the USSR (*Documents on Polish-Soviet Relations*, I, pp. 607–8).

76 Dallin and Nicolaevsky, op. cit., pp. 30–4. For the fate of Jews in Soviet-occupied Europe, compare further Lipper, op. cit., p. 277; Begin, op. cit., pp. 12 *et seq.*

77 Talbott (ed.), op. cit., p. 141. Mrs Roberts saw them in 1939 returning across the San to Przemysl (TS account).

78 Gustav Herling, *A World Apart* (London, 1951), pp. 166–8. Cf. General Keitel's complaint of 5 December 1939 (R. J. Sontag and J. S. Beddie, eds, *Nazi-Soviet Relations* (Washington, 1948), p. 128). The American fellow-traveller Rockwell Kent welcomed the Soviet invasion of Poland, as at least '*those* Jews . . . would be safe'! (David Caute, *The Fellow-Travellers: A Postscript to the Enlightenment* (London, 1973), p. 186.)

79 Ronald Hingley, *Joseph Stalin: Man and Legend* (London, 1974), p. 297. An authoritative Soviet version of events leading up to the conquest of Poland manages to avoid discussion of Soviet-Nazi intrigues by the ingenious method of describing pre-war Anglo-French negotiations in all their not very creditable detail, whilst virtually omitting the role of the Soviet Union (Gromyko *et al.*, eds, op. cit., III, pp. 759–814). The official Soviet explanation of this unsavoury period of her diplomacy is however that the USSR was perfectly aware of Germany's aggressive intentions towards her, but had no alternative to signing the Non-Aggression Pact (Secret Protocol omitted as usual). The evil Men of Munich were in this way foiled in their hopes of inciting Germany and Japan to attack the peace-loving Soviet Union. Needless to say, no documentation is adduced to support these propositions (Gromyko *et al.*, eds, *СССР в Борбе за Мир Накануне второй*

мировой войны (Moscow, 1971), pp. 14–15). At least one Soviet source claims that the Molotov-Ribbentrop Pact was signed *after* the German invasion of Poland! (A. S. Yakovlev, *Цель Жизни* (Moscow, 1966), pp. 207–8). It is in fact well established 'that there is no evidence of . . . alleged British attempts to direct German expansion eastward'. The British rejected the Anti-Comintern Pact and 'deplored the evidence of Russo-German friction'. From Richard Sorge, their agent in Japan, the Soviets were in any case receiving information indicating that Hitler's aggressive preparations were directed against the West, not the Soviet Union (Weinberg, *The Foreign Policy of Hitler's Germany*, pp. 75–6, 104, 551–2).

VII   Digesting the Plunder

1 Arthur Bryant, *The Turn of the Tide 1939–1943* (London, 1957), p. 472. In his radio broadcast of 3 July 1941 Stalin had claimed that the Pact had gained the USSR valuable time (I. V. Stalin, *Сочинения* (Stanford, 1967), II [xv], p. 4). But in another respect his memory deceived him: in 1939 he had deemed the French Army 'worthy of consideration' (Vojtech Mastny, *Russia's Road to the Cold War: Diplomacy, Warfare, and the Politics of Communism, 1941–1945* (New York, 1979), p. 26). It is ironical to note that the most realistic Red Army General Staff plan of resistance to German attack in 1941 required virtual abandonment of all the territories acquired by the Pact (Marshal S. S. Biriuzov, *Когда гремели пушки* (Moscow, 1961), pp. 11–12).

2 Roy Medvedev accepts Stalin's version of events (*Let History Judge: The Origins and Consequences of Stalinism* (New York, 1971), pp. 440–2), as did Sir John Wheeler-Bennett (*Munich: Prologue to Tragedy* (London, 1948), pp. 407–13).

3 Strobe Talbott (ed.), *Khrushchev Remembers* (Boston, 1970), p. 129.

4 Barry A. Leach, *German Strategy Against Russia 1939–1941* (Oxford, 1973), pp. 1–20. For Hitler's earlier musings over policy towards Russia, see Kurt G. W. Lüdecke, *I Knew Hitler* (London, 1938), pp. 422–3.

5 Gerhard L. Weinberg, *Germany and the Soviet Union 1939–1941* (Leiden, 1954), p. 93.

6 Gustav Hilger and Alfred G. Meyer, *The Incompatible Allies: A Memoir-History of German-Soviet Relations 1918–1941* (New York, 1953), pp. 286–7; A. Avtorkhanov, 'Закулисная история пакта "Риббентроп-Молотов"', *Континент* (1975), IV, pp. 303–4.

7 Alfred Seidl (ed.), *Die Beziehungen zwischen Deutschland und der Sowjetunion 1939–1941* (Tübingen, 1949), pp. 156–9; Hilger and

Meyer, op. cit., pp. 316–17. The agreement was renewed a year later (Weinberg, op. cit., p. 147).

8 Ibid., pp. 76–8; Seidl (ed.), op. cit., p. 390; FO 371/24853. The principal Soviet contribution was a hamfisted attempt to blackmail Admiral Feige, who was in charge of the construction work (Talbott, ed., op. cit., p. 131; cf. Admiral N. G. Kuznetsov, 'Перед войной', Октябрь (1965), no. 11, pp. 143–4).

9 Seidl (ed.), op. cit., pp. 390–2; Raymond J. Sontag and James S. Beddie (eds), Nazi-Soviet Relations 1939–1941 (Washington, 1948), pp. 200, 332.

10 Weinberg, op. cit., pp. 150–1, 161, 170; Sontag and Beddie (eds), op. cit., pp. 201, 236; Seidl (ed.), op. cit., p. 391; W. N. Medlicott, The Economic Blockade (London, 1952), I, pp. 633–59. In July 1941 the Soviets supplied the British with a full statistical résumé of German imports from the Soviet Union during the period of the Pact (ibid., pp. 667–71).

11 Gerhard Ritter, The Sword and the Sceptre: The Problem of Militarism in Germany (London, 1973), IV, pp. 113, 119, 229.

12 Francis L. Loewenheim, Harold D. Langley and Manfred Thomas, Roosevelt and Churchill: Their Wartime Correspondence (London, 1975), p. 91.

13 Alan Bullock, Hitler: A Study in Tyranny (London, 1952), p. 483.

14 Weinberg, op. cit., p. 75; cf. Max Beloff, The Foreign Policy of Soviet Russia 1929–1941 (Oxford, 1949), II, pp. 293–5.

15 Cf. Izvestia, 11 January 1941, quoted in Foreign Relations of the United States (Washington, 1941), I, pp. 123–4. Strong Soviet objections to the British blockade of Germany were voiced on 25 October and 11 December 1939 (Jane Degras, ed., Soviet Documents on Foreign Policy (Oxford, 1953), III, pp. 386–8, 411–12).

16 Seidl (ed.), op. cit., p. 151. Compare Stalin's article in Pravda of 30 November 1939 (Stalin, op. cit., I [XIV], p. 404).

17 William L. Shirer, Berlin Diary (London, 1941), p. 208.

18 FO 371/24850, 45.

19 Hilger and Meyer, op. cit., p. 315.

20 Charles E. Bohlen, Witness to History 1929–1969 (London, 1973), p. 96; cf. FO 371/23701, 252–99; 23702, 1–164, 305–7.

21 Weinberg, op. cit., pp. 75–85. In the winter of 1939–40 a Soviet ice-breaker obligingly set out to open the frozen Baltic port of Luleå for the Germans (Winston S. Churchill, The Gathering Storm (London, 1948), p. 430). 'Basis Nord' was constructed by Russian slave-labour, loaned to the Nazis by GULAG (cf. John Murray, A Spy called Swallow (London, 1978), p. 139).

22 The Anti-Comintern Museum in Berlin was closed, and a film of the

Spanish Civil War that might have given offence was shelved (Shirer, op. cit., pp. 193–4, 228).

23 As early as 1933 Foreign Commissar Litvinov assured the German Foreign Office that the USSR 'considers it quite natural that Germany should treat communists in Germany exactly as enemies of the state are treated in Russia' (John L. Heinemen, *Hitler's First Foreign Minister: Constantin Freiherr von Neurath, Diplomat and Statesman* (Los Angeles, 1979), p. 99). Hilger and Meyer, op. cit., p. 311; Sontag and Beddie (eds), op. cit., pp. 88, 175, 177; Talbott (ed.), op. cit., p. 129; Robert Conquest, *The Great Terror: Stalin's Purge of the Thirties* (London, 1968), p. 488; Medvedev, op. cit., p. 443; Stanislaw Kot, *Conversations with the Kremlin and Dispatches from Russia* (London, 1963), p. 160; Victor Kravchenko, *I Chose Freedom* (London, 1947), pp. 332–5; Z. Stypulkowski, *Invitation to Moscow* (London, 1951), p. 15; Solomon Volkov (ed.), *Testimony: The Memoirs of Dmitri Shostakovich* (London, 1979), pp. 96–102. Stalin and Molotov publicly denounced the Allies' cause and issued reasoned defences of Hitler's actions (Degras, ed., III, pp. 389, 406, 436–9). The pejorative epithet 'fascist' simply vanished from Soviet public life (M. I. Gallai, 'Первый бой мы выиграли', *Новый мир* (1966), no. 9, pp. 24–5). It is also interesting to note that the Prussian 'goose-step' still favoured by elite units of the Red Army is a heritage of the alliance with Nazi Germany (ibid.). Fascist Italy had already adopted it in 1937 (Gerhard L. Weinberg, *The Foreign Policy of Hitler's Germany: Starting World War II 1937–1939* (Chicago, 1980), pp. 281–2).

24 W. G. Krivitsky, *I Was Stalin's Agent* (London, 1939), pp. 68–9; Aino Kuusinen, *Before and After Stalin* (London, 1974), pp. 45–6.

25 Hugh Thomas, *John Strachey* (London, 1973), pp. 184–5. Compare the 'argument' of Archibald Robertson in the *Daily Worker* (Bill Jones, *The Russia Complex: The British Labour Party and the Soviet Union* (Manchester, 1977), p. 39; Henry Pelling, *The British Communist Party: A Historical Profile* (London, 1958), pp. 109–19), and the contorted convolutions of Professors Hyman Levy and J. B. S. Haldane (Gary Werskey, *The Visible College: The Collective Biography of British Scientific Socialists of the 1930s* (New York, 1978), pp. 264–5).

26 Pelling, op. cit., p. 40.

27 Weinberg, *Germany and the Soviet Union*, pp. 62–5. Within a few days of Hitler's peace appeal, Soviet Ambassador Maisky put out parallel feelers to the British Government through Eden (The Earl of Avon, *The Eden Memoirs: The Reckoning* (London, 1965), p. 76). On 6 November *Pravda* denounced British and French continuance of the war as a bankers' and reactionaries' plot (A. Kazantsev, *Третья Сила: история одной попытки* (Frankfurt, 1974), p. 68).

28 David Caute, *The Fellow-Travellers: A Postscript to the Enlightenment* (London, 1973), pp. 186–7, 189.

29 Robert E. Sherwood, *Roosevelt and Hopkins: An Intimate History* (New York, 1948), pp. 282, 303; Robert Huhn Jones, *The Roads to Russia: United States Lend-Lease to the Soviet Union* (Oklahoma, 1969), p. 22. The Comintern attempt to throttle Britain's trade supply lines, by inducing seamen to desert or sabotage their ships, etc., was largely frustrated by vigilant anti-Communist American labour-union leaders (Joseph E. Persico, *Piercing the Reich* (New York, 1979), p. 102). Cf. Stanislaw Mikolajczyk, *The Pattern of Soviet Domination* (London, 1948), p. 10.

30 Jean van Heijenoort, *With Trotsky in Exile* (Harvard, 1978), p. 117.

31 A. Rossi, *Les Communistes Français Pendant la Drôle de Guerre* (Paris, 1951), pp. 81–97. Thorez was given passage by the Nazis (cf. Mikhail Koriakov, *I'll Never Go Back* (London, 1948), p. 150).

32 Rossi, op. cit., p. 103.

33 Ibid., p. 348.

34 Ibid., plate IV.

35 Ibid., pp. 74–5.

36 Ibid., pp. 123–4.

37 Ibid., pp. 165–6, 190, 238–52, 334–6, 348–9.

38 Ibid., p. 380.

39 Ibid., pp. 228–33.

40 Talbott (ed.), op. cit., p. 134.

41 Cf. Shirer, op. cit., pp. 131, 342, 343, 365; Arthur Bryant, *The Turn of the Tide 1939–1943* (London, 1957), pp. 51–2; Robert Murphy, *Diplomat Among Warriors* (London, 1964), pp. 53–4; Churchill, op. cit., pp. 436, 511–12.

42 Cf. David J. Dallin, *Soviet Espionage* (Yale, 1955), pp. 25–70. In 1935 the Communist Federation of French Teachers vigorously defended the new Soviet law extending the death penalty down to twelve-year-old children (Alexander Orlov, *The Secret History of Stalin's Crimes* (London, 1954), p. 53).

43 Cf. Milovan Djilas, *Wartime* (New York, 1977), pp. 4–5; Hugh Seton-Watson, *The Pattern of Communist Revolution* (London, 1953), pp. 201–4. The Danish Communist Party similarly postponed resistance to the Germans until after Hitler's invasion of Russia (Beloff, op. cit., II, p. 325).

44 FO 800/276. Trotsky's propaganda organs also opposed support for the British and French war effort (Leszek Kolakowski, *Main Currents of Marxism: Its Origin, Growth, and Dissolution* (Oxford, 1978), III, pp. 208–10).

45 Compare the views of G. Vereker (FO 371/23677, 80–3) and Fitzroy

Maclean (FO 371/24850, 388); FO 371/24855, 54. Even the fellow-traveller Kingsley Martin had come to accept this view by April 1941 (FO 800/279).

46 Compare further Medvedev, op. cit., pp. 442–4; Mastny, op. cit., pp. 25–8; FO 371/66465. For violently anti-British Soviet broadcasts, see FO 371/23678, 167–8, 182, 184, 197, 222, 252–68, 304, etc.; compare also Sir Lancelot Oliphant's realistic view (ibid., 77).

47 John Erickson, 'The Red Army before June 1941', Soviet Affairs (London, 1962), III, pp. 105–9.

48 George F. Kennan, Memoirs 1925–1950 (Boston, 1967), p. 520. In 1937 Polish Foreign Minister Beck declared 'that Poland would fight rather than allow German troops across her territory' to attack the Soviet Union (Weinberg, The Foreign Policy of Hitler's Germany, p. 208).

49 Malcolm Muggeridge (ed.), Ciano's Diary 1939–1943 (London, 1947), p. 170.

50 Seidl (ed.), op. cit., pp. 91, 120–1, 132, 133–42, 145; Sontag and Beddie (eds), op. cit., p. 107; Weinberg, Germany and the Soviet Union, pp. 48, 59–60.

51 Churchill, op. cit., pp. 345, 465. The Soviet version of the escape of the Orzel is given in Degras (ed.), op. cit., III, pp. 376–7.

52 'Estonia 1940–41', The Nineteenth Century and After (London, 1946), CXXXIX, p. 40; cf. Maria Hadow, Paying Guest in Siberia (London, 1978), p. 15. The bedraggled state of the Red Army in Poland had been reported to Hitler, with unpleasant consequences two years later (Albert Speer, Inside the Third Reich (London, 1970), p. 169).

53 Seidl (ed.), op. cit., pp. 121, 122–3; Evald Uustalu, The History of the Estonian People (London, 1952), pp. 238–40; The Baltic States 1940–1972 (Stockholm, 1972), pp. 8–10; Communist Takeover and Occupation of Estonia: Special Report No. 3 of the Select Committee on Communist Aggression (Washington, 1955), pp. 6–8. The text of the Treaty is given in Nazi-Soviet Conspiracy and the Baltic States (London, 1958), pp. 39–41. For Soviet versions of events (which fail to mention the existence of the Nazi-Soviet Pact), compare W. P. and Zelda Coates, Russia, Finland and the Baltic (London, 1940), pp. 48–63; Estonia Between the Two World Wars (Tallinn, 1973), pp. 180–4. The semi-official Soviet version provides a tendentious summary of the Pact, but no mention of the Secret Protocol. Everything is justified by the Soviet Union's need to buy time and 'fulfil its international duty to the international proletariat, to protect the safety of the country of socialism' (A. A. Gromyko et al., eds, История Дипломатия (Moscow, 1965), III, p. 798). On this basis it appears that whatever the Soviet Union does is ipso facto right. A convenient doctrine.

54 For the text of the Latvian Treaty, together with a Stalinist com-

mentary, see W. P. and Z. Coates, op. cit., pp. 63–73. Compare also Seidl (ed.), op. cit., p. 123; Alfreds Berzinsh, *I Saw Vishinsky Bolshevize Latvia* (Washington, 1948), pp. 11–14; Arveds Schwabe, *The Story of Latvia: A Historical Survey* (Stockholm, 1950), pp. 49–50; *The Baltic States 1940–1972*, p. 19. The pretext for the absence of consumer goods in the USSR occupied a venerable place in the Soviet repertory (cf. Thomas, op. cit., p. 86).

55 Text in W. P. and Z. Coates, op. cit., pp. 73–7. Cf. V. Stanley Vardys, *Lithuania under the Soviets* (New York, 1965), p. 48; *The Baltic States 1940–1972*, pp. 29–31.

56 Compare the photocopy and commentary in Agnis Balodis, *Sovjets och Natzitysklands uppgörelse om de baltiska staterna* (Stockholm, 1978), pp. 36–7.

57 Numerous accounts of conditions in Lubianka are preserved by former prisoners and guards; cf. Margarete Buber, *Under Two Dictators* (London, 1949), pp. 10, 26–31; Anatoli Granovsky, *All Pity Choked: The Memoirs of a Soviet Secret Agent* (London, 1955), pp. 76–8; Aino Kuusinen, *Before and After Stalin* (London, 1974); Unto Parvilahti, *Beria's Gardens: Ten Years' Captivity in Russia and Siberia* (London, 1959), pp. 24–8, 37–48; Peter Deriabin and Frank Gibney, *The Secret World* (London, 1960), pp. 135–42; Joseph Czapski, *The Inhuman Land* (London, 1951), pp. 110–13, 118–23, 206–11; *The Memoirs of Ivanov-Razumnik* (Oxford, 1965), pp. 255 *et seq.*, 292–302; Zoltan Toth, *Prisoner of the Soviet Union* (London, 1978), pp. 87–91.

58 Cf. Krivitsky, op. cit., pp. 163–6; 'A. I. Romanov', *Nights are Longest There* (London, 1972), pp. 183–5.

59 For Serov, compare Talbott (ed.), op. cit., p. 115; G. A. Tokaev, *Comrade X* (London, 1956), p. 324.

60 *These Names Accuse: Nominal List of Latvians Deported to Soviet Russia in 1940–41* (Stockholm, 1951), pp. 15–16, 24, 41–8; K. Pelékis, *Genocide: Lithuania's Threefold Tragedy* (Germany, 1949), pp. 30, 273–8.

61 Adam B. Ulam, *Stalin: The Man and his Era* (London, 1974), p. 535; Svetlana Alliluyeva, *Only One Year* (London, 1969), p. 369.

62 Churchill, op. cit., pp. 363–5, 434–5, 458, 550–2; Bryant, op. cit., p. 74. Pre-war Estonia was very much under British influence (Beloff, op. cit., II, p. 79).

63 Andrew Boyle, *The Climate of Treason* (London, 1979), p. 177; E. H. Cookridge, *The Third Man* (London, 1968), pp. 19, 69–70; the *Observer*, 2 December 1979; Gordon Brook-Shepherd, *The Storm Petrels: The First Soviet Defectors, 1928–1938* (London, 1977), pp. 172–80; David Dilks (ed.), *The Diaries of Sir Alexander Cadogan* (London, 1971), pp. 207–8. Yet another source could have been

Krivitsky's 'member of the Council of Imperial Defence' (unidentified): see Richard Deacon, *The British Connection* (London, 1979),
p. 143.

64 Cf. Herbert A. Grant Watson, *The Latvian Republic: The Struggle for
Freedom* (London, 1965), pp. 58, 60–3, 69.

65 The fullest account of the migration is that of Dr Erhard Kroeger, *Der
Auszug aus der alten Heimat* (Tübingen, 1967); compare also Seidl
(ed.), op. cit., p. 126; Heinz Höhne, *The Order of the Death's Head*
(London, 1969), pp. 309–10; Nicholas Bethell, *The War Hitler Won*
(New York, 1972), pp. 150–1; Schwabe, op. cit., pp. 48–9. The Stalinist
writers W. P. and Z. Coates asserted brazenly that the question was
'entirely outside any Soviet-German arrangement'! (*Russia, Finland
and the Baltic*, pp. 88–9). W. P. Coates was the 'indefatigable' secretary
of the 'Friends of the Soviet Union' (Bill Jones, *The Russia Complex:
The British Labour Party and the Soviet Union* (Manchester, 1977),
p. 15).

66 Alliluyeva, op. cit., p. 369.

VIII   David and Goliath

1 Compare Stalin's claim in 1935 (Roy A. Medvedev, *On Stalin and
Stalinism* (Oxford, 1979), p. 76).

2 Max Jakobson, *The Diplomacy of the Winter War* (Cambridge, Mass.,
1961), pp. 55–6, 99–100.

3 Elliot R. Goodman, *The Soviet Design for a World State* (New York,
1960), p. 337.

4 Jakobson, op. cit., pp. 19–93; Väinö Tanner, *The Winter War*
(Stanford, 1950), pp. 3–21; Gerd R. Ueberschär, *Hitler und Finland
1939–1941: Die Deutsch-Finnischen Beziehungen während des Hitler-
Stalin-Paktes* (Wiesbaden, 1978), pp. 42–60.

5 Gerhard L. Weinberg, *Germany and the Soviet Union 1939–1941*
(Leiden, 1954), p. 87.

6 Strobe Talbott (ed.), *Khrushchev Remembers* (Boston, 1970), p. 139.

7 Alfred Seidl (ed.), *Die Beziehungen zwischen Deutschland und der
Sowjetunion* (Tübingen, 1949), pp. 122, 131, 146–9, 153–4, 155, 264–5,
271; Ueberschär, op. cit., pp. 108–22.

8 Milovan Djilas, *Conversations with Stalin* (London, 1962), p. 140.

9 FO 371/236678, 88.

10 The Earl of Avon, *The Eden Memoirs: The Reckoning* (London, 1965),
p. 76.

11 Jakobson, op. cit., pp. 117–18, 141; Tanner, op. cit., pp. 27, 44.

12 'Molotov's Broadcast to the Soviet People', *The U.S.S.R. and Finland*
(New York, 1939), p. 55.

13 Aino Kuusinen, *Before and After Stalin* (London, 1974), pp. 225–32; Roy A. Medvedev, *Let History Judge: The Origins and Consequences of Stalinism* (London, 1971), p. 309.

14 Louis Hagen (ed.), *The Schellenberg Memoirs* (London, 1956), pp. 69–70; Heinz Höhne, *The Order of the Death's Head* (London, 1969), pp. 260–5; Alfred M. de Zayas, *Die Wehrmacht-Untersuchungsstelle: Deutsche Ermittlungen über alliierte Völkerrechtsverletzungen im Zweiten Weltkrieg* (Munich, 1980), pp. 34–6.

15 Eloise Engle and Lauri Paananen, *The Winter War* (London, 1973), pp. 13–14; Tanner, op. cit., pp. 85–7; Jakobson, op. cit., pp. 148–50; Ueberschär, op. cit., pp. 92–6. Professor John Lukacs notes that Stalin had taken a leaf out of Hitler's book (*The Last European War: September 1939/December 1941* (London, 1976), p. 65). For the Soviet version of this incident, see Jane Degras (ed.), *Soviet Documents on Foreign Policy* (Oxford, 1953), III, p. 401.

16 FO 371/24791, 29; William L. Shirer, *Berlin Diary* (London, 1941), p. 209. Many foreign observers shared this view: compare Harold Nicolson, *Diaries and Letters 1939–1945* (London, 1967), p. 47.

17 John Erickson, *The Road to Stalingrad* (London, 1975), pp. 17–18.

18 N. N. Voronov, *На службе военной* (Moscow, 1963), pp. 136–7.

19 Talbott (ed.), op. cit., pp. 150–2.

20 Tanner, op. cit., pp. 89–91; Michael Parrish, 'Command and Leadership in the Soviet Air Force During the Great Patriot War', *Aerospace Historian* (1979), XXVI, p. 194.

21 David J. Dallin and Boris I. Nicolaevsky, *Forced Labor in Soviet Russia* (London, 1948), p. 259.

22 Talbott (ed.), op. cit., p. 153.

23 Ibid., pp. 153–4. On another occasion a Soviet submarine accidentally sank a German freighter (Gustav Hilger and Alfred G. Meyer, *The Incompatible Allies: A Memoir-History of German-Soviet Relations 1918–1941* (New York, 1953), p. 315).

24 Thaddeus Wittlin, *Commissar: The Life and Death of Lavrenty Pavlovich Beria* (London, 1973), pp. 272–4; compare the eye-witness account of Mikhail Soloviev, *My Nine Lives in the Red Army* (New York, 1955), pp. 174–5, 181; FO 371/24791, 7.

25 Engle and Paananen, op. cit., pp. 27, 47, 48; FO 371/24792, 152; FO 371/24795, 174.

26 Victor Kravchenko, *I Chose Freedom* (London, 1947), p. 344.

27 Robert Conquest, *The Great Terror: Stalin's Purge of the Thirties* (London, 1968), pp. 484–92.

28 Erickson, op. cit., p. 14.

IX The Undeclared War

1 *Finland: The Criminal Conspiracy of Stalin and Hitler* (London, 1940), p. 26.

2 R. A. C. Parker, 'Britain, France and Scandinavia', *History* (1976), LXI, pp. 369–79; Sir Llewellyn Woodward, *British Foreign Policy in the Second World War* (London, 1962), pp. 16–26. The Germans were naturally perfectly *au fait* with these Allied plans (*Documents on German Foreign Policy 1918–1945* (London, 1956), Series D, IX, pp. 89–90).

3 Adam B. Ulam, *Stalin: The Man and his Era* (London, 1974), p. 521; Viktor Kalninsh, 'Из Истории Советской Агрессивной Политики', *Факты и Мысли* (New York, November 1979), XV, p. 7; Strobe Talbott (ed.), *Khrushchev Remembers* (Boston, 1970), p. 155.

4 Roy A. Medvedev, *Let History Judge: The Origins and Consequences of Stalinism* (London, 1971), pp. 445–6; Elliot R. Goodman, *The Soviet Design for a World State* (New York, 1960), p. 389. The text of the Soviet-Finnish Treaty is printed in Jane Degras (ed.), *Soviet Documents on Foreign Policy* (Oxford, 1953), III, pp. 421–3; as is that of the Soviet objection of 20 March to the proposed Scandinavian defensive alliance (ibid., p. 424).

5 Max Jakobson, *The Diplomacy of the Winter War* (Cambridge, Mass., 1961), p. 254. Compare the comparison made by Eloise Engle and Lauri Paananen, *The Winter War* (London, 1973), p. 143.

6 Jakobson, op. cit., p. 254. About 415,000 Finns had to leave their homes (Malcolm J. Proudfoot, *European Refugees 1939–52* (London, 1957), p. 41).

7 Alexander Solzhenitsyn, *Архипелаг Гулаг 1918–1956: Опыт Художественного Исследования* (Paris, 1973–5), I, p. 88; Robert Conquest, *Kolyma: The Arctic Death Camps* (London, 1978), p. 97.

8 Charles E. Bohlen, *Witness to History* (London, 1973), pp. 93–5; Jakobson, op. cit., pp. 165–70. A Soviet jurist has since explained the legitimacy of such adventures: 'The U.S.S.R. has a right to defend itself by shifting the boundaries of that state which constitutes an immediate menace to it. In order to secure the frontiers of the U.S.S.R., the territorial problem can be solved by means of a just war, which is the self-defence of the socialist state' (Goodman, op. cit., p. 308).

9 Jakobson, op. cit., pp. 210–15.

10 Väinö Tanner, *The Winter War* (Stanford, 1957), p. 196; Bohlen, op. cit., p. 95. This was the view of the German Ambassador in Moscow (*Documents on German Foreign Policy 1918–1945*, Series D, IX, p. 53), and of the Polish Ambassador in London (*Documents on Polish-Soviet Relations 1939–1945* (London, 1961), I, p. 339).

11 Talbott (ed.), op. cit., p. 155; *Великая отечественная война Советского союза, 1941–1945* (Moscow, 1967), pp. 46–7.

12 Tanner, op. cit., p. 259; FO 371/24794, 30.

13 Nikolai Tolstoy, *Victims of Yalta* (London, 1977), p. 396. From this Russian prisoners in German hands after 1941 were able to deduce their likely fate if they ever returned home ('N.N.N.', *На фронте 1941 года и в плену, воспоминания врача* (Buenos Aires, 1974), p. 75). An effective Finnish propaganda leaflet is preserved in FO 371/24791, 177. An eyewitness saw wounded from the front isolated under guard in hospitals at Sverdlovsk (FO 371/24850, 207); cf. 'A. I. Romanov', *Nights Are Longest There: Smersh from the Inside* (London, 1972), pp. 27–8; Menachem Begin, *White Nights: The Story of a Prisoner in Russia* (London, 1978), p. 186. Their destination was for the most part the slave-labour camps of Pechora (Mikhail Rozanov, *Завоеватели белых пятен* (Limburg, 1951), p. 246).

14 One prisoner, a fish packer from Archangel, related how he was press-ganged in the street by a passing commissar (Engle and Paananen, op. cit., p. 98).

15 David Caute, *The Fellow-Travellers: A Postscript to the Enlightenment* (London, 1973), pp. 60–2.

16 FO 371/24850, 185–208. Captain Tamplin knew Russia well, having lived and worked there before the Revolution (information supplied to me by Col. Tamplin in 1973). Charles Bohlen at the US Embassy in Moscow also noted the dispirited feeling of helplessness and discontent gripping the Russians at this time (Bohlen, op. cit., p. 94). Compare also the gloomy deposition of a Red Army colonel in Finnish hands (Engle and Paananen, op. cit., pp. 102–4). Tamplin and Gatehouse's report confirmed Foreign Office estimates made a year previously (FO 371/23684, 257–83; FO 371/23687, 258–85).

17 Mikhail Soloviev, *My Nine Lives in the Red Army* (New York, 1955), pp. 192–9.

18 Boris Bajanov, *Bajanov révèle Staline* (Paris, 1979), pp. 263–8; Gordon Brook-Shepherd, *The Storm Petrels: The First Soviet Defectors, 1928–1938* (London, 1977), p. 246.

19 *Documents on German Foreign Policy 1918–1945*, Series D, IX, p. 400. On 8 March the Government issued a decree ordering everyone possessing scrap iron to deliver it to the state (William L. Shirer, *Berlin Diary* (London, 1941), p. 233).

20 FO 371/24846, 100–7; cf. FO 371/23678, 285–7.

21 Woodward, op. cit., pp. 28–32; *History*, LXVI, pp. 380–2.

22 FO 371/24850, 5–10.

23 FO 371/24846, 143, 145–6.

24 Constance Babington Smith, *Evidence in Camera: The Story of Photographic Intelligence in World War II* (London, 1958), pp. 129–31; AIR 24/819; AIR 34/717; FO 371/24847, 86–142; CAB 100/3; cf. FO

371/66481. Copies of the reconnaissance report were passed to the French General Staff, and fell into the hands of the Germans when they entered Paris in June 1940 (FO 371/24850, 25–36). They in turn passed them to Moscow. In August Molotov claimed 'that towards the end of March, two foreign aircraft coming from Iran had flown over Baku area'. This was unconvincingly denied by Iran, whose airspace had been violated (ibid., 46–7).

25 FO 371/24852, 41–7.
26 David Irving, *Hitler's War* (London, 1977), p. 835.
27 René Girault, 'Les Relations Franco-Soviétiques après Septembre 1939', *Cahiers du Monde Russe et Soviétique* (Paris, 1976), XVII, p. 37. There appears to be no substance in David Irving's statement that 'Turkey had agreed to allow French aircraft overflights from Syria to bomb the Russian oil fields in the Caucasus' (Irving, op. cit., p. 141): cf. Max Beloff, *The Foreign Policy of Soviet Russia 1929–1941* (Oxford, 1949), II, pp. 301–2.
28 John Lukacs, *The Last European War: September 1939/December 1941* (London, 1976), p. 71. Lukacs is unjustly critical of the Chiefs of Staff Report, the tone of which is distinctly sceptical.
29 Compare the remarks of Robert Boothby and a French scholar in mid-March: Nigel Nicolson (ed.), *Harold Nicolson: Diaries and Letters 1939–1945* (London, 1967), pp. 62, 63.

X Forest Murmurs

1 Sir Llewellyn Woodward, *British Foreign Policy in the Second World War* (London, 1962), pp. 29–31.
2 FO 371/24850, 71.
3 I am grateful to Professor Theodor Oberländer and Dr Ehrenfried Schütte for providing me with details of their service in the German Bergmann unit in the Caucasus in 1942, and later in the Crimea in 1943. The native populations in both regions were overwhelmingly anti-Soviet, welcomed the occupying forces, and actively helped counter Red Army attempts at infiltration. There seems no reason to suppose the British and French would have been accorded a more hostile reception.
4 FO 371/24850, 3–4, 332–63; FO 371/23678, 186–8. Georgian nationalists were said to be ready to welcome an Allied invasion (FO 371/24855, 125–49). It is interesting to note that the War Office had on a later occasion to consider the possibility of sabotaging the oil wells. This was when a Soviet collapse was feared, immediately after the German invasion in June 1941. Fitzroy Maclean was again considered as a likely candidate, and much discussion was spent on whether the action should or should not be taken with Soviet co-operation (FO 371/29594,

18-21, 27, 28, 78; FO 371/29590, 3-4). Max Beloff, *The Foreign Policy of Soviet Russia 1929-1941* (Oxford, 1949), II, p. 48. On 29 March Molotov publicly expressed apprehension over 'extensive and suspicious activity . . . in the creation of Anglo-French, mainly colonial, armies headed by General Weygand' (Jane Degras, ed., *Soviet Documents on Foreign Policy* (Oxford, 1953), III, p. 447).

5 FO 371/24850, 23.

6 *Recalled to Service: The Memoirs of General Maxime Weygand* (London, 1952), p. 40. The young and energetic General Massiet would have commanded the expedition (ibid., pp. 15-17).

7 FO 371/24846, 143. On 13 April Molotov told von Schulenburg that the USSR expected British warships to launch an attack in the Black Sea, and requested a consignment of German magnetic mines (*Documents on German Foreign Policy 1918-1945* (London, 1956), Series D, IX, pp. 151-2).

8 Bill Jones, *The Russia Complex: The British Labour Party and the Soviet Union* (Manchester, 1977), pp. 45, 108, 166; David Caute, *The Fellow-Travellers: A Postscript to the Enlightenment* (London, 1973), pp. 93, 183, 274, 282. Zilliacus was also involved in suspect links with East Germany (Richard Deacon, *The British Connection* (London, 1979), p. 235).

9 NA, RG 84, box 42. In 1937 Zilliacus was in contact with the NKVD agent Rado (Sándor Rado, *Codename Dora* (London, 1977), p. 12).

10 *Le Procès Kravchenko contre Les Lettres Françaises* (Paris, 1949), p. 291.

11 Major-General Sir Guy Salisbury-Jones, then British liaison officer at Weygand's HQ, confirmed this to me.

12 A. Rossi, *Les Communistes Français pendant la Drôle de Guerre* (Paris, 1951), pp. 192-5. British fellow-travellers such as the Webbs, Bernard Shaw and Sybil Thorndike were drawn into the campaign (Caute, op. cit., p. 192).

13 For Soviet fears on this score, compare G. A. Tokaev, *Comrade X* (London, 1956), p. 150.

14 Cf. Milovan Djilas, *Wartime* (New York, 1977), p. 69; Adam B. Ulam, *Stalin: The Man and his Era* (London, 1974), p. 280.

15 Ibid., p. 479.

16 Cf. Alexander Nekrich, *Наказанные Народы* (New York, 1978), pp. 96-108.

17 FO 371/24846, 272-4.

18 Alfred Seidl (ed.), *Die Beziehungen zwischen Deutschland und der Sowjetunion 1939-1941* (Tübingen, 1949), pp. 158, 170-1, 174-6; Gustav Hilger and Alfred G. Meyer, *The Incompatible Allies: A Memoir-History of German-Soviet Relations 1918-1941* (New York,

1953), pp. 315–16; Gerhard L. Weinberg, *Germany and the Soviet Union 1939–1941* (Leiden, 1954), pp. 90–1.

19 Ibid., p. 97.

20 Donald Macintyre, *The Naval War Against Hitler* (London, 1971), pp. 26–34; T. K. Derry, *The Campaign in Norway* (London, 1952), pp. 36–52.

21 Ibid., pp. 78, 144. 'Thus the situation a month after the German invasion of Norway . . . could be summarised as slightly qualified disappointment' (ibid., p. 170). After the first British landings at Harstad and Namsos, 'the military crisis brought Hitler to the verge of a complete nervous breakdown' (David Irving, *Hitler's War* (London, 1977), p. 98).

22 Seidl (ed.), op. cit., pp. 179–80.

23 Weinberg, op. cit., pp. 81–2; Derry, op. cit., pp. 44, 45, 158–9; *Documents on German Foreign Policy 1918–1945*, Series D, IX, p. 135.

24 Hugh Thomas, *John Strachey* (London, 1973), pp. 191–2. Strachey had disassociated himself from the Party's pro-German attitude.

25 Rossi, op. cit., pp. 191–2.

26 Gordon Brook-Shepherd, *The Storm Petrels: The First Soviet Defectors, 1928–1938* (London, 1977), pp. 179–80. Similar co-operation between Nazi and Soviet intelligence existed in the United States (Allen Weinstein, *Perjury: The Hiss-Chambers Case* (London, 1978), p. 328). It was fear of the effects of this co-operation when war broke out in 1939 that induced Whittaker Chambers to inform on the activities of the US Party (Whittaker Chambers, *Witness* (London, 1953), pp. 317–18). He had already been made aware of the profound sympathy felt by Communists for 'a large group in the Nazi party' (ibid., p. 228).

27 FO 371/24846, 243.

28 *The Times*, 20 April 1940.

29 Derry, op. cit., p. 145.

30 Woodward, op. cit., p. 7.

31 George Urban, 'A Conversation with Milovan Djilas', *Encounter* (December 1979), LIII, p. 21.

32 Seidl (ed.), op. cit., p. 120.

33 Jacques Mordal, *La Campagne de Norvège* (Paris, 1949), pp. 45–7; R. A. C. Parker, 'Britain, France and Scandinavia', *History* (1976), LXVI, p. 376.

34 Derry, op. cit., pp. 163, 193; Zygmunt Litynski, *I Was One of Them* (London, 1941), pp. 74–7, 84–8, 91–2; FO 371/24796, 154–64. It was also proposed to enlist Poles who had fled from the Soviet occupation forces to the Baltic States (ibid.); in 1940 the Soviet authorities abducted most of them to the camps of GULAG (Z. Stypulkowski, *Invitation to Moscow* (London, 1951), p. 241). During the invasion in 1939, the Red Army

apparently had strict instructions not to let Polish officers escape from Poland (Nicholas Bethell, *The War Hitler Won* (New York, 1972), pp. 314–15).

35 FO 371/24850, 1–2, 22–4. On 6 February 1940 a detailed Polish military *aide-mémoire* informed the French that Polish forces could be used in Finland, and that Ukrainian and Caucasian émigré nationalists could be brought to co-operate with the Poles in military and political activities directed against Soviet power. '*Cette question contient en germe de très grandes possibilités politiques et militaires. La formation en Syrie d'une unité mixte Ukrainienne et Caucasienne serait fort désirable. Cette unité aurait pour but la lutte avec l'oppresseur soviétique.*' These projects continued under discussion throughout March and April. (Sikorski Historical Institute, A. 12. 851 b/5. I am indebted to Captain W. Milewski for photocopies of these documents.) At the same time negotiations were being conducted between the Russian émigré organization NTS on the one hand, and General Weygand and Alexis Léger of the French Foreign Office on the other with a view to conducting subversive operations within the USSR. Similar talks took place in London between an NTS representative and officials of the Ministry of Economic Warfare. (Information kindly supplied by Dr V. Poremsky, in 1940 NTS representative in Paris.)

36 FO 371/29595, 25–43. On 24 September 1941 General Sikorski suggested that defence of the Caucasian oilfields be entrusted to the Poles (FO 954/19, 386).

37 *The Dark Side of the Moon* (London, 1946), pp. 52–7; Hermann Raschhofer, *Political Assassination: The Legal Background of the Oberländer and Stashinsky Cases* (Tübingen, 1964), p. 205; Maria Hadow, *Paying Guest in Siberia* (London, 1961), p. 16.

38 Louis FitzGibbon, *Katyn: A Crime without Parallel* (London, 1971), pp. 33–51.

39 The evidence that Stalin feared revolution infinitely more than war recurs throughout this book. To provide another telling example, one may recall the NKVD's kidnapping of the White Russian General Miller from Paris in September 1937. This was bound to cause the greatest outrage in France, particularly in view of the reaction to the parallel abduction of General Kutyepov in 1930 (cf. Geoffrey Bailey, *The Conspirators* (London, 1961), pp. 101–2). This was at a time when Litvinov was desperately trying to achieve a united Franco-Soviet policy on intervention in Spain and resistance to Hitler! (Beloff, op. cit., II, 88–102.) Clearly the White plotters ranked higher in Stalin's priorities.

40 FitzGibbon, op. cit., p. 54. General Weygand would have appeared a particularly menacing figure to the NKVD, as he was a prominent

member of the *Comité d'Honneur* of the anti-Soviet organization *Société des Amis de la Russie Nationale.*

41 Ibid., pp. 136, 137, 141.

42 Louis FitzGibbon, *Unpitied and Unknown* (London, 1975), pp. 317, 319, 359, 362, 364. Could this club-house have been identical with the 'trade union retreat at Gniezdovo' at which Party orgies took place in the late 1930s? Cf. Merle Fainsod, *Smolensk under Soviet Rule* (London, 1958), p. 60.

43 Harold Nicolson, *Diaries and Letters 1939–1945* (London, 1967), p. 291.

44 FitzGibbon, *Katyn: A Crime without Parallel*, pp. 183–4.

45 FitzGibbon, *Unpitied and Unknown*, pp. 440–1.

46 Lennard D. Gerson, *The Secret Police in Lenin's Russia* (Philadelphia, 1976), pp. 153–4.

47 Joseph Czapski, *The Inhuman Land* (London, 1951), pp. 35–6. This story would seem to imply that the prisoners were delayed *en route* at a transit camp, as the White Sea is not normally free of ice until May.

48 Roy A. Medvedev, *Let History Judge: The Origins and Consequences of Stalinism* (New York, 1971), p. 13.

49 Typescript memoir, kindly loaned to me by the authoress, Mrs Lucy Roberts, who was told of the practice by a sailor she met when a prisoner at Aya-Guz.

50 'A. I. Romanov', *Nights Are Longest There: Smersh from the Inside* (London, 1972), pp. 136–9. It is said that the commander of NKVD troops at Katyn was a Colonel Pogrebnoi (Anatoli Granovsky, *All Pity Choked: The Memoirs of a Soviet Secret Agent* (London, 1955), p. 229). Professor Swianiewicz describes him as 'a tall, stout, middle-aged man, with dark hair and a ruddy face' (FitzGibbon, *Katyn: A Crime without Parallel*, p. 67).

51 Stalin had great faith in the efficacy of lopping off a nation's leadership, apparently regarding the mass of the population as a mere mob. As is well known, he proposed to Churchill and Roosevelt in 1943 that fifty thousand senior German officers should be liquidated in order that German military strength be extirpated. Churchill was shocked and Roosevelt highly amused (Winston S. Churchill, *Closing the Ring* (London, 1952), p. 330).

52 Seidl (ed.), op. cit., p. 181.

53 When the Germans began to exhume the mass grave in April 1943, a Soviet observation aeroplane was observed circling intently overhead (FitzGibbon, *Unpitied and Unknown*, p. 359).

54 Ibid., pp. 18, 43, 213, 464. Professor Mastny effectively points up objections to explanations of Katyn advanced hitherto: Vojtech Mastny, *Russia's Road to the Cold War: Diplomacy, Warfare, and the Politics of Communism, 1941–1945* (New York, 1979), p. 28.

55 FitzGibbon, op. cit., pp. 38–40; and his *Katyn: A Crime without Parallel*, pp. 53–7.
56 *History*, LXVI, pp. 382–3. For British reservations on action against the Soviet Union (withheld from the French), see David Dilks (ed.), *The Diaries of Sir Alexander Cadogan* (London, 1971), p. 265.
57 E. H. Cookridge, *The Third Man: The truth about 'Kim' Philby, double agent* (London, 1968), pp. 71–3.
58 Andrew Boyle, *The Climate of Treason: Five who Spied for Russia* (London, 1979), pp. 145, 169, 184. I am grateful to Mr Boyle for detailed discussion of these points.

XI Friends and Neighbours

1 FO 371/23678, 298–301. Cf. Malcolm Muggeridge (ed.), *Ciano's Diary 1939–1943* (London, 1947), pp. 179, 180, 192, 197; Max Jakobson, *The Diplomacy of the Winter War: An Account of the Russo-Finnish Conflict 1939–1940* (Harvard, 1961), pp. 187–9.
2 Max Beloff, *The Foreign Policy of Soviet Russia 1929–1941* (Oxford, 1949), II, p. 308; Jane Degras (ed.), *Soviet Documents on Foreign Policy* (Oxford, 1953), III, pp. 412–15.
3 Jakobson, op. cit., pp. 190–7; Robert Dallek, *Franklin D. Roosevelt and American Foreign Policy 1932–1945* (New York, 1979), pp. 208–15; Robert E. Sherwood, *Roosevelt and Hopkins: An Intimate History* (New York, 1948), pp. 137–8; it is amusing to see the selective quotation of another section of this speech, neatly reversing its intent, made by a recent 'revisionist' historian: E. P. King, *The New Internationalism: Allied Policy and the European Peace 1939–1945* (Newton Abbot, 1973), pp. 25–6.
4 Alfred Seidl (ed.), *Die Beziehungen zwischen Deutschland und der Sowjetunion 1939–1941* (Tübingen, 1949), pp. 146–8, 153–4; Väinö Tanner, *The Winter War: Finland Against Russia 1939–40* (Stanford, 1950), pp. 117–23, 144 (cf. p. 178); Gerhard L. Weinberg, *Germany and the Soviet Union 1939–1941* (Leiden, 1954), pp. 88–90, 97, 100, 174–5; Jakobson, op. cit., pp. 184–7.
5 R. J. Sontag and J. S. Beddie (eds), *Nazi-Soviet Relations 1939–1941* (Washington, 1948), pp. 130–1.
6 William L. Shirer, *Berlin Diary: The Journal of a Foreign Correspondent 1934–1941* (London, 1941), p. 203.
7 *Documents on German Foreign Policy 1918–1945* (London, 1956), Series D, IX, pp. 412–14.
8 Seidl (ed.), op. cit., pp. 178–9, 181. The former Kaiser congratulated Hitler on the same day (*Documents on German Foreign Policy*, Series D, IX, p. 598).

9 A. Rossi, *Les Communistes Français pendant La Drôle de Guerre* (Paris, 1951), p. 348. The British Communist Party's attempt to weaken Britain's resistance only resulted in the loss of thousands of members. Diehard followers of the Comintern line, like 'Claud Cockburn' (Frank Pitcairn) soldiered on in virtual isolation, on the principle of 'not leaving the regiment when it is under fire' (Henry Pelling, *The British Communist Party: A Historical Profile* (London, 1958), p. 114).

10 I. V. Stalin, *Сочинения* (Stanford, 1967), II [xv], pp. 14–15, cf. John Lukacs, *The Last European War: September 1939/December 1941* (London, 1976), pp. 293–4.

11 *The Memoirs of General the Lord Ismay* (London, 1960), p. 234; FO 371/29607, 11–12, 15–22, 27–8 ('these soldiers were very badly treated in Russian prisons': 23); FO 371/32981, 27; Tadeusz Wittlin, *A Reluctant Traveller in Russia* (London, 1952), pp. 59–61. An Englishman named Hamilton Gold was in the Zhoutilki Gaol in the summer of 1939 (*Le Procès Kravchenko contre Les Lettres Françaises* (Paris, 1951), p. 559).

12 V. Stanley Vardys, *Lithuania Under the Soviets: Portrait of a Nation, 1940–65* (New York, 1965), p. 49.

13 *The Baltic States 1940–1972* (Stockholm, 1972), p. 31.

14 I. V. Stalin, op. cit., II [xv], p. 5.

15 *Documents on German Foreign Policy*, Series D, IX, pp. 474–5, 548–50, 561, 572–3, 582–3; Vardys, op. cit., pp. 49–52; K. Pelékis, *Genocide: Lithuania's Threefold Tragedy* (Germany, 1949), pp. 38–40; Agnis Balodis, *Sovjets och Nazitysklands uppgörelse om de baltiska staterna* (Stockholm, 1978), pp. 44–6. The Soviet note of 14 June is printed in Degras (ed.), op. cit., III, pp. 453–5.

16 Ibid., III, pp. 455–6; *Documents on German Foreign Policy*, Series D, IX, pp. 574–5; Alfreds Berzinsh, *I Saw Vishinsky Bolshevize Latvia* (Washington, 1948), pp. 15–24; Arveds Schwabe, *The Story of Latvia: A Historical Survey* (Stockholm, 1950), pp. 54–6; Balodis, op. cit., pp. 46–7. Stalin himself played his part in lulling Latvian fears before the attack: cf. Joseph Czapski, *The Inhuman Land* (London, 1951), p. 211.

17 *Documents on German Foreign Policy*, Series D, IX, pp. 581, 589; *Communist Takeover and Occupation of Estonia: Special Report No. 3 of the Select Committee on Communist Aggression* (Washington, 1955), pp. 8–9; Evald Uustalu, *The History of the Estonian People* (London, 1952), pp. 240–1; *Nazi-Soviet Conspiracy and The Baltic States* (London, 1948), pp. 46–8.

18 *Estonia between the two World Wars* (Tallinn, 1973), pp. 184–5.

19 'Estonia 1940–41', *The Nineteenth Century and After* (1946), CXXXIX, p. 40.

20 *Documents on German Foreign Policy*, Series D, IX, pp. 577–80, 687–8.
21 These documents are preserved on file at the Consulate-General of Estonia in New York, to whom I am obliged for the supply of photocopies. For the similar fate of a Latvian Minister, see Czapski, op. cit., pp. 207–8.
22 Roy A. Medvedev, *Let History Judge: The Origins and Consequences of Stalinism* (London, 1972), p. 216.
23 *Documents on German Foreign Policy*, Series D, IX, p. 268. Zhdanov seems to have been angling for a post as a Baltic *Gauleiter* since at least 1936; cf. Max Beloff, *The Foreign Policy of Soviet Russia 1929–1941* (Oxford, 1949), II, p. 78.
24 Robert Conquest, *The Great Terror: Stalin's Purge of the Thirties* (London, 1968), p. 428.
25 Rolfs Ekmanis, *Latvian Literature under the Soviets 1940–1975* (Belmont, Mass., 1978), p. 51.
26 Berzinsh, op. cit., pp. 41–3.
27 Victor Kravchenko, *I Chose Freedom* (London, 1947), p. 344.
28 *The Nineteenth Century and After*, CXXXIX, p. 41.
29 Berzinsh, op. cit., pp. 52–3. A Soviet historian describes it 'as a fact, that Soviet power was "established in a peaceful way, without the bloodshed of armed struggle"' (I. A. Shteiman, *Тактика Компартии Латвии в социалистической революции 1940 года* (Riga, 1977), p. 44).
30 Pelékis, op. cit., pp. 42–58. The assassins live on in honourable retirement in the Soviet Union. A certain Juozas Vildziunas, of the Lithuanian NKVD, has published a proud memoir of his activities in 1940: 'Rudasis lagaminas', *Svyturys* (Vilnyus, August 1968), pp. 20–2. Compare also *The Dark Side of the Moon* (London, 1946), pp. 50–2.
31 Ibid., p. 52; Gustav Herling, *A World Apart* (London, 1951), p. 168. The continuing need for fresh supplies of slave labour for GULAG (David J. Dallin and Boris I. Nicolaevsky, *Forced Labor in Soviet Russia* (London, 1948), p. 104; Mikhail Rozanov, *Завоеватели белых пятен* (Limburg, 1951), p. 274) may account for the abductions, but not for the murders and tortures.
32 Seidl (ed.), op. cit., p. 91.
33 *Documents on German Foreign Policy*, Series D, IX, pp. 396–7, 415–16, 419, 466–70.
34 Seidl (ed.), op. cit., pp. 182–7, 189–92. On 23 June *Izvestia* published an official statement stressing 'that the good-neighbourly relations . . . between the USSR and Germany . . . are based not on opportunist considerations of a transitory character but on the fundamental political interests of the USSR and Germany' (Degras, ed., op. cit., III, p. 457).
35 FO 371/29498, 32–5.
36 Ruta U., *Dear God, I Wanted to Live* (New York, 1978), pp. 77, 84.

37 Albert Konrad Herling, *The Soviet Slave Empire* (New York, 1951), p. 113; Dallin and Nicolaevsky, op. cit., p. 265; Vladimir Petrov, *My Retreat from Russia* (Yale, 1950), pp. 204, 222–3, John A. Armstrong, *Ukrainian Nationalism* (New York, 1955), p. 72.

38 For example, Adam B. Ulam, *Stalin: The Man and his Era* (London, 1974), pp. 524–5; Vardys, op. cit., pp. 48–9.

39 Sontag and Beddie (eds), op. cit., pp. 148, 153–4.

40 Pelékis, op. cit., p. 40.

41 FO 371/29498, 34–5.

42 Ekmanis, op. cit., pp. 66–7. Long after Soviet propaganda claimed that the annexation had been a preventive measure against *Germany*, Khrushchev recalled the atmosphere of the time. 'The way we looked at it, if a full-scale war broke out, and if England, France or Germany tried to launch an invasion against us, they might have tried to use the territories of Lithuania, Latvia, and Estonia as a staging area' (Strobe Talbott, ed., *Khrushchev Remembers* (Boston, 1970), p. 149). The order is significant.

43 Seidl (ed.), op. cit., p. 195. Stalin's view represented long-standing Soviet policy. Back in 1923, Radek had warned: 'If Entente capital, having torn Germany to pieces, were to establish its hegemony over her, on the backs of the conquered German workers, this would signify the greatest danger for Soviet Russia' (Lionel Kochan, *Russia and the Weimar Republic* (London, 1954), p. 83).

XII Clearing the Decks

1 James F. Byrnes, *All in One Lifetime* (London, 1960), p. 383.

2 *Documents on German Foreign Policy* (London, 1956), Series D, IX, pp. 379–83.

3 Max Beloff, *The Foreign Policy of Soviet Russia 1929–1941* (London, 1949), II, pp. 330–1, 335, 341–2; Gerd R. Ueberschär, *Hitler und Finland 1939–1941: Die Deutsch-Finnischen Beziehungen während des Hitler-Stalin-Paktes* (Wiesbaden, 1978), pp. 179–99.

4 Alfred Seidl (ed.), *Die Beziehungen zwischen Deutschland und der Sowjetunion 1939–1941* (Tübingen, 1949), pp. 193–4, 198, 199, 203–4, 212.

5 Ibid., pp. 200–18.

6 Ibid., pp. 218–29.

7 F. H. Hinsley, *Hitler's Strategy* (Cambridge, 1951), pp. 89–95, 116–19, 123–30; David Irving, *Hitler's War* (London, 1977), pp. 133–51.

8 Seidl (ed.), op. cit., pp. 229–97; Paul Schmidt, *Hitler's Interpreter* (London, 1951), pp. 209–20; Gustav Hilger and Alfred G. Meyer, *The Incompatible Allies: A Memoir-History of German-Soviet Relations*

1918–1941 (New York, 1953), pp. 321–4; Gerhard L. Weinberg, *Germany and the Soviet Union 1939–1941* (Leiden, 1954), pp. 140–4; Irving, op. cit., pp. 178–80; V. M. Berezhkov, *С дипломатической миссией в Берлин 1940–1941* (Moscow, 1966), pp. 22–48.

9 Seidl (ed.), op. cit., pp. 298–302; Irving, op. cit., pp. 181–93. On 12 December 1940 Ambassador Dekanozov presented Ribbentrop with a signed photograph of Stalin (*Documents on German Foreign Policy 1918–1945* (London, 1961), Series D, XI, p. 855).

10 Hilger and Meyer, op. cit., p. 291.

11 Stalin related the story to Churchill in 1942 (Winston S. Churchill, *Their Finest Hour* (London, 1949), p. 518). But compare the wary comment of Adam B. Ulam, *Stalin: The Man and his Era* (London, 1974), p. 527.

12 Schmidt, op. cit., p. 210.

13 Hilger and Meyer, op. cit., p. 326.

14 FO 371/29480, 23–8.

15 Seidl (ed.), op. cit., p. 372.

16 Ibid., pp. 372–3.

17 Cripps was one of the few foreign observers who appreciated that Stalin on the whole feared a British victory more than a German one (Sir Llewellyn Woodward, *British Foreign Policy in the Second World War* (London, 1962), pp. 144–50).

18 Seidl (ed.), op. cit., pp. 302–98; Beloff, op. cit., II, pp. 355–84.

19 A. M. Nekrich, *1941: 22 Июня* (Moscow, 1965), pp. 120–1.

20 Winston S. Churchill, *The Grand Alliance* (London, 1950), pp. 319–23.

21 Raymond J. Sontag and James S. Beddie (eds), *Nazi-Soviet Relations 1939–1941* (Washington, 1948), p. 328.

22 Bertram D. Wolfe, *Khrushchev and Stalin's Ghost* (New York, 1957), pp. 164–8.

23 F. W. Deakin and G. R. Storry, *The case of Richard Sorge* (New York, 1966), pp. 228–31; Nekrich, op. cit., pp. 117–19.

24 Ibid., pp. 115–16.

25 *История Великой Отечественной войны Советского Союза 1941–1945* (Moscow, 1965), VI, p. 135.

26 Nekrich, op. cit., pp. 126–41.

27 Hilger and Meyer, op. cit., pp. 331–2.

28 A. I. Chugunov (ed.), *Пограничные Войска в Годы Отечественной Войны 1941–1945* (Moscow, 1968), pp. 53–5.

29 Nekrich, op. cit., pp. 124–5.

30 For further details, compare Barry A. Leach, *German Strategy Against Russia 1939–1941* (Oxford, 1973), p. 170; Heinz Höhne, *Codeword: Direktor: The Story of the Red Orchestra* (London, 1971), p. 237; John Erickson, 'The Red Army before June 1941', *Soviet Affairs* (London,

1962), III, p. 116; his 'The Soviet Response to Surprise Attack: Three Directives, 22 June 1941', *Soviet Studies* (1971–2), XXIII, pp. 519–30; and his *The Road to Stalingrad: Stalin's War with Germany* (London, 1975), pp. 87–97; Roy A. Medvedev, *Let History Judge: The Origins and Consequences of Stalinism* (London, 1972), pp. 447–51.

31 For the NKVD operation in Poland, see *The Dark Side of the Moon* (London, 1946), pp. 52–3.

32 Cf. W. G. Krivitsky, *I Was Stalin's Agent* (London, 1939), pp. 198–201. The main purpose of the decree was to threaten defendants at purge trials with reprisals on their children should they fail to co-operate (Alexander Orlov, *The Secret History of Stalin's Crimes* (London, 1954), pp. 53–4, 88).

33 Hans Becker, *Devil on my Shoulder* (London, 1955), p. 156.

34 *These Names Accuse: Nominal List of Latvians Deported to Soviet Russia in 1940–41* (Stockholm, 1951), pp. 29–30; *The Dark Side of the Moon*, p. 87.

35 Compare the captured record of movements of Latvians in *These Names Accuse*, pp. 52–3.

36 Erickson, *The Road to Stalingrad*, pp. 97–8.

37 Hilger and Meyer, op. cit., p. 336. For the purges immediately preceding the invasion, compare Albert Konrad Herling, *The Soviet Slave Empire* (New York, 1951), pp. 51–61, 72, 79–81, 90–7, 210–17; David J. Dallin and Boris I. Nicolaevsky, *Forced Labor in Soviet Russia* (London, 1948), pp. 265–74; 'Estonia 1940–41', *The Nineteenth Century and After* (1946), CXXXIX, pp. 45–6; Alfreds Berzinsh, *I Saw Vishinsky Bolshevize Latvia* (Washington, 1948), pp. 52–3. Ants Oras, 'Deportations in Estonia', *The Baltic Review* (1947), II, pp. 18–21; *Human Rights and Genocide in the Baltic States* (Stockholm, 1950), p. 20; Antoni Ekart, *Vanished without trace: The story of seven years in Soviet Russia* (London, 1954), pp. 196–7; Ruta U., *Dear God, I Wanted to Live* (New York, 1978), pp. 9–42; C. A. Smith (ed.), *Escape from Paradise* (London, 1954), pp. 41–2; Vladimir and Evdokia Petrov, *Empire of Fear* (London, 1956), p. 119. The melancholy volume *These Names Accuse* contains a list of thirty thousand Latvians deported by the Soviets at this time; see also Jānis Kronlins, *379 Baigā Gada Dienas: Latviešu jaunatnes un tās audzinātāju liktenis Baigajā 1940. un 41. gadā* (1967), pp. 208–341. I am extremely grateful to Mr Arnis Keksis, who collected a great deal of testimony for me on the Baltic purges, both oral and documentary. Only a proportion is quoted here, but that is amply confirmed by the remainder. Large-scale purges also took place in the Ukraine in the days preceding the German invasion (Hermann Raschhofer, *Political Assassination: The Legal Background of the Oberländer and Stashinsky Cases* (Tübingen, 1964), pp. 35, 49).

XIII Friends Fall Out

1 This outline is based on the full accounts provided by A. M. Nekrich (*1941: 22 Июня* (Moscow, 1965), pp. 154–8) and John Erickson (*The Road to Stalingrad* (London, 1975), pp. 112–25). Red Army troops were fraternizing with their Wehrmacht counterparts right up to the last minute (Antoni Ekart, *Vanished without trace: The story of seven years in Soviet Russia* (London, 1954), p. 219).

2 Erickson, op. cit., pp. 14–24, 61, 68.

3 Strobe Talbott (ed.), *Khrushchev Remembers* (Boston, 1970), p. 159. It was only after the invasion that the major effort to move Soviet industries safely eastwards was undertaken: cf. L. S. Rogachevskaya, *Социалистическое Соревнование в СССР: Исторические Очерки 1917–1970гг.* (Moscow, 1977), pp. 177–8; Victor Kravchenko, *I Chose Freedom* (London, 1947), pp. 364–5; A. S. Yakovlev, *Цель Жизни* (Moscow, 1966), pp. 262–3.

4 Alvin D. Coox, 'Japanese Foreknowledge of the Soviet-German War', *Soviet Studies* (1971–2), XXIII, p. 568.

5 Erickson, op. cit., pp. 8–9, 50–1; Nekrich, op. cit., pp. 75–7, 83–4; John Erickson, '1941', *Survey* (1962), XLIV–V, pp. 181–3; Kravchenko, op. cit., pp. 368–78; Otto Preston Chaney, Jr, *Zhukov* (Newton Abbot, 1972), pp. 75–84, 86; Roy A. Medvedev, *Let History Judge: The Origins and Consequences of Stalinism* (London, 1971), pp. 446–54. The British Military Attaché's poor opinion of the Soviet forces is contained in FO 371/23678, 147–64.

6 R. Ya. Malinovsky, 'Двадцатилетие начала Великой Отечественной войны', *Военно-исторический журнал* (1961), no. 6, p. 7; Captain N. F. Rybalko, 'В первый день войны на Черном море', ibid. (1963), no. 6, pp. 63–6; Admiral I. I. Azarov, *Осажденная Одесса* (Moscow, 1962), pp. 16–17.

7 Bertram D. Wolfe (ed.), *Khrushchev and Stalin's Ghost* (New York, 1957), pp. 176–8; Talbott (ed.), op. cit., pp. 166–9, 219; A. Avtorkhanov, *Загадка смерти Сталина, Заговор Берия* (Frankfurt, 1976), pp. 9–15.

8 Roy A. Medvedev, *On Stalin and Stalinism* (Oxford, 1979), p. 123.

9 Svetlana Alliluyeva, *Only One Year* (London, 1969), p. 352.

10 Victor Kravchenko, op. cit., p. 429.

11 Mikhail Soloviev, *My Nine Lives in the Red Army* (New York, 1955), p. 262.

12 Medvedev, *Let History Judge*, p. 457; Talbott (ed.), op. cit., pp. 169–70. Ambassador Maisky in London received no instructions for several days (A. Avtorkhanov, 'Закулисная история пакта "Риббентроп-Молотов"', *Континент* (1975), IV, p. 315).

13 I. V. Stalin, *Сочинения* (Stanford, 1967), III [XVI], p. 6.

14 Adam B. Ulam, *Stalin: The Man and his Era* (London, 1974), pp. 477, 630–1.

15 Cf. Amnon Sella, 'Red Army Doctrine and Training on the Eve of the Second World War', *Soviet Studies* (1975), XXVII, pp. 245–64.

16 Robert Conquest, *The Great Terror: Stalin's Purge of the Thirties* (London, 1968), p. 488. John Erickson too finds this 'difficult to explain' (*The Road to Stalingrad*, p. 77).

17 John Erickson, 'The Soviet Response to Surprise Attack: Three Directives, 22 June 1941', *Soviet Studies* (1971–2), XXIII, pp. 533–4, 537, 549–50. Cf. Wolfe, op. cit., p. 172; Medvedev, op. cit., p. 457. The absurdity of the explanation that any sort of precautions might provoke a German attack was patent to senior commanders at the time; cf. General N. N. Voronov, *На службе военной* (Moscow, 1963), pp. 172–5.

18 Medvedev, *On Stalin and Stalinism*, p. 121.

19 'My Meeting with Stalin', *The American Magazine* (December 1941). Stalin's outrage at Hitler's treaty-breaking was stressed with what seems a marked suggestion of personal betrayal (Robert E. Sherwood, *Roosevelt and Hopkins: An Intimate History* (New York, 1948), p. 328).

20 Stalin, op. cit., II [XV], p. 27.

21 Gustav Hilger and Alfred G. Meyer, *The Incompatible Allies: A Memoir-History of German-Soviet Relations 1918–1941* (New York, 1953), p. 270.

22 Solomon Volkov (ed.), *Testimony: The Memoirs of Dmitri Shostakovich* (London, 1979), p. 72.

23 Boris Bajanov, *Bajanov révèle Staline: Souvenirs d'un ancien secrétaire de Staline* (Paris, 1979), p. 27.

24 Walter Schellenberg, *The Schellenberg Memoirs* (London, 1956), pp. 45–9; 'Geoffrey Bailey', *The Conspirators* (London, 1961), pp. 180–201; Medvedev, *Let History Judge*, pp. 300–1; Nekrich, op. cit., pp. 86–7; Conquest, op. cit., pp. 206–23. As Tukhachevsky had received ominous warnings before his fall (ibid., pp. 171, 212), it is possible he contemplated a pre-emptive *coup*. Indeed, it would be extraordinary if he did not. Professor Ulam thinks 'Stalin at least half seriously believed there was a plot' (op. cit., pp. 452–3). Tukhachevsky's daughter ended up in a camp too (ibid., p. 244).

25 Robert J. O'Neill, *The German Army and the Nazi Party, 1933–1939* (London, 1966), pp. 139–50.

26 F. L. Carsten, 'New "Evidence" against Marshal Tukhachevsky', *The Slavonic and East European Review* (1974), LII, pp. 272–3. Two of Rokossovsky's General Staff Officers were working for the German SD at a later date (Schellenberg, op. cit., p. 307).

27 Ulam, op. cit., pp. 528, 531. This was the view held at the Soviet Embassy in Berlin (*Documents on German Foreign Policy 1918–1945* (London, 1961), Series D, XI, p. 1,036).

28 Nekrich, op. cit., p. 127; George F. Kennan, *Russia and the West under Lenin and Stalin* (Boston, 1961), pp. 334–6. Stalin may also have reflected how much Hitler owed his position to Communist aid and intrigues (ibid., pp. 286–92).

29 Erickson, *The Road to Stalingrad*, p. 91.

30 Ibid., p. 125.

31 General I. V. Tiulenev, Через три войны, (Moscow, 1960), pp. 140–2.

32 Schellenberg, op. cit., pp. 48–9.

33 Talbott (ed.), op. cit., pp. 134, 141.

34 Stalin in 1945 betrayed some apprehension lest Hitler be 'not dead but . . . hiding somewhere' (Charles E. Bohlen, *Witness to History 1929–1969* (London, 1973), p. 220). Martin Bormann could have told more of Nazi-Soviet links, perhaps, had he lived. Bormann favoured a *rapport* with Stalin (Schellenberg, op. cit., pp. 353, 360). An account of Bormann's alleged involvement with the NKVD is provided in 'Ivan Krylov', *Soviet Staff Officer* (London, 1951), pp. 69–70. The work is a forgery (Thomas T. Hammond, ed., *Soviet Foreign Relations and World Communism* (Princeton, 1965), p. 1,099), but emanates from an interesting source (cf. Gordon Brook-Shepherd, *The Storm Petrels: The First Soviet Defectors, 1928–1938* (London, 1977), p. 105), and its circumstantial account deserves further investigation. In 1945 the NKVD took elaborate measures to destroy German records of exchanges concerning the 1939–41 Pact (John Lukacs, *The Last European War: September 1939/December 1941* (London, 1976), p. 530).

35 Vojtech Mastny, *Russia's Road to the Cold War: Diplomacy, Warfare, and the Politics of Communism, 1941–1945* (New York, 1979), p. 34. The Soviet writer Konstantin Simonov finds Stalin's refusal to accept reality 'incomprehensible' (Medvedev, op. cit., p. 453). Hitler's confidence that the Soviet Union would never wage aggressive war so long as Stalin remained in charge suggests he believed he had reason to trust him (cf. Max Beloff, *The Foreign Policy of Soviet Russia 1929–1941* (Oxford, 1949), II, pp. 355–6).

36 Stanislaw Kot, *Conversations with the Kremlin and Dispatches from Russia* (London, 1963), pp. XIX–XX.

37 Ortwin Buchbender, *Das tönende Erz: Deutsche Propaganda gegen die Rote Armee im Zweiten Weltkrieg* (Stuttgart, 1978), pp. 84–5, cf. Kravchenko, op. cit., pp. 357–8; Hitler's claim to have feared Soviet aggression was entirely spurious (Barry A. Leach, *German Strategy Against Russia 1939–1941* (Oxford, 1973), pp. 69–71, 141, 174–5), though he certainly had long-term strategic reasons for going to war

with the USSR (George F. Kennan, *Memoirs 1925–1950* (Boston, 1967), pp. 72, 131).

38 Konstantin Cherkassov, *Генерал Кононов: Ответ перед Историей за одну Попытку* (Melbourne, 1963), I, p. 129. For a similarly tragic family casualty list, see Mikhail Rozanov, *Завоеватели белых пятен* (Limburg, 1951), p. 284.

39 Cf. Wilfried Strik-Strikfeldt, *Against Stalin and Hitler: Memoir of the Russian Liberation Movement 1941–5* (London, 1970), pp. 21–36; David Littlejohn, *The Patriotic Traitors* (London, 1972), pp. 306–7. The deadening effect of Soviet propaganda, abusing with equal zest every political system except one, could lead even a Soviet Jew to disbelieve anti-Nazi propaganda (Bernhard Roeder, *Katorga: An Aspect of Modern Slavery* (London, 1958), p. 63). This propaganda-induced naïveté is well summarized by George Fischer, *Soviet Opposition to Stalin* (Harvard, 1952), pp. 137–42, and A. Kazantsev, *Третья Сила: история одной попытки* (Frankfurt, 1974), pp. 71–6.

40 Richard H. Ullmann, *Britain and the Russian Civil War* (Princeton, 1968), p. 153.

XIV   War on Two Fronts

1 Eugene Lyons, *Stalin: Czar of all the Russias* (London, 1940), p. 250.

2 I. V. Stalin, *Сочинения* (Stanford, 1967), II [XV], pp. 1–10.

3 Gustav Herling, *A World Apart* (London, 1951), p. 175; cf. Alexander Solzhenitsyn, *Архипелаг Гулаг 1918-1956: Опыт Художественного Исследования* (Paris, 1973–5), III, p. 29; Victor Kravchenko, *I Chose Freedom* (London, 1947), p. 359; Adam B. Ulam, *Stalin: The Man and his Era* (London, 1974), pp. 541–2. Russian émigrés listened with cynical amusement (Anatoly V. Baikaloff, 'The Guilty Man', *The Weekly Review* (July 1941), pp. 183–4), whilst the Foreign Office was agitated at Reuter's frank report of Stalin's nervous delivery (FO 371/29467, 12–17). In August 1939 an interpreter at the German Embassy in Moscow was handed a message from a group of peasants she had visited in the countryside near the city. 'How could your Hitler ally himself with our Stalin?' it read; 'we have hoped so much of your Hitler, that he would come and free us!' (Information kindly supplied by Dr Ehrenfried Schütte; Frau Schütte had been the interpreter.)

4 Svetlana Alleluyeva, *Only One Year* (London, 1969), p. 354; Strobe Talbott (ed.), *Khrushchev Remembers* (Boston, 1970), p. 310. Party organization operated under NKVD tutelage (A. Avtorkhanov, 'Закулисная история пакта "Риббентроп-Молотов" ', *Континент* (1975), IV, p. 314).

5 Stanislaw Kot, *Conversations with the Kremlin and Dispatches from Russia* (London, 1963), p. 53.

6 'A. I. Romanov', *Nights Are Longest There: Smersh from the Inside* (London, 1972), pp. 141–2; Oleg Penkovskiy, *The Penkovskiy Papers* (New York, 1965), pp. 37–8; Roy A. Medvedev, *On Stalin and Stalinism* (Oxford, 1979), p. 133.

7 NA 861.00/11897; 'A. I. Romanov', op. cit., pp. 29–30; Antoni Ekart, *Vanished without trace: The story of seven years in Soviet Russia* (London, 1954), p. 261; Robert Conquest, *The Great Terror: Stalin's Purge of the Thirties* (London, 1968), p. 491; Adam B. Ulam, *Expansion and Coexistence: the History of Soviet Foreign Policy, 1917–1967* (London, 1968), p. 322.

8 Boris Bajanov, *Bajanov révèle Staline: Souvenirs d'un ancien secrétaire de Staline* (Paris, 1979), p. 144. Cf. Ulam, *Stalin: The Man and his Era*, p. 281.

9 Cf. Ronald Hingley, *Joseph Stalin: Man and Legend* (London, 1974), pp. 305–6; Conquest, op. cit., p. 488.

10 Jean van Heijenoort, *With Trotsky in Exile* (Harvard, 1978), p. 63. Trotsky's political views at this time were if anything even crazier (Medvedev, op. cit., pp. 135–8).

11 F. W. Deakin and G. R. Storry, *The case of Richard Sorge* (New York, 1966), pp. 199–203; Alexander Orlov, *The Secret History of Stalin's Crimes* (London, 1954), pp. 225–6; Roy A. Medvedev, *Let History Judge: The Origins and Consequences of Stalinism* (London, 1972), pp. 244–5. The fullest account is that of Alvin D. Coox, 'L'Affaire Lyushkov: Anatomy of a Defector', *Soviet Studies* (1967–8), XIX, pp. 405–20.

12 FO 371/23699, 1. The excision must have taken place before the file was deposited in the Public Record Office, as the pagination makes no allowance for the missing pages.

13 Medvedev, op. cit., p. 312; Alliluyeva, op. cit., p. 353; Talbott (ed.), op. cit., p. 170; Conquest, op. cit., pp. 489–90; John Erickson, *The Road to Stalingrad* (London, 1975), pp. 159–60, 176; Michael Parrish, 'Command and Leadership in the Soviet Air Force During the Great Patriot War', *Aerospace Historian* (1979), XXVI, pp. 195–7.

14 Merle Fainsod, *Smolensk under Soviet Rule* (London, 1958), pp. 335–42.

15 Conquest, op. cit., p. 215.

16 Ulam, op. cit., p. 457; Otto P. Chaney, Jr, *Zhukov* (Newton Abbot, 1972), pp. 92–3. The succession of Air Force Chief Commissars remains unclear (*Aerospace Historian*, XXVI, pp. 194–5).

17 General A. B. Gorbatov, 'Годы и Войны', *Новый Мир* (May 1964), XL, p. 113. For examples of the commissars' ceaseless spying and interference, see pp. 117–18, 127–8; Mikhail Soloviev, *My Nine Lives in the Red Army* (New York, 1955), pp. 90–108.

18 Chaney, op. cit., pp. 242–3, 257, 322. A tellingly sarcastic anecdote is given by Victor Nekrassov in his vivid dramatization, *В Окопах Сталинграда* (Moscow, 1955), pp. 145–8. An eye-witness account of the revolting and motiveless murder of a civilian by a *politruk* is provided by 'N.N.N.', *На фронте 1941 года и в плену, воспоминания врача* (Buenos Aires, 1974), pp. 32–4.

19 Vladimir Petrov, *It Happens in Russia: Seven Years Forced Labour in the Siberian Goldfields* (London, 1951), pp. 297–8; Ekart, op. cit., p. 218.

20 A. M. Nekrich, *1941: 22 Июня* (Moscow, 1965), p.113.

21 Vladimir and Evdokia Petrov, *Empire of Fear* (London, 1956), pp. 98–9; 'A. I. Romanov', op. cit., pp. 68–74; Kravchenko, op. cit., p. 369; *Soviet Military Intelligence: Two Sketches*, Research Program on the USSR (New York, 1952), pp. 15–24.

22 Kot, op. cit., p. 53; 'N.N.N.', op. cit., p. 38; Raphael Rupert, *A Hidden World* (London, 1963), p. 94; Soloviev, op. cit., pp. 225, 248–9, 308.

23 Nikolai Tolstoy, *Victims of Yalta* (London, 1977), pp. 33–6, 396–8.

24 Stalin, op. cit., II [xv], p. 13. The statistics are wildly inaccurate.

25 Ibid., pp. 15–16. He returned to this theme two years later (ibid., p. 118).

26 G. A. Tokaev, *Comrade X* (London, 1956), p. 216. Stalin himself was making similarly anxious inquiries in 1942 (ibid., pp. 237–9).

27 FO 371/29499, 38; Kravchenko, op. cit., pp. 353–4, 361–2.

28 CAB 66/54, 125, 126, 127, 131; Vladimir Petrov, *My Retreat from Russia* (Yale, 1950), pp. 40–1; The Earl of Avon, *The Eden Memoirs: The Reckoning* (London, 1965), pp. 301–2; Kravchenko, op. cit., pp. 362–3, 370, 375–7; Chaney, op. cit., pp. 150–2; Anatoli Granovsky, *All Pity Choked: The Memoirs of a Soviet Secret Agent* (London, 1955), pp. 123–4; Soloviev, op. cit., pp. 243–63, 300; Ekart, op. cit., pp. 98–9. It is interesting (and puzzling) to note that the day after the NKVD resumed control in Moscow (19 October) the Moscow (Intelligence) Centre went off the air for six weeks (Alexander Foote, *Handbook for Spies* (London, 1964), p. 98). The US Embassy later discovered confirmation of the destruction of NKVD archives in 1941 (Walter Bedell Smith, *Moscow Mission 1946–1949* (London, 1950), p. 177). For the circumstances of the drafting of the State Defence Committee Decree, see Lieut.-General K. F. Telegin, 'Москва — фронтовой город', *Вопросы исмории КПСС* (1966), no. 9, pp. 104–7.

29 Joseph Czapski, *The Inhuman Land* (London, 1951), pp. 14–17, 138, 222; Kot, op. cit., pp. 53, 62–3, 70, 71, 264. Compare the interesting letter from a Latvian observer published in *The Times*, 12 August 1980; Alexander I. Solzhenitsyn, *The Mortal Danger, How Misconceptions about Russia Imperil the West* (London, 1980), pp. 39–40.

30 Soviet accounts of Baltic and Ukrainian resistance are naturally highly tendentious, but reveal the extent of their concern with the problem by their sheer bulk. Cf. *Soviet Intelligence and Security Services* [1964–72]: *A Selected Bibliography of Soviet Publications, With Some Additional Titles From Other Sources* (Washington, 1972–5), I, items 221–6, 264, 265, 505–6, 509, 522, 668, 692a, 696; II, 173, 202, 265, 453, 524, 669, 832, 908, 961, 1,106, 1,432, 1,502, 1,513.

31 Margarete Buber, *Under Two Dictators* (London, 1949), p. 83; Kot, op. cit., p. 164; Ekart, op. cit., p. 98.

32 Kravchenko, op. cit., pp. 354–7, 367–8, 388; Ekart, op. cit., pp. 94–5; Petrov, op. cit., pp. 27, 83–5.

33 Robert Conquest, *The Nation Killers: The Soviet Deportation of Nationalities* (London, 1970), pp. 59–66, 107–9; Frank H. Epp, *Mennonite Exodus: The Rescue and Resettlement of the Russian Mennonites since the Russian Revolution* (Manitoba, 1962), pp. 352–3; Bernhard Roeder, *Katorga: An Aspect of Modern Slavery* (London, 1958), pp. 140–4; Petrov, op. cit., p. 32.

34 Kravchenko, op. cit., pp. 355–6.

35 Ekart, op. cit., p. 99; Vladimir and Evdokia Petrov, *Empire of Fear*, p. 98.

36 Wilfried Strik-Strikfeldt, *Against Stalin and Hitler: Memoir of the Russian Liberation Movement* (London, 1970), pp. 26–7.

37 Kravchenko, op. cit., pp. 356, 405.

38 Petrov, *My Retreat from Russia*, pp. 125–7.

39 Czapski, op. cit., pp. 69–80. The Pole had yet to comprehend the full extent of the Soviet police world. Twenty degrees below was nothing to the habitués of GULAG; in Kolyma a prisoner at this time noted sardonically that 'the frost fell suddenly to 30 degrees below zero – winter had already ended' (Varlam Shalamov, *Колымские Рассказы* (London, 1978), p. 33).

40 Conquest, *The Great Terror*, pp. 491–2; Medvedev, op. cit., pp. 248–9; Solzhenitsyn, *Архипелаг Гулаг*, I, pp. 88–9; Leonid Plyushch, *History's Carnival: A Dissident's Autobiography* (London, 1979), pp. 188–9; *Communist Takeover and Occupation of Ukraine: Special Report No. 4 of the Select Committee on Communist Aggression* (Washington, 1955), p. 28. Again and again the Germans discovered ghastly relics in death cells (cf. Petrov, op. cit., pp. 110–11, 112–13). Details of the grim find at Dubno are taken from the *Kriegstagebuch* of Herr Wilhelm Heitkampf, then serving with 6 Komp. Panzer-Nachr. Regt 1 (letter kindly passed to me by Dr de Zayas).

41 K. Pelékis, *Genocide: Lithuania's Threefold Tragedy* (Germany, 1949), pp. 54–8.

42 This account draws chiefly on the numerous depositions and other

documents quoted by Hermann Raschhofer, *Political Assassination: The Legal Background of the Oberländer and Stashinsky Cases* (Tübingen, 1964), pp. 32–52, 194–7, 202, 205–6; Unto Parvilahti, *Beria's Gardens: Ten Years' Captivity in Russia and Siberia* (London, 1959), p. 25; John A. Armstrong, *Ukrainian Nationalism 1939–1945* (New York, 1955), pp. 76–7; Alfred M. de Zayas, *Die Wehrmacht-Untersuchungsstelle: Deutsche Ermittlungen über alliierte Völker-rechtsverletzungen im Zweiten Weltkrieg* (Munich, 1980), pp. 333–54. Evidence for numerous comparable massacres behind the retreating firing-line are to be found in ibid., pp. 327–32, 348. The order to effect the massacre bore the initials of Nikita Khrushchev, then Party boss of the Ukraine (Raschhofer, op. cit., p. 49). I am indebted to Mr Bohdan Kazaniwsky, a survivor of the L'vov massacre, for a detailed account of his experiences in the Brigidky prison.

43 Petrov, op. cit., p. 174.

44 Vladimir Petrov, *Escape from the Future: The Incredible Adventures of a Young Russian* (Bloomington, Indiana, 1973), p. 176; 'A. I. Romanov', op. cit., p. 50; Raphael Rupert, *A Hidden World* (London, 1963), p. 119; Soloviev, op. cit., p. 288. Significantly, Beria was the only adviser to whom Stalin turned during the panic-stricken early days after the invasion (A. Avtorkhanov, *Загадка смерти Сталина, Заговор Берия* (Frankfurt, 1976), p. 15).

45 Herling, op. cit., pp. 41, 174–8.

46 Petrov, *My Retreat from Russia*, pp. 1–3; compare the precautions taken in a camp near Vladimir (Ekart, op. cit., p. 88).

47 Joseph Scholmer, *Vorkuta* (London, 1954), pp. 168–9.

48 *Correspondence between the Chairman of the Council of Ministers of the U.S.S.R. and the Presidents of the U.S.A. and the Prime Ministers of Great Britain during the Great Patriotic War of 1941–1945* (Moscow, 1957), I, pp. 21, 24. On 28 September Stalin pressed Beaverbrook on the point in Moscow (FO 371/29470, 57, 62), and Ambassador Maisky re-peated it in London in October (ibid., 116). Stalin was said to be still toying with the idea in mid-December (FO 371/29472, 154); cf. Joan Beaumont, *Comrades in Arms: British Aid to Russia 1941–1945* (London, 1980), pp. 69–70. Even earlier, Stalin had asked Hopkins for 'American troops on any part of the Russian front under the complete command of the American Army' (Robert E. Sherwood, *Roosevelt and Hopkins: An Intimate History* (New York, 1948), p. 343).

49 Cf. Conquest, op. cit., p. 358. This enormous waste of manpower of course continued throughout the war (Solzhenitsyn, op. cit., II, pp. 130, 370–2; III, 9–12, 236).

50 Erickson, op. cit., p. 166.

51 Ibid., pp. 142–3.

52 Jānis Kronlins, *379 baigā gada Dienas: Latviešu jaunatnes un tās audzinātāju liktenis Baigajā 1940. un 41. gada* (1967), pp. 355–6.

53 NA Decimal Files, 861.00/10–246, compare also the appalling incident described by Solzhenitsyn from 1938 (op. cit., II, p. 545).

54 Kravchenko, op. cit., pp. 340, 341.

55 Tadeusz Wittlin, *A Reluctant Traveller in Russia* (London, 1952), p. 132.

56 Petrov, op. cit., p. 4; cf. ibid., pp. 50, 77.

57 Solzhenitsyn, op. cit., III, pp. 239–40; Dimitri Panin, *The Notebooks of Sologdin* (London, 1976), pp. 88–91. Hopes of a further uprising were not extinguished, though (ibid., pp. 103–5, 123–4, 161).

58 Peter Pirogov, *Why I Escaped* (London, 1950), pp. 56, 60–3; Ekart, op. cit., pp. 69–70, 90–1, 98; Herling, op. cit., p. 231; Solzhenitsyn, op. cit., III, pp. 29–34; Petrov, *It Happens in Russia*, pp. 235, 276; C. A. Smith (ed.), *Escape from Paradise* (London, 1954), pp. 45, 236–7, 249–51; Hans Becker, *Devil on my Shoulder* (London, 1955), pp. 163, 208 (compare the bandits' attitude, ibid., p. 187). Some prisoners in 1942 managed to overpower their guards and escaped to join the Germans (David J. Dallin and Boris I. Nicolaevsky, *Forced Labor in Soviet Russia* (London, 1948), p. 23; Roeder, op. cit., p. 21). At least one of these men later fell into the hands of the British, who in 1945 obligingly handed him over to Beria for disposal (FO 371/47897, 111).

59 Roeder, op. cit., pp. 21–2; Scholmer, op. cit., pp. 168–9, 191–2. In 1940 prisoners in Vorkuta were said to have felt strong sympathy for the 'enemy' in the Finnish War (Mikhail Rozanov, *Завоеватели белых пятен* (Limburg, 1951), p. 234).

60 Herling, op. cit., pp. 175–6.

61 Ivan Solonevich, *Russia in Chains: A Record of Unspeakable Suffering* (London, 1938), pp. 23–4.

62 Walter Schellenberg, *The Schellenberg Memoirs* (London, 1956), p. 314.

63 Cf. Panin, op. cit., pp. 104–8.

64 Gerald Reitlinger, *The House Built on Sand: The Conflicts of German Policy in Russia 1939–1945* (London, 1960), pp. 283–4.

65 Cf. Scholmer, op. cit., pp. 169–71.

XV A Pyrrhic Victory

1 Adam B. Ulam, *Stalin: The Man and his Era* (London, 1974), pp. 477, 479–80, 491, 492; and his *Expansion and Coexistence: the History of Soviet Foreign Policy, 1917–1967* (London, 1968), p. 327.

2 Strobe Talbott (ed.), *Khrushchev Remembers* (Boston, 1970), p. 141; John A. Armstrong, *Ukrainian Nationalism 1939–1945* (New York,

1955), pp. 76–7, 83–4; V. Stanley Vardys, *Lithuania under the Soviets: Portrait of a Nation, 1940–65* (New York, 1965), pp. 66–8; Hugh Seton-Watson, *The Pattern of Communist Revolution: A Historical Analysis* (London, 1953), p. 230; Joseph Czapski, *The Inhuman Land* (London, 1951), p. 151.

3 For glimpses of Russian defeatism, see Stanislaw Kot, *Conversations with the Kremlin and Dispatches from Russia* (London, 1963), pp. 62–3, 70, 71; Vladimir Petrov, *My Retreat from Russia* (Yale, 1950), pp. 83–5; Matthew P. Gallagher, *The Soviet History of World War II* (New York, 1963), pp. 148–51. Budenny testified that Stalin nervously checked that Moscow was free from the danger of German bombing before daring to return to the capital to harangue the 6 November parade (A. Avtorkhanov, 'Закулисная история пакта "Риббентроп-Молотов" ', *Континенм* (1975), IV, p. 315).

4 Compare the views of General Sikorski and Sir Stafford Cripps (*Documents on Polish-Soviet Relations 1939–1945* (London, 1961), I, pp. 105–6). Harold Nicolson thought the Red Army would be 'bowled over at a touch', and 80 per cent of the War Office allowed the USSR just ten days of resistance (Harold Nicolson, *Diaries and Letters 1939–1945* (London, 1967), pp. 174, 175). Foreign Office views were similarly gloomy (FO 371/29499, 31–5). Cf. Joan Beaumont, *Comrades in Arms: British Aid to Russia 1941–1945* (London, 1980), pp. 26–7. The Turks thought the Red Army so wretched that it could help neither side (The Earl of Avon, *The Eden Memoirs: The Reckoning* (London, 1965), p. 155).

5 Robert Dallek, *Franklin D. Roosevelt and American Foreign Policy, 1932–1945* (New York, 1979), p. 279.

6 For further details, cf. pp. 281–2 above.

7 Antoni Ekart, *Vanished without trace: The story of seven years in Soviet Russia* (London, 1954), pp. 216–18; Thaddeus Wittlin, *Commissar: The Life and Death of Lavrenty Pavlovich Beria* (London, 1973), pp. 290–1, 293; Victor Kravchenko, *I Chose Freedom* (London, 1947), pp. 368–9, 377, 489–90; *Le Procès Kravchenko contre Les Lettres Françaises* (Paris, 1949), p. 169; G. Tokaev, *Comrade X* (London, 1956), pp. 235, 237; Mikhail Soloviev, *My Nine Lives in the Red Army* (New York, 1955), p. 181. The bravest of officers could still cringe at the mere sight of the green caps of NKVD border guards (Colonel I. T. Starinov, *Мину ждут своего часа* (Moscow, 1964), pp. 211–12; cf. Colonel-General L. M. Sandalov, *Трудные рубежи* (Moscow, 1965), p. 10).

8 David J. Dallin and Boris I. Nicolaevsky, *Forced Labor in Soviet Russia* (London, 1948), pp. 274–81.

9 The treatment of recaptured and returned Russians has been chronicled

in my *Victims of Yalta* (London, 1977), and that of the Crimean Tartars and other 'punished peoples' by Robert Conquest (*The Nation Killers: The Soviet Deportation of Nationalities* (London, 1970)) and Alexander Nekrich (*Наказанные Народы*) (New York, 1978)). Compare also Tokaev, op. cit., pp. 256–70; Talbott (ed.), op. cit., p. 312; Ekart, op. cit., pp. 221–3; Bertram D. Wolfe, *Khrushchev and Stalin's Ghost* (New York, 1957), pp. 190, 196; Unto Parvilahti, *Beria's Gardens: Ten Years' Captivity in Russia and Siberia* (London, 1959), pp. 119–22.

10 I. V. Stalin, *Сочинения* (Stanford, 1967), II [xv], pp. 1–35.

11 Roy A. Medvedev, *On Stalin and Stalinism* (Oxford, 1979), p. 124. Medvedev relates this anecdote to Stalin's 3 July broadcast, but the context clearly suggests the 7 November speech, which is a simplified version of that delivered to the Moscow Soviet on the previous day.

12 Merle Fainsod, *How Russia is Ruled* (Harvard, 1959), pp. 112–13. The rank of general had been reintroduced after the Finnish War (Ulam, *Stalin: The Man and his Era*, p. 523) and that of ambassador in May 1941 (Alfred Seidl, ed., *Die Beziehungen zwischen Deutschland und der Sowjetunion 1939–1941* (Tübingen, 1949), p. 388).

13 NA, RG 84, box 5. Harriman concluded wryly that 'he would never make such a statement today' (27 November 1945). For the replacement of ideology by patriotism in Party propaganda, see the report of Ronald Mathews of the *Daily Herald* (CAB 66, 125).

14 As noticed by the British and US Ambassadors (FO 800/301, 110; NA 861.22/98).

15 John Lukacs, *The Last European War: September 1939/December 1941* (London, 1976), p. 157.

16 Arthur Koestler, *The Yogi and the Commissar and other Essays* (London, 1945), pp. 196–8; Kravchenko, op. cit., pp. 420–1; Tokaev, op. cit., pp. 253–4; Gregory Klimov, *The Terror Machine: The inside story of the Soviet Administration in Germany* (London, 1953), pp. 29, 80–3, 314.

17 Nikolai Tolstoy, *Victims of Yalta*, p. 124.

18 Koestler, op. cit., pp. 198–9. Even the Leningrad streets were re-christened with their pre-Revolutionary names (Klimov, op. cit., pp. 22–3).

19 Tokaev, op. cit., pp. 223–7.

20 Medvedev, op. cit., pp. 124–6, 132; Koestler, op. cit., p. 195; CAB 66, 130; FO 371/29549, 35–7, 144. Shostakovich believed that Stalin's deeply superstitious nature helped to make this religious revival acceptable (Solomon Volkov, ed., *Testimony: The Memoirs of Dmitri Shostakovich* (London, 1979), pp. 144–7, 149). Roy Medvedev extols Stalin's statecraft (op. cit., p. 126). Solzhenitsyn makes a rather sharper

comment (*Архипелаг Гулаг 1918-1956: Опыт Художественного Исследования* (Paris, 1973–5), III, p. 19).

21 Kravchenko, op. cit., pp. 425–6; Tokaev, op. cit., pp. 249–52. When the concessions were in large part withdrawn after the war, Malenkov was skilfully made the Party scapegoat for having supposedly initiated them (Boris I. Nicolaevsky, *Power and the Soviet Elite* (New York, 1965), p. 259).

22 Elinor Lipper, *Eleven Years in Soviet Prison Camps* (London, 1951), pp. 142–6.

23 Kot, op. cit., p. 176.

24 Bernhard Roeder, *Katorga: An Aspect of Modern Slavery* (London, 1958), p. 258. Cf. CAB 66, 126; Lev Kopelev, *No Jail for Thought* (London, 1979), pp. 96, 121, 311; Peter Deriabin and Frank Gibney, *The Secret World* (London, 1960), pp. 45, 49; Kravchenko, op. cit., pp. 382–5; Petrov, op. cit., p. 92; 'Voinov', *Outlaw: The Autobiography of a Soviet Waif* (London, 1955), p. 205. 'Believe me', a senior Red Army officer threatened in his cups, 'let us just finish with Hitler, then we'll fix those bastards, the N.K.V.D. devils' (Menachem Begin, *White Nights: The Story of a Prisoner in Russia* (London, 1978), p. 238).

25 Barry A. Leach, *German Strategy Against Russia 1939–1941* (Oxford, 1973), pp. 152, 155–7, 196; *Documents on German Foreign Policy 1918–1945* (London, 1964), Series D, XIII, pp. 79, 92–3, 395, 910; Tolstoy, op. cit., pp. 35–8.

26 *Documents on German Foreign Policy*, Series D, XI, pp. 370–2.

27 *Hitler's Table Talk 1941–1944* (London, 1953), p. 400.

28 Soloviev, op. cit., pp. 205–6, 249; Klimov, op. cit., pp. 52–60, 218; Petrov, op. cit., pp. 87–9; Ekart, op. cit., pp. 134, 218–20; Roeder, op. cit., pp. 63–4; 'A. I. Romanov', *Nights are Longest There: Smersh from the Inside* (London, 1972), pp. 36, 89–90; Czapski, op. cit., p. 145; Kravchenko, op. cit., pp. 365–7; Stalin, op. cit., II [xv], pp. 22–4; Molotov's Diplomatic Notes of 6 January and 27 April 1942 (*Documents on Polish-Soviet Relations 1939–1945* (London, 1961), I, pp. 259–61, 340–2).

29 FO 371/48004. Some Nazi leaders, from enlightened self-interest, came to criticize the policy of brutality and extermination: cf. Louis P. Lochner (ed.), *The Goebbels Diaries 1942–1943* (New York, 1948), pp. 330, 347–8; Louis Hagen (ed.), *The Schellenberg Memoirs* (London, 1956), pp. 310–11.

30 Stalin, op. cit., II [xv], p. 53.

31 *Континент*, IV, p. 318.

32 Tokaev, op. cit., p. 150.

33 WO 106/3268, 32. Hitler feared the use of gases and poisons (David Irving, *Hitler's War* (London, 1977), p. 264).

34 Hermann Raschhofer, *Political Assassination: The Legal Background of the Oberländer and Stashinsky Cases* (Tübingen, 1964), p. 34.

35 The background of the notorious *Kommissarbefehl* is fully discussed in Helmut Krausnick, Hans Buchheim, Martin Broszat and Hans-Adolf Jacobsen, *Anatomy of the SS State* (London, 1968), pp. 356–7, 505–35.

36 Tolstoy, op. cit., pp. 33–4, 55–6. In this context it is interesting to note the extraordinarily lenient treatment accorded by Soviet authorities to Gauleiter Koch, the Butcher of the Ukraine (Gerald Reitlinger, *The House Built on Sand: The Conflicts of German Policy in Russia 1939–1945* (London, 1960), pp. 226–7). 'Only 4 percent of the British and Americans captured by the Germans died before their release' (Walter Scott Dunn, Jr, *Second Front Now – 1943* (Alabama, 1980), p. 113).

37 In 1944 an NKVD officer admitted that Russia in 1941 was in a state of total chaos, when one 'could easily move about the country and reach any place unmolested' (David J. Dallin, *Soviet Espionage* (Yale, 1955), pp. 268–9).

38 Cf. *Le Procès Kravchenko*, p. 166; Soloviev, op. cit., p. 260.

39 Roy A. Medvedev, *Let History Judge: The Origins and Consequences of Stalinism* (London, 1972), pp. 454–65; Ronald Hingley, *Joseph Stalin: Man and Legend* (London, 1974), pp. 315–20, 322–3, 325–6, 337–8; Bertram D. Wolfe, *Khrushchev and Stalin's Ghost* (New York, 1957), pp. 176–86.

40 Soloviev, op. cit., pp. 26–9. Many Red Army generals were astoundingly ignorant (ibid., pp. 19–34), but few were quite as awful as Marshal Golovanov, Commander of the (non-existent) Long Range Aviation (Michael Parrish, 'Command and Leadership in the Soviet Air Force During the Great Patriot War', *Aerospace Historian* (1979), XXVI, p. 197).

41 Gallagher, op. cit., p. 18.

42 Medvedev, op. cit., p. 312; Ekart, op. cit., p. 91; Lipper, op. cit., pp. 239–41; Aino Kuusinen, *Before and After Stalin: A Personal Account of Soviet Russia from the 1920s to the 1960s* (London, 1974), p. 173; Robert Conquest, *The Great Terror: Stalin's Purge of the Thirties* (London, 1968), pp. 486, 489–90; Z. Stypulkowski, *Invitation to Moscow* (London, 1951), p. 357.

43 Compare Arthur Koestler's telling remarks in *The Yogi and the Commissar*, pp. 137–41.

44 Soloviev, op. cit., pp. 5–6.

45 A. V. Gorbatov, 'Годы и войны', *Новый Мир* (April 1964), XL, pp. 116, 118–19, 129.

46 Ibid. (March 1964), XL, pp. 148–56.

47 Cf. John Erickson, *The Road to Stalingrad* (London, 1975), p. 310.

48 Eve Curie, *Journey Among Warriors* (London, 1943), pp. 184–9.

49 Wilfried Strik-Strikfeldt, *Against Stalin and Hitler: Memoir of the Russian Liberation Movement* (London, 1970), p. 93; A. Kazantsev, Третья Сила: история одной попытки (Frankfurt, 1974), p. 149.

50 Parvilahti, op. cit., pp. 153–4; FO 371/47957, 121–38; Anatoli Granovsky, *All Pity Choked: The Memoirs of a Soviet Secret Agent* (London, 1955), pp. 193, 194–5, 198; Talbott (ed.), op. cit., pp. 140–1; Armstrong, op. cit., pp. 174–6; Roeder, op. cit., pp. 60–2; Vardys, op. cit., pp. 85–108. In 1948–9 thousands of Lithuanians were deported to Siberia in consequence of continuing resistance by partisans (NA 860 M. 4016/8–3149). Already in 1944 Stalin told the Polish Premier that he had liquidated 20,000 Ukrainians and conscripted another 200,000 suspects into the Red Army (Stanislaw Mikolajczyk, *The Pattern of Soviet Domination* (London, 1948), p. 111).

51 Cf. Mikolajczyk, op. cit., pp. 117, 148; Granovsky, op. cit., p. 197. Stalin's designate for the Presidency of occupied Poland was appropriately an ex-NKVD 'interrogator', i.e. torturer (Alexander Orlov, *The Secret History of Stalin's Crimes* (London, 1954), p. 102). For evidence of Soviet fears of 'abroad' on susceptible Red Army men, see Walter Bedell Smith, *Moscow Mission 1946–1949* (London, 1950), pp. 279–80).

52 Czapski, op. cit., pp. 242–3; cf. Mikolajczyk, op. cit., p. 23.

53 A. Spekke, *Latvia and the Baltic Problem* (London, 1952), pp. 84–5. For a horrible example of the Red Army at its usual work – bayoneting wife, mother, baby, etc. – see Parvilahti, op. cit., pp. 255–7.

54 Albert Konrad Herling, *The Soviet Slave Empire* (New York, 1951), pp. 102–15; C. A. Smith (ed.), *Escape from Paradise* (London, 1954), pp. 3–23; Parvilahti, op. cit., pp. 152–3.

55 Herling, op. cit., pp. 143–4; Zoltan Toth, *Prisoner of the Soviet Union* (London, 1978), pp. 4–7; Granovsky, op. cit., pp. 200–4; NA Decimal Files, 861.00/1–1546.

56 Smith (ed.), op. cit., pp. 127–56; Granovsky, op. cit., pp. 218–32; NA Decimal Files, 861.00/4–1648.

57 Fitzroy Maclean, *Eastern Approaches* (London, 1949), pp. 505–6. Mr Constantine Fitzgibbon has kindly supplied me with a similar first-hand description. German prisoners were of course massacred in droves (Maclean, op. cit., pp. 507–8).

58 Milovan Djilas, *Wartime* (New York, 1977), pp. 415–16, 420; and his *Conversations with Stalin* (London, 1962), pp. 81–5.

59 Djilas, *Conversations with Stalin*, pp. 101–2.

60 Alfred M. de Zayas, *Die Wehrmacht-Untersuchungsstelle: Deutsche Ermittlungen über alliierte Völkerrechtsverletzungen im Zweiten Weltkrieg* (Munich, 1980), pp. 39–40; and his *Die Anglo-Amerikaner und die Vertreibung der Deutschen* (Munich, 1977), pp. 79–97; Kopelev,

op. cit., pp. 63, 65, 66, 78–9, 81, 97; Mikhail Koriakov, *I'll Never Go Back* (London, 1948), pp. 60–73; Tokaev, op. cit., pp. 291–2; Peter Pirogov, *Why I Escaped* (London, 1950), pp. 190, 194–5; George F. Kennan, *Memoirs 1925–1950* (Boston, 1967), p. 265; article in *Daugavas Vanagu Mēnešrakts* (1978), VI, p. 25 (kindly translated by Mr J. Treijs and sent to me by Mr Arnis Keksis); Ortwin Buchbender, *Das tönende Erz: Deutsche Propaganda gegen die Rote Armee im Zweiten Weltkrieg* (Stuttgart, 1978), p. 305.

61 Cf. Klimov, op. cit., p. 223. Crimes on a similar scale of enormity were committed during the expulsion and dragooning of the Sudeten Germans, though for this crime the Soviets were only partially responsible, the main role being played by Stalin's protégé, Dr Beneš (cf. Wilhelm K. Turnewald, ed., *Documents on the Expulsion of the Sudeten Germans* (Munich, 1953)).

62 Kopelev, op. cit., pp. 67, 82, 83–4; Kennan, op. cit., p. 240; Klimov, op. cit., pp. 174–5.

63 Kopelev, op. cit., pp. 115–17.

64 Djilas, op. cit., p. 102. The ravaging of eastern Germany was not the USSR's last destructive act in the Second World War. In August Soviet forces incurred severe losses in their race to grab territory from the defeated Japanese. Red Army behaviour was as uncivilized as ever, and nearly a million Japanese were taken away into slavery: Adam B. Ulam, *Expansion and Coexistence: the History of Soviet Foreign Policy, 1917–1967* (London, 1968), p. 477; Arthur Bryant, *Triumph in the West 1943–1946* (London, 1959), p. 508; Dallin and Nicolaevsky, op. cit., pp. 277–8.

65 Kravchenko, op. cit., pp. 427–8; Dallin and Nicolaevsky, op. cit., p. 137; Lipper, op. cit., pp. 170–1, 278–9; Stypulkowski, op. cit., pp. 186–208, 357–8; Solzhenitsyn, op. cit., II, pp. 535–6.

66 Elliot R. Goodman, *The Soviet Design for a World State* (New York, 1960), p. 293.

67 Cf. Harold Nicolson's perceptive remarks (*Diaries and Letters 1939–1945* (London, 1967), p. 388). Hitler was determined to take the German people with him if he fell (Walter Schellenberg, *The Schellenberg Memoirs* (London, 1956), p. 427).

68 George Urban, 'A Conversation with Milovan Djilas', *Encounter* (December 1979), LIII, p. 21.

69 Ulam, *Stalin: The Man and his Era*, pp. 298, 597.

70 Stalin's refusal to help the insurgents (for which see Andrzej Korbonski, 'The Warsaw Rising Revisited', *Survey* (summer 1970), LXXVI, pp. 95–8) may have been premised on memories of Chiang Kai-shek's similar abandonment of the Shanghai uprising in 1926 (George F. Kennan, *Russia and the West under Lenin and Stalin* (Boston, 1961),

p. 271). There is some evidence of a revival of Soviet aid to the Nazis in face of the common threat (cf. J. K. Zawodny, *Nothing but Honour: The Story of the Warsaw Uprising, 1944* (London, 1978), p. 56). The Germans, unlike the Soviets, granted combatant status to the Poles (ibid., p. 62). Recent evidence reveals the extent to which the NKVD co-operated with the Gestapo throughout the war years in betraying and combating the Polish patriotic Home Army (*Armija Krajova*): Robert Moss, 'Moscow's Link with Gestapo', *Daily Telegraph*, 25 August 1980.

71 General S. M. Shtemenko, *The Last Six Months: Russia's Final Battles with Hitler's Armies in World War II* (London, 1978), pp. 260–77; Marshal R. Y. Malinovsky (ed.), *Будапешт Вена Прага: Историко-мемуарный труд* (Moscow, 1965), pp. 77–172.

72 Ibid., pp. 367–74.

73 Ewald Osers, 'The Liberation of Prague', *Survey*, LXXVI, pp. 99–111.

74 Mikolajczyk, op. cit., p. 87.

75 Klimov, op. cit., pp. 212, 224.

76 Granovsky, op. cit., pp. 209–11; Smith (ed.), op. cit., pp. 163–4. On the Danish island of Bornholm the Soviet garrison was confined to quarters built in the woods (Mary Dau, 'The Soviet Union and the Liberation of Denmark', *Survey* (summer 1970), LXXVI, pp. 77–8).

77 John R. Deane, *The Strange Alliance: The Story of American Efforts at Wartime Co-operation with Russia* (London, 1947), p. 155.

78 Ibid., pp. 180–1, 214–17; Kennan, op. cit., pp. 240–2; NA, RG 84, box 11 (report from George Kennan).

79 'A. I. Romanov', op. cit., pp. 145–6.

80 Klimov, op. cit., pp. 65–7, 69–78, 121, 211. This euphoria had been increasing as victory approached (ibid., pp. 18–19).

81 Ulam, op. cit., p. 595; A. Avtorkhanov, *Загадка смерти Сталина, Заговор Берия* (Frankfurt, 1976), pp. 16–17.

82 'A. I. Romanov', op. cit., pp. 144–6, 226, 230, 238; Stypulkowski, op. cit., pp. 355–6; *The Report of the Royal Commission Appointed under Order in Council P.C. 411 of February 5, 1946* (Ottawa, 1946), pp. 638, 639, 664–5; Koriakov, op. cit., p. 159; Mikolajczyk, op. cit., pp. 248–9.

83 Otto Preston Chaney, Jr, *Zhukov* (Newton Abbot, 1972), pp. 307, 348–52.

84 'A. I. Romanov', op. cit., pp. 163–9.

85 Peter Deriabin and Frank Gibney, *The Secret World* (London, 1960), pp. 63–8; Nicolaevsky, *Power and the Soviet Elite*, p. 239; Solzhenitsyn, op. cit., III, pp. 36–9; Dallin and Nicolaevsky, op. cit., pp. 281–98.

86 Cf. Ulam, op. cit., p. 618.

87 Solzhenitsyn, op. cit., III, pp. 26, 29; Klimov, op. cit., p. 291; Czapski,

op. cit., p. 20; Smith (ed.), op. cit., p. 40; Ekart, op. cit., p. 135; Kravchenko, op. cit., pp. 358, 409; *Le Procès Kravchenko*, p. 169; FO 371/24850, 195; FO 371/29499, 92.

88 Eliot B. Wheaton, *Prelude to Calamity: The Nazi Revolution 1933–35* (London, 1969), p. 332. In October 1938, after the Munich crisis, Stalin and Hitler again agreed to muzzle press criticism of their respective regimes (Gerhard L. Weinberg, *The Foreign Policy of Hitler's Germany: Starting World War II 1937–1939* (Chicago, 1980), p. 531).

89 Seidl (ed.), op. cit., p. 126; R. J. Sontag and J. S. Beddie (eds), *Nazi-Soviet Relations 1939–1941* (Washington, 1948), pp. 145, 177; Herbert von Dirksen, *Moskau Tokio London: Erinnerungen und Betrachtungen zu 20 Jahren deutscher Aussenpolitik 1919–1939* (Stuttgart, 1949), p. 126.

90 Cf. Lukacs, op. cit., pp. 308–26, 345.

91 Stalin, op. cit., II [xv], pp. 21–3.

92 FO 800/415. Cf. FO 800/302, 12–13, 18, 59–69, 72, 95–6; CAB 65/54, 124; Joan Beaumont, *Comrades in Arms: British Aid to Russia 1941–1945* (London, 1980), pp. 37, 42–3, 125–6, 134–5, 152, 159–65; Arthur Bryant, *The Turn of the Tide 1939–1943* (London, 1957), pp. 376–7, 461–2, 463; Donald Macintyre, *The Naval War Against Hitler* (London, 1971), pp. 309, 349.

93 Evidence of Stalin's peace feelers towards Germany is to be found in his speech of 23 February 1942 (*Сочинения*, II [xv], pp. 43–4); for other evidence, compare Vojtech Mastny, *Russia's Road to the Cold War: Diplomacy, Warfare, and the Politics of Communism, 1941–1945* (New York, 1979), pp. 73–6, 77–83; Ulam, op. cit., p. 589; Paul Schmidt, *Hitler's Interpreter* (London, 1951), pp. 269–70; Lukacs, op. cit., pp. 148–50.

94 Compare the OSS report 'Russia and the question of a separate Russo-German peace' (14 September 1943), NA, R & A No. 1193.

95 Cf. *Конференция Представителей СССР, США и Великобритании в Думбартон-Оксе: Сборник Документов* (Moscow, 1978), pp. 102–6.

96 NA, RG 84, box 11.

97 NA Decimal Files, 861.00/6–2146.

98 Vojtech Mastny, 'The Cassandra in the Foreign Commissariat: Maxim Litvinov and the Cold War', *Foreign Affairs* (1976), LIV, p. 375.

99 Talbott (ed.), op. cit., p. 262.

100 Cf. Ulam, 'Communist Doctrine and Soviet Diplomacy', *Survey* (1970), LXXVI, p. 4.

XVI Western Attitudes

1 John Lukacs, *The Last European War: September 1939/December 1941* (London, 1976), pp. 411–13; Joan Beaumont, *Comrades in Arms:*

British Aid to Russia 1941–1945 (London, 1980), pp. 43, 147; Bill Jones, *The Russia Complex: The British Labour Party and the Soviet Union* (Manchester, 1977), pp. 62–5.

2 Harold Nicolson, *Diaries and Letters 1939–1945* (London, 1967), p. 250. For British press glozing of Soviet misdeeds and ill intentions, cf. Elisabeth Barker, *Churchill and Eden at War* (London, 1978), pp. 229–30.

3 Victor Kravchenko, *I Chose Freedom* (London, 1947), pp. 466–72.

4 Nearly ten thousand corpses were uncovered at Vinnitsa in 1943 – victims of Stalin's purges of the 1930s (cf. *Amtliches Material zum Massenmord in Winniza* (Leipzig, 1943). I am indebted to Mr W. Bolubash for a photocopy of this grim report, with its pages of terrifying photographs. Compare also Alfred M. de Zayas, *Die Wehrmacht-Untersuchungsstelle: Deutsche Ermittlungen über alliierte Völkerrechtsverletzungen im Zweiten Weltkrieg* (Munich, 1980), pp. 362–5.

5 Report from General Sir Andrew Thorne of 3 April 1945 (PREM 3.364/17.790).

6 Compare 5 Corps Intelligence Summaries nos 71, 509, 517 (WO 170/4240). This was the view of their commander, Field Marshal Kesselring (see *Kesselring: A Soldier's Record* (New York, 1954), p. 331). Evidence accumulated from the earliest days of the invasion of Soviet atrocities against German prisoners-of-war (cf. de Zayas, op. cit., pp. 136–7, 198–200, 273–324). The Nazis were no laggards in this sort of competitive barbarity; Hitler and Stalin shared an interest in setting an unbridgeable gulf of hatred between their respective subjects.

7 Cf. Adam B. Ulam, *Stalin: The Man and his Era* (London, 1974), pp. 564–5; George C. Herring, Jr, *Aid to Russia 1941–1946: Strategy, Diplomacy, The Origins of the Cold War* (New York, 1973), p. 301. In 1942 Beaverbrook believed that 'the Russian dead stand in the way' of a Soviet-German peace! (A. J. P. Taylor, *Beaverbrook* (London, 1972), p. 535.)

8 Herring, op. cit., p. 297; Isaac Deutscher, *Stalin: A Political Biography* (Oxford, 1949), p. 550. Cf. Stalin's own claim (FO 181/1012).

9 A. Avtorkhanov, "Закулисная история пакта "Риббентроп-Молотов"", *Континент* (1975), IV, pp. 318–19.

10 Warren W. Eason, 'The Soviet Population Today: An Analysis of the First Results of the Soviet Census' in Herbert Muller (ed.), *Population Movement in Modern European History* (New York, 1964), pp. 108–16.

11 Roy A. Medvedev, *On Stalin and Stalinism* (Oxford, 1979), p. 139.

12 Gerald Reitlinger, *The House Built on Sand: The Conflict of German Policy in Russia 1939–1945* (London, 1960), p. 448. A further 1,200,000 prisoners-of-war failed to return home after the war (ibid., p. 449).

13 Medvedev, op. cit., p. 140.
14 Nikolai Tolstoy, *Victims of Yalta* (London, 1977), p. 38.
15 Ibid., pp. 34–5.
16 Cf. Helmut Krausnick, Hans Buchheim, Martin Broszat and Hans-Adolf Jacobsen, *Anatomy of the SS State* (London, 1968), pp. 472–3, 523–31.
17 Leonard Schapiro and Peter Reddaway (eds), *Lenin: The Man, the Theorist, the Leader; A Reappraisal* (New York, 1967), p. 172.
18 Information from the late Brigadier R. C. Firebrace.
19 Gregory Klimov, *The Terror Machine: The inside story of the Soviet Administration in Germany* (London, 1953), pp. 19–20; Mikhail Soloviev, *My Nine Lives in the Red Army* (London, 1955), pp. 286–93; Walter Millis (ed.), *The Forrestal Diaries* (London, 1952), p. 260; Antoni Ekart, *Vanished without trace: The story of seven years in Soviet Russia* (London, 1954), p. 91; Peter Pirogov, *Why I Escaped* (London, 1950), p. 71; 'A. I. Romanov', *Nights are Longest There: Smersh from the Inside* (London, 1972), pp. 72–4; C. A. Smith (ed.), *Escape from Paradise* (London, 1954), p. 129; Vladimir Petrov, *My Retreat from Russia* (Yale, 1950), pp. 145–6; Alexander Solzhenitsyn, *Архипелаг Гулаг 1918-1956: Опыт Художественного Исследования*, I, p. 92; Peter J. Huxley-Blythe, *The East Came West* (Caldwell, Ohio, 1964), pp. 180–1; cf. Albert Konrad Herling, *The Soviet Slave Empire* (New York, 1951), pp. 61–3; Ruta U., *Dear God, I Wanted to Live* (New York, 1978), pp. 35–6. Sometimes men from Penal Battalions were mingled with regular troops but not issued with camouflage so as to draw the enemy's fire (compare the illustration between pp. 296–7 in Alan Clark, *Barbarossa* (London, 1965)). The Germans employed Russian prisoners in the same way (Reitlinger, op. cit., pp. 235, 242), a practice impudently condemned by the Soviet 'jurist' Professor A. N. Trainin, *Hitlerite Responsibility under Criminal Law* (London, 1945), p. 49.
20 Svetlana Alliluyeva, *Only One Year* (London, 1969), p. 353.
21 'A. I. Romanov', op. cit., pp. 167–8, 209, 228.
22 Reitlinger, op. cit., pp. 283, 448–9.
23 On 31 October 1939 Molotov claimed that 2,599 Soviet troops had died in the invasion of Poland (Jane Degras, ed., *Soviet Documents on Foreign Policy* (Oxford, 1953), III, p. 393).
24 Medvedev, op. cit., p. 133.
25 Kravchenko, op. cit., p. 405; 'A. I. Romanov', op. cit., pp. 116–17, 228–9; Ronald Hingley, *Joseph Stalin: Man and Legend* (London, 1974), pp. 346–8. A typical example is that of an entire village near Odessa razed to the ground because it had abandoned collective farming under the German occupation (Smith, ed., op. cit., p. 153).

26 Cf. Robert Conquest, *The Nation Killers: The Soviet Deportation of Nationalities* (London, 1970), pp. 64–6.

27 Medvedev, op. cit., p. 145; David J. Dallin and Boris I. Nicolaevsky, *Forced Labor in Soviet Russia* (London, 1948), p. 262; Solzhenitsyn, op. cit., II, pp. 131–2, 216–17, 410, 542–3, 587.

28 In 1942 large-scale massacres took place in the camps (Svetlana Alliluyeva, *Twenty Letters to a Friend* (New York, 1967), p. 79).

29 Dimitri Panin, *The Notebooks of Sologdin* (London, 1976), p. 90. Panin further estimates that another five million died in the succeeding war years (ibid., p. 93).

30 Malcolm J. Proudfoot, *European Refugees: 1939–52; A Study in Forced Population Movement* (London, 1957), pp. 218–19.

31 Tolstoy, op. cit., pp. 408–9.

32 For Lillian Hellman's support for Stalin, see Sidney Hook, 'Lillian Hellmann's Scoundrel Time', *Encounter* (February 1977), XLVIII, pp. 82–91. A recent bibliography lists 79 books and articles describing Soviet prisons and camps, published in the West between 1919 and 1945. By the year of Stalin's death the number had increased to 209, the majority based on first-hand experience (Libushe Zorin, *Soviet Prisons and Concentration Camps: An Annotated Bibliography 1917–1980* (Newtonville, Mass., 1980), pp. 7–51).

33 *The Times*, 23 November 1979.

34 Compare Professor Robert Skidelsky's excellent exposition, 'Exploding Certain Convenient Myths of the 1930's', *Encounter* (June 1980), LIV, pp. 23–8.

35 Hugh Thomas, *John Strachey* (London, 1973), p. 36.

36 Cf. Lewis S. Feuer, 'Marx and the Intellectuals', *Survey* (October 1963), XLIX, pp. 102–12.

37 Whittaker Chambers, *Witness* (London, 1953), pp. 66–8.

38 Eugene Lyons, *Assignment in Utopia* (London, 1937), pp. 324–32.

39 Cf. Anthony Storr, *Human Aggression* (London, 1968), pp. 26–7.

40 Michael Grant, *Gladiators* (London, 1967), pp. 115–16.

41 Alfred Adler, *The Neurotic Constitution: Outlines of a Comparative Individualistic Psychology and Psychotherapy* (London, 1918), pp. 127–33, 140, 192, 324–5, 328.

42 C. G. Jung, *Essays on Contemporary Events* (London, 1947), p. 51.

43 Storr, op. cit., pp. 91–2. Hitler was instinctively aware of man's propensity to cruelty, and the use that could be made of it. 'Why babble about brutality and be indignant about tortures? The masses want that. They need something that will give them a thrill of horror' (Hermann Rauschning, *Hitler Speaks* (London, 1939), pp. 89–90).

44 Melvin J. Lasky, 'In the Margin: From Sartre to Solzhenitsyn', *Encounter* (July 1975), XLV, p. 94.

45 Solomon Volkov, *Testimony: The Memoirs of Dmitri Shostakovich* (London, 1979), pp. 152–5; Kravchenko, op. cit., pp. 252–3; Klimov, op. cit., pp. 278–9; Lyons, op. cit., pp. 226–8.

46 Berhard Roeder, *Katorga: An Aspect of Modern Slavery* (London, 1958), pp. 247–8.

47 Henry Pelling (*The British Communist Party: A Historical Profile* (London, 1958), pp. 80–3, 88–9) has described the recruitment of young intellectuals to the Party in the 1930s. According to Krivitsky, their support played a crucial part in helping Stalin to impose and survive the purges from 1936 onwards (Walter Krivitsky, *I Was Stalin's Agent* (London, 1939), p. 99).

48 Cf. Nicolson, op. cit., p. 308; David Caute, *The Fellow-Travellers: A Postscript to the Enlightenment* (London, 1973), p. 158.

49 Cf. Charles E. Bohlen, *Witness to History, 1929–1969* (London, 1973), pp. 125–6; George F. Kennan, *Russia and the West under Lenin and Stalin* (Boston, 1961), pp. 349–50, 358–9; John Lewis Gaddis, *The United States and the Origins of the Cold War, 1941–1947* (New York, 1972), pp. 37–42. A vocal minority in the USA, however, continued to express dislike of Soviet policies and ideology (ibid., pp. 42–6, 53–6; Nicolson, op. cit., p. 295).

50 Winston S. Churchill, *The Grand Alliance* (London, 1950), p. 737. In 1945 General Brooke was relieved that the Empire had been saved, but feared its days were numbered (Arthur Bryant, *Triumph in the West 1943–1946* (London, 1959), pp. 502, 516, 517–18). Harold Nicolson saw the Empire as a moth-eaten lion (op. cit., pp. 218–19).

51 John Harvey (ed.), *The War Diaries of Oliver Harvey* (London, 1978), p. 267. (Harvey considered Stalin's Russia was 'at the dawn of sudden freedom and enlightenment': p. 174.) Harold Macmillan had held gloomy views in the 1930s (Andrew Boyle, *The Climate of Treason: Five who Spied for Russia* (London, 1979), p. 18).

52 Nicolson, op. cit., pp. 170, 174.

53 Harvey (ed.), op. cit., pp. 57, 62–3, 116–17.

54 Beaumont, op. cit., pp. 74, 97–9; Taylor, op. cit., pp. 476, 492.

55 Harvey (ed.), op. cit., pp. 30, 47, 155, 293. Compare Eden's misery when he found his Russian visit in 1941 had received less publicity than Beaverbrook's (ibid., pp. 80–1).

56 Ibid., p. 242. Unhappy during his 1943 visit to the White House, Eden confessed 'he felt more at home in the Kremlin. There at least they meant business' (p. 229).

57 Ibid., pp. 86, 288.

58 FO 800/301, 23. The FO advised successive Heads of the Military Mission to Moscow 'to give in to them whenever one could reasonably do so' (Lt-Gen. Sir Giffard Martell, *The Russian Outlook* (London,

1947), p. 46; Bryant, op. cit., p. 149).

59 Nicolson, op. cit., pp. 404, 421. Eden in turn was admired by Soviet Ambassador Maisky in 1941 as the one sensible British statesman (ibid., p. 189).

60 FO 371/56887. The FO 'agreed that there was little evidence to support this theory'. Eden had gained a largely spurious reputation as an opponent of appeasement of Hitler: cf. David Dilks (ed.), *The Diaries of Sir Alexander Cadogan* (London, 1971), p. 415; Telford Taylor, *Munich: The Price of Peace* (London, 1979), pp. 135, 137, 241, 243. For his continuing appeasement of Stalin, see Dilks (ed.), op. cit., pp. 446, 449–50; Arthur Bryant, *The Turn of the Tide 1939–1943* (London, 1957), p. 460; and his *Triumph in the West*, pp. 289–90; Martell, pp. 87, 108–9, 112–13, 117, 118–21, 125–7; Stanislaw Kot, *Conversations with the Kremlin and Dispatches from Russia* (London, 1963), p. 176; FO 800/301, 225, 229; FO 371/29471, 156–64, 173–4A; Tolstoy, op. cit., pp. 428–30.

61 Harvey (ed.), op. cit., p. 30.

62 Stanislaw Mikolajczyk, *The Pattern of Soviet Domination* (London, 1948), p. 89.

63 Boyle, op. cit., pp. 195–8.

64 FO 800/301, 43, 48. The Ambassador noticed Wilson's ability for 'making contacts' at this time (ibid., 23, 27).

65 Compare the account by Wilson's colleague John Balfour (FO 371/37057, 9–39); ibid., 5; Raphael Rupert, *A Hidden World* (London, 1963), pp. 7–8; Fitzroy Maclean, *Eastern Approaches* (London, 1949), p. 49; Lyons, op. cit., pp. 318, 424–7. John Murray, *A Spy called Swallow: The true love story of Nora, the Russian agent* (London, 1978), pp. 115, 137, 143–4.

66 FO 800/302, 73.

67 Ibid., 53–7. Wilson had toyed with the idea of persuading the Ambassador in Moscow, Clark Kerr, to issue the note under his name (ibid., 29). Cf. Barker, op. cit., pp. 289–91.

68 FO 371/43335.

69 FO 371/36923, 28–9; FO 800/301, 48. For Zinchenko's NKVD association, cf. David J. Dallin, *Soviet Espionage* (Yale, 1955), p. 478.

70 FO 800/302, 29, 30, 73. For Soviet moves at this time in eastern Poland, cf. George H. Janczewski, 'The Origin of the Lublin Government', *The Slavonic and East European Review* (1972), I, pp. 410–33.

71 FO 800/301, 102; FO 800/302, 29–30.

72 Field Marshal Brooke was strongly critical of the Foreign Office attitude (FO 371/43288, 135).

73 Mikolajczyk, op. cit., pp. 58, 73; Robert Moss, 'Moscow's Link with Gestapo', *Daily Telegraph*, 25 August 1980.

74 FO 371/43288, 125; FO 371/43290, 14, 140.
75 Ibid., 231–40.
76 FO 371/43288, 58, 65; FO 800/302, 74.
77 Ibid., 219; FO 371/43291, 41, 68.
78 John R. Deane, *The Strange Alliance: The Story of American Efforts at Wartime Co-operation with Russia* (London, 1947), pp. 154, 203.
79 FO 800/302, 73–4, 219; FO 371/43382, 138. For Chichaev, cf. FO 371/47709, N 1109, N 1184. In May 1945 he was transferred to Prague as 'Minister-Counsellor' (NA 861.00/1–1546).
80 Christopher Warner, Head of the Northern Department, was in March 1944 'finding his faith in the Russians is being subjected to ever new strains' (FO 800/302, 220).
81 FO 800/302, 220.
82 Tolstoy, op. cit., pp. 43, 137, 148, 421. Guy Burgess was serving in the FO News Department at this time (Boyle, op. cit., pp. 253, 264, 278).
83 The *Manchester Guardian*, 16 September 1946. I am grateful to Mr Edward Pearce for supplying me with this and the next reference.
84 The *Daily Herald*, 17 January 1947. The patently fraudulent nature of Soviet 'land redistribution' in Poland is described by Stanislaw Mikolajczyk, himself leader of the Polish Peasant Party (op. cit., pp. 243–5).
85 FO 371/47987, 4.

XVII   Close Designs and Crooked Counsels

1 General S. M. Shtemenko, *Генеральный Штаб в годы войны* (Moscow, 1973), II, pp. 449–50. For an earlier discussion of the subject-matter of this chapter, cf. Chapter Eleven of my *Victims of Yalta*. I have not thought it necessary to repeat references to material already reproduced there.
2 Shtemenko was a general particularly closely associated with Stalin (Ronald Hingley, *Joseph Stalin: Man and Legend* (London, 1974), p. 421; Oleg Penkovskiy, *The Penkovskiy Papers* (New York, 1965), pp. 70, 89–90).
3 NA, RG 59, 711.62114/1C–744. A similarly uncompromising instruction arrived on 19 February 1945 (WO 32/11119, 230A).
4 On 12 May 1945 AFHQ informed the Soviet authorities that 'the disposal of Soviet citizens will continue to be regulated in accordance with the present agreements between the United States, British and Soviet Governments' (WO 204/1596).
5 WO 170/4183, 487.
6 General V. Naumenko (ed.), *Великое Предательство: Выдача казаков в Лиенце и других местах (1945–1947)* (New York, 1962–70), I, p. 140;

Jozef Mackiewicz, *Kontra* (Paris, 1957), pp. 144–5; Peter J. Huxley-Blythe, *The East Came West* (Caldwell, Idaho, 1964), p. 121.

7 WO 32/11119, 230A. For other examples of Macmillan's involvement in the question of Soviet citizenship, cf. ibid, 138c, 142A; WO 32/11137, 62c, 78A, 388A; WO 32/11681, 98A; WO 204/2877.

8 Here it may be pertinent to allude to the fate of 30,000 Yugoslav refugees, handed over in May 1945 by 5 Corps to Tito's partisans and massacred in cold blood at Bleiburg. This was described by a Foreign Office official at Belgrade as a 'ghastly mistake', and a later memorandum referred to a 'slip up'. One can only remark on the series of unusual 'slip ups' committed at this particular time and place. Cf. David Floyd, 'How Britain sent 30,000 refugees to their death', *Now!* (16 November 1979), pp. 57–8. On 19 May Col. Rose Price of the 3rd Bn Welsh Guards noted in his War Diary: 'Evacuation of Croats begin. Order of most sinister duplicity received i.e. to send Croats to their foes i.e. TITS to Yugoslavia under the impression that they were to go to ITALY. TIT guards on trains hidden in guards van' (WO 170/4982).

9 PREM 3. 364, 750–2.

10 WO 170/4183, 487.

11 WO 170/4183, 460.

12 For details of the interpreters and forms, cf. Naumenko (ed.), op. cit., II, p. 169; A. I. Delianich, *Вольфсберг -373* (San Francisco, 1975), p. 105. The incident is related in detail in my *Victims of Yalta* (Corgi Books, London, 1979), pp. 299–308, 325–7.

13 'A. I. Romanov', *Nights are Longest There: Smersh from the Inside* (London, 1972), pp. 169–74. It was NKVD troops who received the Cossacks at Judenburg (Naumenko, ed., op. cit., II, p. 300).

14 'A. I. Romanov', op. cit., pp. 148–9. The brutal killing of a legless Cossack officer at SMERSH HQ is described in Naumenko (ed.), op. cit., II, p. 185.

15 Ibid., I, p. 183.

16 Cf. Roy A. Medvedev, *On Stalin and Stalinism* (Oxford, 1979), pp. 134–5; Unto Parvilahti, *Beria's Gardens: Ten Years' Captivity in Russia and Siberia* (London, 1959), pp. 76, 128; Z. Stypulkowski, *Invitation to Moscow* (London, 1951), pp. 211–32.

17 Naumenko (ed.), op. cit., I, p. 141.

18 WO 170/5034.

19 Delianich, op. cit., p. 59.

20 Naumenko (ed.), op. cit., II, p. 300.

21 'Conc and Collecting Pts and Transit Camps as at 16 May 45', kindly loaned to me by Major R. C. Taylor, then a staff officer with 78 Infantry Division.

22 A retired officer named Shaun Stewart declared in 1978 that he had no

regrets for the part he played in vigorously rounding up the Cossacks and their families. 'I certainly did not and do not now', he asserts (*Victims of Yalta*, pp. 20–1).

23 Thaddeus Wittlin, *Commissar: The Life and Death of Lavrenty Pavlovich Beria* (London, 1973), pp. 21–3, 38, 289; Robert Conquest, *The Great Terror: Stalin's Purge of the Thirties* (London, 1968), p. 465; 'A. I. Romanov', op. cit., p. 138; David J. Dallin and Boris I. Nicolaevsky, *Forced Labor in Soviet Russia* (London, 1948), p. 269.

24 Gustav Hilger and Alfred G. Meyer, *The Incompatible Allies: A Memoir-History of German-Soviet Relations, 1918–1941* (New York, 1953), p. 322; Adam B. Ulam, *Stalin: The Man and his Era* (London, 1974), p. 526.

25 N. N. Krasnov, *Незабываемое* (New York, 1957), pp. 75–81.

26 Cf. Naumenko (ed.), op. cit., II, pp. 36–8.

27 Cf. E. H. Cookridge, *The Third Man: The truth about 'Kim' Philby, double agent* (London, 1968), pp. 113–16.

28 Huxley-Blythe, op. cit., pp. 202–10.

Postscript. Direct evidence of Field-Marshal Alexander's hostility to the surrender of the Cossacks has recently been supplied to me by Mrs Louise Buchanan, who in 1945 stayed with neighbours and friends of the Alexanders in Northern Ireland. On leave at Hillsborough Alexander unburdened himself of the many frustrations bedevilling him in the Mediterranean theatre. 'Certainly,' writes Mrs Buchanan, 'the return of . . . the Cossacks was mentioned and I remember being puzzled by hearing that "Alex's" protests were absolutely ignored and how sick and furious it made him. Like Wavell and Tedder, he was something of a romantic in his soldiering, you know. And that is hard to explain in 1980.'

I am grateful for information and help received in writing this chapter to Professor John Erickson, Mr Peter J. Huxley-Blythe and Brigadier C. E. Tryon-Wilson.

XVIII Hands Across the Sea

1 Henry Pelling, *The British Communist Party: A Historical Profile* (London, 1958), pp. 105–7; David Caute, *The Fellow-Travellers: A Postscript to the Enlightenment* (London, 1973), p. 10.

2 FO 371/37019, 2; FO 800/301, 29.

3 Elliot R. Goodman, *The Soviet Design for a World State* (New York, 1960), pp. 44–5; W. G. Krivitsky, *I Was Stalin's Agent* (London, 1939), pp. 43–92; Victor Kravchenko, *I Chose Freedom* (London, 1947), p. 422; *The Report of the Royal Commission . . . to Investigate the Facts Relating to . . . the Communication . . . of Secret and Confidential Information to Agents of a Foreign Power* (London, 1946), p. 640; Pelling, op. cit., pp. 122–4.

4 'A. I. Romanov', *Nights are Longest There: Smersh from the Inside* (London, 1972), p. 238. Exactly similar threats were uttered at this time by Abakumov's colleague, V. N. Merkulov: cf. Nikolai Tolstoy, *Victims of Yalta* (London, 1977), p. 193.

5 Cf. David J. Dallin, *Soviet Espionage* (New York, 1955), pp. 14–21, 25–70; Krivitsky, op. cit., pp. 88, 90–1.

6 Ibid., p. 90; Whittaker Chambers, *Witness* (London, 1953), pp. 265–6.

7 Dallin, op. cit., pp. 202, 416; 'A. I. Romanov', op. cit., pp. 68–9; Gordon Brook-Shepherd, *The Storm Petrels: The First Soviet Defectors, 1928–1938* (London, 1977), p. 236; Elisabeth K. Poretsky, *Our Own People: A Memoir of 'Ignace Reiss' and His Friends* (Oxford, 1969), p. 145; Victor Serge, A. Rosmer and Maurice Wullens, *L'assassinat d'Ignace Reiss* (Paris, 1938), p. 17 (reference kindly supplied by Professor Robin Kemball).

8 Hermann Rauschning, *Hitler Speaks: A Series of Political Conversations with Adolf Hitler on his Real Aims* (London, 1939), pp. 17–19. Hitler's cynical boast is exactly paralleled by the actual instructions for recruiting traitors issued by NKGB General Sudoplatov in 1946 (John Barron, *KGB: The Secret Work of Soviet Agents* (London, 1974), p. 309).

9 Cf. Henri Noguères, *Munich: or the Phoney Peace* (London, 1965), pp. 364–5; John Lukacs, *The Last European War: September 1939/December 1941* (London, 1976), pp. 213–15.

10 'A. I. Romanov', op. cit., p. 59. Cf. George F. Kennan, *Russia and the West under Lenin and Stalin* (Boston, 1961), p. 225.

11 For Pontecorvo, cf. *Joint Committee on Atomic Energy, Soviet Atomic Espionage* (Washington, 1951), pp. 12, 38–9.

12 F. W. Deakin and G. R. Storry, *The case of Richard Sorge* (New York, 1966), pp. 139–40, 141, 143.

13 Guy Burgess stole cigarettes from friends and looted bombed houses – crimes not committed for gain but for substitute accomplishment (Kim Philby, *My Secret War* (London, 1968), p. 8; Andrew Boyle, *The Climate of Treason: Five who Spied for Russia* (London, 1979), p. 335).

14 Cf. Poretsky, op. cit., pp. 222–6.

15 *Soviet Atomic Espionage*, pp. 11–12, 26.

16 Chambers, op. cit., p. 299.

17 Ibid., pp. 265–6; Krivitsky, op. cit., pp. 90–2; *Soviet Atomic Espionage*, pp. 82, 101–2, 103, 106–7, 109–10, 160; *The Report of the Royal Commission*, pp. 104, 543; Dallin, op. cit., pp. 20–4; Vladimir and Evdokia Petrov, *Empire of Fear* (London, 1956), p. 275.

18 David Dilks (ed.), *The Diaries of Sir Alexander Cadogan* (London, 1971), p. 383; FO 800/301, 84–5; Dallin, op. cit., p. 427.

19 Ibid., pp. 217–18, 230–1, 270–1; John R. Deane, *The Strange Alliance:*

The Story of American Efforts at Wartime Co-Operation with Russia (London, 1947), pp. 50–5; Tolstoy, op. cit., pp. 64–8; Joseph E. Persico, *Piercing the Reich: The Penetration of Nazi Germany by American Secret Agents during World War II* (New York, 1979), p. 335.

20 FO 371/43361, 2–11. Further details of espionage work at Archangel are given in Petrov, op. cit., p. 161; for the recording of foreigners' weak points, cf. p. 264.

21 John Murray, *A Spy called Swallow: The true love story of Nora, the Russian agent* (London, 1978), pp. 57–68; FO 371/24856, 344–76.

22 Peter Deriabin and Frank Gibney, *The Secret World* (London, 1960), pp. 91, 199; Kravchenko, op. cit., pp. 148–66; C. A. Smith, *Escape from Paradise* (London, 1954), p. 26; Milovan Djilas, *Conversations with Stalin* (London, 1962), pp. 93–4; and his *Wartime* (New York, 1977), pp. 429, 434; Eugene Lyons, *Assignment in Utopia* (London, 1937), p. 239; Robert Conquest, *The Great Terror: Stalin's Purge of the Thirties* (London, 1968), p. 410; Gustav Hilger and Alfred G. Meyer, *The Incompatible Allies: A Memoir-History of German-Soviet Relations, 1918–1941* (New York, 1953), p. 162.

23 Robert Conquest, *Kolyma: The Arctic Death Camps* (London, 1978), pp. 194–5. The girls were also employed as call-girls for high Party and military functionaries, Colonel-General Serov of the NKVD acting as pimp (Mikhail Soloviev, *My Nine Lives in the Red Army* (New York, 1955), p. 35).

24 FO 800/301, 62.

25 Richard Deacon, *The British Connection: Russia's Manipulation of British Individuals and Institutions* (London, 1979), pp. 50–1; Vojtech Mastny, *Russia's Road to the Cold War: Diplomacy, Warfare, and the Politics of Communism, 1941–1945* (New York, 1979), p. 99; Caute, op. cit., p. 274; Sir Giffard Martel, *The Russian Outlook* (London, 1947), pp. 138–40; Z. Stypulkowski, *Invitation to Moscow* (London, 1951), p. 337; Arthur Koestler, *The Yogi and the Commissar and other Essays* (London, 1945), p. 152.

26 Gregory Klimov, *The Terror Machine: The inside story of the Soviet Administration in Germany* (London, 1953), pp. 260–1; Strobe Talbott (ed.), *Khrushchev Remembers* (Boston, 1970), p. 131; Kravchenko, op. cit., pp. 185–6, 317, 451.

27 FO 800/300, 154.

28 Information supplied by Mr L. H. Manderstam, then an SOE officer. Perhaps Hill's hopes were based on his experiences of twenty-five years earlier, when as a British agent in Russia he had made use of a prostitute as a secret courier (Geoffrey Bailey, *The Conspirators* (London, 1961), p. 33).

29 Philby, op. cit., p. 8.

30 FO 371/43382, 138-42.

31 Lyons, op. cit., p. 458. By Khrushchev's time Jews had been largely purged from the intelligence services (Oleg Penkovskiy, *The Penkovskiy Papers* (New York, 1965), p. 358).

32 Boyle, op. cit., pp. 318-19, 351. As early as 1930 Mr Alan Walker, First Secretary at the Legation for the Baltic States, was told by his chief, Sir Joseph Addison, 'Remember this, my dear Alan, that the one thing the old women of both sexes who are behind the Private Secretary detest is anything straightforward or natural. Never, unless you are rich and can tell them to . . . themselves, get the reputation of liking women; anything so natural is anathema to them; but be a bugger, a drunk or a red and you can': put a foot wrong.' (Information kindly supplied by Mr Walker.)

33 E. H. Cookridge, *The Third Man: The truth about 'Kim' Philby, double agent* (London, 1968), pp. 116, 125.

34 Deacon, op. cit., pp. 51-2; Lyons, op. cit., pp. 331, 511; Boyle, op. cit., p. 115.

35 *Radio Times* (12-18 January 1980), p. 4.

36 Alastair Hamilton, *The Appeal of Fascism: A Study of Intellectuals and Fascism 1919-1945* (London, 1971), pp. 237-8; Lukacs, op. cit., pp. 388-9.

37 Richard Hanser, *Prelude to Terror: The Rise of Hitler 1919-1923* (London, 1971), p. 292.

38 Rauschning, op. cit., p. 23.

39 R. G. L. Waite, *Vanguard of Nazism: The Free Corps Movement in Postwar Germany 1918-1923* (Cambridge, Mass., 1952), pp. 222-3; Konrad Heiden, *Hitler: A Biography* (London, 1936), pp. 216-20, 384, 400; Saul Friedländer, *Counterfeit Nazi: The Ambiguity of Good* (London, 1969), p. 42.

40 Richard Grunberger, *A Social History of the Third Reich* (London, 1971), pp. 63, 335, 347-9, 384. One may note in particular the homosexual overtones of the *Hitlerjugend* and kindred organizations, who were 'banded together for the sake of a mystic, manly ideal that overrode all family ties' (D. J. West, *Homosexuality* (London, 1960), p. 24; cf. Grunberger, op. cit., pp. 252-3, 259; David L. Schoenbaum, *Hitler's Social Revolution: Class and Status in Nazi Germany* (London, 1967), pp. 187-92).

41 Boyle, op. cit., p. 368.

42 Cf. *The Report of the Royal Commission*, pp. 93, 617-18, 693-5.

43 Chambers, op. cit., p. 288; Allen Weinstein, *Perjury: The Hiss-Chambers Case* (London, 1978), p. 172.

44 Ibid., pp. 351-7, 449, 361-3.

45 In strong contrast to Professor Weinstein's magisterial indictment is

the extreme weakness of the defence put up by Hiss's supporters. Cf. ibid., p. 589; Sidney Hook, 'The Case of Alger Hiss', *Encounter* (August 1978), LI, pp. 48–55; 'Arguments (New & Old), about the Hiss case', ibid. (March 1979), pp. 80–90.

46 James F. Byrnes, *All in One Lifetime* (London, 1960), p. 322.

47 Weinstein, op. cit., p. 510.

48 Djilas, op. cit., p. 77. The anonymous 'well-wisher' who was keeping Stalin informed of highly secret Allied negotiations with the Germans in March 1945 must surely have been a highly-placed official of the Foreign Office or State Department: cf. Adam B. Ulam, *Stalin: The Man and his Era* (London, 1974), p. 611.

49 Cf. Elisabeth Barker, *Churchill and Eden at War* (London, 1978), p. 223.

50 David Rees, *Harry Dexter White: A Study in Paradox* (London, 1974), pp. 116–18, 180–2, 191, 212–14, 244–76. The Morgenthau Plan was warmly espoused by the Soviets (ibid., pp. 298–301, 309, 476).

51 Ibid., pp. 214–20; Weinstein, op. cit., p. 455.

52 Rees, op. cit., pp. 94–7.

53 Cf. Dallin, op. cit., pp. 389–492.

54 Deriabin and Gibney, op. cit., p. 180. Soviet atomic research had been greatly set back by purges of leading scientists (Alex Weissberg, *Conspiracy of Silence* (London, 1952), p. 359), whilst others were obliged to work for the GULAG administration (Smith, op. cit., pp. 82–3). Both the traitors abroad and atomic research in the USSR conveniently came under Beria's direction ('A. I. Romanov', op. cit., p. 178).

55 William Boyce Thompson used the American Red Cross as a 'cover' for his dealings (Robert C. Williams, *Russian Art and American Money, 1900–1940* (Cambridge, Mass., 1980), pp. 18–20).

56 Ibid., pp. 168–9.

57 Ibid., pp. 196, 197, 201, 209, 218–19; NA 861.00/10–246. For the significance of the Hammers' business relationship with the Soviet Union, as active today as ever, see the important study by Charles Levinson, *Vodka-Cola* (London, 1980), pp. 7, 126, 138, 194, 195, 247. Armand Hammer was convicted for making illegal contributions to Richard Nixon's presidential campaign fund, and has been accused of persistent bribery on an international scale (ibid., p. 252).

58 Williams, op. cit., pp. 219–24.

59 Cf. Robert Dallek, *Franklin D. Roosevelt and American Foreign Policy 1932–1945* (New York, 1979), pp. 78–81.

60 Williams, op. cit., pp. 229–62; John Lewis Gaddis, *The United States and the Origins of the Cold War, 1941–1947* (New York, 1972), pp. 34–7, 48, 73, 143, 302.

61 George F. Kennan, *Memoirs, 1925–1950* (Boston, 1967), pp. 84–5;

Charles E. Bohlen, *Witness to History 1929–1969* (London, 1973), pp. 40–1; Dallek, op. cit., pp. 144–5. For a similarly sinister-seeming action a few years later, cf. Brook-Shepherd, op. cit., p. 168.

62 David Martin, *Patriot or Traitor: The Case of General Mihailovich* (Stanford, 1978), pp. 83–90, 99–119, etc. MI6 sources seem also to have been tainted (ibid., pp. 108–17). Compare also Staniša Vlahović, 'Audiatur et Altera Pars – British Wartime Policy towards Yugoslavia', the *South Slav Journal* (1979), II, pp. 5–8; Deacon, op. cit., pp. 162–70; Rebecca West's review of Martin's book in the *South Slav Journal*, II (no. 2), pp. 18–19; ibid. (1980), III (no. 2), pp. 52–5.

63 Cookridge, op. cit., p. 16; Boyle, op. cit., pp. 66, 69, 72, 75, 77, 100; Pelling, op. cit., pp. 151–2; Deacon, op. cit., pp. 77–8, 92.

64 The *South Slav Journal*, II, p. 8 (reference to FO 371/48865, 159).

65 Cf. Cookridge, op. cit., pp. 14–15, 19, 38; Boyle, op. cit., pp. 102, 213–14; Deacon, op. cit., pp. 96–7, 137–8; Pelling, op. cit., pp. 111, 125–6; FO 371/37000, 24–36; FO 371/37007, 103–4.

66 FO 371/71661.

67 Compare my review, '"Victims of Yalta" – an Inquiry?', *Encounter* (1980), LIV, pp. 89–92.

68 Nicholas Bethell, *The Last Secret: Forcible Repatriation to Russia 1944–7* (London, 1974), p. 53. Strachey was a friend of Blunt, Burgess and Springhall (Hugh Thomas, *John Strachey* (London, 1973), pp. 202, 205), and on at least one occasion betrayed his country to aid foreign interests (ibid., p. 229).

69 Cf. Tolstoy, op. cit., pp. 104–5.

70 Petrov, op. cit., p. 211.

71 'A. I. Romanov', op. cit., p. 170.

72 Nikolai Krasnov, *The Hidden Russia* (New York, 1960), pp. 77, 249, 325–6.

73 'A. I. Romanov', op. cit., pp. 151, 236, 248.

74 Bertram D. Wolfe, *Khrushchev and Stalin's Ghost* (New York, 1957), p. 46.

Epilogue

1 Cf. Arthur M. Schlesinger, Jr, 'The Cold War Revisited', the *New York Review of Books* (October 1979), XXVI, pp. 46–52.

2 Schlesinger, Jr, 'Origins of the Cold War', *Foreign Affairs* (1967), XLVI, pp. 46–7. For Stalin's consistent attachment to the concept of international Communist revolution, cf. Robert C. Tucker, 'The Emergence of Stalin's Foreign Policy', *Slavic Review* (1977), XXXVI, pp. 568–71; Elliott R. Goodman, *The Soviet Design for a World State* (New York, 1960), pp. 36–41.

3 Bernard Pares, *A History of Russia* (London, 1949), p. 612. Even so shrewd a commentator as Professor Schlesinger suggested by implication that Stalin was motivated by concern for the twenty million Russian war dead (*Foreign Affairs*, XLVI, pp. 29–30). As has been shown, most of the twenty million were killed on Stalin's instructions.

4 Quoted in ibid., pp. 29–30.

5 Cf. Joseph Czapski, *The Inhuman Land* (London, 1951), p. 225; Charles E. Bohlen, *Witness to History 1929–1969* (London, 1973), pp. 91, 197; Winston S. Churchill, *Triumph and Tragedy* (London, 1954), p. 323.

6 Strobe Talbott (ed.), *Khrushchev Remembers* (Boston, 1970), pp. 307, 361.

7 So wrote Fitzroy Maclean in 1941 (FO 371/29479, 15). Cf. Robert E. Sherwood, *Roosevelt and Hopkins: An Intimate History* (New York, 1948), pp. 327–30, 343–5; John R. Deane, *The Strange Alliance: The Story of American Efforts at Wartime Co-operation with Russia* (London, 1947), pp. 20, 258, 300–1; Walter Bedell Smith, *Moscow Mission 1946–1949* (London, 1950), p. 188; David Dilks (ed.), *The Diaries of Sir Alexander Cadogan* (London, 1971), pp. 219, 656, 747; Stanislaw Kot, *Conversations with the Kremlin and Dispatches from Russia* (London, 1963), p. xviii.

8 So the Turkish Ambassador reported of his meeting on 2 March 1940 (FO 371/24843, 334).

9 Alexander Orlov, *The Secret History of Stalin's Crimes* (London, 1954), pp. 129–30.

10 Milovan Djilas, *Conversations with Stalin* (London, 1962), p. 105.

11 George Kennan, *Russia and the West under Lenin and Stalin* (Boston, 1961), p. 351; Adam B. Ulam, *Stalin: The Man and his Era* (London, 1974), p. 571.

12 Vojtech Mastny, *Russia's Road to the Cold War: Diplomacy, Warfare, and the Politics of Communism, 1941–1945* (New York, 1979), pp. 273–9.

13 Talbott (ed.), op. cit., p. 156; Ulam, op. cit., pp. 522, 598. At Teheran Churchill had made strong representations on behalf of Finland (Winston S. Churchill, *Closing the Ring* (London, 1952), pp. 351–4). The preservation of Finnish independence enabled pro-Soviet writers in the West to lull suspicions of Soviet intentions in Europe (cf. Walter Duranty, *Stalin & Co.: The Politburo – the Men who run Russia* (London, 1949), pp. 143–4).

14 Djilas, op. cit., p. 70; Mary Dau, 'The Soviet Union and the Liberation of Denmark', *Survey* (summer 1970), LXXVI, pp. 75–81. Stalin had always possessed a realistic sense of compromise (cf. Robert Conquest, *The Great Terror: Stalin's Purge of the Thirties* (London, 1968), p. 428).

15 Djilas, op. cit., p. 71. Stalin's anxiety over the possibility of US air bases in the Kurile Islands was an indication of his fears (Ulam, op. cit., p. 628).

16 Djilas, op. cit., p. 95; Victor Kravchenko, *I Chose Freedom* (London, 1947), pp. 419–20; *Correspondence between the Chairman of the Council of Ministers of the U.S.S.R. and the Presidents of the U.S.A. and the Prime Ministers of Great Britain During the Great Patriotic War of 1941–1945* (London, 1958), I, pp. 41–5; Willi A. Boelcke (ed.), *The Secret Conferences of Dr Goebbels October 1939–March 1943* (London, n.d.), p. 236; David Irving, *Hitler's War* (London, 1977), p. 211; Winston S. Churchill, *The Grand Alliance* (London, 1950), p. 736; and his *The Hinge of Fate* (London, 1951), pp. 179–80, 294–5.

17 Werner Maser, *Hitler* (London, 1973), pp. 92–3.

18 General S. M. Shtemenko, *The Last Six Months: Russia's Final Battles with Hitler's Armies in World War II* (London, 1978), p. 41.

19 Nikolai Tolstoy, *Victims of Yalta* (London, 1977), p. 104.

20 Svetlana Alliluyeva, *Twenty Letters to a Friend* (New York, 1967), p. 134; Gregory Klimov, *The Terror Machine: The inside story of the Soviet Administration in Germany* (London, 1953), p. 147; Talbott (ed.), op. cit., p. 221.

21 *Внешняя политика Советского Союза в период Отечественной войны* (Moscow, 1946), II, p. 105.

22 Cf. Mastny, op. cit., pp. 133–44.

23 David J. Dallin and Boris I. Nicolaevsky, *Forced Labor in Soviet Russia* (London, 1948), pp. 296–8; Albert Konrad Herling, *The Soviet Slave Empire* (New York, 1951), pp. 168–96; *The Dark Side of the Moon* (London, 1946), pp. 229, 296–7. For the personal account of a Pole dispatched to Vorkuta at this time, see Edward Buca, *Vorkuta* (London, 1976), pp. 17–46.

24 Tolstoy, op. cit., pp. 408–9.

25 For the Caucasian and Crim Tartar deportations, cf. Alexander Nekrich, *Наказанные Народы* (New York, 1978), pp. 96–9; Robert Conquest, *The Nation Killers: The Soviet Deportation of Nationalities* (London, 1970), pp. 64–6.

26 V. Stanley Vardys, *Lithuania under the Soviets: Portrait of a Nation, 1940–65* (New York, 1965), pp. 85–108; Talbott (ed.), op. cit., pp. 140–1; Unto Parvilahti, *Beria's Gardens: Ten Years' Captivity in Russia and Siberia* (London, 1959), pp. 153–4; *Communist Takeover and Occupation of Ukraine: Special Report No. 4 of the Select Committee on Communist Aggression* (Washington, 1955), pp. 30–2.

27 J. G. Frazer, *The Scapegoat* (London, 1913), p. 105.

28 Ulam, op. cit., p. 683.

29 Talbott (ed.), op. cit., pp. 280–1, 308. When his daughter Svetlana

pleaded to be allowed to discard her bodyguard, Stalin's immediate reaction was: 'To hell with you then. Get killed if you like' (Alliluyeva, op. cit., p. 134).

30 Adam B. Ulam, in *Slavic Review*, XXXVI, p. 307; George F. Kennan, *Memoirs 1925–1950* (Boston, 1967), pp. 537, 543–4.
31 Mastny, op. cit., p. 272.
32 Cf. G. A. Tokaev, *Comrade X* (London, 1965), pp. 321–2; Klimov, op. cit., p. 306.
33 John H. Backer, *The Decision to Divide Germany: American Foreign Policy in Transition* (Durham, NC, 1978), pp. 151–2; Djilas, op. cit., p. 106; Talbott (ed.), op. cit., p. 233.
34 Compare Stalin's realistic assessments of relative Soviet and American strength (Djilas, op. cit., pp. 62, 138, 141, 164).
35 Adam B. Ulam, *Expansion and Coexistence: the History of Soviet Foreign Policy, 1917–1967* (London, 1968), pp. 425–8; and his *Stalin: The Man and his Era*, pp. 638–40; Djilas, op. cit., pp. 164–5; Backer, op. cit., pp. 145, 149–55; James F. Byrnes, *Speaking Frankly* (New York, 1947), pp. 188–92.
36 John Barron, *KGB: The Secret Work of Soviet Agents* (London, 1974), pp. 309–10; Vladimir and Evdokia Petrov, *Empire of Fear* (London, 1956), p. 257.
37 Nikolai Krasnov, *The Hidden Russia* (New York, 1960), pp. 208–9, 223; Bernhard Roeder, *Katorga: An Aspect of Modern Slavery* (London, 1958), p. 156.
38 NA 800.20261/9–946; Robert Conquest, *Kolyma: The Arctic Death Camps* (London, 1978), pp. 25, 64, 154–8; Elinor Lipper, *Eleven Years in Soviet Prison Camps* (London, 1951), pp. 290–1; Zoltan Toth, *Prisoner of the Soviet Union* (London, 1978), pp. 92–3, 109–13, 115–19; Parvilahti, op. cit., pp. 205–7, 253–4; Roeder, op. cit., pp. 21–7; Dimitri Panin, *The Notebooks of Sologdin* (London, 1976), pp. 88–91, 103–5, 123–4, 161; Varlam Shalamov, 'Последний Бой Майора Пугачева', *Колымские Рассказы* (London, 1978), pp. 833–47; Edward Buca, *Vorkuta*, pp. 231–74.
39 Mikhail Soloviev, *My Nine Lives in the Red Army* (New York, 1955), pp. 106–7; Tokaev, op. cit., pp. 245, 280–1.
40 Karel Kaplan, 'Segretissimo dall' Est', *Panorama* (26 March 1980), pp. 164–89. Cf. *The Times* (6 May 1977); *Le Monde* (6 and 20 May 1977).
41 Svetlana Alliluyeva, *Only One Year* (London, 1969), pp. 150–1; Tokaev, op. cit., pp. 331–2; Boris I. Nicolaevsky, *Power and the Soviet Elite* (New York, 1965), pp. 118, 170–1, 248–9. The 'dissident' historian Roy Medvedev chides Stalin for his excessive caution in missing chances of expanding Soviet post-war power (*Let History Judge: The Origins and Consequences of Stalinism* (London, 1972), pp. 469–74).

42 Ulam, *Stalin: The Man and his Era*, p. 668.

43 *Panorama* (26 April 1977), pp. 174–7; cf. Bill Jones, *The Russia Complex: The British Labour Party and the Soviet Union* (Manchester, 1977), pp. 127, 128, 131–2.

44 For Laski's admiration of the Purge trials, see Conquest, *The Great Terror*, p. 506.

45 Klimov, op. cit., p. 306. Klimov, an advisory expert on the Soviet side of the Allied Control Commission in Berlin, was present at the conversation.

46 A. Avtorkhanov, *Загадка смерти Сталина, Заговор Берия* (Frankfurt, 1976), p. 219.

Index

N.B. Page numbers in italics refer to the Notes

INDEX

Vladivostok: transit camp, 14; UN forces
approach, 358
Vlasik, 'General' Nikolai, 61, 62
Vlasov, Gen. Andrei, 264; 'Vlasov' army,
271, 356
Volga-German Republic, 242, 283
Vologda camp, 31, 252
Volokolamsk, 263
Vorkuta, 17, 243, 248, *425*; death-rate, 16;
rebellion, 357
Voronov, N. N., 136, *380*
Voroshilov, Kliment Yefremovich, 38,
136, 141–2, *370*, *393*
Vyshinsky, Andrei Yanuaryevich, 12,
192, 232, 255

Walküre, *see* Operation Walküre
Warner, Christopher, 292, *439*
Warsaw: fall of, 97; Home Army, 270
Webb, Beatrice, 10, *407*
Webb, Sidney, 10, *407*
Weinstein, Prof. Allen, 337
Weizsäcker, Ernst von, 93, 200
Weygand, Gen. Maxime, 164, *409*
White, Harry Dexter, 337
White Russians, 297–322
Wilson, Geoffrey, 290–4, 333, 343, *438*
Wolfsberg, 297, 306, 320

Yagoda, Genrikh Grigoryevich, 40, 43,
52, *376*

Yalta Conference, 293, 296–7, 337, 343,
352
Yamashita, Gen., 223
Yartsev, Boris, 127
Yenukidze, Abel, 39
Yeowell, John, 188
Yezhov, Nikolai Ivanovich, 29, 61, *383*
Yudenitch, Gen., 300
Yugoslavia: Communist Party, 114;
Yugoslav-Soviet Treaty (1941), 209;
German invasion of, 209; USSR breaks
diplomatic relations with, 214; Soviet
occupation of, 267; Communists seize
power in, *379*

Zapadnaya Litza Bay, 110
Zaporozhye, 244
Zelyony Myss, 36
Zemlyanki, 8
Zhdanov, Andrei, 192, *390*, *391*, *413*
Zhukov, Marshal Georgi
Konstantinovich, 222, 273
Zilliacus, Konni, 165, *407*
Zinchenko, Constantin, 291, 293, *438*
Zinoviev, Grigory Yevseyevich, 39, *372*
Zionists: treatment under Stalin, 16, 27;
killed during German invasion, 247;
persecution began under Lenin, *373*;
see also Jews
Zubalov (industrialist), 39
Zuvalovo, 35